THE FRANCIS FORD COPPOLA ENCYCLOPEDIA

James M. Welsh
Gene D. Phillips
Rodney F. Hill

THE SCARECROW PRESS, INC.
Lanham • Toronto • Plymouth, UK
2010

Published by Scarecrow Press, Inc.
A wholly owned subsidiary of The Rowman & Littlefield Publishing Group, Inc.
4501 Forbes Boulevard, Suite 200, Lanham, Maryland 20706
http://www.scarecrowpress.com

Estover Road, Plymouth PL6 7PY, United Kingdom

British Library Cataloguing in Publication Information Available

Library of Congress Cataloging-in-Publication Data

Welsh, James Michael.
  The Francis Ford Coppola encyclopedia / James M. Welsh, Gene D. Phillips, Rodney F. Hill.
    p. cm.
  Includes bibliographical references and index.
  ISBN 978-0-8108-7650-7 (hardback : alk. paper) — ISBN 978-0-8108-7651-4 (ebook)
  1. Coppola, Francis Ford, 1939—Encyclopedias. I. Phillips, Gene D. II. Hill, Rodney, 1965–.
III. Title.
  PN1998.3.C67H55 2010
  791.4302'33092—dc22   2010010472

Printed in the United States of America

CONTENTS

FOREWORD
Life under the Hood—An Appreciation of Francis Ford Coppola

John C. Tibbetts

THERE'S A memorable scene in Francis Ford Coppola's *Tucker*, when automobile entrepreneur Preston Tucker (Jeff Bridges) proudly steps on stage to introduce to the press his newly designed "car of the future," the Tucker Torpedo. Through the curtains and down the ramp glides the gleaming red beauty. Flashbulbs pop. Reporters rush forward. A bevy of beauteous "Tuckerettes" blow kisses. Members of the Tucker clan exchange hugs.

However, few in attendance could have suspected that the "car of the future" is a fake, a sham, a collection of hastily assembled body parts.

The Francis Ford Coppola Encyclopedia takes a fresh look under the hood, as it were, at the technological dazzle and the dramatic machinery of Coppola's world. A reassembly of those body parts is in order. Once the darling of the so-called New Hollywood in the late 1960s and 1970s, Coppola and his brethren, Martin Scorsese, Brian De Palma, Robert Altman, and Hal Ashby, had portended a generation that breathed new life and conviction into auteurist theory and practice, while reviving, revising, and extending a faltering film industry. "The way to come to power," declared Coppola, speaking for his generation, "is not always to merely challenge the Establishment, but first make a place in it and then challenge, double-cross, the Establishment." Brave words, indeed. But after the spectacular box office successes of the first two *Godfather* films (1972, 1974) and the critical praise lavished on *The Conversation* (1974), the "debacles" (so-called by some critics) of *Apocalypse Now* (1979); *One from the Heart* (1982); *The Cotton Club* (1984); and most recently, *Youth without Youth* (2007) and *Tetro* (2009) suggest that Coppola has left the building, deserted his agenda, and betrayed his public. Indeed, more than a few critics have stated flatly that since *One from the Heart*, he has never fulfilled his promise, and that his mastery of style and technique has merely made him a slave to it. Nothing could be more devastating than Pauline Kael's critique of *The Cotton Club*: "He's watching his brain cells twinkle. . . . His expansiveness has become strictly formal; emotionally, he seems to have shrunk."

However, coming away from this book, we might find, as critic David Thomson has noted in his *New Biographical Dictionary of Film*, that "no American career has had such endless, entertaining turmoil, or says as much about making movies in America now. No one retains so many jubilant traits of the kid moviemaker, or has inspired darker comments."

The Francis Ford Coppola Encyclopedia is a compendium of all things Coppola, accumulated and architected by a team of indefatigable and knowing inquisitors and Coppola specialists led by James M. Welsh, Rodney Hill, and Fr. Gene D. Phillips. Through this "labyrinth of letters"—the sort of thing Borges envisioned in his story "The Library of Babel"—we can stroll down endless corridors, examine the shelves, pause before a particularly intriguing subject and title, and pluck out, by turns, a sublime passage and a foolish anecdote.

For example, there are the neglected and overlooked films of his youthful apprenticeship with Roger Corman in the early 1960s (*Dementia 13*); those first New Wave–influenced films, such as *You're a Big Boy Now* (1966) and *The Rain People* (1969); the canonical works, particularly the *Godfather* films, *The Conversation*, and *Apocalypse Now*; the troubled history of the first American Zoetrope productions, including the disastrous *One from the Heart* (1982); the admirable series of Coppola-produced titles, including *The Black Stallion* (1979); later projects as a director-for-hire, including the undervalued *Tucker* and *The Rainmaker*; and the negative reception of his most recent films, *Youth without Youth* (2007) and *Tetro* (2009).

During our stroll, best recall the dictum, "The glance reveals what the gaze obscures." Thus, quick glimpses reveal some choice nuggets about Coppola's world. Regarding his familial connections, in 1961 his father, Carmine, a classically trained musician, scored the first of several films for his son, *Tonight for Sure*, a "nudie" exploitation flick; Coppola's wife, Eleanor, not only witnessed the filming of *Apocalypse Now* but co-produced with him the profitable wineries and eco-friendly boutique hotels. And his son, Roman, directed a curious film called *CQ* (2001), concerned with—naturally—the travails of making movies. Moreover, who remembers that Coppola once teamed up with producer

George Lucas, famed cinematographer Vittorio Storaro, and superstar Michael Jackson to make for Disney the innovative 3-D *Captain EO*; that CBS Cable presented in 1981 a documentary about Coppola's participation in the restoration of Abel Gance's epic *Napoleon*? Regarding *Apocalypse Now*, that the *Redux* version restores a twenty-four-minute "French plantation" scene, which includes a political discussion of the French involvement in Indo-China; that a frustrated Coppola had to trick a reluctant Marlon Brando into a screen test by submitting to a fake "makeup check"; that journalist Michael Herr not only wrote the articles that inspired the film but served as a writer of the narration for both it and for *The Rainmaker* (1997)? And what about *The Godfather*? We read about the legendary tussles Coppola had with producer Robert Evans (ultimately Evans's faith in Coppola to direct stemmed from his belief that Coppola "knew the way [Italian] men ate their food, kissed each other, and talked"); that author Mario Puzo envisioned Don Corleone after Pope Alexander during the time of the Borgias; and that Sterling Hayden, who portrayed McCluskey, organized during World War II covert operations behind German lines in Croatia. And who knew that since 1997 Coppola has edited a magazine of fiction and film, *Zoetrope: All-Story*, which has featured noted contributors Margaret Atwood, Kurt Vonnegut, and Sherman Alexie?

Is there a pattern, an arc, a trajectory, a *meaning* to be discerned in this vast, storied tapestry of lights, sounds, words, and colors? What about their many rude collisions, their contrasts of fragile dreams and hallucinatory nightmares, promises of enterprise and disasters of apocalypse, shock-cuts of editing, clashing color palettes of hot crimsons and mordant, bruised greens, and the gritty, realistic textures transformed by the unabashed theatricality of broad-brushed, self-indulgent sentimentality? Nowhere is all of this more preposterously apparent than in the gloriously improbable *One from the Heart*. Here was Coppola's bête noire, a rejection of realism and genre revisionism, embracing self-conscious artifice and a nostalgia for classical Hollywood conventions. Take the concluding scene, to cite just one example: Coppola stages a reunion of separated lovers in high-flying style. After two days of searching for each other, those errant lovers, Franny and Hank (Teri Garr and Frederic Forrest), are at last reunited. Hank, distraught after a fruitless dash in the rain to the airport to stop his lover's departure, has returned to his rain-swept street and his shadow-haunted apartment. But as he crouches in the darkness, about to set fire to a pile of mementoes, Franny suddenly appears stage right. The spell is broken. A pink and golden dawn quickly floods the room. The crawling shadows vanish. We are in Wonderland. The tears of the lovers spangle their cheeks. "Oh, you silly boy," sings Crystal Gayle on the soundtrack. . . . Outside, a yellow light twinkles over the blue neon, studio-bound streets. The Curtains close on the scene. The $27 million production was such a disastrous failure that it bedeviled Coppola for more than a decade and destroyed Zoetrope Studios.

For a reexamination of this film, one that may ultimately be considered one of his most significant works, turn these pages. . . .

By getting agreeably lost in the labyrinthine corridors of thought and image in this book, while thinking and rethinking, fussing and fretting over its fractured, kaleidoscopic portrait of Coppola, I've been coming to the conclusion that Coppola and his work might be considered quintessentially *American*. He is essentially a child of American transcendentalism—at least in the sense that those brash idealists Nathaniel Haw-

thorne and Ralph Waldo Emerson deployed an "omniscient eye" to regard the American temper with a philosophical as well as poetic attitude, audaciously trusting in their own "infallibility" to read all Nature as a "sublime alphabet." (Stanley Cavell talks about these "Emersonian moments" in his philosophical musings in *The World Viewed*; and I propose they may constitute a key to "reading" films like *Tucker*, *Rumble Fish*, and *Youth without Youth*.) Moreover, how finely observed and how potently relevant here are Emerson's own observations in his essay "Self-Reliance"—with their compact utterances and twenty-one-gun bursts of rhetoric (sometimes verging on incoherency)—that the American observer is a *poet of action*, whose power "ceases in the instance of repose"; rather, "it resides in the moment of transition from a past to a new state, in the shooting of the gulf, in the darting to an aim. . . . Good for that and good for nothing else . . . A War; an earthquake, the revival of letters, the new dispensation by Jesus, or by Angels, Heaven, Hell, power, science . . . exist only to him as colors his brush." And Hawthorne, likewise, might have been predicting Coppola's own peculiar American audacity when he observed that the Transcendental artists seem always "careening on the utmost verge of a precipitous absurdity," seeking "the neutral ground where the Actual and the Imaginary meet, coming as close as possible without actually tumbling over."

But to what degree does Coppola inscribe *himself* in these neon conflagrations, montage-collisions, and phantasmagoric dreams? The best of Coppola, David Thomson suggests, does not reside in his "furious efforts" and "fearful fantasies" of "trying to be everything for everyone." Rather, Thomson continues, "he is at his best when secretly telling a part of his own story, or working out his fearful fantasies." Is Coppola, then, like the failed Tucker automobile, merely an empty shell; or is he, like Tucker himself, the artificer of dreams so intensely personal and so stubbornly visionary that they can't be denied?

In this wise, it seems like I keep coming back to those recent films, *Youth without Youth* and *Tetro*. In a column in the *Economist*, dated May 16, 2009, *Tetro* was described as "the film of a free man starting again." Similarly, *Youth without Youth* meditates on time and opportunities once lost, now recaptured. Its extravagantly romantic style recognizes the onrush of time and the regeneration of artistic vision in the face of imminent mortality. The aging Dominic, stricken by a finger of lightning, recaptures a lost youth and a lost love, gains preternatural powers of mind and body, and survives the repressions of the dictatorial Nazi regime. Consumed by nothing less than the search for the wellsprings of religious philosophy and language, he is almost literally split in two, his identity a counterpoint of conflicting voices. Ultimately, his time runs out, and, transformed again into an old man, he dies, a self-confessed failure. "I will never finish my life's work," he admits, "and I will die alone." In the sympathetic opinion here of co-editor James M. Welsh, it is the closest Coppola has come to his own cinematic testament. "After bringing the Godfathers to life," writes Welsh, "after peering into the heart of darkness and finding some illumination out of chaos, the man has more than earned the right to take chances." If the parallels with the life, mind, and ambitions of Coppola—himself struck by a finger of light, as it were—are apparent enough, the meaning of it all is not so clear. Either its meaning "is *so*, or it is *not* so," Dominic is counseled, "or it is *so* and *not-so* combined, or it is neither so nor not-so combined." By now, Coppola admits with disarming modesty, "What I've learned is that this phase of shooting isn't really making the film; you're gather-

ing pieces. It's not really a performance. . . . That was always very important to me when I was younger, because I wanted to be a really good director and that meant I should have a good, set manner—which means nothing, absolutely nothing. All that matters is you get the components that ultimately you're going to make into a beautiful film."

A personal note: I met Coppola just once, in the Sheraton-Center in New York City in June 1981. As a board member of the National Film Society, I had invited him to come to our annual Artistry in Cinema Awards ceremony to recognize Gwen Verdon's lifetime achievement in musical comedy. As it happened, he had cast her in the role of "Tish Dwyer" in his upcoming *The Cotton Club*. Of course, he arrived a few minutes late—standard behavior, I had been told—and was slightly out of breath. When I joked with him that he was not wearing his customary white coat and slacks, he apologized with a wry smile: "We just wrapped *The Cotton Club* about twenty minutes ago. I'm late because when we were changing the lighting awhile ago, I decided to cook a quick dinner. But I spilled tomato sauce on my white pants, so I had to change. And right now I really want to go to bed, but if there's one person I would take this time for—and put on this suit—it's Gwen Verdon!"

Quickly, he went to podium amid loud applause from the packed audience. It was a memorable moment, seeing him and Gwen Verdon together on the podium.

"In case you're wondering why I'm here," he began to the packed house, "I was raised in a musical comedy family. Both my uncle and father were musical comedy conductors for shows. My father was the chief arranger for the Radio City Music Hall and my uncle was the conductor. So even when I was a kid, I was very interested in musical theatre. One of my greatest idols was Gwen Verdon. So when we did *The Cotton Club* and I had the opportunity to have her in the cast, I was really thrilled. It has been an exceptional experience." He then read her a congratulatory telegram from Verdon's friend, the song-and-dance man Gene Nelson.

Verdon came to the podium. "I want to thank Mr. Coppola for putting me in *The Cotton Club*," she said, "because that was truly the beginning of the recognition of dance, both in New York and in Culver City, California, which is where my mother danced."

It was just a tiny moment. But I later learned this was the sort of gesture that was typical of his fabled loyalty to family and friends.

The point is, I wonder if *we* have been loyal to *him*. I think we're like the epony-mous "Wakefield" in a curious story by Hawthorne. Ever the faithful husband, Wakefield one day suddenly quits his wife and home to take up an anonymous residence a few blocks away. For twenty years he keeps a wary distance, avoiding all direct contacts with her. Then, one day, just as suddenly, he again ascends the porch steps and returns to his patiently waiting spouse. Similarly, we realize it wasn't Coppola who left us; it was *we* who deserted *him*. We stepped aside for a moment and, like Wakefield, "exposed ourselves to the fearful risk of losing [our] place forever." No, this book confirms that Coppola has been waiting for our return all along. "Don't get too close to people," Tucker had been warned by his friend Abe; "you'll catch their dreams." It's time we come home again, close the gap, and catch more than a few of Coppola's dreams. They have been waiting for us, all along.

ACKNOWLEDGMENTS

JAMES M. WELSH wishes to thank the Rev. Gene D. Phillips for thirty-plus years of cooperation, generosity, and goodwill; Rodney Hill for coordinating these entries ever so thoughtfully and cheerfully; Mary Graham for her hospitality in Chicago and for permitting all three editors to meet at her condo on the Loop; Kate and Bart Ideker for their hospitality in Atlanta and the use of their splendid table; John Tibbetts for getting the ball rolling in the first place and for his introductory comments here; Randy Neil and Allyn Miller of Kansas City for helping me to make connections all those many years ago in Los Angeles and elsewhere; Kevin Brownlow in London and Robert Harris in Rye, New York, for sharing information and materials about Abel Gance, Claude Lelouch, and Francis Coppola; Don Whaley for insights into the Monomyth and the mysteries of Zen and anarchism as practiced by John Milius; Chris Meissner and all of those trained at the University of Kansas who helped us get through the day; and, most especially, my colleague at Scarecrow Press, Stephen H. Ryan, senior editor for arts and literature.

Gene D. Phillips is grateful to Francis Ford Coppola for agreeing to be interviewed at the Cannes International Film Festival and for reading through all of his published interviews to check for factual errors. Research materials were provided by: the Paramount Collection of the Margaret Herrick Library of the Academy of Motion Picture Arts and Sciences in Hollywood; the Department of Special Collections of the Research Library of the University of California at Los Angeles; the Billy Rose Collection of the Theater and Film Collection of the New York Public Library for the Performing Arts, at Lincoln Center; the Film Archive of George Eastman House in Rochester, New York; and the Warner Bros. Collection in the Archives of the University of Southern California Library. Thanks to Rodney Hill and James M. Welsh for their invaluable support and for making this collaborative effort both pleasant and rewarding.

Rodney F. Hill wishes to thank his home institution, Georgia Gwinnett College, for its support during the completion of this volume. Specifically, thanks are due to Dr. Daniel J. Kaufman, president of the College; Dr. Stanley Preczewski, vice president of academic and student affairs; Dr. Jo Galle, associate vice president of academic affairs; and Dr. Lois Richardson, dean of the School of Liberal Arts. At the GGC Library, my research efforts were made easier thanks to the work of Gene Ruffin, Vicki Parsons, Holly Heitman, Maxine Small, and all of their associates. I would also like to thank my GGC colleagues who contributed individual entries to this volume: Jason Mosser and Thomas Clancy. My sincere thanks also go to our other contributors, whose essays I count among the best pieces in the book: Fernando Arenas, Tom Dannenbaum, Heidi Kenaga, Christofer Meissner, Paul

B. Ramaeker, Manuel Pérez Tejada, Billy Budd Vermillion, and Donald M. Whaley. A large measure of thanks is due to John C. Tibbetts, not only for his insightful foreword to this volume, but also for his years of friendship and guidance. Finally, I wish to offer my profound gratitude to James M. Welsh and Gene D. Phillips for allowing me to join them in this venture, for setting such high standards with their research, and for being such congenial and supportive collaborators.

INTRODUCTION
So Why Does Francis Coppola Deserve His Own Encyclopedia?

James M. Welsh

> Creativity, after all, is the ability to see connections between seemingly dissimilar elements.
>
> —Francis Coppola, *Zoetrope: All-Story*, vol. 3, no. 2

THE *ECONOMIST*, a smart, international weekly magazine, usually doesn't pay much attention to movies or moviemakers, but on May 16, 2009, it devoted half a page to the release at the Cannes Film Festival of Francis Ford Coppola's *Tetro* in an anonymous piece entitled "Starting Over," noting that, at the age of seventy, the (now more than ever) indie director of *The Godfather* "is back at the helm" (p. 92). In this film, "mined from the imposing mythology of the Coppola family," about a theatrical genius, who, working in Buenos Aires has been unable to finish his magnum opus, the director reminds his audience of what he can achieve "with actors, when he isn't distracted by technique," creating "the film of a free man starting again." Though the film fell far short of being a blockbuster and occasioned predictable spasms of confusion and displeasure among certain spasmatic reviewers, it appeared to have been inspired by the ambitious optimism of a master craftsman, and that in itself was reason to cheer. DeSica, Fellini, and Antonioni are no longer among

us, but the Italian spirit and sensibility lives on in the transplanted work and the person of Francis Coppola. Of course, a new film by Coppola may not exactly equal a new film by Fellini—that sometimes grotesque and gaudy Roman *god*—but, by God, Coppola's later work certainly stands up to the later work of the late Fellini.

On the one hand, then, there is the larger-than-life filmmaker and entrepreneur; on the other hand, there is the person, who can be incredibly kind, forgiving, and generous. My friend John Tibbetts remembers meeting Francis Coppola in person at an awards ceremony in New York, honoring Gwen Verdon in 1981, when Coppola was at the time involved in shooting *The Cotton Club*. Well, I was there, too, but I remember meeting Mr. Coppola differently, from my perspective. The director was late arriving at the hotel after a long and difficult day of shooting. The award had been named for the late Eleanor Powell, and the banquet dragged on as the attendees waited, listening to a song rendered by "The Street Singer," Arthur Tracey, whose most famous standard had been "Pennies from Heaven," alternating with "Ellie" stories told by the secretary of Eleanor Powell. This pleasant entertainment had been going on for a very long time when Mr. Coppola finally arrived. John had sent me to the lobby to serve as a "runner" and to get Francis to the ballroom as quickly as possible. And so I accompanied the Great Man up the elevator to the ballroom, and we arrived at the back of the room just as the latest round of "Ellie" stories was in progress. John Tibbetts frantically waved his long arms, like a basketball player trying to prevent a shot, to get the lady's attention, as he finally did. Immediately understanding the situation, Eleanor Powell's former secretary excitedly announced: "And now, ladies and gentlemen, here he is, the man who directed . . . *The Deer Hunter!*" This was followed by something of a gasp from some of us in the audience, but Francis Coppola took the gaffe in stride, perfectly, and acknowledged his bearded presence without saying a word about Michael Cimino, whose film had been mistaken for *Apocalypse Now*, a kind and graceful conclusion, I thought, to what might have been an awkward moment, improvised by Coppola on the spot.

But John and I were both delighted to see Mr. Coppola attending the award ceremony at an event sponsored by the National Film Society out of Kansas City. We had worked many such "events," in New York, in Washington, D.C., and (mainly) in Los Angeles, before we went on (years later) jointly to edit a series of movie encyclopedias for Facts On File, New York: We started the ball rolling with our two-volume *Encyclopedia of Filmmakers*; but the first book out of the gate treating an individual director was Tom Leitch's magnificent *Encyclopedia of Alfred Hitchcock*, which was very favorably reviewed by Ken Moog on the MacGuffin website as one of the best Hitchcock books of the year. The second volume in the series was *The Encyclopedia of Stanley Kubrick*, edited by Rodney Hill and Father Gene D. Phillips, S.J., assisted by John Tibbetts and Jim Welsh working on the sidelines and behind the scenes. All together we did about a dozen titles for Facts On File before that series

closed down. But we knew that there were many other directors whose work was important enough to deserve coverage, and of these, Francis Ford Coppola was certainly one of the most important. Scarecrow Press agreed, fortunately, and work commenced three years ago, even though Laurence Raw's *The Ridley Scott Encyclopedia* was the first title out of the gate in 2009 for the Scarecrow Press series. One essential difference in the series concept is that the present series extends to directors who are still active, such as Ridley Scott and Francis Coppola.

Coppola is a very special case, however, a generational "cousin" to some and "uncle" to others, as an antiestablishment maverick. His work is movie infused. It's difficult not to "read" *Tucker* as both autobiographical and allegorical, for example, with Preston Tucker standing up to the Detroit auto industry as Francis Coppola would later stand up to the Hollywood industry. Then there is Francis Ford Coppola as the auteur cinephile (he has written screenplays, after all, and is "author" of his own work as well as the work of others), not only respectful of masters like Abel Gance and Akira Kurosawa, but also promoting their work; as producer, Coppola has been a steady advocate of "serious" cinema, inviting Wim Wenders to California and then standing behind the Wenders *Hammett* project. And then Coppola became editor and publisher of *Zoetrope: All-Story* magazine, which started as a tabloid and then morphed into a gorgeously produced glossy showcase for the creative work of other writers and designers. In *Zoetrope: All-Story* (vol. 11, no. 3, Fall 2007) you'll find a better (or at least a more readable) translation of Mircea Eliade's novella "Youth without Youth" than the earlier English translation published under the title "Rejuvenation by Lightning" in volume 2 of the Classics of Romanian Literature Series (Eastern

European Monographs, 1992), edited by Kurt W. Treptow. That same issue of *Zoetrope: All-Story* includes a piece with Coppola interviewing himself about the Eliade project, and Eleanor Coppola interviews Tim Roth (Domenic Matei) and Alexandra Maria Lara, who played the dual roles of Veronica and Laura in the film. In the Summer 2009 issue, *Zoetrope: All-Story* featured Coppola's original story treatment that he later transformed into the screenplay of *Tetro*, which debuted at the 2009 Cannes Film Festival. "Originally, I planned to write out the entire piece in prose to refresh and evolve my ideas about the story," Coppola explained. "I've been writing in screenplay format for so many years now that I usually fall back on that; however, I often suspect that prose is better for composing a story in that it allows a writer to map a character's thoughts and other elements that are not included in a screenplay but might be helpful to explore."

Coppola has been a multitalented artistic leader throughout his career, a Renaissance man in postmodern America, and a *necessary* presence. A shorter book was once published to demonstrate *Why Sinatra Matters*. This book is intended to provide a similar demonstration for why Francis Coppola also matters to a later generation.

We especially appreciate the portrait John Tibbetts draws in his foreword of Francis Coppola as a magnanimous dream catcher, one who mastered the mainstream and then, after something of a cinematic sabbatical, eclipsed it, returning to simpler formulas and learning from his children, especially Sofia, how to shoot on a more intimate scale while telling stories of family honor and integrity and stories of soaring metaphysical and philosophical overreaching. And for all that, I personally don't consider the more recent films "debacles," for Coppola is in a perfectly protected position. He can tell his stories now without having to "prove" anything to anybody. After bringing the Godfathers to life, after peering into the heart of darkness and finding some illumination out of chaos, the man has more than earned the right to take chances. If certain critics scoff, that is their misfortune and embarrassment. And that, I think, is the ultimate meaning of all the information collected here, bits and pieces of a life and career assembled, one hopes, in such a way that some manner of meaningful pattern may be discerned, perhaps the paradigm of a particularized American dream. It's been a difficult "project" because it covers a huge and meaningful career, stretching across a transformative period for Hollywood and the entertainment industry. Our goal was to cover the territory in an interesting and informative way. We hope we have managed to do it some justice, and that Mr. Coppola and his fans will forgive us any indiscretions or shortcomings.

Note: Throughout this volume, cross-references within entries are indicated in ALL CAPS.

ABEL GANCE'S NAPOLEON (1927)

A reconstruction by KEVIN BROWNLOW of the original silent version of Gance's spectacular five-hour epic film, not seen in its complete form since 1927 when it premiered at the Paris Opéra. The reconstruction was first exhibited in its complete form at the Twenty-fourth London Film Festival on Sunday, November 30, 1980, at the Empire Cinema, Leicester Square, with a new score composed by Brownlow's collaborator at Thames Television, Carl Davis, performed by the Wren forty-three-piece orchestra, conducted by Carl Davis himself. This epic spectacular was first brought to the Telluride Film Festival in America in 1979, with ABEL GANCE himself in attendance in Colorado at a screening that lasted until 3 AM. Introducing Kevin Brownlow as recipient of the Mel Noikoff Award at the San Francisco Film Festival in 2007, Milestone Film & Video founder Dennis Doros called Brownlow "the godfather of modern film archiving practices." Doros noted that Brownlow's "magnificent restoration" of Abel Gance's 1927 classic Napoleon "wasn't just the film preservation event of the decade when it was rereleased in a gloriously restored version in 1981, but a cultural phenomenon. Many people have taken credit for the resurrected Napoleon's success," Doros added, "but it was all Kevin's doing. For nearly 40 years, he assembled every scrap of celluloid he could find, searching Paris flea markets and the world's most exclusive archives. He championed the film and Gance at every opportunity, even when no one else cared. And he is still restoring the film. Like the 'Flying Dutchman,' the film is his curse—and the world's blessing."

Born in Sussex on June 2, 1938, Kevin Brownlow was educated at a boarding school in Crowborough, Sussex, where he developed an interest in film preservation and collecting at an early age. His oral history concerning early Hollywood professionals, The Parade's Gone By . . . (1968) helped to define the interests of the "Film Generation" of the 1960s. He later formed a production company in London with the late David Gill, Photoplay Productions, one that released award-winning television documentary series, notably, Hollywood: The Pioneers, The Unknown Chaplin, and Cinema Europe: The Other Hollywood. Brownlow also had made a documentary entitled Abel Gance: The Charm of Dynamite (1968) and wrote and published the definitive book on the subject, entitled in England Napoleon: Abel Gance's Classic Film (London: Jonathan Cape, 1983).

At the time the Brownlow restoration was shown in America, ROBERT A. HARRIS had the rights to an alternative, awkwardly expanded version of Napoleon, called Bonaparte and the Revolution, that Gance had made with director Claude Lelouch in 1972 and that Robert Harris was then distributing in the United States. So negotiations were put into play between Harris and Coppola, and consequently the 1981 Radio City Music Hall *Napoleon* spectacular was mounted, billed as "Francis Ford Coppola Presents *Napoleon*: Abel Gance's 1927 Masterpiece," though the program stated in fine print at the end "We would like to thank Kevin Brownlow, The British Film Institute, Clyde Jeavons, David Francis, Thames Television, [and] Liz Sutherland for their kind permission to reprint and borrow passages from their London Film Festival program for *Napoleon*." Purists knew that Brownlow needed to be thanked, however, for more than the program. Thus FRANCIS COPPOLA, working with TOM LUDDY of the Pacific Film Archives, and ultimately with Robert A. Harris of Images Film Archive in Rye, New York, mounted their successful revival of "*Napoleon*: Abel Gance's 1927 Masterpiece" at the Radio City Music Hall in New York City, accompanied by a full orchestra conducted by CARMINE COPPOLA, Francis's father, playing a score he had composed to accompany the film rather than the Carl Davis score that had been used in London. When the film was screened in Washington, D.C., at the Kennedy Center's American Film Institute Theatre, musicologist Arthur Kleiner, an expert on music to accompany silent cinema, was flown in from Minneapolis to accompany the film on piano and theatre organ. At the New York premiere, the theatre organ at Radio City (played by Leonard Raver, the official organist of the New York Philharmonic from the faculty at the Juilliard School) took over from the orchestra to enable the orchestra to rest during what was a four-and-a-half-hour screening. Sources close to Kevin Brownlow alleged that Coppola and Harris had shortened Gance's film by as much as thirty minutes in order to satisfy union regulations and avoid overtime charges at Radio

City. The ninety-one-year-old director was unable to attend either the London Festival premiere or the Radio City Music Hall opening, but Gene Kelly was there, holding up a telephone receiver so that Gance, in his Paris apartment, could hear the enthusiastic applause. This silent premiere, backed by Coppola and Zoetrope, took New York by storm and proved to be unexpectedly popular. What was originally scheduled for a three-day run had to be extended. As a consequence, the film eventually toured other major American cities, across the country to Los Angeles. It played the Midland Theatre in Kansas City, for example, accompanied by the Kansas City Philharmonic, conducted by Carmine Coppola. The success nationwide of this restoration and revival set an important precedent. Eventually Robert Harris would restore Hitchcock's *Vertigo*, for example, followed by David Lean's *Lawrence of Arabia*, and, in 1989, the fiftieth-anniversary "edition" of *Gone with the Wind*, "restored and publicized at a total cost of about $350,000, earned $2.5 million at the box office and sold 220,000 copies in videocassette, for a total profit of about $7 million," according to the *New York Times* (April 25, 1991). By 1986, the Cinémathèque Française in Paris had completed a restoration of Gance's other five-hour silent masterpiece *La Roue* (1920–1923), under the editorial supervision of Marie Epstein. However, Kevin Brownlow had set the standard in London and Paris, and Francis Coppola had set the standard in America.—JAMES M. WELSH

References

Lenny Borger, "'Napoleon' Wows London," *Variety*, December 3, 1980, 7; see also Lenny Borger, "Restored by the Cinémathèque, Reviewed by *Variety*," *Variety*, October 1, 1986, 36; Kevin Brownlow, "'Napoleon'—A Triumphal Return," *New York Times*, October 11, 1981, sec. 2: 1; Kevin Brownlow, *Napoleon*:

Abel Gance's Classic Film (London: Jonathan Cape, 1983); Annette Insdorf, "'Napoleon'— Rescuing an Epic Film," *New York Times*, January 18, 1981, sec. 2: 1; James M. Welsh, "Napoleon," *Films in Review* 32, no. 3 (March 1981): 156–60.

ACORD, LANCE (1964–)

Cinematographer who worked with SOFIA COPPOLA on *LOST IN TRANSLATION* (2003), for which he was nominated for a BAFTA Award from the British Academy of Film and Television Arts. On that project, Acord was instrumental in helping to resolve problems between the American and Japanese crews. Lance Acord previously collaborated with Sofia Coppola as cinematographer on her short film, *Lick the Star*. After studying photography and filmmaking at the San Francisco Arts Institute, the Northern California native began his career with acclaimed photographer/ filmmaker Bruce Weber. Together they made documentaries, commercials, and music videos. Acord won the MTV Video Music Award for Best Cinematography for his work on Fatboy Slim's "Weapon of Choice," directed by SPIKE JONZE. Acord also has shot numerous television commercial campaigns for clients such as Levi's, Volkswagen, and Nike. He made his first foray into narrative feature filmmaking as the cinematographer on VINCENT GALLO's *Buffalo 66*. Since then, he has been the director of photography on Spike Jonze's multi-award-winning features *Being John Malkovich* and *Adaptation*, as well as Peter Care's *The Dangerous Lives of Altar Boys*.—RODNEY HILL/JAMES M. WELSH

ALLEN, JOAN (1956–)

Respected stage and screen actress cast in the roles of Maddy Nagle in Coppola's *PEGGY SUE GOT MARRIED* (1986) and Vera Tucker in *TUCKER: THE MAN AND HIS DREAM* (1988). Hailing from Rochelle,

Illinois, she was a theatre major at Northern Illinois University and at Eastern Illinois University, Allen (born August 20, 1956) soon became a member of the Steppenwolf Theatre Company in Chicago, where she performed in over thirty productions. Off-Broadway she performed in Christopher Durang's *The Marriage of Bette & Boo* (for which she won an Obie Award) and her Jefferson Award–winning role in the Steppenwolf production of *And a Nightingale Sang . . .*, for which she also won the Clarence Derwent, Drama Desk, Outer Critics Circle, and Theatre World Awards, bringing her to the attention of FRED ROOS, who cast her in FRANCIS COPPOLA's *Peggy Sue Got Married*. Allen received the Best Actress Tony Award for her performance opposite John Malkovich in Lanford Wilson's *Burn This*, and was nominated in the same category for her role in *The Heidi Chronicles*. Her film work also received high recognition. She was nominated for the Best Supporting Actress Academy Award for her role as Pat Nixon in Oliver Stone's *Nixon* (1996) and again the following year for her role opposite Daniel Day-Lewis in the film adaptation of Arthur Miller's *The Crucible* (1997).—JAMES M. WELSH

AMERICAN GRAFFITI (1973)

Outside of his own films as a director, FRANCIS FORD COPPOLA is perhaps best known as an early mentor of director GEORGE LUCAS. That mentorship reached its climax with the making and subsequent success of Lucas's 1973 film *American Graffiti*.

Coppola's involvement in *American Graffiti* resulted from a couple of factors that were in play in the latter part of 1972. First, Coppola was basking in the success of *THE GODFATHER*—a success that gave him quite a bit of momentum, leverage, and cachet in Hollywood studio circles. Second, Lucas was coming off of the relative critical and commercial failure of his first feature, *THX 1138*, and he was having trouble gaining backing for *American Graffiti*, a nostalgic coming-of-age story based on his youth in the early 1960s. The two circumstances combined to involve Coppola in the production of the film that would end up launching the lucrative and influential subsequent career of his erstwhile protégé.

Lucas had encountered resistance—if not complete disinterest—from studios regarding the *American Graffiti* project. Studios objected to several potential pitfalls in making the film: the marketability of a period piece of its kind, the necessity of casting unknowns in the film's many teenage roles, the licensing costs of Lucas's plan to fill the soundtrack with period songs from the late 1950s and early 1960s. Lucas had been able to develop the screenplay via an option at United Artists, but the studio passed on the film after the script was completed. Ultimately, Universal agreed to produce the film at a low cost, and then only with a seasoned filmmaker supervising the production.

Coppola was a natural choice to fill this role. He was, as always, interested in shepherding the careers of other filmmakers. In addition, he wanted to exercise his newfound clout within the studio system. The ability to do both while helping Lucas to realize a personal project like *American Graffiti* sealed the deal for Coppola—he saw his involvement as a matter of "friendship, love, and belief in George." With Coppola vouching for the film creatively and financially, *American Graffiti* went into production.

Coppola ended up being mostly an absentee overseer whose name lent the production prestige, both with the studio suits at Universal and for audiences once the film was released. He was determined not to act the studio meddler that he had so often encountered in his own work. He tried to stay out of Lucas's way during production of the film, although he did make occasional visits to the set. Coppola's most useful work as *American Graffiti*'s guardian came only when the film was finished and ready for presentation to test audiences and studio executives.

In a now-legendary public confrontation with Universal executive Ned Tanen, Coppola ferociously defended his friend's film—and saved it from extensive cuts and reediting. After a test screening of *American Graffiti* in San Francisco in January 1973, Tanen told Lucas and Coppola that he found the film unfit for release in its present form. Right there in the theatre, Coppola exploded at Tanen (much to Lucas's disbelief and dismay), reminding Tanen how Lucas had completed the film on budget and on schedule (which he did) and predicting that it would become a huge hit (which it would). Follow-up discussions with Universal on Coppola's part, in which he further defended the film in the form Lucas had submitted it, resulted in only minor cuts to the film prior to its release (Schumacher, 1999, 146–47).

American Graffiti was released to theatres on August 1, 1973, and almost immediately, it found an audience receptive to its nostalgia and stories of teenage high jinks. The film's marketing tagline—"Where were you in '62?"—had resonance for audiences as well, as the film was credited with helping to launch the fifties nostalgia fad of the 1970s (later exemplified by the stage production and film of *Grease* as well as by the TV sitcom hits *Happy Days* and *Laverne and Shirley*). *American Graffiti*'s cast of then relative unknowns now reads like a Who's Who of American cinema and television of the subsequent three decades: Ron Howard, Cindy Williams, Richard Dreyfuss, HARRISON FORD, Mackenzie Phillips, Charles Martin Smith, Suzanne Somers. Howard and Dreyfuss portrayed the film's two main characters, Steve and Curt, respectively. Along with a host of friends and acquaintances, the two boys spend their final night before departing for college cruising the strip in their small hometown, enjoying some final high school–era adventures, and pondering their future, all to a soundtrack of music from the film's early-1960s period.

The story and structural elements of *American Graffiti* both drew from earlier films and influenced films that followed. The film shows influences from 1960s beach-party films as well as earlier films portraying 1950s drag racing and juke joint subcultures. Lucas, an astute student of film history, was even said to have borrowed plot elements for *American Graffiti* from as unlikely a source as Federico Fellini's *I Vitelloni* (1953). Lucas, of course, would gain greater fame and success through his subsequent *Star Wars* films, which borrowed heavily from genre and serial films of the 1930s and 1940s; this tendency to rework tropes and story elements from earlier film culture found its first flowering in *American Graffiti*. *American Graffiti* influenced a host of later films that had coming-of-age plots or featured music from the late 1950s and early 1960s, including *Diner* (1982), *Stand By Me* (1986), *La Bamba* (1987), *Dirty Dancing* (1987), *Hairspray* (1988), and *Mermaids* (1990).

Another later film that was influenced by *American Graffiti*'s fifties nostalgia was Coppola's own *PEGGY SUE GOT MARRIED*, from 1986. This influence on one of his later, lesser films was only one of the benefits Coppola received from his association with *American Graffiti*. Coppola drew from the large cast of *American Graffiti* for his next project, *THE CONVERSATION*, giving Cindy Williams and Harrison Ford key roles in that film. *American Graffiti* established Coppola as an effective and successful producer of other direc-

tors' films, a role that has become somewhat of a second career for him and that he has carried out on such films as *THE BLACK STALLION* (1979), *HAMMETT* (1982), Kenneth Branagh's *FRANKENSTEIN* (1994), and his daughter Sofia's *THE VIRGIN SUICIDES* (1999) and *LOST IN TRANSLATION* (2003). Finally, Coppola also got an unexpected financial windfall from his association with *American Graffiti*—his participation in the film's profitable success earned him a $3 million payday. —CHRISTOFER MEISSNER

References
John Belton, *American Cinema/American Culture*, 3rd ed. (Boston: McGraw-Hill, 2009); Peter Cowie, *Coppola* (New York: Charles Scribner's Sons, 1989); Michael Schumacher, *Francis Ford Coppola: A Filmmaker's Life* (New York: Crown Publications, 1999).

AMERICAN ZOETROPE
FRANCIS FORD COPPOLA's own production company/movie studio, founded in San Francisco in 1969, idealistically, in the words of *New Yorker* critic Michael Sragow, to permit artists "to share ideas and equipment, and eventually to transform their native cinema." After noting that the last credit of *THE RAIN PEOPLE* reads "produced by American Zoetrope, San Francisco," Ronald Bergan explains the derivation: "The Greek word Zoetrope means 'life movement,' but it was also the name of the 19th-century toy invented by William George Horner, which was a revolving drum with images that spun around rapidly, giving the impression of movement." American Zoetrope became a magnet for movie mavericks and friends of Coppola's, such as JOHN MILIUS, GEORGE LUCAS, Coppola's UCLA classmate Carroll Ballard (*THE BLACK STALLION*), John Korty (*The Crazy Quilt*), and Haskell Wexler (*Medium Cool*). John Milius told Sragow that "None

of those other guys—Lucas, Spielberg, all of them—could have existed without Francis's help." Over the years, the facility that Coppola originally named American Zoetrope has undergone various kinds of reorganization with attendant variations of name (e.g., it was temporarily called Omni Zoetrope in the 1980s). For the sake of consistency and to avoid confusion, Coppola's production company is referred to as American Zoetrope throughout this book.—GENE D. PHILLIPS/JAMES M. WELSH

References

Ron Bergan, *Francis Coppola Close Up: The Making of His Movies* (London: Orion Media, 1998); Michael Sragow, "Godfatherhood," *New Yorker*, March 24, 1977, 44–52.

APOCALYPSE NOW (1979)

DIRECTOR: Francis Ford Coppola. SCREENPLAY: John Milius and Francis Ford Coppola. Produced by Francis Coppola for Zoetrope Studios. PHOTOGRAPHY: Vittorio Storaro. EDITING: Lisa Fruchtman, Gerald B. Greenberg, and Walter Murch. ORIGINAL MUSIC: Carmine Coppola. PRODUCTION DESIGN: Dean Tavoularis. ART DIRECTION: Angelo Graham.
CAST: Marlon Brando (Kurtz), Martin Sheen (Willard), Robert Duvall (Lt. Col. Kilgore), Frederic Forrest (Chef), Sam Bottoms (Lance), Larry Fishburne (Clean), Albert Hall (Chief), Harrison Ford (Col. Lucas), Dennis Hopper (Photojournalist), G. D. Spradlin (Gen. Corman), Scott Glenn (Colby), Cynthia Wood (Playmate of the Year), Colleen Camp (Playmate).
RUNNING TIME: 153 minutes. Color.
RELEASED THROUGH: United Artists. PREMIERE: May 10, 1979 (Cannes International Film Festival).
ACADEMY AWARDS: Cinematography, Sound.
DVD: Paramount.

In 1975 FRANCIS FORD COPPOLA announced that he intended to make a film about the Vietnam War. Hollywood filmmakers had avoided that subject, fearing that a movie about the war would be too controversial and financially risky, but a poll commissioned by Coppola found that Americans would accept a "non-didactic" film about Vietnam. The resulting movie was *Apocalypse Now*, directed by Coppola and cowritten by Coppola and JOHN MILIUS. The film was an adaptation of JOSEPH CONRAD's novella "HEART OF DARKNESS," updating the novella's setting from the Belgian Congo in the 1890s to Vietnam in the 1960s.

Coppola had difficulty making his film. The military refused to assist (Pentagon officials objected to the script); a typhoon hit the Philippines, where the film was being shot; and one of the principal actors, MARTIN SHEEN, suffered a heart attack. The film ran millions of dollars over budget and took four years to complete: *Apocalypse Now* was not released until 1979.

The film tells the story of Captain Willard (Martin Sheen), a CIA assassin ordered to find Colonel Walter Kurtz (MARLON BRANDO), a Green Beret accused of murdering four suspected Vietcong agents. Kurtz has escaped, gathered a force of Montagnard tribesmen, and moved into Cambodia, where he is waging a private war, "operating," an American General says, "without any decent restraint, totally beyond the pale of any acceptable human conduct." Kurtz's superiors have concluded that he is insane, and they order Willard to "terminate" Kurtz "with extreme prejudice." A navy patrol boat carries Willard upriver into Cambodia. Along the way, he and the crew experience adventures that become more and more surreal: a helicopter assault on a village, an encounter with a tiger in the jungle, a USO Playboy Bunny show, the killing of civilians in a sampan, a battle at an isolated bridge, and an attack by natives with arrows and spears. Eventually, Willard finds Kurtz and assassinates him.

Apocalypse Now is a rewriting of the traditional adventure story, a kind of story told in every culture, the story that comparative mythologist Joseph Campbell has called "the monomyth." The plot of the monomyth always begins in the world of common, ordinary, everyday life. The hero is pulled out of this world into the adventure, goes through a series of episodes in which he overcomes difficulties, and wins a climactic final victory, which spiritually transforms him. He returns from the adventure with the "boon," the power to regenerate society. Versions of the monomyth include, says Campbell, various tales of a journey to the underworld, as in Dante's *Inferno*, Aeneas visiting the land of the dead to consult his father and learn the future, or the story of Jesus, who leaves the world, ascends to heaven, and returns with the boon—the Good News of life after death. The victory won may be the gaining of wisdom or enlightenment (the story of the Buddha is a version of the monomyth, Campbell argues) or the killing of a tyrannical father-figure (which Campbell says is a version of the Oedipus story in which the son kills his father and takes his place).

John Milius, in writing his screenplay, had different versions of the monomyth in mind. Milius has said that he based Willard on Aeneas and Dante. The film begins, as does Dante's *Inferno*, with the protagonist alone, in midlife, having lost his moral and spiritual compass and undergoing a tortured, agonizing dark night of the soul. The descent into the Underworld is symbolized in the film by the image of Willard's helicopter descending in Nha Trang to meet with the officers who will give him his mission. The Nung River in the film corresponds to the rivers of the Underworld and, as Frank Tomasulo has pointed out,

the scene at the Do Lung Bridge in which soldiers stand in water and beg for the patrol boat to pick them up calls to mind Canto XII of *The Inferno*, in which the makers of war are submerged in a river of blood. Milius also has said that he based Willard on Jesus and Oedipus. The identification of Willard with these two figures is established in the opening scene of the film. As two soldiers drag a drunken Willard to the shower in his Saigon hotel room, Willard is in a crucifixion posture and the shower into which they put him becomes a symbolic baptism. The Oedipal theme is announced in the opening scene of the film by the use of the Doors' song, "The End," about a son who kills his father and sleeps with his mother.

Apocalypse Now is a non-didactic film that takes no clear moral or political stand on the Vietnam War. Willard returns with two things from his journey. One is a manuscript written by Kurtz. The other is Lance, one of the sailors from the boat. Depending on which of these we take to be the boon, the film can be understood as either pro-war or anti-war, an ambiguity that reflects the different positions taken on the war by Milius and Coppola.

Milius believed the decision to go to war in Vietnam was a mistake, but that once in the war, the United States should have done whatever was necessary to win, quickly and decisively. Conrad's narrator in "Heart of Darkness," Milius has argued, failed to recognize Kurtz's wisdom. For Milius, Kurtz is crazy, but he is also telling the truth. The wisdom that Willard is bringing back with him, the wisdom that will regenerate society, is the message of Kurtz's manuscript: "Drop the bomb. Exterminate them all."

Coppola opposed the war. In his view the Vietnam War had descended into primitivism and savagery, and America had become the mirror image of what it was supposed to be against. By killing Kurtz, Willard takes his place, becomes the new Kurtz and the leader of Kurtz's Montagnard army. Willard lays down his weapon at the end, and the Montagnards do the same. Willard is leading them, Coppola says, into a future without war. In this interpretation, the boon is Lance. Lance has given in to the primitivism and savagery represented by Kurtz, but Willard pulls Lance away from savagery and brings him home, symbolically ending the war.

Initial reviews of *Apocalypse Now* were mixed. Critic Stanley Kauffmann hailed the film as the ultimate Vietnam War movie. The film won praise for its cinematography and for individual scenes, especially the helicopter assault (acclaimed as one of the greatest battle scenes ever filmed). Some critics, however, charged that the film lacked well-defined characters; critics especially disliked the performances of Sheen and Brando. Others criticized the film for

its self-contradiction and political emptiness. Almost all regarded as a failure Coppola's attempt to use myth and allegory.

Whatever the initial critical reaction, the film's reputation has grown as the years have passed. In 2007 the American Film Institute listed *Apocalypse Now* among the 100 greatest American films ever made. —DONALD M. WHALEY

References

Tony Chiu, "Coppola's Cinematic Apocalypse Is Finally at Hand," in *Francis Ford Coppola: Interviews*, ed. Gene D. Phillips and Rodney Hill (Jackson: University Press of Mississippi, 2004); Francis Ford Coppola, Introduction to *Apocalypse Now Redux: The Screenplay*, by John Milius and Francis Ford Coppola (New York: Hyperion, 2000); John Milius, "A Soldier's Tale," in *Rolling Stone: The Seventies*, ed. Ashley Kahn, Holly George-Warren, and Shawn Dahl (Boston: Little-Brown, 1998); Frank P. Tomasulo, "The Politics of Ambivalence: *Apocalypse Now*

Apocalypse Now.

as Prowar and Antiwar Film," in *From Hanoi to Hollywood: The Vietnam War in American Film*, ed. Linda Dittmar and Gene Michaud (New Brunswick, NJ: Rutgers University Press, 1990); Donald M. Whaley, "Adaptation Studies and the History of Ideas: The Case of *Apocalypse Now*," in *The Literature/Film Reader: Issues of Adaptation*, ed. Peter Lev and James M. Welsh (Lanham, MD: Scarecrow Press, 2007).

APOCALYPSE NOW REDUX (2001)

This expanded version of FRANCIS COPPOLA's Vietnam War epic includes fifty-three minutes that had been cut from the original film, bringing the new running time to a total of three hours and seventeen minutes. Completed by Coppola and his close associates WALTER MURCH, VITTORIO STORARO, and Kim Aubry in the fall of 2000, the reedit includes an expansion of the Air Cavalry sequence (with ROBERT DUVALL as Capt. Kilgore), as well as three entire sequences that had been deleted from the 1979 cut: a second segment involving the Playboy Bunnies; a "French plantation" sequence, featuring Aurore Clément and the late Christian Marquand; and a scene with Willard (MARTIN SHEEN) confined to a metal container, where Kurtz (MARLON BRANDO) lucidly reads him passages from *Time* magazine's coverage of the war.

Most of the cuts that were made in the 1979 version came about after an early screening for distributors in Japan, where the film came across as being too strange and surreal. Coppola explains that, in response to the distributors' reactions to the film, "We pretty much stripped out some of the surreal elements . . . we made it much more a kind of forward, linear movie, more like a war movie of that time. . . . We decided that we had to shorten it and make it more normal if we were going to save our skins."

According to Coppola's longtime friend and associate, GEORGE LUCAS: "Francis works in a very intuitive way; so he . . . just likes it to flow. And whenever you do that, you end up with a problem, of having a film at times that is way too long, and a film that doesn't have a really strong narrative line in it [to] keep the audience hooked in."

After the original 1979 release, Coppola revisited the film over the years and found *APOCALYPSE NOW* to be somewhat less strange than he had initially thought; so he began to toy with the idea of restoring some of the deleted scenes. Walter Murch recalls: "Francis and I had long talked about the possibility of going back and retrieving many scenes that we just didn't quite have the nerve to include in the original release. Perhaps it was a conservative streak, but there was real concern in 1979 that audiences weren't going to put up with the amount of material in the original script." Thus, the director characterizes *Apocalypse Now Redux* as "The real picture as it might have been," had he not been discouraged by that group of distributors in 1979. As for the diminishing strangeness of the picture, Coppola points out that sometimes "the far-out art of the past becomes the wallpaper of the future."

In the late 1990s, Paramount's plans for a new DVD release of *Apocalypse Now* gave Coppola and his Zoetrope company the opportunity to consider an expanded version of the film. Kim Aubry explains, "We wanted to be closely involved because we had seen what had been done in various DVD releases up to that point, and didn't like the results."

Once Aubry had located all the image and audio elements, Murch reviewed the original negative and found twelve new sections that were complete enough to be considered for inclusion; that number was narrowed down to eight. According to Aubry, the added scenes were selected based on "the strength of the performances, and if the scenes had been fully shot and covered."

"It was not only a matter of addition," Murch noted, "but of restructuring, and sometimes placing certain scenes at different points. The additions also clarify some points, as when Clean, played by LAURENCE FISHBURNE, is killed. In the original, we never see him buried. Now, we do, at the French plantation."

Although the restoration and expansion was intended initially only for DVD release, it soon became clear to Coppola that there should be a theatrical release. Cinematographer Vittorio Storaro was called in from Rome to examine the negative, and he determined that the image had degraded to an unacceptable extent. He argued that only a Technicolor-style dye-transfer process would suffice to restore and preserve the rich color scheme of the film. According to Storaro, "It was essential that we were able to restore not only all the colors to full saturation, but that we achieved pure blacks and pure whites. True tones are degraded by one percent per year. Only dye-transfer prints remain intact and pristine through time."

Most notable among all the changes reflected in *Apocalypse Now Redux* are those affecting four sequences in particular: the Air Cavalry section, an additional scene with the Playboy Bunnies, the French plantation, and Kurtz's interactions with Willard.

According to Coppola, the beginning and ending of the Air Cavalry segment were cut largely for the sake of pacing. *Apocalypse Now Redux* restores a short introduction of Capt. Kilgore (Robert Duvall) as he and his men arrive by helicopter, preceding Coppola's own brief appearance as the documentary filmmaker. (Incidentally, joining Coppola in that cameo are DEAN TAVOULARIS and Vittorio Storaro.)

A more dramatically significant addition comes at the end of the Air Cavalry segment, as Willard steals one of Kilgore's surfboards and brings it onto the boat for Lance (SAM BOTTOMS). In a subsequent added scene, a patrol helicopter flies overhead blaring a taped message from Kilgore, urging Willard to return the board. Coppola has said of the Air Cavalry scenes: "These scenes began to be so surreal to me that I think the whole direction of *Apocalypse Now* began to change, and it began to go from a so-called war film into this 'journey into the surreal.'"

In a sequence completely excised from the original version of the film, Willard and company encounter the Playboy Bunnies a second time, finding their helicopter stranded without fuel in a rainstorm at a medevac camp. These scenes in *Apocalypse Now Redux* occur between Willard's revisiting Kurtz's dossier while continuing upriver and the sampan massacre. GENE D. PHILLIPS points out that "the exteriors for the second bunny scene were shot during the torrential rains that caused the production to be shut down in 1976" (169). (Coppola admits that, at this point in the production, he kept thinking up many possible new scenes, often inspired by "HEART OF DARKNESS," partly as a way of deferring the film's ending, which he still did not have scripted.)

As the Bunny sequence begins, when Willard realizes that the Playboy helicopter needs fuel, he barters with the Bunnies' agent (Bill Graham), trading some fuel from the boat in exchange for giving the men some time alone with the Bunnies. There were supposed to be three vignettes, but Coppola only shot two before the typhoon necessitated that filming be stopped. Coppola explained, "Even though we hadn't shot the entire scene . . . I made the decision to go for it and to try to put this sequence together as best I could, with the footage I had."

One of the two completed scenes involves an encounter between Chef (FREDERIC FORREST) and a former "Playmate of the Year" (Colleen Camp), in which he awkwardly and tragicomically tries to recreate her centerfold pose. The other features a more bittersweet interlude between Lance and another Playmate (Cindy Wood). Here Coppola explores a parallel that he saw between the exploitation of young men (by sending them off to what he calls "the obscenity of war") and the sexual exploitation of young women. A third scene, never shot, was to have yet another Playmate doing a tarot reading of Willard's future, symbolically laying out the last third of the movie. In *Variety,* Todd McCarthy calls the restored Playmates scene a "passage striking for its utter newness as well as for its exceedingly sad, poignant tone."

By far the most extensive addition to *Apocalypse Now Redux* (at roughly twenty-four minutes in length) is a sequence in which Willard and the patrol boat crew stop off at a French plantation that seems to emerge from the fog, as though from a dream. Coppola explained: "My idea was that as they progressed up the river, they were like going back more and more in time in a funny kind of way, that we were revisiting the history of Vietnam in reverse, and the first stop was in the '50s . . . we now are with the French. That was what I was looking for in the French plantation. It was a kind of ghostly afterview of something—almost like they talk about the light from the stars: we see it, but the star's already dead."

Upon going ashore at the plantation, the first order of business for Willard and

the crew is to give the fallen "Mr. Clean" a military burial, in a ceremony that combines French and American traditions. Afterward they all join their hosts for a full dinner of French cuisine, a meal that is dominated by talk of history and politics. (Incidentally, the dinner scene features brief appearances by Coppola's two sons, Gio and Roman, with the latter reciting a poem by Baudelaire.)

In its original, 1979 cut, the dinner scene featured the following voiceover by Willard (which still exists in the documentary, *HEARTS OF DARKNESS: A FILM-MAKER'S APOCALYPSE*): "It was like having dinner with a family of ghosts. There were still a few hundred of them left on plantations all over Vietnam, trying to keep themselves convinced that it was still 1950. They weren't French anymore, and they'd never be Vietnamese. They were floating loose in history without a country. They were hanging on by their fingernails, but so were we; we just had more fingernails in it." For the expanded version, Walter Murch reedited the entire sequence from scratch, a fact that explains why the voiceover is no longer present.

Dinner is followed by a romantic scene, conceived as a kind of "break" in the film, in which Willard and the young widow Roxanne (Aurore Clément) smoke an opium pipe and prepare to make love. The sequence ends with Roxanne's musings on Willard's dual nature, as both someone who kills and someone who loves, as she is about to join him in bed.

Although Coppola has offered a few reasons for the removal of the French plantation scenes from the original release, perhaps the most practical explanation is that the segment is a self-contained chunk that could be deleted wholesale, trimming almost twenty-four minutes from the film's overlong running time. Add to that the perceived didacticism of the dinner scene, which in 1979 seemed too much like a history lesson.

Another arguably didactic (although thoroughly engaging) scene deleted from the original release but restored here occurs after Willard has reached Kurtz's compound in Cambodia. Held captive in a cramped, metal container, Willard is observed through narrow openings, first by a crowd of children and then by Kurtz. Then Kurtz opens the door of the container, allowing more light to enter, and reads aloud from *Time* magazine's coverage of the war, which offers an absurdly optimistic view of the situation in Vietnam.

This unscripted performance, in which Brando reads actual articles from *Time*, reflects an overall approach of improvisation that Coppola felt he had to take with the veteran actor. Coppola describes Brando (with whom he had worked on *THE GODFATHER*) in this way: "A man of incredible intellect . . . one of the few really brilliant men I've ever met. But he has a lot of techniques to sabotage the situation. . . . I don't know why, but maybe he feels that if he can break up and disrupt everything, then it should be [disrupted]."

In the case of the *Time* magazine scene, at least, the improvisational approach seems to have paid off. The scene fits particularly well with what Coppola terms an "anti-lie" theme of the film (and its source novella): "If the government, if the publications, if people lie about things, then there can be no morality; because the lie does away with the natural check that would happen. If people really had to deal with what the truth was, they wouldn't permit it. So governments over history, organs of state and what have you, are often lying, and really that's the theme of 'Heart of Darkness.' He has the line, I think, where he says something like, 'I hate the stench of a lie.'"

One major scene not restored in *Apocalypse Now Redux* is the demolition of Kurtz's jungle lair. "We shot it because we had to destroy it," Coppola explains. "So I said, 'Let's blow it up and take shots of it.'" Coppola did initially include some of the scene as "mere decorative backdrop to the closing credits," but after a preview screening he realized that audiences might misinterpret these shots as an alternate ending. Finally, he removed the images, and now the closing credits play over a black screen. Coppola adds that he "did not want to send the message that the film ends in destruction and death."

Apocalypse Now Redux premiered in May 2001, at the CANNES INTERNATIONAL FILM FESTIVAL, where in 1979 the original version won the Palme d'Or. Miramax distributed the film theatrically in the United States, but Paramount retained video, DVD, and television rights (where the bulk of the profits lie with any motion picture). According to former Miramax executive Harvey Weinstein, the company knew that taking on the theatrical distribution was a financial risk (and indeed, it ultimately grossed only $4.61 million at the domestic box office). "We can't make any money on it," Weinstein said. "We may lose money on it. But this is what all the Miramaxes of the world should be doing."

Writing in *Variety*, Todd McCarthy found that, "Despite the new running time of nearly 3¼ hours, 'Apocalypse Now Redux' still goes by quickly. . . . It retains its brilliance and its mysteries. . . . It's a richer experience now, still breathtaking at times and more gratifying."—RODNEY HILL

References

Jonathan Bing, "'Apocalypse' Again in New York: Coppola Joins Cast Members for 'Redux,'" *Variety*, July 25, 2001; *Hearts of Darkness: A Filmmaker's Apocalypse*, dir. Fax Bahr, George Hickenlooper, and Eleanor Coppola (documentary footage) (American Zoetrope and Cineplex-Odeon Films, 1991); *Indochina Chronology* 20, no. 2 (April–June 2001): 32; Robert Koehler, "Apocalypse New: Coppola's Seminal Vietnam Pic Returns to Cannes," *Variety*, May 2, 2001; Todd McCarthy, "Apocalypse Now Redux," *Variety*, May 13, 2001; Michael Ondaatje, *The Conversations: Walter Murch and the Art of Editing Film* (New York: Knopf, 2002); Gene D. Phillips, *Godfather: The Intimate Francis Ford Coppola* (Lexington: University of Kentucky Press, 2004).

ASTAIRE, FRED (1899–1987)

Iconic American actor, singer, and luminous dancer who played the lead role of Finian McLonergan in *FINIAN'S RAINBOW* (1968). Astaire left his graceful mark on the Hollywood musical in such films as *Easter Parade* (1948) and *The Band Wagon* (1953). He wanted his musical numbers to be an extension of the plot, not a mere interruption of the story, as usually was the case with the numbers in "backstage musicals." Moreover, his dance numbers were more intimate and less spectacular than was common in movie musicals. Astaire insisted that the camera stay on the principal dancers throughout the number and photograph them in full figure. In this way they would not get lost among the chorus and decor. Indeed, by integrating the movement of the dancers with that of the camera, Astaire was able to accomplish a blend of sight and sound that influenced even nonmusical films. In short, his musical numbers were characterized by restraint and simple eloquence.

FRANCIS COPPOLA agreed to direct *Finian's Rainbow* because it afforded him the opportunity of directing one of the screen's legendary hoofers, Fred Astaire. But what finally clinched the deal for Coppola was the score: lyricist E. Y. HARBURG and composer Burton Lane had served up in *Rainbow* a score that boasted songs like "Old Devil Moon" and "If This Isn't Love." Several of these songs had become standards, and they went a long way in explaining why the musical had racked up 725 performances on Broadway.

Astaire biographer Joseph Epstein writes that Astaire's musicals were often freighted with "daft stories which don't bear thinking about." *Finian's Rainbow* is no exception. Coppola was appalled when he read the "cockamamie" screenplay. The creaky plot of the twenty-five-year-old formula musical, which was set in a never-never-land, was far-fetched at best.

Coppola did his best to turn out a respectable movie musical within the limitations of the stringent budget and tight schedule imposed on him—for what was supposed to be a large-scale musical. To make matters worse, Coppola was dissatisfied with the choreography supplied by Hermes Pan. A veteran of vintage Astaire musicals like *Blue Skies* (1946), Pan had been hired at Astaire's behest. Simply put, Coppola found Pan's dance routines too sophisticated for a "folksy" musical filled with simple, good-hearted rustics like *Finian's Rainbow*. Coppola accordingly fired Pan and in desperation was forced to stage most of the musical numbers himself, though he had no training as a dance director.

Be that as it may, the bulk of the production numbers were filmed without any set choreography once Pan had walked off the picture. Coppola would play back the music for a dance routine and instruct the dancers from behind the camera. Astaire, who was accustomed to plotting out each dance routine in meticulous detail with a choreographer, had to make do with Coppola telling him, "We'll put the camera here; Fred, go over there and do something. Then let's have two girls block in this space." Astaire, old trouper that he was, would then oblige with a little impromptu routine.

Coppola would shoot about eight takes of a musical number and have Astaire and the other dancers improvise their way through the number each time, so that each take varied somewhat from all the others. During editing, Coppola pasted together the best bits from each take into the final version of the number.

Withal, *Finian's Rainbow* was being groomed by the studio brass to be a road show attraction, with reserved-seat performances at advanced prices, complete with an overture and an intermission. The studio even opted to blow up the film to 70 mm for the road show engagements; and the wide-screen ratio dictated that the top and the bottom of the frame had to be cropped, thereby cropping off the feet of Astaire and the other dancers while they were dancing. When the film was processed in 70 mm, Coppola moaned, "no one bothered to check the top and bottom of the frame."

David Thomson opines that *Finian's Rainbow* is a "mediocre" musical which nevertheless pays "respectful, nostalgic tribute to Astaire's greatness." At its best, *Rainbow* is an amiable if lightweight musical. Nevertheless, Fred Astaire understandably termed *Finian's Rainbow* overall the biggest disappointment of his long career. Not surprisingly, it was the sixty-eight-year-old Astaire's last appearance as a lead in a musical.—GENE D. PHILLIPS

References

Jean-Paul Chaillet and Elizabeth Vincent, *Francis Ford Coppola*, trans. Denise Jacobs (New York: St. Martin's Press, 1984); Joseph Epstein, *Fred Astaire* (New Haven, CT: Yale University Press, 2008); David Thomson, *The New Biographical Dictionary of Film* (New York: Knopf, 2004).

ASTORIA STUDIOS, QUEENS, NEW YORK

Further evidence that FRANCIS COPPOLA should be regarded as a premiere cineaste was provided when he decided to restore Astoria Studios to working order for the filming of *THE COTTON CLUB* in 1983. The Astoria, located at 34–31 Thirty-fifth Street in the borough of Queens, fell vacant in 1972, though it had been utilized by other directors besides Coppola after 1972: Sidney Lumet made *The Wiz* there in 1977, with Michael Jackson and Diana Ross, for example, and *The Verdict* in 1982 with Paul Newman and James Mason, and Bob Fosse made *All That Jazz* there in 1979. "The 'return' of feature-film production to New York is no accident," historian Richard Koszarski wrote in his book *The Astoria Studio and Its Fabulous Films* (1983): "The movies are only coming home." In fact, over 100 silent films had been produced there, showcasing the talents of Lillian Gish, Gloria Swanson, Clara Bow, Rudolph Valentino, Paul Robeson, Claudette Colbert, Gary Cooper, W. C. Fields, and the Marx Brothers, among others. In fact, the first two Marx Brothers films were shot at the Astoria facility: *The Cocoanuts* (1929) and *Animal Crackers* (1930). During World War II, the United States Army Signal Corps took over the facility and used it until 1971 to make training films. The old Astoria facility was given new life as the Kaufman-Astoria Studios Motion Picture and Television complex, comprising fifteen buildings on a ten-acre site, with a 27,000-square-foot main stage and seven additional film and television stages, along with "service facilities ranging from makeup, wardrobe, and dressing rooms to carpentry and art shops and screening rooms and a remodeled commissary, and a full equipped sound and music recording stage large enough to hold a full orchestra," according to *New York Times* reporter Leslie Bennetts. "I think it is the key to film making in New York," said investor Alan King, who moved his own company's production offices from Manhattan to Queens. "New York was always used as a back lot; people came here, shot their locations and went back to California to finish their pictures. That move alone adds a lot of expense to a picture. But the Astoria studio will be a complete service. You'll do all your preproduction work, everything from that base," adding, "It used to cost you 10 to 20 percent more to shoot in New York. That won't be true any more. We're putting in the highest state-of-the-art equipment, and I think we'll get a big piece of the action." In 1983, Rochelle Slovin, executive director of the Astoria Motion Picture and Television Foundation, announced that The Museum of Motion Pictures and Television at Astoria was scheduled to open in the winter of 1985–1986. This then became the American Museum of the Moving Image, which opened on September 10, 1988, in what had been the East Coast offices of Paramount Pictures and became the first American museum devoted to the history, art, and technology of film and video. —JAMES M. WELSH

References

Leslie Bennetts, "Astoria Studio Revives Film Era in New York," *New York Times*, August 3, 1983; Richard Koszarski, *The Astoria Studio and Its Fabulous Films* (New York: Dover Publications, 1983).

BALLHAUS, MICHAEL (1935–)

Award-winning German cinematographer, born in Berlin, August 5, 1935, the son of actors Oskar Ballhaus and Lenna Huter. Learning his craft with Max Ophüls, Ballhaus went to work as an assistant television cameraman and was promoted to director of photography by 1960; he then found work with several directors of The New German Cinema (*Das neue Kino*), especially R. W. Fassbinder, Schlöndorff, and Geissendörfer. Moving to the United States, Ballhaus worked on several pictures with Martin Scorsese, including *GoodFellas* (1990), for which he won the Los Angeles Film Critics' Award, and with FRANCIS COPPOLA on *BRAM STOKER'S DRACULA.*—James M. Welsh

BASS, RONALD JAY (1942–)

Screenwriter who worked with Coppola adapting NICHOLAS PROFFITT's 1983 novel *GARDENS OF STONE* to the screen. Several reviewers blamed Bass directly for the film's shortcomings. "In adapting the Proffitt novel," Vincent Canby wrote for the *New York Times*, for example, "Ronald Bass hasn't written a screenplay but a collection of synopses for three or four films. In addition to the relationship between Clell [Hazard, the JAMES CAAN character] and Jackie Willow [the D. B. SWEENEY character who wants to serve in Vietnam, not in THE OLD GUARD at Arlington National Cemetery],

the film is also about Clell's affair with an antiwar newspaper reporter [ANJELICA HUSTON], and Jackie's romance with the daughter [MARY STUART MASTERSON] of a colonel who doesn't approve of her alliance with an enlisted man." Canby considered it a "mystery why Mr. Coppola, one of the most efficient writers in Hollywood, came to direct such a screenplay, one that's alternately lame and utterly confusing. Possibly he tried to improve things, but the movie builds to no point. It unravels." Writing for *The Washington Post Weekend*, Desson Howe seemed to agree with Canby, but blamed the director rather than the writer: "James Earl Jones, James Caan, and D. B. Sweeney turn in superior performances in *Gardens of Stone*, but it's all for naught. FRANCIS COPPOLA sabotages their efforts with a handsome but fragmentary film that can't decide which story to tell." For his *Washington Post* review, Hal Hinson wrote that the film was "written for the screen [by Ronald Bass, who also wrote *Black Widow*] in a flatfooted comic-book style, and about halfway through the whole thing collapses in a heap," but added, helpfully, that "for a while at least, it's eminently watchable." In his *Newsweek* review, David Ansen complained that "Ronald Bass's adaptation of Nicholas Proffitt's novel sets up the relationships, then doesn't seem to know what to do with them." Ronald Jay Bass was born in Los Angeles on March 26, 1942, and educated at

Stanford, Yale, and Harvard, where he graduated with a degree in law in 1967. He went on to become a novelist, screenwriter, and film producer, and won an Academy Award for Best Original Screenplay for *Rain Man* in 1988. His screenwriting credits include *Black Widow* (1987), *Dangerous Minds* (1995), *What Dreams May Come* (1998), and dozens of other pictures.—JAMES M. WELSH

References

David Ansen, "Vietnam, Seen from the Grave," *Newsweek*, May 8, 1987; Vincent Canby, "Film: 'Gardens of Stone' Portrays Vietnam Era," *New York Times*, May 8, 1987, C12; Hal Hinson, "'Gardens' Random Harvest," *Washington Post*, May 8, 1987, D1, D10; Desson Howe, "Lines of Lead in 'Gardens of Stone,'" *Washington Post Weekend*, May 8, 1987, 25.

BECK, JULIAN (1925–1985)

The poet, abstract expressionist painter, theatre director, designer, and stage and screen actor Julian Beck was born in the Washington Heights area of Manhattan on May 31, 1925, the son of Irving Beck and Mabel Lucille (Blum). After briefly attending Yale University and the College of the City of New York, he became an abstract expressionist painter during the 1940s, but his career took an important turn in 1943 after he met Judith Malina, who became his open-marriage partner. Beck and Malina founded the Living Theatre in 1947, experimenting first with naturalism, then with anarchism in theatre. Their experimental theatre troupe became influential during the late 1950s and on into the 1960s. As committed political activists, Beck and Malina's acts of civil disobedience led to arrests and jail terms, both at home and abroad. After their Greenwich Village theatre was closed down by the IRS in 1974, the Living Theatre continued to perform in cities abroad to high acclaim. In 1984 the troupe returned to New York City for the first time in ten years to present *The Archaeology of Sleep*. Beck's reward, after having alienated Benedict Nightingale, theatre critic for the *New Statesman* and contributor for the *New York Times*, was to be cast as Sol Weinstein in *THE COTTON CLUB* (1984), linking Coppola to a theatrical legend. The Living Theatre received many awards, including early on the Lola D'Annunzio, 1959; the Obie, 1960; and, in Paris, the Grand Prix of the Théâtre des Nations, 1961. Beck's last film role was as the evil Reverend Henry Kane in *Poltergeist II*, released in 1986. Beck was planning to reopen the Living Theatre in New York when he succumbed to cancer at Mount Sinai Hospital in New York on September 14, 1985.—JAMES M. WELSH

THE BELLBOY AND THE PLAYGIRLS (1962)

DIRECTOR: Fritz Umgelter and Francis Ford Coppola. SCREENPLAY: Fritz Umgelter and Francis Ford Coppola. PRODUCER: Wolfgang Hartwig. PHOTOGRAPHY (color): Jack Hill. EDITING: Jack Hill. ORIGINAL MUSIC: Klaus Ogermann. ART DIRECTION: Albert Locatelli.

CAST: Karen Dor (Dinah), Don Kenney (George), Willie Fritsch (Gregor), June Wilkinson (Madame Whimplepoole).

RUNNING TIME: 94 minutes. Color and B&W.

After completing *TONIGHT FOR SURE*, Coppola was commissioned to work on another skin flick. A producer had bought the American distribution rights to a 1958 German picture entitled *Mit Eva Fing Die Sünde* (*Sin Began with Eve*), which had already been dubbed into English. He commissioned Coppola to interpolate some nudie footage in color into the black-and-white film. The final film was retitled *The Bellboy and the Playgirls*. Since Coppola's color footage is easily identifiable in the finished film, it is possible to state that the five Coppola sequences add up to nearly fifty minutes of screen time, thereby accounting for about half of the total ninety-four-minute running time of the finished product.

The plot of the German portions of the present film concerns Dinah (Karen Dor), a young actress who refuses to do a seduction scene during rehearsals for a stage play. She claims that she is too "old-fashioned" to appear in such a compromising scene on stage before a live audience. Gregor, the director (Willie Fritsch), endeavors to loosen her up and take away her inhibitions by telling her randy stories about sexual relations throughout the centuries. There is a flashback to ancient Greece in which a young maiden is advised by a Don Juan with a wink, "Men believe that wives are for procreation and mistresses are for recreation." Gregor eventually coaxes Dinah into going through with the love scene in the play.

Into the German film's tedious plot Coppola inserted a naughty storyline about George (Don Kenney), the bellboy from the Happy Holiday Hotel next door to the theatre. George, addressing the camera, informs the viewer that he is taking a correspondence course in how to be popular with women. He is observing the rehearsals of Gregor's play from the catwalk in the rafters above the stage in order to learn how the young man in the play ingratiates himself with his unwilling girlfriend. He then goes back to the hotel and seeks to gain entrance to room 299—which is occupied by Madame Whimplepoole (June Wilkinson) and her Pink Lace Girls—in order to make time with the girls.

Masquerading as a telephone repair man, he attempts to install surveillance equipment in room 299 (shades of Coppola's later feature THE CONVERSATION). At one point the girls, who are fed up with George's

obsession with them, finally manage to discourage George's attentions by luring him to participate in a game of strip poker—after they have stacked the deck against him. So it is George who loses his clothes. He flees from room 299 in his shorts after wrapping himself in a window curtain.

At the fade-out the chastened George is watching the lovemaking on the theatre stage below as he sits once more in the rafters. Once again addressing the camera, he says that he is aware that he has failed to become a Lothario—for now at least—but he is going to continue his correspondence course in how to be popular with women.

Coppola provides plenty of door slamming and misunderstandings, after the manner of old-fashioned French farce, for his segments of the movie. In any event, it is not the stag movie its title seems to suggest. In fact, by today's standards, the film has no more nudity than an R-rated commercial film is allowed.

Coppola does not apologize for his exploitation films. "It was the only way for me to work with a camera and actually make a movie," he explains. He was still officially a student at the UCLA film school, and he was severely criticized by his classmates "for deciding to go into exploitation films," as he puts it. "I was called a cop-out because I was willing to compromise." —GENE D. PHILLIPS

References

Jean-Paul Chaillet and Elizabeth Vincent, *Francis Ford Coppola*, trans. Diane Jacobs (New York: St. Martin's Press, 1984); Jon Lewis, *Whom God Wishes to Destroy: Francis Ford Coppola and the New Hollywood* (Durham, NC: Duke University Press, 1997).

BILL, TONY (1940–)
A very adaptable actor, producer, and director who played Raef for FRANCIS

COPPOLA in *YOU'RE A BIG BOY NOW* (1966). Born in San Diego, California, on August 23, 1940, and college educated at Notre Dame (earning BA and MA degrees), Bill made his acting debut in *Come Blow Your Horn* in 1963, playing Frank Sinatra's younger brother. His acting career then led to his becoming a creative coproducer of *The Sting* at Universal in 1973 and then briefly on the *Taxi Driver* project, partnered with Julia and Michael Phillips. In 1980 he reinvented himself as director of the coming-of-age film *My Bodyguard,* followed by other directing assignments, such as *Six Weeks* (1982) and *Crazy People* (1990). —JAMES M. WELSH

BISKIND, PETER (1938?–)

Historian of the "new" Hollywood and author of *Easy Riders, Raging Bulls* (1998) and *Down and Dirty Pictures* (2004), Biskind authored *The Godfather Companion,* published by HarperCollins in 1990. After serving as editor-in-chief of *American Film* magazine for the American Film Institute, Biskind, an industry "insider," also served as executive editor of *Premiere* magazine. *The Godfather Companion* was praised by *Variety* (January 28, 1991) for Biskind's "exhaustive research and documentation," and, despite some "small errors" caused by Biskind's having to rely on scripts while writing the last part of the book on *Godfather III,* declared the book to be "irresistible fun." The reviewer added that "for hardcore fans, Biskind's effort is an impossible offer to refuse." Surprisingly, Nick Browne's Cambridge University Press casebook, *Francis Ford Coppola's "The Godfather" Trilogy,* published ten years later in 2000, fails to list Peter Biskind in the index. Biskind's most recent book, *Star: How Warren Beatty Seduced America* (2010) claims that the actor seduced over 12,000 women during the course of his astonishing career.—JAMES M. WELSH

BLACK, KAREN (1942–)

Actress who played the role of Amy in Coppola's *YOU'RE A BIG BOY NOW* (1966) and also appeared as Myrtle in *THE GREAT GATSBY* (1974), scripted by Coppola, for which she won a Golden Globe Award as Best Supporting Actress. (Although *Variety* lists her year of birth as 1942, other sources indicate 1939.)

Karen Black was a key figure in the "Hollywood Renaissance," appearing in such landmark films as DENNIS HOPPER's *Easy Rider* (1969), Bob Rafelson's *Five Easy Pieces* (1970), John Schlesinger's *Day of the Locust* (1975), and Robert Altman's *Nashville* (1975). Black is also well remembered as the blonde-wigged femme fatale in Alfred Hitchcock's final film, *Family Plot* (1976), and as a woman terrorized by a demonic doll in Dan Curtis's TV movie, *Trilogy of Terror* (1975).

Her work in *Five Easy Pieces* earned Black multiple awards as Best Supporting Actress, from such organizations as the New York Film Critics' Circle, the National Board of Review, and the Golden Globes, as well as an Oscar nomination. Although JACK NICHOLSON's star turn in that film threatens to overshadow all else, critic Andrew Culbertson notes that "Karen Black's performance as the clinging, dim-witted waitress aspiring to be a country singer is as good as any in the film."

The *Variety* review of *You're a Big Boy Now* mentions Black by name and notes that in general Coppola has drawn top-flight performances from his talented cast. Bosley Crowther, writing in the *New York Times,* is less generous in his estimation of most of the film's performances, but he acknowledges that Karen Black does "well enough" in her role as "a nice girl from the library." Roger Ebert saw the film as the first example of a trend that he called "Eros 101," involving young, inexperienced men being seduced by older women—culminating in Mike Nichols's *The Graduate* (1967).

After her career peaked in the 1970s, Karen Black turned more toward the independent sector of the film business, with mixed results. Still, she has worked consistently in the industry, with more than 100 films to her credit. The producers of one such independent feature, *Red Dirt* (2000) have this to say about working with Black: "We were first struck by Karen's boundless positive energy. She is an amazing life force. On the set, she exuded this spirit of free will and selflessness as she traveled from location to location, usually singing along the way."—RODNEY HILL

References

Bosley Crowther, "Growing Pains: You're a Big Boy Now," *New York Times*, March 21, 1967; Andrew Culbertson, "Auspicious Beginnings: Nicholson's Leitmotif in *Five Easy Pieces*," *Bright Lights Film Journal* 57 (August 2007), www.brightlightsfilm.com/57/jack.html; Roger Ebert, "You're a Big Boy Now," *Chicago Sun-Times*, July 17, 1968; "Karen Black," *Variety* Profiles, www.variety.com; *Red Dirt*, official website, www.reddirt.com.

THE BLACK STALLION (1979)

DIRECTOR: Carroll Ballard. SCREENPLAY: Melissa Mathison, Jeanne Rosenberg, and William D. Wittliff. PRODUCERS: Fred Roos and Tom Sternberg. EXECUTIVE PRODUCER: Francis Ford Coppola. CINEMATOGRAPHY: Caleb Deschanel. FILM EDITING: Robert Dalva. ORIGINAL MUSIC: Carmine Coppola. ART DIRECTION: Aurelio Crugnola and Earl G. Preston. ART DEPARTMENT: Maria-Teresa Barbasso (asst. art director), Robert Blackgoat (storyboards), and Kevin Hughes (asst. property manager). ASSISTANT DIRECTOR: Doug Claybourne. SECOND ASST. DIRECTORS: David Earl, Jim Kaufman, and Robert McCart. PRODUCTION MANAGEMENT: Ted Holliday, Ned Kopp, and Alessandro von Norman.
CAST: Kelly Reno (Alec Ramsey), Mickey Rooney (Henry Dailey), Teri Garr (Alec's Mother), Hoyt Axton (Alec's Father), Michael Higgins (Neville). RUNNING TIME: 118 minutes. Technicolor. RELEASED THROUGH: Metro Goldwyn Mayer. NEW YORK CITY PREMIERE: October 13, 1979. U.S. THEATRICAL RELEASE: October 17, 1979. DVD: MGM.

The Black Stallion (1979) is based on the first novel of Walter Farley's book series that began publication in 1941. The series details the adventures of young Alec Ramsey and his Arabian horse, Black. This film version was directed by Carroll Ballard and was adapted by screenwriters MELISSA MATHISON (nominated for an Academy Award for screenwriting, *E.T.: The Extra-Terrestrial*, 1982), Jeanne Rosenberg, and William D. Wittliff. The film stars Kelly Reno as Alec, country-western singer Hoyt Axton, and TERI GARR (*Close Encounters of the Third Kind*; *Oh, God!*) as his father and mother, and Mickey Rooney as the former jockey and horse trainer.

The film garnered an array of nominations and awards for both cast and crew members. Chief among these was a Special Achievement Academy Award, given to Alan Splet for his sound editing. Certainly, in the first part of the film, the combination of CARMINE COPPOLA's music and the scenes of the boy and the horse on the beach create a magical element. Splet's editing creates an even stronger impression in the climactic race in the film. As the final lap is run, the suspense is heightened with the camera staying even with the lead horses and an increasing rhythm of pounding hooves and panting snouts makes the race a physical sensation for the viewer.

Other honors that the film received include Los Angeles Film Critics Awards for Carmine Coppola, Best Music, and Caleb Deschanel, Cinematography, and Academy Award nominations for Mickey Rooney, Best Actor in a Supporting Role, and for Robert Dalva, Editing. These awards emphasize the strongest aspects of the film—its extraordinary poetic beauty and its strongly sentimental storyline.

FRANCIS FORD COPPOLA chose his UCLA classmate Carroll Ballard to direct the film. In the same vein as *The Black Stallion*, Ballard went on to direct the animal-centered *Never Cry Wolf* (1983), a conservation adventure set in Alaska. Following *The Black Stallion*, Coppola executive-produced Akira Kurosawa's *KAGEMUSHA*, Paul Schrader's *Mishima: A Life in Four Chapters*, and many other films.

The opening credits of the film appear in front of blowing sand, which reveals the image of a horse figurine, with an eerie flute-like melody on the soundtrack. This mysterious preface fades into another enigmatic image—the screen is divided between a solid surface across its bottom quarter and rushing movement filling its upper three-quarters. We are uncertain of our perspective, but then the second shot gives a similar but more recognizable view. The camera is anchored on a ship's rail at the extreme right of the frame, and we have the ocean rushing off to the left. These shots combine to set the stage in an environment in which Nature and natural power are dominant, and people are its pawns, as we next see an Arab figure, a woman, and Alec each in single shots on deck, at the mercy of the ship's rocking, rising, and falling to the sea's movement.

Against relative silence, with only the sound of the waves and a simple musical soundtrack, Alec's character is established. He enjoys the wild movement of the ship, leaning out from its extremities on the ship

and over the railing. This way, he catches the sound of arguing and runs to find a wild black stallion, fighting against the restraints of five men and the woman we had seen before on deck. From here, Alec runs to his father's card game to share the news, and we see one of the players place the horse figurine from the credits into the pot. Alec returns to where the stallion has been contained, and they have their first encounter over sugar cubes Alec has brought from the card game.

Later, Alec's father is sharing his winnings from the card game and gives Alec a pocketknife, which will play an essential role, and the horse figurine: "Bucephalus, the magic horse of Alexander the Great," a horse Alexander acquired through a challenge to ride him. That night, the chaos of a shipboard fire results in the stallion jumping into the sea and Alec falling overboard. He finds a rope trailing from the horse, hangs on, and awakens the next morning on a beach, thus beginning the second part of the film.

This portion of the film, running approximately the second twenty minutes, is nearly without speech and contains the mix of beautiful music and natural sights between the boy and the stallion, as mentioned above. The film will forever be marketed and remembered for this stunning part of the film. The rescue of both Alec and the Black, as he has named the horse, from their island segues into Alec back at school, telling his tale at a special welcome-home ceremony. Thus the third section of the film details Alec's readjustment to home life with his mother (Teri Garr), the Black becoming quartered at former-jockey Henry Dailey's (Mickey Rooney) farm, and Alec and Henry's growing relationship. This pairing brings an idyllic sense back into the film, with shots of Alec running and riding the Black as they did on the beach, and as we learn of Henry's past and see his growing idealism about the Black as a champion. This section of the film climaxes with the Black's nighttime track run in the rain for the reporter who can initiate the challenge between the Black and the two legitimate racing contenders. This "test race" is another example of remarkable editing of sound and image, as the sound of the Black's hoof-beats circles the track, and the sound of the pouring rain and the darkness limit our perception. As the run ends, Henry has to cut the mane from Alec's grip, as he has passed out from exhaustion.

After this amazing demonstration and "resurrection," the championship race is on, and the final part of the film, making full use of the audio and visual effects noted above, returns Alec and the Black to their earlier glory, even with the Black being injured and starting the race from a deficit. As they cross the finish line, the camera centers on their shadow, which becomes their shadow once again in the surf, and they burst past the other horses, Alec with arms raised in victory.

The sequel *The Black Stallion Returns* was released in 1983, also starring Reno as Alec Ramsey. The television series *Adventures of the Black Stallion* ran from 1990 to 1993, starring Richard Ian Cox and Mickey Rooney.—THOMAS CLANCY

BOTTOMS, SAM (1955–2008)
Actor Sam Bottoms played surfer-soldier Lance B. Johnson for FRANCIS COPPOLA in *APOCALYPSE NOW* (1979), taking reckless orders from the mad surfer Lt. Col. Bill Kilgore, played by ROBERT DUVALL. In 1987 Coppola would cast him again in *GARDENS OF STONE*. Bottoms was born in Santa Barbara, California, in 1955, the son of sculptor James "Bud" Bottoms. He was "discovered" by director Peter Bogdanovich, who cast him to play a mute, mentally handicapped boy in *The Last Picture Show* (1971), along with his better-known

brother, Timothy Bottoms. He also acted for Clint Eastwood in *The Outlaw Josie Wales* and *Bronco Billy* and appeared more recently in the popular film, *Seabiscuit*. Bottoms died of brain cancer in Los Angeles on December 16, 2008.—JAMES M. WELSH

BRAM STOKER'S DRACULA (1992)

DIRECTOR: Francis Ford Coppola. SCREENPLAY: James V. Hart. PRODUCERS: Francis Ford Coppola, Fred Fuchs, and Charles Mulvehill. PHOTOGRAPHY: Michael Ballhaus, A.S.C. EDITING: Anne Goursaud, Glen Scantlebury, and Nicholas C. Smith. MUSIC: Wojciech Kilar. PRODUCTION DESIGN: Thomas Sanders. ART DIRECTION: Andrew Precht. COSTUME DESIGN: Eiko Ishioka. SECOND UNIT DIRECTOR AND VISUAL EFFECTS: Roman Coppola.

CAST: Gary Oldman (Dracula), Winona Ryder (Mina Murray/Elisabeta), Anthony Hopkins (Van Helsing), Keanu Reeves (Jonathan Harker), Tom Waits (Renfield), Sadie Frost (Lucy Westenra), Richard E. Grant (Jack Seward), Cary Elwes (Arthur Holmwood), Bill Campbell (Quincey Morris).

RUNNING TIME: 130 minutes. Technicolor.

ACADEMY AWARDS: Sound, Costume, Makeup.

DVD: Columbia.

Bram Stoker's ultimate vampire fantasy, *Dracula*, had been adapted to stage and screen many times before FRANCIS COPPOLA considered his adaptation. The first "unofficial" screen version of Stoker's novel was F. W. Murnau's silent classic *Nosferatu*, loosely adapted by Murnau in 1922, changing the European locale from England to the continent and even changing Stoker's Dracula to the Germanic Graf Orlak. Murnau changed the story substantially because he had not obtained the rights to the novel from Stoker's estate. Stoker himself had worked unsuccessfully on a stage adaptation that was simply too long and cumbersome, until it was later reshaped by Hamilton Deane's stage adaptation, set entirely in England. The Deane version toured England in 1926 before opening in London in 1927. The later American stage version was revised by the London-based American journalist John L. Balderston. This version opened on Broadway on October 5, 1927, and was the basis for the 1931 Tod Browning film, starring the forty-six-year-old Hungarian expatriate actor Bela Lugosi (Bela Blasko), whose appearance epitomized the image fabricated by Deane. Other films, such as the one directed by John Badham in 1978, followed the Deane-Balderston stage adaptation.

Although Coppola intended to go back to Stoker's novel, his film was not to be shot on location. His notion of authenticity was to have the characters set in his mythical "Romania" speak in Romanian. The project originated with screenwriter JAMES V. HART, who had worked with Steven Spielberg on the movie *Hook* (1991, loosely adapted from James M. Barrie's *Peter Pan*). Hart's "Dracula: The Untold Story," was a cable television project when actress WINONA RYDER, reading for the role of Mina, was sufficiently impressed by the screenplay to pass it along to Coppola, who then became interested. Coppola's film, claiming to be "*Bram Stoker's Dracula*," begins with a "back story" to explain to how Dracula became Dracula. Beginning in fifteenth-century Romania (though the country as we know it was not founded until 1859), this Gothic fabrication shows Vlad the Impaler (GARY OLDMAN) leaving his castle to do battle with the Turks, but leaving behind his beloved spouse, Elisabeta (Winona Ryder). She is tricked by the Turks into believing that her husband has been killed and in grief and desperation commits suicide by leaping from the castle wall. When Vlad returns home to find his beloved wife

dead, he is then told by an Orthodox priest (ANTHONY HOPKINS) that, as a suicide, she cannot be buried in consecrated ground. Devastated and outraged, he renounces God and the holy church and forms a bizarre pact with the Devil that turns him into the mythic vampire. None of this fanciful and spectacular back story is to be found in the novel, though legend has it that Vlad's wife committed suicide in the way suggested at Castle Dracula. But this back story gives Dracula a context that seriously distorts Bram Stoker's original design, shifting the story from one of Gothic terror to one of Gothic romance. The novel begins with solicitor Jonathan Harker (the memorably anguished KEANU REEVES) being sent on a mission to Transylvania to visit Count Dracula, leaving his betrothed Mina (Winona Ryder) behind in England. In the film, but not in the novel, Mina seems to be Elisabeta reincarnated; not only is the Count attracted to her, therefore, but she seems to have medieval memories of her former marriage to Vlad before he became Dracula. Moreover, the priest, whose ruling concerning Elisabeta's burial drove Vlad to the Devil, seems to be reincarnated as Dr. Abraham Van Helsing (overplayed by Anthony Hopkins, with little restraint), the peculiarly obsessed scientist and metaphysician.

As played by Gary Oldman, Coppola's Dracula has a sense of power and majesty. We next see him hundreds of years later, when Jonathan Harker arrives at his haunted castle in Transylvania, a passage filmed with eerie effectiveness. Made up to look three hundred years old, Oldman's Count arguably recalls Bela Lugosi. Otherwise, however, the visual conception is strikingly original. Harker completes his real estate transaction with the Count but is then imprisoned in Dracula's castle for a month as arrangements are made to transport Dracula and his strange retinue to the ruined Abbey the Count has purchased on

Gary Oldman seduces Winona Ryder in *Bram Stoker's Dracula*.

the outskirts of London. (But why, one wonders, would this Prince of Darkness choose to settle upon consecrated ground?) Left behind, Harker eventually manages to escape via the river to a convent, where he is gradually nursed back to health. Meanwhile, in England, Dracula has seen a photograph of Harker's fiancée, Mina, whom he immediately recognizes as the reincarnated Elisabeta. When he stalks, then seeks her out in London, he appears to her as a much younger man (his youthful appearance is consistent with Stoker's novel), but this shifty devil also appears as a bestial wolfman for the rape of Mina's aristocratic best friend, Lucy. Oldman undergoes eight different changes of makeup in the film.

Coppola's film attempts to be inventive while moving toward multiple excesses, working a rather scrambled metaphor involving extravagant sexual behavior and the exchange of contaminated blood, probably involving a potentially repulsive allusion to the AIDS dilemma. At one point

Van Helsing is seen giving a lecture on vampire bats, diseases of the blood, venereal diseases, and civilization. In the film Van Helsing apparently works in Oxford, and doesn't have to be sent for in Amsterdam. Coppola works in other ways to move the narrative forward in time, as he attempts to show how much of an anachronism Dracula has become in the early twentieth century, dominated by science and technology rather than religion and superstition. Mina uses a typewriter (invented in 1859), for example, to keep her journal. The learned doctors in England use a recording device to keep their notes. Then there are the microscopes that magnify blood platelets and a device for blood transfusion. Some of this technology can be traced to the novel, but by no means all of it. The modern, mechanized world revealed by the film has changed so much that an ancient demon from a more superstitious era seems not only awkward and out of place but a pathetic misfit.

The action is set in 1898 (though the novel was published in 1897), about the time the movies were born, and Coppola sets up a meeting between Vlad and Mina at a Cinematograph, since the age of mechanical reproduction has just begun. This gives Coppola an excuse to indulge in his own enthusiasm for early cinema and the visual flamboyance of film pioneer ABEL GANCE, imitating Gance's shock-cutting techniques and breathtaking camera movements. The film's visual effects, created by second-unit director ROMAN COPPOLA and intentionally avoiding computer-generated images, replicate Gance's pendulum-swing camera work, for example, as the spirit of Dracula speeds up a staircase, then withdraws, just as rapidly. The mysterious passage of Dracula's coffin over the sea vaguely recalls the famous double-tempest sequence of Gance's *Napoleon.* Gance also seems to have inspired matte work and various iris effects Coppola uses throughout the film.

Coppola's cinematographer MICHAEL BALLHAUS began his career in Germany with Rainer Werner Fassbinder and Volker Schlöndorff and would have been well aware of the techniques required for creating Coppola's visual spectacle, which takes precedence over the international cast.

The narrative framework of Stoker's novel is epistolary. The story is told through letters, journal entries by Mina Murray and Jonathan Harker recounting his journey to the Carpathians, and newspaper clippings. In the film, the backstory is narrated by Anthony Hopkins using one peculiar accent, which is later replaced by another, still in the Hopkins voice, which voices over the captain's log of the *Demeter*, the ship that carries Dracula to England. The Hopkins narrator intrudes at other times, giving vampire lore, as when, for example, he says, "Contrary to popular belief, the vampire can move by day, though it is not his natural time, and his powers are weak." The voice is consistently that of Anthony Hopkins but not consistently that of the same character. There is also a comic bluntness about the film's Van Helsing that is not really in keeping with the novel. Hopkins plays him as something more than Stoker's Van Helsing.

The film is governed by a different context than the novel and a whole different logic determines the behavior of the main characters, Dracula and Mina, who are locked into a beauty-and-the-beast relationship that tends to leave Jonathan out of the loop. The film also gets the tone of the novel and of Victorian England wrong by turning Mina's aristocratic friend Lucy into a randy tart. Coppola's version is consistent with the mores of the late twentieth century rather than those of the late nineteenth century. The moral atmosphere of the film may be "wrong," but not at the expense of box office revenue. The compounded complications are astonishing. History has been adapted to legend, a perverse exercise in

mythic biography that has produced a film representation of a fifteenth-century Wallachian *Voivod* (prince) as a mythic vampire, the "son of the devil," notorious for his cruelty, as adapted from history to novelistic fiction to the theatre to cinema, many times over, until "Bram Stoker's Dracula" morphs into Francis Ford Coppola's *Dracula*, telescoping F. W. Murnau's *Nosferatu* (originally plagiarized in 1922 from Stoker's novel) and Bela Lugosi's *Dracula*, shaped for the stage by John Balderson's dramatic adaptation. To even think about discussing the popular culture implications of the Dracula myth and its many permutations one must attempt to do justice to these complications. So what about old-fashioned notions of the "fidelity"? One could argue that too much has disappeared into this intertextual maze. Of course, that is only to be expected in a Hollywood treatment of popular myth and legend that is still encountering intertextual permutations, but aside from the metaphorical-metaphysical tacked-on wrap-around, the film is true in its way to the source novel.—JAMES M. WELSH

BRANDAUER, KLAUS MARIA [KLAUS GEORG STENG] (1943–)

Actor who portrays Carlo, the Tetrocini family patriarch in *TETRO* (2009). Although FRANCIS FORD COPPOLA has admitted that the story of *Tetro* draws from his own experiences, he stops short of calling it "autobiographical." In terms of Brandauer's character, Coppola told *The Hollywood Reporter*: "The father in the film is kind of a monster more in keeping with *Desire Under the Elms* or *Cat on a Hot Tin Roof*. He's more of a mythological Greek tragedy father in competition with his sons. My father was nothing like that."

Brandauer was born in Bad Aussee, Austria, educated in Stuttgart, Germany, at the Academy of Music and Dramatic

Arts. Thereafter, he performed in repertory theatres in Tubingen, Dusseldorf, and elsewhere, before being hired by the respected Burgtheater troupe in Vienna.

After several appearances on French and West German television, Brandauer made his big-screen debut in 1972 in *The Salzburg Connection.* His international screen breakthrough, however, came nearly ten years later, with Istvàn Szàbo's Oscar-winning Hungarian-German coproduction, *Mephisto* (1981), for which Brandauer was named Best Actor at the Cannes Film Festival and nominated for the BAFTA Award for Best Actor. He then gained mainstream exposure opposite Sean Connery in the James Bond movie, *Never Say Never Again* (1983), as the villain Maximilian Largo. Brandauer won the Golden Globe Award and was nominated for an Oscar for his supporting role in Sydney Pollack's *Out of Africa* (1985), starring Meryl Streep and ROBERT REDFORD. In 1990 Brandauer was cast as Dante, the Soviet scientist, along with Ken Russell, J. T. Walsh, James Fox, Roy Scheider, Michelle Pfeiffer, and Sean Connery in the all-star adaptation of John le Carré's *The Russia House,* directed by Fred Schepisi. In 1989 Brandauer directed his first film with himself in the lead, *Georg Elser—Einer aus Deutschland,* about a loner who intends to assassinate Hitler. He made his American television debut in HBO's *Introducing Dorothy Dandridge* (1999), portraying film director Otto Preminger. —RODNEY HILL/JAMES M. WELSH

References

American Zoetrope, *Tetro,* official website, www.tetro.com; Gregg Kilday, "Q & A: Francis Ford Coppola," *Hollywood Reporter,* May 13, 2009, www.hollywoodreporter.com.

BRANDO, MARLON (1924–2004)

Signature "Method" actor who portrayed Don Vito Corleone in *THE GODFATHER* (1972) and Col. Kurtz in *APOCALYPSE NOW* (1979). The appeal of Brando's acting style and of his most enduring characters lies in their complexity and apparent self-contradiction: alternately harsh and kind, selfish and generous; alienated yet sympathetic; inarticulate yet attractive; brutal yet vulnerable; possessing extreme physical power tempered by gentle restraint. These qualities served Brando extremely well in both of his roles for FRANCIS FORD COPPOLA.

Born Marlon Brando, Jr., in Omaha, Nebraska, on April 3, 1924, the actor made his Broadway debut in 1944 but became famous in 1947 for his searing portrayal of Stanley Kowalski in Tennessee Williams's *A Streetcar Named Desire,* under the direction of Elia Kazan. Taking that role to the screen in 1951, Brando was nominated for an Academy Award, and he would later win the Oscar for his portrayal of Terry Malloy in Kazan's film *On the Waterfront* (1954).

As a young man, Marlon Jr. moved to New York and enrolled in the Dramatic Workshop of the New School for Social Research. There, while appearing in the long-running play *I Remember Mama,* Brando studied acting with the noted coach Stella Adler, who chiefly is credited with influencing his technique. Brando adopted the "Method" approach, which emphasizes a character's motivations for actions. Brando said of Adler's influence, "If it hadn't been for Stella, maybe I wouldn't have gotten where I am—she taught me how to read, she taught me to look at art, she taught me to listen to music."

In 1961 Brando starred in and produced *One-Eyed Jacks,* a film that he ultimately directed after a falling out with Stanley Kubrick, who had originally been hired to direct. Brando spent the remainder of the 1960s in a string of commercial failures that somewhat diminished his reputation among critics and audiences.

Marlon Brando as Don Corleone.

In 1972, however, his career bounced back with the role of mafia boss Don Vito Corleone in Francis Ford Coppola's masterpiece, *The Godfather*. Brando was the top choice of both Francis Coppola and novelist Mario Puzo, but Paramount was opposed to the idea. Studio executives demanded that Brando provide a screen test (knowing that he would refuse); but Coppola tricked the actor by pretending that he just needed a makeup check.

In the opinion of *Washington Post* critic Stephen Hunter (writing in 2004), Brando's turn as Don Corleone constituted "the single greatest film performance" in the "single greatest American movie" ever made. Brando won his second Best-Actor Oscar for the role, but he refused to accept it. In a notorious moment that has gone down in Oscar history, Brando sent an actress named Maria Cruz, claiming to be a Native American named Sacheen Littlefeather, to reject the award on his behalf; and "Littlefeather" used the occasion to speak at length in protest of Hollywood's degradation of Native Americans. *Variety* was shocked by Brando's "unforgivable rudeness."

On the heels of Brando's triumph in *The Godfather* came another critically acclaimed role—considered by some to be the definitive performance of Brando's mature career—in Bernardo Bertolucci's *Last Tango in Paris* (1973). The great Brando, it seemed, was back. However, acting in *Last Tango* proved too strenuous for Brando, as he explained in his autobiography: "*Last Tango in Paris* required a lot of emotional arm wrestling with myself, and when it was finished, I decided that I wasn't ever again going to destroy myself emotionally to make a movie."

For his appearance in Francis Coppola's magnum opus, *Apocalypse Now*, Brando demanded a salary of $1 million for three weeks of work, and he showed up on location grossly overweight and woefully unprepared. When Brando arrived for his three weeks of shooting, he had not even read "HEART OF DARKNESS" and thus did not understand the character of Kurtz or his motivations. As producer Fred Roos explained: "The whole company was sitting up on the set around the camera, the crew all poised to go and shoot, and Francis and Marlon would be talking about the character, and whole days would go by. And this was at Marlon's urging, and yet he's getting paid for it."

Coppola became so frustrated with Brando that he told his wife, Eleanor: "What I should do is just shoot for the next three weeks irrationally. If I did an improvisation every day between Marlon Brando and Marty Sheen, would I at that time have more magical [and in a way telling] moments than if I just close down for three weeks and write a structure that then they act? . . . I'm much better off to do an improvisation every day."

Even though *Apocalypse Now* crystallized Brando's notoriety for being extraordinarily difficult, the actor still was able to command top dollar, even for very brief appearances, such as his cameo role in *Superman* (1979); and his ability to earn large sums with relatively little effort led Brando to accept roles purely for the money, with little regard for the quality of the films. He admitted in *Songs My Mother Taught Me*, "I've made stupid movies because I wanted the money."

Brando's last notable film appearances include Andrew Bergman's *The Freshman* (1990), in which Brando offers a comedic variation on Don Corleone; *DON JUAN DE-MARCO*, with Faye Dunaway and Johnny Depp, with Coppola as executive producer; *The Score* (2001), in which he appears alongside ROBERT DE NIRO; and truly one of his most bizarre renditions, as the title character in John Frankenheimer's remake of *The Island of Dr. Moreau* (1996), with Val Kilmer.—RODNEY F. HILL/JAMES M. WELSH

References

Marlon Brando and Robert Lindsey, *Songs My Mother Taught Me* (New York: Random House, 1994); *Hearts of Darkness: A Filmmaker's Apocalypse*, dir. Fax Bahr, George Hickenlooper, and Eleanor Coppola (documentary footage) (American Zoetrope and Cineplex-Odeon Films, 1991); Gene D. Phillips and Rodney Hill, *The Encyclopedia of Stanley Kubrick* (New York: Facts On File, 2002).

BRIDGES, JEFF (1949–)

American actor who starred as PRESTON TUCKER in *TUCKER: THE MAN AND HIS DREAM*. Bridges brilliantly captured the script's upbeat, can-do attitude, according to a very positive *Variety* review (August 3, 1988): "Flashing his charming smile and oozing cocky confidence, his Tucker is inspiring because he won't be depressed or defeated by anything." Still, there was a problem because "the viewer can't claim to know him at all, for nothing resembling a 3-dimensional human being ever emerges." Since the film of Tucker's career presents

so many parallels to Coppola's own career, the story submerges into self-absorbed allegory, and allegorical characters are always, by definition, one-dimensional. Born in Los Angeles on December 4, 1949, the son of actor LLOYD BRIDGES and the younger brother of actor Beau Bridges, he attended University High School and then went to New York City to study acting at the Berghoff Studios. He made his acting debut in his father's television series *Sea Hunt* in 1963 and his feature film acting debut in *Halls of Anger* (1970). His first Academy Award nomination was for Best Supporting Actor for his performance in *The Last Picture Show* (1971), directed by Peter Bogdanovich. A

Jeff Bridges as Preston Tucker.

second Oscar nomination for Best Supporting Actor came in 1974 for his performance in Michael Cimino's *Thunderbolt and Lightfoot*. A third Oscar nomination came for his performance as an alien in the film *Starman*. He also performed for Michael Cimino in *Heaven's Gate* (1980), for John Huston in *Fat City* (1972), and for Robert Benton's debut film as director, *Bad Company* (1972). Major roles during the 1990s included *The Fisher King* (1991), Walter Hill's *Wild Bill* (1995), Ridley Scott's sea adventure, *White Squall* (1996), and his iconic performance for the Coen Brothers' cult picture *The Big Lebowski* (1997), followed by the political thriller *Arlington Road* (1999). In 2000 Bridges earned an Oscar nomination for his portrayal of Jackson Evans, the president of the United States in *The Contender*. In 2010 Jeff Bridges won several critics awards, the Golden Globe, and the Academy Award for Best Actor for his career-topping portrayal of an alcoholic country & western singer in the film *Crazy Heart* (2009).—JAMES M. WELSH

BRIDGES, LLOYD VERNET, JR. (1913–1998)

American actor who plays Michigan senator Homer Ferguson, known as "the senator from Detroit" because of his ties to the automobile industry, who, in *TUCKER: THE MAN AND HIS DREAM* (1988), triggers investigations of the entrepreneur Preston Tucker by the Securities and Exchange Commission and by the Internal Revenue Service, apparently intending to ruin the man. Lloyd Bridges was born in San Leandro, California, on January 15, 1913, and educated at Petaluma High School and UCLA. His first role on Broadway came in 1939, in Shakespeare's *Othello*. After serving in the Coast Guard, Bridges eventually became a contract player for Columbia Pictures. His movie debut was in *The Lone Wolf Takes a Chance* (1941). His breakthrough roles came later in *Home of the Brave* (1949)

and as Gary Cooper's opportunistic deputy in *High Noon* (1952). *New York Times* reviewer Janet Maslin called his cameo appearance in FRANCIS COPPOLA's *Tucker: The Man and His Dream* as "the Senator who spearheads the auto industry's anti-Tucker campaign" an "inspired bit of casting," because his son, JEFF BRIDGES, played the eponymous PRESTON TUCKER and because this was the first film ever to enable father and son to work together. But *New York Times* critic John Gross was troubled by the apparent logic of the Ferguson role: "The prime villain of the movie, the one we actually see, is a politico rather than a bureaucrat, the scheming Senator Ferguson; and behind Ferguson and the forces he mobilized lurk the big car makers of Detroit. The ultimate enemies at whose hand Tucker suffers defeat are fellow capitalists." For the most part during the 1980s and beyond, however, Lloyd Bridges often opted for comedy, following the lead of actor Leslie Nielson, taking comic roles in *Airplane* (1980), *Joe vs. the Volcano* (1990), *Hot Shots!* (1991), and in *Jane Austen's Mafia!* a 1998 spoof of the *GODFATHER* trilogy. Lloyd Bridges died in Los Angeles on March 10, 1998.—JAMES M. WELSH

References

John Gross, "A Movie That Cannily Celebrates the American Businessman as a Hero," *New York Times*, September 4, 1988, sec. 2: 29; Janet Maslin, "Behind the Wheel of a Grand Obsession," *New York Times*, August 12, 1988, C-8.

BROWNLOW, KEVIN (1938–)

British archivist, historian, filmmaker, and television producer whose lifetime dedication to the silent cinema enabled him to restore ABEL GANCE's epic *Napoleon* (1927) to the five-hour version that premiered at the Paris Opéra in 1927, in consultation with Gance himself. The story of that restoration and of the making of the original epic film is told in Kevin Brownlow's book, *Napoleon: Abel Gance's Classic Film* (London: Jonathan Cape, 1983) and in Brownlow's documentary film about Gance, entitled *The Charm of Dynamite* (1968) [See also *ABEL GANCE'S NAPOLEON*].—JAMES M. WELSH

BUTLER, BILL (1921–)

Cinematographer, notably on Coppola's *THE CONVERSATION*. (He is not to be confused with the film editor Bill Butler, who edited Stanley Kubrick's 1971 film, *A Clockwork Orange*.) Butler was one of the cast and crew whom FRANCIS COPPOLA brought together to shoot *THE RAIN PEOPLE* totally on location. The film unit traveled cross-country in a convoy of five autos, plus a Dodge minibus that carried the technical equipment.

One of the difficulties posed by shooting the film entirely on location was that Butler, as director of photography, had to make do with the minimum of lighting equipment that had been brought along in the minibus. Butler had come from Chicago TV and was shooting his first Hollywood feature. His experience in making TV documentaries had taught him how to shoot quickly and efficiently with a small crew.

In the film, Gordon (ROBERT DUVALL), the motorcycle policeman to whom Natalie (Shirley Knight) is sexually attracted, lives in a trailer park; and Butler had to light a night sequence there. For an interior scene in the trailer, he simply screwed photoflood lamps into the lighting fixtures already available in the trailer in order to provide sufficient lighting for shooting the scene. For exterior shots, as the characters walked around the trailer park at night, Butler hid lights behind bushes on the grounds in order to provide illumination for shooting. "It's a real challenge when you have a minimum number of lights to work with," he comments. "You really have to be inventive." He liked working with Coppola on this film and on *The Conversation* because "he gives you a lot of freedom. He lets your creativity work for him."

Coppola initially engaged Haskell Wexler as the director of photography on *The Conversation* but was irritated by the length of time it took Wexler to light a scene. Wexler stubbornly contended that some of the exteriors Coppola had selected were well-nigh impossible to light; for example, the opening scene in San Francisco's Union Square at high noon.

Coppola finally shut down the picture for ten days, during which he sent word to Wexler that his services were no longer required and secured another cinematographer. He eventually replaced Wexler with Bill Butler, who had done yeoman's service in photographing *The Rain People* on the road.

The critical acclaim accorded *The Conversation* helped Butler's career to take off—his next assignment was the blockbuster *Jaws* (Steven Spielberg, 1975). In addition, he was nominated for an Academy Award for his work on *One Flew over the Cuckoo's Nest* (Milos Forman, 1975). —GENE D. PHILLIPS

References

Dennis Schaefer and Larry Salvati, *Masters of Light: Conversations with Contemporary Cinematographers* (Los Angeles: University of California Press, 1984); Michael Schumacher, *Francis Ford Coppola: A Filmmaker's Life* (New York: Crown, 1999); David Thomson, *Have You Seen. . . ? 1,000 Films* (New York: Knopf, 2008).

CAAN, JAMES (1940–)

James Caan met and became friends with FRANCIS FORD COPPOLA while the two were attending Hofstra University in the late 1950s. In 1960, Caan was bitten by the acting bug and enrolled in New York's Neighborhood Playhouse School of the Theatre. In the 1960s, he appeared on stage and in numerous television series, landed a small part in Billy Wilder's *Irma La Douce*, and eventually moved on to starring roles in films by the likes of Howard Hawks and Robert Altman. Coppola's working relationship with Caan began when he picked him to star in his dramatic 1969 road movie, *THE RAIN PEOPLE*, as Jimmy "Killer" Kilgannon, an ex-football player suffering from brain damage who travels across country with the film's emotionally scarred female protagonist, only to be fatally shot trying to protect her from what he perceives as an attempted assault.

Caan's most famous performance in a Coppola film—and probably the most celebrated performance of his career—came in 1972, when he portrayed Santino "Sonny" Corleone, the elder son of MARLON BRANDO's character and temporary head of the Corleone crime family, in *THE GODFATHER*. According to *Vanity Fair*'s Mark Seal, Caan has become so identified with this role that "he is constantly tested in public" by fans who wonder if he will explode with rage as Sonny would. Accord-

ing to Caan, he has been taken for a real-life mobster several times and was twice declared "Italian of the Year," despite the fact that he is the son of Jewish immigrants who fled Hitler's Germany in the 1930s. As Caan told Mark Seal, his interpretation of Sonny flowed naturally from his experiences growing up in New York and his familiarity with gangster types. The bitter, sarcastic delivery of Don Rickles (a friend of Caan's) was an influence on the role, and Caan added a number of memorable elements to the character through improvisation. One key improvised line discussed by Seal is delivered sneeringly by Caan to AL PACINO's Michael Corleone after Michael decides he wants to kill a cop who has wronged the family: "What do you think this is, the army, where you shoot 'em a mile away? You gotta get up close, like this—and *bada-bing!* You blow their brains all over your nice Ivy League suit." Another key moment—the tossing of the twenty dollar bill after smashing the photographer's camera at his sister's wedding—was likewise improvised: "When I grabbed that poor extra as he took the picture, the guy must've had a heart attack. None of that was scripted. Then I remembered my neighborhood, where guys could do anything as long as they paid for it afterwards. I had this guy choked. Luckily, Richie [Castellano] grabbed me. Then I took out a 20, threw it on the ground, and

James Caan in *The Rain People*.

walked off." Coppola also played a vital role in nurturing his actors and helping them get in character. In a 1997 interview with Michael Sragow, Caan pointed out that Coppola helped him feel protective toward TALIA SHIRE's Connie: "Francis would tell me, 'Someone's bothering Talia,' and it wouldn't have anything to do with the movie, but I'd take care of it. The s.o.b. must have done it on purpose."

The casting of Caan had a great deal to do with his star-making performance as Chicago Bears running back and cancer victim Brian Piccolo in the ABC television movie *Brian's Song* (1970), a role that garnered him an Emmy nomination. On the strength of this performance and his new-found notoriety, Caan was nearly given the role of Michael Corleone. His was one of many names floated for the role (along with ROBERT REDFORD, Warren Beatty, and other major stars of the day), and he did perform a screen test for the part. As Coppola said years later, "We were ready to go into production before we found our Michael Corleone. The studio guys wanted Jimmy Caan to play him. I love Jimmy, but I felt he'd be wrong for Michael—and perfect for Sonny." Coppola has said that he had Caan, as well as Pacino and ROBERT DUVALL, in mind for *The Godfather* from early on, as he was still wrangling with ROBERT EVANS over the casting of Marlon Brando. However, the part of Sonny was at one point promised to Carmine Caridi, an Italian American actor, which was the result of an agreement between Coppola and casting director FRED ROOS to cast real-life Italians in all the Italian roles. When Coppola began to wrangle with producer Robert Evans over casting Al Pacino in the role of Michael, Evans demanded that if Coppola had to have Pacino in the film, then the more bankable Caan should be given the part of Sonny instead of a less visible role. The casting decision worked remarkably well, earning Caan an Oscar nomination.

Caan reprised the role of Sonny in a few flashback scenes in *THE GODFATHER: PART II*, but after a series of flops in the late 1970s, Caan suffered the death of his sister and has since admitted to substance abuse problems that sidelined his acting career for a number of years in the 1980s. Caan returned to the screen in 1987 in Coppola's *GARDENS OF STONE*, as Sergeant Clell Howard, a Vietnam veteran who serves in the ceremonial honor guard at Arlington National Cemetery and becomes more and more disillusioned and disappointed with America's involvement in the conflict as the film progresses. Since his reappearance in motion pictures, Caan has acted steadily and often brilliantly in many films and television programs, including *Misery* (1990), *Mickey Blue Eyes* (1999), *Dogville* (2003), *Elf* (2003), and *Las Vegas* (2003–2007).—BILLY BUDD VERMILLION

References

"The Godfather," Wikipedia, www.wikipedia.org; "James Caan," Wikipedia, www.wikipedia.org; "James Caan Biography," Leninimports.com, http://www.leninimports.com; "James Caan: Biography from Answers.com," www.answers.com; Peter Keough, "Coppola Carves a Cinematic Elegy: *Gardens of Stone*," in Gene D. Phillips and Rodney Hill, eds., *Francis Ford Coppola: Interviews* (Jackson: University Press of Mississippi, 2004), 125–31; William Murray, "*Playboy* Interview: Francis Ford Coppola," in Phillips and Hill, 17–44; Gene D. Phillips, "Francis Ford Coppola Interviewed," in Phillips and Hill, 143–66; Mark Seal, "The Godfather Wars," *Vanity Fair*, March 2009, www.vanityfair.com; Michael Sragow, "Godfatherhood," in Phillips and Hill, 167–83.

CAGE, NICOLAS
[NICHOLAS COPPOLA] (1964–)

Actor and nephew of FRANCIS FORD COPPOLA, born in Long Beach, California, on January 7, 1964, the son of August Coppola, a professor of comparative literature at California State University, and Joy Vogelsang, a dancer and choreographer. He dropped out of high school to become an actor, first appearing as Nicholas Coppola in *Fast Times at Ridgemont High* in 1982 and as Nicolas Cage thereafter. In 1983 Cage played Smokey for his uncle in *RUMBLE FISH* and went on to star as Vince Dwyer in *THE COTTON CLUB* (1984) and in *PEGGY SUE GOT MARRIED* (1986). But, arguably, his best early roles were for other directors, including memorable performances with Sean Penn in Richard Benjamin's wonderfully modulated *Racing with the Moon* and then as one of the leads in Alan Parker's *Birdy* (both 1984, *Birdy* took the Grand Prix Jury Prize at Cannes); as H. I. McDonnough in the Coen Bros. romp, *Raising Arizona*, and as Danny Aiello's younger brother in Norman Jewison's

Moonstruck (both 1987); and then as the psychopath lead for David Lynch's *Wild at Heart* (1990, which took the Palme d'Or at Cannes). In 1995 Cage's suicidal performance in *Leaving Las Vegas* won all of the Best Actor accolades, including the Oscar, but his goofball performance in *Honeymoon in Vegas* two years earlier in 1993, though silly, was a definite crowd-pleaser. During that decade Cage also brought off an unlikely transition to action-adventure star and was even somewhat convincing with Sean Connery in the absurd *Con-Air* (1997) and also with John Travolta in John Woo's even more absurd *Face/Off.* Cage was amusingly flamboyant in Brian De Palma's *Snake Eyes* (1998), and effective as well in the action thriller *8mm* (1998). His career choices got more interesting in the following decade, however, with *Captain Correlli's Mandolin*, which was disappointing only to those who had read the source novel and knew what to expect, and with *Adaptation* (2002), in which Cage played dual roles as the brothers Kaufman.—JAMES M. WELSH

CAMPBELL, BILL [WILLIAM O.] (1959–)

Stage and screen actor who played Quincy Morris in *BRAM STOKER'S DRACULA* (1992) after starring in his feature film debut, *The Rocketeer* (1991). Born in Charlottesville, Virginia, on July 7, 1959, and raised in Virginia, Campbell first studied commercial art in Chicago at the American Academy of Art, before turning to acting, studying at the Ted Liss Studio for the Performing Arts and at Second City. His West Coast television roles include *Family Ties, Dynasty, Star Trek: The Next Generation, Law & Order*, and opposite James Woods on the series *Shark*, though he is probably best known for his work on the ABC series *Once and Again.* His stage roles have varied from musicals (e.g., *Carousel* and *Guys and Dolls*) to Shakespeare (*The Taming of the*

Shrew, Macbeth, The Tempest, and *Hamlet*).—JAMES M. WELSH

CANNES INTERNATIONAL FILM FESTIVAL

This most prestigious cinematic "event" in France was instrumental in furthering the career of FRANCIS COPPOLA. New generational directors began to make their presence felt when François Truffaut won the Best Director Award at Cannes in 1959 for daring to be different and for setting the standard for alternative cinema with *The 400 Blows.* Other "New Wave" directors— such as Godard, Chabrol, Rohmer, Rivette, and even Resnais—were not so fortunate when it came to the grand prize at Cannes, the Palme d'Or. Marcel Camus beat out *The 400 Blows* for the Palme in 1959 with *Black Orpheus.* Jacques Demy won the Palme d'Or in 1964 for *The Umbrellas of Cherbourg* and Claude Lelouch in 1966 for *A Man and A Woman*, both commercially successful films. In general, American films and directors were ignored, however. In 1955 *Marty* won the Palme, but that was the exception then, not the rule. A paradigm shift came after 1968 at Cannes, as English-language counterculture pictures began to flourish. In 1969 Lindsay Anderson's *If . . .* won the Palme, and Dennis Hopper's *Easy Rider* was launched worldwide at Cannes. In 1970 Robert Altman's *M*A*S*H* won the Palme d'Or. In 1974 Francis Coppola's *THE CONVERSATION* won the Palme, and two years later Martin Scorsese took the top award for *Taxi Driver*; but, as *Variety* reported in its 1989 Cannes "Special Issue," Coppola was "the only director of the modern era to have captured the Palme twice," the second time as co-winner for *APOCALYPSE NOW.* In 2001 Coppola released an expanded version of *Apocalypse Now*, with fifty-three minutes of original footage that had been cut from the film the first time around. *APOCALYPSE NOW REDUX* was appropriately unveiled at Cannes in May 2001. Although the film was not in competition this time, it was still generally regarded as one of the best films on display at the festival that year.—JAMES M. WELSH AND GENE D. PHILLIPS

CAPTAIN EO (1986)

> DIRECTOR: Francis Ford Coppola. SCREEN-PLAY: George Lucas, Rusty Lemorande, and Francis Coppola. PRODUCER: Rusty Lemorande. PHOTOGRAPHY: Peter Anderson. EDITING: Lisa Fruchtman and Walter Murch. ORIGINAL MUSIC: James Horner. PRODUCTION DESIGN: Geoffrey Alan Kirkland. SET DECORATION: Cheryal Kearney and John Sweeney.
> CAST: Michael Jackson (Captain EO), Anjelica Huston (Supreme Leader), Dick Shawn (Commander Bog), Tony Cox (Hooter).
> RUNNING TIME: 17 minutes. Color.
> RELEASED THROUGH: Walt Disney Attractions. PREMIERE: September 12, 1986.

Captain EO is a short 3-D science fiction film made in 1986, starring Michael Jackson and directed by FRANCIS FORD COPPOLA. The production was a hugely expensive undertaking, costing more per minute—over a million dollars for every minute shot (estimates for the total range from $17 to $30 million)—than any film made up to that point in time. A joint venture between Eastman Kodak, Lucasfilm, and the Walt Disney Company, *Captain EO* was made as an attraction for Disney's theme parks and was produced by Rusty Lemorande, with Coppola's friend GEORGE LUCAS serving as executive producer. The screenplay was written by Lucas, Lemorande, and Coppola, based on a story developed by Walt Disney Imagineering. Unsurprisingly, given the involvement

of Lucas and Coppola, the credits for the film read like a Who's Who of the movie brat generation: WALTER MURCH was an editor on the project (working under Lisa Fruchtman, who, unlike Murch, received screen credit), James Horner did the score, VITTORIO STORARO was a lighting consultant, and Rick Baker worked on makeup and creature effects.

Captain EO represented the Walt Disney Company's goal of forging ahead into a new era of synergy and cross-promotion. In the early to mid-1980s, Disney's new CEO, Michael Eisner, began working to revitalize the company and the brand, a strategy that included developing new attractions for Disney's theme park empire. In 1984 and 1985, Michael Jackson's *Thriller* album and John Landis's epic music video for the title song demonstrated Jackson's appeal not only as a singer but as an all-around performer who could carry a long-form, high-concept music video. Eisner and Disney sought to capitalize on this and "create something with Michael Jackson, who appealed to teenagers, but also to young kids, and even their parents." According to Eisner, this was something of a no-brainer, as "Jackson was a huge fan of our parks, sometimes visiting several times a month, in and out of disguise." Disney's COO at the time, Frank Wells, echoed these sentiments at the film's opening, pointing out that when he first heard about Jackson's tours of Epcot Center, "that day began our heads a-scratching." The result was an expensive but tremendously popular and long-running show that provided an immersive and entertaining experience for millions of guests at Disneyland and the company's other parks over the next several years.

Captain EO built on Michael Jackson's mega-stardom, the phenomenal success of Hollywood's recent science fiction blockbusters, and the revival of 3-D mov- ies in the early 1980s (*Friday the 13th Part III, Jaws 3D*). Jackson was almost certainly the biggest draw for audiences at the time, given his immense popularity, but also central to the film's appeal (and certainly to its style) is the innovative use of 3-D technology. In a 1987 interview with Peter Keough, Coppola discussed the use of 3-D technology in *Captain EO*: "When we fin- ished, I asked my collaborator, the photog- rapher Vittorio Storaro, what he thought. 'Now we have 3-D,' Vittorio said. 'When I go back to Italy, I make a film, it is only 2-D. I lose one D!'" Some commentators would go so far as to claim that *Captain EO* gained a "D" when it was screened in the Disney theme parks, where smoke machines and laser light show elements were part of the show, making it a more interactive experience. The inaccurate but evocative term "4-D" began to be used in marketing the film and other attractions like it around this time, and Richard Cor- liss memorably referred to the experience of watching the film as taking a trip to "the feelies."

Coppola's film borrows stylistic and narrative elements from Lucas's *Star Wars* franchise, telling the story of a heroic small- scale rebellion against an evil intergalactic empire, complete with rusted and worn- down spaceships of varying classes and sizes, cute robots, alien creatures intended to appeal primarily to younger audience members, and dynamic laser battles in the heart of space. Beyond the interstellar dogfights, puppets, and special effects, the spectacle also includes elaborate musical set-pieces. Jackson's singing and dancing are integrated into the film's plot and are (with perhaps too little logic or explana- tion) EO's weapons of choice in the battle of good versus evil, light against dark.

The film opens on an image of a distant spiral galaxy as an asteroid spins toward the viewer from the depths of space. A somber voice intones, "The cosmos: a universe of good and evil, where a small group struggles to bring freedom to the countless worlds of despair—a ragtag band, led by the infamous Captain EO." The asteroid explodes, and Captain EO's ship flies into view. A comic scene with the crew—a two-headed, bird- like pilot named Idee and Odee; a clumsy, elephantine alien slob called Hooter; Fuzz- ball, a little flying monster; the mustachioed robot Major Domo and his smaller coun- terpart, Minor Domo—ends as they trip an intruder alarm outside the orbit of a small planet, and EO arrives on deck to lead them in. The ship is then chased by enemy vessels and crash lands on the surface of a dark, dystopian, industrial wasteland, where the holographic visage of the rebel commander (Dick Shawn) urges them to seek out the Supreme Leader (ANJELICA HUSTON). The crew is soon captured by the Supreme Leader's guards and brought before her to await their judgment for trespassing. The Supreme Leader hangs suspended with cables from a huge black edifice, her body melded with the machinery, as she hisses and claws at the intruders, looking very much like a cyborg version of the Wicked Witch of the West.

At this point, the film shifts from a relatively traditional space opera into some- thing much closer to Landis's *Thriller*, as EO offers the Supreme Leader a "gift" that will "unlock" the beauty within her. Through stop-motion animation, the robotic assis- tants of Captain EO transform themselves into musical instruments and a synthesized beat begins to play, just before Hooter slips and falls on EO's cape and knocks over the keyboard, giving the Supreme Leader a chance to send in her sinister warriors to capture the meddlesome band. Suspense builds as the soldiers advance on EO, but when Hooter reassembles the keyboard, EO begins to shoot beams of light from his hands at the black-clad enemies, transforming them into backup dancers dressed in bright orange and yellow. With EO standing in front, the dancers begin to gyrate and move toward the Supreme Leader, and the film cuts between closer views of Jackson, long shots of all the dancers, and overhead views that highlight the choreography. As the song—"We Are Here to Change the World"—kicks into high gear, shots of the band playing along and reaction shots of the horrified Supreme Leader are worked into the mix. The Supreme Leader tries to stop EO with her Whip Warriors, dark-armored centurions with formidable weaponry, but EO is able to win them to his cause and they begin to follow him. Dark, metallic machine-men stand dormant along the walls of the hall leading to the exit of the Supreme Leader's chambers, and as EO marches back toward the Supreme Leader he transforms these figures into white-costumed dancers, making his army virtually unstoppable. Suddenly, EO rises into the air and shoots beams of blue light at the Supreme Leader herself. The screen is filled with color as the evil empress emerges from the light a beautiful woman in a flowing rainbow-hued dress, and the blackened husk of a planet becomes a wonderland of color. The dance resumes, and EO begins to sing "Another Part of Me." As he and the crew walk away during the song, Fuzzball flies toward the camera and waves, cooing, "Bye-bye." Outside, the camera rises over the glorious, living planet, and viewers are given one last look at EO's spaceship as it disappears before the credits roll over the rest of Jackson's final number.

Captain EO opened initially at Epcot Center and Disneyland in September of 1986, then at Tokyo Disneyland the following spring. A few years later, in 1992, it was unveiled at the new Disneyland Park in Paris. In 1994, Disney canceled *Captain EO* at Epcot Center, but kept it running at its other theme parks. Although the cancellation occurred in the wake of allegations about child abuse by Jackson and the ensuing criminal investigation of the pop star, Disney officially denied that concerns about Jackson's behavior or the shattering of his reputation had anything to do with their decision. Spokesman David Herbst pointed out that the company had "to keep offering something new." Herbst did acknowledge that Disney "may have gotten some complaints. But that is not why we are replacing the film." At Epcot Center, the show was replaced with a new attraction, *Honey, I Shrunk the Audience*, based on the popular science fiction family comedy, *Honey, I Shrunk the Kids*.

Following Michael Jackson's death in the summer of 2009, rumors began to circulate on Disney fan sites and elsewhere on the Internet, suggesting that *Captain EO* might reopen in 2010. A Reuters report in September 2009 cited a press conference held by Disney CEO Bob Iger, who denied the rumors but left open the possibility for *Captain EO*'s return. According to Iger, while no concrete plans had been made as of September and questions about who owned the product existed, Disney was nonetheless "looking at it." Iger said, "It's the kind of thing that, if we did it, would get a fair amount of attention and we'd want to do it right." With the success of Michael Jackson's final concert film, *This Is It*, in November 2009, rumors again began circulating about *Captain EO*'s return to Disneyland in early 2010. —BILLY BUDD VERMILLION

References

Associated Press, "Disney Drops Jackson Show at Epcot Center," *Chicago Tribune*, City Edition, February 27, 1994, p. 20; "Captain EO," Wikipedia, www.wikipedia.org; "Captain EO at Yesterland," Yesterland.com, http://www.yesterland.com/eo.html; Richard Corliss, "Let's

Go to the Feelies," *Time*, September 28, 1986, 80; Michael D. Eisner, with Tony Schwartz, *Work in Progress: Risking Failure, Surviving Success* (New York: Hyperion, 1998); Roger Friedman, "Michael Jackson's 'Captain EO' Will Return to Disneyland," Showbiz411, November 16, 2009, www.showbiz411.com; Peter Keough, "Coppola Carves a Cinematic Elegy: *Gardens of Stone*," in Gene D. Phillips and Rodney Hill, eds., *Francis Ford Coppola: Interviews* (Jackson: University Press of Mississippi, 2004); Jon Lewis, *Whom God Wishes to Destroy: Francis Coppola and the New Hollywood* (Durham, NC: Duke University Press, 1995); Graeme McMillan, "Maybe Michael Jackson Will Live Again After All," io9, September 12, 2009, www.io9.com; Peter Sciretta, "Captain EO to Return to Disneyland?" */Film*, September 2, 2009, www.slashfilm.com; Peter Sciretta, "Disney Denies the Return of Captain EO," */Film*, September 10, 2009, www .slashfilm.com; Tribune Wire Services, "Captain EO Brings a New Era to Video," *Chicago Tribune*, City Edition, September 18, 1986, p. 11; Sue Zeidler, "Disney Says No Plans to Bring Back Jackson 3-D film," Reuters, September 10, 2009, www.reuters.com.

CAZALE, JOHN (1936–1978)

American character actor who plays Fredo Corleone in both *THE GODFATHER* and *THE GODFATHER: PART II* and Stanley in *THE COVERSATION*. Born in Boston, Massachusetts, in 1936, John Cazale was educated at Oberlin College and at Boston University. In 1968 he won an Obie Award for his performance in the off-Broadway production of *The Indian Wants the Bronx* (written by Israel Horovitz) and went on to appear in five of the top films of the 1970s, three of them directed by FRANCIS FORD COPPOLA, and all of which were nominated for a Best Picture Oscar: *The Godfather* (1972), *The Conversation* (1974), *The Godfather: Part II* (1974), *Dog Day Afternoon* (1975), and *The Deer Hunter* (1978). Cazale, best remembered, perhaps, for his portrayal of Fredo Corleone for Francis Coppola, was an actor's actor: he appeared with AL PACINO in three plays and three films, and, after meeting Meryl Streep at a Shakespeare in the Park production of *Measure for Measure*, he told Pacino: "I've met the greatest actress in the history of the world!" Reminding audiences that, had he lived, Cazale would have been in a league with ROBERT DE NIRO, GENE HACKMAN, his friend Al Pacino, and Meryl Streep (with whom he became romantically involved until his death from cancer on March 12, 1978), director Richard Shepard's forty-minute HBO-produced documentary film *I Knew It Was You* was released on July 29, 2009, as part of a New York retrospective of all five of Cazale's greatest films. "I learned more about acting from John than from anybody," Al Pacino noted to Shepard in the documentary. The title of Adam Sternbergh's profile for *New York* magazine (August 3, 2009, p. 58) sums up the achievement of this "Zelig of the Seventies"—"The Godfather: John Cazale got famous playing Fredo Corleone. Was he also the Greatest Actor of his Generation?" According to *New Yorker* critic Hilton Als, Cazale "married a Brando-influenced naturalism to a nearly mute, neurotic poeticism that was all his own." Cazale should be valued for the way this character actor "taught us something about marginalization with his intense introspection and physical awkwardness." Cazale was the Italian American counterpart of the first-generation American Jewish actor John Garfield, who embodied a particular "jittery post-war Angst," in the words of Hilton Als.—JAMES M. WELSH

References

Hilton Als, "Flashbacks," *New Yorker*, November 5, 2007, 100–101; Adam Sternbergh, *New York*, August 3, 2009, 58.

CHOWN, JEFFREY (N.D.)

Professor of Communication Studies at Northern Illinois University, educated at the University of Oklahoma (MA) and the University of Michigan (PhD in American Studies). Chown is the author of *Hollywood Auteur: Francis Coppola* (1988), a critical examination of the "auteur theory" with reference to the films and career of FRANCIS COPPOLA, paying particular attention to production accounts, collaborators, script material, and the commercial considerations that influence what might be described as "a film by Francis Coppola." Chown concludes by writing that "in the final analysis," he feels "a great deal of compassion for this man I do not personally know." The book is awash with irony.—JAMES M. WELSH

CLARK, PETULA [SALLY OLWEN] (1932–)

Singer, composer, and actress who played the lead role of Sharon McLonergan opposite FRED ASTAIRE in *FINIAN'S RAINBOW* (1968). One of the most internationally known and influential pop singers of the 1960s, Petula Clark set the tone for a generation with her songs, "I Know a Place" and "Downtown." By the time she was featured in *Finian's Rainbow* (and nominated for a Best Actress Golden Globe), Clark had appeared in nearly thirty films and was already a huge international talent. Born on November 16, 1932, in Ewell, Surrey, England, she made her radio debut on BBC in 1942 and was a star by age eleven, known as the "British Shirley Temple." She also sang in music halls and performed for British troops during World War II. In 1964 her recording of the song "Downtown" (written by composer-arranger Tony Hatch), originally recorded in 1963, was rereleased in four different languages and became a hit, first in the United Kingdom, then in France; by January of 1965 it was number one on the U.S. charts, and setting records for Britain. Still performing in her seventies, Petula Clark holds many records of distinction in the performing arts. In 1998 she was honored by Queen Elizabeth II by being designated CBE (Commander of the Order of the British Empire).—JAMES M. WELSH AND THOMAS CLANCY

COLES, CHARLES "HONI" (1911–1992)

Veteran tap dancer, Broadway star, Vaudevillian, and TV and film performer, who served from 1960 to 1976 as production manager of the legendary Apollo Theater, played the dancer "Sugar Coates" in *THE COTTON CLUB* (1984). Born in Philadelphia on April 2, 1911, he was the son of George and Isabel Coles.

Charles Coles made his New York debut in 1931 at the Lafayette Theatre, as a member of "The Three Millers," known for their acrobatic feats of dance. Later in that decade, at the Apollo Theater and the Harlem Opera House, he garnered the reputation as having the "fastest feet in show business." Coles and dancing partner Cholly Atkins often appeared as a team, under the name "Coles and Atkins." They met in 1940, while Coles was dancing with the Cab Calloway Orchestra, and formed a partnership after World War II. Coles and Atkins appeared in the original Broadway run of *Gentlemen Prefer Blondes* (1949–1952), in which they reportedly "stopped the show" with the Jule Styne number, "Mamie Is Mimi."

In 1983 at age 72, Coles received the Tony Award, the Drama Desk Award, and the FRED ASTAIRE Award for his featured acting and dance work in the Broadway Musical, *My One and Only.* He received the National Medal of the Arts in 1991 and was posthumously inducted into the Tap Dance Hall of Fame in 2003.

Charles Coles's other film work includes appearances in *Rocky II* (1979),

Dirty Dancing (1987), and as a character called "Old Shady" in the NBC TV movie, *Charleston* (1979), which *Variety* describes as a "tacky road-company version of 'Gone with the Wind.'" In 1944, Coles married Marion Evelyn Edwards (1915?–2009), with whom he had two children. Marion Coles was also a renowned professional dancer and had appeared on stage with various big bands, including those of Jimmie Lunceford, Duke Ellington, Count Basie, and Cab Calloway. Charles Coles died in New York City on November 12, 1992.—RODNEY HILL

References

"Charleston," *Variety* Profiles, www.variety.com; Constance Valis Hill, "Charles 'Honi' Coles," American Tap Dance Foundation website, www .atdf.org/awards/honi.html.

COLLABORATION (ARTISTIC)

A concept central to FRANCIS COPPOLA's approach to filmmaking, involving relationships with cast and crew. In *ZOETROPE: ALL-STORY* (vol. 11, no. 3, Fall 2007), Coppola described the process of working with his Academy Award–nominated editor WALTER MURCH as being "fully collaborative. He comes up with very eccentric ideas that I like, ideas that hadn't been considered in the original material. I come up with eccentric ideas too that he's also able to appreciate. So the two of us doing that creates really effervescing possibilities of evolving the story, of making it clearer on one level, more adventurous on another, and more cinematic in that we are putting things together in a metaphoric context." In that same issue of *Zoetrope: All-Story*, commemorating the release of *YOUTH WITH-OUT YOUTH*, ELEANOR COPPOLA interviewed lead actor TIM ROTH, who told her that "Francis really likes collaboration, particularly in the visual aspects of the film. Once I gained a sense of the imag-ery he was seeking, if something occurred to me, I would suggest it to him and quite often he was very pleased about that, I think." He added that quite often Coppola would have the frame set before the actor arrived: "If the moment he's asking you to do isn't organic to you, you have to take his intentions and make them your own. What made it less frustrating was that he pretty much knew where I'd want to go, toward the end of the filming especially." Eleanor Coppola remarked that seeing Roth "on the set all the time with Francis—it seemed like ensemble theater, or a family almost." Roth responded, "I think our relationship definitely grew. At the beginning, there was the director and there was the actor, and we communicated when we needed to; but as the filming went on, I found that I could talk to him about any work-related problem, any scene. If I stayed close to him, I learned a lot, so there was no reason for me to go anywhere. . . . It's wonderful to watch. Making shots look like they're multimillion-dollar shots when you know damn straight they're not. Our relationship really blossomed toward the end." One sup-poses that this appreciation of the collab-orative process late in Coppola's career also reflects a tendency that was present earlier, before being leavened by the wisdom of age. —JAMES M. WELSH

CONRAD, JOSEPH [JÓZEF TEODOR KONRAD KORZENIOWSKI] (1857–1924)

Born in Ukraine and raised Polish, his homeland occupied by Russia, Conrad was sent into exile as a child with his family and went to sea at the age of seventeen, sailing the world for nearly two decades. By 1878 he had signed on to an English ship, and by 1886 he had become a naturalized Brit-ish subject. He taught himself to write in a foreign language, which he had mastered by 1895, when *Almayer's Folly* was published. By 1899 Conrad had written "HEART OF

DARKNESS," recounting a voyage up the Congo in 1890, an autobiographical narrative involving an "experience pushed a little [and only very little] beyond the actual facts of the case." This voyage was later to be updated and adapted by FRANCIS FORD COPPOLA into his filmed masterpiece, *APOCALYPSE NOW.* A creative flood of novels would follow: *Outcasts of the Islands* (1896), *The Nigger of the "Narcissus"* (1897), and *Youth* (1898) preceded "Heart of Darkness," which was followed by *Lord Jim* (1900), *Typhoon* (1903), *Nostromo* (1904), *The Secret Agent* (1907). Other novels, such as *Chance* (1913) and *Victory* (1915) would follow, but those written during and after World War I fell short of the brilliance Conrad had achieved before the war. By the twenty-first century, "Heart of Darkness" had risen in popularity with critics and readers. The most recent update for The Norton Critical Edition took 70 pages to reprint Conrad's text, then added 400 pages of critical commentary. Conrad died in 1924 at the age of sixty-seven at Bishopsbourne in Kent and was buried at Canterbury in Kent. By the mid-twentieth century, Conrad's literary reputation was secure, as demonstrated when he was included in J. I. M. Stewart's *Eight Modern Writers* (Oxford: The Clarendon Press, 1963), completing the multivolume *Oxford History of English Literature.*

In the spring of 1975, Francis Coppola told an interviewer that his next film would deal with the Vietnam War. As a starting point for his screenplay Coppola noted that he had selected a six-year-old scenario done by writer-director JOHN MILIUS (*The Wind and the Lion*) in 1969, based on Conrad's "Heart of Darkness."

For the record, "Heart of Darkness" does not appear in the screen credits of *Apocalypse Now* as the literary source of the film. As a matter of fact, a reference to Conrad's novella was originally listed in the screen credits, but Milius complained to the Screen Writer's Guild, and the reference to the book was removed. Milius vetoed the presence of Conrad's novella in the film's credits because he felt that citing Conrad's book as the source of the movie would minimize the importance of the material contributed to the screenplay by the scriptwriters.

At any rate, years later, Milius told Peter Cowie that he felt differently about the matter. He freely conceded that "Heart of Darkness" is indeed the source story for the film. "It was my favorite Conrad book," he said, and hence he wanted very much to bring it to the screen. Significantly, the Academy Award nomination for the film's screenplay was in the category of Best Screenplay based on material from another medium—the only official acknowledgment that "Heart of Darkness" was the movie's literary source.

Indeed, Coppola states in his audio commentary on the DVD of *Apocalypse Now* (released in 2006), that "I took my paperback of "Heart of Darkness," in which I made many notations, to the set every day. I had "Heart of Darkness" in one hand and the script of *Apocalypse Now* in my other hand on the set."

On the surface it seems that Conrad's novella is very different from Coppola's film. For instance, Conrad's story takes place in the Belgian Congo in the 1890s and focuses on Charles Marlow, a British sailor employed by a European trading firm as captain of one of their steamboats. By contrast, Coppola's film is set in Southeast Asia in the 1960s, and centers on Benjamin Willard, an American army officer. Yet, as film scholar Linda Cahir points out, although the settings and backgrounds of novella and film are quite different, the manner in which the story is narrated in each instance is "splendidly similar." Here is a brief summary of the fundamental parallels between book and film.

For example, "each tale-proper begins with the protagonist's explanation of how he got the appointment which necessitated his excursion up river," Cahir points out. Marlow is dispatched to steam up the Congo in order to find Mr. Kurtz, an ivory trader who disappeared into the interior and never returned. Willard is mandated to journey up the Mekong River in a navy patrol boat to find Col. Kurtz, who has recruited his own renegade army to fight the Vietcong. Furthermore, the last stop for both Marlow and Willard, concludes Cahir, "is the soul-altering confrontation with the mysterious Kurtz."

Moreover, one of the elements of Coppola's film that serves to bring it closer to the original story is employing Willard as the narrator of the film, just as Marlow is the narrator of the novella. Hence the screenplay of *Apocalypse Now* remains most faithful to its source in its attempt to depict the action through flashback, with the narrator's comments on the action heard as voiceover on the soundtrack.

Apocalypse Now, when it finally reached the screen in 1979, turned out to be a mammoth spectacle, which Coppola shot almost entirely on location in the Philippines. As mentioned, the setting of the story is updated from the late nineteenth century to the time of the Vietnam War. As we know, Captain Benjamin Willard, played by MARTIN SHEEN (*The Subject Was Roses*), who is the central character and narrator of the movie, is ordered by his superior officers to penetrate into the interior of the jungle and track down Col. Walter E. Kurtz (MARLON BRANDO), a renegade officer who has raised an army composed of deserters like himself and of native tribesmen, in order to fight the war on his own terms. When he locates Kurtz, Willard is to "terminate his command with extreme prejudice," which is military jargon meaning that Willard should assassinate

Kurtz. Col. Kurtz, it seems, rules over his followers like a fanatical warlord, and has taken to employing brutal tactics to attain his objectives. Willard's first reaction to his mission is that liquidating someone for killing people in wartime seems like "handing out speeding tickets at the 'Indy 500.'" He therefore decides to withhold judgment about Kurtz until he meets up with him personally.

As Willard chugs up the Mekong River in a patrol boat in search of Kurtz, his journey becomes a symbolic voyage backward in time. In entering Kurtz's outpost in the wilderness. Willard has equivalently stepped back into a lawless, prehistoric age where barbarism holds sway. The compound, then, becomes a graphic visual metaphor that reflects Kurtz's gradual descent into primitive barbarism.

In fact, the severed heads that lie scattered around the grounds testify to the depths of pagan savagery to which Kurtz has sunk during his sojourn in the jungle. The severed heads, shown in long shot, recall the scene in the novel when Marlow is shocked to see that Kurtz has shrunken heads stuck on pikes in front of his lodgings.

Furthermore, it is painfully clear to Willard that, despite the fact that Kurtz's native followers revere him as a god, Kurtz is incurably insane. Willard also discovers, when he at last meets Kurtz, that Kurtz is slowly dying of malaria; hence his physical illness is symbolic of his moral sickness.

By now Willard has definitely made up his mind to carry out his orders by killing Kurtz; and Kurtz, who has sensed from the beginning the reason why Willard was sent to find him, finally makes no effort to stop him. For one thing, Kurtz presumably prefers a quick death, as meted out by Willard, to a slow death from malaria. More importantly, as Willard explains in his voiceover commentary on the soundtrack, Kurtz wants to die bravely, like a soldier, at the hands of another soldier, and not be ignominiously butchered as a wretched renegade. Indeed, in order to die like a soldier, Kurtz dons his Green Beret uniform, while he is waiting for Willard to come and assassinate him. Willard accordingly enters Kurtz's murky lair and ceremoniously slays him with a machete. (Kurtz dies of natural causes in the book.)

Willard's killing of Kurtz is intercut with shots of the Cambodian tribe that is part of Kurtz's army slaughtering a sacrificial water buffalo, a scene that suggests that Willard implicitly sees his "execution" of the diabolical Kurtz for his hideous war crimes as a kind of ritual slaying.

After Willard has slain Kurtz, he pauses at Kurtz's desk and notices a typescript lying on it. We see in close-up that, scrawled in red across one page is the statement, "Drop the Bomb. Exterminate them all!" This is Kurtz's manner of indicating his way of ending the Vietnam War: he would like to have seen all of the North Vietnamese, soldiers and non-combatants alike, destroyed from the air. Col. Kurtz's cold-blooded remark recalls a similar passage in the novella, in which Marlow peruses a report that Kurtz had prepared for the International Society for the Suppression of Savage Customs. The report ends with a postscript, presumably added much later: "Exterminate the brutes."

When Willard leaves Kurtz's quarters, Kurtz's tribesmen submissively lay their weapons on the ground as he passes among them. Clearly they believe that the mantle of authority has passed from their deceased leader to the man he has allowed to slay him. But Willard, his mission accomplished, walks out of the compound and proceeds to the river bank, where his patrol boat awaits him to take him back to civilization, Coppola commented to me. "Willard has carried out his mission, and so the film ends with Willard returning to his patrol boat," just as a cleansing rain washes over his body; and he sails downriver to salvation, a sadder but wiser man.

As the boat pulls away from the shore, Willard hears the voice of Kurtz uttering the same phrase he had spoken just before he met his Maker: "The horror, the horror." At the end Kurtz was apparently vouchsafed a moment of lucidity, in which he realized what a depraved brute he had become.

Hence the theme of the movie is the same as that of Conrad's novel. In *Apocalypse Now*, just as in "Heart of Darkness," the central journey is both a literal and a metaphoric one, writes Jorn Hetebrugge; it is fundamentally "a voyage of discovery into the dark heart of man, and an encounter with his capacity for evil." In harmony with this observation, Coppola says that he too sees Willard's journey upriver as a metaphor for "the voyage of life that each of us takes within ourselves and during which we choose between good and evil."—GENE D. PHILLIPS/JAMES M. WELSH

References

Linda Cahir, "Narratological Parallels in Joseph Conrad's *Heart of Darkness* and Francis Ford Coppola's *Apocalypse Now*," *Literature/Film Quarterly* 20, no. 3 (Summer, 1992): 181–87; Peter Cowie, *Coppola: A Biography*, rev. ed. (New York: Da Capo, 1999); Roger Ebert, *The Great Movies* (New York: Broadway Books, 2003); Jorn Hetebrugge, "*Apocalypse Now*," in *Movies of the Seventies*, ed. Jurgen Muller (Los Angeles: Taschen, 2005), pp. 602–7.

THE CONVERSATION (1974)

DIRECTOR: Francis Ford Coppola. SCREEN-PLAY: Francis Ford Coppola. PRODUCERS: Francis Ford Coppola and Fred Roos for American Zoetrope. PHOTOGRAPHY: Bill Butler. SUPERVISING EDITOR, SOUND MONTAGE, AND RERECORDING: Walter Murch. EDITING: Richard Chew. MUSIC:

David Shire. PRODUCTION DESIGN: Dean Tavoularis. SET DECORATION: Doug Von Koss. COSTUME DESIGN: Aggie Guerard Rodgers. TECHNICAL ADVISERS: Hal Lipset, Leo Jones, Jim Bloom.
CAST: Gene Hackman (Harry Caul), John Cazale (Stan), Allen Garfield (Bernie Moran), Frederic Forrest (Mark), Cindy Williams (Ann), Michael Higgins (Paul), Elizabeth MacRae (Meredith), Harrison Ford (Martin Stett, Assistant to the Director), Robert Duvall (the Director), Mark Wheeler (Receptionist), Teri Garr (Amy), Robert Shields (Mime in Union Square), Phoebe Alexander (Lurleen).
RUNNING TIME: 113 minutes. Technicolor.
RELEASED THROUGH: Paramount. PREMIERE: April 7, 1974.
DVD: Paramount.

Like *THE RAIN PEOPLE*, *The Conversation* (1974) was based on Coppola's original screenplay. After making *The Rain People*, he told me, he was thinking of "leaving Hollywood and making low-budget films in San Francisco." One low-budget, high-quality movie he made there was *The Conversation*.

He envisioned the film, he said, as centering on a nightmarish situation that had developed in our society, "a system that employs all the sophisticated tools that are available to intrude upon our private lives." Not surprisingly, Coppola invited the gifted WALTER MURCH, who had first joined Coppola's "filmmaking family" when he served as sound engineer on *The Rain People*, to work on the film. Coppola needed an inventive sound technician like Murch because several scenes in the movie were sound oriented.

At first Coppola hired cinematographer Haskell Wexler (*In the Heat of the Night*) as director of photography, but the headstrong Wexler did not get along with the equally strong-minded Coppola.

When the director complained that the painstaking Wexler was taking too long to set up a shot, Wexler shot back that Coppola had chosen some locations—such as the opening sequence in a crowded public square—that were almost impossible to light and to shoot. Coppola responded that, if Erich von Stroheim could shoot *Greed* in the streets of San Francisco in 1924, he did not see why he could not shoot *The Conversation* in the streets of San Francisco in 1972. He eventually replaced Wexler with BILL BUTLER, who had done yeoman's service in photographing *The Rain People* on the road.

One can understand Wexler's problems with the sequence that took place in Union Square at high noon. When principal photography commenced there on November 26, 1972, Coppola and Wexler had to photograph the two lovers, Ann (Cindy Williams) and Mark (FREDERIC FORREST), while they walk around Union Square surrounded not only by extras but by innumerable passersby on their lunch break. This sequence required six cameras, plus a battery of long-distance microphones.

Still the opening scene was worth all the trouble. It starts out with a slow, three-minute overhead zoom shot that gradually moves in on the milling crowds in Union Square, then finally zeroes in on Ann and Mark, who are conversing about Ann's husband, the wealthy director of a corporation (ROBERT DUVALL).

The movie focuses on Harry Caul (GENE HACKMAN), a surveillance expert, who bugs a conversation between Ann and Mark as they converse about Ann's husband. It seems that the Director has discovered their illicit affair and may be planning to kill them.

Harry Caul, who has supervised the surveillance operation, takes the tapes of Ann and Mark's conversation back to his workshop, a loft in an otherwise empty warehouse. Coppola states in his commentary on the DVD of *The Conversation* (released in 2000) that "the warehouse where Harry does his work is like a citadel, with fence-like partitions separating the high-security areas where he keeps his personally designed technological devices locked away from the rest of the workshop," so that no one, not even his assistant, Stan (JOHN CAZALE), can enter there. On the master tape, Mark is overheard to say, "He'd kill us if he got the chance." Harry finds this revelation very disturbing.

Since Harry is a Catholic, he heads for his parish church, where he goes to confession. He confesses to the priest that he still feels some lingering moral guilt about an earlier case in which two people were murdered as a result of his disclosures to his client, even though he was not legally responsible for their deaths. Now he feels that he should intervene in his present case in order to save two young people from being murdered and, thus, atone for the previous deaths. It is evident that Harry is ambivalent about the morality of spying on people.

Harry attends a convention for surveillance experts and invites some of them back to his loft for a party. Meredith, a call girl, also comes along and lingers after everyone else is gone. Harry and Meredith inevitably bed down together. When he awakens, Meredith and the tapes are gone.

The lovers are to have a rendezvous with the Director at a local hotel in order to hash things out. Harry, intent on protecting Ann and Mark from the wrath of her husband, shows up at the designated hotel room—only to find the Director dead. He discovers that Ann and Mark arranged to liquidate him so that they could possess his wealth and power. Too late, Harry realizes that he misunderstood the conversation

Gene Hackman listens in on Frederic Forrest and Cindy Williams.

that he overheard between Mark and Ann: they were planning to kill the Director before he got the opportunity to murder them. While examining the bathroom, he flushes the toilet—only to have it disgorge bloody rags and paper towels, which spill out all over the floor.

Murch recalls in his commentary on the DVD, "In this scene in *The Conversation*, the toilet regurgitates the evidence of guilt. It slowly overflows with blood. The guilty pair had tried to force the evidence of the murder down the toilet in order to clean up the hotel room, but it came flooding back up like an accusing finger."

Completely shattered by this revelation, Harry is even more distraught when he receives a threatening phone call, in which he is warned, "We know that you know, and we are watching you." The movie ends with Harry in despair, unable to find the surveillance device that has been planted in his own apartment. When Harry is himself under surveillance, writes Anne Pohl, "he freaks out like a wild animal that suddenly realizes it's been caged."

Coppola observes on the DVD that he has often been asked where the bug was planted in Harry's apartment. "I always imagined that it was in the strap of his saxophone, which was hanging around his neck and was fastened with a clasp to his sax. Harry often forgot to take the strap off after he finished playing," so he absentmindedly wore it around his neck like a necklace that he was unaware of.

Murch was really "a full collaborator on the film," says Coppola. He edited the picture, assisted by Richard Chew, and mixed the soundtrack. One narrative link that Murch made during editing concerned Meredith, the call girl, and the theft of the tapes. In the screenplay "Meredith slept with Harry and simply disappeared the next morning," Murch comments. In a separate scene, Harry discovered that the tapes had been snatched by some minion of Stett, the Director's chief assistant (HARRISON FORD). "I thought that, if we insinuated that Meredith took the tapes, it would make things hang together better." It would be more interesting to identify the thief as the call girl, rather than make the thief some anonymous henchman of Stett's. Hence, Murch combined the two incidents so that it is evident that Meredith seduced Harry in order to steal the tapes for Stett. "But that tie-up was constructed during editing," Murch concludes. "That was not in the script."

Murch made an even more significant contribution to the film while he was mixing the soundtrack. He discovered a crucial bit of tape that he had previously overlooked: it was an alternate reading of the line in the opening sequence in which Frederic Forrest as Mark altered the emphasis from "He'd *kill* us if he got the chance" to "He'd kill *us* if he got the chance." Murch decided to employ both readings of the line in the film at different points—the more innocuous one in the first scene, and the more sinister one when Harry later hears the remark again late in the movie. Coppola completely agreed with Murch when the latter pointed out that it was the only way to clinch the idea for the audience that Harry had finally uncovered the truth (i.e., that Mark and Ann were planning to murder her husband, and not vice versa). Murch explains that he wanted to clarify for the audience that the first time Harry hears Mark's statement, Harry thinks of Mark and Ann as two potential victims who need his protection. But when Murch employed the second reading of the line with a different inflection, which emphasizes *us* rather than *kill*, he wanted to indicate to the filmgoer that the phrase now takes on a new emphasis for Harry. As Murch puts it, "Harry hears the line in his mind as it must have been all along": "He'd kill *us* if he got the chance." This implies: If he is going to kill them, they should kill him first. At last Murch dug out the old recording of Forrest's reading of the line that he had disregarded months before and used it.

In the course of mixing the soundtrack Murch noticed the significance of Coppola arranging to have a single piano to provide the underscore for the film. The background music was composed and played by DAVID SHIRE, who at that time was married to Coppola's sister, TALIA SHIRE. *The Conversation* is one of the few mainstream films to have a background score played by a solo instrument (the zither accompaniment for Carol Reed's *The Third Man* [1949] also comes to mind). Because the background music was scored for piano alone, the music has a lonely and haunting sound: "a single instrument for a film about a single, lonely man," says Murch.

Although *The Conversation* was not a box office hit, it went on to win the Palme d'Or (Golden Palm), the Grand Prize at the CANNES INTERNATIONAL FILM FESTIVAL, and to become Coppola's favorite among his movies. When I asked him why it was his favorite, he replied that *The Conversation* "is a personal film based on my own original screenplay; it represents a personal direction I wanted my career to take. I have always preferred to create my own story material, as I also did with *DEMENTIA 13* and *The Rain People*," rather than make films derived from literary works.
—GENE D. PHILLIPS

References
Richard Blake, *After Image: The Catholic Imagination of Six Filmmakers* (Chicago: Loyola Press, 2000); Roger Ebert, *The Great Movies—II* (New York: Broadway Books, 2005); Scott Foundas, "Coppola Rising," *DGA Quarterly* 3, no. 1 (Spring, 2007): 1–9; Vincent LoBrutto, *Sound on Film: Interviews with Creators of Film Sound* (New York: Praeger, 1994); Walter Murch, "Stretching Sound Conversation to Help the Mind See," *New York Times*, October 1, 2000, sec. 2: 1, 24–25; Anne Pohl, "The Conversation," in *Movies of the Seventies* (Los Angeles: Taschen, 2005), 290–93.

COPELAND, STEWART (1952–)
Stewart Copeland, composer for Coppola's *RUMBLE FISH* (1983), was born in Alexandria, Virginia, the son of a CIA officer, and spent his formative years in the Middle East. An accomplished percussionist, Copeland began his musical career in 1975 with the British rock band Curved Air, but he is best known as the drummer and one of the original members of the Police, the 1980s rock band among whose best known songs are "Roxanne" (1978), "Message in a Bottle" (1979), "Don't Stand So Close to Me" (1980), "Every Little Thing She Does Is Magic" (1981), "Every Breath You Take" (1983), and "King of Pain" (1983). Copeland was responsible for some of the band's more eccentric, experimental compositions like "On Any Other Day" for the album *Reggatta de Blanc* (1979) and "Miss Gradenko" for *Synchronicity* (1983). His brother is Miles Copeland III, founder of I.R.S. Records and manager of the Police. In 1980 he released a solo album, *Music Madness from the Kinetic Kid*, under the pseudonym Klark Kent. In 1989 he formed a jazz combo, Animal Logic, with bassist Stanley Clarke.

Copeland received a Golden Globe nomination for *Rumble Fish*, FRANCIS COPPOLA's black-and-white adaptation of the S. E. HINTON novel about alienated youth in Tulsa, Oklahoma. Copeland wrote a heavily percussive, Reggae-influenced soundtrack to accompany Coppola's narrative. The songs that Copeland wrote for the soundtrack to *Rumble Fish*, especially the song "Don't Box Me In," share some of the quirkiness of the songs he wrote for the Police. After scoring *Rumble Fish*, Copeland composed the scores for seventy films and television shows. Some of the better known films Copeland scored are *Wall Street* (1987), *Talk Radio* (1988), *Raining Stones* (1993), *Four Days in September* (1997), *West Beirut* (1998), *Pecker* (1998), and *She's All That* (1999). His television work includes episodes of *The Equalizer* (1985–1987), *Highlander* (1991), *Dead Like Me* (2003–2004), for which he was nominated for an Emmy for the title song, and *Desperate Housewives* (2004), for which he won a BMI TV Music Award. In addition to the songs he wrote for *Rumble Fish*, Copeland wrote the songs "Cannes" for *Nine ½ Weeks* (1986), "Strange Things Happen" for *The Texas Chainsaw Massacre 2* (1986), "Straight Boys" for *Pecker* (1998), and "Wait Gecko" and "I Just Know" for *The Boiler Room* (2000).

Copeland worked as director, cinematographer, producer, and editor of *Everybody Stares: The Police Inside Out* (2006), a documentary about the band. His film, *The Rhythmatist* (1985), chronicles Copeland's own musical quest to Africa. One of Copeland's rare acting roles is as American Soldier #1 in *South Park: Bigger, Longer, and Uncut* (1999).—JASON MOSSER

COPPOLA, CARMINE (1910–1991)

Musician, composer, and father of August Coppola, FRANCIS FORD COPPOLA, and of the actress TALIA SHIRE, the elder Coppola composed the music for several of his son's films and conducted his own score for the American release of ABEL GANCE's epic *Napoleon* (1927), which, after opening at Radio City Music Hall, with a full, sixty-piece American Symphony Orchestra, then toured the whole country. Trained at Juilliard and the Manhattan School of Music, during the 1940s he played first flute for the NBC Symphony Orchestra conducted by Arturo Toscanini. Carmine Coppola was born in New York on June 11, 1910, and married actress Italia Pennino, who died in 2004. In 1975 Carmine Coppola won an Academy Award with the Italian composer NINO ROTA for their original dramatic score for *THE GODFATHER: PART II*. In 1979 Coppola won a Golden Globe Award for his score for *APOCALYPSE NOW*. In 1989 Francis Coppola cast his father to play a street musician in "LIFE WITHOUT ZOE," Coppola's contribution to the omnibus film *NEW YORK STORIES*. The elder Coppola, grandfather of NICOLAS CAGE, SOFIA COPPOLA, JASON SCHWARTZMAN, and Robert Schwartzman, died in Northridge, California, at the age of eighty on April 26, 1991.—JAMES M. WELSH

COPPOLA, CHRISTOPHER (1962–)

Son of August Coppola and Joy Vogelsang, born in Los Angeles County on January 25, 1962. This film director and producer is the nephew of FRANCIS FORD COPPOLA and the older brother of NICOLAS CAGE, who was to star as a con man along with hero Val Kilmer in the film *Deadfall*, which Christopher Coppola co-produced and directed in 1993. It is described as a *film noir* environment with "lots of shadows and basically everybody's sort of enmeshed in this world where there's no hope." Christopher Coppola's debut film as director was *Dracula's Widow* (1989).—JAMES M. WELSH

COPPOLA, CRITICISM, AND CONTROVERSY

FRANCIS FORD COPPOLA has often seemed larger than life. If he were a liar, he would have specialized in whoppers. If he were a writer (and he *was*, has been, and continues to be), he would want to become an editor and publisher (as he has in fact become with *ZOETROPE: ALL-STORY*), maybe even run an empire. If he had been a playwright in the nineteenth century, he would have surpassed the extravagance of David Belasco. But he wasn't just one of these possibilities, he was *all* of them. To be sure, Coppola has made more than his share of mistakes and miscalculations. *How* would *APOCALYPSE NOW* end? *When* would it end? How much would it cost? How does one capture a dream? How could one set that dream to music and make it sing and soar? Could it be "filmed in its entirety on the stages of Zoetrope Studios," as *ONE FROM THE HEART* claimed to be? Who could afford to take such chances? Is the unexamined life worthwhile? To the distress of Paramount Pictures, Coppola rented Radio City Music Hall *on his own* and without consulting with Paramount, in order to premiere *One from the Heart* to a sold-out audience of 6,000 spectators (some of them friends and industry insiders). At a press conference afterward, one cheap-shot radio reporter claimed that everyone he had asked had disliked the film Coppola had overspent himself making and promoting. *Time* magazine recorded Coppola's reasoned response (January 25, 1982): "I'm very proud, and I imagine that years from now, just as with my other films, people will see something in it. It was an original work. It's not a copy of anything. And by the end, you're supposed to feel something—something innocent, something sweet, something romantic." Prophetic words? People might indeed see "something in it," decades later. But at the time of its release? Listen to Vincent Canby of the *New York Times*: "*One from the Heart* has no characters, no performances, no story, no comedy and no romance, only what Hollywood calls 'production values.' These are Mr. Tavoularis's sets representing a gaudy downtown Las Vegas thoroughfare and assorted cafes, offices, streets, houses, motels and nightclubs in the vicinity. . . . *One from the Heart* appears to have been originally conceived as a series of sets, then as a story to go with the sets, even though this isn't the way it happened."

The public image of Coppola in the 1980s was that of a somewhat arrogant *Wunderkind*: "I feel that I'm an object of both faith and scorn," Coppola told Tom Shales of the *Washington Post* in 1982. "I don't know to what extent, but I do feel I am not understood by my critics, that they can't believe that I could really be what I am. And so they choose to make me what they can accept, which is something of a charlatan." When asked about his least understood qualities, Coppola said: "My sincerity. And, maybe, my innocence." Coppola called *New Yorker* critic Pauline Kael "one of those critics who, when they give you a really wonderful review they almost feel that they've made you, and then when they request to see your unfinished film and you say, 'We are not showing it,' or do not invite her in an intimate way into your life, she chooses to unmake you. And Pauline Kael cannot unmake me!" Coppola added, "There's a reason why Pauline liked *THE GODFATHER* so much. 'Cause she's into power."

Over a lifetime of criticism, however, Francis Coppola has developed a wise tolerance for his would-be critics, and a certain forbearance. When asked as early as 1988 in an interview for *Mother Jones* what role the media played in covering Zoetrope's troubles, Coppola replied: "As I look at it now, the troubles I had with Zoetrope or the troubles I had with *Apocalypse* weren't so much the media's fault. I think it was more the fact that I tended to talk too much, to tell too many of my dreams too early. I disclosed too much, and thereby just left myself open to all levels of failure, if the things I said I was trying to do did not come true, or if I was not able to sell people on the idea that they were coming true. If people are armed with too much information about something, that something usually doesn't get to come true." But media critics *have* treated Coppola harshly.

Writing for *The Village Voice* (August 16, 1988), for example, David Edelstein, who found *TUCKER: THE MAN AND HIS DREAM* "so dazzling and so deeply uninteresting," opined that men "like Coppola and Lucas like to rationalize their failures. They see themselves as visionaries, men ahead of their time in a country frightened by new ideas; they blame big business for sabotaging them and the press for smearing them, and there might be some truth to all those charges. But the result of their thinking is *Tucker*, which is the ultimate Zoetrope movie in more ways than Coppola intended. Attempting to account for Zoetrope's failure, it ends up exemplifying that failure—you watch it and you know what went wrong, even if you missed *One from the Heart*, HAMMETT, *The Escape Artist*, and the others." Fortunately, other reviewers were more pleased, even charmed, by what Janet Maslin called the film's "cockeyed optimism." *New Yorker* critic Terrence Rafferty thought *Tucker* had "marvelous moments throughout," although he claimed that ultimately "the movie collapses in nostalgia, bad faith, and Capra-style populism." Rita Kempley of the *Washington Post* called *Tucker* "an Edsel of a movie," adding that, "at least it isn't a Hyundai. Coppola, bless him, would never do anything small-spirited—or for that matter economical," and concluded, "Coppola's failures are often more interesting than other directors' best efforts." In the 1988 *Mother Jones* interview, Coppola described himself as "a person who puts a lot of stock in intuition and love and feelings." Coppola added, by way of explanation, "The important thing is not so much the facts of the world around us . . . who's the president or whether Roger Ebert didn't like my film. Those things seem like little details compared to what I do know, which is that there is such a thing as passionate feeling. You take on that point of view

a little more when you're in the country by yourself, especially when you've had a couple of years like I've had." Sitting for a joint interview with Coppola for the *Washington Post*, GEORGE LUCAS claimed "I've never come across anything written about me that was very accurate." Coppola interjected with an idea he had also expressed elsewhere: "Often reporters come with the story they already want to write about us. I open up, reveal my true feelings and then without exception, wish I hadn't. My frankness is used against me."—JAMES M. WELSH

References
Vincent Canby, "Obsession with Technique," *New York Times*, February 21, 1982, sec. 2, 13; David Edelstein, "Wheeler Dealer," *The Village Voice*, August 16, 1988, 55; Jill Kearney, "Francis Ford Coppola: He's Far from Tuckered Out," *Mother Jones*, September 1988, 19–24; Rita Kempley, "Coppola in Overdrive," *Washington Post*, August 12, 1988, B1, B8; Janet Maslin, "Behind the Wheel of a Grand Obsession," *New York Times*, August 12, 1988; Donna Rosenthal, "Movie Mavericks Lucas & Coppola, Together Again," *Washington Post*, August 7, 1988, G1–G3; Tom Shales, "Master at the Brink," *Washington Post*, February 10, 1982, C1, C13; John Skow, "Going for the Cheeky Gamble," *Time*, January 25, 1982, 70.

COPPOLA, ELEANOR NEIL (1936–)
The talented wife of FRANCIS FORD COPPOLA, who worked with him on *DEMENTIA 13*, married him, bore his children, and sacrificed some of her own artistic ambitions in order to stabilize their domestic lives. She was with him in the jungle during the ordeals of filming *APOCALYPSE NOW* and kept a diary that she later published, then went on to write and partially direct *HEARTS OF DARKNESS: A FILMMAKER'S APOCALYPSE*, an award-winning documentary about the making of her husband's epic Vietnam film.

"After *Hearts of Darkness*, I shot a 'making of' [documentary] for Francis's film *THE RAINMAKER*, Sofia's film *THE VIRGIN SUICIDES*, and Roman's film *CQ*," she explained in her memoir, *NOTES ON A LIFE* (2008). These were followed in 2005 by yet another documentary on the making of Sofia's third feature film, *MARIE ANTOINETTE*.—JAMES M. WELSH

COPPOLA, FRANCIS FORD (1939–)

Auteur filmmaker; entrepreneur; and, later, vintner, who came to settle in Napa Valley, California, Francis Coppola has been called everything from "maverick" to "megalomaniac." His career has been dominated by extremes, from the phenomenal successes of the 1970s (especially *THE GODFATHER*, 1972, and *THE GODFATHER: PART II*, 1974) to some bitter disappointments in the 1980s (notably *ONE FROM THE HEART*, 1982). This pronounced duality is characteristic of Coppola's "love-hate relationship" with the Hollywood system, in which his personal vision often has been compromised for the sake of commerce.

Coppola has enjoyed some of the top honors in the film industry: two Palme d'Or Awards at the CANNES INTERNATIONAL FILM FESTIVAL, five Oscars, two Golden Globes, three Directors' Guild of America Awards, three Writers' Guild of America Awards, the British Academy Award, Best Director from the National Society of Film Critics, and a career Golden Lion from the Venice Film Festival, among others. Journalists in *Time*, *Newsweek*, and elsewhere have likened Coppola to *Wunderkind* directors ORSON WELLES and Stanley Kubrick.

Of course such praise has its sting, given the well-known turbulence of Welles's career and the gross misrepresentations that Kubrick suffered in the press. Regrettably, the same has held true for Coppola. His worst publicity was dished out around two of his most daring, unconventional projects, *APOCALYPSE NOW* (1979) and *One from the Heart*. During the filming of *Apocalypse Now* in the Philippines, a production that was running long and over budget, the press depicted Coppola as a megalomaniacal madman. Similarly, well before the release of *One from the Heart*, the press largely had deemed it a fiasco, an excessive vanity project by a director who had perhaps gotten too big for his britches. By and large, Coppola has taken such treatment in stride: "I've never been portrayed as anything but a guy on a tightrope, which is an interesting story, but it's not the whole story. I've been on a tightrope for twenty-five years."

The son of composer and musician CARMINE COPPOLA and his wife, Italia, Francis Coppola was born in Detroit, Michigan, on April 7, 1939; but he grew up in the suburbs of New York City. Coppola's career in entertainment began—as he has said he would like it to end up—as an amateur. During a childhood illness that kept him bedridden for almost a year, he occupied himself with various gadgets and puppets, making up stories and shows. As a child he also edited home movies and added sound to them. (Coppola's early affinities for puppetry and film—as well as his tendency to vacillate between intensely personal projects and films for hire—oddly parallel those of another great, visionary filmmaker, Jacques Demy.) The young Coppola was influenced by the films of Sergei Eisenstein, and he was inspired to pursue the study of theatre at Long Island's Hofstra University (alongside actors LAINIE KAZAN and JAMES CAAN), where he directed and wrote numerous plays. Then he enrolled in the master's program at UCLA's film school, where he studied with Dorothy Arzner. While at UCLA he became an assistant to B-movie king ROGER CORMAN, for whom he made his first commercial feature, the low-budget horror movie *DEMENTIA 13* (1963). His next film, *YOU'RE A BIG BOY NOW* (1966), earned him a Master of Fine Arts degree.

In the mid-1960s, Coppola wrote a number of scripts for Seven Arts, including an adaptation of Carson McCullers's *Reflections in a Golden Eye*, eventually filmed by John Huston in 1967. Around that same time he wrote *PATTON*, a screenplay that was finally filmed in 1970. After a couple of rewrites, it was primarily Coppola's version that made it to the screen, and it would win him his first of several Academy Awards.

In 1969, frustrated by his experience the year before in making the studio musical *FINIAN'S RANBOW*, Coppola founded his own production company, AMERICAN ZOETROPE. Through it, he helped launch the careers of other young filmmakers like GEORGE LUCAS, JOHN MILIUS, and Carroll Ballard. Milius told Michael Sragow: "None of those other guys—Lucas, Spielberg, all of them—could have existed without Francis's help." Furthermore, films produced by American Zoetrope over the years have introduced at least two generations of new stars to Hollywood, including AL PACINO, DIANE KEATON, ROBERT DE NIRO, ROBERT DUVALL, HARRISON FORD, ROB LOWE, EMILIO ESTEVEZ, and others.

Ironically, Coppola was reluctant to take on the project that was to become his breakthrough film: *The Godfather*. His initial reaction to MARIO PUZO's bestselling novel was one of distaste, but after a second look, Coppola saw the appeal in its fundamental study of family and power, two subjects that have always interested him immensely. After a series of uphill battles over casting decisions, cinematographic style, and other issues, the resulting film met with staggering critical and financial success.

Oddly enough, in Coppola's own view, that success may have been the worst thing that ever happened to him, as he told Sragow: "In some ways [*The Godfather*] ruined me. It just made my whole career go this way instead of the way I really wanted it to go, which was into doing original work as a writer-director. . . . The great frustration of my career is that nobody really wants me to do my own work."

On the other hand, *The Godfather* did bring about the chance for Coppola to do exactly the kind of film he wanted to make. When Paramount asked him to make *The Godfather: Part II*—an idea that he says initially "seemed horrible"—Coppola agreed only on the condition that the studio finance a smaller, more personal project, *THE CONVERSATION* (1974), which remains his favorite among all of his films.

During the mid- to late-1970s, Coppola produced and directed his most notorious film, *Apocalypse Now*, a project plagued by negative rumors for much of its production. A seemingly chaotic series of preview screenings arguably predisposed critics and audiences alike to beware of the film. Despite winning the prestigious Palme d'Or at the Cannes International Film Festival—making Coppola the first director ever to win the award twice—*Apocalypse Now* took several years to break even on its $31 million budget. In subsequent years, the film has garnered a reputation as an acknowledged masterpiece.

Still enjoying the windfall of his success with *The Godfather* and *The Godfather: Part II*, Coppola took some of the biggest chances of his career in the late 1970s and early 1980s. In 1979, largely with money he had earned from his profit-participation in the *Godfather* films, Coppola purchased the old Hollywood General Studios and formed Zoetrope Studios. The idea was

Coppola on the set of *Tucker: The Man and His Dream*.

to create an updated studio system, with a stable of players, writers, and technicians, along with a few old-school consultants and "artists in residence," such as Gene Kelly and Michael Powell.

The first (and only) film that Coppola would produce and direct at Zoetrope Studios was his ill-fated musical fantasy, *One from the Heart*, probably the biggest disappointment of his career. The film suffered from distribution problems, compounded by reports in the press about the perceived excesses of the production—echoes of *Apocalypse Now*. Coppola expressed his

frustrations with these misrepresentations: "*One from the Heart* suffered from the perception of me as some wild, egomaniac Donald Trump type of guy, and once they think about you that way, it's just so many months before you're brought down."

The commercial failure of *One from the Heart*, together with the disappointing box office performance of other films produced by Zoetrope Studios, left Coppola saddled with tremendous debt by the mid-1980s. He had bet big and lost big, and in 1984 he was forced to sell the studio real estate at auction. Still, determined as ever to stay in the game, he took on the role of director-for-hire on a number of films, with the aim of pulling out of debt and resurfacing to make his own kind of pictures.

A few of those works for hire have enjoyed considerable commercial and even critical success, notably *PEGGY SUE GOT MARRIED* (1986), starring KATHLEEN TURNER and Coppola's nephew, NICOLAS CAGE. Although these were not the kind of personal films that Coppola would have preferred to make, he insists that he "never took on anything with the attitude that it was going to be terrible. It may have turned out that way, but I thought it was great while I was doing it."

A curious trend in Francis Coppola's career is that his films often bear uncanny parallels to his own life. For example, the story of *TUCKER: THE MAN AND HIS DREAM* (1988) could very well describe Coppola's problematic relationship with the Hollywood system. More strikingly, at the time when Coppola was shooting *GARDENS OF STONE* (a 1987 film about the loss of young soldiers in the Vietnam War), his oldest son, Gian-Carlo (Gio), was killed in a boating accident. Coppola candidly told GENE PHILLIPS: "I was doing a movie about the burying of young boys and suddenly found that my own boy died right in the midst of it; and his funeral was held in the same chapel where we shot similar scenes of deceased veterans in *Gardens of Stone*. My son is gone, but his memory is not."

In the 1990s, Coppola continued to work sporadically as a director-for-hire on such films as *JACK* (1996), starring ROBIN WILLIAMS, and *THE RAINMAKER* (1997), a compelling David-and-Goliath courtroom drama starring MATT DAMON and DANNY DEVITO; but subsequently he hit a directorial dry spell in which he did not complete a film for ten full years. During that time, however, Coppola continued to be active in the film business as a producer and executive producer, notably on a few projects directed by his children, Sofia and Roman: *THE VIRGIN SUICIDES* (2000), *LOST IN TRANSLATION* (2003), and *CQ* (2002), among others.

In 2007, Coppola returned to directing with *YOUTH WITHOUT YOUTH*, a low-budget literary adaptation starring TIM ROTH, shot on location in Bucharest. Coppola's next project, *TETRO* (2009) was his first original screenplay since 1974. The film stars VINCENT GALLO and newcomer ALDEN EHRENREICH as estranged brothers from a competitive, artistic Italian American family, who reunite in Buenos Aires and somewhat reluctantly dig up the family's buried skeletons.

Fascinated with gadgetry since childhood, Coppola has tended to employ the latest technology in his work. Indeed, for most of his career Coppola has been just as interested in new cinematic technologies as he has been in narrative techniques. His forward-thinking hopes for an "ELECTRONIC CINEMA," articulated numerous times since the 1970s, may finally be fulfilled with the current, ongoing digital revolution. Coppola articulated his astonishingly prescient ambitions in 1979: "I believe we'll be the first all-electronic movie

studio in the world. . . . We won't shoot on film or even on tape; it'll be on some other memory—call it electronic memory. And then there's the possibility of synthesizing images on computers, of having an electronic facsimile of Napoleon playing the life of Napoleon."

In 1992, Coppola said that he had been "sure that the motion picture industry was going to turn into a worldwide electronic communications industry, that television was going to be international, that satellites were going to make any part of the world as viable as any other part of the world, that advanced editing and forms of high-definition television were going to allow filmmakers to cook up what they had in their heads cheaper and easier, and there was going to be a great golden age of communication." Now, almost two decades later, most of Coppola's predictions have come to pass, and with the benefit of hindsight we can see more clearly the potential that Coppola foresaw a generation ago.
—RODNEY HILL

References

"Francis Ford Coppola," *Variety* Profiles, www .variety.com; Gene D. Phillips and Rodney Hill, eds., *Francis Ford Coppola: Interviews* (Jackson: University Press of Mississippi, 2004).

COPPOLA, GIAN-CARLO ["GIO"] (1963–1986)

Born September 17, 1963, in Los Angeles, the first son of Francis and Eleanor Coppola, who worked with his father as associate producer for *RUMBLE FISH* and *THE OUTSIDERS*; second-unit director for *THE COTTON CLUB* and the Michael Jackson short, *CAPTAIN EO*, for Disney; and video editor on *ONE FROM THE HEART*. Disaster struck when Gian-Carlo was assigned as second-unit director for *GARDENS OF STONE*. He was killed at the age of 22 in a Memorial Day boating accident near

Annapolis, Maryland, on May 26, 1986, while taking a day off from the filming of *Gardens of Stone* at Arlington National Cemetery. Griffin O'Neal, the son of actor Ryan O'Neal, first reported by *Variety* as a passenger on the boat who was also injured, was, according to other sources, at the helm and later "convicted of reckless endangerment and gross negligence" for having caused the accident. At the time Gian-Carlo died, his fiancée, Jacqui de la Fontaine, was two months pregnant with their daughter, Gian-Carla Coppola, who was born on January 1, 1987.—JAMES M. WELSH

Reference

"Coppola's Son Dies in Boating Mishap," *Variety*, May 28, 1986, 4, 96.

COPPOLA ON ADAPTATION

FRANCIS COPPOLA is a visionary auteur, if ever any American director has earned that designation. "I had always approached my career thinking that I was going to be a writer-director—that I was one of the few guys that *could* write an original screenplay," Coppola told interviewer Michael Sragow, and, to be sure, both *THE RAIN PEOPLE* (1969) and *THE CONVERSATION* (1974) were based on original screenplays by Francis Coppola. His original scripts have earned accolades, and he has had a hand in writing the screenplays of all of his most famous films. GENE D. PHILLIPS notes that Coppola was hired by the independent producing company Seven Arts and was the credited cowriter for two of their films in 1966: Tennessee Williams's *THIS PROPERTY IS CONDEMNED* (which Coppola coscripted with Fred Coe and Edith Sommer) and *IS PARIS BURNING?* (which Coppola wrote with novelist GORE VIDAL). Early on, Coppola's work as adaptor-writer with Edmund H. North on Franklin J. Schaffner's *PATTON* (not released until 1970 by 20th Century-Fox,

but deemed Oscar-worthy by the Academy for Best Adapted Screenplay) and later on *THE GREAT GATSBY* helped him to gain entry into the Hollywood fraternity. Of course *APOCALYPSE NOW* was a complicated adaptation, but, then, so was *THE GODFATHER*, championed by ROBERT EVANS, chief of production at Paramount Studios, who controlled the movie rights and nursed along the project. Evans told interviewer Michael Sragow that Coppola "was not the only Italian-American director I knew, but the brightest young director I knew." *The Godfather* was not titled "MARIO PUZO's *The Godfather*," however, though (or perhaps *because*) the novelist's involvement was so ongoing and obvious. Later on, there was a trend to attach the original author's names to film adaptations—*BRAM STOKER'S DRACULA*, for example, in 1992, even though it was *really* "Francis Ford Coppola's *Dracula*," despite the screen credit given to JAMES V. HART (who apparently cooked up the odd backstory), soon to be followed by another Zoetrope production, *MARY SHELLEY'S FRANKENSTEIN*, and later, in 1997, by *JOHN GRISHAM'S THE RAINMAKER*. When Coppola returned to filmmaking after a ten-year hiatus in 2007, it was with an adaptation (though one written by an author most mass-cult Americans would not recognize), MIRCEA ELIADE's *YOUTH WITHOUT YOUTH*. *The Godfather*, cowritten by Mario Puzo and Francis Ford Coppola, who earned a second Best Adapted Screenplay Oscar for his work, presents a very interesting model for adaptation that Coppola openly has discussed with interviewers. Just as Mario Puzo had written the novel to make money, financial constraints also prompted Coppola to direct this Mafia-related film project. Coppola at first rejected the novel after first trying to read it, but he later warmed to the project when he came to understand its potential as a *family* drama—"the story of the family, this father and his sons, and questions of power and succession"—this, Coppola told *Playboy* in 1975, *this* "was a terrific story, if you could cut out all the other [vulgar] stuff. I decided it could be not only a successful movie but also a *good* movie." Coppola gave Puzo full credit for having created the story and the characters, "even in *Part II*, which I wrote more of than *Part I*," Coppola confessed. The two worked separately on the screenplay: "I would do the first draft and send it to him," Coppola told *Playboy*, "and he would make corrections and rewrite and change anything he wanted to and send it back to me, and then I'd rework it again, and it went back and forth. We work in totally different ways," Coppola said, but, clearly, this was a matter of full creative cooperation. "Like me," Coppola concluded, "Mario went after the money at first. He's very frank about that. But if the two movies are strong, it's because of what Mario originally put in his book that was strong and valid." Has there ever been a more effective example of successful cooperation between a novelist and auteur screenwriter?—JAMES M. WELSH

Reference

Gene D. Phillips and Rodney Hill, eds., *Francis Ford Coppola Interviews* (Jackson: University Press of Mississippi, 2004).

COPPOLA, ROMAN (1965–)

Second-unit director with his father, FRANCIS COPPOLA, on the following films: *BRAM STOKER'S DRACULA, JACK, THE RAINMAKER, YOUTH WITHOUT YOUTH,* and *TETRO.* Also did second-unit direction for *MARIE ANTOINETTE,* written and directed by his sister, SOFIA COPPOLA. At the age of sixteen he was the sound recordist on *The Black Stallion Returns* (1983) and worked as production assistant on location for *THE OUTSID-*

ERS and associate producer of *RUMBLE FISH.* After three years of study in film at New York University, he founded Commercial Pictures, an independent film company. Roman Coppola, co-owner of the company Directors Bureau, shot commercials (for Toyota Prius, for example), and music videos for bands like The Strokes and the French pop group, Phoenix, whose music is featured in his sister's feature film, *LOST IN TRANSLATION.* His own directorial debut feature film *CQ* was a nostalgic homage to 1969 from the vantage point of the year 2001. Written and directed by Roman Coppola, *CQ* (2002) tells the story of a spy movie called *Dragonfly* being shot in Paris in 1969 by a temperamental director, played by Gérard Depardieu, who is replaced by younger playboy (JASON SCHWARTZMAN); meanwhile, the fictional film's editor and second-unit director Paul (Jeremy Davies) is working on his own, personal film, but having problems completing it. Although *CQ* was "pilloried" after its premiere at the CANNES INTERNATIONAL FILM FESTIVAL, Elvis Mitchell's *New York Times* review of the recut American release was more generous.—JAMES M. WELSH

Reference

Elvis Mitchell, "How Contradictory Parts Go Together," *New York Times*, May 24, 2002, B18.

COPPOLA, SOFIA (1972–)

Actress; writer; and, later, director daughter of FRANCIS FORD COPPOLA, who cowrote her father's segment of the omnibus film *NEW YORK STORIES* (1989). In 1990 when WINONA RYDER pulled out of *THE GODFATHER: PART III*, Sofia Coppola agreed to replace her in the role of Mary Corleone, but she was mauled by hostile critics. When *THE VIRGIN SUICIDES*, directed and adapted by Sofia Coppola from the novel by Jeffrey Eugenides, was released in 2000, unforgiving *Washington Times* reviewer Gary Arnold remembered her as having been miscast by her father "a decade ago as the martyred ingénue of his *Godfather III*." Coppola conceded at the time that being a member of the Coppola clan helped to open doors for her: "It opens doors, but you don't just get everything handed to you," she added. By the time *The Virgin Suicides* opened at the Sundance Film Festival, the twenty-eight-year-old director had been married for a year to filmmaker SPIKE JONZE, recipient of an Oscar nomination for his directing debut film *Being John Malkovich*. She was born while her father was shooting *THE GODFATHER* and made her film debut in 1972 as the baby boy in the christening scene toward the end of that movie. Growing up, she traveled with her family to the Philippines (*APOCALYPSE NOW*), Tulsa (*THE OUTSIDERS* and *RUMBLE FISH*), Manhattan (*THE COTTON CLUB*), Los Angeles (*ONE FROM THE HEART*), and, finally, the Napa Valley, where the permanent family home and vineyards were. Her father told an interviewer: "At the very beginning of my own career, I had resolved that I would never travel to any location without taking my kids along. Although it makes academic skills suffer, it compensates with a sense of the world culture beyond one's own." She turned down an offer to attend film school at New York University, choosing instead to study painting at the California Institute of the Arts in Valencia. Her father's company helped her to find funding for her first feature film, which was screened at the Director's Fortnight section of the CANNES INTERNATIONAL FILM FESTIVAL in 1999, then purchased for distribution by Paramount Spotlight. Her next film, *LOST IN TRANSLATION*, starring Bill Murray and Scarlett Johansson, was an unexpected breakthrough success, earning Oscar nominations in 2003 for star Bill Murray and for Coppola herself

for direction, and winning for her the award for Best Original Screenplay. According to ELEANOR COPPOLA, Sofia "wrote *Lost in Translation* quickly as a little project to do while she gave herself time" before turning to the screenplay adapting Antonia Fraser's biography of the French Queen that was originally intended to be her second feature film. Consequently, *MARIE ANTOINETTE* (2006) was her third film, directed and adapted by Coppola from Antonia Fraser's book, *Marie Antoinette: The Journey*. It starred JASON SCHWARTZMAN (Coppola's cousin) as the sexually clueless Louis XVI, and Kirsten Dunst (who had worked with Coppola on *The Virgin Suicides*), perfectly cast as what *Variety* called a "famous royal airhead who in the end lost her head" (May 29–June 4, 2006). The film premiered at Cannes (where it was not admired) May 24, 2006, and played in France, though its American release was delayed until October. It offered a spectacle of flamboyant costumes designed by Milena Canonero, accompanied by catchy pop tunes. *Variety* critic Todd McCarthy wrote that "on its own terms, the approach succeeds." Stuart Klawans wrote in *The Nation* (November 6, 2006): "The honor of France was at stake last spring when Sofia Coppola's *Marie Antoinette* premiered at Cannes to a continuous accompaniment of hoots and whistles—'a welcome,' *Le Monde* reported, 'even colder than the one reserved for *The Da Vinci Code*.'" But more sympathetic reviewers took it to be a film "about superficiality rather than a superficial film." By 2006 Coppola was married to French rocker Thomas Mars (of the band Phoenix, that provided music for *Lost in Translation*) and was expecting a child, daughter Romy.
—JAMES M. WELSH

COPPOLA—THE AUTEUR AS VINTNER

When Rita Kempley interviewed FRANCIS COPPOLA for the *Washington Post* in 1987, grapes were considered merely "a sideline for the Californian, who vints wine on his 1,500-acre Napa Valley estate. He is to Bordeaux what Paul Newman is to salad dressing, with 80 acres of vineyard and his own vats burbling." By the time Francis Coppola directed *BRAM STOKER'S DRACULA* in 1992, however, the auteur director none too modestly identified himself in the press kit for that film as chairman of AMERICAN ZOETROPE, "the San Francisco–based film and television production company infused with his distinctive independent spirit of innovation and creativity," but he also boasted about being at that point "the proprietor of the Neibaum-Coppola Estate Winery in the Napa Valley [of] California, which makes Rubicon, one of America's premier wines, and where the Coppola family makes its home." How *Italian*! Francis Coppola bought the Inglenook estate, located in Rutherford, California, in the Napa Valley and turned it into the Niebaum-Coppola winery, which would later produce Francis's signature wines, such as Rubicon, described by the *Wine Spectator* as "an intense, full-flavored blend of Cabernet Sauvignon, Cabernet Franc and Merlot." The premium line as of this writing was the Francis Ford Coppola Director's Cut Cinema 2007, but for cineastes it would be the Francis Ford Coppola Sofia Rose 2008, named for his celebrity daughter. After Coppola went to Romania to film *YOUTH WITHOUT YOUTH*, one could hope that he might have developed a taste for fine Romanian vintages and might eventually import some of the better ones, such as Cotnari Grassa, from the north of Moldavia. In fact, *Variety* reported that he had been investigating Romanian vineyards.—JAMES M. WELSH

Reference

Rita Kempley, "Francis Coppola and the Creative Bond," *The Washington Post*, May 8, 1987, D1, D9.

CORMAN, ROGER WILLIAM (1926–)

Producer of *DEMENTIA 13* (1963), the film FRANCIS FORD COPPOLA directed after having worked for two years as a Corman assistant. Corman also appeared in a cameo role as a senator in *THE GODFATHER: PART II* (1974). Born in Detroit, Michigan, on April 5, 1926, the son of William Corman, an engineer who had served in the navy in World War I, and his wife, Anne. In 1940, Roger Corman moved with his family to Beverly Hills, California, and attended Beverly Hills High School, graduating in 1943, and then enrolling at Stanford University, intending to become an engineer and earning a degree in industrial engineering in 1947. In 1948 Corman went to Baillol College, Oxford, to read English literature for a term, and then traveled in Europe. Back in California in 1951, Corman found work, first reading, then writing scripts, and, finally, directing and producing. Corman ultimately became the main producer for American International Pictures, where he encouraged and mentored many gifted younger directors. In 1970 Corman founded the successful production and distribution company New World Pictures. In December of 1976 the British Film Institute at the National Film Theatre, London, ran a retrospective called "The Corman Connection," featuring films made by Corman-tutored writers and directors, including Robert Towne, Francis Ford Coppola, JOHN MILIUS, Richard Rush, Martin Scorsese, Monte Hellman, and others. The BFI program notes selected Coppola as "arguably the most successful graduate of the Corman school." Corman's biographer notes that Coppola was the first Corman alumnus "to hire his former boss as an actor, casting him as a U.S. senator in *The Godfather: Part II* (1974)." On November 12, 2009, the Associated Press reported that Corman, eighty-three, as director and producer of 350 movie credits, would receive an honorary Oscar for lifetime achievement.—JAMES M. WELSH

Reference

Beverly Gray, *Roger Corman: An Unauthorized Biography of the Godfather of Indie Filmmaking* (Los Angeles: Renaissance Books, 2000).

THE COTTON CLUB (1984)

DIRECTOR: Francis Ford Coppola. SCREEN-PLAY: William Kennedy, Francis Coppola, from a story by William Kennedy, Francis Coppola, and Mario Puzo. PRODUCER: Robert Evans for American Zoetrope-Orion. PRODUCER CONSULTANT: Milton Forman. COPRODUCERS: Silvio Tabet, Fred Roos. EXECUTIVE PRODUCER: Dyson Lovell. LINE PRODUCERS: Barrie M. Osborne, Joseph Cusumano. PHOTOGRAPHY: Stephen Goldblatt. EDITING: Barry Malkin, Robert Q. Lovett. MUSIC: John Barry, Bob Wilber. PRODUCTION DESIGN: Richard Sylbert. ART DIRECTION: David Chapman, Gregory Bolton. COSTUME DESIGN: Milena Canonero. SOUND EDITING: Edward Beyer. MONTAGE AND SECOND UNIT DIRECTOR: Gian-Carlo Coppola. PRINCIPAL CHOREOGRAPHER: Michael Smuin. TAP CHOREOGRAPHER: Henry Le Tang.
CAST: Richard Gere (Dixie Dwyer), Gregory Hines (Sandman Williams), Diane Lane (Vera Cicero), Lonette McKee (Lila Rose Oliver), Bob Hoskins (Owney Madden), James Remar (Dutch Schultz), Nicolas Cage (Vincent Dwyer), Allen Garfield (Abbadabba Berman), Fred Gwynne (Frenchy), Gwen Verdon (Tish Dwyer), Lisa Jane Persky (Frances Flegenheimer), Maurice Hines (Clay Williams), Julian Beck (Sol Weinstein), Novella Nelson (Madame St. Claire), Larry Fishburne (Bumpy Rhodes), John Ryan (Joe Flynn), Tom Waits (Irving Stark), Ron Karabatsos, Glenn Withrow, Jennifer Grey, Wynonna Smith,

Thelma Carpenter, Charles "Honi" Coles, Larry Marshall, Joe Dallesandro. RUNNING TIME: 128 minutes. Technicolor. PREMIERE: December 14, 1984. DVD: MGM.

ROBERT EVANS, who was production chief at Paramount when FRANCIS FORD COPPOLA filmed *THE GODFATHER* there, in due course left his position to become an independent producer. By the early 1980s, Evans's career was in dire straits, and he hoped to get back on top by making *The Cotton Club*.

In 1982 Evans optioned James Haskins's *The Cotton Club*, a coffee-table book that was a nonfiction picture-history of the famous Harlem nightclub that enjoyed its heyday in the Roaring Twenties, a cabaret where the drinks were cold and the jazz was hot.

The Cotton Club was designed as a musical about the famed Harlem nightspot that flourished in the Prohibition Era, where the entertainers were black and the customers were white. Because the club was run by a racketeer named Owney Madden and his cohorts, the plot at times takes on the dimensions of a gangster picture, thereby recalling the director's *Godfather* films. The concept of blending the format of the movie musical with that of the gangster movie—the two most popular film genres during the period of the early talkies—seemed like a dandy idea in theory; but it did not work out satisfactorily in practice.

Evans planned to finance the picture through private investors. He eventually made a deal with Ed and Fred Doumani, owners of the Tropicana and El Morocco casinos in Las Vegas. The brothers were reputed to have links to the Mafia in Vegas, but Evans believed that their checkbooks were as good as anyone else's.

Since the present film was to some extent a gangster picture, Evans commissioned MARIO PUZO— who by this time had cowritten the screenplays of *The Godfather* and *THE GODFATHER: PART II*— to do the first draft of the script. But Evans was dissatisfied with the screenplay Puzo submitted in the summer of 1982. Although Evans and Coppola had had multiple clashes during the filming of *The Godfather*, Evans was confident that Coppola would be glad to make a fast buck revising Puzo's *Cotton Club* screenplay. Evans was convinced that the new picture would be "*The Godfather* with music," and would prove to be another winner.

After filming *RUMBLE FISH* (1983) Coppola was brought in at the eleventh hour to collaborate on *The Cotton Club*. By the time he signed on to rewrite the script and to direct the movie, the project was plagued with a variety of production problems, as well as with an unviable screenplay; Coppola did his best to improve matters. He decided that the only way to make more room for the white gangster plot in the scenario was to have the story of the Cotton Club's black entertainers simply provide a backdrop for the melodrama about the white mobsters. Evans bought the concept.

Coppola decided that the screenplay was still not up to par and called in Pulitzer Prize–winning novelist WILLIAM KENNEDY, who had written a trilogy of novels about the Roaring Twenties.

One of the major obstacles they met in rewriting the script, according to Kennedy, was the "perpetual task of enhancing RICHARD GERE's role." Since Gere as Dixie Dwyer, the lone white musician at the Cotton Club, was the male lead, he had to be central to the story. So Dixie became an employee of the infamous Dutch Schultz (JAMES REMAR), a sadistic real-life mobster who frequented the club.

In addition to Richard Gere and GREGORY HINES (as Delbert "Sandman" Williams), the cast now included BOB HOSKINS as Owney Madden; DIANE LANE, who had appeared in two previous Coppola films, as Vera Cicero, Dixie's inamorata; and Lonette McKee as Lila Rose Oliver, Hines's love interest. Gregory Hines's own brother, Maurice, played Delbert's brother Clayton Williams. Julian Beck, cofounder of New York's Living Theater, was cast as Sol Weinstein, Dutch Schultz's grizzled, world-weary enforcer. NICOLAS CAGE was given a meatier role than he had had in *Rumble Fish*, that of Gere's tough younger brother, Vincent "Mad Dog" Dwyer.

Coppola selected Michael Smuin, of the San Francisco Ballet, as choreographer; British cinematographer Stephen Goldblatt as director of photography; and BARRY MALKIN, by now a Coppola regular, as editor. Principal photography commenced on August 28, 1983, at the historic ASTORIA STUDIOS in Queens, where the Marx Brothers made *The Cocoanuts* in 1929.

Recalling Evans's constant interference during the shooting of *The Godfather*, when Evans was studio boss at Paramount, Coppola took the precaution of barring him from the set of *The Cotton Club*. He was able to make this stricture stick by threatening to quit.

Since Coppola found it helpful to have his co-scripter S. E. HINTON on the set of *Rumble Fish* for last-minute rewrites, he decided to keep Kennedy on salary while *The Cotton Club* was in production. Still, the endless script revisions caused delays in shooting. As a result, filming fell increasingly behind schedule. As DEAN TAVOULARIS quipped, "For Francis a script is like a newspaper; a new one comes out every day."

Nicolas Cage became so frustrated by the delays that one day he angrily trashed his dressing room. "I was slated for three weeks' work," he explains. "I was there for six months, in costume, in makeup, on the set" in case Coppola got around to doing a scene in which Cage was scheduled to appear. Francis Coppola tactfully explained his nephew's behavior by saying that Cage's fit of rage was meant to help him in preparing to play the ruthless "Mad Dog" Dwyer in the picture, a character based on the real gangster "Mad Dog" Coll.

Finally, when the film's triumvirate of investors threatened to cut off the cash flow, Coppola announced posthaste that he was going to draw on his early experience working on ROGER CORMAN's low-budget flicks. He would abandon any further rewrites and shoot the remaining scenes with maximum efficiency. Three days in a row he did a dozen camera setups per day, whereas he had previously been averaging two to three setups a day. On December 22, Coppola took the unit to Grand Central Station to film the final scene, which he and Kennedy had not had time to script. Coppola kept the cameras rolling for nearly twenty hours and wrapped the picture at 6:00 AM on December 23, 1983.

The shooting period for *The Cotton Club* eventually ran to eighty-seven days, spread over twenty-two months. By the end of shooting, the budget had skyrocketed to $48 million, nearly double the original figure. In his own defense Coppola emphasized that a substantial part of the overage was due to the fact that Evans had been mismanaging the funds during preproduction for six months before he got involved.

At any rate, Coppola's rough cut ran 140 minutes; Orion, the film's distributor, insisted on a film closer to a conventional length of two hours. One way of shortening the film was to condense the songs and dances performed by the black entertainers at the Cotton Club and leave the main plot about the white mobsters pretty much

intact. In retrospect, Coppola acknowledges that "we eliminated about twenty minutes or so" of the musical numbers "that probably should not have been cut out." Coppola thought *The Cotton Club* would have been more successful in a longer version. The film was finally released at 128 minutes.

The plot of *The Cotton Club* as released revolves around the lives of two pairs of brothers, and their stories are told in parallel fashion. The white brothers are Dixie and Vincent Dwyer. Dixie Dwyer, a cornet player, is the token white musician at the Cotton Club and is allowed to sit in with the band. He is also a minion of beer baron Dutch Schultz and secretly falls for Dutch's teenaged gun moll, Vera Cicero. His younger brother Vinnie is an inexperienced hood who hopes to gain the Dutchman's favor by becoming Dutch's bodyguard. The two black brothers are Delbert "Sandman" Williams and Clayton Williams, a dance team at the Cotton Club. Sandman longs to make it big as a solo act in order to impress Lila Rose Oliver, a satiny torch singer at the club. Clay is hurt when Sandman goes off on his own, but they eventually are reconciled.

A fair amount of screen time is spent in portraying how Dixie uses his association with Dutch Schultz to snag the title role in a Hollywood gangster picture called *Mob Boss*, in which he imitates his erstwhile boss Dutch Schultz. To that extent, Dixie is based on George Raft, a dancer in New York nightclubs who, by his own admission, got help from top underworld figures in his struggle to make it in pictures. He gained overnight success as a coin-flipping gangster in *Scarface* (1932). Gere even had his hair brushed back flat with brilliantine just to look more like Raft. (Dixie's parlaying his mob connections into a screen career recalls the episode in *The Godfather* when Vito Corleone fostered the movie career of Johnny Fontane, who, as we know, was modeled in some ways on Frank Sinatra.)

Richard Gere and James Remar in *The Cotton Club*.

At film's end Vera is free of Dutch, who perishes in a gangland killing, and can marry Dixie; and Sandman has likewise won the heart of Lila. Coppola accordingly stages a grand finale that cuts between Grand Central Station and a Grand Central set on the Cotton Club stage—a sequence that is not in the shooting script and, consequently, was created by Coppola during filming. On stage, Clay Williams leads the Cotton Club company through a dance number set in the depot, and the action shifts to Sandman and Lila at Grand Central Station going off on their honeymoon, while Dixie is reunited with Vera on the depot platform. The two couples travel off on the Twentieth Century Limited toward marital bliss, to the tune of Duke Ellington's "Daybreak Express." Pianist-humorist Oscar Levant once described the movie musical as a series of catastrophes ending in a floor show. That description certainly fits *The Cotton Club*, which has its share of catastrophes and yet concludes with a dazzling production number.

The Cotton Club premiered in New York City on December 8, 1984. Pauline Kael condemned the present film as "a composite of the old Warner Bros. gangster pictures and musicals of the 1930s. It seems that Coppola had skimmed the top off every 1930s movie he had ever seen, added seltzer, stirred it with a swizzle stick, and called it a movie."

Admittedly, *The Cotton Club* has its share of eye-filling musical numbers, featuring the celebrated dancer Gregory Hines, plus some exciting action sequences built around harrowing gangland shootouts between rival mobs of bootleggers. Nevertheless, despite Coppola's conscientious efforts to whip the movie into shape, *The Cotton Club* remains a hybrid, a mixture of two disparate screen genres that, in the last analysis, never quite coalesce into a unified work of art. Still *The Cotton Club* is a film worth watching, and it has attracted on DVD some of the wider audience it deserves.—GENE D. PHILLIPS

References

Peter Biskind, *Easy Riders, Raging Bulls: Coppola, Scorsese, and Other Directors* (New York: Simon & Schuster, 1999); Michael Daly, "A True Tale of Hollywood: *The Cotton Club*," *New York*, May 7, 1984, 43–60; Robert Evans, *The Kid Stays in the Picture: A Memoir* (Beverly Hills, Dove, 1995); Lawrence Grobel, *Above the Line: Conversations with Robert Evans and Others* (New York: Da Capo, 2000); Noel Isaacs, "*The Cotton Club*: A Reverie," *Literature/Film Quarterly* 24, no. 1 (Winter, 1996): 109–10; Pauline Kael, *State of the Art* (New York: Dutton, 1985).

COTTON CLUB MURDER CASE

ROBERT EVANS, who had been studio chief at Paramount when FRANCIS COPPOLA made *THE GODFATHER*, eventually became an independent producer. In 1982 Evans decided to make *THE COTTON CLUB*, about the famous nightclub in Harlem during the Jazz Age that catered to a high-class white clientele. He decided to make a peace treaty with Coppola, with whom he had constantly battled during the making of *The Godfather*, and ask him to write and direct the movie.

Evans opted to obtain financial backing for the picture from private investors, and got Ed and Fred Doumani, owners of two Las Vegas casinos, to back the film. The Doumanis were linked to the Mafia in Vegas, but no matter, Evans was desperate for financing. The Doumanis, in turn, recruited Denver oilman Victor Sayyah as a coinvestor. Like the Doumanis, Sayyah was known to be a tough customer and to drive a hard bargain.

During production, the trio of investors constantly pressured Coppola to cut expenses; but, as Coppola periodically reminded them, the production had been running full speed ahead for six months before he came on board, when Evans was supervising preproduction—and overspending. The Doumanis eventually threatened to withdraw from the project, which was going considerably over schedule and over budget, unless things improved.

Evans panicked and frantically cast about for additional investors. He got to hear about Elaine Jacobs (aka Karen Jacobs-Greenberger), a rich, blonde divorcée from Texas, who was interested in getting into the film business. She was in fact involved in dubious dealings with the underworld, and had ties to a Colombian drug cartel. But Evans at this juncture felt that "beggars couldn't be choosers" and agreed to let Jacobs put him in touch with Roy Radin, a sleazy variety show promoter from New York. Radin arranged a multimillion-dollar loan from some of his disreputable financial sources, in order to provide Evans with additional backing for *The Cotton Club*.

Shortly afterward, Radin had a major falling out with Jacobs, who discovered that he had surreptitiously possessed himself of 200 kilos of cocaine from her private stash. Radin was last seen on May 13, 1983, getting into Jacobs's limo, on his way to a dinner meeting with her at La Scala, at which they were presumably going to bury the hatchet. As a matter of fact, the hatchet, so to speak, was buried in Radin; his decomposed corpse turned up a month later in a remote canyon on the outskirts of Los Angeles. He had been shot several times through the head, and a stick of dynamite had been shoved into his mouth and the fuse lit. Evans, aware that the drug dealings between Radin and Jacobs had gone sour, went ballistic. A detective on the case later testified that Evans confided to the Doumanis, "That bitch killed Radin; and I'm next"—though there was no evidence that Jacobs was a threat to Evans.

Still, Evans was inevitably dragged into the case as a material witness, and so Jacobs's trial was dubbed by the tabloids the *Cotton Club* murder case. He was eventually exonerated of any involvement in Radin's death, while Jacobs was convicted of the kidnapping and killing of Radin in retaliation for the theft of the cocaine. Needless to say, the loan Radin had engineered for Evans never materialized. Brett Morgen and Nanette Burstein's documentary *The Kid Stays in the Picture*, based on Evans's autobiography of the same title, is riveting in its coverage of the *Cotton Club* murder case. It includes newsreel footage of the murder scene and of Jacobs's trial.

Meanwhile Coppola, who staunchly contends that he was completely ignorant of Evans's negotiations with Jacobs and Radin, soldiered on with the screenplay, and the Doumanis stayed on board. Toward the end of filming, the Doumanis and Sayyah, who had no previous experience in the picture business and who had had no luck in dealing with Coppola, were finally fed up. In fact, Sayyah got so infuriated during a cost-accounting conference with associate producer Melissa Prophet, Coppola's liaison with the investors, that he went berserk and hurled her through a plate glass window. A wag quipped that a Prophet is not known in her own country. With that, Sayyah sheepishly repaired to Vegas.

Hearing about Evans's negotiations with racketeers, one trade paper commented that Evans was willing to make deals with individuals whom the most reputable producers would hesitate to shake hands with.—GENE D. PHILLIPS

References

John Connolly, "Man of a Thousand Lives: Robert Evans," *Premiere* 14, no. 8: 93–97, 119; Michael Daly, "A True Tale of Hollywood: *The Cotton Club*," *New York*, May 7, 1984, 43–60; Robert Evans, *The Kid Stays in the Picture: A Memoir* (Beverly Hills: Dove, 1995); Jon Lewis, *Whom God Wishes to Destroy: Francis Coppola and the New Hollywood* (Durham, NC: Duke University Press, 1997).

CQ (2001)

DIRECTOR: Roman Coppola. SCREENPLAY: Roman Coppola. PRODUCER: Gary Marcus. EXECUTIVE PRODUCERS: Willi Bär and Francis Ford Coppola. PHOTOGRAPHY: Robert D. Yeoman. EDITING: Leslie Jones. MUSIC SUPERVISOR: Brian Reitzell. ADDITIONAL MUSIC: Roger Neill. PRODUCTION DESIGN: Dean Tavoularis. ART DIRECTION: Luc Chalon and Oshin Yeghiazariantz. SET DECORATION: Philippe Turlure. COSTUME DESIGN: Judy Shrewsbury.
CAST: Jeremy Davies (Paul), Angela Lindvall (Valentine/Dragonfly), Élodie Bouchez (Marlene), Gérard Depardieu (Andrezej), Giancarlo Giannini (Enzo), Massimo Ghini (Fabrizio), Jason Schwartzman (Felix DeMarco), Billy Zane (Mr. E.), Dean Stockwell (Dr. Ballard).
RUNNING TIME: 88 minutes. Color.
RELEASED THROUGH: United Artists. PREMIERE: May 12, 2001.
DVD: MGM.

Written and directed by ROMAN COPPOLA, this retro-mod art film was financed by AMERICAN ZOETROPE, with FRANCIS FORD COPPOLA as executive producer. ELEANOR COPPOLA made a documentary about the making of *CQ*, just as she had done for *THE VIRGIN SUICIDES* (her daughter Sofia's first feature film) and *APOCALYPSE NOW*. Generally dismissed by critics, *CQ* has a great deal of charm, and it is exactly the sort of small, personal project that Roman's father has striven repeatedly to make himself.

Jeremy Davies stars as Paul, an aspiring American filmmaker working in Paris in 1969 as an editor on a sci-fi art film, *Codename: Dragonfly*, directed by the temperamental Andrezej (Gérard Depardieu). At the same time, Paul is working on a no-budget, independent, and very personal film of his own, chronicling his difficult relationship with his live-in Parisienne girlfriend, Marlene (Élodie Bouchez). After an explosive confrontation, *Dragonfly*'s producer, Enzo (GIANCARLO GIANNINI) fires Andrezej and replaces him with the eccentric Felix DeMarco (JASON SCHWARTZMAN). Before he can even start working on the picture, DeMarco is injured in a car wreck, and Enzo desperately turns to Paul to rescue the production. Andrezej, believing that his artistic vision will be compromised for the sake of commercial viability, attempts to sabotage the completion of the film; but Paul assures him that the ending of the film will preserve Andrezej's antiestablishment point of view. As Paul gets more and more involved with *Codename: Dragonfly* and its sexy star, Valentine (Angela Lindvall), his relationship with Marlene falls apart, and his own independent film suffers as well. *CQ* ends with Paul attempting to balance the success of *Dragonfly* with his desire to continue making smaller, more personal films. Director Roman Coppola told *Variety*: "I wanted my first film to express my own voice, a film that was personal to me. I wanted to be the only director who could have made this movie."

References abound to other films and filmmakers— including Godard's *Alphaville* (1965), Truffaut's *Day for Night* (1973), Kubrick's *2001* (1968) and *Dr. Strangelove* (1964), and Franju's variations on Feuillade. Of course, Roman Coppola has also been influenced by the career of his father, as Eleanor Coppola explains in her documentary: "You never know what your kids are going to remember from their childhood. Once Francis put his fist through a door in frustration during a production, and . . . the crew framed it and gave it to him as a present." (Such an episode occurs with Andrezej in *CQ*.) Francis Coppola adds: "Roman incorporated many of his impressions as well as his memories of being in a family that was involved in filmmaking and of the many

colleagues that I had during the time that he was a little boy, and somehow took all of these impressions and fashioned them into this ingenious piece."

Far from being simply a throwaway string of postmodern pastiche, however, these references are deftly handled and come across as genuinely affectionate homages that attest to Roman Coppola's wide-ranging taste in film. He told one interviewer, "I like more arty, brainy movies; I also like stupid, playful, fun movies." A big part of *CQ*'s appeal is its funky, groovy quality, coupled with its self-aware interrogation of realism versus stylization in the cinema.

The film premiered at the fifty-fourth CANNES INTERNATIONAL FILM FESTIVAL in 2001 and was fairly ravaged by critics, leading Roman Coppola to recut the picture. One of the few rave reviews came from Elvis Mitchell in the *New York Times*: "There's nothing like love to give a movie a B-12 shot, and 'CQ' shimmers with it. Mr. Coppola extends an invitation to audiences to join his retro love-in to become helplessly caught in the thrall of a dazed sexiness reminiscent of 60's pop, which the score by Mellow evokes thoroughly and beautifully. Don't fight the undertow. Go along with it."

Other reviewers acknowledged *CQ*'s visual stylishness but seemed to miss the fun and substance that it has to offer, suggesting that the film ultimately falls flat. Perhaps as a result of this general critical misunderstanding, *CQ* was a commercial failure, with a cumulative box office gross of less than half a million dollars. Luckily, however, Roman Coppola seems to have learned an important lesson from his father's career and has not let this setback deter him from forging ahead. In the years since *CQ*, the younger Coppola has continued to work as a director of music videos and a producer on a number of film and video projects.—Rodney Hill

References
Eleanor Coppola, "CQ—4 Documentaries from 5 Different Filmmakers: Ellie," *CQ* DVD Special Features (MGM, 2002); Elvis Mitchell, "How Contradictory Parts Go Together," *New York Times*, May 24, 2002; Matthew M. Ross, "Less Can Be More," *Variety*, January 8, 2002.

CRUISE, TOM [THOMAS CRUISE MAPOTHER IV] (1962–)

Arguably the most successful actor of the so-called "brat pack," Cruise played Steve Randle in FRANCIS FORD COPPOLA's 1983 film, *THE OUTSIDERS*. Born in Syracuse, New York, on July 3, 1962, Thomas Cruise Mapother IV was the son of an electrical engineer, Thomas Cruise Mapother III, originally from Canada. When his father left in 1973, Cruise's mother, Mary Lee Mapother, moved her family to Louisville, Kentucky, where she remarried; the family finally settled in Glen Ridge, New Jersey. There, in 1980, Cruise joined the high school production of *Guys and Dolls* when a leg injury forced him off the school's wrestling squad. He later recalled: "All of a sudden, I felt like I knew what I was doing. I got all this attention, and it just felt right."

Within a year, he was appearing on the big screen, with a small role in Franco Zeffirelli's *Endless Love* (1981), followed by a more substantial part in *Taps* that same year. Next came a role in Francis Ford Coppola's *The Outsiders*, which Cruise was filming when he tested for his breakthrough role as Joel Goodson in Paul Brickman's *Risky Business*, the sleeper hit of 1983. For that film, Cruise won the Golden Globe Award for Best Actor. His next major role came in *All the Right Moves* (1983), in which he portrays a young man hoping that his football prowess will help him escape life in the depressed steel town in which he grew up. Following his role in Ridley Scott's *Legend* (1985), Cruise portrayed a fearless jet pilot in Tony Scott's *Top Gun*, and he became the top box office star of 1986.

Subsequently Cruise began to establish a more serious reputation as an actor, costarring with Paul Newman in Martin Scorsese's *The Color of Money* (1986); with Dustin Hoffman in Barry Levinson's *Rain Man* (1987), a performance that Molly Haskell called "magnificent, generous"; and starring in Oliver Stone's *Born on the Fourth of July* (1989) as paralyzed Vietnam veteran Ron Kovic, and in Neil Jordan's 1994 adaptation of Anne Rice's *Interview with the Vampire*.

One of Cruise's most profusely lauded performances was in the title role in Cameron Crowe's *Jerry Maguire* (1996) which earned Cruise the Golden Globe Award nomination, and National Board of Review Award for Best Actor, among many other awards. So far, the Oscar has eluded Tom Cruise, but he remains one of the top male stars, in terms of box office draw, in the world; and Janet Maslin calls Cruise a real, "old-fashioned movie star." Cruise's tremendous star appeal made him Stanley Kubrick's top choice for the male lead in *Eyes Wide Shut* (1999), the great director's under-appreciated swan song.

In recent years Tom Cruise has branched out into producing, and beginning with *Mission: Impossible* (1996) he has served as producer or executive producer on a number of films in which he also stars. They include *Vanilla Sky* (2001), *The Last Samurai* (2003), and *Valkyrie* (2008).—JAMES M. WELSH/RODNEY HILL

References
James Cameron-Wilson, *Young Hollywood* (London: B.T. Batsford, 1994); Gene D. Phillips and Rodney Hill, *The Encyclopedia of Stanley Kubrick* (New York: Facts On File, 2002).

D

DALLESANDRO, JOE (1948–)

Actor who appears as Lucky Luciano in Coppola's *THE COTTON CLUB* (1984). Joe Dallesandro is perhaps best known for his scantily clad roles in various underground skin flicks produced by Andy Warhol and directed by Paul Morrissey, including *Flesh* (1968) and *Trash* (1970), and later the horror parodies *Flesh for Frankenstein* (1973) and *Blood for Dracula* (1974).

Prior to his work with Warhol, Dallesandro modeled for various homoerotic publications produced by the Athletic Modeling Guild, and he purportedly appeared in a pornographic "loop" circa 1965. Because of this early visibility in the gay subculture, Dallesandro has remained a cult gay icon, even though his own sexuality is difficult to pin down. (In a 1993 interview with the *Advocate*, he suggested that he was bisexual.) John R. Burger characterizes Dallesandro as "an inadvertent embodiment of the post-1960 development of gay male sexual representation."

Dallesandro's appeal as a sexual icon seemed to dwindle after the mid-1970s, at which time he embarked on a series of appearances in European films, including Serge Gainsbourg's *Je t'aime, moi non plus* (1976). Since then he has taken on minor roles in numerous American films, including Coppola's *The Cotton Club*, John Waters's *Cry Baby* (1990), and Stephen Soderbergh's *The Limey* (1999).

In 2009 a documentary on Dallesandro's career, *Little Joe*, appeared, with Dallesandro himself credited as writer and one of the producers. The film's tagline none-too-subtly hints at its subject's sex appeal: "Andy Warhol made him famous. The underground films made him a sexual icon. His body made him a legend."—RODNEY HILL

References

John R. Burger, *One-Handed Histories: The Eroto-Politics of Gay Male Video Pornography* (Binghamton, NY: Haworth, 1995); "Joe Dallesandro, " Internet Movie Database, www.imdb.com/name/nm0198072/

DAMON, MATT (1970–)

Award-winning American screenwriter and actor who played Rudy Baylor, an idealistic young attorney in Coppola's adaptation of John Grisham's *THE RAINMAKER* (1997). Damon also played an uncredited cameo as *Life* magazine reporter Ted Jones in *YOUTH WITHOUT YOUTH* (2007). He was born Matthew Paige Damon in Cambridge, Massachusetts, on October 8, 1970. Educated at Harvard University, Damon earned his earliest acting experience at the American Repertory Theatre and at other Boston-based theatre venues. His feature film debut came with a small role in *Mystic Pizza* in 1988. Ten years later Damon won an Academy Award for Best Original Screenplay, written with his friend Ben Affleck, for the critically

Matt Damon in *The Rainmaker*.

acclaimed coming-of-age drama *Good Will Hunting*, as well as a Best Actor Academy Award nomination for his performance in the title role of that film, directed by Gus Van Sant. Also in 1998 Damon starred in the title role of Steven Spielberg's World War II drama, *Saving Private Ryan*. In 1999 he played John Grady Cole in *All the Pretty Horses*, adapted by Ted Tally and Billy Bob Thornton from Cormac McCarthy's novel. By 2002 Damon had achieved superstar status with his role as the murderously programmed amnesiac Jason Bourne in *The Bourne Identity*, directed by Doug Liman. He was also part of an all-star ensemble in *Ocean's Eleven* (2001) and its sequels, *Ocean's Twelve* (2004) and *Ocean's Thirteen* (2007).—James M. Welsh

DANES, CLAIRE (1979–)

American actress featured in Oliver Stone's *U-Turn* and FRANCIS COPPOLA's *THE RAINMAKER*, adapted from JOHN GRISHAM's novel, both films made in 1997. She was born on April 12, 1979, the daughter of Chris and Carla Danes, and raised in New York City. At the age of four she was enrolled in modern dance classes, before attending Dalton High School and the Professional Performing Arts School. Also as a youngster she enrolled at the LEE STRASBERG Theatre Institute to study acting, preparing her for what was to come, but her Broadway debut was delayed until October 19, 2007, when she played Eliza Doolittle in the revival of George Bernard Shaw's *Pygmalion*; her earliest acting success was to be on television. Playing a teenager named Angela Chase for the ensemble series *My So-Called Life*, Danes earned an Emmy nomination and a Golden Globe Award for Best Actress in a Television Drama. Early film roles included daughter Beth in the Gillian Armstrong adaptation of Louisa May Alcott's *Little Women* (1994). Other films soon followed, including Jocelyn Moorhouse's *How to Make an American Quilt* (1995) and Jodie Foster's comedy *Home for the Holidays* (1995); but Australian director Baz Luhrmann made her a star by casting her as a fetching Juliet opposite Leonardo DiCaprio's brooding Romeo in his freewheeling, postmodern adaptation of *Romeo + Juliet* (1996). *Washington Post* critic Rita Kempley declared them "a gorgeous couple," a notion surely confirmed by the box office grosses. Danes was a radiant sixteen at the time and a very affecting Juliet. The next year, she played Jenny in Oliver Stone's *U-Turn* and Kelly Riker for Francis Coppola in *The Rainmaker* (1997). Claire Danes is a close personal friend of Coppola clansman JASON SCHWARTZMAN, Francis Coppola's nephew and the son of TALIA SHIRE. Danes obviously knows how to talk the talk, since she has appeared with Jay Leno on *The Tonight Show* and on *The Late Show with David Letterman*, but she also must know how to think, since she has also appeared on *Charlie Rose*. She completed two years as a psychology major at Yale University, where her grandfather, Gibson Andrew Danes (1910–1992), once served as dean of the School of Art and Architecture. Oliver Stone is said to have written a recommendation supporting her admission to Yale. In 2002 Claire Danes played Meryl Streep's daughter in the highly regarded film adaptation of *The Hours* (though the following year, perhaps following a lapse of judgment, she also appeared in *Terminator 3*). In September of 2009 she married Hugh Dancy, whom she first met on the set of *Evening* in 2007. In 2009 Danes played Sonja Jones in the cult picture *Me and Orson Welles*, to the delight, perhaps, of her more serious fans. This celebrity's star rose fast, and is apparently still rising.—JAMES M. WELSH

DEMENTIA 13 (1963, BRITISH TITLE: THE HAUNTED & THE HUNTED)

DIRECTOR: Francis Ford Coppola. SCREENPLAY: Francis Ford Coppola. PRODUCER: Francis Ford Coppola for Roger Corman Productions. PHOTOGRAPHY: Charles Hannawalt. EDITING: Stewart O'Brien. MUSIC: Ronald Stein. ART DIRECTION: Albert Locatelli.
CAST: William Campbell (Richard Haloran), Luana Anders (Louise Haloran), Bart Patton (Billy Haloran), Mary Mitchell (Kane), Patrick Magee (Justin Caleb), Eithne Dunn (Lady Haloran), Peter Reed (John Haloran), Karl Schanzer (Simon), Ron Perry (Arthur), Derry O'Donovan (Lillian), Barbara Dowling (Kathleen). PREMIERE: September 25, 1963. RUNNING TIME: 97 minutes, B&W. DVD: Good Times Video.

While he was enrolled in the Masters Program in Film at UCLA, FRANCIS COPPOLA accepted employment from independent producer-director ROGER CORMAN, known as the "King of the Bs," along Hollywood's Poverty Row, which churned out low-budget pictures. Corman was looking for a production assistant who would work for peanuts; Coppola was his man.

Coppola was the first of several young filmmakers to whom Corman provided an entry into the film business in Hollywood. To his credit, Corman showed his fledgling filmmakers the ropes and taught them his efficient penny-pinching methods for making a movie on the double and on the cheap.

Coppola was second-unit director on *THE YOUNG RACERS* (1963), which Corman produced and directed in Europe. After the location shooting on this movie was completed in England, with the Grand Prix at Liverpool, Corman remembers, "I decided to finance a second film," but not direct it.

Shooting two movies back-to-back and employing the same crew and some of the same actors would really be a money-saving enterprise. Corman had brought over to Europe a Volkswagen minibus that he had outfitted with the technical equipment needed to shoot a film. "The most logical place to shoot the picture was Dublin," he explained, "because we could just ferry the minibus over from Liverpool." Moreover, an independent filmmaker could make movies more economically in Ireland.

Corman told Coppola that "if he could come up with an idea for a film in Ireland, he could direct it." Coppola came up with the concept of a psychological thriller and pitched it to Corman. It was a slasher-type picture, obviously designed to cash in on Hitchcock's highly successful *Psycho* (1960). Corman responded enthusiastically, "You've got a picture, kid!" Coppola entitled the movie *Dementia 13*, incorporating the legendary unlucky number in the title.

Coppola, with a minimal crew of nine, shot the picture on a limited budget at Ardmore Studios in Dublin for nine days. He did two additional days on location in the Irish countryside. He thus completed principal photography in a record eleven days.

A group of Coppola's fellow students from the UCLA film school came over to Dublin at their own expense to help out with the production. One of them was the set director, Eleanor Neil, who became Coppola's wife when the film unit returned to the States.

The cast of *Dementia 13* not only included some of the actors from *The Young Racers*, such as William Campbell and Patrick Magee, but also some of the members of Dublin's distinguished Abbey Theater, such as Eithne Dunn, whom Coppola coaxed into playing character parts.

Since the film has not been widely seen, a rather detailed synopsis is in order. The plot that Coppola conjured up for *Dementia 13* initially centers on John Haloran and his wife, Louise. While John rows Louise, a brassy blonde, on a pitch-dark lake,

they argue about his mother's will, which stipulates that Louise will profit from Lady Haloran's will only as long as John, who has a weak heart, remains alive. John, exhausted from the strain of rowing as well as from the quarrel, abruptly succumbs to a heart attack before they return to shore. The scheming Louise pushes John's corpse overboard in order to hide his death and subsequently informs Lady Haloran (Eithne Dunn) and her other two sons, Richard (William Campbell), a sculptor, and Billy (Bart Patton), that John has flown to New York on business.

Lady Haloran, who presides over Castle Haloran, continues to mourn morbidly for her daughter, Kathleen, seven years dead, who perished in the lake as a child. Louise goes for a midnight swim in the lake; when she rises to the lake's surface close to the shore, she is inexplicably bludgeoned to death by an unseen attacker.

Lady Haloran pays a visit to Kathleen's dollhouse, which she has turned into a musty shrine to her dead daughter. There she discovers a wax effigy of Kathleen, which has been placed in the playhouse as an eerie reminder of Kathleen's death. Just then the ax-wielder appears and savagely smashes the dollhouse to pieces. Lady Haloran flees the premises and narrowly escapes being murdered.

Richard's fiancée, Kane (Mary Mitchell), endeavors to convince him to leave the doom-ridden estate. Justin Caleb, the family doctor (Patrick Magee), then devises a scheme to smoke out the killer. Dr. Caleb orders the lake to be drained, and a gravestone turns up, bearing the inscription "Forgive me, Kathleen dear." Caleb recalls that Billy has been suffering from nightmares ever since Kathleen's death, so the doctor strongly suspects that Billy knows more about Kathleen's death than he has ever divulged. Accordingly, at the wedding reception for Richard and Kane on the lawn of the estate, Caleb confronts Billy with the wax figure of Kathleen's corpse, which had turned up in the dollhouse earlier.

He forces Billy to admit that he accidentally pushed Kathleen into the pond when they were scuffling about, playing a children's game on the shore. In fact, the effigy of Kathleen is really a wax doll Billy made to "relieve his guilt for her death," as the doctor puts it. With that, Billy goes berserk and is thereby revealed to be a homicidal maniac whose obsession with death has led him to murder Louise and others. Just as he is about to attack Kane with an ax lying conveniently on the lawn, Dr. Caleb shoots him dead. Caleb then melodramatically buries Billy's hatchet in the skull of the effigy, to dramatize the fact that the curse on the Haloran family has been shattered at last.

It is easy to pick flaws in *Dementia 13*. For one thing, Dr. Caleb's explanation of Billy's psychosis is "cookbook Freud," a bizarre elaboration on Freud's theory of neurotic guilt. The screenplay has an interesting premise, but it presents a pinwheeling series of murders without enough transitional material to link them together into a coherent narrative. On the other hand, the film's pace never lags, since the suspenseful story is punctuated with not only scenes of violence but smatterings of piquant sex (the steamy love scenes between Richard and Kane), designed to bolster the picture's commercial potential for the drive-in trade. When the picture opened in New York in September, 1963, most film critics dismissed it as the sort of teen-oriented "exploitation film" that was typical of the Corman film factory. One reviewer opined that the characters were mostly cardboard cutouts and another criticized the wooden dialogue.

Be that as it may, *Dementia 13* did show a modest profit and has been judged more benignly by film historians who have

Luana Anders and William Campbell in *Dementia 13*.

reassessed it over the years. Cowie sees the picture as a bellwether of Coppola's future career and astutely observes that *Dementia 13* prefigures Coppola's later work by introducing his interest in the family as a source of strife and tragedy— from the neurotic Lady Haloran's endless mourning for Kathleen to her criminally insane son Billy's multiple homicides. Looking back on the movie, Coppola seems satisfied with it. "I think it showed promise; it was imaginative," he comments, appraising it as more than a mere accumulation of clichés. It is worth noting that there is a homage of sorts to the film in an episode of *The Sopranos* (2001), a TV series about the Mafia. In it the daughter of a Mafia don and her date attend a screening of *Dementia 13* at a New York revival house and are appropriately frightened.

Shortly after Coppola finished his chores on *Dementia 13*, he decided to sever his relationship with Corman. He appreciated the firsthand experience he had obtained as a tyro filmmaker while working under Corman's tutelage.—GENE D. PHILLIPS

References

Roger Corman with Jim Jerome, *How I Made a Hundred Movies and Never Lost a Dime* (New York: Random House, 1990); Peter Cowie, *Coppola: A Biography*, rev. ed. (New York: Da Capo, 1994); Michael Gordimer and Naomi Wise, *On the Edge: The Life and Times of Francis Coppola* (New York: Morrow, 1989).

DE NIRO, ROBERT (1943–)

Leading American actor trained for the stage by Stella Adler and LEE STRASBERG, De Niro received the Academy Award for Best Supporting Actor for his portrayal of Vito Corleone in *THE GODFATHER: PART II* (1974). De Niro was born in New York City on August 17, 1943, the son of painters Robert De Niro, Sr., and Virginia Admiral; he grew up in Greenwich Village and was educated at the Rhodes School and the High School of Music and Art in New York. He left school at sixteen to begin acting professionally and studied with acting coaches Stella Adler, Luther James, and Lee Strasberg. In 1968 De Niro appeared at the Public Theater and then on Broadway in the play *Cuba and His Teddy Bear*. De Niro made his motion picture debut in *The Wedding Party*, with Jill Clayburgh in 1963 (though the film was not released until 1969). Film director Brian De Palma cast De Niro in other early film roles, including *Greetings* (1968) and *Hi, Mom!* (1970), but the actor's greatest success came in a number of signature Martin Scorsese films, especially *Mean Streets* (1973), *Taxi Driver* (1976), *The King of Comedy* (1983), *GoodFellas* (1990), *Cape Fear* (1991), and, perhaps most famously, *Raging Bull* (1980), which earned De Niro an Academy Award for his portrayal of the boxer Jake La Motta. De Niro also earned Academy Award nominations for his work in four additional films, notably his role as Travis Bickle in Scorsese's *Taxi Driver* (1976), his Vietnam vet in Michael Cimino's *The Deer Hunter* (1978), the catatonic patient Leonard in

Robert De Niro as the young Vito Corleone in *The Godfather: Part II*.

Penny Marshall's *The Awakening* (1990), and as Max Cady, the revenge-seeking ex-con in Scorsese's 1991 remake of *Cape Fear*. His performance as young Vito Corleone for Coppola earned the actor his second Oscar for Best Supporting Actor. In 1988 De Niro founded a production company with Jane Rosenthal, TriBeCa Productions, and the TriBeCa Film Center. *A Bronx Tale*, which marked De Niro's directorial debut in 1993, was a TriBeCa production, as were *Cape Fear*, *Wag the Dog*, and the screen adaptation of the hit musical *Rent*, among other films. De Niro did not direct another film until 2006, *The Good Shepherd*, starring MATT DAMON and Angelina Jolie, about the origins of the CIA. De Niro married twice, first to actress Diahnne Abbott (two children, Drena and Raphael), then to former flight attendant Grace Hightower; three children: Aaron and Julian (twins), and Elliot.—James M. Welsh

DEVITO, DANNY (1944–)

Comedian turned producer, director, and actor who plays Deck Schifflet in *THE RAINMAKER* (1997). Born in Neptune, New Jersey, on November 17, 1944, DeVito was educated at Oratory Prep School and the Wilfred Academy of Hair and Beauty Culture, and, finally, at the American Academy of Dramatic Arts, making his stage debut in 1969. In 1975 he was part of the film cast of *One Flew over the Cuckoo's Nest*, repeating a performance he had honed on stage off-Broadway. In 1981 DeVito won a Best Supporting Actor Emmy for his television portrayal of the character of Louie De Palma in the popular series *Taxi* (1978–1983). He turned to directing in 1987 with *Throw Momma from the Train*, followed by *The War of the Roses* (1989) and *Hoffa* (1992); but he also continued to act in all the films he directed. In 1989 DeVito was named NATO Star of the Year.—James M. Welsh

DILLON, MATT (1964–)

Popular actor who played Rusty James in *RUMBLE FISH* (1983) and Dallas Winston in *THE OUTSIDERS* (1983). Born in New Rochelle, New York, on February 18, 1964, Dillon was "discovered" by a casting

Matt Damon and Danny DeVito in *The Rainmaker*.

director when he was fourteen years old and still in junior high school. Jonathan Kaplan gave him his first role in a feature film in *Over the Edge* (1979), which *New York Times* film critic Vincent Canby included in his list of the best films of 1980 after the film's New York premiere screening at Joseph Papp's Public Theatre. Tim Hunter, who had coscripted *Over the Edge*, directed *Tex* in 1982, adapted from S. E. HINTON's novel, for which Dillon was a natural and which, in turn, set Dillon up for his role in *The Outsiders*. Hinton was so impressed by Dillon's performance in *Tex* that she went directly to Coppola, urging him to cast Dillon as Dallas. Including *Tex*, Dillon had appeared in five films before being cast in Francis Coppola's S. E. Hinton adaptations. In Italy Dillon earned the Best Actor of 1984 Award for his portrayal of Rusty James in *Rumble Fish*. In 1984, *Washington Post* critic Paul Attanasio was charmed by the way Dillon performed in a marginal film, *The Flamingo Kid*,

Matt Dillon, C. Thomas Howell, and Ralph Macchio in *The Outsiders*.

directed by sitcom auteur Garry Marshall: "In a strange, oddly affecting performance, Matt Dillon plays against his image as a troubled teen idol," he wrote. "In *The Outsiders* and *Rumble Fish*, Dillon made a style out of inarticulateness. But in *The Flamingo Kid* that style is attached to a theme—he's dumbfounded by the wealth around him," effectively adapting that style to comedic purposes. That same year, two Japanese magazines, *Roadshow* and *Screen*, chose Dillon as the Most Popular Foreign Actor of 1984. Matt Dillon is the older brother of the actor Kevin Dillon, featured in Oliver Stone's *Platoon* (1986).—JAMES M. WELSH

Reference

Paul Attanasio, "Flimsy 'Flamingo,'" *Washington Post*, December 22, 1984, F4.

DONAHUE, TROY [MERLE JOHNSON, JR.] (1936–)

American actor and former teen idol who had starred in two television series, *Surfside Six* (1960–1962) and *Hawaiian Eye* (1962–1963); was cast to play Merle Johnson in *THE GODFATHER: PART II*, ironically, since Merle Johnson was the actor's actual name. He and FRANCIS COPPOLA had attended the same military school. The actor was born in New York City on January 27, 1936, and turned to acting while a journalism student at Columbia University. He married and divorced the actress Suzanne Pleshette in 1964, then married actress Valerie Allen in 1966.—JAMES M. WELSH

DONAT, PETER [PIERRE COLLINGWOOD DONAT] (1928–)

Canadian American, Yale-trained stage actor cast to play Questadt in *THE GODFATHER: PART II* (1974) and Prosecuting Attorney Kerner in *TUCKER: THE MAN AND HIS DREAM* (1988). Donat was born on January 20, 1928, in Kentville, Nova Scotia, Canada, the son of Marie and Philip

Ernst Donat, and the nephew of the British actor Robert Donat. He immigrated to the United States in 1950 in order to study drama at Yale University Drama School. Primarily a man of the theatre, Donat has performed at the Stratford Ontario Shakespeare Festivals in his native Canada, as well as in Broadway and off-Broadway productions. In 1961 he played the lead in the first Canadian play performed at the Stratford Festival, Donald Jack's *The Canvas Barricade*. In 1957 he received the Theatre World Award for Best Featured Actor of 1957. He was a member of Ellis Rabb's legendary APA Repertory Company, and, in 1968, he joined the American Conservatory Theatre in San Francisco. Beyond his films for FRANCIS COPPOLA, Donat appeared in the following (selected) films: *Cyrano De Bergerac* (1972, with Marsha Mason), *The Hindenburg* (1975), *The China Syndrome* (1979), Norman Jewison's *F.I.S.T.* (1978, with Sylvester Stallone), *Little Nikita* (1988, with Sidney Poitier and River Phoenix), DANNY DEVITO's *The War of the Roses* (1989), *School Ties* and *The Babe* (both 1992), David Fincher's *The Game* (1997, with Sean Penn and Michael Douglas), among other titles. On television he played Bill Mulder, Agent Mulder's father on *The X-Files*, as well as many roles in some of the most popular TV mystery and drama series, including *Mission Impossible*, *The Waltons*, *Hawaii Five-O*, *Charlie's Angels*, *Dallas*, *Quincy*, *Hill Street Blues*, and *Murder, She Wrote*.—JAMES M. WELSH

DON JUAN DEMARCO (1995)

This romantic fantasy produced by FRANCIS FORD COPPOLA (directed by Jeremy Leven) might seem at first an odd fit in the repertoire of a filmmaker often regarded as an auteur. The willingness of AMERICAN ZOETROPE to produce a romantic fantasy about a delusional young man claiming to be the relentless lover Don Juan has to do

in part, of course, with business. Yet, it is possible to identify parallels in and around *Don Juan DeMarco* with Coppola's interests and vision as a filmmaker, even as an author. Considering these connections and parallels, *Don Juan DeMarco* hardly constitutes an outlier in Coppola's eclectic oeuvre. Rather, it is yet another example of the sort of quirky, independent-minded filmmaking that Coppola has supported consistently through his American Zoetrope production company.

Don Juan DeMarco tells the story of a twenty-one-year-old man (Johnny Depp) who believes he is the legendary seducer who has made love to more than a thousand women. However, when the centerfold beauty Dona Aña breaks his heart, this Don Juan is ready to end his life in a last duel fought on the precipitous heights of a billboard's catwalk. The middle-aged, semi-retired psychiatrist, John Mickler (MARLON BRANDO), playing along as Don Octavio, convinces Don Juan to desist in this endeavor. Soon afterward, the delusional youth enters a psychiatric clinic that he believes to be Don Octavio's villa.

Mickler ends up having one last assignment in his long career: to diagnose in ten days the flamboyant patient's mental state and determine if he requires medication and a longer treatment. DeMarco not only becomes Mickler's patient, but also his inspiration, as the psychiatrist begins to understand the idea that passion can conquer everything. Don Juan's detailed and extravagant chronicles of his sexual encounters energize the therapist. Revitalized, Mickler rekindles his marriage with Marilyn (Faye Dunaway), a relationship that had become bogged down in stale routine.

DeMarco's tales are replete with implausible moments and sketchy facts. As he narrates his outlandish backstory, viewers discover a series of bizarre, often incongruent, and sanitized episodes in the sexual life of the unexpected Don Juan. The very notion that his ideal love was once the centerfold of a men's magazine seems ludicrous. Other flaws and inconsistencies abound in Don Juan's stories. The depiction of the Mexican countryside is as fake as Depp's Castilian accent when he inflects (or inflicts) his lines. In an interesting move, the film leaves space for ambiguity about the veracity of DeMarco's tales of his own life by presenting contradictory pieces of evidence, suggesting that the stories of this Don Juan deserve at least the benefit of the doubt.

The film's notable cast performs at an uneven level. Johnny Depp's acting is commendable as he carries the interpretation of his character with a charming, deadpan seriousness. Brando delivers a lightweight performance, arguably well suited to the farcical spirit of the narrative. At times, however, the renowned actor seems to lack energy as he goes through the motions, almost in a mechanical fashion; and the erstwhile great actress Faye Dunaway delivers an adequate performance at best.

Several film critics have noted a weak narrative and directorial hand in *Don Juan DeMarco*, salvaged only by the three stars. The critic Janet Maslin describes the film as "cheesy," sustained by "Mr. Brando's peculiar presence" and Johnny Depp's performance that confirms "a brilliantly intuitive young actor with strong ties to the Brando legacy," but in a production "with a serious potential to be a third-rate movie." More benevolently, Emmanuel Levy makes some concessions to the film. Levy describes *Don Juan DeMarco* as an "inconsequential but immensely likable two-generational comedy." He also considers the cast as "the most memorable and—marketable—dimension," overshadowing the movie's "small-scale, rather slight narrative." These and other critics have also commented on Brando's lukewarm performance in contrast to Depp's more engaging work.

Despite these critiques, *Don Juan DeMarco* fared well at the box office. With a modest budget estimated around $23 million, the movie had an above-average theatrical run in 1995. It was clear that the film would break even, at least. After fifteen weeks, *Don Juan* had collected close to $22 million in ticket sales. Later, *Don Juan* would conquer audiences overseas, accumulating around $65 million. For New Line Cinema and American Zoetrope, the film was a commercial success.

Coppola announced the news that he would embark in the production of *Don Juan DeMarco* in early 1994. Almost a decade before, after the debacle of *ONE FROM THE HEART* (1982), the closing of Zoetrope Studios, and the debts left by *APOCALYPSE NOW* (1979), Coppola had surprised everyone with a commercially successful romantic comedy with enough merits to deserve a few Academy nominations: *PEGGY SUE GOT MARRIED* (1986). Coppola once acknowledged that the risk in investing his own money in *Apocalypse Now* could mean that he might end up making "Goldie Hawn movies" to pay the bills, but he welcomed that chance as an exciting experience. By the time he backed up *Don Juan DeMarco*, Coppola had enjoyed the enormous success of *BRAM STOKER'S DRACULA* (1992); but even with regained confidence, and once again a millionaire filmmaker, Coppola knew that in order to make more personal films, he needed to direct and produce the commercial ones now and then. This was the Coppola who agreed to deliver a third installment of *THE GODFATHER* once he found himself swamped in debts, a filmmaker who, according to Jon Lewis, "saw himself as at once an outsider wanting in and insider wanting out."

In this context, it makes sense that Coppola would be inclined to back the directorial debut of the author and screenwriter Jeremy Leven, an aspiring director who believed he was the most adept to capture the vision of his *Don Juan* on film. Like Coppola, Leven was also an "outsider," a psychiatrist turned novelist and screenwriter.

Thematically, *Don Juan DeMarco*'s narrative offers a series of motifs that correlate with some of Coppola's films and life experiences. For instance, Coppola has referred to *Peggy Sue Got Married* and *JACK* (1996) as fables. As noted by Michael Schumacher, Coppola sees in this narrative form a means to tell entertaining and whimsical stories with meaningful subtexts. Like *Peggy Sue Got Married* and *Jack, Don Juan DeMarco* is also a fable, as overtly noted in Mickler's voiceover narration toward the end of the film. The fable in *Don Juan* is a likable and lighthearted allegory, a vehicle to deliver a simple but noble "moral." In this sense, it is possible that Coppola saw more than an economic opportunity in producing Leven's script. Coppola may have spotted a few commonalities with the films mentioned above and perhaps even identified with Leven's story himself.

The fable of an outcast who rebels against the world, the lunatic *Don Juan* in Leven's film, echoes Coppola's life and own quest in Hollywood. Polio struck Francis Ford Coppola when he was nine. The experience of seclusion in a hospital, and the sense of isolation for being different, is a traumatic experience that has recurred through several of Coppola's films, including *THE CONVERSATION* (1974) and *Jack*. The notion of a maverick who wants to change the world appears in Coppola's biopic of the infamous carmaker, Preston Tucker, in *TUCKER: THE MAN AND HIS DREAM* (1988). GENE D. PHILLIPS observes that, even in those films for hire like *Peggy Sue* or *Jack*, Coppola is an auteur, the kind of filmmaker who strives to imprint his vision, at times attempting to appropriate the story at a personal level. As *Don Juan DeMarco*'s producer, Coppola likely saw in the screenplay a resemblance, even if small, to some of his own preoccupations and recurrent themes as a filmmaker and storyteller. Like Tucker and Jack, the insane Don Juan is an outcast who tries to find his place in a world that seems against him.

Of course, *Don Juan DeMarco* offered a viable commercial project for Coppola and his Zoetrope film company, since New Line Cinema and Johnny Depp were already onboard. Nobody expected Brando to accept the role as John Mickler, but the veteran actor did so for purely financial reasons.

As noted above, the film does have its flaws. It is telling that later, rather than pursuing a career in directing, Leven would prefer to focus on honing his writing skills, adapting novels for the screen. (Recently, Leven has adapted Nicholas Sparks's *The Notebook* and Jodi Picoult's *My Sister's Keeper*.) But even if critics have regarded the film as a lightweight romantic fable and deemed Leven's directing skills as weak, *Don Juan DeMarco* presents an exuberant and unusual narrative that carries good-natured ideals with ties to Coppola's universe. It seems fitting that Coppola should have felt inclined to support and produce such a project, the story of one against the world, where courage and passion in what one believes make the protagonist indomitable against adversity. In a sense, it is Coppola's own story, a tale that the filmmaker has told more than once in his cinematic oeuvre.—MANUEL PÉREZ TEJADA

References

Tony Chiu, "Coppola's Cinematic *Apocalypse* Is Finally at Hand," in *Francis Ford Coppola: Interviews*, ed. Gene D. Phillips and Rodney Hill (Jackson: University Press of Mississippi, 2004); D. Gritten, "Taking on Big, Bad Brando," *Herald*

Sun, July 27, 1995, 35; Stanley Kauffmann, "*Don Juan DeMarco* directed by Jeremy Leven," *The New Republic*, May 1, 1995, 29; Emmanuel Levy, "*Don Juan DeMarco*," *Daily Variety*, March 27, 1995; Jon Lewis, *Whom God Wishes to Destroy: Francis Ford Coppola and the New Hollywood* (Durham, NC: Duke University Press, 1997); Janet Maslin, "Johnny Depp with a Don Juan Complex," *New York Times*, April 7, 1995; Gene D. Phillips, *Godfather: The Intimate Francis Ford Coppola* (Lexington: University Press of Kentucky, 2004); Michael Schumacher, *Francis Ford Coppola: A Filmmaker's Life* (New York: Crown Publishers, 1999); Mark Woods, "O'seas Auds in 'Seven' Heaven; 'Babe' Climbs," *Daily Variety*, February 12, 1996, 14.

DRACULA (1992)

See entry above for *BRAM STOKER'S DRACULA*. For a reasonably complete listing of Dracula films, including the Coppola adaptation, see "Filmography on Dracula, Vampires, and the Undead," in Raymond T. McNally and Radu Florescu, *In Search of Dracula* (Boston: Houghton Mifflin, 1994), pp. 257–92.—JAMES M. WELSH

DRACULA, VLAD (C. 1430–1476)

Born in Sighişoara (Schassberg in German), a fortified Saxon town in Transylvania, about the year 1430, the historic "Dracula" was also known as Vlad Tepes (meaning "Vlad the Impaler," so named for his brutal treatment of Turkish prisoners he captured). The Holy Roman Emperor Sigismund had granted Vlad's father the throne of Wallachia and invested him with "The Order of the Dragon" (*Dracul* in Romanian means "Dragon"; *Dracula* means "son of the Dragon"), this as a consequence of the father's bravery in fighting Czech Hussites and the Turks. The father seized the Wallachian throne in 1436 and was put to death in 1447. In 1453 Constantinople fell to the Turks. The son, Vlad Dracula, ruled Wallachia with

an iron hand from 1456 to 1462. He was imprisoned by the Hungarian King Matthias Corvinus for twelve years, from 1462 until 1474, and was released after he finally converted from Orthodox Christianity to Roman Catholicism. He again became supreme ruler of Wallachia from 1474 to 1476, when he was killed, fighting the Turks.—JAMES M. WELSH

References
R. T. McNally & Radu Florescu, *In Search of Dracula: The History of Dracula and Vampires* (Boston: Houghton Mifflin, 1994); Kurt W. Treptow, *Vlad III Dracula: The Life and Times of the Historical Dracula* (Iasi: The Center for Romanian Studies, 2000).

DUVALL, ROBERT (1931–)

Distinctive, award-winning, American actor, cast to play Tom Hagen in *THE GODFATHER* and again in *THE GODFATHER: PART II*. Duvall also worked with FRANCIS COPPOLA in *THE RAIN PEOPLE* (1969) and *THE CONVERSATION* (1974). The *Godfather* performance earned Duvall an Academy Award nomination for Best Supporting Actor, and in 1979 Duvall earned his second Oscar nomination as Best Supporting Actor in Coppola's *APOCALYPSE NOW*. Born in San Diego, California, on January 5, 1931, Duvall moved east with his family at age ten and settled on the Atlantic Seaboard, living in Annapolis, Maryland. He earned a degree in drama at Principia College in Elsah, Illinois, and served a two-year tour of duty with the United States Army. By 1955 he was in New York, enrolled in the Neighborhood Playhouse on the G.I. Bill. The celebrated acting coach Sanford Meisner cast Duvall in Tennessee Williams's *Camino Real* and in Horton Foote's *The Midnight Caller*. Horton Foote then recommended Duvall for his 1963 screen debut in *To Kill a Mockingbird* for the role of the mysterious and misunderstood Boo Radley. On Broadway Duvall starred in *Wait until Dark* and won an Obie Award for his performance as the hero in the Broadway revival of Arthur Miller's *A View from the Bridge*. After a standout performance on the live television series *Naked City*, Duvall went on to other television roles. Besides continuing working relationships with Horton Foote (on *Tender Mercies*, earning a Best Actor Academy Award in 1983, for example) and Francis Coppola, Duvall played Major Frank Burns in Robert Altman's *M*A*S*H* (1970), and also worked with GEORGE LUCAS on *THX 1138*, with Sam Peckinpah on *The Killer Elite*, with Sidney Lumet on *Network*, and playing Conan Doyle's Dr. Watson for Herbert Ross in *The Seven-Per-Cent Solution*. Duvall earned a Golden Globe for his portrayal of the Soviet dictator in the HBO film *Stalin*. In 1980 Duvall was nominated for a Best Actor Oscar for his portrayal of the Marine pilot Bull Meechum in *The*

Great Santini. One of the actor's favorite roles was that of Gus in the television miniseries *Lonesome Dove*, which also earned him an Emmy nomination. In 1977 Duvall made his directorial debut with a documentary film about a Nebraska rodeo family entitled *We're Not the Jet Set*. In 1983 he directed his second film, *Angelo, My Love*, concentrating on New York's Gypsy community. But perhaps Duvall's breakthrough film as director was *The Apostle* (1998), in which he was involved in all phases of production as writer, director, executive producer, and star, portraying Euliss "Sonny" Dewey, a popular and colorful Pentecostal preacher from Texas, and "The Apostle" of the title.—JAMES M. WELSH

DUVALL, SHELLEY (1949–)

Actress born in Houston, Texas, on July 7, 1949, and discovered by director Robert Altman, who cast her in the oddly allegorical *Brewster McCloud* (1970) and in numerous

Robert Duvall, Diane Keaton, and Al Pacino in *The Godfather: Part II*.

other productions, most notably *Nashville* (1976) and *Popeye* (1981). She was named Best Actress at the Cannes Festival for her performance in Altman's haunting *Three Women* (1977), and that same year she made a cameo appearance in Woody Allen's Oscar-winning *Annie Hall*. Duvall is equally known for her often misunderstood performance as Wendy Torrance in Stanley Kubrick's *The Shining* (1980), a production that was particularly difficult for the actress.

During the 1980s she turned to producing children's television programming through her own company, Platypus Productions. Her first venture was the *Faerie Tale Theatre* series on Showtime, for which FRANCIS FORD COPPOLA directed the "RIP VAN WINKLE" episode. In 1988 Duvall formed another production company, Think Entertainment, which was the first such enterprise devoted entirely to cable television productions—resulting in her being named one of "ten to watch"

in cable television by the trade journal, *Channels: The Business of Communication*. Subsequent Showtime series produced by Duvall include *Shelley Duvall's Tall Tales and Legends* and *Shelley Duvall's Bedtime Stories*. Furthermore, she has produced shows for the three major TV networks, as well as PBS, TNT, Nickelodeon, and the Disney Channel.

Shelley Duvall's acting career saw a moderate resurgence in the 1990s, with roles in Stephen Soderbergh's *The Underneath* (1995), Jane Campion's *The Portrait of a Lady* (1996), and Guy Maddin's *Twilight of the Ice Nymphs* (1997).—RODNEY HILL/JAMES M. WELSH

References

"Shelley Duvall," *Variety* Profiles, www.variety .com; Billy Budd Vermillion, "Shelley Duvall," in *The Encyclopedia of Stanley Kubrick*, ed. Gene D. Phillips and Rodney Hill (New York: Facts On File, 2002).

EHRENREICH, ALDEN (1990–)

The talented, teenaged actor who portrays Bennie in FRANCIS FORD COPPOLA's film, *TETRO* (2009), Alden Ehrenreich has been compared favorably to a young Leonardo DiCaprio. *Rolling Stone* characterizes him as a "gifted newcomer" and his performance in *Tetro* as "stellar."

Ehrenreich grew up in Pacific Palisades, California, the son of an interior-designer mother and orthodontist stepfather. At the age of fourteen, he made a short, comedic video for a friend, in which he breaks into her house, "trying on her clothes and just being ridiculous." That video, among others, was shown at the friend's bat mitzvah party, and in attendance was Steven Spielberg, who took note of Ehrenreich's screen presence. As a result, Ehrenreich was called in to meet with DreamWorks casting executives, eventually landing roles in episodes of *CSI* and *Supernatural* before being cast in *Tetro*.

When asked about Coppola's approach with young actors, Ehrenreich told the *New York Times*: "The atmosphere Francis creates around him is extremely warm, inviting and collaborative. . . . It's like he provides the map, but you find what countries you want to visit. He doesn't give you a specific laundry list, he invites you into the environment, and you decide how to interact." Ehrenreich told *Interview* magazine,

"[Coppola] has been my favorite director for a long time."

Coppola seemed to identify particularly with the character of Bennie, as he told the *New York Times*: "I think I am all the characters, but the kid is who I was. That's my story."

In 2008–2009, Alden Ehrenreich completed his freshman year of college, studying studio acting at New York University. He has roles in several feature films currently in production as of 2010.—RODNEY HILL

References

American Zoetrope, *Tetro*, official website, www.tetro.com, Michael Martin, "Alden Ehrenreich," *Interview*, February 1, 2009, 24; Todd McCarthy, "Tetro," *Variety*, May 14, 2009, www.variety.com; Larry Rohter, "Family Dynamics, without the Bullets," *New York Times*, June 3, 2009, www.nytimes.com; Nicole Sperling, "Hollywood Insider," *Entertainment Weekly*, November 23, 2007, 12; "Tetro," *Rolling Stone*, June 25, 2009, 83.

ELECTRONIC CINEMA

Innovative concept that FRANCIS COPPOLA attempted to put into practice in making *ONE FROM THE HEART* (1982), which, as contemptuously described by an unusually hostile Vincent Canby, Coppola promised would "eventually revolutionize filmmaking by using computers and video equipment in various combinations to cut down both pre- and post-production work time, in this way to save money." Canby added, "The one thing Electronic Cinema doesn't yet do, obviously, is write a screenplay that can be directed, acted, and edited into a coherent piece of popular entertainment." Canby's intent was to use *One from the Heart* as a negative example of what he saw as an objectionable new trend of films attempting to achieve a "highly stylized, mostly studio-created unreality," films that "appear to be returning to the controlled conditions of studio production and, more important, to the kind of films that celebrate special looks and effects that can only be achieved within those fantasy-factories." Foolishly, it would appear, Canby was objecting to what would become the future standard of filmmaking in America.

Reporting for *Variety* a month before Canby's "Obsession with Technique" piece appeared in the *New York Times*, Thomas M. Pryor predicted that Francis Coppola "might well turn out to be the Lee De Forest of the motion picture business—a technical innovator who is bypassed by the commercial mainstream which, ironically, will capitalize on the fruits of his restless creativity." Pryor complained that the industry "always has been penny-pinching in terms of research and development, all the while squandering millions on pictures which never should have been started, or shut down when the original budget had to be doubled and tripled." Well, *One from the Heart* went over budget, but Pryor speculated that this happened because Coppola "was exploring new technology. Obviously, no advancement in technology can be achieved without paying a price. So let's just agree that Coppola poured most of his budget into not only developing but bringing to a high point of technical proficiency, a means of marrying the best of motion picture film and electronic photography

and all the editing versatility that thus can be united." As a consequence, Hollywood "should now realize that it can reproduce the world with unbelievable reality right on the sound stage." Thus Thomas Pryor saw the possibilities that Vincent Canby could not see, noting that Coppola appeared "to be in serious jeopardy" because of *One from the Heart*, since "the industry at large will benefit hugely from the technical innovativeness that he has explored," other studios should come to his financial rescue "as an expression of gratitude for boldness in doing research and development that they have failed to understand over the years."

Other journalists noticed the Airstream van, called "The Silverfish," from which Coppola was working in the 1980s, "containing his personalized 'electronic cinema' movie-making system," as Christian Williams wrote in the *Washington Post* (August 29, 1982), but failed to explore the significance fully, beyond Coppola's description: "Movies have always been thought of in three stages," Coppola explained. "There's pre-production, production, and then post-production, where you actually put the movie together. The whole point of our system is to make it possible to do all that at once—cheaper, faster and better." Then the kicker, which should have been the focus of the whole piece: "People will still make the movies, but technology will permit the art form to advance. Someday, for example, we'll be making movies with no sets at all. We'll work with only a stage. And it will look totally realistic." Shades of *Avatar*? Coppola clearly was decades ahead of the visionary curve.—JAMES M. WELSH

References

Vincent Canby, "Obsession with Technique," *New York Times*, February 21, 1982, sec. 2: 13; Thomas M. Pryor, "Cost Aside, Coppola's 'Heart' Reflects Top Technical Research," *Variety*, January 27, 1982, 3, 35; Christian Williams,

"Coppola's New Terrain," *Washington Post*, August 29, 1982, D1, D8.

ELIADE, MIRCEA (1907–1986)

Prominent Romanian intellectual, scholar, and writer, author of the story "Youth without Youth," published under the title "Rejuvenation by Lightning" in Eliade's *Mystic Stories* collection, and adapted to cinema by FRANCIS COPPOLA in 2007. Eliade was born in Bucharest in 1907 and graduated with a degree in philosophy from the University of Bucharest in 1928. Postgraduate study at the University of Calcutta in India until 1932 prepared him for his scholarly work concerning the history of religions. In 1939 Eliade entered diplomatic service, working in England and Portugal during World War II. After the communist takeover of Romania, Eliade taught in Paris at the École des Hautes Études and never returned to his homeland. Eventually he taught the history of religions at the University of Chicago, until his death in 1986. His academic works include *Traité d'histoire des religions* (1949), *Le Mythe de l'eternel Retour* (1949), *Images et Symboles* (1952), and *Le Sacré et le Profane* (1956). Some of his finest fictional work, such as *Miss Christina* (1936) and *Doctor Honigberger's Secret* (1940) was written in Romania; later work such as *The Gypsies* (1959) and "Youth without Youth" (1976) were written in exile, but in Romanian, because, Eliade told an interviewer, "From time to time, I feel the need to seek out my roots, the land of my birth. In exile, the native land is the language, is a dream. And it is then that I wrote my novels." The myth of the eternal return seems central to the story of "Youth without Youth," and also the scholar's fascination with language and comparative religion.—JAMES M. WELSH

ELWES, CARY (1962–)

London-born actor, the son of painter Dominic Elwes and interior designer Tessa Kennedy, Cary Elwes plays Arthur Holmwood in *BRAM STOKER'S DRACULA* (1992). After moving to New York to attend college, he studied acting at Sarah Lawrence College, the LEE STRASBERG Institute, and the Actors Studio. Elwes made his film debut in England in Marek Kanievska's *Another Country* (1984) then went on to act with Helena Bonham-Carter in *Lady Jane* (1985). His breakthrough in America was the leading role in Rob Reiner's comedic fairy-tale adventure, *The Princess Bride* (1987); and he later played a similar lead in Mel Brooks's *Robin Hood: Men in Tights* (1993). Both films made good use of Elwes's blond, innocent, good looks and dashing air. Despite these notable starring turns, Elwes's career has been defined chiefly by supporting roles, in films such as *Days of Thunder* (1990), as TOM CRUISE's rival; *Twister* (1996); *Liar Liar* (1997) alongside Jim Carrey; *Kiss the Girls* (1997); Tim Robbins's *Cradle Will Rock* (1999), portraying John Houseman; *Shadow of the Vampire* (2000), about the making of the 1922 classic *Nosferatu*; Peter Bogdanovich's *The Cat's Meow* (2001), as filmmaker Thomas Ince; *Saw* (2004), which represents a darker turn in Elwes's repertoire; and Disney's animated film, *A Christmas Carol* (2009), in which Elwes voices several characters.—RODNEY HILL/JAMES M. WELSH

References
"Cary Elwes," *Variety* Profiles, www.variety.com; "Cary Elwes," Internet Movie Database, www.imdb.com/name/nm0000144/.

ESTEVEZ, EMILIO (1962–)

American actor, born in New York City on May 12, 1962, the first son of the actor MARTIN SHEEN, and raised in Los Angeles, he got his first acting role in a television special entitled *Seventeen Going on Nowhere*, right after graduating from high school. Among his friends were Sean and

CHRISTOPHER PENN and Rob and Chad Lowe. His debut performance was in the television film *In the Custody of Strangers* (1982). His first feature film role was *Tex*, adapted from the novel by S. E. HINTON and directed by Tim Hunter in 1982. Hinton suggested that Estevez would be perfect for the role of Mark Jennings, the protagonist of her book *That Was Then, This Is Now*, which Estevez promptly optioned, wrote, and starred in when it was made in 1985. For FRANCIS COPPOLA, Estevez played "Two-Bit" Matthews in *THE OUTSIDERS* (1983), which, along with *The Breakfast Club* and *St. Elmo's Fire* (both in 1985), made him a charter member of the so-called "brat pack." In 1986 Estevez, said to be the youngest star ever to direct and write his own screenplay, wrote and directed *Wisdom* (a film later savaged by a *Variety* review) and again, in 1990, he also wrote and directed *Men at Work*. He was more commercially successful, however, in films directed by others: John Badham's police drama, *Stakeout* (1987), for example, and *Young Guns* (1988), playing Billy the Kid, and its sequel, *Young Guns II* (1990).
—JAMES M. WELSH

Reference

James Cameron-Wilson, *Young Hollywood* (Lanham, MD: Madison Books, 1994).

EVANS, ROBERT (1930–)

Evans was associated as a producer with *THE GODFATHER* and *THE COTTON CLUB*. He was born Robert Shapera on June 29, 1930, in New York City. He worked as a child actor on radio, but when he finished his schooling he became sales director of a sportswear company. At age twenty-six he met retired screen actress Norma Shearer in Hollywood, and she selected him to play her deceased husband, the legendary movie mogul Irving Thalberg, in the Lon Chaney biopic *Man of a Thousand Faces* (1957).

Evans took supporting roles in other films, such as *The Sun Also Rises* (1957), until he decided to move up to film production.

In 1966 he joined Paramount and in due course became vice president in charge of production. During his tenure at Paramount the studio turned out blockbusters like *Rosemary's Baby* (1968) and *Love Story* (1970).

Evans approached FRANCIS COPPOLA, believed to be the only Italian director in Hollywood at the time, and asked him to direct *The Godfather*. Several other directors, such as Peter Yates, John Frankenheimer, and Constantin Costa-Gavras, had declined because they thought the novel glamorized the Mafia. Coppola also hesitated, knowing that the Mafia had tainted Italian Americans, but it was also politically advisable for Evans to get Coppola on board in order to appease the Italian lobby. Even so, the Italian American Civil Rights League threatened to picket the film unless they were assured that neither "Cosa nostra" nor "Mafia" would be used. Ronald Bergan quotes Evans as saying he had faith in Coppola because he believed Coppola "knew the way these men ate their food, kissed each other, [and] talked. He knew the grit." When Coppola hesitated, Evans described himself as "on my knees, begging the director who had made three features [four and a half, actually], all flops, to please, please put *The Godfather* on the screen." Coppola finally agreed to write and direct the picture for $150,000, plus 7.5 percent of net profits, so long as the film would be made as a family chronicle rather than as a gangster epic.

The Godfather was the last major hit to be released by Paramount while Evans was studio chief (1967–1973). The studio had mandated that Coppola deliver a rough cut of *The Godfather* running two hours; but Coppola's first cut was three hours. The front office demanded that he condense the film to two hours, and he dutifully cut it to two hours and twenty minutes. He recalls that he did so "by cutting all the footage that wasn't germane to the story."

Evans then complained that Coppola had excised all the scenes focusing on character development and had nothing but the plot left. With Evans's support, Coppola accordingly restored the original three-hour version. Forever after, Evans maintained that he personally supervised Coppola's reediting of the movie, a boast that Coppola flatly denied.

A decade after the release of the film Coppola read an interview with Evans in which Evans again claimed that he personally masterminded the final edit of *The Godfather*. Coppola shot off a vehement telegram to Evans dated December 13, 1983, stating in part: "Your stupid blabbing about cutting *The Godfather* comes back to me and angers me for its ridiculous pomposity." Evans replied in a telegram dated the following day that he did not deserve "the venomous diatribe."

The consensus of those involved in the release of *The Godfather*, including Frank Yablans, president of Paramount, was to side with Coppola. Indeed, Yablans remembers Evans lobbying with him in support of Coppola's three-hour version of the film, but he affirms pointedly: "Evans did not save *The Godfather*; Evans did not make *The Godfather*. That is a total figment of his imagination." Producer Albert Ruddy assured me in conversation that the release version of *The Godfather* "was Francis's cut, frame for frame."

Brett Morgen and Nanette Burstein's documentary on Robert Evans's life, *The Kid Stays in the Picture*, premiered at the 2002 CANNES INTERNATIONAL FILM FESTIVAL; in it Evans continues to maintain that he had an artistic influence on *The Godfather*. In the directors' commentary

included on the DVD of the documentary, Morgen acknowledges that Coppola contests Evans's claims about his role in shaping *The Godfather*.

In 1974 Evans became an independent producer, with *Chinatown* (1974) and *Marathon Man* (1976) to his credit. After that came *Black Sunday* (1977) and some other box office flops. Evans's career began to unravel in the early 1980s, starting with his conviction on a charge of cocaine possession, which was followed by various scandals.

Evans decided to produce *The Cotton Club* (1984), a movie about the famed Harlem nightclub, and persuaded Coppola, who had directed Evans's biggest hit at Paramount, to direct. But he and Coppola feuded throughout production. "Francis," says Evans, "is a fat fuck."

Evans had trouble financing the picture and desperately turned to Roy Radin, a business man of dubious reputation, with mob connections. After Radin was murdered in a gangland slaying, Evans was dragged into the case as a material witness. This is because Radin was a backer of *The Cotton Club*; Evans was, however, cleared of any involvement in Radin's death (see the entry on "*THE COTTON CLUB* MURDER CASE" in this book). As things turned out, Evans wound up being producer of the movie in name only. When it was finally completed, *The Cotton Club* was a failure at the box office.

Evans's name was attached to some mediocre movies in the 1990s, such as *Jade* (1995). But the documentary *The Kid Stays in the Picture* brought Evans back into prominence for a while, since it portrayed him as a "Hollywood legend."—Gene D. Phillips/James M. Welsh

References

John Connolly, "Man of a Thousand Lives," *Premiere* 14, no. 8 (August 2001), 93–97, 119;

Michael Daly, "A True Tale of Hollywood: *The Cotton Club*," *New York*, May 7, 1984, 43–60; Robert Evans, *The Kid Stays in the Picture: A Memoir* (Beverly Hills: Dove, 1995); Lawrence Grobel, *Above the Line: Conversations with Robert Evans and Others* (New York: Da Capo, 2000); David Thomson, *The Biographical Dictionary of Film*, rev. ed. (New York: Knopf, 2004).

F

FINIAN'S RAINBOW (1968)

DIRECTOR: Francis Ford Coppola. SCREEN-PLAY: E. Y. Harburg and Fred Saidy, based on the Broadway play. BOOK: E. Y. Harburg and Fred Saidy. LYRICS: E. Y. Harburg. MUSIC: Burton Lane. PRODUCER: Joseph Landon. ASSOCIATE PRODUCER: Joel Freeman. PHOTOGRAPHY: Philip Lathrop. EDITING: Melvin Shapiro. MUSIC DIRECTION: Ray Heindorf. ASSOCIATE MUSIC SUPERVISOR: Ken Darby. PRODUCTION DESIGN: Hilyard M. Brown. COSTUME DESIGN: Dorothy Jeakins. CHOREOGRAPHY: Hermes Pan. SOUND: M. A. Merrick, Dan Wallin.

CAST: Fred Astaire (Finian McLonergan), Petula Clark (Sharon McLonergan), Tommy Steele (Og), Don Francks (Woody), Barbara Hancock (Susan the Silent), Keenan Wynn (Senator Billboard Rawkins), Al Freeman Jr. (Howard), Ronald Colby (Buzz Collins), Dolph Sweet (Sheriff), Wright King (District Attorney), Louil Silas (Henry), Brenda Arnau (Sharecropper), Avon Long, Roy Glen, Jerster Hairston (Passion Pilgrim Gospellers).

RUNNING TIME: 144 minutes. Technicolor, Panavision, 70 mm.

RELEASED THROUGH: Warner Bros.–Seven Arts. PREMIERE: October 9, 1968.

DVD: Warner Home Video.

Although *YOU'RE A BIG BOY NOW* was not a financial success, it garnered some positive reviews. Consequently Seven Arts, which by this time had merged with Warner Bros, was sufficiently impressed with Coppola's handling of *Big Boy* that the company asked the promising young director to make *Finian's Rainbow* (1968), a large-scale movie musical starring FRED ASTAIRE. Coppola accepted the offer mostly because the Burton Lane–E. Y. HARBURG score boasted a bumper crop of songs, including standards like "If This Isn't Love."

Still Coppola had to contend with the screenplay, adapted from the script of the stage play. *Finian's Rainbow* takes place in Rainbow Valley, Missitucky, a mythical Southern village. Finian McLonergan (Fred Astaire) and Sharon, his daughter (PETULA CLARK), have fled to America from Glocca Mora, Ireland, to elude Og, a leprechaun (TOMMY STEELE), whose magical pot of gold Finian has stolen. Woody Mahoney (Don Francks), a sharecropper, sells Finian a plot of land, on which Finian buries the pot of gold that has the power to grant three wishes to whoever possesses it.

Sharon uses one of the wishes to teach a lesson to the racist Senator "Billboard" Rawkins (KEENAN WYNN). She temporarily transforms him into a black man to let him experience racial bigotry. Sharon uses the second wish to restore the senator to his status as a white man. Meanwhile, Howard, a black friend of Woody's, has invented a way of growing menthol tobacco, which

Fred Astaire as Finian.

brings prosperity to Rainbow Valley when he and Woody form the Tobacco Cooperative with the black and white sharecroppers. Og the leprechaun eventually becomes human so that he can woo Susan the Silent, Woody's mute sister (Barbara Hancock). Og himself invokes the third and final wish that the crock of gold can grant in order to give Susan the power of speech. By then Woody has fallen in love with Sharon, and they are married. At the fade-out Finian departs, continuing to "follow the rainbow" wherever it will lead him. The theme of the story seems to be that gold is merely a base metal, while people constitute the world's true wealth—a rather banal notion not calculated to keep the moviegoer up nights pondering it.

As noted, Coppola was appalled when he read the "cockamamie" script. The creaky plot of the twenty-year-old formula musical simply did not hold up. One of the principal elements of the plot concerns the blustering Senator Rawkins who threatens to disrupt the racially integrated community of sharecroppers. The social commentary implied in this situation was at odds with the never-never-land atmosphere of the rest of the story, which revolved around

Og, the fanciful leprechaun whose crock of gold can make people's dreams come true. The two strands of the story had been combined in what was nothing less than a shotgun marriage.

Coppola therefore overhauled the screenplay in an effort to "make it acceptable for contemporary audiences" and yet remain faithful to the spirit of the original show. Thus the film ends with emphasis on the whites and blacks working together with good old American know-how, raising mentholated tobacco and bettering their communal existence in the bargain. In sum, Coppola thought *Rainbow* was a marvelous show of yesteryear: "I tried to make it work on its own terms and not get fancy." He endeavored to give it a "timeless" dimension so that the period in which the story is set is never really defined. Coppola did his best to turn out a respectable movie musical within the limitations of schedule and budget imposed on him.

Coppola had petitioned the studio brass to permit him to shoot the picture on location in Kentucky, but they refused. They wanted him to film the movie on the backlot and to employ an enormous forest set they had spent a lot of money to build for an earlier musical, *Camelot* (1967). It would stand in for rustic Missitucky, thereby enabling the studio to get its money's worth out of the forest set. In effect, that meant that the dancers had to perform on soft grass and muddy earth—instead of on the hard surfaces of a proper dance floor—as Astaire led the jolly inhabitants of Rainbow Valley in merry dances through fields and streams. Coppola was not satisfied with veteran dance director Hermes Pan's choreography, and Pan contended that it was the best he could do with a principal set that had not even been designed for the present film. He asked to have more rehearsal time, but Coppola could not grant his request since there was no margin in the tight production schedule.

"The choreography was abysmal; let's be honest," says Coppola bluntly. "We fired the choreographer halfway through the picture." Coppola staged most of the musical numbers eventually.

Coppola, after all, would be the first to admit that he was no dance director. Nevertheless, he did develop a concept for each number in the wake of Pan's departure from the film. "I dreamed up the way the numbers were going to be done," he explains. For example, "If This Isn't Love" would be done with children's games. Coppola would play back the music for a dance routine and instruct the dancers to "move with the music" while he directed them from behind the camera. Astaire, old trouper that he was, would then oblige with a little impromptu soft shoe routine as he danced his way around a rustic backyard or shuffled off down a country road. Pan did, however, retain his screen credit as choreographer, though what passed for choreography in the picture was largely Coppola's work.

In the end Warners–Seven Arts permitted Coppola to shoot on location for a scant eight days. This footage was carefully interspersed throughout the film to enliven the bulk of the footage that was shot at the studio. It was used to particularly good advantage in the opening credit sequence. Coppola assigned Carroll Ballard, a fellow film school alumnus, to do second-unit photography for the title sequence. During the opening credits the camera roams over a field of flowers and then pans up to Finian and Sharon hiking through the fields. The camera then takes in a rainbow as Sharon sings, "Look to the Rainbow" (recalling Harburg's lyrics for a song in *The Wizard of Oz*, "Over the Rainbow"). There follows a succession of quick shots, wherein the pair pass several legendary American landmarks, including the Statue of Liberty, Mount Rushmore, the Golden Gate Bridge, and Glacier National Park, in the course

of their journey to Rainbow Valley, where they arrive at the close of the credits.

At all events, the skimpy production numbers, coupled with the dated storyline (with the racist senator experiencing a miraculous change of heart), coalesced to make the movie decidedly not a favorite with audiences or with critics. Coppola's brave effort to yoke liberal social attitudes about Southern racism to a quaint, threadbare Irish fable about leprechauns just did not come off. Even the tune-bank of charming songs could not save the picture. Coppola simply shrugs, "I was brought in to direct a project that had already been cast and structured."

One unexpected dividend that did come out of Coppola's travails in making the picture was that it provided him with the opportunity of meeting GEORGE LUCAS, with whom he would collaborate in the years ahead. Lucas, a University of Southern California film student, had won a scholarship that entitled him to an internship at Warners–Seven Arts, whereby he could observe a film in production for six months. Lucas showed up daily on Coppola's set. He was aware that Coppola was the first film school graduate to go big-time. They sensed that they were kindred souls from the outset, and Coppola made Lucas his administrative assistant on the picture. Lucas was a fledgling filmmaker and Coppola was his mentor, and this relationship would continue on Coppola's next film, *THE RAIN PEOPLE*.—GENE D. PHILLIPS

References

Peter Biskind, *Easy Riders, Raging Bulls: Coppola, Scorsese, and Other Directors* (New York: Simon & Schuster, 1999); Laurie Fink, "*Finian's Rainbow*," in *The Encyclopedia of Stage Plays into Film*, ed. James Welsh and John Tibbetts (New York: Facts On File, 2001), 473–74; Joseph Gelmis, *The Director as Superstar* (Garden City, NY: Anchor 1970).

FISHBURNE, LAURENCE, III (1961–)

Stage-trained actor, praised by *New Yorker* critic John Lahr in 2008 as "one of America's finest actors." Born on July 30, 1961, in Augusta, Georgia, raised in Brooklyn, Fishburne made his screen debut on the daytime serial *One Life to Live*, at the age of twelve, then got cast as a character named "Clean" in *APOCALYPSE NOW* (1979) by lying about his age; he was fourteen years old at the time, and he is listed in the credits as "Larry Fishburne." He later played Midget in *RUMBLE FISH* (1983), and other roles for Coppola including Bumpy Rhodes in *THE COTTON CLUB* (1984) and Flanagan in *GARDENS OF STONE* (1987), though he is probably best known on-screen for his later portrayal of Morpheus in the cult science-fiction *Matrix Trilogy* (1999–2003). John Singleton helped to advanced Fishburne's career in 1991 when he wrote the role of Furious Styles, a single father attempting to raise a teenage son (Cuba Gooding, Jr.) in South Central Los Angeles for his film *Boyz 'n the Hood*.

At the age of thirty-four in 1995, Fishburne broke another color barrier when he became the first African American to play the lead in *Othello* for Oliver Parker's adaptation of Shakespeare's play. On stage Fishburne won a Tony Award for August Wilson's *Two Trains Running*, and was noticed by playwright George Stevens, Jr., in his Pasadena Playhouse production of August Wilson's *Fences*, who cast him as Thurgood Marshall on Broadway, replacing James Earl Jones, who introduced the role in tryouts. Consequently, Fishburne was nominated for a Tony Award in 2008 for his portrayal of Thurgood Marshall on Broadway in *Thurgood*, a one-man play by George Stevens, Jr. about the first African American appointed to the United States Supreme Court. Director Leonard Foglia told *New York* magazine, "It's thrilling, to be bringing a discussion of race to Broadway at a time when Obama is running for president."

Fishburne's television experience includes *The Tuskegee Airmen* and an Emmy Award for *Miss Evers' Boys*. In August of 2008 CBS announced that Fishburne would be joining the team of television crime fighters on the popular police series *CSI: Crime Scene Investigation*, replacing the retiring William Petersen, who played professor turned detective Dr. Raymond Langston, setting a precedent for the casting of a minority lead actor in a major television drama series. Fishburne's character, a former pathologist turned college lecturer who examines why people turn violent, was scheduled to begin appearing in the 2008–2009 season's ninth episode.
—James M. Welsh

Reference

John Lahr, "The Fight Back," *New Yorker*, May 12, 2006, 128–29.

FORD, HARRISON (1942–)

American actor celebrated for his work with GEORGE LUCAS and Steven Spielberg, cast by Coppola to play Martin Stett in *THE CONVERSATION* (1974) and Colonel Lucas in *APOCALYPSE NOW* (1979), on which project he met MELISSA MATHISON, the writer of *E.T.*, in 1976, whom he married, after divorcing his first wife in 1979. (Ford and Mathison were legally separated in 2001, after having had two children, Malcolm and Georgia.) The popular actor who would play Han Solo in *Star Wars* before going on to become Indiana Jones, was born in the Chicago suburbs the son of a Roman Catholic advertising executive and a Jewish mother. Ford graduated from Maine Township High School in Park Ridge, Illinois, in 1960 and enrolled in Ripon College in Wisconsin, where he took a drama course in his junior year. He married college sweetheart Mary

Marquardt (a marriage that lasted for fifteen years and produced two children, Willard, a teacher, and Benjamin, a chef) and worked in summer theatre before moving to California in 1964.

Cast in a production of *John Brown's Body* at the Laguna Beach Playhouse, Ford was noticed by a Columbia Pictures talent scout and signed into the studio's New Talent program. After eighteen months at Columbia, Ford signed with Universal and was cast first for television, then as a minor character in Clive Donner's *Luv* (1967) and the Richard Rush movie *Getting Straight* (1970). French New-Wave auteur Jacques Demy wanted Ford to star in his only American film, *Model Shop*, in 1969, but executives at Columbia did not see much potential in Ford at that time and opted for Gary Lockwood instead. Neither successful nor especially happy with his acting career, Ford became a carpenter and built a recording studio for the Brazilian musician and composer, Sergio Mendes.

George Lucas persuaded Ford to return to acting for *AMERICAN GRAFFITI* (1973), which turned out to be an unexpected hit. Roles for Coppola in *The Conversation* and *Apocalypse Now* then followed before Ford's astonishing breakthrough success in *Star Wars*. Ford went on to star in over twenty movies, nine of which grossed over $100 million each, setting a record for a film actor. He has developed a likable on-screen presence and has handled his success reasonably well.—JAMES M. WELSH

References

Alan McKenzie, *The Harrison Ford Story* (New York: Arbor House/Priam Books, 1984); Dotson Rader, "I Found Purpose," *Parade Magazine*, July 7, 2002, 4–5.

FORREST, FREDERIC (1936–)

Actor who played Mark in *THE CONVER-SATION*, played Jay 'Chef' Hicks in *APOC-ALYPSE NOW*, played Hank in *ONE FROM THE HEART*, and played Eddie Dean in *TUCKER: THE MAN AND HIS DREAM*. Born in Waxahachie, Texas, Forrest studied acting in New York City with Irene Daly, Sanford Meisner, and LEE STRASBERG. Forrest moved to Los Angeles in 1970 to star in the play *Silhouettes*, by Ted Harris. His movie debut was in *When the Legends Die*, in which he played opposite Richard Widmark and was nominated for a Golden Globe. Forrest became a member of the repertory company of contract players Coppola assembled for the Zoetrope Studios in Hollywood in 1980. Forrest starred in *HAMMETT*, directed by WIM WENDERS, and also acted opposite Bette Midler in *The Rose*, winning the National Film Critics Award for Best Supporting Actor, as well as Golden Globe and Oscar nominations.—JAMES M. WELSH

FROST, SADIE (1965–)

London-born actress who made her American film debut playing Lucy Westenra in *BRAM STOKER'S DRACULA* (1992). She studied with the Talia Conti Theatrical School and began her theatrical career at the age of eleven. At age nineteen, she had joined Manchester's Exchange Theatre, and she was featured in director Matthew Jacob's debut short feature, *Vardo*, in 1986, based on Jonathan David's prize-winning entry in the *London Sunday Times* Screenplay Competition. Her earlier film roles include Peter Medak's *The Krays* (1990) and Nick Broomfield's *Dark Obsession* (1990). Following her work with FRANCIS COPPOLA, Frost was cast in the comedy *Splitting Heirs* (1993), with John Cleese, Eric Idol, Rick Moranis, Barbara Hershey, and Catherine Zeta-Jones. Later films included *Bent* (1997) and *An Ideal Husband* (1998). She was at one time married to the actor Jude Law.—JAMES M. WELSH

FRUCHTMAN, LISA (N.D.)

Award-winning film editor whose first assignment with FRANCIS COPPOLA was in 1974 as assistant editor for *THE GODFA-THER: PART II.* In 1990 she was editor for *THE GODFATHER: PART III,* and in 1979 for *APOCALYPSE NOW,* earning both Oscar and BAFTA Award nominations. She also edited the Disney short film, *CAPTAIN EO.* Lisa Fruchtman received an Academy Award for her work on *The Right Stuff* (1983). She was born in New York City, earned a BA degree from the University of Chicago, then moved to San Francisco in 1974, where she began her career as an editor at the National Film Board of San Francisco. She also worked on the following titles: *Heaven's Gate* (1980), *Children of a Lesser God* (1986), and *My Best Friend's Wedding* (1997), among other films.—JAMES M. WELSH

GALLO, VINCENT (1961–)

American actor, artist, and musician born in Buffalo, New York, who plays the title role in *TETRO* (2009). Gallo moved to New York City in 1978 and joined the musical group, Gray, along with the legendary artist, Jean-Michel Basquiat. Along with Basquiat, Gallo exhibited his paintings and sculptures in New York galleries and became a fixture in the downtown art scene. From 1978 to 1981, Gallo also gained notoriety for his performance art pieces, staged on the streets of New York City, which shocked passersby but impressed his invited friends. Filmmaker Eric Mitchell witnessed some of these performances and offered Gallo the leading role in his film, *The Way It Is* (1985), which also featured newcomer Steve Buscemi. *The Way It Is* marked Vincent Gallo's feature film debut, although he had directed himself previously in several short films.

To date, Gallo has appeared in more than thirty films, including Claire Denis's *Trouble Every Day* (2001) and *Nénette et Bonni* (1996), the independent comedy *Palookaville* (1995), and Abel Ferrara's *The Funeral* (1996), as well as films that Gallo himself wrote, produced, and directed: *Buffalo 66* (1998), *The Brown Bunny* (2003), and *Promises Written in Water* (set for a 2010 release).

Gallo has created a reputation for himself as being outspoken and often offensive. He has told interviewers that he prostituted himself as a teenager in New York City. He has freely badmouthed critics, as well as fellow actors and directors. And he has shocked audiences with his films, especially *Brown Bunny*, which ends with Chloe Sevigny performing oral sex on Gallo. Roger Ebert characterized the film as the worst in the history of the CANNES INTERNATIONAL FILM FESTIVAL; and in retaliation, Gallo referred to Ebert as a "fat pig." Such a record is very interesting, to say the least, for a man who characterizes himself (perhaps in jest?) as a conservative, rightwing Republican.—RODNEY HILL

References

American Zoetrope, *Tetro* official website, "Vincent Gallo," www.tetro.com; Liese Spencer, "Handpicked to Be a Wiseguy," *Independent*, October 1, 1998, www.independent.co.uk; "Vincent Gallo," *Variety* Profiles, www.variety.com.

GANCE, ABEL (1889–1981)

Pioneering and inventive French film director of the epic *Napoléon*, which FRANCIS FORD COPPOLA revived in America, building upon the restored five-hour reconstruction that had been a lifetime project for the British film archivist, historian, filmmaker, and television producer KEVIN BROWNLOW, whose careful reconstructive work was done in consultation with Gance himself. Coppola shortened the film to conform to union regulations at the Radio City Music Hall in New York, commissioned CARMINE COPPOLA to compose a new American score (the Brownlow reconstruction had already premiered in London and Paris with a score composed by Carl Davis), and coordinated a very successful run in New York, with a live orchestral accompaniment; Coppola then toured the spectacle to other major American cities as well, to further acclaim. Abel Gance, the French pioneering counterpart to the American director D. W. Griffith, was born in Paris, October 25, 1889. Like Griffith, an early interest in performing and writing led Gance to the stage. This interest in acting first took him to the Théâtre du Parc in Brussels in 1907; by 1909 he had become a film actor in Paris for Léonce Perret and was writing film scenarios, and by 1911 he had formed his own film production company, Le Film Français. Gance directed six major films—*J'Accuse* (two versions: 1919 and 1938), *La Roue* (1921), *Napoléon* (1927), *Un grande amour de Beethoven* (1938), *Cyrano et d'Artagnan* (1963)—and many lesser ones, such as *La Fin du monde* (1930, featuring "Perspective Sound," invented by Gance and André Debrie for the film, patented August 13, 1929), *La Dame aux camellias* (1934), *Lucrèce Borgia* (1935), and *Louise* (1938). His experimental montage work in the early 1920s was influential for other filmmakers, such as Sergei Eisenstein in the Soviet Union. Though Gance had difficulty funding his film projects in later life, he collaborated with Claude Lelouch on his final "version" of *Napoleon*, which was entitled *Bonaparte et la Révolution*, released in 1972, but not a very well-unified feature. Gance lived to see the Brownlow reconstruction of his *Napoléon* projected under the stars at night for the Telluride Film Festival in the mountains of Colorado, but by the time the Coppola spectacular opened at Radio City, M. Gance was too ill to travel.

He was able to hear the audience applause via trans-Atlantic telephone, however, and he was able to offer his apologies for not attending through his telephone partner, the likable actor Gene Kelly, explaining that he did not have the "pep" to travel.
—JAMES M. WELSH

References
Kevin Brownlow, *Napoleon: Abel Gance's Classic Film* (London: Jonathan Cape, 1983); Steven Philip Kramer and James Michael Welsh, *Abel Gance* (Boston: Twayne Publishers, 1978).

GANZ, BRUNO (1941–)
International leading German-Swiss actor, fluent in four languages, who plays Professor Stanciulescu in FRANCIS COPPOLA's *YOUTH WITHOUT YOUTH* (2007). Ganz was born in Zurich, Switzerland, on March 22, 1941, but after Swiss military service, he began his stage career in Germany, becoming in 1970 a founder and leading star of the Schaubühne am Halleschen Ufer, a Berlin-based, left-wing theatrical company directed by Peter Stein. He was featured on stage in *Hamlet*, Ibsen's *Peer Gynt*, Brecht's *Jungle of Cities*, Heinrich von Kleist's *Prince of Homburg*, and Peter Handke's *The Ride across Lake Constance* and *They Are Dying Out*. The Austrian writer Peter Handke, a friend and colleague of WIM WENDERS, would later direct Ganz as the spurned husband in his 1977 film adaptation of Handke's own novel, *Die linkshändige Frau* (*The Left-Handed Woman*), playing opposite Edith Clever, the leading actress of the Theater am Halleschen Ufer in Berlin. Ganz's first film appearance, however, came as the writer Yakov Schalimov in Peter Stein's screen adaptation of Maxim Gorky's *Summer Guests* in 1975. The following year he would save the heroine from dishonor in Eric Rohmer's *The Marquise of O.* (1976). Other roles soon followed, making him the lead actor of *Das neue Kino*, the

New German Cinema. In 1976 he played a supporting role in Jeanne Moreau's directorial debut picture, *Lumiere*, and in Hans W. Geissendörfer's screen adaptation of Ibsen's *The Wild Duck*. Claiming to be "tired of theatre" in 1976, Ganz left the Schaubühne to concentrate exclusively on his film career. Ganz claims his role as the assassin in Wim Wenders's *The American Friend* (1977) was "my first real film . . . a test of whether or not I could become a *real* movie actor." He played a truly spooky Jonathan Harker for Werner Herzog's *Nosferatu—Phantom der Nachts* (1979) and the chess prodigy for Wolfgang Petersen's *Black and White Like Day and Night*, also in 1979. He later went on to be featured in Wim Wenders's masterpiece *Wings of Desire* (1987). His first English-speaking role was for Franklin Schaffner's *The Boys from Brazil* (1978), as the scientist who explains cloning. It is highly appropriate, therefore, that Ganz eventually found his way into a Coppola film at exactly the time Coppola

was reinventing himself as an experimental filmmaker.—JAMES M. WELSH

GARCIA, ANDY [ANDRÉS ARTURO GARCIA Y MENENDEZ] (1956–)

The actor who plays Vincent Mancini in *THE GODFATHER: PART III*, the illegitimate son of Sonny Corleone, who finds himself a candidate to succeed his uncle Michael, just as Michael had succeeded his father Don Vito Corleone. FRANCIS COPPOLA cast Garcia to play Vincent, presumably because Garcia resembled ROBERT DE NIRO, who played Vito in *THE GODFATHER: PART II*, Vincent's grandfather. Garcia received both Academy Award and Golden Globe nominations for his work in *Godfather III*. Garcia was born in Bejucal, La Habana Province, Cuba, and moved to Miami Beach, Florida, with his family at the age of five after the failed Bay of Pigs invasion. He was educated at Miami Beach Senior High School, then attended Florida International University to study

Andy Garcia and Talia Shire in *The Godfather: Part III*.

acting. He got acting experience by performing in local theatres before moving to Los Angeles in the late 1970s. Garcia made his television acting debut in the 1981 premiere episode of the police drama *Hill Street Blues*. Impressed by Garcia's performance in Hal Ashby's film *8 Million Ways to Die* (1986), director Brian De Palma cast him in *The Untouchables* (1987), a breakthrough for the actor's career. Film roles for Paramount Studios followed, including *Internal Affairs* (1989), *Black Rain* (1989), *Dead Again* (1991), *Ocean's Eleven* (2001), *Ocean's Twelve* (2004), and *Ocean's Thirteen* (2007), which kept Garcia visible in a long-running popular string of caper movies as part of an all-star ensemble. Hal Ashby and Brian De Palma launched Garcia's career; Francis Coppola made him a star. —JAMES M. WELSH

Reference

James Cameron-Wilson, *Young Hollywood* (Lanham, MD: Madison Books, 1994).

GARDENS OF STONE (1987)

DIRECTOR: Francis Ford Coppola. SCREENPLAY: Ronald Bass, based on the novel by Nicholas Proffitt. PRODUCERS: Michael I. Levy and Francis Coppola for Zoetrope Studios. EXECUTIVE PRODUCERS: Stan Weston, Jay Emmett, and Fred Roos. COEXECUTIVE PRODUCER: David Valdes. PHOTOGRAPHY: Jordan Cronenweth. EDITING: Barry Malkin. MUSIC: Carmine Coppola. PRODUCTION DESIGN: Dean Tavoularis. ART DIRECTION: Alex Tavoularis. COSTUME DESIGN: Willa Kim, Judianna Makovsky. SOUND DESIGNER: Richard Beggs.

CAST: James Caan (Clell Hazard), Anjelica Huston (Samantha Davis), James Earl Jones (Goody Nelson), D. B. Sweeney (Jackie Willow), Dean Stockwell (Homer Thomas), Mary Stuart Masterson (Rachel Feld), Dick Anthony Williams (Slasher Williams), Lonette McKee (Betty Rae), Sam Bottoms (Lt. Webber), Elias Koteas (Pete Deveber), Larry Fishburne (Flanagan), Casey Siemaszko (Wildman), Peter Masterson (Colonel Feld), Carlin Glynn (Mrs. Feld), Erik Holland (Colonel Godwin), Bill Graham (Don Brubaker).
RUNNING TIME: 112 minutes, color (De Luxe).
RELEASED THROUGH: Tri-Star. PREMIERE: May 8, 1987.
DVD: Sony Pictures.

After the excesses that marked the making of *APOCALYPSE NOW*, Coppola, after finishing the film in 1979, said, "Sometimes I think, why don't I just make my wine" (he owns a vineyard near his Napa estate) "and do some dumbbell movie every two years?" But Coppola continued making movies that mattered to him. Thus he made another film about the Vietnam War, *Gardens of Stone*. It has no stunning battle sequence, since it takes place stateside. In contrast to a king-size war epic like *Apocalypse Now*, *Gardens of Stone* tells what Coppola calls a more intimate, personal story. While *Apocalypse Now* depicts the Vietnam War itself, *Gardens of Stone*, its companion piece, is concerned with the home front during the same period.

In the spring of 1985 Victor Kaufman, chief executive of Tri-Star Pictures, invited Coppola to direct *Gardens of Stone*, which Ronald Bass had adapted from the novel by NICHOLAS PROFFITT. The novelist had served three years in THE OLD GUARD, the venerable army unit that oversees military burials at Arlington National Cemetery near Washington, D.C. Proffitt's novel centers on the Old Guard. Coppola explains that he decided to make this muted, elegiac film about the special ceremonial unit of the army because he has been interested in the role of ritual in army life ever since he attended a military school as a youngster. Besides, he also valued the opportunity to present an in-depth portrayal of servicemen as a sort of family whose members are bound together by a traditional code of honor and by mutual loyalty and affection. In short, his goal in making the film was to limn military men, not as conventional movie stereotypes, but as complicated human beings.

Gardens of Stone presents the benign image of the army as a large family and shows how the elders in the family endeavor to give the younger members the benefit of their experience—only to lose some of them in battle. The message Coppola extracted from the story was that "we are sworn to protect our children" and yet we keep putting them in circumstances that make that impossible, so that "you end up burying them, all dressed up in military ritual."

Coppola, we remember, had had a falling out with the Pentagon over the script for *Apocalypse Now*, and he had therefore been denied the army's cooperation in making the movie. In the present instance, Coppola literally could not afford to alienate the Pentagon a second time, since *Gardens of Stone* simply could not be made without access to Arlington National Cemetery and the military training base at Fort Myer that figures prominently in the story, not to mention the equipment and personnel that the army could make available.

While reworking the script, Coppola points out, "I was trying to be faithful to the book. I didn't want to juice the film up with superfluous plot and conflict." That explains the absence of battle scenes in the film. The war is depicted solely by a series of newsreel clips shown on television back home: close-ups of the anguished faces of suffering soldiers, shots of the wounded

being stowed aboard helicopters by their comrades at arms.

As usual, Coppola enlisted crew members from his previous pictures, including production designer DEAN TAVOULARIS, editor BARRY MALKIN, and composer CARMINE COPPOLA, who scored the music for the military band. GIAN-CARLO "GIO" COPPOLA, the elder of Coppola's two sons, was again in charge of videotaping rehearsals so that the director could discuss various scenes with the actors. He was assisted by his buddy Griffin O'Neal, the troubled son of actor Ryan O'Neal, who had just finished a year in a drug rehabilitation program.

Once again, Coppola called on actors who had appeared in his other films. JAMES CAAN, cast as an old-timer, Sergeant Clell Hazard, was emerging from a five-year hiatus from films, during which he had successfully controlled his substance abuse (something O'Neal had so far failed to do.) Shooting started in May 1986. The eight-week shoot wrapped on August 5, 1986, right on schedule and just slightly over the $13.5 million budget. When Coppola moved into postproduction, he collaborated closely with editor Barry Malkin, who had worked on *Apocalypse Now* (uncredited).

In filming the burial rites, Coppola had been at pains to capture the grandeur and pace of the ritual, but preview audiences found these scenes tedious. "A young audience—and young audiences are pretty much what you get in these previews—saw these scenes" as just a lot of marching, he explains, "so we had to modulate these drills." In the end, adds Malkin, "we were allowed" by the military advisors "to skip over parts of the ceremonies because they took too long."

Gardens of Stone opens with Lieutenant Jackie Willow's military funeral at Arlington

National Cemetery, near the Tomb of the Unknown Soldier, complete with a twenty-one-gun salute. There follows an extended flashback that covers the events leading up to his funeral, and it is to his funeral that the movie returns at the film's conclusion. Hence, Jackie's obsequies serve as the narrative frame for the entire picture.

The film focuses on Sergeant Clell Hazard (James Caan), a combat veteran who has become increasingly demoralized as he observes the army futilely waging a war in Vietnam he is convinced is unwinnable. "I care about the U.S. Army," he says to a friend; "that's my family. And I don't like it when my family is in trouble."

After four years in Vietnam, Hazard is now a member of the Old Guard, a special unit that serves as the honor guard for the burials of servicemen killed in Vietnam at Arlington National Cemetery (the gardens of stone). In practice, this can involve participation in as many as fifteen funerals a day. Depressed by the continuing loss of so many young lives, Hazard sardonically tells

Jackie Willow, a young recruit in the Old Guard (D. B. SWEENEY), that burying is their business and business has never been better. Bright-eyed, impetuous Jackie insists that the war is not lost and that the right kind of soldier could make a difference. Hazard, on the other hand, thinks Jackie far too idealistic and tells him so repeatedly. Nonetheless, the rambunctious lad is itching to plunge into the fray, in order to do whatever he can to help win the war.

Jackie in due course is shipped overseas, where he is killed in action just a few weeks before he was to complete his tour of duty. During the ceremonies at graveside for Jackie, we can hear a couple of the younger members of the Old Guard muttering their favorite jingle: "Ashes to ashes and dust to dust; / Let's get this over and get back in the bus." Jackie no doubt recited this same impish little ditty when he was part of the ceremonial guard.

Hazard, who had become a surrogate father for Jackie during their time together in the Old Guard, feels as if he has indeed

James Caan, D. B. Sweeney, and James Earl Jones.

lost a son when Jackie is killed. The aging soldier remembers that Jackie had dreamed of winning the Combat Infantry Badge while he was in Vietnam, but did not live long enough to receive one. Hence Hazard places his own CIB on Jackie's coffin before the interment, equivalent to a gift from father to son. Hazard also decides, in the wake of Jackie's death, to return to the battleground in Vietnam, in the hope that he can teach other young fighting men everything he knows about how to survive under fire, since he never got the chance to help Jackie in this way.

Critical reaction to *Gardens of Stone* was very reserved, indeed, with most reviewers praising individual aspects of the film, but not the whole show. For example, Jordan Cronenweth's cinematography was lauded for giving the movie a mellow, autumnal look with its muted, pastel tints. But the film as a whole was thought to rely too much on character and mood and not enough on dynamic storytelling. Coppola himself confessed that he was aware of this problem from the get-go: "I was trying to orchestrate a piece that didn't have a strong narrative," and it showed.

Inevitably, *Gardens of Stone* was compared to *Apocalypse Now*, much to the later film's disadvantage. Referring to Jackie's funeral, Richard Blake asked, "Why did Coppola, whose own strong *Apocalypse Now* presented a searing portrait of Vietnam and its corrosive effects on human values, turn to sentimentality in *Gardens of Stone*?" The film's somber vision was to some degree responsible for its dismal performance at the box office. Coppola consoled himself with a "Certificate of Appreciation for Patriotic Civilian Service" from the U. S. Army, which endorsed the film as displaying the devotion to duty and strong leadership that characterizes army.

Coppola experienced a personal tragedy during the making of *Gardens of Stone*. During the first week of filming, his twenty-two-year-old son Gian-Carlo was killed in a boating accident on Chesapeake Bay near the location site. The driver of the speedboat was Griffin O'Neal, who was convicted of reckless endangerment and gross negligence. This writer, like numberless people in the film world, extended condolences to Coppola. Later on he commented in his journal, "It's true that movies you work on become part of your life at the time. They raise questions about family and friends. I was doing a movie about the burying of young boys and suddenly found that my own boy died right in the midst of it; and his funeral was held in the same chapel where we shot similar scenes of deceased veterans in *Gardens of Stone*. My son is gone, but his memory is not."
—Gene D. Phillips

References

Richard Blake, "Overgrown Gardens," *America*, June 17, 1987, 506; Eleanor Coppola, *Notes on a Life* (New York: Doubleday, 2008); Francis Ford Coppola, "Journal: 1989–93," in *Projections: Three Filmmakers on Filmmaking*, ed. John Boorman and Walter Donohue (Boston: Faber and Faber, 1994), 3–43; Peter Keough, "Coppola Carves Out a Cinematic Elegy," *Chicago Sun-Times Show*, May 16, 1987, 5; Robert Lindsey, "Coppola Returns to the Vietnam War," *New York Times*, May 3, 1987, sec. 2: 34; Gabriella Oldham, *First Cut: Conversations with Film Editors* (Los Angeles: University of California Press, 1995).

GARFIELD, ALLEN
[ALLEN GOORWITZ] (1939–)

American character actor who had appeared in forty-seven motion pictures by 1990, including Robert Altman's *Nashville* (1975, playing the protective husband of C&W singer Ronee Blakely) and FRANCIS COPPOLA's *THE COTTON CLUB* (1984, playing Abbadabba Berman), his third role for Coppola after *THE CONVERSATION* (1974, as Bernie Moran) and *ONE FROM THE HEART* (1982). Garfield, who reverted to using his birth name, Allen Goorwitz, after 1979, was born and raised in Newark, New Jersey, where he began a newspaper career as a copy boy for the *Newark Star Ledger* and then advanced to sports reporter. He later served as managing editor of the *Linden Leader* in Linden, New Jersey. Garfield made his Broadway debut in 1970 in Donald Freed's play, *Inquest: The Trial of Julius and Ethel Rosenberg*. This followed his film debut in Brian De Palma's high-spirited film about draft evaders, *Greetings* (1968). He played a screenwriter to Peter O'Toole's director in Richard Rush's *The Stunt Man* (1980) and two years later played a movie producer for WIM WENDERS's *The State of Things* (1982). A lifetime member of the Actors Studio in New York, he studied acting with LEE STRASBERG, Harold Clurman, and Elia Kazan. Eventually, Garfield moved to Beverly Hills, where he directed his own acting school, The Actor's Shelter.—JAMES M. WELSH

GARR, TERI (1944–)

Dancer, comedienne, and actress who plays Amy Fredericks in *THE CONVERSATION* (1974) and Frannie in *ONE FROM THE HEART* (1982), a quasi-musical, romantic fantasy about a Las Vegas couple (Garr and FREDERIC FORREST) who fall out of love and then fall in love again. Teri Garr was born in Lakewood, Ohio, on December 11, 1944, the daughter of actor Eddie Garr and his wife Phyllis Lind (née Emma Schmotzer), who had been a dancer with the Radio City Music Hall Rockettes. After the death of Garr's father, her mother moved to Hollywood and found work as a wardrobe mistress. A graduate of North Hollywood High School, Garr then majored in speech and dance at California State, Northridge.

Garr has often played "a spirited comedienne of the Joan Blondell mold," writes Ephraim Katz, for example, as the wide-eyed girlfriend of Dr. Frankenstein in Mel Brooks's *Young Frankenstein* in 1974. That same year Garr took a small, meaty role in Coppola's *The Conversation*.

Throughout the film Harry Caul (Gene Hackman), a surveillance expert, wears a translucent plastic raincoat, a visual symbol that he is insulated inside his own private world. At one point "Harry lies down on the bed next to his mistress Amy [Teri Garr] without removing his transparent raincoat," says Coppola. Amy asks him to share something personal with her. "I don't have any secrets," he replies cagily. "I'm a secret," she says. Coppola comments, "When she asks him personal questions about himself, he bristles. She equivalently wants to look through the transparent raincoat at the man underneath," and he accuses her of prying. Amy is fed up with Harry, and sadly but firmly says that she does not want to see him anymore.

Garr went on to costar in Steven Spielberg's hugely successful *Close Encounters of the Third Kind* (1977) and other films, and then Coppola put her in *One from the Heart*, a romantic comedy set in Las Vegas. Teri Garr was cast as Frannie; Frederic Forrest (*APOCALYPSE NOW*) as Hank, her live-in lover; RAUL JULIA as Ray, a lounge waiter that Frannie is enamored with; and NASTASSJA KINSKY as Leila, a high-wire artist who has run away from the circus, to whom Hank is attracted.

When shooting commenced on February 2, 1981, Coppola had a silver Airstream trailer, which he christened the "Silverfish," stationed near the set. It was filled with high-definition TV monitors, control boards, and microphones. Coppola explained that, after shooting a scene, "I can review each shot and know right away whether I want to . . . make a change in a scene." The system, which he dubbed "ELECTRONIC CINEMA," allowed Coppola to make a preliminary edit of each scene when it was filmed.

For the record, Scott Haller, who visited the set, observed that Coppola all too often directed scenes from inside the Silverfish. In directing a scene from the trailer, according to Haller, Coppola's disembodied voice issued directions, which were relayed to cast members on the set "via a loud speaker, for everyone to hear." Teri Garr told me (during a brief interview when she was working on another film) that some of the actors complained that they found it disturbing that the director was sequestered in an off-stage control booth. His voice was amplified over a public address system, as if he were Zeus on Mount Olympus or the Wizard of Oz. Garr herself felt somewhat uneasy with a "remote-control" director; "We couldn't talk back to him. We just listened and took direction. We felt like puppets."

Coppola later countered that he was on the set to rehearse the actors before a scene was filmed and only retreated to the Silverfish when they were ready to do a take so he could watch it on the monitor. Be that as it may, as shooting progressed, this method of directing generated so much tension on the set that some of the cast whispered that "Big Brother is watching you." Consequently, Coppola gradually tapered off from using this technique toward the end of filming, much to Garr's relief. Pauline Kael writes, "In interviews Coppola talked about directing the movie from inside a trailer while watching the set on video equipment. This movie feels like something directed from a trailer. It's cold and mechanized, it is a remove from the action."

One from the Heart was a failure (a wag christened it "One from the Glands"). But Garr quickly snapped back afterward with her Oscar-nominated role as Sandy, the wimpish girlfriend of Michael (Dustin Hoffman), in *Tootsie* (Sydney Pollack, 1982).

According to one source, Garr's career as a dancer started with the San Francisco Ballet, before she turned to film and television acting during the 1960s. She appeared as a dancer in nine Elvis Presley movies, made frequent appearances on "The Sonny and Cher Comedy Hour" (1973–1974), and later became a regular guest on "Late Night with David Letterman." In 2002 Garr disclosed that she suffered from multiple sclerosis, and she later became a spokesperson for the National Multiple Sclerosis Society.—GENE D. PHILLIPS/JAMES M. WELSH

References
Roger Ebert, *The Great Movies II* (New York: Broadway Books, 2005); Scott Haller, "Francis Coppola's Biggest Gamble," *Saturday Review*, July 1981, 20–26; Pauline Kael, *Taking It All In* (New York: Holt, Rinehart, and Winston, 1984); Ephraim Katz, *The Film Encyclopedia*, ed. Ronald Nolan, rev. ed. (New York: Harper Collins, 2008).

GENIUSES (1982)
Goofball satirical play about a group of filmmakers on location in the Philippines, twenty-eight days behind schedule, working on a multimillion-dollar epic film called *Parabola of Death*. The play was written by JONATHAN REYNOLDS, who spent three months in the Philippines with Coppola working on *APOCALYPSE NOW*. The play opened off-Broadway in 1982 and played Arena Stage in Washington, D.C., in 1983. "Rarely have I cared less about a group of characters on the stage," *Washington Post* reviewer David Richards wrote. Although the play inspired "a fair amount of laughter, the laughter is mean-spirited and without generosity," the reviewer complained. Most impressive was "the rotten weather," as the result of how a typhoon was staged to end Act One.—JAMES M. WELSH

Reference

David Richards, "Low-Grade 'Geniuses,'" *Washington Post*, April 1, 1983, D1, D4.

GENTRY, CURT (N.D.)

Friend of FRANCIS COPPOLA and author of the bestseller *J. Edgar Hoover: The Man and the Secrets* (1991). When the Quincy Jones Entertainment Company bought the rights to Gentry's book, it was rumored that Coppola would direct the picture.—JAMES M. WELSH

GERE, RICHARD (1949–)

American star actor who played Dixie Dwyer in *THE COTTON CLUB* (1984). Born in Philadelphia but raised on a farm in upstate New York near Syracuse, his father, Homer, was an insurance salesman, and his mother, Doris, was a homemaker. A talented musician, Gere got his professional start in New York's musical theatre in the early 1970s, and a highlight of his early stage career was his starring role as Danny Zuko in the Broadway production of *Grease* (1973). His first notable screen role came in Richard Brooks's *Looking for Mr. Goodbar* (1977), in which Gere portrays DIANE KEATON's hustler-beau.

The following year, Richard Gere landed his first two leads in major films, Terrence Malick's masterpiece *Days of Heaven* and Robert Mulligan's *Bloodbrothers*; but full-blown movie stardom followed two years later, with Paul Schrader's *American Gigolo* (1980). Then in 1982 Gere reached new heights with the highly successful *An Officer and a Gentleman*.

The remainder of the 1980s saw a falling off in Gere's stardom, with a series of commercial failures, including *The Cotton Club*. Still, Gere's performance in that film found favor with some critics, including Roger Ebert: "Richard Gere is especially good as Dixie Dwyer, maybe because the camera has a way of seeing him off-balance, so that he doesn't dominate the center of each shot like a handsome icon; Coppola stirs him into the action." Despite some critical praise, *The Cotton Club* was a commercial disappointment, with its budget of $47 million and a domestic box office gross of only $25 million.

In 1990, Richard Gere resurrected and redefined his stardom in Mike Figgis's thriller, *Internal Affairs*, and in Garry Marshall's romantic comedy, *Pretty Woman*, costarring Julia Roberts. Gere's newfound appeal as a "silver fox" in the latter film has been compared by some critics to the late career of Cary Grant. The following year, Gere appeared in Akira Kurosawa's penultimate film, the gentle, multigenerational drama, *Rhapsody in August* (1991). Throughout the 1990s and since then, Gere has been an outspoken advocate for Tibetan and Taiwanese independence, and he has become closely allied with the Dalai Lama in these efforts.

In 2002 Gere returned to his musical roots in the Oscar-winning film version of *Chicago*, which won him the Golden Globe as Best Actor. His other notable films of the decade include *The Mothman Prophecies* (2002), *Shall We Dance?* (2004) with Jennifer Lopez, and Robert Altman's *Dr. T and the Women* (2000).—RODNEY HILL

References

"The Cotton Club," *Variety* Profiles, www.variety.com; Roger Ebert, "The Cotton Club," *Chicago Sun-Times*, 1984, www.rogerebert.suntimes.com; "Richard Gere," Turner Classic Movies Database, www.tcmdb.com.

GIANNINI, GIANCARLO (1942–)

Italian international superstar who anchors FRANCIS COPPOLA's episode, "LIFE WITHOUT ZOE," in the omnibus film *NEW YORK STORIES* (1989), and later played Enzo in *CQ* (2001), directed by ROMAN COPPOLA. Giannini was born on August 1, 1942, in Spezia, Italy, and attended the National Academy of Dramatic Arts (Accademia Nazionale d'Arte Dramatica) in 1961 in Rome. He made his stage debut in 1962 as Puck in Shakespeare's *Midsummer Night's Dream* and then was chosen to play Romeo in Franco Zeffirelli's famous stage production of *Romeo and Juliet*. Giannini later co-starred with Anna Magnani in Zeffirelli's stage production of *The Sea Wolf*. In 1965 he made his television debut as David Copperfield in the Dickens-inspired RAI television miniseries. Giannini's long association with Italian film director Lina Wertmüller began when he was cast for her stage play, *Two and Two are No Longer Four*, also directed by Zeffirelli. Though he would be featured in films by other internationally famous directors—he co-starred with Robert Mitchum in Edward Dmytryk's *Anzio!* (1968), for example, in Stanley Kramer's *The Secret of Santa Vittorio* (1969), and in the great Luchino Visconti's last film, *The Innocent* (1977)—Giannini rose to fame mainly because of his continued association with Wertmüller, featured as a tragicomic emblem of forlorn, frustrated, and abused Italian manhood. Ultimately, he became her partner in Wertmüller's film production company, Liberty Films. Wertmüller led him to international acclaim for his performance in *The Seduction of Mimi* in 1971, then three roles followed in 1972 with other directors: *It Was Me* and *The Sensual Man*, directed by Alberto Lattuada, and *Paolo il Caldo*, produced and directed by Marco Vicario. But Giannini was most famous in America for his work with Wertmüller. In 1974 he won the award for Best Actor at the CANNES INTERNATIONAL FILM FESTIVAL for his performance in Wertmüller's *Love and Anarchy*, and he was also featured in *Swept Away*, an art-house success in 1974; then

in 1976 Giannini was nominated for the Academy Award for Best Actor for his performance in *Seven Beauties*, even though his performance was entirely in Italian. Most recently Giannini played the French agent René Mathis in two James Bond features, *Casino Royale* (2006) and *Quantum of Solace* (2008).—JAMES M. WELSH

GLOVER, DANNY [LEBERN] (1947–)

Leading African American actor of film, stage, and television, cast to play Judge Tyrone Kipler in *THE RAINMAKER* (1997). Danny Glover was born in San Francisco, California, on July 12, 1947. His parents, James and Carrie Glover, were postal workers, union organizers, and activists in the NAACP. Glover was educated at San Francisco State University and the Black Actors Workshop of the American Conservatory Theatre, as well as the American University in Washington, D.C. He made his off-Broadway debut in a 1980 revival of Athol Fugard's *The Blood Knot*, and he also appeared in the original Broadway production of Fugard's *Master Harold . . . and the Boys* (1982). His breakthrough film role came in 1984, in Robert Benton's *Places in the Heart*, but his first starring role in a theatrical film was in Steven Spielberg's *The Color Purple* (1985), in which he portrayed "Mister," the abusive husband of Whoopi Goldberg's character. Starting in 1987, his comedic action roles in the *Lethal Weapon* series made him an international star. Since that time, Glover has used his star power to get behind a number of progressive films dealing with African and African American themes, including: *To Sleep with Anger* (1990), with Glover as executive producer and supporting actor, playing the Devil—a role that won him an Independent Spirit Award; and *A Rage in Harlem* (1991), in which Glover costarred with executive producer Forest Whitaker.—RODNEY HILL/ JAMES M. WELSH

Reference

"Danny Glover," Turner Classic Movies Database, www.tcmdb.com.

THE GODFATHER (1972)

DIRECTOR: Francis Ford Coppola. SCREEN-PLAY: Mario Puzo, Francis Ford Coppola, based on the novel by Puzo. PRODUCER: Albert S. Ruddy (Alfran Productions). ASSOCIATE PRODUCER: Gray Frederickson. PHOTOGRAPHY: Gordon Willis. EDITING: William Reynolds, Peter Zinner. MUSIC: Nino Rota (additional music by Carmine Coppola). PRODUCTION DESIGNER: Dean Tavoularis. ART DIRECTION: Warren Clymer. COSTUME DESIGN: Anna Hill Johnstone. SOUND: Walter Murch and Christopher Newman.
CAST: Marlon Brando (Don Vito Corleone), Al Pacino (Michael Corleone), James Caan (Sonny Corleone), Richard Castellano (Clemenza), Robert Duvall (Tom Hagen), Sterling Hayden (McClusky), John Marley (Jack Woltz), Richard Conte (Barzini), Al Lettieri (Sollozzo), Diane Keaton (Kay Adams), Abe Vigoda (Tessio), Talia Shire (Connie), Gianni Russo (Carlo Rizzi), John Cazale (Fredo Corleone), Rudy Bond (Cuneo), Al Martino (Johnny Fontane), Morgana King (Mama Corleone), Lenny Montanna (Luca Brasi), John Martino (Paulie Gatto), Salvatore Corsitto (Bonasera), Richard Bright (Neri), Alex Rocco (Moe Greene), Tony Giorgio (Bruno Tattaglia), Vito Scotti (Nazorine), Tere Livrano (Theresa Hagen), Victor Rendina (Philip Tattaglia), Jeannie Linero (Lucy Mancini), Julie Gregg (Sandra Corleone), Ardell Sheidan (Mrs. Clemenza), Simonetta Stefanelli (Apollonia), Angelo Infanti (Fabrizio), Corrado Gaipa (Don Tommasino), Franco Citti (Calo), Saro Urzi (Vitelli).
RUNNING TIME: 175 minutes. Technicolor.
RELEASED THROUGH Paramount. PREMIERE: March 11, 1972.

ACADEMY AWARDS: Best Picture, Adapted Screenplay, Actor (Marlon Brando). DVD: Paramount.

Because FRANCIS COPPOLA's early films did not fare well at the box office, he experienced some difficulty in launching film projects. When he won an Academy Award for coauthoring the script for the epic war film *PATTON* (1970), however, Paramount Pictures decided to entrust him with the direction of a gangster picture about the Mafia they were going to make called *The Godfather*, based on the best-selling novel by MARIO PUZO. Paramount production chief ROBERT EVANS became increasingly convinced that only an Italian American director could supply the creative tissue to make a Mafia movie work. "It must be ethnic to the core," he said. "You must smell the spaghetti." Coppola was a director of Italian ancestry. Furthermore, Evans assumed that, as a young director, Coppola would be very tractable.

Coppola initially thought the book read like a lurid potboiler by the likes of Irving Wallace (*The Chapman Report*)—books that he considered below the belt and beneath discussion. Besides, Coppola wanted to avoid doing formula pictures. GEORGE LUCAS, Coppola's colleague, remembers that Coppola asked, "George, should I make this gangster movie?" Lucas reminded Coppola that AMERICAN ZOETROPE was floundering. "Francis, we're in debt," he said; "you need a job. I think you should do it. Survival is the key thing here." So Coppola took Paramount up on its offer.

When he got further into the book, Coppola saw that it was "the story of a family, this father and his sons; and I thought it was a terrific story, if you could cut out all the other stuff." So, once he had scraped away the dispensable subplots, he concluded that "it wasn't a piece of trash." Coppola lent the narrative dignity, performing a job of alchemy in turning Puzo's novel into art on the screen.

Coppola says in the indispensable documentary that accompanies the DVD of the *Godfather Trilogy* (released 2008), "I did my own version of the screenplay, then I contacted Mario and we collaborated." Puzo adds in the same documentary, "We wrote separately. I sent my stuff to him, and he sent his stuff to me. Then he made the final decision as to what would be in the shooting script." Coppola was able to whittle Puzo's gargantuan novel down to a screenplay of 163 pages for a film of about three hours.

Coppola never backed off from indicating in the script that the mobsters were of Italian descent. He wished to show the Italian American community with understanding and candor, to indicate that Don Corleone, the godfather of the title, was convinced that organized crime was the passport to the American dream for downtrodden immigrants. He further emphasized that *The Godfather* was focusing on a group of fictitious Italian criminals and not defaming the entire Italian community.

Coppola added a minor but telling incident early in the film, when one of Don Corleone's capos, Peter Clemenza (Richard Castellano), is leaving home to arrange the murder of Paulie Gatto, the don's treacherous bodyguard who is in the pay of another mob. Coppola had Clemenza's wife say to him, "Don't forget to bring home some cannoli." Then in the scene where Clemenza has a hit man liquidate Paulie in a car on a remote country road, Clemenza says to him, "Leave the gun. Take the cannoli." Clemenza's thinking about the dessert his wife told him to bring home—immediately after a killing—provides a chilling moment in the film.

Robert Evans appointed Albert Ruddy to produce the picture. It was generally known that Ruddy had a reputation for bringing B pictures in on budget. Evans had declared that *The Godfather* was to be a low-budget movie, shot at the studio and using the back lot. Moreover, it was to be set in the present, rather than after World War II (which is the time frame of the book) in order to avoid the extra expense of making a period picture. The movie, in brief, was designed to be made on the double and on the cheap for $1 million.

Coppola balked at these restrictions. To begin with, he maintained that the story simply would not work if set in the present. For example, mob members no longer shot each other in the streets like rabbits the way they did during the gang wars in the old days. "I made a big point of saying to the studio that the story was immersed in the postwar period and had to take place there," he says. When the book became a runaway hit with the public, Coppola, who was turning out to be a good deal less tractable than the front office had anticipated, strongly urged the studio to upgrade the production to an A picture, as befitted the movie adaptation of a bestseller.

He ultimately succeeded in getting the studio to change its tune: The picture was to be set in period and he would be allowed to film the bulk of the picture on location in New York, and even to shoot the scenes set in Sicily on location in Sicily. The budget was finally increased to $6.5 million.

When the question of casting came up, both Coppola and Puzo agreed that their first choice to play Don Vito Corleone, the sixty-five-year-old godfather, was MARLON BRANDO. Nevertheless, Evans rejected Brando out of hand since the actor had a reputation for being temperamental and cranky on the set. Moreover, Brando had in recent years been in a string of flops.

Coppola made an eloquent plea on the actor's behalf—while standing on the conference table—during a meeting with the studio brass. Evans relented and ultimately approved Brando for the part.

After principal photography commenced on March 23, 1971, at the old Filmways Studio in New York, Coppola was aware that some disgruntled studio executives were fed up with fencing with him about production and casting decisions; Coppola sensed that some of them would like to be rid of him. They backed off only after viewing the superbly directed scene in which Michael Corleone (AL PACINO) commits his first two murders in a Bronx restaurant, to avenge an attack on his father. "This scene certainly saved me," notes Coppola.

But there was still dissonance in the ranks about Coppola's competency as a director. GORDON WILLIS, the director of photography, did not cotton to Coppola from the get-go. The director had what he terms "a touch-and-go relationship" with Willis on *The Godfather*. "To him I was just some kid," while Willis saw himself as a seasoned veteran. Willis grew increasingly impatient waiting around for Coppola to finish lengthy rehearsal periods before he could finally photograph a scene.

One day, after Coppola and Willis had an especially acrid altercation, Willis walked off the set and refused to photograph the scene. Work stopped. Coppola was beside himself. "Fuck this picture!" he shouted. "I've directed four movies without anyone telling me how to do my job." He then stalked off the set. Shortly afterward, a resounding bang reverberated from the direction of Coppola's office. "Oh my God!" the assistant director exclaimed. "He's shot himself!" In actual fact, Coppola, while blowing off steam, had kicked a hole in his office door.

An uneasy truce was established between the director and the cinematographer, and filming went on. Despite their differences, they did work well together. Thus, they devised a sinister, shadowy atmosphere for the interiors, in which dangerous people like the godfather are only partially visible. The don is the personification of evil, says Willis, so he wanted to keep him in menacing shadows. Filming in dark settings earned Willis the nickname of "The Prince of Darkness." At all events, principal photography wrapped on July 2, 1971.

The Godfather begins in 1945, on the wedding day of Connie Corleone (TALIA SHIRE, Coppola's sister), who is the daughter of Don Vito Corleone (Marlon Brando), the chieftain of one of the most powerful of the New York Mafia "families." The jubilant wedding reception in the sunny garden of the Don's estate offers a sharp contrast to the somber scene in his study, where the godfather sits in semidarkness, stroking his cat and listening to the petitions being presented to him by his associates. (He is following a custom which dictates that a godfather must seriously consider any request for help made to him on such a festive occasion.) Film historian Jenny Jones comments that the don's cat suggests that Vito Corleone is "a gentle man with hidden claws."

Vito Corleone is a calculating man who has always run his empire of crime with the efficiency of a business executive. Whenever he encountered resistance from someone with whom he wanted to make a deal, the don simply extended to him what he ominously terms "an offer he couldn't refuse," and he got what he wanted.

The filmgoer is afforded a salient example of how the don implements this policy in the episode in which Don Corleone intimidates Hollywood producer Jack

Wolz (John Marley) into giving a part in a picture to singer-actor Johnny Fontane (Al Martino), one of the don's "godsons." He does so by arranging to have the producer's prize stallion decapitated, and its head placed in Woltz's bed.

"In the book the horse's head was on the bedpost," Coppola points out in his commentary, "but I thought it would be more horrible if he at first sees some wet blood on the bed sheets and fears that *he* has been stabbed. Then he pulls back the blankets and sees the horse's head." Coppola's staging of this scene is an improvement on the manner in which Puzo handled it in the book, as the novelist was the first to admit.

There was another problem associated with the Woltz sequence. When the novel was published, it was widely rumored that the Johnny Fontane character was based on Frank Sinatra. When Johnny entreats Vito to get him a part in a war movie that he needs to resuscitate his ailing career, many readers thought of how Sinatra lobbied to get the role of Maggio in Fred Zinnemann's film *From Here to Eternity* (1953) in order to revive his fading career. Sinatra personally berated Puzo, when he encountered him in a restaurant, for apparently implying that he got the role he wanted in *From Here to Eternity* through the intervention of the Mafia. Director Fred Zinnemann told me that he cast Sinatra in that picture because he admired Sinatra's acting skills. Indeed, Sinatra won an Academy Award for the film.

The awesome Don Vito is the object of the envy and the hatred of some other Mafiosi, who fear that he is becoming too powerful. Accordingly, an assassination attempt is made on his life, which leaves him incapacitated for some time. Sonny, his oldest son (JAMES CAAN), rules in his stead for the duration of his illness. Michael, Don Vito's youngest son, just home from serving in the army during World War II, is anxious to prove himself to his father. He gets the chance to do so when he convinces Sonny to let him even the score with the family's enemies by killing the two individuals responsible for the attempt on their father's life: a leading mobster and a corrupt cop.

In one of the most riveting scenes in the picture, Michael successfully carries out his plan to gun down both men in a Bronx restaurant. He then escapes into temporary exile in Sicily, in order to be out of the reach of reprisals. While in Sicily Michael meets and marries Apollonia, a beautiful peasant girl. Despite the bodyguards that surround Michael and his new bride, Apollonia dies in an explosion that had been intended to kill Michael. Embittered and brutalized by this never-ending spiral of revenge, Michael returns to America, where his tough methods of dealing with other Mafiosi continue to impress his father; and he gradually emerges as the heir apparent of the aging Don Vito.

Al Pacino and Marlon Brando.

Friction between the Corleones and the other Mafia clans continues to mount, and the volatile Sonny is gunned down as the result of a clever ruse. He is lured into making a hurried trip to New York from the Corleones' compound on Long Island without his bodyguard. En route he stops to pay the toll on a causeway, where he is pulverized by an execution squad with submachine guns. A barrage of bullets blasts Sonny's Lincoln Continental and riddles Sonny's body as he writhes in agony.

Coppola still had to do the don's death scene. In the course of the scene Vito is playing with his grandson Anthony in his tomato patch. While rehearsing the scene Brando said, "I have a little game I sometimes play with my kids." He made fangs out of an orange peel, wedged them in front of his teeth, and growled like a bear. Coppola set up two cameras in order to be sure that he captured the scene: "Brando shoved the orange peel into his mouth, and the lad playing his grandson really got scared." Here was the godfather "dying as a monster!" says Coppola, for shortly afterward the old man keels over and expires among the tomato plants. It is a touching scene, he concludes.

Then, when the ailing Don Vito dies, the Corleone family closes ranks under Michael's leadership, and the new don effects the simultaneous liquidation of their most powerful rivals by having them all killed on the same day and at the same hour. Coppola intercuts these murders with shots of Michael acting as godfather at the baptism of his little godson (played by Coppola's baby daughter, SOFIA COPPOLA). The ironic parallel between Michael's solemn role as godfather in the baptismal ceremony and the stunning "baptism of blood" he has engineered to confirm his position as godfather of one of the most formidable Mafia clans in the country is unmistakable.

William Reynolds was assigned to cut the first half of the picture and PETER ZINNER to edit the second half. Accordingly, Coppola worked closely with Zinner to create the baptism scene. "Intercutting the baptism with the slaughter was not in the script," Coppola explains. The two sequences were to be presented separately. When he opted to intercut the two sequences, Peter Zinner suggested that they add the powerful organ theme, which then became the unifying force that tied the two sequences together musically. In short, the montage choreographed mayhem with religion by intercutting multiple murders with the baptism of Michael Corleone's godson, Michael Rizzi, the son of Connie and Carlo. The baptism sequence illustrates the immeasurable gap between the sacred rituals of the Church and the unholy rites of the murderous Corleone mob.

By this time Michael has married again; and the movie ends with his second wife Kay (DIANE KEATON) standing in the doorway of the study where Don Vito once ruled, watching the members of the Corleone Mafia family kissing Michael's hand as a sign of their loyalty to him. The camera draws away and the huge door of Don Michael's study closes on the scene, shutting out Kay—and the filmgoer—from any further look at the inner workings of the Mafia. Coppola did the rough cut of the film in his editing facility in San Francisco. His principal concern about the rough cut of the picture during editing was the running time. "Bob Evans said that, if it was over two hours, I would have to cut the film at Paramount in Los Angeles," meaning that the studio brass would supervise the shortening of the rough cut, probably with a meat cleaver. "My first cut was in fact three hours, so I cut all the footage that wasn't germane to the study and got it down to two hours and twenty minutes," he recalls. Evans called the short version "a two-hour trailer" for the movie. "You've cut all the human stuff out, and you've only got the plot left. All the best stuff was left on the cutting room floor."

So Evans ordered Coppola to bring the rough cut down to Paramount in Los Angeles and restore the footage he had eliminated from his first cut. "Basically I simply put back everything that I had cut from my first version, which was three hours. But there was no problem about my simply putting it all back, because it had all been there in the first place."

Some of the scenes Coppola excised from the rough cut during postproduction were not reinstated. All of these deleted scenes can be viewed in a special section of the DVD. The only one that I wish that Coppola might have found a place for in the final cut of the film is the scene in which Kay is praying for Michael in church—a scene that Coppola had originally intended to use as the ending of the film. It shows Kay lighting a candle and praying for her husband's lost soul. Puzo favored this ending since this is the way the book ends. But Evans and others thought that the ending would be more effective if the picture concluded with Michael closing the door on Kay as he takes his place as the head of the Corleone dynasty, and Coppola eventually went with that ending. Still the brief scene of Kay praying fervently in church might have been inserted elsewhere in the film, since it proves a significant contrast to Michael's hypocritical participation in the baptism ceremony.

Coppola's continuing preoccupation with the importance of family in modern society is once again brought into relief in the present picture. As a matter of fact, the thing that most attracted Coppola to the project in the first place was that the book is really the story of a family. It is about "this father and his sons," he says, "and questions of power and succession." In essence, *The Godfather* offers a chilling depiction of the way in which Michael's loyalty to his flesh-and-blood family gradually turns into an allegiance to the larger Mafia family to which they in turn belong, a devotion that in the end renders him a cruel and ruthless mass killer.

With this film, Coppola definitely hit his stride as a filmmaker. He tells the story in a straightforward, fast-paced fashion that holds the viewer's attention for close to three hours. Under his direction the cast members without exception give flawless performances, highlighted by Brando's Oscar-winning performance in the title role. *The Godfather* also received Academy Awards for the best picture of the year and for the screenplay, which Coppola coauthored with Puzo. The picture was an enormous critical and popular success. And when the American Film Institute honored the best one hundred American films made during the first century of cinema in 2007, *The Godfather* followed only *Citizen Kane* at the head of the list.

Nevertheless, a few reviewers expressed some reservations about the film. The movie was criticized in some quarters for subtly encouraging the audience to admire the breathtaking efficiency with which organized crime operates. Coppola counters that such was never his intent. He feels that he was making an especially harsh statement about the Mafia at the end of *The Godfather*, when Michael makes a savage purge of all of the Corleone clan's known foes. If some reviewers and moviegoers missed the point he was trying to make, however, he looked upon the sequel, which Paramount had asked him to make, as "an opportunity to rectify that." For in the sequel Coppola would see to it that Michael was shown to be manifestly more cold-blooded and cruel than his father ever was.—GENE D. PHILLIPS

References

Nick Browne, ed., *Francis Ford Coppola's Godfather Trilogy* (New York: Cambridge University Press, 2000); Robert Evans, *The Kid Stays in the Picture: A Memoir* (Beverly Hills: Dove, 1995); Jenny Jones, ed., *The Annotated Godfather: The Complete Screenplay* (New York: Black Dog and Leventhal, 2007); Dave Kehr, "*The Godfather*: The Coppola Restoration on DVD," *New York Times*, September 23, 2008, B 2; Harald Keller, "*The Godfather*," in *Movies of the Seventies* (Los Angeles: Taschen, 2005), pp. 108–17; Harlan Lebo, *The Godfather Legacy* (New York: Simon & Schuster, 1997); Mario Puzo, *The Godfather Papers* (Greenwich, CT: Fawcett Crest, 1973).

THE GODFATHER: PART II (1974)

DIRECTOR: Francis Ford Coppola. SCREENPLAY: Francis Ford Coppola, Mario Puzo, based on the novel by Puzo. PRODUCERS: Francis Ford Coppola, Gray Frederickson, and Fred Roos. ASSOCIATE PRODUCER: Mona Skager. PHOTOGRAPHY: Gordon Willis. EDITING: Barry Malkin, Richard Marks, Peter Zinner. MUSIC: Nino Rota (ADDITIONAL MUSIC by Carmine Coppola). PRODUCTION DESIGNER: Dean Tavoularis. ART DIRECTION: Angelo Graham, George R. Nelson. COSTUME DESIGN: Theadora Van Runkle. SOUND: Walter Murch and Chuck Wilborn.

CAST: Al Pacino (Michael Corleone), Robert Duvall (Tom Hagen), Diane Keaton (Kay Corleone), Robert De Niro (Vito Corleone), John Cazale (Fredo), Talia Shire (Connie), Lee Strasberg (Hyman Roth), Michael V. Gazzo (Frankie Pentangeli), G. D. Spradlin (Sen. Pat Geary), Richard Bright (Al Neri), Gaston Moschin (Don Fanucci), Tom Rosqui (Rocco Lampone), Bruno Kirby (young Clemenza), Frank Sivero (Genco Abbandando), Francesca De Sapio (young Mama Corleone), Morgana King (Mama Corleone), Marianna Hill (Deanne Corleone), Leopoldo Trieste (Signor Roberto), Dominic Chianese (Johnny Ola), Amerigo Tot (Michael's Bodyguard), Troy Donahue (Merle Johnson), James Caan (Sonny Corleone). RUNNING TIME: 200 minutes. Color. RELEASED THROUGH: Paramount. PREMIERE: December 12, 1974. ACADEMY AWARDS: Best Picture, Director, Adapted Screenplay, Supporting Actor (Robert DeNiro), Original Score, Art Direction/Set Decoration. DVD: Paramount.

Given the staggering financial success of *THE GODFATHER* (which grossed $129 million worldwide, having cost roughly $6 million to produce), it is no wonder that Paramount tried repeatedly to persuade FRANCIS FORD COPPOLA to come up with a sequel, something in which the director/producer had little to no interest at first. Charles Bludhorn, the head of Paramount's parent company, Gulf+Western, purportedly lamented, "You've got the recipe for Coca Cola, and you don't want to make any more bottles!" Coppola finally relented, and the resulting film not only was one of the triumphs of the year, winning multiple Academy Awards (including Best Picture) and other accolades, but is also widely regarded as one of the masterpieces of American cinema.

The Godfather: Part II came in at a production cost of more than $15 million, about two and a half times the cost of its predecessor, but delivered a box office gross of only about one-third of the original's. Still, according to Jon Lewis, the film had turned a profit well before its first public screenings, thanks to exhibitor advances of some $26 million. Furthermore, compared to the original, critics have lavished equal or greater praise onto the sequel. In a review for *Variety*, A. D. Murphy wrote: "'The Godfather, Part II' far from being a spinoff followup to its 1972 progenitor is an excellent epochal drama in its own right providing bookends in time—the early part of this century and the last two decades—to the earlier story. AL PACINO again is outstanding as Michael Corleone, successor to crime family leadership. . . . The Paramount release has everything going for it to be an enormous b.o. winner."

Production began October 1, 1973; and as director, producer and cowriter, Coppola was to receive $1 million plus 13 percent of gross rentals. GENE D. PHILLIPS quotes Coppola as saying, "I knew I could never top *Godfather I* in terms of financial success, but I did want to make a film that topped it as a really moving human document." In another interview, Coppola characterizes the whole endeavor as "a risky proposition, now that I look back at it. . . . So many of my pictures . . . are really on the brink of disaster all the time, and it takes a gigantic leap of faith, when you look at the script, to think that we're gonna pull off these projects. Some we do, I suppose, some we don't; but they're all a leap of faith."

Luckily, Coppola was able to reassemble many key members of the cast and crew from the first film, and he freely attributes much of what works about the combined saga to those talents, especially the actors. Al Pacino (identified by *Screen World* as one of the top box office draws of 1974) chillingly transforms the character of Michael Corleone from the idealistic war hero of the first film into an increasingly paranoid, power-hungry, corrupt, and ultimately damned antihero in the second.

ROBERT DUVALL and JOHN CAZALE return, as Tom Hagen (consigliere and adoptive brother of Michael Corleone) and Fredo Corleone (Michael's weak, older brother), respectively, and these two characters serve to illustrate Michael's turning away from his close family members as he enters a greater arena of power and corruption and begins to trust no one. Michael thoughtlessly humiliates

Hagen by questioning his loyalty in front of "family" associates, when in fact Tom is one of Michael's few real friends (Coppola really wanted Duvall for *Part III* as well, and he has said that the Hagen character was "a missing dimension that that film was meant to have"). Similarly, Michael allows himself to be so consumed with paranoia and revenge that he commits the grievous sin of fratricide, having Fredo killed for his unwitting complicity with rival mobster Hyman Roth (LEE STRASBERG).

As Michael's wife, Kay, the marvelous DIANE KEATON also returns from the original cast. At the end of Part I, it becomes clear that Michael has shut Kay out of any meaningful role in his life as he takes over the position of Don. The motif of his literally closing the door on her is repeated in *The Godfather: Part II* after their divorce—brought about by Kay's defiant admission that she chose to abort her pregnancy rather than bring another Corleone son into the world. According to Coppola, this particular plot element, Kay's abortion, was suggested to him by his sister, TALIA SHIRE, who reprises her role as Michael's sister, Connie.

Connie's role takes on more weight in Part II: she begins the film as a spoiled Mafia princess, deliberately trying to hurt Michael by way of her promiscuous, carefree lifestyle. Despite Michael's strong objections, she insists that she will go ahead with her plans to marry Merle Johnson (TROY DONAHUE), whose fortune-hunting motives are all too apparent, both to Michael and to the film's audience. Near the end of the film, however, Connie matures noticeably, due in large part to the death of Mama Corleone (jazz *chanteuse* Morgana King). At the matriarch's wake, Connie reconciles her differences with Michael and expresses her desire to come back to the family. Shire's role as Connie would become even more central to

Al Pacino.

Coppola's final installment in the series, *The Godfather: Part III* (1990).

The most important newcomer to the cast is the magnificent ROBERT DE NIRO, who portrays the young Vito Corleone in the flashback scenes in Little Italy. Coppola, among others, found De Niro's performance to be quite believable as the young man who would grow into the older Don Vito (MARLON BRANDO) seen in the original film. De Niro imbues the character with a sense of honor and genuine love for his family. As an immigrant from Sicily, Vito tries to live honestly but finds that he must resort to a life of crime in order to avoid being exploited by the ruthless "Black Hand" organization.

One scene in particular illustrates the subtlety of De Niro's performance: after having been let go from his job as a grocery store clerk (replaced by a nephew of the local crime boss), rather than coming home angry or frustrated, Vito enters his flat with a smile and greets his wife warmly, gently placing a single pear on the kitchen table, presenting the perfectly shaped treasure to her as if it were a Fabergé egg. In turn, she seems delighted to receive it. This simple but moving scene beautifully illustrates Vito's love for his family and the idea that, despite whatever problems he may be facing out in the world, he is determined to have a happy home life.

JEFFREY CHOWN and other commentators have remarked on the brilliant contrast throughout *The Godfather: Part II* between the ascension of young Vito as family man and mob boss in the 1910s and 1920s and the downfall of his son, Michael, in the film's "present-day" of the 1950s. The alternating plot structure seemed rather unconventional and even daring at the time, certainly for the sequel to such a blockbuster hit as *The Godfather*. Coppola explained: "I thought it would be interesting to juxtapose the decline of the Family with the ascension of the Family; to show that as the young Vito Corleone is building this thing out of America, his son is presiding over its destruction."

Coppola sets up the dual time structure early on, and he elegantly moves from flashbacks to the "present" by way of graphically and/or thematically motivated dissolves. For example, when Vito as a child is quarantined on Ellis Island, he sings a song as he looks out the window of his hospital room. We dissolve to the first communion of Anthony Vito Corleone, son of Michael and Kay, at roughly the same age; and the same song is being performed at the ceremony. Similar transitions later in the film take us from Michael kissing Anthony good night to Vito (De Niro) gazing upon the infant Santino, by way of a graphic dissolve, and from Michael learning that Kay has had a "miscarriage" to young Vito worrying over the health of baby Fredo. As the plot moves forward, Coppola cuts back and forth between the two eras less frequently, allowing each of the two stories to progress in longer durations as the film goes along. When preparing a television version that combined Part I and Part II, Coppola tried rearranging all the scenes in chronological order; but he found that the two stories told in Part II were "nowhere near as good alone as when they are told in parallel." Near the end of *The Godfather: Part II*, with the flashback scene where a young Michael announces his plans to volunteer for military service in World War II, Coppola had hoped to bring the two stories together by having Brando present in that scene as Don Vito. Brando however would not agree to be in the film; so Coppola had to settle for suggesting Vito's arrival offscreen.

One reason that Coppola gave *The Godfather: Part II* the double structure was "to give it another dimension beyond just sort of making the first *Godfather* over again." He explained, "I would imagine that every scene in *Godfather II* has a precedent in a scene from the first *Godfather*. In a funny way, the story, to take it further, inevitably repeats it."

Indeed, several key aspects of Part II recall Part I. Each film opens with a religious ritual and celebration (Connie's wedding in Part I, Anthony's first communion in Part II). Each film also features a surprise attack on the Don, an attempted assassination in a hospital, and a series of killings that wrap up loose ends of the plot, presented in parallel editing. Although the setting of Part II has moved westward, even Michael's Lake Tahoe compound (filmed on location at the Henry Kaiser estate) parallels but extends the Long Island house of Part I.

Similarities between the two films continue even to the elements of visual style, such as the production design by DEAN TAVOULARIS. The meticulous attention that Tavoularis gave to historical detail is quite evident in the Ellis Island sequence, where the young boy Vito first arrives in the United States. The set designs were based on historical photographs, and Tavoularis recreated the Ellis Island facilities in a fish market in Trieste. Equally convincing are the scenes where Michael deals with Hyman Roth in Havana, which were actually filmed in Santo Domingo, Dominican Republic.

Another key artistic contributor who returned for Part II (and later, Part III) is cinematographer GORDON WILLIS. Coppola has said that Willis was very firm in his ideas about the color structure of the films. Willis told *American Cinematographer*, "It's yellow-red in much of the lighting as well as the lab work, and that ties all three films together. . . . The repeatability of the visual structure really has to do with making the right choices. The initial choice is taste, and maintaining the look is craft. There's great elegance in simplicity. My choices in lighting and the overall color were designed to create a mythic, retrospective feel, [one] without clutter."

Nick Browne describes the film's aesthetic as being simultaneously realist and theatrical. One might add that the film's approach at times is rather operatic, in terms of its grand subject matter and mannered style, which approaches pageantry. The film's operatic qualities are hardly accidental, as Coppola had been exposed to this kind of story from his childhood onward, thanks to the musical professionals in his family. The film freely acknowledges its debt to opera in the scene where Vito and Genco attend the operetta *Sensa Mamma* (composed by Coppola's maternal grandfather, Francesco Pennino). The title song, "Sensa Mamma," was quite popular in its day, according to Gene Phillips, and in the film it foreshadows the family tragedies to come in the Corleone clan.

Another of the film's family musical connections, of course, is CARMINE

COPPOLA, who wrote the "source music," while NINO ROTA composed the bulk of the score. The elder Coppola's contribution was more significant in Part II than in Part I, and he also received higher recognition: he and Rota jointly received the Oscar that year for Best Music.

In a manner befitting its grand, operatic style, *The Godfather: Part II* casts its subject matter of organized crime in a large-scale, mythological light. As Coppola explained: "For me, the Mafia is just a metaphor for America. It is transplanted from Europe; it is a capitalistic, profit-seeking body; it believes that anything it does to protect and sustain itself and its family is morally good." Elsewhere, he elaborates: "The career of Michael Corleone was the perfect metaphor for the new land. Like America, Michael began as a clean, brilliant young man endowed with incredible resources and believing in a humanistic idealism. . . . But then he got blood on his hands. He lied to himself and to others about what he was doing and why."

This notion of the American mythos in *The Godfather: Part II* is strengthened by the film's plot connections to major historical and cultural phenomena, specifically U.S. relations with Cuba in the 1950s, and the rise of Las Vegas as a center of gambling and other "vices." A key player in both of these arenas is Miami-based mobster Hyman Roth, a fictionalized version of Meyer Lansky, who had been closely aligned with dictator Fulgéncio Batista in pre-Castro Cuba and also ran the "Bugs and Meyer Mob" together with Bugsy Siegel (the basis for the Moe Green character in Part I). Furthermore, Coppola included a reference to the legendary story about the head of ITT giving Batista a solid gold telephone, which the director found symbolic of capitalism in pre-Castro Cuba: the Mafia organizations were "graduating up" to be like corporations, operating on a higher-level playing field. In this regard, the corrupt senator, Pat Geary (G. D. SPRADLIN), represents for Coppola the "next level of villain."

One thing that Nick Browne finds so outstanding about Part II is "its outlook, so rare in American films from the early 1970s, on a flawed American protagonist as an emblem of American empire." Browne continues: "Moreover, the first two films amounted to a social phenomenon—they entered into every level of American culture—high and low—sometimes by attitude, sometimes by quotation, and sometimes through their iconic, signature scenes. The first two films entered not only movie history, but American mythology as well." There they have remained for nigh on forty years.—RODNEY HILL

References

Stephanie Argy, "Post Focus: Paramount Restores *The Godfather*," *American Cinematographer* 89 no. 5 (May 2008); Nick Browne, ed., *Francis Ford Coppola's Godfather Trilogy* (Cambridge: Cambridge University Press, 2000); Jeffrey Chown, *Hollywood Auteur: Francis Coppola* (New York: Praeger, 1988); Richard Combs, "Coppola's Family Plot," *Film Comment* 38 no. 2 (2002): 38; Peter Cowie, "Francis Ford Coppola," *International Film Guide* (London: Tantivy Press, 1976), 51–58; Peter Cowie, *The Godfather Book* (London: Faber and Faber, 1997); Jon Lewis, "If History Has Taught Us Anything . . . Francis Coppola, Paramount Studios, and *The Godfather Parts I, II, and III*," in Browne, *Francis Ford Coppola's Godfather Trilogy*, 23–56; A. D. Murphy, "The Godfather, Part II," *Variety*, 9 December 1974; Gene D. Phillips, *Godfather: The Intimate Francis Ford Coppola* (Lexington: University of Kentucky Press, 2004); Phoebe Poon, "The Corleone Chronicles: Revisiting The Godfather Films as Trilogy," *Journal of Popular Film & Television* 33, no. 4 (2006): 187–95; John Willis, *Screen World*, vol. 26 (London: Frederick Muller, 1975).

THE GODFATHER: PART III (1990)

DIRECTOR: Francis Ford Coppola. SCREEN-PLAY: Mario Puzo and Francis Ford Coppola. PRODUCER: Francis Ford Coppola for Zoetrope Studios/Paramount. CO-PRODUCERS: Fred Roos, Gray Frederickson, Charles Mulvehill. ASSOCIATE PRODUCER: Marina Gefter. EXECUTIVE PRODUCERS: Fred Fuchs, Nicolas Cage. PHOTOGRAPHY: Gordon Willis. EDITING: Barry Malkin, Walter Murch, Lisa Fruchtman. MUSIC: Carmine Coppola. PRODUCTION DESIGN: Dean Tavoularis. ART DIRECTION: Alex Tavoularis. COSTUME DESIGN: Milena Canonero. SPECIAL EFFECTS COORDINATOR: Larry Cavanagh. PRODUCTION SUPERVISOR: Alessandro von Normann.

CAST: Al Pacino (Michael Corleone), Talia Shire (Connie Corleone), Diane Keaton (Kay), Andy Garcia (Vincent), Franc D'Ambrosio (Anthony Corleone), Sofia Coppola (Mary), John Savage (Andrew Hagen), Eli Wallach (Altobello), Donal Donnelly (Archbishop), Richard Bright (Al Neri), Al Martino (Johnny Fontane), Joe Mantegna (Joey Zasa), George Hamilton (B. J. Harrison), Robert Ciechini (Lou Penino), Terri Liverano Baker (Theresa Hagen), Bridget Fonda (Grace), Raf Vallone (Lamberto), Mario Donatone (Mosca), Vittorio Duse (Don Tommasino), Rogerio and Carlos Miranda (Best Twins), Jeanne Savarino (Francesa Corleone), Janet Savarino Smith (Kathryn Corleone), Helmut Berger (Keinszig), Carmine Caridi (Old Don), Don Castello (Parisi), Al Ruscio (Volpe), Vito Antuofermo ("The Ant"), Rick Aviles (Masked Man #1), Michael Bowen (Masked Man #2), Jeannie Linero (Lucy Mancini), Mickey Knox (Frank Romano), Julie Gregg (Sandra), James Chan Leong, Kellog Smith, John Abineri, Brian Freilino (Stockholders), Don Novello (Dom), Peter Schweitzer (Vatican Journalist), Morgan Upton (TV Newscaster), Franco Citti (Calo).

RUNNING TIME: 163 minutes. Technicolor.

RELEASED THROUGH: Paramount. PREMIERE: December 25, 1990.
DVD: Paramount.

It was sixteen years before FRANCIS COPPOLA made the third and final installment of the *GODFATHER* trilogy. In the intervening years, while he busied himself with other projects, he steadfastly resisted all efforts on the part of successive regimes at Paramount to cajole him into making another sequel. "I couldn't see doing a third *Godfather* film," Coppola explains in the indispensable documentary that accompanies the DVD of the *Godfather Trilogy* (released 2001), "because Michael has damned himself in the second movie. He has lost his family and everything that he values. When I finished that film, with Michael in the hell he had created for himself, I thought I was done with *The Godfather*. There seemed to be nothing further to be said."

Nevertheless, the enormous critical and financial success of the first two *Godfather* films encouraged Paramount to extend to him a free rein in creating *The Godfather: Part III* (1990). In conceding to Coppola a substantial amount of control over the script and direction of *Godfather III*, the studio in effect "made him an offer he couldn't refuse," to cite an oft-repeated line from the first *Godfather* that has become part of our language. Indeed, Coppola wanted to link the final act of Michael's story to the tragic grandeur of Shakespearean tragedy. He refers to Michael's affinity with King Lear—the tormented, aging man whose empire is slipping from his grasp—as a source of inspiration for the film.

Coppola would again be collaborating with MARIO PUZO on the screenplay of *Godfather: Part III*. They introduced Sonny Corleone's illegitimate son Vincent, who, in *The Godfather*, had been conceived at

Connie's wedding reception during Sonny's sexual encounter with bridesmaid Lucy Mancini.

While casting about for story ideas, Coppola began to read press accounts of the Vatican Bank scandal, in which the Mafia figured. He created the character of Archbishop Gliday—based on Bishop Marcinkus, an American bishop stationed in Rome who was implicated in some questionable Vatican financial transactions. (The real bishop happened to hail from Cicero, Illinois, Al Capone's old stomping grounds.) Archbishop Gliday is a highly fictionalized version of Bishop Marcinkus. Coppola and Puzo followed their customary procedure of writing separately and then revising each other's work. Coppola composed the first half, Puzo the second half, and then they nailed them together.

In order to ensure continuity between the third film of the trilogy and its predecessors, Coppola reassembled most of the members of his production crew. This team of regulars included cinematographer GORDON WILLIS, editor WALTER MURCH, production designer DEAN TAVOULARIS, and composer CARMINE COPPOLA. Furthermore, some of the key actors were once more on deck, including AL PACINO, DIANE KEATON, and TALIA SHIRE. Working closely with each of his creative collaborators unquestionably enabled Coppola to place on all three films, not the stamp of the studio, but the unmistakable stamp of his own directorial style.

The one major cast member from the first two films who did not return this time around was ROBERT DUVALL. He found the salary he was offered to be unacceptable and was likewise dissatisfied with the size of his part. The actor felt that Tom Hagen simply did not play the vital role in *Godfather: Part III* that he did in the previous two films. "Not having Duvall in *Godfather-III*,"

Coppola notes, "was a profound loss to me and to this movie."

Duvall was replaced by George Hamilton, in the role of B. J. Harrison, an unctuous corporate attorney. Another new member of the cast besides Hamilton was ANDY GARCIA as Vincent Mancini, Sonny's bastard son. "Vinnie is an outsider," says Garcia, and Michael Corleone takes him in. "The closer he comes to Michael, the more Vinnie becomes like him." Indeed, Garcia comes across in the movie like the young Al Pacino of *The Godfather*—very intense, very serious, and somewhat dangerous.

"The thing that is different about *Godfather-III*," Coppola recalls, "is that Michael is different." The third film begins in 1979, twenty years after the close of the second film. Michael is getting ready for death, and he wants to rehabilitate himself. "So I wanted him to be a man who was older and concerned with redemption," Coppola continued. "Michael Corleone realized that he had paid very dearly for being a cold-blooded murderer, and was a man now who wanted to make peace" with God. In brief, Michael is aware that his final reckoning is drawing near.

Elaborating on this point, Peter Cowie explains that the screenplay "deals with the themes of redemption and reconciliation close to Coppola's heart." *Godfather: Part III* depicts Michael as "a Mafia boss yearning to achieve respectability, and craving forgiveness from the Church for his manifold sins," as Douglas Brode writes. To the dismay of the other Mafiosi, Michael is determined to sell off his casinos and other Mafia-related enterprises, and to assume the role of a respectable international financier.

The movie's opening sequence accordingly depicts Michael receiving a papal honor: he is named a Knight of the Order of St. Sebastian, in return for a handsome donation from the "Vito Corleone Foundation." Brode wryly remarks that the solemnity of the elaborate ritual is effectively undercut by the cynical implication that a gangster like Michael Corleone can buy himself "such a majestic honor." What's more, Michael's apparent generosity to the church is not as altruistic as it might appear, adds Cowie: "Michael intends, not so much to relinquish his ill-gotten gains, but rather to launder them." Michael therefore becomes implicated in a crafty scheme to launder the Corleone funds by filtering large sums of cash through the Vatican Bank, in exchange for saving the Vatican Bank from bankruptcy.

Furthermore, Michael's partnership with the Vatican enables him to purchase a controlling interest in Immobilare, a consortium of investors and politicians who are as corrupt as any of the lower-class Mafiosi whom Michael consorted with in New York City. By getting the Corleone family entangled with these upper-class European crooks, Michael remarks wryly, "We're back with the Borgias!" He realizes that he has once more been drawn into conniving with unsavory characters in some dirty business deals, just when he had hopes of going completely legitimate. He moans, "Just when I thought I was out, they pull me back in!"

Commenting about the Vatican's willingness to make an unholy alliance with a Mafia chieftain like Michael Corleone, Coppola points out that history has shown the Vatican to be not only a spiritual community of the faithful but also a secular institution. "I respectfully submit that everything I put into the movie about the Vatican as a business organization, being venal and mercenary because of its involvement in financial improprieties, is true."

Principal photography commenced on November 27, 1989, at Cinecittà Studios in Rome where there would also be extensive location work around the city. When shooting in Europe was completed, the production moved to New York for more location work.

Coppola would sometimes experience periods of discouragement in the stressful atmosphere of shooting a major commercial picture on a tight schedule. ELEANOR COPPOLA records in her notes on the making of the film that on March 6, 1990, while Coppola was still filming at Cinecittà, she discovered her husband "sitting on a sofa in Michael Corleone's living room, very depressed." He spoke of "how he hated that he was doing the same material he had done nearly twenty years ago," how he hated the great amount of time it took to make the movie, "and that it's about shooting people."

Shooting wore on until May 25, 1990. The director then had to supervise the editing of the film for its premiere on December 25. He had only six months to whittle a mountain of footage down to a final cut of just under three hours running time. The pressure on Coppola increased as he worked around the clock to meet Paramount's deadline. He collaborated with principal editors Walter Murch, BARRY MALKIN, and LISA FRUCHTMAN. For the record, Coppola met the studio-imposed deadline, and the film opened on Christmas Day, 1990.

The movie begins with the celebration of Michael's papal knighthood, which is his bid for respectability. During the reception it seems likely that Vinnie will be Michael's heir as head of the Corleone crime family. (Peter Cowie mistakenly refers to Vinnie in his Coppola book as the illegitimate son of Michael, rather than of his brother Sonny.) Vinnie cleverly insinuates himself into the family business by methodically liquidating members of rival Mafia clans who are plotting against Michael and by seducing Michael's daughter Mary (SOFIA COPPOLA, the director's daughter).

"Connie emerges as a strong figure in this film," Coppola says. Now far removed from the victimized wife she was in *The Godfather*, she has evolved into "a combination of Lady Macbeth and Lucrezia Borgia." Connie, a malevolent figure wrapped in a black shawl, is out for blood. She schemes to control and murder the Corleones' enemies with the pitiless efficiency once displayed by her brother Michael and by her father Vito. She sees Vinnie as her ally. With Connie as Vinnie's sponsor, it is not surprising that Michael eventually recognizes him as a surrogate son, made clear when Michael officially changes Vinnie's surname from Mancini to Corleone.

Vinnie arranges to have his minions slaughter the Corleones' enemies while the family attends an opera performance. The film's finale, then, takes place during a majestic performance in Palermo of Mascagni's opera *Cavalleria Rusticana*, a brutal revenge drama, which, appropriately enough, is about a vendetta in a Sicilian village. The melodramatic events onstage parallel the violent events offstage.

The intercutting of the opera performance with the baroque orgy of murder Vinnie has orchestrated recalls the montage of violence and death that climaxes *The Godfather* and *THE GODFATHER: PART II*. In quick succession we once again see a series of murders. For example, the nefarious banker, Keinszik, is smothered with a pillow by Vinnie's hoodlums, and his corpse is discovered hanging from a bridge in Rome.

Some of Michael's underworld enemies want him dead, and an assassin attempts unsuccessfully to murder him in the course of the opera performance. The assassin in the present film makes his second desperate effort to kill Michael outside the opera house after the performance. Tragically, Mary stops the bullet aimed at Michael and dies in the arms of her anguished father. With dreadful irony Michael unwittingly brings about what William McDonald terms "the last act of this tragedy of family power and ruin": the death of Michael's daughter on the steps of the opera house— cut down by the bullet that was meant for him. The scene brings to mind Michael's observation, made earlier in the film: "The only wealth in this world is children, more than all of the money and power on earth." As Michael crumples on the steps of the opera house, his mouth gapes open in a silent scream of agony and despair. "Walter Murch removed Michael's scream from the sound track, making it seem so much more agonizing," says Coppola.

In the original script, Michael, and not Mary, was supposed to be struck down by the assassin's bullet, Coppola confides in the documentary. "I finally came up with an ending which was worse for Michael than just dying"—he is left to live with the horrors his life has wrought.

The Godfather: Part III premiered with a strong box office, despite mixed reviews. One recurring source of criticism for the film was the casting of Coppola's daughter Sofia as Mary, Michael's daughter. Coppola chose her while she was visiting the set in Rome during the Christmas holidays. "I only put her in the role because the day before we were to shoot a scene with WINONA RYDER as Mary, Winona dropped out," due to illness. Granted Sofia was not an experienced actress; but "it was Sofia that I had in mind when I created the character of Mary, the apple of her father's eye," a girl who is "sweet and kind," Coppola explains.

Coppola did not want to endure the costly delay involved in waiting for the studio to send over a replacement for Winona Ryder from Hollywood. "My decision was vilified by some critics, but I never regret-

On the set of *The Godfather: Part III*: Joe Mantegna, Francis Ford Coppola, Al Pacino, Eli Wallach (seated), and Andy Garcia.

ted it. I was thrilled to have her play the part . . . because I saw her as just like the vulnerable kid Mary was supposed to be." Sofia Coppola is certainly adequate as the young, awkward daughter of a powerful man. At times she is touching, as in her love scenes with Andy Garcia, who is quite tender with her.

The release prints of the film run 161 minutes, while the version available on DVD is 170 minutes. The additional nine minutes are accounted for by scenes that mostly feature Sofia Coppola. Apparently Francis Coppola wanted to restore scenes with Sofia that he had been prevailed upon to delete from the original version. For example, there is a scene reinstated on DVD in which Mary asks her father to reassure her that the Vito Corleone Foundation is genuinely legitimate. Michael assures her that it is not the money-laundering operation it is rumored to be. Harlan Lebo quotes Michael Wilmington's balanced assessment of *Godfather: Part III*: Wilmington grants

that the movie has "grand moments to match either of its predecessors," but adds, "the complex financial conspiracy that underlies the story never becomes clear. . . . And yet, it is a wonderful movie."

In writing on the *Godfather Trilogy*, on the occasion of its release on DVD in 2008, Dave Kehr stated, "Eighteen years after the sting of disappointment has passed, *Part III* no longer seems the total disaster it once did. . . . Connie seems to possess the calm, dark resolve that has abandoned her increasingly sentimental brother," a Godmother capable of carrying the plot forward better than he. To say that *Godfather: Part III* is not in a class with masterpieces like its two predecessors is merely to recognize that it suffers only by comparison with the standard Coppola had set for himself by his previous achievements.—GENE D. PHILLIPS

References

Nick Browne, ed., *Francis Ford Coppola's Godfather Trilogy* (New York: Cambridge University

Press, 2000); Douglas Brode, *Money, Women, and Guns: Crime Movies* (New York: Carol, 1995); Eleanor Coppola, *Notes on a Life* (New York: Doubleday, 2008); Peter Cowie, *Coppola: A Biography*, rev. ed. (New York: Da Capo, 1994); Barbara Harrison, "Godfather-III," *Life*, November 1990, 50–65; Dave Kehr, "*The Godfather*: The Coppola Restoration on DVD," *New York Times*, September 23, 2008, B2; Harlan Lebo, *The Godfather Legacy* (New York: Simon & Schuster, 1997); William MacDonald, "Thicker Than Water and Spilled by the Mob: *The Godfather*," *New York Times*, May 21, 1995, sec. 2: 11.

THE GODFATHER: THE GAME (2006)

Videogame released by Electronic Arts, themed to Coppola's *THE GODFATHER* (1972), enhanced by NINO ROTA's music and by the voices of MARLON BRANDO, JAMES CAAN, and ROBERT DUVALL, but, according to *Variety* (April 10–16, 2006) "truer to the letter than the spirit of the movie." AL PACINO chose not to participate, according to *Variety*, and Coppola not only refused but called the game "a misuse of film."—James M. Welsh

GOODWIN, MICHAEL (1941–)

Screenwriter and film journalist, coauthor with NAOMI WISE of *On the Edge: The Life and Times of Francis Coppola* (1989), an unauthorized biography, criticized for indulging in pop psychoanalysis and irresponsible speculation, but significant as the first book-length Coppola biography. *Variety* opined that the book provided "a fascinating overview," but "little in the way of original material."—James M. Welsh

Reference

Kimm, "Literati," *Variety*, November 22, 1989, 111.

GRANT, RICHARD E. [RICHARD GRANT ESTERHUYSEN] (1957–)

Star actor, novelist, screenwriter, and director Richard E. Grant played Dr. Jack Seward for FRANCIS COPPOLA in *BRAM STOKER'S DRACULA* (1992) well enough to persuade American viewers that he was British. In fact, Richard Grant Esterhuysen was born and raised in Mbabane, Swaziland, in southeast Africa, the son of Afrikaner Henrik Esterhuysen, head of education for the British Protectorate of Swaziland. After attending secondary school at Waterford Kamhlaba, he went on to study English and drama at the University of Cape Town, where he cofounded the multiracial Troupe Theatre Company, along with fellow students, and then became involved in the Space Theatre group, founded by playwright Athol Fugard and Yvonne Bryceland. He appeared in a wide range of productions over two years (*Oedipus, Agamemnon, Othello, The Threepenny Opera, Fanshen*, and *Total Eclipse*, for example) before moving on to England in 1982, where he was nominated the most promising newcomer by *Plays and Players* magazine for his work in *Tramway Road* at the Lyric Theatre in Hammersmith, a West-London suburb. When he registered with the British Actors' Equity Association in the United Kingdom, he changed his name to become Richard E. Grant. After acting in London fringe theatre, Grant appeared in the British television series *Sweet Sixteen*, then starred in the made-for-television film *Honest, Decent, Legal & True*, which led to his being cast as the unemployed, alcoholic 1960s actor Withnail in writer-director Bruce Robinson's *Withnail & I* (1986). He went on to become a distinctive leading man for top American directors, such as Robert Altman in *The Player* (1992), *Ready to Wear* (1994), and *Gosford Park* (2001), for example, and for Martin Scorsese in *The Age of Innocence* (1993). Earlier film roles include *Mountains of the Moon* (1990), *Henry & June* (1990), and *L.A. Story* and *Hudson Hawk* (both 1991). In 1996 this classically trained actor would play Sir Andrew Aguecheek in the film adaptation of *Twelfth Night*. In 1991 he wrote *By Design: A Hollywood Novel*, published by Picador in Britain. In 2005 he wrote the film *Wah-Wah*, starring Nicholas Hoult in the lead, supported by Gabriel Byrne, Miranda Richardson, Emily Watson, and Julie Waters. The next year he published *The Wah-Wah Diaries: The Making of a Film*. Thus has Richard Grant found success in several genres, and in several media on several continents.—James M. Welsh

THE GREAT GATSBY (1974)

FRANCIS COPPOLA worked as a screenwriter for hire during the mid-1960s. Nevertheless, after he became a full-fledged movie director, he wrote only one more script for a film that he did not personally direct.

After the successful launching of *THE GODFATHER* in March 1972, ROBERT EVANS, Paramount's production chief, asked Coppola to compose the screenplay for the film adaptation of F. Scott Fitzgerald's celebrated novel of the Roaring Twenties, *The Great Gatsby*, which would be directed by Jack Clayton (*Room at the Top*). It seems that the muddled script submitted by Truman Capote, filled with confusing dream sequences and flashbacks, was not acceptable. Evans wanted Coppola to provide a more straightforward rendition of the plot.

Coppola took on the task in order to provide himself with a change of pace from working on *The Godfather* and hammered out a serviceable script in five weeks. In the story, Jay Gatsby (ROBERT REDFORD) crystallizes the American Dream for himself in Daisy (Mia Farrow), the girl he lost to millionaire Tom Buchanan a few years earlier. Gatsby, of course, is deeply hurt by Daisy's rejection. But he eventually decides to mount a campaign to win her back by attempting to amass a fortune by racketeering. Nonetheless, Gatsby is doomed never to win Daisy away from Tom. He is eventually killed by a lunatic who mistakenly assumes that Gatsby is responsible for his wife's death. Evans remembers that "Coppola delivered a screenplay that really worked."

"Francis came in and did an absolute miracle job," Clayton said, adding that he made only minor alterations in the screenplay that Coppola turned over to him. Clayton did admit to putting into the screenplay some material from the book that Coppola had not originally included; but anything that was added to the film, Clayton emphasized, "was *always* in the book." Yet it is precisely Clayton's additions to his screenplay that Coppola afterward contended were responsible for extending the duration of the finished film to the point where the movie seemed, in his estimation, "interminable."

One salient example will suffice to illustrate Coppola's point. On the one hand, Coppola had included in his script the scene from the novel in which Gatsby's father, Henry Gatz, comes to town for his son's funeral. He included this scene because he thought it important for the viewer to see that, ironically enough, in the eyes of at least one person, Gatsby had really grown up to be the great Gatsby, for, as far as Henry Gatz could tell, his son had become a distinguished man of business who had possessed at the time of his death an enormous estate complete with all the luxuries that money could buy. On the other hand, Coppola did not believe that the film should continue on to depict the funeral itself, in spite of the fact that that scene is in the book, because he felt that playing out such a scene in detail would needlessly protract the running time of a film he was hoping could be kept down to a manageable length. Coppola had planned instead to have the movie conclude with a further touch of irony. As Coppola describes the final scene as he envisioned it, Gatsby's father, while looking around his son's bedroom, "sees the picture of Daisy, and he says, 'Who's the girl?'" That, Coppola maintains, should really have been the end of the movie.

Had Mr. Gatz's remark about the photograph been used to conclude the film, Coppola continues, it would have neatly tied in with the shot of this same photograph of Daisy that appears in the course of the movie's opening credits. In this manner the movie would have both begun and ended with the picture of Daisy, Gatsby's most cherished possession and the symbol of his dreams and ambitions. "So what I had set up at the beginning," Coppola concludes, would have gone "all the way to the end." By adding the lengthy funeral sequence to the script as a replacement for his own much more terse finale to the movie, Coppola contends that Clayton made the closing scenes of the movie that follow Gatsby's death seem less like an epilogue than an anticlimax.

Regardless of which side one takes in the matter of Clayton's adding the funeral episode to Coppola's script, it must be conceded that all of the interpolations Clayton made in the screenplay, taken together, eventually resulted in a motion picture that in the last analysis seems at times slow-paced and overlong. Despite the fact that some Hollywood wags had dubbed the film "The Great Ghastly," Redford's box office appeal made the movie a commercial success. Katja Kirate writes in *Movies of the Seventies* that "Coppola's script stays true to the novel"; he accomplished his aim of capturing the spirit of the book, "Fitzgerald's masterly evocation of the Roaring Twenties," despite Clayton's rejuggling of the script.

When Coppola saw the way that Clayton spent time "fidgeting" with his screenplay for *Gatsby* without his knowledge or consent, he realized the strong influence a director has on the way a film turns out. Coppola therefore resolved regularly to direct the scripts he wrote. He then moved on to write and direct *THE CONVERSATION*.—GENE D. PHILLIPS

References

Robert Evans, *The Kid Stays in the Picture: A Memoir* (Beverly Hills: Dove, 1995); Katja Kirate, "*The Great Gatsby*," in *The Movies of the Seventies*, ed. Jurgen Muller (Los Angeles: Taschen, 2005), 274–79; Gene Phillips, *Fiction, Film, and F. Scott Fitzgerald* (Chicago: Loyola University Press, 1986).

GRISHAM, JOHN [RAY] (1955–)

Popular American novelist whose novel *THE RAINMAKER* was adapted to the screen and directed by FRANCIS FORD COPPOLA. Bernard Weinraub wrote in the *New York Times* (November 7, 1997) that Coppola had never read a Grisham novel and bought *The Rainmaker* at Kennedy International Airport, a number one best seller, out of curiosity. "I became a sucker for Grisham just like everyone else," Coppola said, and by the time he got to Paris, Coppola had decided to adapt the book and direct the film, released in November of 1997. John Ray Grisham was born in Jonesboro, Arkansas, on February 8, 1955. He was educated at Southaven High School, DeSoto County, Mississippi (where he would later practice criminal and civil law for a decade), and continued on to earn a BS degree at Mississippi State University in 1977 and a JD degree from the University of Mississippi School of Law in 1981. From 1984 to 1990 he served as a Democratic delegate to the Mississippi House of Representatives. His first novel, *A Time to Kill*, was published modestly in 1988, but by the time his second novel, *The Firm*, was published, it became the best-selling novel of 1991, followed by another success, *The Pelican Brief*, in 1992. Film adaptations followed both *The Firm* and *The Pelican Brief* in 1993, and *A Time to Kill* was filmed later, in 1996. *The Rainmaker*, filmed by Francis Coppola in 1997 was published in 1995. Grisham has averaged over a book a year thereafter, but he seems to be well grounded. He has called himself "a famous writer in a country where nobody reads," which makes him seem to be a man of engaging modesty.—JAMES M. WELSH

GWYNNE, FRED (1926–1993)

American character actor who makes an instant impression as Frenchy, Owney Madden's sidekick in Coppola's *THE COTTON CLUB* (1984). (Big Frenchy, who oversaw the nightly operation of the Cotton Club, was kidnapped by the Dutch Schultz mob in 1931.) Gwynne's first line in the film, a sinister "and me," drew gasps of recognition from audiences in the film's initial release, due no doubt to the familiarity of Gwynne's voice and imposing presence from years of syndicated reruns of the classic 1960s sitcom, *The Munsters.*

The New York City native studied portrait painting before serving in the U.S. Navy during World War II. After the war, he attended the Phoenix School of Design before going to Harvard, where he was president of the *Harvard Lampoon*, drawing cartoons for the publication. Gwynne's stint at Harvard also included a membership in the famed Hasty Pudding Club. Gwynne pursued acting after graduation, joining Cambridge's Brattle Repertory Company, and making his Broadway debut in Mary Chase's *Mrs. McThing* opposite Helen Hayes. Gwynne can also be glimpsed in *On the Waterfront* (1954), his film debut.

During a dry spell, Gwynne worked at the J. Walter Thompson agency, where he is credited with coining the slogan "the world's most beautifully proportioned car." Real popularity came with an appearance on *The Phil Silvers Show*, which led to his being cast as Lt. Francis Muldoon on the popular TV comedy *Car 54, Where Are You?*, where he first worked with his future *Munsters* co-star, Al Lewis. *The Munsters* gave Gwynne his most enduring role as the iconic Herman Munster, a comic version of the Frankenstein monster living with his family in the suburbs. The show became a syndication

staple. Gwynne was later quoted as saying, "I love old Herman Munster. Much as I try not to, I can't stop liking that fellow."

Gwynne also made notable impressions in Thornton Wilder's *Our Town*, as Big Daddy in a famed Broadway revival of Tennessee Williams's *Cat on a Hot Tin Roof*, and for his work as the wheelchair-bound Col. Kincaid in Preston Jones's *A Texas Trilogy.*

FRANCIS COPPOLA's casting of Gwynne in the role of Frenchy caused already-tense relations between Coppola and producer ROBERT EVANS to collapse when Evans forbade Gwynne in the role. Coppola prevailed, citing his "artistic control" over the project, and Gwynne got the role of Frenchy, the mobster pal and virtual sidekick of BOB HOSKINS's Owney Maddin. Gwynne and Hoskins share a terrific chemistry, building to one of the most effective scenes in the film, after Frenchy's return from captivity with NICOLAS CAGE's gang. Hoskins has paid the ransom for his safe return. Gwynne pretends a rage at the apparently low ransom paid, and breaks Hoskins's watch in the process. When Hoskins reveals the large sum actually paid and says he would have paid ten times as much, Gwynne reaches into his pocket and produces a gift-wrapped new watch as a present. Hoskins's mock furious "You asshole!" and their warmly affectionate embrace are arguably the emotional highlight of the film.

Gwynne made several films after *The Cotton Club*, with notable appearances in *Fatal Attraction*, *Pet Sematary*, and *My Cousin Vinny*. Gwynne also found time to write and illustrate several well-received children's books. He died on July 2, 1993, of pancreatic cancer.—TOM DANNENBAUM

References
Bruce Lambert, "Fred Gwynne, Popular Actor, is Dead at 66," *New York Times*, July 3, 1993; Michael Schumacher, *Francis Ford Coppola: A Filmmaker's Life* (New York: Crown Publishers/ Random House, 1999).

H

HACKMAN, GENE (1930–)

Highly respected American actor and star, who distinguished himself for his portrayal of Harry Caul in FRANCIS COPPOLA's *THE CONVERSATION* (1974). Born in San Bernardino, California, Hackman was raised in Danville, Illinois, the son of a journalist. He went from high school into the Marine Corps and was stationed in China as a radio operator. After being discharged from the Marines, Hackman worked for a number of television stations before enrolling in the Pasadena Playhouse on his way to Broadway. His stage debut was with ZaSu Pitts in *The Curious Miss Caraway*; his first starring role on Broadway was with Sandy Dennis in the comedy *Any Wednesday*.

Hackman's motion picture career began with Warren Beatty in *Lilith* (1964), and his association with Beatty led to his being cast in *Bonnie and Clyde* as Clyde's slow-witted brother, Buck Barrow, which resulted in Hackman's first Academy Award nomination. A second Oscar nomination came for his performance in *I Never Sang for My Father*, and the Award itself came in 1972 for his stellar performance as Jimmy "Popeye" Doyle in *The French Connection*. Then in 1993 Hackman swept the Academy Awards, Golden Globes, British Academy Awards, and the Los Angeles and New York Film Critics Awards for Best Supporting Actor for his performance as the brutal gunfighter turned sheriff Little

Bill Daggett in Clint Eastwood's *Unforgiven*. Hackman was also nominated for a Best Actor Academy Award for his FBI agent Rupert Anderson in *Mississippi Burning* (1988). Before starring with John Travolta and Rene Russo in Barry Sonnenfeld's adaptation of Elmore Leonard's *Get Shorty* in 1995, Hackman returned to the New York stage to star with Glenn Close and Richard Dreyfuss in Mike Nichols's theatrical production of *Death and the Maiden*.

A veteran of eighty films, Hackman's roles are certainly too numerous to mention here, but he distinguished himself many times over in both prestige and

Gene Hackman as Harry Caul in *The Conversation*.

popular films, such as *The Poseidon Adventure* (1971), *A Bridge Too Far* (1977), Warren Beatty's *Reds* (1981), as Lex Luthor in *Superman: The Movie* (1978) and its sequels, as Coach Norman Dale in *Hoosiers* (1986), as Captain Frank Ramsey in *Crimson Tide* (1995), right up to Monroe Cole in *Welcome to Mooseport* (2004), apparently his last film. In 2008 Hackman announced to CNN interviewer Larry King his intention to retire from filmmaking.
—James M. Welsh

HAMMETT (1982)

FRANCIS COPPOLA opened his own studio, Zoetrope Studios, in Hollywood, in 1980. The short-lived facility went belly-up in 1982, in the wake of the flop of the two films produced there. The first was *ONE FROM THE HEART* (1982), which was directed by Coppola himself. The other picture that hastened the demise of Zoetrope Studios was *Hammett*, a Zoetrope production directed by the respected German filmmaker WIM WENDERS (*The American Friend*, 1977). Coppola was executive producer of the film.

The script was based on a novel by Joe Gores, *Hammett* (1975), set in 1928, in which Dashiell Hammett, the famed author of hardboiled detective fiction like *The Maltese Falcon*, solves a real-life mystery involving a missing Chinese prostitute. Wenders collaborated on the script with a string of screenwriters, who complained that he insisted on departing substantially from the original story line. Finally Coppola ordered him to stop the multiple rewrites of the script and to commence principal photography. On February 4, 1980, Wenders began filming, with FREDERIC FORREST in the title role. But Wenders continued revising the script nonstop throughout the production period. Coppola ultimately decided that Wenders had reworked the screenplay to the point where it involved

an impenetrable mystery that was not adequately solved at the end. Wenders had not been shooting the approved screenplay, Coppola explains, "and I could not dissuade Wim from this path. . . . So I stopped production" and postponed the remainder of filming indefinitely.

During the hiatus Coppola had the screenplay totally overhauled by still another scriptwriter, who attempted to steer the story back to the original plotline and provide a coherent ending. The new script entailed the reshooting of 80 percent of the picture. Coppola summoned Wenders back to finish the shoot in the fall of 1981, after Coppola had himself completed the filming of *One from the Heart*. Wenders finished filming in a record twenty-three days. Coppola monitored the reshoot by regularly viewing the retakes done by Wenders and offering him suggestions. But Coppola did not reshoot any scenes himself, as Leonard Maltin mistakenly asserts.

Recalling the troubled production period of *Hammett*, Gregory Solomon observes, "Just ask Wim Wenders, who worked for Coppola, the executive producer on *Hammett*, how little the latter values a director's artistic freedom—unless he happens to be the director." This statement is severely unfair to Coppola when one considers that he had to scrap much of what Wenders originally shot because it departed significantly from the official script—at a considerable financial loss to Coppola. In the end *Hammett* wound up costing $10 million, and was considerably over schedule and over budget.

Hammett, which was to be distributed by Warner Bros., had its world premiere at the CANNES INTERNATIONAL FILM FESTIVAL on June 6, 1982, where it received a poor press. Many of the press corps complained that *Hammett*'s convoluted plot yielded only a murky solution to the mystery about the missing Chinese call girl. She turned out to be embroiled in a complex conspiracy to blackmail some corrupt city officials, which was never adequately explained. In sum, the film was dismissed as an undistinguished detective yarn, mere "private eye-wash." Warners accordingly gave the film a token release and then shelved the picture.

Seeing the film on home video today, one notices an effective performance by Forrest as Dashiell Hammett. And the picture is further enhanced by Philip Lathrop's moody cinematography. With all its shortcomings, *Hammett* is a treat for mystery fans.

During the time that shooting on *Hammett* was suspended, Wenders returned to Europe and made *The State of Things* (1983), a movie about a hapless German director named Friedrich (clearly modeled on Wenders), who is making a picture for an eccentric American producer who is short of funds. Gordon, the producer, who is played by Allen Garfield (*THE CONVERSATION, One from the Heart*) seems to be based on Coppola. Adding credence to this theory that is widely held in film circles is the fact that, like Coppola, Garfield has a stocky build. In addition, there are parallels between the movie that Friedrich is making for Gordon and *Hammett*, the picture that Wenders was making for Coppola. When Friedrich's film goes over budget, Gordon shuts down the production.

Friedrich confronts Gordon about abandoning the production in the producer's mobile home, which obviously recalls Coppola's Airstream trailer. While arguing with Friedrich, Gordon exclaims in exasperation that the investors would not put up more funds to keep the picture afloat because the script was too muddled—precisely Coppola's complaint about Wenders's much-rewritten screenplay for *Hammett*.

Wenders maintains that the producer in *The State of Things* "is really not Fran-cis Coppola. I don't think you can find any traces of *Hammett* or Coppola in *The State of Things*." On the contrary, given the many references in *The State of Things* to Coppola's dealings with Wenders on *Hammett*, enumerated above, it seems slightly disingenuous for Wenders to maintain that he did not have Coppola in mind when he created the character of Gordon. After all, when Wenders made *The State of Things* Coppola had suspended filming on *Hammett*, and Wenders had no guarantee that it would ever be finished.

At all events, after both *One from the Heart* and *Hammett* had tanked at the box office, Coppola inevitably had to shutter Zoetrope Studios in Hollywood. Coppola returned his entire operation to the AMERICAN ZOETROPE offices in the Sentinel Building in San Francisco, which he continued to run as an independent production unit, producing films in partnership with major Hollywood studios. But he no longer owned his own studio.—GENE D. PHILLIPS

References

John Gallagher, *Film Directors on Film Directing* (New York: Greenwood Press, 1989); Jon Lewis, *Whom God Wishes to Destroy: Francis Coppola and the New Hollywood* (Durham, NC: Duke University Press, 1997); Robert Lindsey, "Promises to Keep," *New York Times Magazine*, July 24, 1988, 23–27; Leonard Maltin, et al., eds., *Movie Guide*, rev. ed. (New York: New American Library, 2009); Greg Solomon, "Walter Hill's *Supernova*," *Film Comment* 36, no. 4 (July–August, 2000): 22–23.

HARBURG, E. Y. "YIP" (1896–1981)

One of the great lyricists of American popular song, Harburg cowrote the "book" for the 1947 Broadway musical *FINIAN'S RAINBOW*—considered by some to be his masterpiece—as well as the screenplay for FRANCIS FORD COPPOLA's 1968 film adaptation. Born Isidore Hochberg, Harburg wrote the lyrics for more than 500 songs, including such well-known titles as "April in Paris," "It's Only a Paper Moon," and the classic "Over the Rainbow," cowritten with Harold Arlen for the iconic 1939 MGM film, *The Wizard of Oz*, starring Judy Garland.

Although Harburg's lyrics often have a light, playful feel, they also tend toward serious themes, as with the 1932 hit, "Brother, Can You Spare a Dime?" regarded as an anthem of the Depression era. Similarly, *Finian's Rainbow* delves into social issues such as race, prejudice, and political corruption in its none-too-subtle Southern setting of Missitucky. Largely due to the political satire of *Finian's Rainbow*, Harburg ended up being named in the McCarthy-era pamphlet, *Red Channels*, as among 150 people in the entertainment industry who had promoted left-wing causes, and he was subsequently blacklisted in Hollywood.

Nevertheless, Harburg continued to work well into the 1960s, renewing his collaboration with Harold Arlen on a number of projects. They wrote songs for Judy Garland at the end of her career, for the films *Gay Purr-ee* and *I Could Go on Singing*; and in 1968, to commemorate the death of Martin Luther King, Jr., they cowrote the song, "Silent Spring." Harburg died in Los Angeles in 1981 in an automobile accident on Sunset Boulevard.—RODNEY HILL

References

Sandra Brennan, "E. Y. 'Yip' Harburg," All Movie Guide, http://www.allmovie.com/artist/ey-yip-harburg-93402; "E. Y. Harburg: Biography," The Songwriters Hall of Fame website, www.songwritershalloffame.org; Steven Suskin, "Finian's Rainbow," *Variety*, March 27, 2009; John S. Wilson, "E. Y. Harburg, Lyricist, Killed in Car Crash," *New York Times*, March 7, 1981.

HARRIS, JULIE (1925–)

Actress who played Miss Thing, the landlady who operates a rooming house in FRANCIS FORD COPPOLA's *YOU'RE A BIG BOY NOW* (1966). One of the most renowned American stage performers of her generation, Julie Harris has enjoyed a prolific career in the theatre, film, and television, spanning six decades.

Born in Grosse Pointe Park, Michigan, Julie Harris received her professional training at the prestigious Yale School of Drama and at the legendary Actors Studio. Her breakthrough on Broadway was in Carson McCullers's *The Member of the Wedding* (1950) as troubled teenager Frankie "F. Jasmine" Addams, a role that she repeated in the 1952 film version (her big-screen debut) with Ethel Waters and Brandon De Wilde. Another career highlight for Harris was her one-woman show, *The Belle of Amherst*, in which she portrayed the poet Emily Dickinson. In the 1990s, Harris returned to Broadway in a revival of Tennessee Williams's *The Glass Menagerie*.

Harris's most notable films include *East of Eden* (1955), directed by Elia Kazan and starring James Dean; the chilling psychological horror film, *The Haunting* (1963), directed by Robert Wise and adapted from Shirley Jackson's novel; John Huston's *Reflections in a Golden Eye* (1967), again adapted from Carson McCullers; and *Gorillas in the Mist* (1988). Her recent big-screen appearances include roles in *The Golden Boys* (2008) and *The Lightkeepers* (2010).

In the late 1940s, Julie Harris made her first television appearance on *Actor's Studio*, an early ABC production featuring other talent from the eponymous thespian group, including Eva Marie Saint and MARLON BRANDO. Since then Harris has appeared in dozens of series and made-for-TV movies, perhaps most notably the night-time soap *Knots Landing* (a spinoff of *Dallas* that ran from 1979 to 1993) in which she portrayed the recurring character Lillimae Clements, the mother of Valene Ewing (Joan Van Ark).

Julie Harris is the most honored performer in the history of the American Theatre Wing's Tony Awards, holding the record for the most wins (six) as well as the most nomination (ten). She also has won three Emmys, a Grammy, and the Drama Desk Award.—RODNEY HILL

References

"Julie Harris," Internet Movie Database, www .imdb.com/name/nm0364915/; "Julie Harris," *Variety* Profiles, www.variety.com; "Tony Legacy: Facts and Trivia," http://www.tonyawards.com.

HARRIS, ROBERT A. (1945–)

American film archivist and preservationist who worked with FRANCIS FORD COPPOLA on ABEL GANCE'S *NAPOLEON*. Harris had obtained the rights to the 1972 *Napoleon* restoration put together by Abel Gance and Claude Lelouch, entitled *Bonaparte and the Revolution* (1972), comprised of footage from both the silent and sound versions of *Napoleon*, and newly shot footage as well, but unfortunately this remake was unable to match the dynamic power of the original 1927 masterpiece. Harris, who had founded a 16 mm film distribution company, Images, in Rye, New York, claimed the exclusive rights for Gance's *Napoleon* in America, which had to be negotiated with Coppola.

One of the country's leading practitioners of motion picture restoration, Harris has supervised some of the best-known and most financially successful restorations of film classics. They have included: *Spartacus*; *My Fair Lady*; David Lean's *Lawrence of Arabia* (with Jim Painten, Harris's fellow producer on *The Grifters*); and Alfred Hitchcock's *Vertigo* and *Rear Window* (both with James C. Katz).

Harris refers to himself as an activist, a member of the "restoration police," in the effort to save deteriorating classic films. Together with Katz, he has reportedly com-

piled a list of two dozen large-format films, including *Around the World in 80 Days* (1956), *Ben-Hur* (1959), and *The Alamo* (1960) that he would like to see restored.

Harris was also coauthor, with Michael S. Lasky, of *The Films of Alfred Hitchcock* (1976), a sort of nostalgic reaction against the academics and critics following François Truffaut and Robin Wood who were determined to elevate the reputation of Hitchcock as artist rather than a "mere" entertainer.—JAMES M. WELSH/RODNEY HILL

References

Robert A. Harris, "Resurrecting Spartacus," interview with Gary Crowdus and Duncan Cooper, *Cineaste* (undated clipping file); Gene D. Phillips and Rodney Hill, *The Encyclopedia of Stanley Kubrick* (New York: Facts On File, 2002); "Rear Window to Get a Cleaning," *StudioBriefing*, September 29, 1997.

HART, JAMES V. (1960–)

Writer-producer James V. Hart was coproducer of *BRAM STOKER'S DRACULA* (1992) and also worked with Coppola's AMERICAN ZOETROPE as coproducer for the screen adaptation of *MARY SHELLEY'S FRANKENSTEIN* (1994), directed by Kenneth Branagh and starring Branagh as Victor and ROBERT DE NIRO as the Creature, as well as Tom Hulce and Branagh regulars Helena Bonham-Carter, Richard Briers, and Ian Holm, and featuring Branagh composer Patrick Doyle's music. *Variety* called the film a "major disappointment," however, even though it was "based on alluring marquee elements and the success of *Bram Stoker's Dracula*. Coppola's *Bram Stoker's Dracula* originated with screenwriter James V. Hart, who had worked with Steven Spielberg on the movie *Hook* (1991, freely adapted from James M. Barrie's *Peter Pan*), his first produced screenplay. This "success" enabled him to become coproducer on the *Dracula* project. Born (apparently) in Fort Worth, Texas, in 1960 and educated at Southern Methodist University, Hart studied finance and economics as an undergraduate before taking his master's degree in film and broadcasting. He started working on what he called "the real Dracula" project during the 1970s, greatly influenced by Leonard Wolf's *Annotated Dracula* (1975), and claims to have been "completely spellbound" by Stoker's writing. His first-draft screenplay, entitled *Dracula: The Untold Story*, was about to become a cable television movie when actress WINONA RYDER read for the role of Mina and was so impressed by the screenplay that she passed it along to FRANCIS COPPOLA, who also became interested, because he believed, with reason, no one had ever really filmed the *book*. When Hart began producing films in the 1970s, he was working toward a master's degree in broadcast film arts. Hart's later produced screenplays include *Muppet Treasure Island* (1996), *Contact* (1997), *Tuck Everlasting* (2002), and *Lara Croft, Tomb Raider: The Cradle of Life* (2003), among other projects. In 2005 he wrote a children's novel entitled *Capt. Hook: The Adventures of a Notorious Youth*, said to be a sort of prequel to James M. Barrie's *Peter Pan*. His screenplay adapting Ayn Rand's *Atlas Shrugged* was apparently in development for a film to be released in 2011.—JAMES M. WELSH

Reference

Brian Lowry, "Branagh Looses Monster," *Variety*, November 6, 1994, 88.

HARTMAN, ELIZABETH (1941–1987)

A fragile, high-strung actress who customarily played sensitive roles. After she garnered an Academy Award nomination for her first movie part, as a blind girl in *A Patch of Blue* (1965), FRANCIS COPPOLA opted to cast her as a young femme fatale in *YOU'RE A BIG BOY NOW*.

Hartman by then had appeared in a couple of pictures, usually as a mousy, inhibited girl. In giving her an unsympathetic role Coppola was showing his willingness to cast an actor against type. The late Elizabeth Hartman told me during a brief conversation that when Coppola phoned and asked her to play the sexy Barbara Darling she nearly cried. "Do you know what I look like?" she asked. He did, and he stuck to his choice.

In the film Bernard Chanticleer (Peter Kastner) secures a job working in the stacks at the New York Public Library; so he decides to move from Long Island into his own apartment in New York City.

As things develop, Bernard becomes interested in Amy Prentiss (KAREN BLACK), a coworker at the library. But he soon transfers his attachment to Barbara Darling (Elizabeth Hartman), one of the library's patrons. Given the fact that Barbara is a go-go dancer at a Greenwich Village discotheque and an actress in offbeat, off-Broadway plays, it is hard to imagine her as a regular library patron—but no matter. In any case, the promiscuous Barbara eventually sheds Bernard for the more attractive Raef, Bernard's raffish friend.

Hartman's movie career never really got off the ground. After playing opposite Clint Eastwood in the Civil War drama *The Beguiled* (1971), her parts in pictures all but dried up. She became "increasingly depressed," according to Ephraim Katz, and eventually became an outpatient in a Pittsburgh mental institution. Finally she took her own life by jumping out of her fifth floor apartment; she was 45. —GENE D. PHILLIPS

References

Jeffrey Chown, *Hollywood Auteur: Francis Coppola* (New York: Praeger, 1988); Ephraim Katz, *Film Encyclopedia*, ed. Ronald Nolan, rev. ed. (New York: Harper Collins, 2008).

***THE HAUNTED AND THE HUNTED* (1963)**
British title for *DEMENTIA 13* (1963).

HAYDEN, STERLING
[STERLING RELYEA WALTER,
A.K.A. JOHN HAMILTON] (1916–1986)
American star actor, mariner, adventurer, and OSS spy, born on March 16, 1916, in Montclair, New Jersey, the son of a newspaper advertising executive who died when the boy was nine; thereafter, when his mother remarried, he adopted his stepfather's name of Hayden. Sterling Hayden was a seafarer before going to Hollywood to become an actor, notably for Stanley Kubrick in *The Killing* (1956) and, perhaps most memorably, his fluid performance as the demented General Jack D. Ripper, who orders a B-52 bomber group to launch an aerial attack on the Soviet Union in Kubrick's *Dr. Strangelove* (1964). He plays McCluskey, a corrupt policeman, in Coppola's *THE GODFATHER* (1972). Hayden became first mate on a schooner voyage around the world in 1936 and captained a ship from Gloucester, Massachusetts, to Tahiti in 1939 before joining the Marine Corps and the Office of Strategic Services in 1941 under the assumed alias of John Hamilton. Based in Italy, he organized secret shipping operations, was attacked by the Germans, and operated behind German lines in Croatia. According to OSS records released in August 2008, the following commendation was written for Hayden in April of 1944: "Lt. Hamilton conducted a reconnaissance of the Dalmation Islands to plot alternate shipping routes in [the] event of [a] German invasion, which was then starting. He was strafed by German planes, and . . . conducted himself in a brave manner." A later commendation dated December 21, 1944, added: "He has great courage and has shown an almost reckless disregard of his own life where duty is involved." Hayden's acting career began before his wartime service, with the film *Virginia* (1941), which also featured Madeleine Carrol, to whom Hayden was married for four years. After the war, Hayden returned to Hollywood in 1947, and by 1950 was working for director John Huston in *The Asphalt Jungle*. After his *Godfather* role for Coppola, Hayden played an alcoholic writer modeled after Ernest Hemingway for director Robert Altman in *The Long Goodbye* (1973). He died at his home in Sausalito, California, on May 23, 1986.—JAMES M. WELSH

References
Josh White, "OSS Records Bristle with Details about Agents," *The Washington Post*, August 15, 2008, A19; Todd McCarthy, "Sterling Hayden, 70, Succumbs; Eccentric Lead, Character Actor," *Variety*, May 28, 1986, 4, 24; Gene D. Phillips and Rodney Hill, eds., *The Encyclopedia of Stanley Kubrick* (New York: Facts On File, 2002).

"HEART OF DARKNESS" (1899)
Novella by JOSEPH CONRAD that served as the basis of the screenplay for *APOCALYPSE NOW*. In 1969 JOHN MILIUS conferred with FRANCIS COPPOLA about his scenario for *Apocalypse Now*, a film about the Vietnam War. In discussing the script with Milius, Coppola recalled Joseph Conrad's 1899 novella, "Heart of Darkness."

In the novella Charles Marlow, the narrator, is charged with the task of tracking down Kurtz, an ivory trader who has disappeared into the interior of the African jungle. Coppola suggested that Milius use the search for a mysterious ivory trader named Kurtz, which provides the fundamental structure of "Heart of Darkness," as the basis of the screenplay. Milius agreed that "it would be interesting to transplant Conrad's 'Heart of Darkness' to Vietnam," and he proceeded to write a screenplay loosely based on Conrad's novella.

Coppola went on to other projects and did not return to *Apocalypse Now* until 1975. He reached back to Milius's six-year-old scenario. Milius's script had updated the story to the Vietnam War and turned Kurtz from an ivory trader into a Green Beret officer who defects from the U.S. Army and sets up his own army across the Cambodian border, where he proceeds to conduct his own private war against the Vietcong.

In rewriting the screenplay, Coppola planned "to take John Milius's script and mate it with 'Heart of Darkness.' Consequently, my script is based on 'Heart of Darkness' to an even greater extent than the original screenplay." Thus Coppola derived the character of the flipped-out freelance photojournalist in his screenplay from the young Russian sailor who is a disciple of Kurtz in "Heart of Darkness." Coppola even gives the photographer some of the Russian's dialogue verbatim from the book. For example, the photojournalist says to Willard, the Marlow character in the film, that Kurtz "has enlarged my mind; you don't judge him as you would an ordinary man." In brief, Coppola made the photojournalist the equivalent of the harlequin Russian sailor from Conrad.

After examining Milius's first-draft script for *Apocalypse Now* (dated December 5, 1969), film scholar Brooks Riley points out in *Film Comment* that Coppola stuck very close to Milius's original scenario when he revised it for production six years later. If the revised script "strayed from the first draft," she writes, "*it was not so much away from Milius's conception*" of the plot "*as toward Milius's source, the Conrad novel.*" (Emphasis added.) In fact, JEFFREY CHOWN, in his book on Coppola, cites the director as claiming that at one point he had seriously considered changing the film's title to that of the novella. Little wonder "Heart of Darkness" is the spine of *Apocalypse Now.*

Brooks Riley notes two major alterations that Coppola made in Milius's ver-

sion of the script that are particularly significant. One change that Coppola made concerned the very beginning of the screenplay. Milius begins his script with a scene set in Kurtz's stronghold in the jungle, from which his rebel band makes its forays into the jungle against the Vietcong; and in this scene there is a glimpse of Kurtz himself, exhorting his disciples. By contrast, Coppola chose to follow Conrad in this matter by withholding our first sight of Kurtz until Willard finally tracks him down late in the film. Kurtz's absence from the film throughout most of its running time steadily builds suspense in the viewer who continually wonders what this strange and mysterious individual will really be like, once he finally makes his appearance. "To have shown Kurtz first, only to have abandoned him for the next two-thirds of the film," Riley explains, would have proved to be "a dilution of the film's carefully planned unveiling of the man."

The other crucial revision that Coppola made in Milius's screenplay concerned the film's conclusion. In Milius's conception of the film's finale, Willard is so mesmerized by the overpowering personality of Col. Kurtz that he succumbs to the corrupting influence of this barbarous war lord. That is, Willard decides to join the native Cambodian tribesmen and the runaway American soldiers who comprise Kurtz's army. Shortly afterward, the Vietcong attack Kurtz's compound; and Kurtz and Willard fight side by side until Kurtz is killed in battle.

Coppola was thoroughly dissatisfied with Milius's ending for the film. As Coppola describes this ending, Kurtz, "a battle-mad commander," wearing two bands of machine gun bullets across his chest, takes Willard by the hand and leads him into battle against the North Vietnamese.

Needless to say, this finale of the film, as conceived by Milius, departs to a greater degree from Conrad's ending to the story than Coppola's ending for the film does. In Coppola's film Willard recoils from Kurtz's savage practices in the same manner that Marlow does in the book. Hence neither Marlow nor the film's Willard fall under Kurtz's sway in the way that Milius's Willard does. In the novella, Kurtz expires with the cryptic words on his lips, "The horror, the horror."

Presumably Kurtz's repetition of the phrase, "the horror," when he was on the point of death reflects that, before he succumbed to the deadly tropical disease that took his life, he got a flash of personal insight into his life that forced him to see the hideous horror of his moral corruption.

When Marlow returns home, he goes to see Kurtz's fiancée, who has remained faithful to Kurtz, despite his prolonged sojourn in the Congo. Marlow gently tells her of Kurtz's demise. With supreme irony Marlow reassures her that "his end . . . was in every way worthy of his life." When she asks him what her fiancé's last words were, Marlow cannot bring himself to inform her that Kurtz's final painful utterance was "the horror, the horror." He rather tells her that Kurtz died speaking her name. Marlow, after all, does not wish to destroy her fond memories of her deceased fiancé, which are all she has left of him.

As Catharine Rising writes, Marlow's lie preserves the young woman's "deluded love of the dead. To suppress Kurtz's actual words . . . signifies not only Marlow's compassion," but his admiration for a woman "who strikes him as beautiful, and in whom . . . he lauds a mature capacity for fidelity" to her beloved.

Andrew Gillon observes that Marlow emerges from his encounter with Kurtz in the wilderness a wiser if sadder man. Marlow thus learns from Kurtz's moral deterioration that one can only cope with one's personal capacity for evil by recognizing it for what it is. In sum, Conrad portrays human nature in the novella with a potential for greatness, which is coupled with an inclination toward evil that can finally undermine that capacity for good—which is precisely what happened to Kurtz.

In the film Willard is what Avrom Fleishman calls in his book *Narrated Films* an internal (subjective) narrator, because Willard gives his personal reactions to his own experiences as he narrates them over the soundtrack.

It is more difficult to imply in a movie, than it is in a work of fiction, that a given account of past events is being presented from the subjective point of view of one of the characters—as when Willard recalls in his voiceover commentary his initial misgivings about carrying out his secret orders to assassinate Kurtz when he finds him. This is because a film audience is always conscious that it is watching what is being dramatized in flashback on the screen—*not* through the eyes of the character who is narrating the events in question—but through the eye of the camera.

But the viewer still does not have the sense that he is seeing the flashback from the point of view of the character who is retelling the event. It is true that the central character remains on the screen more than anyone else in the movie, and his comments are often there on the soundtrack. But we still don't see others completely from his point of view, as we do in the novella.

Therefore *Apocalypse Now* is robbed of some of the emotional intensity that one feels when one reads "Heart of Darkness," simply because in the book the narrator frequently communicates to the reader his subjective reaction to the episodes from the past he is narrating. For example, the filmgoer never grasps the extent to which Willard, the narrator of the film, is profoundly touched by Kurtz's tragedy in the movie, since many of the sage reflections about

Kurtz's life and death which Marlow makes in the book are simply not in the film.

Near the beginning of the trip, Willard and the crew of his small craft witness an air attack on a North Vietnamese village carried out by Lieutenant Colonel Kilgore (ROBERT DUVALL), which utilizes all the facilities of modern mechanized warfare, from helicopters and rockets to radar-directed machine guns. By the time that Willard's boat reaches Kurtz's compound in the heart of the dark jungle, the modern weaponry has been replaced by the weapons of primitive man, as Kurtz's native followers, wearing war paint, attack Willard's small vessel with arrows and spears in an attempt to scare off the intruders. (The attack of the natives is taken directly from the novella.)

When Kurtz takes Willard into custody, Kurtz, in his malarial delirium, spends hours rambling to Willard about his theories of war and politics, which he maintains lie behind his becoming a rebel chieftain. Kurtz does this, not only because he wants a brother officer to hear his side of the story, but also because he ultimately wants Willard to explain to Kurtz's son his father's reasons for acting as he has. Significantly, even in the depths of his madness, Kurtz has not lost sight of the preciousness of family attachments. (Kurtz is not married in the novella, so Marlow goes to comfort Kurtz's fiancée, not his son, once he gets to Europe.)

As mentioned above, although some film critics found those scenes in which Kurtz theorizes about the motivation for his unspeakable behavior wordy and overlong, most agreed that the movie contains some of the most extraordinary combat footage ever filmed. The battle scene that particularly stands out is the one in which the officer who is aptly named Kilgore systematically wipes out a strongly fortified enemy village from the air, described above.

It is spectacular scenes like this one that have prompted some commentators on the film to rank *Apocalypse Now*, which won one of the two Grand Prizes awarded at the 1979 CANNES INTERNATIONAL FILM FESTIVAL, among the great war movies of all time. Moreover, this writer feels that the film can likewise be numbered among the major adaptations of Conrad to the screen.—GENE D. PHILLIPS

References

David Blakesley, "Heart of Darkness," in *Novels into Film*, ed. John Tibbetts and James M. Welsh, rev. ed. (New York: Facts On File, 2005), 178–80; Jeffrey Chown, *Hollywood Auteur: Francis Coppola* (New York: Praeger, 1988); Andrew Gellan, *Joseph Conrad* (Lubbock: Texas Tech University Press, 1994); Jorn Hettebrugge, "*Apocalypse Now*" in *100 All-Time Favorite Films*, ed. Jurgen Muller (Los Angeles: Taschen/BFI, 2008), 2:634–39; Brooks Riley, "Heart Transplant," *Film Comment* 15, no. 1 (September–October, 1979): 26–27; Catherine Rising, *Darkness at Heart: Fathers and Sons in Conrad* (New York: Greenwood Press, 1990).

HEARTS OF DARKNESS: A FILMMAKER'S APOCALYPSE (1991)

Award-winning documentary film, written and directed by Fax Bahr and George Hickenlooper with documentary footage shot by ELEANOR COPPOLA in 1977 and 1978. The documentary was telecast on the pay-cable network Showtime, premiering on October 12, 1991, before its feature-film premiere at the New York Film Forum on November 27, 1991. "We were in the jungle, there were too many of us, we had access to too much money, too much equipment—and little by little we went insane," is the way FRANCIS COPPOLA describes the experience. Serious complications included a major monsoon, civil unrest in the Philippines, the firing of one leading actor (HARVEY

KEITEL), and the heart attack suffered by his replacement, MARTIN SHEEN. *New York Times* reviewer Janet Maslin wrote that screenwriter JOHN MILIUS claimed that "the film was meant to resemble 'The Odyssey,' with Playboy Bunnies substituting for Sirens" and quoted Coppola, who was never "exactly sure what he was after," as calling it 'The Idiodyssey.'" Maslin concluded that "Even allowing for the aggrandizing nature of a film largely shot by his wife, Mr. Coppola emerges from this portrait in legitimately heroic terms." Although Coppola might "have brought on much of the trouble and confusion," the director "also provided the inspiration and the vision to cut through utter chaos and create perhaps a better film than the one he had originally intended." *Washington Post* television critic Tom Shales considered the documentary a "better movie than Apocalypse itself" because "it contains some of the most revealing backstage footage ever—harrowing and funny and painful."
—James M. Welsh

References
Janet Maslin, "Coppola's 'Apocalypse' Then," *New York Times*, November 27, 1991, C9, C14; Tom Shales, "Francis Ford Coppola's Folly," *Washington Post*, October 12, 1991, D1, D9.

HERR, MICHAEL (1940–)
Journalist whose article "The Battle for Khe San" inspired the creation of *APOCALYPSE NOW* (1979), for which Herr wrote the narration for FRANCIS COPPOLA, as well as served as an advisor. Herr also later provided the narration for Coppola's adaptation of *JOHN GRISHAM'S THE RAINMAKER* (1997). Herr's experience in Vietnam and his obvious talents as a writer also led to a collaboration with director Stanley Kubrick and combat writer Gustav Hasford on Kubrick's *Full Metal Jacket* (1987), adapted from Hasford's combat novel *The Short-Timers*. Born

in Syracuse, New York, Michael Herr was sent to Vietnam in 1967 by *Esquire* magazine to work as a civilian war correspondent. He later collected his magazine articles, which provided vivid verbal snapshots of the war, into his book, *Dispatches* (1977), considered one of the best first-person accounts of the Vietnam conflict. At the same time that Herr's articles were appearing in *Esquire* in the late 1960s, JOHN MILIUS was working on his script for *Apocalypse Now*. WALTER MURCH, who designed the sound for that film and edited it, claimed that Herr was hired to write the film's narration because Milius had borrowed so much from Herr's articles.

Specific scenes in the movie are taken from Herr's essays, including the opening sequence in a Saigon hotel room in which Willard looks out the window on the city and lies on the bed watching the ceiling fan and including the scene at the Do Lung bridge in which an American soldier locates by sound an enemy caught in the wire at the base's perimeter and kills him with an M-79 grenade launcher. Coppola has said that the photographer, played by DENNIS HOPPER in *Apocalypse Now*, is based in part on combat photographer Sean Flynn (son of actor Errol Flynn), who figures prominently in Herr's book. More importantly, Herr's book inspired the way the war is portrayed in the film, as a drug-soaked, rock-and-roll, psychedelic war.

In one of his essays, Herr refers to Vietnam as "a California corridor cut and bought and burned deep into Asia." That line probably inspired Milius to conceive of the Vietnam War as, he described it, "a California war," a "sort of East-meets-West thing, an ancient Asian culture being assaulted by this teenage California culture" and accounts for all the references in the film to Southern California and its culture—Charles Manson, Disneyland, Beverly Hills (the name of the command bunker at the Do Lung bridge), the music of the Doors, and surfing.

Other elements of the articles and dispatches were incorporated into *Apocalypse Now*. Herr's reference to the tigers in the hills of Vietnam most probably inspired the film's scene of the encounter with a tiger in the jungle. Herr also tells stories of "irregulars" in the Vietnam War who were "lost to headquarters," on their own without supervision, who exercised absolute authority over hamlets in which they operated; he tells of people driven insane by the war, of "mad colonels" who were "nonchalant about the horror," and of Americans who wanted to drop the bomb on Vietnam, who "wanted a Vietnam they could fit into their car ashtrays." These references in *Dispatches* suggest the Vietnam story in *Apocalypse Now* that Milius grafted onto the plot of JOSEPH CONRAD's novella, "HEART OF DARKNESS."

Through his work on *Apocalypse Now* and *Full Metal Jacket* and through his book *Dispatches*, Herr has been instrumental in shaping how the Vietnam War has been remembered.—DONALD M. WHALEY/JAMES M. WELSH

HINES, GREGORY (1946–2003)

Dancer, choreographer, and actor who played Sandman Williams in *THE COTTON CLUB* (1984). Born in New York on February 14, 1946, Gregory Hines began training as a dancer at an early age with choreographer Henry LeTang, who taught both Gregory and his older brother, Maurice. When Gregory turned five, the two brothers went professional as "The Hines Kids," performing in nightclubs. Backstage at New York's Apollo Theater they were advised by tap-dancing legends, such as CHARLES "HONI" COLES, Sandman Sims, The Nicholas Brothers, and Teddy

Maurice and Gregory Hines in *The Cotton Club*.

Hale. Gregory made his Broadway debut with his brother, Maurice, in *The Girl in Pink Tights* (1954). When he turned eighteen, Gregory and his brother joined their drummer father, Maurice Sr., to become "Hines, Hines, and Dad," a hugely popular touring act. His fame was established two decades later when he was nominated for three Tony Awards for his performances in *Eubie* (1978, a tribute to the great Baltimore Ragtime piano player Eubie Blake, for which he won the Theatre World Award), *Comin' Uptown* (1980), and Duke Ellington's *Sophisticated Ladies* (1981). Hines danced with his brother Maurice in *Eubie*, *Sophisticated Ladies*, and in Coppola's *The Cotton Club*. In 1992 Hines won the Tony Award for Best Actor in a Musical for his portrayal of jazz great Jelly Roll Morton in *Jelly's Last Jam*, and also won the Drama Desk Award. In 1981 Hines made the transition from dancer to motion picture actor, appearing in the Mel Brooks comedy *History of the World—Part I*, followed that same year by his costarring role with Albert Finney in the thriller, *Wolfen*. His film career continued with *Deal of the Century* in 1983; *White Nights*, with Mikhail Baryshnikov, in 1985; the acclaimed musical drama *Tap* in 1989; the psychological thriller *Eve of Destruction* in 1991; and *The Tic Code* in 1998. In 1997, after frequent appearances on the NBC television series "Will and Grace," Hines starred in his own CBS sitcom, "The Gregory Hines Show." The versatile Gregory Hines, who had been called "the Pied Piper of Modern Tap," died in Los Angeles in 2003.—JAMES M. WELSH

HINTON, S. E. [SUSAN ELOISE HINTON INHOFE] (1948–)

Novelist who wrote her first teen novel, *THE OUTSIDERS*, while she was still enrolled as a junior in Will Rogers High School in Tulsa, Oklahoma; remarkably, it became a best-selling young-adult novel after its publication in 1967, selling several million copies. *The Outsiders* was adapted for the screen by Kathleen Knutson Rowell, but Hinton had an active role in adapting her later novel, *RUMBLE FISH*, cowriting the screenplay with FRANCIS COPPOLA; she also played a prostitute in the film adaptation. Hinton similarly appeared in a cameo role as a nurse in Dally's room in *The Outsiders*.

Born in Tulsa on July 22, 1948, Susan Hinton was educated at the University of Tulsa, earning a BS degree in 1970. Her 1975 novel, *Rumble Fish*, was originally published as a short story in the Tulsa literary journal, *Nimrod*, in 1968. Her 1979 novel, *Tex*, was adapted to film by Tim Hunter in 1982, and her 1971 novel *That Was Then, This Is Now* was adapted to film in 1985 by Christopher Cain, scripted by EMILIO ESTEVEZ, who played Mark Jennings; it was the only film adaptation in which Hinton herself was not involved, according to Jay Daly's *Presenting S. E. Hinton* (1987), the first critical treatment of Hinton's fiction.

She used the pen name S. E. Hinton because she feared that young people might be put off by a novel depicting male adolescence if they were aware that the author was a female. As a matter of fact, her readership never guessed that the author was a young woman, probably because when she was growing up most of Susie Hinton's close friends were the group of boys that she regularly hung out with.

The Outsiders, in the words of journalist Lizzie Skurnick, is "an iconic work, still read in classrooms across the country." Indeed, parents who had read the book in high school now give it to their own kids to read. The novel, by way of its narrator Ponyboy Curtis, introduces us to the greasers, "the genial hoods Hinton will follow for most of her career," and the socs (short for *social*), a rival gang composed of wealthy preppies, Skurnick continues. The two groups make up the East Side/West Side dichotomy of Tulsa's youth. "I went to Will Rogers High School in Tulsa," Hinton recalls. "I was mad about the cliques, so I used the two extreme groups, the greasers and the socs, in my book." Thus *The Outsiders* is an excellent introduction for teens to class strife.

Coppola was convinced that *The Outsiders* was written with the authentic voice of a youngster, as she told the story of three brothers who endeavor to maintain themselves as a family after both their parents have died in an auto accident. "As I was reading the book, I realized that I wanted to make a film about young people, and about belonging," says Coppola, "belonging to a peer group with whom one can identify and for whom one feels real love. Even though the boys are poor and to a certain extent insignificant, the story gives them a kind of beauty and nobility." *Tex* was the first of Hinton's novels to be filmed; it was directed by Tim Hunter in 1982.

"Adults are noticeably absent in this world," Skurnick notes (Were the boys hatched?). The gaping absences of parents—killed in a car wreck, dead in a hospital, "leave holes in the boys' lives." What is left for the "fractured families" is an older brother who can rise to be a proto-father, as Darrel (Patrick Swayze), the elder brother of Ponyboy (C. Thomas Howell) does in Coppola's film of *The Outsiders*.

In a world where adults are in short supply, the youngsters depend on the brotherhood of the gang. "Passing through a principal's office, to the back of a police car, an ambulance or a holding cell," Skurnick concludes, "Hinton's heroes become more loyal—to their friends."

"When I met Susie," Coppola says, "it was confirmed to me that she was not just a young people's novelist, but a real American novelist. For me the primary thing about her books is that the characters come across as very real. Her dialogue is memorable, and her prose is striking. Often a paragraph of her descriptive prose sums up something essential and stays with you."

Because of his esteem for Hinton as a novelist, Coppola involved her in the shoot. "Once I sold the book," she observes, "I expected to be asked to drop off the face of the earth. But that didn't happen. I know that I had extremely rare experiences for a writer. Usually the director does not say, 'Boys, these are important lines, so you've got to know them word for word,' which is what Francis said to the actors." In addition to monitoring the script, Miss Hinton was on the set every day, supervising haircuts and wardrobe. "The boys depended on me a lot," she says. "I was a kind of a greaser den mother, and they were always consulting me."

After finishing the feature film of *The Outsiders*, Coppola followed it immediately with the screen adaptation of another Hinton novel. While he was shooting *The Outsiders* in Tulsa, Coppola got the idea that he would like to employ the same crew and locations for a second teen movie. As Hinton tells it, "Halfway through *The Outsiders*, Francis looked up at me one day and said, 'Susie, we get along great. Have you written anything else I can film?'" She said frankly, "I've got this weird book that no one understands." Hinton told him about *Rumble Fish*, and he read the book and loved it.

Coppola said, "I know what we can do. On our Sundays off, let's write a screenplay, and then as soon as we can wrap *The Outsiders*, we'll take a two-week break and start filming *Rumble Fish*." She said "Sure, Francis, we're working 16 hours a day, and you want to spend Sundays writing another screenplay?" She concludes, "But that's what we did."

Susie Hinton wrote the book five years after *The Outsiders*, when she was more mature, and consequently, "it had tremendously impressive vision and dialogue and characters," says Coppola. Stephen Farber records, "Coppola actually co-wrote the screenplay. Mr. Coppola concentrated on structure and visual imagery, while Miss Hinton wrote all the dialogue. She found to her surprise that she had certain talents for screenwriting."

Hinton begins the novel in the present and then has Rusty James narrate the story in flashback, a device she had likewise utilized in *The Outsiders*. Coppola rejected the flashback structure—which he had employed in his film of *The Outsiders*—for the movie version of *Rumble Fish*, presumably because he wanted to take a different approach to the material than he had taken in his previous Hinton film. Otherwise, the shooting script for *Rumble Fish* follows the novel quite faithfully.

"I get the same kind of letters today that I got forty years ago," Hinton told the *Chicago Tribune*. A boy will say, "I didn't know that anybody else felt like this." Hinton mentions that every time she got a letter from a youngster who said *Rumble Fish* was his favorite novel the return address was invariably a reformatory. This is understandable, since the novel portrays youthful angst and rebellion even more frankly than *The Outsiders*. *Rumble Fish* has a darker, grittier quality than *The Outsiders*. Hence, Coppola chose to shoot it in black-and-white.

Matt Dillon once again plays a troubled teen, as he had in *The Outsiders*; here he is called Rusty James.

During filming, Hinton was herself impressed with her ability to rewrite material under the gun. "Working with Francis," she recalls, "I could never tell when he was going to turn to me and say, 'Susie, we'll need a new scene here to make this play.' I could

have it for him in three minutes, and it was pretty good, too." This sort of emergency writing on the set yielded some memorable bits of dialogue. Some of the nifty lines one hears spoken from the screen are not in the final shooting script and, therefore, must have been supplied by Hinton on the set, perhaps with the help of the cast during improvisations. For example, Motorcycle Boy, Rusty James's older brother (Mickey Rourke), expresses his fatherly concern for his troubled younger brother in terms that remind one of Darrel dealing with his surrogate son Ponyboy in *The Outsiders*. David Thomson maintains that *Rumble Fish*, as much as *The Outsiders*, is "a haunting evocation of the teenage years."

On June 7, 2008, S. E. Hinton accepted the *Chicago Tribune*'s Young Adult Book Prize as a pioneer in literature for young adults. She said that she was pleased with the movies derived from her work and enjoyed doing cameos in both of the Coppola films. "I've kept my Screen Actors Guild card up to this day," she noted. "If Francis calls, I'm ready."—Gene D. Phillips/James M. Welsh

References

Jay Daly, *Presenting S. E. Hinton* (Boston: Twayne Publishers, 1987); Stephen Farber, "Directors Join the S. E. Hinton Fan Club," *New York Times*, March 20, 1983, sec. 2: 19; S. E. Hinton, *Some of Tim's Stories* (Norman: University of Oklahoma Press, 2007); Lizzy Skurnick, "The Brotherhood of S. E. Hinton," *Chicago Tribune Books*, May 30, 2008, 6–7; Elizabeth Taylor, "Interview with S. E. Hinton," *Chicago Tribune Books*, May 30, 2008, 7; David Thomson, *Have You Seen . . . ? 1,000 Films* (New York: Knopf, 2008).

HOPKINS, ANTHONY (1937–)

Honored British stage actor who played Dr. Van Helsing in *BRAM STOKER'S DRACULA*, born on December 31, 1937, the son

Cary Elwes, Richard E. Grant, and Anthony Hopkins in *Bram Stoker's Dracula.*

of Richard Arthur Hopkins and Muriel Anne (Yeats) Hopkins, in Port Talbot, South Wales. Educated at Cowbridge Grammar School, Glamorgen, and the Welsh College of Music and Drama in Cardiff, then, after two year's service in the military, at London's Royal Academy of Dramatic Art, where he was admitted on scholarship and graduated in 1963. His apprenticeship was served at the Phoenix Theatre in Leicester and the Liverpool Playhouse before he was invited to audition for Sir Laurence Olivier, director of the National Theatre at the Old Vic. His film debut came in 1967 when Peter O'Toole selected him to play Richard the Lionhearted in *The Lion in Winter.* The next year he played Claudius to Nicol Williamson's Hamlet in the groundbreaking Round House Theatre production directed by Tony Richardson. In 1974 he played the psychiatrist Dr. Martin Dysart on Broadway in the National Theatre production of Peter Shaffer's *Equus,* winning both the New York Drama Desk Award and the New York Outer Critics Circle Award. He won the British Theatre Association's Best Actor Award for his role in David Hare's play *Pravda* at the National Theatre. And of course he won the 1991 Academy Award for Best Actor for his portrayal of Dr. Hannibal Lecter in Jonathan Demme's *The Silence of the Lambs.* In June of 1987 Hopkins was awarded the Commander of the Order of the British Empire in the Queen's Honor List.—JAMES M. WELSH

HOPPER, DENNIS (1936–2010)

Distinctive American counterculture writer, director, character actor, and star who played the photojournalist in *APOCALYPSE NOW* and the father in *RUMBLE FISH* (1983). Hopper also appeared in ELEANOR COPPOLA's *HEARTS OF DARKNESS: A FILMMAKER'S APOCALYPSE* (1991). Dennis Hopper was born on May 17, 1936, in Dodge City, Kansas, the son of Marjorie Mae and Jay Millard Hopper. His family later moved to San Diego. He was educated at the Wooster School, Danbury, Connecticut, and at Helix High School, La Mesa, California (near San Diego). Hopper broke into filmmaking with James Dean in both Nicholas Ray's *Rebel without a Cause* and George Stevens's *Giant* in 1956 (though his first acting role was in the noir western *Johnny Guitar* in 1954). He then helped to shape the movies of the protest generation by writing and directing *Easy Rider* (1969), costarring with Peter Fonda and setting the tone for a particular kind of free-spirited filmmaking typical of his generation. *Easy Rider* earned Hopper the Best New Director Award at the 1968 CANNES INTERNATIONAL FILM FESTIVAL. *The Last Movie*, which he also wrote and directed in 1971, was generally neither so successful nor so iconic (though the film did win a major award at the 1971 Venice Film Festival). But his career and legend continued as character actor in films as varied as *Cool Hand Luke* (1967) and *True Grit* (1989), on the one hand, and *Hoosiers* (1986) and cult favorites *The River's Edge* (1986) and David Lynch's *Blue Velvet* (1986), on the other. He was nominated for an Academy Award for Best Supporting Actor in *Hoosiers* and won the Best Actor Award from the Los Angeles Film Critics Association for *Blue Velvet*. No less impressive was his performance for the cult German director WIM WENDERS in *The American Friend* (1977), adapted from the Patricia Highsmith novel, *Ripley's Game*. On television Hopper costarred early on with Natalie Wood in *King's Row* and *Carnival* on the "Kaiser Aluminum Hour," both directed by George Roy Hill. Hopper was still doing commercials as a counterculture "character" in his seventies, and was featured in the TV series *Crash* as a drug-addicted music producer prior to his death on May 29, 2010.—JAMES M. WELSH

HOSKINS, BOB (1942–)

British character actor who appeared in *THE COTTON CLUB* (1984). He began his career on the London stage and moved on to British films. He was eventually cast in Hollywood movies because of his uncanny ability to impersonate American characters with an authentic-sounding accent. Thus

he played the racketeer Owney Madden, owner of the Cotton Club, in FRANCIS COPPOLA's film.

Hoskins remembers that endless script revisions caused delays in shooting. After all, substantially reworking a scene with the actors prior to shooting was time consuming. As a result, filming fell increasingly behind schedule. Thus actors would show up on the set in makeup and costume to do a scheduled scene, only to find by the end of the day that Coppola would not get to that scene until the next day at the earliest. This situation was repeated throughout the shoot with some regularity. Bob Hoskins's scenes were delayed so often that he really got bored sitting around his dressing room day after day, "waiting for something to happen." Eventually, he says, "you forgot what you do for a living."

David Thomson writes that Hoskins has made an "explosive impact" appearing as a gangster in films like *The Long Good Friday* and *Mona Lisa*, as well as *The Cotton Club*.—GENE D. PHILLIPS

References
Michael Daly, "A True Tale of Hollywood: *The Cotton Club*," *New York*, May 7, 1989, 43–60; David Thomson, *The New Biographical Dictionary of Film* (New York: Knopf, 2004).

HOWELL, C. THOMAS (1966–)

Born on Pearl Harbor Day, December 7, 1966, in Van Nuys, California, Christopher Thomas Howell experienced thrills in front of a crowd from a young age. Following his father's example as a stunt coordinator, Howell began acting at the age of four and did some work as a child stunt player. He also worked as a child rodeo performer, winning the "All-Around-Cowboy" award at the California Junior Rodeo Association at the age of twelve.

Continuing with his stunt work and breaking into acting, Howell moved into doing commercials and, at sixteen, was a stunt actor in Steven Speilberg's *E.T.: The Extra-Terrestrial* (1982) as a bicycle rider near the end of the film. Exposure from that hit brought him the lead role in FRANCIS FORD COPPOLA's ensemble film *THE OUTSIDERS* (1983). Howell's rebel character Ponyboy Curtis won him a Young Artist Award. He next appeared with his *Outsiders* costar PATRICK SWAYZE in the demolition-derby racing film *Grandview U.S.A.* (1984), also starring Jamie Lee Curtis. Howell immediately worked again with Swayze in the apocalyptic *Red Dawn* (1984).

Another starring role followed in the romantic screwball comedy *Secret Admirer* (1985), but Howell's next completed project proved to be controversial. The thriller-horror film *The Hitcher* (1986) received wide attention, but was most noteworthy for its over-the-top violence. Roger Ebert awarded the film "zero stars," referring to the "particularly sick" plot elements. Howell reprised his role fifteen years later in *The Hitcher II: I've Been Waiting* (2003).

The same year as *The Hitcher*, Howell starred in *Soul Man* (1986), in which, for much of the film, his character appears in blackface, attempting to pass himself off as an African American who has received a scholarship to Harvard Law School. Although his character eventually regrets and apologizes for his charade, the NAACP and student groups protested the film's racial humor. Howell met his first wife, Rae Dawn Chong, on that film. After marrying in 1989, they divorced in 1990.

Since the late 1980s, Howell's career has been dominated by television, with appearances on such series as *Moonlighting* and *E.R.* Perhaps capping off his celebrity status in 2008, Howell appeared on the celebrity reality show *Celebracadabra*. He won as the most believable and proficient magician and received his honorific "Great-

est Celebrity Magician." The title seems apropos for the son of a stuntman, a professional who has demonstrated his talent within every aspect of Hollywood product over his lifelong career.—THOMAS CLANCY

HUSTON, ANJELICA (1951–)

Actress, star player, and daughter of writer-director John Huston (1906–1987) and granddaughter of actor Walter Huston (1884–1950), she played her first lead role in a feature film for FRANCIS COPPOLA, as Samantha Davis, an antiwar *Washington Post* reporter in *GARDENS OF STONE* (1987). She also starred with Michael Jackson in *CAPTAIN EO*, the 3-D Disneyland film attraction. Anjelica Huston was born in California but raised in Ireland (St. Clerans, County Galway), England, and France. She made her film debut at the age of fifteen in *A Walk with Love and Death*, a medieval romance directed by her father. Her performance for director Stephen Frears in *The Grifters* earned the Best Actress Awards from the National Society of Film Critics and the Los Angeles film critics, as well as an Oscar nomination. John Huston directed her performance in *Prizzi's Honor* in 1985, for which she earned an Academy Award for Best Supporting Actress. She was radiant as the melancholy Gretta Conroy, her role in her father's adaptation of James Joyce's last story from *The Dubliners*, entitled *The Dead*, which won her an Independent Spirit Award. Her performance in the CBS miniseries *Lonesome Dove* earned her an Emmy nomination. She also had a knack for comedy, as witnessed by her portrayal of the Grand High Witch for director Nicolas Roeg's adaptation of Roald Dahl's *The Witches* (1990).—JAMES M. WELSH

HUYCK, WILLARD (1945–)

Screenwriter, director, and producer Willard Huyck was born on September 8, 1945. Huyck became a friend of JOHN MILIUS and protégé of USC classmate GEORGE LUCAS, who introduced him to FRANCIS COPPOLA, who, in turn, signed Huyck and his partner and wife, Gloria Katz, to write and direct six pictures for his then newly created company, AMERICAN ZOETROPE. Though none of these pictures were made, Huyck and Katz had written the Academy Award–nominated screenplay for the extraordinarily successful *AMERICAN GRAFFITI* in 1973 with and for George Lucas. Their later screenplay, *Lucky Lady*, directed by Stanley Donen in 1975 and starring Burt Reynolds, Liza Minnelli, and GENE HACKMAN, was, in the words of *Washington Post* critic Gary Arnold (November 9, 1979), "sunk by a fatal lack of comic authenticity." Likewise, their feature *French Postcards* (1979), which Huyck directed and Katz produced and both of them wrote, was doomed by what Gary Arnold called a "hopelessly trivial-minded screenplay." Huyck enjoyed a revival of fame and success with *Indiana Jones and the Temple of Doom* in 1984, but another reversal after directing the ill-fated and notoriously bad *Howard the Duck* two years later in 1986.—JAMES M. WELSH

INGLENOOK WINERY

Located in Rutherford, California, in the Napa Valley. FRANCIS COPPOLA took the Inglenook estate and turned it into the Niebaum-Coppola winery, which later produced his signature wines. —JAMES M. WELSH

IS PARIS BURNING? (1966)

FRANCIS COPPOLA was engaged in earning a master's degree in film at UCLA when Seven Arts, an independent production unit, employed him as a screenwriter. Ray Stark, his immediate boss at Seven Arts, was pleased with his work on various projects. Indeed, Coppola's reputation as an accomplished "script doctor" spread around the Seven Arts film unit. He was often called in to help to try and save a project when the screenplay was in trouble.

Such a troubled project was the war film *Is Paris Burning?* a joint American-French coproduction based on the book *Paris, Brûle-t-il?* by Larry Collins and Dominique Lapierre, to be directed by French director René Clément (*Purple Noon*) and released by Paramount. In early 1965 Stark sent Coppola to Paris to collaborate with the ailing screenwriter Anthony Veiller (*The Night of the Iguana*). Stark saw Coppola as Seven Arts' insurance policy—in the event of the aging Veiller's demise, Coppola was to take over for him. "I was to take the pencil from his hand when it fell out," Coppola states. Veiller was not aware of Coppola's private arrangement with Stark. He saw Coppola as a mere neophyte screenwriter who was to learn his trade from Veiller. "For five weeks, I would go to him every morning at his hotel, and he would mock my work," Coppola recalls. Finally, just as Coppola got fed up with bickering with Veiller, the elderly screenwriter did expire, and Coppola found himself saddled with a mammoth project—a bewildering, multistoried account of the liberation of Paris in 1944, a bloated war epic with an all-star cast, including Charles Boyer, ORSON WELLES, and Kirk Douglas.

Screenwriter GORE VIDAL (*Suddenly Last Summer*) was brought in to help Coppola finish the script, since it was clear that it was too much for a young writer to cope with alone. Like Veiller, Vidal saw their collaboration as a junior-senior relationship, Coppola remembers, but Vidal was much more gracious than Veiller. He would have him work out a scene and then they would go over it.

The film's French producer, Paul Graetz, had made an agreement with the city officials in Paris that the historical events would be depicted in the screenplay in a manner that pictured General Charles de Gaulle as a gallant French leader. In return, they would allow the film unit to shoot on location all over Paris. At this juncture, de Gaulle, as president of France, was still a world figure. Therefore, to ensure that he would not be offended in any way by the movie, some French screenwriters, including Claude Boulé, Jean Aurenche, and Pierre Bost, were appointed to kibitz on the script at the behest of government bureaucrats. The script conferences inevitably deteriorated into shouting matches. Coppola ultimately realized that it was hopeless to endeavor to pacify the Gaullist writers on the film, who staunchly maintained that every Frenchman was a hero. In the end no less than ten screenwriters worked on the screenplay. The intransigence of the French writers contributed in no small way to the script turning out to be fragmented and lacking in continuity. The final shooting script was principally a collation of the work of Coppola, Vidal, Boulé, Aurenche, and Bost. The Screenwriters Guild in Hollywood, however, awarded sole screen credit to Coppola and Vidal. As a result, several critics blamed Coppola and Vidal because the script bulldozed the complexities of the historical events the movie presented. The film was damned as an incoherent, ponderous, and shallow tribute to the liberation of Paris, one of the great experiences of World War II.

Veiller was not the only casualty during the period the film was being made. Producer Graetz, worn out from all of the infighting, suffered a heart attack and died during the final days of shooting. As for Coppola, in the wake of the debacle that was *Is Paris Burning?* he and Seven Arts decided to part company. After laboring as a script doctor on ten scripts in all at Seven Arts, Coppola recounts that he both quit and was fired at the same time. Still, the failure of this picture was not laid at Coppola's door by industry insiders. Consequently, he then moved on to work as a screenwriter at Twentieth Century-Fox.—Gene D. Phillips

References

Jean-Paul Chaillet and Elizabeth Vincent, *Francis Ford Coppola*, trans. Denise Jacobs (New York: St. Martin's Press, 1984); Leslie Halliwell, *Film Guide*, ed. David Gritten, rev. ed. (New York: Harper Collins, 2008); Robert Johnson, *Francis Ford Coppola* (Boston: Twayne, 1977).

J

JACK (1996)

DIRECTOR: Francis Ford Coppola. SCREEN-
PLAY: James DeMonaco and Gary
Nadeau. PRODUCERS: Ricardo Mestres,
Fred Fuchs, and Francis Ford Coppola
for American Zoetrope, Buena Vista.
EXECUTIVE PRODUCER: Doug Claybourne.
PHOTOGRAPHY: John Toll. EDITING: Barry
Malkin. MUSIC: Michael Kamen. PRO-
DUCTION DESIGN: Dean Tavoularis. ART
DIRECTION: Angelo Graham. COSTUME
DESIGN: Aggie Guerard Rodgers. SOUND:
Agamemnon Andrianos.
CAST: Robin Williams (Jack Powell),
Diane Lane (Karen Powell), Jennifer
Lopez (Miss Marquez), Brian Kerwin
(Brian Powell), Fran Drescher (Dolo-
res Durante), Bill Cosby (Lawrence
Woodruff), Michael McKean (Paulie),
Don Novello (Bartender), Allan Rich
(Dr. Benfante), Adam Zolotin (Louis
Durante), Todd Bosley (Edward),
Seth Smith (John-John), Mario Yedidia
(George), Jeremy Lelliott (Johnny Duf-
fer), Rickey O'Shon Collins (Eric), Hugo
Hernandez (Victor).
RUNNING TIME: 113 minutes. Technicolor.
RELEASED THROUGH: Buena Vista. PREMIERE:
August 9, 1996.
DVD: Walt Disney Video.

Walt Disney Pictures, for whom FRANCIS
COPPOLA had filmed "LIFE WITHOUT
ZOE" for *NEW YORK STORIES*, brought
him a script by Gary Nadeau and James
De Monaco entitled *Jack*, in which the title
character has the mind of a ten-year-old in
a forty-year-old body. Coppola was immediately attracted to the material because
it called up some childhood memories of
his own.

Jack is afflicted with a fictitious disease that makes him age at four times the
normal rate, a factor that cuts him off from
normal children. The screenplay caused
Coppola to remember his bout with polio
as a boy: "When I was nine I was confined
to a room for over a year with polio, and
because polio is a child's illness, they kept
every other kid away from me. I remember being pinned to this bed, and longing
for friends and company," says Coppola.
"When I read *Jack*, I was moved because
that was precisely his problem; there were
no children in his life."

In addition, *Jack* reminded him of an
earlier film: "*PEGGY SUE GOT MARRIED*
was a kind of sweet fable," he explained,
"and in a way *Jack* is like that." (In *Peggy
Sue* the situation that obtains in *Jack* is
reversed: she is a forty-year-old woman
who finds herself in her teenage body.)
"Even though *Jack* didn't originate with me,
I tried to tackle the story with as much feeling and love as I could." He adds, "It's like
an arranged marriage; slowly I find ways to
care about it."

The film begins with a precredit
sequence in which a woman is rushed in

to labor, crying, "It's too soon. It's not even two months!" She then gives birth to a premature baby. "Now that's a pretty serious kind of opening for such a whimsical movie," says Coppola. "So I added a thing where the mother is at a *beaux-arts* ball; when they rush her into the hospital," she and her husband are wearing bizarre costumes straight out of *The Wizard of Oz*. This gives a wacky kind of "Preston Sturges" feeling to the scene.

For his production team Coppola was able once more to bring back production designer DEAN TAVOULARIS and editor BARRY MALKIN, with John Toll as director of photography. ROBIN WILLIAMS was set to take the title role, and Coppola heartily approved. Williams can be childlike, Coppola stated, "but he's such an extraordinarily intelligent man that I knew he could pull off the illusion" of being a child trapped in an adult's body. DIANE LANE, whose association with Coppola dated way back to *THE OUTSIDERS*, took the part of Jack's mother, Karen Powell. Principal photography started in September 1995 and proceeded in a routine fashion.

The concept of a boy with a man's body had been done before, most notably in the Tom Hanks vehicle *Big* (1988), in which a twelve-year-old gets his wish to grow "big" granted temporarily by a carnival wishing-machine. In *Jack* the boy's rapid growth is not caused by magic but by an irreversible disease. That gives the present film some poignancy. It is evident that, since Jack ages physically four years for each calendar year that he lives, he may not reach twenty.

In the film's prologue, Jack is born fully developed after a two-month pregnancy. After the prologue the story leaps ahead a decade, whereby Jack is ten and looks like a robust adult of forty. His parents, Brian and Karen Powell, in the intervening years have kept him at home. A kindly school teacher, Lawrence Woodruff (Bill Cosby), has come

to the house regularly to tutor Jack. Since Jack has no ordinary contact with other children, Brian, with Woodruff's support, persuades Karen to liberate Jack from his cloistered existence and let him go to elementary school with other children his age. "Just because a person is different," says Woodruff, "he shouldn't be an outcast." Be that as it may, Jack's classmates initially see him as a freak and ridicule him during class and in the schoolyard. The other kids gradually accept him, however, when they realize that his size can benefit them. He is a topnotch basketball player at recess, and he looks old enough to buy them *Penthouse* magazine at the local drugstore.

But Jack's adult body, coupled with his child's mind and emotions, can present drawbacks for him. He nurses a schoolboy crush on his teacher, Miss Marquez (Jennifer Lopez), and he asks to be her escort to a school dance, since she is tall enough to dance with him. She tactfully declines his invitation, calling herself an elderly lady, too old for school dances.

Jack gets into real trouble when he goes to a café, hoping to find a girl tall enough for him to dance with and Dolores Durante (Fran Drescher), a promiscuous divorcée, sidles into the club. When she takes a shine to Jack, a jealous drunk resents the attention that she is giving him and punches him out. Jack gets into a slugfest with the drunk and knocks him flat. So he spends the night in the slammer, to the chagrin of his parents. The tavern scene, a high spot in the movie, is sparked by vibrant performances from Drescher and Williams.

Jack's physician dutifully warns Jack's parents that "Jack's internal clock is ticking faster than normal," and that premature signs of aging will regularly occur, which will indicate that his time is running out. In short, Jack will grow old and sick and inevitably have a short life span. At this moment Coppola cuts to a butterfly landing on

Jack's windowsill. Jack picks it up—it is dead. The image, implying that life is short for a butterfly and for Jack too, once more demonstrates the strong visual sense that is characteristic of Coppola's films.

In the epilogue, set seven years later, an aging, somewhat feeble Jack, who by this time is going on seventy, is valedictorian when his class graduates from high school. "My life has been short," he begins, "but in the end none of us has very long on this earth. Life is fleeting—it's like a shooting star: it passes quickly. But while it is here it lights up the sky. So we must live life to the fullest while we are still here." He concludes, "When you see a shooting star, think of me."

Jack's final speech struck a chord in Coppola: "The idea is that it really isn't how long you live; it's how completely you live your life that is important. . . . My son Gio only lived twenty-three years, but it was a complete twenty-three years." The picture ends with a dedication to Coppola's granddaughter Gia, Gio's daughter: "To Gia, 'When you see a shooting star . . .'"

Coppola was thoroughly lambasted by the reviewers for *Jack*. Gene Siskel, one of Coppola's biggest fans in the past, took great exception to *Jack*, as did most of his colleagues. Apparently Siskel noticed that one of the revelers at the costume party in the movie's opening sequence was dressed up as a bottle of wine from Coppola's vineyard. "But *Jack* is anything but vintage Coppola. Williams takes over the movie and basically does some talk show riffs on what it's like being a boy. . . . My advice: Buy the wine; put a cork in the movie." Michael Wilmington's more benign appraisal of the picture called it "sunny, humane, and high-spirited."

Coppola's direction is competent but not inspired. Lacking the invention or the fluency of his other films, *Jack* suffers by comparison. Coppola has always had

a predilection for youth flicks, but with *Jack* he has not progressed much beyond his earlier "coming of age" movies like *YOU'RE A BIG BOY NOW*, *The Outsiders*, *RUMBLE FISH*—or *Peggy Sue Got Married*, the picture that *Jack* most resembles as a mild fantasy. Overlong at 113 minutes, *Jack* finally wears out its welcome. The milk of human kindness has curdled in this dark comedy about a youngster who grows old before his time because of an incurable disease. Still, the movie takes some imaginative risks as it veers between stark drama (Jack growing old) and knockabout farce (the barroom brawl).

ELEANOR COPPOLA records in her *NOTES ON A LIFE* that, after the picture opened, a young man stopped Francis on a Paris street and said accusingly, "Why did you do *Jack*?" Coppola brooded over the young man's question and asked himself "why he did so many commercial films" like *Jack*, instead of making more personal films like *THE CONVERSATION*.

Critics had come to have substantial expectations of a director with Coppola's elegant craftsmanship. "Coppola is one of the greatest of the post-war American filmmakers," Wilmington writes, "and though you can't expect him to give us a *Godfather Trilogy* or an *APOCALYPSE NOW* every time out, you can expect more ambition and ideas" than are evident in *Jack*.

As things turned out, nobody liked *Jack* but the public. When it opened across the United States on August 9, 1996, it obviously reached its target audience of youngsters. By the end of the year it was one of the top box office attractions of 1996, with $60 million as a domestic gross.
—GENE D. PHILLIPS

References

Eleanor Coppola, *Notes on a Life* (New York: Doubleday, 2008); Michael Schumacher, *Francis Ford Coppola: A Filmmaker's Life* (New York:

Crown, 1999); Gene Siskel, "Tiresome *Jack*," *Chicago Tribune*, August 9, 1996, B2; Michael Wilmington, "Trapped in the *Jack* Box," *Chicago Tribune*, August 9, 1996, B1.

JACKSON, JOE
[DAVID IAN JACKSON] (1954–)

British-born singer-songwriter and composer who composed and arranged the music for *TUCKER: THE MAN AND HIS DREAM* (1988). Jackson first became popular for his "power pop" and new wave music. Later in his career, along with Elvis Costello and Graham Parker, Jackson challenged punk rock. Jackson was born in Burton-upon-Trent in Staffordshire, England, on August 11, 1954, and a year later moved with his family to Portsmouth. An asthmatic child, Jackson found solace in music and began violin lessons at age eleven. At age sixteen he started to perform in public. In 1972 Joe Jackson was accepted into the Royal Academy of Music in London, where he studied piano, percussion, composition, and orchestration for three years. While in school he played piano and vibes for the National Youth Jazz Orchestra. He also played keyboards for the Royal Academy Big Band, conducted by John Dankworth. After his graduation Jackson formed the band "Arms and Legs" with his friend, Mark Andrews, and the band, which lasted until 1976, released two singles in the United Kingdom. After he signed with A&M Records, Jackson's first LP, *Look Sharp* (1979) delivered his first gold record with the top-20 single, "Is She Really Going Out with Him?" His second LP *I'm the Man* also earned Jackson Holland's Edison Award. His next album, *Night and Day*, won another Edison Award and also received two Grammy Award nominations. From 1979 to 2001 Jackson earned five Grammy Award nominations, including one for his soundtrack for *Tucker*, nominated for Best Album of

Original Instrumental Background Score Written for a Motion Picture or TV.
—JAMES M. WELSH

JOHN GRISHAM'S
THE RAINMAKER (1997)

See entry below for *THE RAINMAKER*. The novelist's name was included in the title of the film adaptation by the same logic that *Dracula* was released as *BRAM STOKER'S DRACULA* and also to separate Coppola's adaptation of Grisham's novel from the similarly titled Burt Lancaster film about a Midwestern con man "miracle worker," released in 1956.

JOHNSON, ROBERT KENNETH (1936?–)

Film scholar, born in New York City, educated at Queens College, New York University, and Hofstra College, thence to graduate education at Cornell University (MA, 1960). He was teaching at Suffolk University, Boston, when he wrote one of the first books dealing with FRANCIS COPPOLA's career up to 1976 for the Twayne Series: *Francis Ford Coppola* (Boston: Twayne, 1977). Johnson later became a poet widely published by the small presses. One critic called him "the poet-laureate of the ordinary moment in time."

JONZE, SPIKE [ADAM SPIEGEL] (1970–)

Eccentric, experimental filmmaker and video artist who was married to SOFIA COPPOLA from 1999 to 2004, when they divorced. "Spike" (so nicknamed by his friends because of his unruly hair) is the son of Art Spiegel III, grandson of the founder of the Spiegel catalog company in New York. When he was two years old, his parents divorced, and the boy moved with his mother to Bethesda, Maryland, a Washington, D.C., suburb.

Completing high school in 1987, Spike migrated to the West Coast, where he found work as a journalist and, later, as a video artist. Jonze was one of the first directors to rise through music videos to be named three-time best director at the MTV Music Video Awards, after producing the videos "Sabatoge" (Beastie Boys, 1994), "California" (Wax, 1995), "Buddy Holly" (Weezer, 1995), "It's So Quiet" (Bjork, 1995), "Elektrobank" (Chemical Brothers, 1997), "Sky's the Limit" (Notorious B.I.G., 1997), "Weapon of Choice" (Fatboy Slim, 2001), and "Fully Flared" (skateboard video competition, 2007).

His first feature film was *Being John Malkovich* (1999, earning three major Academy Award nominations, including Best Director), a film he could not have made without the cooperation of the actor John Malkovich. According to a *New York Times* profile written by Saki Knafo, FRANCIS COPPOLA called Malkovich in the south of France in December of 1997 and asked Malkovich if he would meet with Jonze in Paris to discuss the project, and, as a consequence, *Being John Malkovich* went into production in 1998, financed by PolyGram (which soon after merged with Universal). The film was successful, and by the age of twenty-nine Spike Jonze was both well connected and sought after as a director. His next successful film was *Adaptation* (2002, four Academy Award nominations, and one Oscar for Chris Cooper as Best Supporting Actor), involving a story about the impossibility of telling stories on film, with NICOLAS CAGE (another Coppola link) playing a screenwriter frustrated about adapting a book without a plot.

This challenge was later to be followed by a film adaptation of Maurice Sendak's children's book, *Where the Wild Things Are* (2009). At first Jonze was puzzled, asking "How do you adapt a poem?" He then turned to the novelist Dave Eggers for help with the screenplay. Jeff Rubinov at Warner Bros. approved the script and production began in Australia in 2006. Delays ensued when Warner Bros. objected to the darkness of the story ("too weird" and "too scary"), a conflict between what Saki Knafo called "plot versus attitude," taking the lead from Sendak and enabling Jonze to inhabit a world in which one can "skip from fantasy to reality in the conviction that both exist."—JAMES M. WELSH

Reference

Saki Knafo, "Wild Life," *New York Times Magazine*, September 6, 2009, 30–35, 44–46.

JULIA, RAUL (1940–1994)

Celebrated actor, probably best known for his performance opposite William Hurt in *Kiss of the Spider Woman*, who plays Ray in *ONE FROM THE HEART*. Born and raised in Puerto Rico, Julia went to New York to pursue an acting career in 1964, making his New York debut in *Life Is a Dream*. Performing off-Broadway for the next two years, Julia appeared in *Macbeth*, the first of fourteen New York Shakespeare Festival productions. Julia was a four-time Tony nominee for *Nine*, *The Threepenny Opera*, *Where's Charley?*, and *Two Gentlemen of Verona*. His film performance in *Kiss of the Spider Woman* earned a Golden Globe nomination and the National Board of Review Award for his performance.—JAMES M. WELSH

K

KAGEMUSHA: THE SHADOW WARRIOR (1980)

DIRECTOR: Akira Kurosawa. SCREENPLAY: Masato Ide and Akira Kurosawa. PRODUCERS: Akira Kurosawa and Tomoyuki Tanaka for Kurosawa Film/Toho, in association with Twentieth Century-Fox Film Corporation. ASSISTANT PRODUCER: Teruyo Nogami. PHOTOGRAPHY: Takao Saito and Masaharo Ueda. PHOTOGRAPHY SUPERVISORS: Kazuo Miyagawa and Asakazu Nakai. MUSIC: Shinichiro Ikebe. PRODUCTION COORDINATOR: Ishio Honda, ART DIRECTION: Yoshiro Muraki. PRODUCTION ADVISERS: Shinobu Hashimoto and Masato Ide. PRODUCERS (International Version): Francis Ford Coppola and George Lucas. ASSISTANT PRODUCER (International Version): Audie Bock. SUBTITLE SUPERVISOR (International Version): Donald Richie.
CAST: Tatsuya Nakadai (Lord Shingen and his Double), Tsutomo Yamazaki (Nobukado), Kenichiro Hagiwara (Katsuyori), Kota Yui (Takemaru), Hideji Otaki (Masakage), Hideo Murata (Nobuharu), Takayuki Shiho (Masatoyo), Shuhei Sugimori (Masanobu), Noboru Shimizu (Masatane), Koji Shimizu (Katsusuke), Sen Yamamoto (Nobushige), Daisuke Ryu (Nobunaga), Masayuki Yui (Ieyasu).
ORIGINAL RUNNING TIME: 180 minutes; International Version: 162 minutes. Panavision, Eastmancolor.

U.S. RELEASE: Twentieth Century-Fox Film Corporation. PREMIERE: Japan, 1980. DVD: Criterion.

Japan, 1573. Shingen Takeda, one of the powerful warlords disputing the dominion of Japan during its historical *Sengoku* (Warring States) Period, is about to take a castle from his enemy, Ieyasu Tokugawa (future founder of the Tokugawa dynasty which governed the country from c. 1600 to 1868). Suddenly, Lord Shingen is fatally wounded by an enemy sniper, and his retainers must turn to a bold plan: to have their lord replaced by a double, or *Kagemusha*, as they try to keep friends and foes alike from learning the bad news.

Kagemusha was director Akira Kurosawa's return to the *Jidaigeki* or period drama, the genre that gave him widespread fame and success, after several years of box office failures—only relieved by the Soviet coproduction of *Dersu Uzala* (1975)—and increasing bureaucratic difficulties to produce his films.

Kurosawa's funding troubles had started with the long and problematic shooting of his film *Red Beard* in 1965, which gave him a reputation in the industry as a tyrannical figure who was extremely difficult to work with. They were compounded by the box office failure of his next project, *Dodeskaden* (1970), a look at contemporary life in a Tokyo slum, a work that Joan Mellen has called "a low-budget, minor film that compares with Kurosawa's great works only as a shadow resembles substance." The director's bad reputation and declining fortunes were only compounded by a disagreement with Fox over the Japanese segments of the big budget World War II film *Tora! Tora! Tora!* (1970). Kurosawa and Fox's chief, Darryl F. Zanuck, did not agree on the pace and method of production and neither his footage nor his credit were included in the final release of the film. Things came to a head for Kurosawa in December 1971, when he attempted suicide.

Some years later, the Soviet production organization, Mosfilm, invited Kurosawa to direct a project in the Soviet Union. The result was *Dersu Uzala* (1975), an award-winning film about the life of a Siberian mountain man. His long-cherished project of *Kagemusha*, for which he had drawn numerous exquisitely detailed sketches and storyboards, had to remain on paper, facing the reluctance of Japanese studios to provide its funding.

It took the influence of GEORGE LUCAS and FRANCIS FORD COPPOLA with the 20th Century Fox studio in the United States to convince Kurosawa's former production home, Toho, to greenlight this project. According to Michael Schumacher, "Coppola was especially pleased by his association with the Kurosawa film. The Japanese director had been a hero of Coppola's for as long as he could remember." Coppola served as coexecutive producer of the international version of the picture, together with his friend George Lucas, whose influence over Fox had recently been solidified by the success of *Star Wars* (1977). Lucas's own admiration for the Japanese master is evident in the fact that Kurosawa's *The Hidden Fortress* (1958) gave the American director

the idea for the characters who would later become C3PO and R2D2 in the science-fiction epic and its sequels.

With Coppola and Lucas's help, Kurosawa secured the roughly $2 million needed to finance the completion of *Kagemusha*. The result—after a difficult shoot that included the illness of Kurosawa's customary camera operator, Kazuo Miyagawa, and the departure of his longtime composer, Masaru Sato—is at once a thrilling, epic samurai film, the director's first one shot in color, a display of Kurosawa's painterly training and taste, and a fine psychological study that prefigures his 1985 film, *Ran*, also starring Tatsuya Nakadai. In turn, Coppola would draw from *Kagemusha* for the first battle scene in his own 1992 epic horror film, *BRAM STOKER'S DRACULA.*—FERNANDO ARENAS VÉLEZ

References

Peter Grilli, "*Kagemusha*: From Painting to Film Pageantry," essay written for the Criterion Collection DVD, www.criterion.com/current/posts/360; Donald Richie, *The Films of Akira Kurosawa*, revised ed. with additional material by Joan Mellen (Berkeley: University of California Press, 1984); Michael Schumacher, *Francis Ford Coppola: A Filmmaker's Life* (New York: Crown Publishers, 1999).

KAZAN, LAINIE (1940–)

Singer and entertainer who seriously turned to acting in 1980 after a successful career as a nightclub entertainer who had hosted her own variety program for NBC. Lainie Kazan was born Lanie Levine in Brooklyn, New York, on May 15, 1940. Kazan made her Broadway debut in 1961 in *The Happiest Girl in the World*. As a young singer Kazan got her big break when she understudied Barbra Streisand in the Broadway production of *Funny Girl*. After she replaced Streisand for one matinee and one evening performance, offers started to pour in, and concerts were to follow. In 1976 she opened Lainie's Room at the Los Angeles Playboy Club; the following year she opened Lainie's Room East in New York City. Kazan was nominated for an Emmy Award for her performance in the NBC television series *St. Elsewhere* and an ACE Award nomination for the Showtime cable series *The Paper Chase*. FRANCIS COPPOLA "discovered" Kazan as a blues singer at the Fairmont Hotel in San Francisco. Besides her on-screen appearance in Francis Ford Coppola's *ONE FROM THE HEART* (1982), Kazan appeared in the Paul Bartel cult comedy *Lust in the Dust* (1985) and in the Disney drama *The Journey of Natty Gann* (1985). Her portrayal of a typical Jewish mother in *My Favorite Year* earned Kazan a Golden Globe nomination in 1982, but her blockbuster hit film was to come much later, *My Big Fat Greek Wedding*, which grossed over $600 million after its release in 2002.—JAMES M. WELSH

KEATON, DIANE (1946–)

Actress featured as Kay Adams in *THE GODFATHER* trilogy. Born Diane Hall and raised in Santa Ana, California, she left college and moved to New York to pursue a singing career. However, it was her acting that really paid off, and Keaton made her Broadway debut in *Hair* in 1968, then starred with Woody Allen in his Broadway production of *Play It Again, Sam* (1970), beginning a long collaboration and romance with Allen, resulting in a string of films, including *Annie Hall*, the 1977 Best Picture Oscar winner, which also earned Keaton the Academy Award for Best Actress (and which was shot by another Coppola collaborator, cinematographer GORDON WILLIS). In a wonderful moment of comical reflexivity in *Annie Hall*, Woody Allen's character, Alvy, is harassed by a pair of Italian American men in front of a theatre as he is waiting for Annie (Keaton) to join

him. When she finally arrives, he quips that he has been "standing here with the cast of *The Godfather*!"

Following *Annie Hall*, Keaton worked with Allen in his next two films, the dramatic *Interiors* (1978) and the comedy/drama *Manhattan* (1979), even though their romantic relationship had subsided by then. In 1993 Keaton teamed up with Woody Allen again in *Manhattan Murder Mystery*, a hilarious romp that relied heavily on their undiminished screen chemistry.

Throughout her career, Keaton has moved apparently effortlessly from comedy to drama, with major successes in the latter category including Warren Beatty's *Reds* (1981), *Looking for Mr. Goodbar* (1977) with RICHARD GERE, and *Crimes of the Heart* (1986), as well as Coppola's *Godfather* trilogy.

Since the late 1980s, Keaton has become more and more active behind the camera in the capacities of director and/or producer on numerous projects. These include her directorial debut, the documentary *Heaven* (1987); the critically acclaimed TV series *Pasadena* (2001); and an episode of *Twin Peaks* (1991).

In addition to her Oscar for *Annie Hall*, Keaton's other major awards include the Golden Globe for Best Actress for her performance in *Something's Gotta Give* (2003) in which she costars with JACK NICHOLSON. Keaton also was a recipient of the National Board of Review Award for Best Acting by an Ensemble, for *The First Wives Club* (1996).—RODNEY HILL/JAMES M. WELSH

Reference

"Diane Keaton," *Variety* Profiles, www.variety.com.

KEITEL, HARVEY (1939–)

American actor, born in Brooklyn May 13, 1939, who became a regular for director Martin Scorsese and who was seriously considered by FRANCIS COPPOLA for *APOCALYPSE NOW*. His parents, Miriam and Harry Keitel, were Jewish immigrants from Romania and Poland. After serving in the Marine Corps, Keitel was tutored for the stage by Frank Corsaro and by LEE STRASBERG and Stella Adler at the Actors Studio, making his off-Broadway debut in 1965 in Arthur Miller's *Death of a Salesman*. Keitel returned to the stage in 1984 in David Rabe's *Hurleyburly*, directed by Mike Nichols, and in 1985 to appear in Sam Shepard's *A Lie of the Mind*. Harvey Keitel was with Scorsese from the beginning, playing J. R. in *Who's That Knocking at My Door?* (1965–1969), Charlie in *Mean Streets* (1973), Ben in *Alice Doesn't Live Here Anymore* (1974), Sport in *Taxi Driver* (1976), and Judas in *The Last Temptation of Christ* (1988). Keitel's talent also enhanced the work of several other major directors, including Ridley Scott (*The Duellists* in 1977 and *Thelma & Louise* in 1991), Nicolas Roeg (*Bad Timing—A Sensual Obsession*, 1982), Abel Ferrara (*Bad Lieutenant*, 1992), Quentin Tarantino's iconic *Reservoir Dogs* (1992), and Jane Campion's *The Piano* (1993). David Thomson described Keitel as an actor "so good, so persistent, yet so regularly denied at the highest table," but perhaps that has changed over time. Keitel earned an Academy Award nomination for Best Supporting Actor for his portrayal of Mickey Cohen for director Barry Levinson in *Bugsy* (1991), and in 2002 he got the Stanislavsky Award presented by the Moscow International Film Festival. Harvey Keitel was originally cast to play Willard in *Apocalypse Now*, after negotiations had failed with a number of other actors, including Steve McQueen, AL PACINO, JAMES CAAN, and JACK NICHOLSON. By April 16 of 1976, however, Coppola had decided to replace his leading man. According to biographers Michael Goodwin and Naomi Wise, Keitel hated the

jungle and was beginning to hate the assignment when he was replaced by MARTIN SHEEN. Together with his partner Peggy Gormley, Keitel formed his own film production company, The Goatsingers, serving as executive producers on Tony Bui's *Three Seasons*, winner of the Grand Jury Prize and Audience Award at the 1999 Sundance Film Festival, and Wayne Wang and Paul Auster's *Blue in the Face*, both of which Keitel appeared in. Always a dependable character actor, Keitel played Agent Jack Crawford in the Brett Ratner/Ted Tally adaptation of Thomas Harris's *Red Dragon* (2002). In 2008 Keitel was perfectly chosen to play the brutal police lieutenant (DCI Hunt, played by Phil Glenister in the original British series) in the short-lived American remake of the cult television series *Life on Mars*.
—JAMES M. WELSH

References
Michael Goodwin and Naomi Wise, *On the Edge: The Life and Times of Francis Coppola* (New York: Morrow, 1989); David Thomson, *A Biographical Dictionary of Film*, 3rd ed. (New York: Knopf, 1994).

KENNEDY, WILLIAM JOSEPH (1928–)
American journalist, novelist, and screenplay writer who collaborated with FRANCIS COPPOLA on the screenplay for *THE COTTON CLUB* (1984). Kennedy was born on January 16, 1928, and grew up in Albany, New York, a city he later made famous in his "Albany cycle" of novels. One of the best of these novels, *Ironweed*, was published in 1983 and won the Pulitzer Prize for Fiction in 1984; in 1987 it was then adapted to the screen by the novelist himself, for a film starring JACK NICHOLSON and Meryl Streep, playing lowlife characters attempting to survive hard times during the Great Depression. What Kennedy's writing did for Albany has been compared to what Saul Bellow did for Chicago and what

James Joyce did for his native Dublin. The first novel in the Albany cycle, *Legs* (1975), set during the 1920s and 1930s and telling stories about the fictional Irish American Phelan family, presented a fictional portrait of a Jack "Legs" Diamond, a dancer turned gangster, a story that convinced Francis Coppola to invite Kennedy, who had at the time never written plays, to collaborate with him on the screenplay for *The Cotton Club* (1984). Born and raised in Albany's North End, Kennedy attended Public School No. 20, the Christian Brothers Academy, and then Siena College in Loudonville, New York, before turning to a career in journalism. He worked as a journalist in Albany and in Puerto Rico, where he became managing editor of the *San Juan Star* in 1959, a position he held for two years before he decided to become a full-time, celebrated writer.—JAMES M. WELSH

KILAR, WOJCIECH (1932–)

Symphonic composer, born in Lwow, Poland, in 1932, educated at the Higher School of Music in Katowice, where he studied with piano master W. Markiewiczowna and with composition tutor B. Woytowicz, before going on to Paris to study composition with Nadia Boulanger. Heavily influenced by classical compositions and Polish folk music, he has composed music for European films for over thirty years, working with directors Krzysztof Zanussi and Andrzej Wajda, before working with FRANCIS COPPOLA on *BRAM STOKER'S DRACULA*. Coppola favored Kilar because he wanted the music to underscore the Eastern European atmosphere of Stoker's Gothic romance. —JAMES M. WELSH

KINSKI, NASTASSJA [NASTASSJA AGLAIA NAKSZYNSKI] (1961–)

German-born actress who plays Leila in *ONE FROM THE HEART* (1982), she is the daughter of legendary actor Klaus Kinski (1926–1991) and his second wife, Ruth Brigitte Tocki (1941–?), a former shopgirl turned writer. Klaus Kinski left his wife for another woman when Nastassja was around eight years old. She rarely saw her father after that, and their strained relationship was never reconciled.

Nastassja Kinski's first feature film role came at the age of thirteen, playing a young mute girl in WIM WENDERS's *The Wrong Move* (1975). Since then she has made two other films with Wenders: *Paris, Texas* (1984) alongside HARRY DEAN STANTON, and *Faraway, So Close!* (1993). At the age of fourteen Kinski had a leading role in the German TV movie *Reifenzeugnis*, directed by Wolfgang Petersen (*Das Boot*), playing a high school student having an affair with one of her teachers. At age fifteen, already famous, she served three months in a juvenile prison for shoplifting.

Kinski's breakthrough motion picture role came in 1979, with Roman Polanski's *Tess*, adapted from Thomas Hardy's *Tess of the d'Urbervilles* (1891), a novel introduced to the director by his late wife, Sharon Tate. In order to improve Kinski's English and soften her accent, Polanski sent her to study for six months at LEE STRASBERG's studio. "[Polanski] took a lot of time, two years," she told the *Guardian*, "preparing me for that film. . . . He was strict with me, but in a good way. He made me feel smart, that I could do things." Some sources report a long romantic involvement between Kinski and Polanski, but the actress denies such a relationship. For her work in *Tess*, Kinski was awarded a Golden Globe as "Best New Star of the Year."

In 1981, she was the subject of a famous still photograph by Richard Avedon, "Nastassja Kinski and the Serpent," in which she appears nude except for a python draped suggestively around her body. Avedon's photo sold widely as a poster, cementing Kinski's status as a sex symbol of the 1980s.

She made her first American film appearances in 1982, with FRANCIS FORD COPPOLA's *One from the Heart* and Paul Schrader's remake of *Cat People*, which also starred Malcolm McDowell.

Kinski was married to Egyptian filmmaker Ibrahim Moussa for eight years, and they have two children together. She left him in 1991 for legendary music producer Quincy Jones, who is the father of her third child.

During Kinski's first pregnancy in 1984, she went into semiretirement from acting, but she has continued to appear in films and on television, both in the United States and in Europe. Her other screen credits include such notable films as the Taviani brothers' *The Sun Also Shines at Night* (1990), Lina Wertmüller's *As Long as It's Love* (1989), and David Lynch's *Inland Empire* (2006).—RODNEY HILL

References

"Biography for Nastassja Kinski," Turner Classic Movies Database, www.tcm.com/tcmdb/participant.jsp?spid=351350&apid=0; Tom Gliatto, et al., "One Night Stand," *People Weekly*, November 17, 1997, 22; Suzie Mackenzie, "Daddy's Girl," *Guardian*, July 3, 1999, www.guardian.co.uk.

KIRBY, BRUNO (1949–2006)

Bruno Giovanni Quilaciolu was born in New York City April 28, 1949. The date was also his father's birthday, a coincidence for which the son attributed his special closeness with his actor father, Bruce Kirby (*The Late Late Show*). Following his first film work in *The Young Graduates* (1971), Bruno Kirby's career took off with his auspicious casting in the pilot of the TV series, *M*A*S*H* (1972). Within two years, his young career reached a pinnacle opportunity. After *The Harrad Experiment* and

Cinderella Liberty (both 1973), Kirby next worked with FRANCIS FORD COPPOLA and ROBERT DE NIRO in *THE GODFATHER: PART II* (1974), playing the young Peter Clemenza, the main influence upon Vito Corleone (De Niro) to contest the corrupt neighborhood boss and begin his rise to power.

As strong as his presentation of young Clemenza was, though, Kirby did not have another significant role until playing Albert Brooks's film editor buddy in *Modern Romance* (1981). Although the film is Brooks's from start to finish, Kirby's tone-perfect, Quaalude-providing straight man, skewering the Hollywood stereotype, confirms his own comic talent. Director Rob Reiner used Kirby's subtle comedic talent in casting him as a limousine driver in *This Is Spinal Tap* (1984). The character of the Frank Sinatra aficionado who could not communicate with the "hip" band was a perfect fit for Kirby.

In the mid-1980s, Kirby's career continued upward with modest films (*Birdy* 1984) and working with Barry Levinson (*Tin Men* 1984). He and Levinson reunited with *Good Morning, Vietnam* (1984), starring ROBIN WILLIAMS, and would work together again in 1995 on Levinson's television series *Homicide: Life on the Streets* and in the film *Sleepers* (1996). But it was the success of *Vietnam* that brought Kirby back to Reiner with his next important role, again as a supporting buddy, in *When Harry Met Sally* (1989). From that high point, his career scored two more hits—*The Freshman* (1990), a charming send-up of the *Godfather* films, and *City Slickers* (1991).

During this time, Kirby also did television work, most notably nine episodes on the comedy series *It's Garry Shandling's Show* (1989–1990). He would reprise his work with Garry Shandling in five episodes of Shandling's next series *The Larry Sanders Show* (1993–1998). But his talent played equally well in comedy or drama. The mid-1990s brought him dramatic roles with Leonardo DiCaprio (*The Basketball Diaries* 1995) and AL PACINO (*Donnie Brasco* 1997). As with many other modern actors, Kirby had his turn in animation (*Stuart Little* 1999), a television movie (as prosecutor Vincent Bugliosi in *Helter Skelter* 2004), and an impressive one-time guest star appearance (as a producer on *Entourage* 2006).

On April 25, 1995, Kirby's fans enjoyed a unique look into his career and family history when he appeared as a guest on Tom Snyder's *The Late Late Show*. He recalled how his actor-father would come home after midnight, awaken him, bundle him up, and take him to an all-night movie theatre. He also shared a memory of his mother, and her connection to his first meeting Elvis Presley, when Kirby worked as an usher in a theatre.

Kirby passed away from leukemia on August 14, 2006, less than three weeks after he had been diagnosed. His final appearance is in a scene on Garry Shandling's DVD collection, *Not Just the Best of The Larry Sanders Show*. After having appeared on earlier episodes of *The Larry Sanders Show*, Kirby had been "bumped" from the lineup of Sanders's final show, and Shandling gave him the spot of honor, at the end of the DVD-extra documentary "The Making of The Larry Sanders Show." Kirby arrives in the studio to discuss his hosting the documentary, but an embarrassed Shandling tells him that Greg Kinnear has hosted the feature in his place. Kirby acts mortified and angry at being "bumped from a DVD" and storms out, with a freeze-frame on the stage curtain he races past, yelling, "Lose my number!" Seconds later, a slide, bearing Shandling's remarks, appears onscreen: "My good friend Bruno Kirby unexpectedly passed away 9 weeks after we shot this scene. This was the last work he did. He was a genius, and a kind, giving man. I wish you all could have met him. I will miss him dearly."—THOMAS CLANCY

References

Not Just the Best of The Larry Sanders Show, Sony Pictures Television, 4-Disc DVD Set, 2007; *The Late Late Show* with Tom Snyder, CBS Television, April 25, 1995.

KOYAANISQATSI (1982)

DIRECTOR: Godfrey Reggio. WRITERS: Ron Fricke, Michael Hoenig, Godfrey Reggio, and Alton Walpole. PRODUCER: Godfrey Reggio. EXECUTIVE PRODUCER: Francis Ford Coppola. ASSOCIATE PRODUCERS: Mel Lawrence, Roger McNew, T. Michael Powers, Lawrence Taub, and Alton Walpole. CINEMATOGRAPHY: Ron Fricke. EDITING: Ron Fricke and Alton Walpole. ORIGINAL MUSIC: Philip Glass.
RUNNING TIME: 86 minutes.
RELEASED THROUGH: Metro Goldwyn Mayer and Francis Ford Coppola Presents.
PREMIERE: New York Film Festival October 4, 1982. U.S. THEATRICAL RELEASE: September 14, 1983.
DVD: MGM.

"It was like looking at the world for the first time."

—Composer Philip Glass

Director Godfrey Reggio's first film is a documentary of sorts, but one that uses compelling, mesmerizing images and music instead of narrative. Drawing upon the Hopi term meaning "life out of balance," the film is an eighty-six-minute work of art that informs us of our world's transformation from natural harmony to technological blight—although a similarly striking beauty is found in both. Reggio's purpose was to create a film that was "meant to provoke . . . to offer an *experience* rather than an idea or information or a story . . . fundamentally, to stir up enough to actually . . . to create an experience of the subject. It is up to the viewer to take for herself what that means." The result is a Rorschach-like mirror that is at first confusing but ultimately stunning.

The film opens with somber organ music, the title appearing slowly from top to bottom, red letters against black background, and bass voices chanting the Hopi word *koyaanisqatsi* (*koyaanis*—disorganized, chaotic, crazy; *qatsi*—way of life), as an Anasazi (the Hopi ancestors) cave drawing comes into view—a famous grouping of figures that some believe might suggest extraterrestrial contacts within their culture. The tallest tube-shaped figure in the drawing is distinctly different from the others. Are there flames or exhaust at the bottom? Does the top have two large eyes, or is it a helmet? We are left guessing its meaning and significance. This ancient scene transforms, with the somber music and chanting still underlying, into the black and red clouds of a massive explosive force, launching a rocket, shown rising in slow motion. Where, and when, are we? Have we spanned centuries of time, the history of the human race and technology, with one dissolve?

This prologue then seems to carry us back; we are flying over a barren landscape, somewhere in the desert. The sun is low; this could be a prehuman dawn. Whenever it is, the scene is of breathtaking natural beauty, undisturbed, stark, and awesome in its harmony of earth and sky formations. Natural forces and processes occur through slow-motion and fast-motion photography. The music changes and accelerates as we swoop low over land and water and high above roiling clouds.

At about the twenty-minute mark, different explosions, slow-motion dirt explosions, and an earth-moving truck belching black smoke announce the rise of the machine age, of electrification, assembly lines, factories, refineries, dams, atom bomb tests, soaring skyscrapers, and nuclear

energy plants next to beach sunbathers. The subject of the film has changed, but Glass's score and Ron Fricke's photography continue their hypnotic pace. Now we are swept along with moving images of technology, seeming to have its own natural pulse and rhythm. The dance of traffic movement on multilane highways, seen dizzyingly from above, becomes a terrible ballet of war armaments, followed by abandoned cityscapes and scenes of urban poverty, followed by buildings being brought down.

In the DVD extra features, Reggio comments on his stance vis-à-vis technology in the film: "So it's not the effect of [technology], it's that everything exists within [technology]. It's not that we *use* technology; we *live* technology. Technology has become as ubiquitous as the air we breathe, so we're no longer conscious of its presence." Although the images suggest that we are dehumanized by technology, made into automatons, slaves to our machines and routines, perhaps the poetic beauty of our cohabitation with technology is the point.

Another transition in the film reminds us of that beauty, again with startling images. We are now viewing the turmoil of a crowded subway station, several hundred bodies seen from above, automatically jockeying for space and moving forward at many times normal speed, then we cut to crowded sidewalks with tides of people moving in slow motion, and then back to traffic again, now at night and sped up, with headlights and taillights appearing as elongated streams of color, pulsing to Glass's electronic score accompanied by an etheric choir. The pace only quickens from here; traffic scenes are followed by daytime traffic *and* crowds interweaving through the city streets and by people rushing through Grand Central Station.

The pattern of quickly intercutting scenes of people-traffic-TV broadcast images-more people repeats and accelerates until finally a return point comes near the end of the film. Just as we started with a rocket launch after the opening title screen and men's voices begin chanting "Koyaanisqatsi," the same happens now, except this time the rocket explodes after take-off and a few seconds of flight. The camera follows its burning, falling, spinning apex in slow motion until a freeze-frame dissolves into another Anasazi cave drawing. Now, all the figures are in tube-like shapes, as only the tallest was before, and some of them appear to float in the air. The film ends with a screen of director Reggio's definitions of the term *koyaanisqatsi* and a screen of Hopi predictions that were sung in the film.

Reggio followed *Koyaanisqatsi* with two films to complete his trilogy: *Powaqqatsi* ("Life in Transformation," 1988), and *Naqoyqatsi* ("Life as War," 2002).
—THOMAS CLANCY

Reference

"Essence of Life," Special feature on *Koyaanisqatsi* DVD, Metro Goldwyn Mayer Home Entertainment, 2002.

L

LANDAU, MARTIN (1928–)

Trained stage actor and Hollywood regular who plays Abe Karatz (and the voice of Walter Winchell) in FRANCIS COPPOLA's *TUCKER: THE MAN AND HIS DREAM*. Landau imagined Karatz, a character drawn from real life, as being a lonely, New York Jew, an amiable hustler who becomes PRESTON TUCKER's partner, advisor, friend, and ally in battling the government and Detroit's Big Three. "In size and dimension, it's probably the best role I've had since *Cleopatra*, and my ten best scenes in *Cleopatra* weren't even in the movie," Landau told the *New York Times* (August 7, 1988): "This role allowed me *to act*. I loved it." Landau added, "Abe grows radically during the film; it allowed me to create a character with many dimensions, one who is cold and rather callous at the beginning and grows into a warm, feeling and caring human being." Born in Brooklyn, New York, on June 20, 1928, Landau attended James Madison High School and the Pratt Institute before getting a job at the age of seventeen at the New York *Daily News*, where he worked for five years as an editorial artist and cartoonist and helping Gus Edson produce his comic strip, *The Gumps*. In 1955 he auditioned for admission to the Actors Studio and was one of two applicants admitted. Chosen to join the Actors Studio, Landau was trained by LEE STRASBERG, Elia Kazan, and Harold Clurman. Landau eventually became an executive director of the Actors Studio, along with directors Mark Rydell and Sydney Pollack. Landau played one of the major villains in Alfred Hitchcock's *North by Northwest* who fights Cary Grant on the "face" (or faces) of Mount Rushmore, and was also wonderfully effective as Judah Rosenthal, a seriously conflicted character in Woody Allen's *Crimes and Misdemeanors* (1989); but he was probably best known to the general public for his starring role on the hit television series *Mission Impossible* (1966–1969) with his wife, the actress Barbara Bain. Landau was apparently grateful to Coppola and producer (and former brilliant casting director) FRED ROOS for the opportunity to play Abe Karatz. "I've spent a lot of time playing roles that didn't really challenge me," Landau told the *New York Times*. "You want roles that have dimension. The role of Abe gave me that." Landau was nominated for an Academy Award for Best Actor in a Supporting Role for *Tucker: The Man and His Dream*, and won the Golden Globe Award.
—JAMES M. WELSH

Reference

Robert Lindsey, "Martin Landau Rolls Up in a New Vehicle," *New York Times*, August 7, 1988, sec. 2: 1, 19.

LANE, DIANE (1965–)

Actress who appeared repeatedly in films by FRANCIS COPPOLA, playing Cherry Valance in *THE OUTSIDERS* (1983), Patty in *RUMBLE FISH* (1983), Vera Cicero in *THE COTTON CLUB* (1984), and Karen Powell in *JACK* (1996). Born into theatre, her father was New York drama coach Burt Lane. She played the role of Medea's daughter in Andrei Serban's theatrical production of that classic play at La Mama Experimental Theatre and stayed with that company for the next five years. She later appeared in the Joseph Papp production of *Agamemnon* and the Lincoln Center production of *The Cherry Orchard*. Her appearance in Liz Swado's Public Theatre production of *Runaways* led to her motion picture debut with director George Roy Hill in *A Little Romance* (1979), alongside Sir Laurence Olivier. Years later after *The Outsiders* and *Rumble Fish*, she costarred again with MATT DILLON and Tommy Lee Jones in *The Big Town* (1987). In 1988 Lane married actor Christopher Lambert, whom she had met at the age of nineteen and with whom she costarred in *Knight Moves* (1992); a year after the birth of a daughter, Eleanor, they divorced in 1994; ten years later, she married the actor Josh Brolin. Lane's later films included *The Perfect Storm* (2000), with George Clooney, and two with the actor RICHARD GERE, *Unfaithful*, which earned a Best Actress Academy Award nomination for 2002, and *Nights in Rodanthe* (2008). —JAMES M. WELSH

LEICHTLING, JERRY (1948–)

Screenwriter for FRANCIS COPPOLA's *PEGGY SUE GOT MARRIED* (1986), a melancholy but entertaining comedy that helped to restore the director's box office standing. In the plot (coscripted with Arlene Sarner), forty-three-year-old Peggy Sue (KATHLEEN TURNER) loses consciousness at her twenty-fifth high school

class reunion and finds herself transported back to the 1960s in her high school prime, giving her a chance to not only reenact but to revise and emend her teenage decisions. *Variety* judged the picture a "marked improvement over anything else" director Francis Coppola had done lately and predicted that it was "sure to bring many disenchanted Coppola fans back to the theatre." Though the film appears to be a pleasantly "sentimental, lighthearted, adult version" of *Back to the Future*, in fact both films were in production at the same time. In the words of the *Variety* review, "First-time scriptwriters Jerry Leichtling and Arlene Sarner have written a nice mix of sap and sass for Peggy Sue's character, a melancholy mother of two facing divorce who gets all dolled up in her 1950s-style ball gown to make a splash at her 25th high school reunion." Leichtling, also identified as a journalist, speechwriter, political consultant, and playwright, grew up in New York and graduated from Martin Van Buren High School in Queens Village, New York. His other screenwriting credits include director Tony Richardson's last film, *Blue Sky* (1994), which he coscripted with Arlene Sarner and Rama Laurie Stagner, the film's associate producer, who wrote the original story as a semiautobiographical account of her own parents' turbulent relationship and her father's forced institutionalization by the U.S. Army.—JAMES M. WELSH

"LIFE WITHOUT ZOE" (episode in *New York Stories*) (1989)

DIRECTOR: Francis Ford Coppola. SCREENPLAY: Francis Ford Coppola, Sofia Coppola. SEGMENT PRODUCERS: Fred Roos and Fred Fuchs for Touchstone Pictures Buena Vista. PHOTOGRAPHY: Vittorio Storaro. EDITING: Barry Malkin. MUSIC: Carmine Coppola. PRODUCTION DESIGN: Dean Tavoularis. ART DIRECTION: Speed

Hopkins. Costume Design: Sofia Coppola.
Sound Recording: Frank Graziadei.
Cast: Heather McComb (Zoe), Talia Shire
(Charlotte), Gia Coppola (Baby Zoe),
Giancarlo Giannini (Claudio), Paul Her-
man (Clifford, the Doorman), James
Keane (Jimmy), Don Novello (Hec-
tor), Bill Moor (Mr. Lilly), Tom Mard-
irosian (Hasid), Jenny Bichols (Lundy),
Gina Scianni (Devo), Diane Lin Cosman
(Margit), Selim Tlili (Abu), Robin Wood-
Chapelle (Gel), Celia Nestell (Hillry),
Alexdra Becker (Andrea), Adrien Brody
(Mel), Michael Higgins, Chris Elliott
(Robbers), Thelma Carpenter (Maid),
Carmine Coppola (Street Musician),
Carole Bouquet (Princess Soroya), Jo Jo
Starbuck (Ice Skater).
Premiere: February 26, 1989.
Running Time: 34 minutes (of 124 total).
Technicolor.
DVD: Touchstone Pictures.

"Life without Zoe" is FRANCIS COPPO-
LA's segment in the omnibus film *NEW
YORK STORIES*, a fantasy concerning the
spoiled but somehow endearing twelve-
year-old daughter of a celebrity father and
a jet-setting mother. The short film developed into a family project: seventeen-year-
old SOFIA COPPOLA not only cowrote
the screenplay with her father, but she also
designed the costumes. Her aunt, TALIA
SHIRE (from the *GODFATHER* films)
would have a featured role, and her grandfather, CARMINE COPPOLA, composed
the score. In addition, some old hands
from other Coppola films were recruited:
production designer DEAN TAVOULARIS,
editor BARRY MALKIN, and cinematographer VITTORIO STORARO. The director
of photography, in tandem with Coppola,
chose a luscious color palette to approxi-
mate the world of luxury the film depicts.

Zoe (Heather McComb) points out,
"My parents named me Zoe because Zoe
means life in Greek." Zoe, of course, was

associated in Coppola's mind with the
name of his independent film unit, AMERI-
CAN ZOETROPE, since Zoetrope means in
Greek "the movement of life," a reference
to primitive motion pictures.

Zoe's father, Claudio Montez
(GIANCARLO GIANNINI) is a renowned
flautist, who frequently goes on concert
tours around the world and is seldom home.
Claudio is separated from Zoe's mother,
Charlotte (Talia Shire), a fashion photographer who likewise travels a lot. Zoe, who is
sophisticated beyond her years, lives at the
Sherry-Netherland Hotel where Hector, the
family butler (DON NOVELLO), pampers
her in her parents' absence. Zoe attends an
exclusive private school, but yearns to see
her parents reunited so that they can form
a family once more (another reference to
Coppola's constant theme).

In June 1988 Coppola transported the
Silverfish, his minibus trailer, complete
with its TV monitors and other audiovi-
sual accessories, to New York, where he
would film "Life without Zoe" on location
in Manhattan. The ritzy Apthorp apartment building on the Upper West Side was
employed for some scenes.

Zoe at one point meets a mysterious, beautiful Arab princess, the wife of a
wealthy sheik, who had given one of her
priceless earrings to Claudio as a token of
her esteem for his musical virtuosity. On
second thought she fears that her jealous
husband might suspect that she is romantically involved with Claudio, so she wants
to get the earring back. Because Claudio is
away, the princess hopes Zoe can retrieve
the jewel from the hotel safe where Claudio has placed it for safekeeping. Zoe thus
becomes involved in a bogus robbery of the
safe when some of the princess's retainers
"steal" the earring, which Zoe then smug-
gles back to the princess.

When her father returns from his
travels, Zoe proudly explains what she has

done. She obviously wants to impress her dad favorably. He is indeed relieved that the precious earring has been returned to the princess—since Charlotte might have otherwise thought that the gift of the earring betokened that there was something between Claudio and the princess. "This is the wrong time for a misunderstanding between your mother and me," he tells Zoe, who he knows wants her parents to reconcile. "Little Miss Fixit" eventually decides to cement the reconciliation between her parents by arranging to fly to Greece with Charlotte to attend Claudio's concert at the Acropolis in Athens. So the little film ends with a family reunion.

Editor Barry Malkin characterizes "Life without Zoe" as a "contemporary fairy tale," a kind of fable out of the Arabian Nights, in which the Arab princess is a damsel in distress saved by the timely intervention of an imaginative young girl. But Malkin was dissatisfied with the way the segment turned out. At the behest of the Disney organization, the parent company of Touchstone, "we abbreviated the episode and removed some material from the film. I was sorry that a number of things wound up on the cutting room floor. And I know Francis feels that way too."

Indeed he does. Coppola emphasizes that the script had more character development, especially in terms of Zoe's relationship with her father. She finds it burdensome to cope with a famous father who is emotionally unavailable to her. The Disney executives wanted the episode to be a lightweight anecdote, not a character study. "In an attempt to make the story delightful and charming," Coppola concludes, this material was largely eliminated.

It is not surprising, therefore, that when *New York Stories* was released on February 26, 1989, some reviewers found "Life without Zoe" woefully rushed and bursting with loose ends and unfulfilled promises. Yet it is still a visually arresting, engaging rite-of-passage comedy. Critic Stuart Klawans speculated in the *Nation* (March 27, 1989) that the "spoiled but magical Zoe shares her name with the studio Coppola founded and then ran into the ground, 'Zoetrope,'" interpreting the film as "an allegory about Coppola's loss of the studio," with "the spendthrift little girl" representing the studio, while "the fatally talented but absent father represents Coppola."—Gene D. Phillips

References

David Breskin, *Inner Voices: Filmmakers in Conversation*, rev. ed. (New York: Da Capo, 1997); Stuart Klawans, "*New York Stories*," *Nation*, March 27, 1989, 23; Robert Lindsey, "Promises to Keep," *New York Times Magazine*, July 28, 1988, 23–27; Gabriella Oldham, *First Cut: Conversations with Film Editors* (Los Angeles: University of California Press, 1995).

LOST IN TRANSLATION (2003)

Director: Sofia Coppola. Screenplay: Sofia Coppola. Producers: Sofia Coppola and Ross Katz. Executive Producers: Francis Ford Coppola and Fred Roos. Associate Producer: Mitch Glazer. Line Producers: Callum Greene and Kiyoshi Inoue. Photography: Lance Acord. Editing: Sarah Flack. Music: Kevin Shields. Production Design: K. K. Barrett and Anne Ross.

Cast: Scarlett Johansson (Charlotte), Bill Murray (Bob), Akiko Takeshita (Mrs. Kawasaki), Kazuyoshi Minamimagoe (Press Agent), Giovanni Ribisi (John), Anna Faris (Kelly).

Running Time: 102 minutes. Color.

Released through: Focus Features. Premiere: August 23, 2003 (Telluride Film Festival).

Academy Awards: Best Original Screenplay.

DVD: Universal Studios.

Bob Harris (Bill Murray) and Charlotte (Scarlett Johansson) are two Americans in Tokyo. Bob is a movie star in town to shoot a whiskey commercial, while Charlotte is a young woman tagging along with her workaholic photographer husband (Giovanni Ribisi). Unable to sleep, Bob and Charlotte cross paths one night in the luxury hotel bar. This chance meeting soon becomes a surprising friendship. Charlotte and Bob venture through Tokyo, having often hilarious encounters with its citizens, and ultimately discover a new belief in life's possibilities.

For this her second feature film, SOFIA COPPOLA began the scripting process in 2000, shot the film in Japan starting in the fall of 2002, and cast Bill Murray and Scarlett Johansson to star. Thanks to ICM agent Bart Walker's presales of the Japanese, French, and Italian rights, Coppola was able to complete the production and postproduction phases before her American distributor, Focus Features, saw any of the film—thus maintaining an unusual level of control for a filmmaker at such an early stage in her career. A gradual, platform release to U.S. theatres in the fall of 2003, supported by careful attention to marketing and publicity strategies, resulted in a steadily building box office return, which only improved after the film's wider release in January 2004. With a production budget of less than $5 million, the film ended up grossing some $44.5 million.

On top of its surprising success at the box office, Lost in Translation turned out to be rather highly acclaimed. The film earned five Golden Globe nominations, four Oscar nominations (winning for Best Original Screenplay), three BAFTA Film Awards, for Best Editing, Best Actor, and Best Actress; four Independent Spirit Awards, honoring films made for under $15 million, winning for Best Actor, Best Screenplay, Best Director, and Best Film; the French César

for Best Foreign Film; and two awards at Venice, one for Sofia Coppola and one for Scarlett Johannson.

Reacting to the Golden Globe nominations for his daughter's second feature film, executive producer FRANCIS FORD COPPOLA told Variety: "This beautiful slip of a girl—she's only 31—is holding up the family name in the company of such wonderful people. She's started to have a distinct voice. You can see her style. She wrote it out of her heart." He continued with a reminder that Lost in Translation contains "no violence or sex—just pure human feelings."

Critical reviews tended to note the excellent performances, deft direction, and writing. Peter Rainier in New York magazine, for instance, writes: "Bill Murray has become an actor of extraordinary range. [Sofia Coppola] accomplishes the difficult feat of showing people being bored out of their skulls in such a way that we are never bored watching them. She does this by creating such empathy for Bob and Charlotte that our identification with them is almost total. Coppola has hit on a metaphor for modern alienation that is so mundane it's funny."

Roger Ebert similarly raved: "I think that we're looking at an Academy Award nomination here, maybe for both of them. This is certainly one of the year's best movies. One thing I especially admired was the way Bill Murray dials down his gift for comedy, and finds just the right tired and subdued note. Any comedian can be really funny, but it takes a certain genius to be just a little funny, kind of quietly funny, kind of wearily funny. It's quite a movie."

Even the great novelist Kurt Vonnegut weighed in, providing this blurb for the film's publicity: "Lost In Translation is my favorite film this year. I loved it."

Shortly after the film's release, Sofia Coppola was honored at the annual "Work in Progress" benefit hosted by the Museum of Modern Art, an event intended to recognize an emerging cinema artist possessing a distinct directorial voice and creative vision. In conjunction with the honors, MoMA also acquired prints of *Lost in Translation* and *THE VIRGIN SUICIDES* for its permanent film collection.—RODNEY HILL/ JAMES M. WELSH

References
Army Archerd, "Hollywood Family Celebrating," *Variety*, December 22, 2003, www.variety.com; Focus Features, *Lost in Translation*, official website, http://www.filminfocus.com/focusfeatures/film/lost_in_translation/overview; Dana Harris, "New Film Legends of the Fall," *Variety*, October 12, 2003, www.variety.com; David Rooney, "Museum Hails 'Lost' Helmer Coppola," *Variety*, December 18, 2003, www.variety.com.

LOWE, ROB (1964–)
American actor and "Brat Pack" star who played "Sodapop" Curtis, the brother of C. THOMAS HOWELL and PATRICK SWAYZE, in FRANCIS COPPOLA's *THE OUTSIDERS* (1983). Robert Helper Lowe was born in Charlottesville, Virginia, March 17, 1964, the son of trial lawyer Charles Lowe and his wife, Barbara, the eldest of three children. Raised in Dayton, Ohio, Rob Lowe's parents divorced and his mother remarried and moved to Malibu, California, when her son was twelve years old. Together with his younger brother, Chad, Rob went to Santa Monica High School with EMILIO ESTEVEZ and CHARLIE SHEEN, Sean and CHRISTOPHER PENN, and Robert Downey Jr. Rob Lowe started his acting career early in summer stock productions and in two afterschool television specials, "Schoolboy Father" and the Emmy Award–winning "A Matter of Time." He also appeared in the series *A New Kind of Family* and with Gena Rowlands in the television movie *Thursday's Child* (1983), a role that earned the nineteen-year-old a

Golden Globe nomination for Best Actor in a TV Movie or Miniseries. He would later earn a second nomination for his portrayal of a twenty-one-year-old mentally challenged Texan in *Square Dance* (1987). *The Outsiders* marked his feature film debut in 1983, and he went on to star as Jodie Foster's brother in *The Hotel New Hampshire* (1984), adapted from John Irving's novel and directed by Tony Richardson. Other roles followed: In 1985 he starred along with Emilio Estevez in Joel Schumacher's *St. Elmo's Fire* and the following year he was featured in *About Last Night . . .* (1986). Lowe was later successful for his portrayal of Sam Seaborn, originally considered the lead character of *The West Wing* (1999–2003), earning an Emmy and two Golden Globe nominations for Best Actor in a Drama Series.—JAMES M. WELSH

LUCAS, GEORGE (1944–)
Executive producer of *TUCKER: THE MAN AND HIS DREAM*; associate producer, *THE RAIN PEOPLE*, and early Hollywood friend and colleague of FRANCIS COPPOLA. Lucas was born in Modesto, California, and attended Modesto Junior College before enrolling at the USC film school, where he made several short films, including *THX 1138*, which won first prize at the National Student Film Festival. Lucas won a Warner Bros. scholarship in 1968 enabling him to observe Coppola's direction of *FINIAN'S RAINBOW*, and Lucas advanced from Polaroid cameraman to film editor by the time Coppola invited Lucas to work as his assistant on his road movie *The Rain People* in 1969. Lucas also made a documentary about the making of that film.

Lucas persuaded Coppola to move to San Francisco in order to establish AMERICAN ZOETROPE, an independent film production company with Coppola as major shareholder and Lucas as vice president. The first American Zoetrope project was a full-length version of *THX 1138*, produced by Coppola and directed by Lucas. The same team made *AMERICAN GRAFFITI*, which Lucas directed in 1973, a surprise hit that earned five Academy Award nominations, including cowriting, direction, and Best Picture. In 1976 Lucas wrote and directed *Star Wars*, following up as producer of its sequels, *The Empire Strikes Back* and *The Return of the Jedi*. Lucas and Coppola worked as executive producers of *KAGEMUSHA*, enabling the celebrated Japanese director Akira Kurosawa to finance, produce, and distribute his film. Lucas was also the executive producer and cowriter of *Raiders of the Lost Ark*, directed by Steven Spielberg, which started the Indiana Jones series of adventure films and won five Academy Awards. Lucas was producer of the Disney short film *CAPTAIN EO*, directed by Coppola. Lucas and Coppola were also executive producers of *Mishima*, a film directed by Paul Schrader about the life and writings of Yukio Mishima. When the industry later blackballed Zoetrope, Lucas left in 1971 to start Lucasfilm, Ltd.

Despite the man's tremendous popular success, Lucas, long considered America's master mythmaker, has had trouble telling a coherent story, according to critic Ann Hornaday, since his plots are driven by spectacle, not character. If *THX 1138* flopped in 1971, it's because Lucas was "more interested in creating effects and exploring intellectual notions of totalitarianism and free will than deepening character or connecting with the audience." ROBERT DUVALL's THX is a "singularly unengaging hero" because Lucas is "content to let his characters function as ideas. He doesn't do flesh and blood." With *Star Wars*, Lucas's "weakness became his greatest strength. Who needed story when the audience would be satisfied with spectacle?" According to Peter Biskind, Lucas was "the only New Hollywood director

who succeeded in establishing his financial independence from Hollywood." But what did George Lucas achieve with all that independence? JOHN MILIUS, speaking of Lucas and Coppola for the book *Easy Riders, Raging Bulls* (p. 424), told Peter Biskind "Francis really tried to do things with his power. He made movies with WIM WENDERS, produced *THE BLACK STALLION*, produced George Lucas. George built Lucasland up there, his own private little duchy—which was producing what? A bunch of pap." Speaking with Biskind Coppola himself was critical of Lucas (p.381): "I'm the only one of his friends who never had a piece of *Star Wars*. Although I was the one whom he would talk to about it. I helped him, but clearly, once he went on, he went on. It was clear to me he just wanted his own show. I had brought him along with me everywhere I went, but he didn't bring me along with him."

But there may be two sides to this story and friendship, since George Lucas helped Coppola to bankroll the *Tucker* project, after four major studios had rejected it. Coppola told the *Washington Post* that it was difficult for him to approach Lucas, his former apprentice, for help: "It was a role-reversal, like going to a very successful and busy younger brother. I didn't want George to feel I was intruding, trying to capitalize on his success." Lucas responded: "I went through the same thing with Francis. After *THX-1138* [produced by Coppola in 1971] I said, 'I'm not going to live under your shadow. I'm going to be my own man.' So I went off on my own and couldn't get [*American Graffiti*] off the ground. It was embarrassing to come back and say, 'Gee, Francis, I need your help.'" Interviewed with Coppola at the time of *Tucker*'s release, Lucas told the *Washington Post*: "All our movies are Tuckers. They overcame a lot of opposition to get made." And for that both

Lucas *and* Coppola deserve a whole lot of credit.—James M. Welsh

References

Peter Biskind, *Easy Riders, Raging Bulls* (New York: Simon & Schuster, 1998); Ann Hornaday, "The Lord of the Light Side," *Washington Post*, August 10, 2008, M1, M5; Donna Rosenthal, "Movie Mavericks Lucas & Coppola, Together Again," *Washington Post*, August 7, 1988, G1–G3.

LUDDY, TOM (N.D.)

Tom Luddy, director and programmer of the Pacific Film Archives of the University of California Art Museum at Berkeley, and also one of the organizers of the Telluride Film Festival in Colorado, was an associate of FRANCIS COPPOLA since 1979 and went on to serve as director of special projects at AMERICAN ZOETROPE. Coppola first met Luddy when he was editing *THE GODFATHER: PART II.* The first of Luddy's "special" projects was the revival of the pioneering French director ABEL GANCE's epic *Napoleon* (1927). The 1972 San Francisco Film Festival's "Homage to Abel Gance," which featured the four-hour 1972 Gance-Lelouch *Napoleon* remake entitled *Bonaparte and the Revolution*, first sparked a renewed interest in Gance on the West Coast. Later that year KEVIN BROWN-LOW's restored *Napoleon* was shown at the Avenue Theatre in San Francisco, with Robert Vaughn playing a portion of Arthur Honegger's original score on the Wurlitzer. Luddy attended the San Francisco screening and suggested to Coppola that Zoetrope should distribute Brownlow's restoration of *Napoleon.* Coppola was receptive to this suggestion and commissioned his father to compose a full orchestral score. In January of 1981 Zoetrope, with the sponsorship of the Film Society of Lincoln Center and the Museum of Modern Art scheduled the *Napoleon* spectacle for a three-day run at the Radio City Music Hall, a 6,000-seat sell-out at $25 a ticket for the premiere on January 23. The screening was sensational, and the run was extended; the fifty-year-old film grossed $800,000 over eight screenings, and was then circulated with live orchestration to other major American cities. Other special projects included the seven-hour *Our Hitler—A Film from Germany*, directed by Hans-Jürgen Syberberg; sponsorship of Godfrey Reggio's *KOYAANISQATSI*; and two collaborations with French director Jean-Luc Godard: *Every Man for Himself* and *Passion.* Luddy also worked as coproducer with Fred Fuchs and FRED ROOS on American Zoetrope productions such as *The Secret Garden*, directed by Agnieszka Holland in 1993.—James M. Welsh

M

MACCHIO, RALPH [GEORGE] (1961–)

Juvenile Italian American actor who plays Johnny Cade in *THE OUTSIDERS* (1983). Ralph George Macchio was born in Huntington, Long Island, on November 4, 1961, the son of Ralph and Rosalie Macchio, and attended Half Hollow Hills High School West. Famous for his youthful good looks, he was discovered by a talent scout and appeared in television commercials at an early age. In 1980, according to James Cameron-Wilson, Macchio "beat out 2,000 candidates for the part of Betty Buckley's troubled nephew Jeremy" in the ABC television series *Eight Is Enough* (1980–1981), kick-starting his acting career. Roles followed in Robert Downey's *Up the Academy* and the television film *Dangerous Company*, in which, with Beau Bridges, he played an "outsider," which led then to his role for the FRANCIS COPPOLA film. He became even more famous the following year, however, when, after playing a juvenile delinquent in *Teachers*, with Nick Nolte, Macchio was chosen to play the lead role in *The Karate Kid* (1984) and its sequels. His character, Daniel LaRusso, coached in the martial arts by the gardener Miyagi (wonderfully played by Noriyuki "Pat" Morita) became an overnight sensation and was brought back time and again in two sequels, *The Karate Kid Part II* (1988) and *The Karate Kid Part III* (1989). Fortune smiled again in 1992, when Ralph Macchio played UCLA student Bill

Gambini in the low-budget comedy hit *My Cousin Vinny*, stuck in Alabama and accused of a crime he did not commit, but saved by his cousin, Brooklyn lawyer Vinny LaGuardia Gambini (brilliantly played by Joe Pesci). Though he outgrew the youthful roles that made him famous, Macchio continued to work in film and television.
—JAMES M. WELSH

Reference

James Cameron-Wilson, *Young Hollywood* (Lanham, MD: Madison Books, 1994).

MALAIMARE, MIHAI JR. (1975–)

Romanian cinematographer who worked with FRANCIS FORD COPPOLA on two films: *YOUTH WITHOUT YOUTH* (2007) and *TETRO* (2009), he is the son of the theatre actor, director, and politician, Mihai Malaimare (b. 1950). Beginning at the age of fifteen, the younger Malaimare recorded family life and made short narrative videos using a camera he had received as a gift. He enrolled in an after-school program for still photography and went on to study cinematography at the Universitatea Nationala de Arta Teatrala si Cinematografica in Bucharest.

While casting for the more than fifty roles in *Youth without Youth*, Coppola decided to use the screen-testing process not only to select his actors but also to select his director of photography. "[E]ach time I shot a test with an actor, I'd use a different photographer," he explained. "They were all fine, but I chose Mihai Malaimare, Jr. The movie was about becoming young again. I liked the fact that Mihai was so young, had a gentle personality, and was tremendously talented."

Coppola wanted to shoot *Youth without Youth* using his own Sony F900 HD camera; but Malaimare's prior feature experience had been on film cameras, so Coppola sent him to Los Angeles for additional training at Sony's facilities there. Although critics overwhelmingly panned *Youth without Youth*, some reviews did praise Malaimare's images, which are dominated by a cool, blue, moonlit look and a golden glow similar to that achieved by GORDON WILLIS in *THE GODFATHER* and its sequels. Malaimare and Coppola worked so well together on *Youth without Youth* that Coppola engaged him on his next project, *Tetro*.

This was to be quite a different challenge, however, as Malaimare explains: "In Argentina, Francis and I were both trying to get our bearings in a foreign country. Finding locations in Romania was easier for me because I was familiar with a lot of places. The production designer and I were always coming up with places that we knew. In contrast, here we had to discover everything and scout out each location. It was a great journey of discovery."

Coppola's decision to shoot *Tetro* primarily in black-and-white was influenced partly by the cinematic "masterworks" that he had discovered during his film-school days. He says, "Mihai and I watched many beautiful films together, studying the styles of *La Notte* [1961] by Michelangelo Antonioni, *Baby Doll* [1956], and *On the Waterfront* [1954] by Elia Kazan. From these films, we settled on a very vivid and contrasted black-and-white look."

While the majority of *Tetro* is shot in black-and-white, color cinematography also serves a couple of important functions in the film, as Malaimare explains: "For the flashback scenes, Francis wanted to try something like Ansochrome [the 1970s 8 mm home-movie film stock]. He was thinking how a memory looks. Certain moments from the past are related to photos or home movies. We thought it would be nice to have this feeling . . . and we reproduced that look in the HD camera. . . . The other big color part is the ballet. Those images were meant to be tributes to [Emeric Pressburger and] Michael Powell's *Tales of Hoffmann* and *The Red Shoes*, so we simulated the Technicolor look [high saturation of the primary colors] in the HD camera."

On working with Malaimare, Coppola says: "I think that he was born to make beautiful cinematic images. I feel very comfortable working with him. Now that we've collaborated on two films, I've begun to ask myself, 'Would Mihai like this?' and if he likes it, then I know that it's good."—RODNEY HILL

References
American Zoetrope, "*Tetro*," official website, www.tetro.com; "Mihai Malaimare Jr.," Internet Encyclopedia of Cinematographers, www.cinematographers.nl/PaginasDoPh/malaimare.htm; Sony Pictures Classics, "*Youth without Youth*," official website, www.sonyclassics.com/youthwithoutyouth/main.html.

MALKIN, BARRY (C. 1940–)
Film editor on several of FRANCIS COPPOLA's films, beginning with *THE RAIN PEOPLE* (1969). Malkin is a very private man who never discusses his personal life. As a result, we do not even know when he was born. The best guess is sometime around 1940.

Barry Malkin was a boyhood acquaintance of Coppola's from Queens. "We lived in the same neighborhood as teenagers," says Malkin, but they had not seen each other for years. Malkin visited fellow editor Aram Avakian while the latter was working on *YOU'RE A BIG BOY NOW*, and he noted that the screenplay bore the name of Francis Ford Coppola. "I used to have a friend when I was a kid named Coppola," he exclaimed. "I wonder if it's the same guy."

When Avakian got around to inquiring if Coppola knew Malkin, he answered, "I knew a guy named Blackie Malkin," which was Malkin's nickname as a youngster. Coppola eventually asked Malkin to edit *Rain People*. "It was my opportunity to edit a class feature film," Malkin states, after working on a forgettable programmer called *Fat Spy* (1966). *Rain People* was being released by a major studio. Coppola and Malkin went on to collaborate on several features thereafter, because Malkin found Coppola an easy director to work with: "For starters, we don't have discussions about which take to use; our tastes are similar, and there is a mutual trust."

The Rain People was made while Coppola, his cast, and crew traveled cross-country in a Dodge mobile home that had been modified to carry the film unit's technical equipment. Malkin edited the film en route on a Steenbeck editing machine. The Steenbeck at which he worked, he recalls, was wedged into the original kitchenette space of the mobile home, which also doubled as the dressing room.

The last two months of shooting were in Nebraska, so Coppola took over an abandoned shoe shop in Ogallala and transformed it into his command post. The production team occupied an empty store, says Malkin. He started a full-scale editing of the footage into a rough cut before the production unit returned to Los Angeles.

Coppola was convinced that making *Rain People* 15,500 miles away from the Hollywood studio "shark pool" was the prototype of how he would like to make movies in the future. He in due course established a production facility, AMERICAN ZOETROPE, with state-of-the-art editing equipment, in San Francisco.

Malkin coedited *THE GODFATHER: PART II* (1974) at American Zoetrope. During a preview in San Diego, Coppola observed that the audience began to fidget noticeably as the movie unspooled. He and his editors therefore had to make some adjustments in the final cut and still meet the studio's target date for the movie's premiere. Barry Malkin, PETER ZINNER, and Richard Marks were the principal film editors. Malkin recalls: "We were working day and night to get the final mix finished. I remember sleeping on the floor of the editing room, just getting catnaps." Malkin says that Coppola made no substantial alterations in the film at this juncture: "it was mostly a lot of tightening up."

Malkin subsequently edited *RUMBLE FISH* (1983). Coppola collaborated closely with Barry Malkin on the edit of the movie. Malkin particularly enjoyed cutting together the rumble scene that occurs near the beginning of the movie when RUSTY JAMES takes on the leader of an opposing gang. The fight comprised eighty-one shots in two minutes of screen time. "It's generally easier to cut . . . a flashy, razzle-dazzle action sequence," explains Malkin, "than it is to edit a dialogue sequence with a lot of characters sitting around a table," which can seem quite static and boring to the viewer.

The following year, Malkin coedited *THE COTTON CLUB* with Robert Lovett—Coppola's movie musical–gangster picture about the renowned Harlem nightspot. Coppola held a private screening of a 140-minute rough cut. The reaction was mildly favorable, but several of the viewers thought the film overlong. Accordingly, Coppola decided that the movie should be edited down close to two hours. He shortened the musical numbers performed by the black entertainers at the Cotton Club and left the main plot involving the gangsters fairly intact.

Barry Malkin, for one, was not in harmony with this decision. "*The Cotton Club* was a film that got compressed to its detriment," he contends. "Right from the very beginning, there's a dance piece involving the Cotton Club girls, and it's intercut with the titles." Originally this dance routine, shot in smoky color, was a self-contained sequence, and some of it was lost when it was combined with the opening credits, which are in black-and-white. This number displayed the sassy, high-kicking chorines as they paraded across the screen, accompanied by the original recording of Duke Ellington's band playing "The Mooche," all wailing clarinets and sultry strings. "I preferred it when it was . . . a separate sequence," Malkin concludes.

The studio sponsored three sneak previews of the picture. There was no indication in the preview cards from these advance screenings that the audience wanted more of the performers at the Cotton Club. On the contrary, the younger members of the preview audiences consistently complained that there was too much tap dancing. As a result, the dance routines were further truncated as one of the ways of bringing the film in at two hours. "The response of the test audiences is paramount," adds Malkin—"it becomes the bottom line; the tail wags the dog." In sum, Malkin thought *The Cotton Club* "would have been more successful in a longer version."

After editing *PEGGY SUE GOT MARRIED* (1986) for Coppola, Malkin took on *GARDENS OF STONE* (1987), Coppola's second film about the Vietnam conflict. Coppola collaborated closely with Malkin, who had worked on *APOCALYPSE NOW*. Malkin agreed with Coppola that the film "was an elegy of sorts, since it was about death. . . . It's brooding, purposely so. In my first cut I constructed certain sequences to exactly document the way the honor guard did their ceremonies" when burying their fallen comrades at Arlington Cemetery. This is because "it was impressed on me that in the end the army . . . would look at the cuts and make sure we had done them properly. So the first time I put the sequences together, I followed the ceremonial rites to a tee." The younger members of the preview audiences found the military burial rites dull. In the end, Malkin recalls, Coppola had him skip over some parts of the funeral ceremonies because they went on too long.

Malkin went on to edit "LIFE WITHOUT ZOE," Coppola's segment of *NEW YORK STORIES* (1989); to coedit *THE GODFATHER: PART III* (1990) with Coppola veteran WALTER MURCH; and to edit *JACK* (1996) and *THE RAINMAKER* (1997). That brings the number of Coppola movies that Malkin collaborated on to an astonishing eleven films.—GENE D. PHILLIPS

References

Peter Keogh, "Coppola Carves a Cinematic Elegy," *Chicago Sun-Times Show*, May 10, 1988, 5; Vincent LoBrutto, *Selected Takes: Film Editors on Editing* (New York: Praeger, 1991); Gabriella Oldham, *First Cut: Conversations with Film Editors* (Los Angeles: University of California Press, 1995); Michael Schumacher, *Francis Ford Coppola: A Filmmaker's Life* (New York: Crown, 1999).

MANTEGNA, JOE
[JOSEPH ANTONIO, JR.] (1947–)

Tony Award–winning Italian American stage and screen actor, producer, writer, and director, but above all an actor often affiliated with the Chicago playwright and director David Mamet. When approached to play Joey Zasa in *THE GODFATHER: PART III*, Mantegna found it an offer he couldn't refuse. After all, the first two *Godfathers* had amassed nine Oscars, twenty-one nominations, and $700 million in grosses. Joe Mantegna was born on November 13, 1947, in Chicago, the son of Joseph Anthony Mantegna Sr. and his wife, Mary Ann. He was educated at the J. Sterling Morton High School East in Cicero, Illinois, and graduated from the Goodman School of Drama (DePaul University Theatre School) in 1969. His acting debut was in a stage production of *Hair* in 1969. His Broadway acting debut was in the play *Working* in 1978. Mantegna won a Tony Award for his portrayal of super-salesman Richard Roma on stage in the original production of David Mamet's *Glengarry Glen Ross*. Mantegna's film debut came in *The Medusa Challenge* in 1977, but some of his best work on film was done for David Mamet in *House of Games* (1987) and *Things Change* (1988), winning the Best Actor Award at the Venice Film Festival for the latter. In 1991 he starred in David Mamet's film, *Homicide*. Mantegna earned Emmy Award nominations for three miniseries: *The Last Don* (1997), *The Rat Pack* (1999, for his portrayal of the singer Dean Martin), and *The Starter Wife* (2007). In 2004 Mantegna received the Lifetime Achievement Award of the Los Angeles Italian Film Festival. In 2007 Mantegna replaced Mandy Patinkin as the lead character of the popular CBS television drama series, *Criminal Minds*.—James M. Welsh

MARIE ANTOINETTE (2006)

DIRECTOR: Sofia Coppola. SCREENPLAY: Sofia Coppola. PRODUCERS: Sofia Coppola, Ross Katz. EXECUTIVE PRODUCERS: Francis Ford Coppola, Paul Rassam, Fred Roos. CO-PRODUCER: Callum Greene. LINE PRODUCER: Christine Raspillere. PHOTOGRAPHY: Lance Acord. EDITING: Sarah Flack. PRODUCTION DESIGN: K. K. Barrett. CAST: Kirsten Dunst, Jason Schwartzman, Judy Davis, Rip Torn, Rose Byrne, Asia Argento, Molly Shannon, Shirley Henderson, Danny Huston. RUNNING TIME: 123 minutes. Color. DVD: Sony Pictures.

Based on a biography by Antonia Fraser, *Marie Antoinette* was SOFIA COPPOLA's third feature film as director, after *THE VIRGIN SUICIDES* (1999) and *LOST IN TRANSLATION* (2003). FRANCIS FORD COPPOLA's AMERICAN ZOETROPE produced the picture, and it was released through Columbia Pictures. The film examines the young Austrian princess's betrothal and marriage to Louis XVI in the years leading up to the French Revolution, depicting her world as one isolated from the problems of ordinary French citizens and the political turmoil seething outside the royal court. As Roger Ebert puts it in his glowing review of the film, Sofia Coppola's Versailles "is a self-governing architectural island, like Kane's Xanadu, that shuts out politics, reality, poverty, society."

In his harsh yet perceptive analysis, Alexander Zevin sees Sofia Coppola's movie as part of a broader cultural reassessment of Marie Antoinette as something other than an uncaring, out-of-touch monarch, citing Caroline Weber's book, *Queen of Fashion*, and Sena Jeter Naslund's novel, *Abundance*, as similarly sympathetic portraits of the infamous queen. The film certainly does not present her as a villain of history, though Kirsten Dunst's performance makes the character seem (perhaps appropriately) vacuous and out of touch. The sympathy we feel for this woman emerges from the ways in which her world is depicted as one of stifling rules and regulations. Courtly tradition and propriety override human emotions, desires, needs, and seemingly natural reactions to events throughout the film. Coppola has also tried to suggest Marie's relation to modern viewers: "Here's this lonely wife whose husband is not paying attention to her and staying out partying and shopping. We've heard that story before."

Writing in *Sight and Sound*, Pam Cook identifies the key stylistic feature of *Marie Antoinette* as "travesty": "Travesty, a common device in theatre and literature, irreverently wrests its source material from its historical context, producing blatantly fake fabrications that challenge accepted notions of authenticity and value. It brazenly mixes high and low culture, and does not disguise its impulse to sweep away tradition." For Cook, this not only works as postmodern fun, but also serves to link the present day with the past, to demonstrate that we can only conceive of the world that was through eyes that have only seen the world that is. Indeed, modern pop, punk, and new wave music dominates the film's soundtrack, and Sofia Coppola indulges in creative anachronism throughout the movie—most notably, in a panning shot depicting Marie's shoes that reveals pairs of Manolo Blahniks and baby blue Converse All-Stars among the period footwear. The world of Marie Antoinette depicted in the film may not look or sound exactly like the world of the ancien régime, but it manages to capture the spirit of an age and of one woman's experience of it through Sofia Coppola's perspective: that of a young, privileged woman obsessed with fashion. The film is not entirely ahistorical, however; as Dunst points out, "[S]he didn't say, 'Let them eat cake'" (a point echoed by Marie in the film). The fact that such a memorable yet ultimately inconsequential quotation is given pride of place in *Marie Antoinette* might be another sign of the film's postmodern sensibility, wherein rock music and scenes shot (by special permission) in the palace of Versailles are seamlessly interwoven.

While the film did receive some very positive reviews and eventually won an Academy Award for Best Costume Design, it was infamously booed at its world premiere at the CANNES FILM FESTIVAL, which Francis Ford Coppola attended. *USA Today*'s Harlan Jacobson pithily wrote of this incident and Sofia Coppola's response to it, "Marie Antoinette lost her head. Coppola kept hers." The director seemed to understand: "We always knew that the French are protective of their history, and that's one of the challenges. . . . But I wanted to show it in France first, because we made it here and it takes place here."
—Billy Budd Vermillion

References

Associated Press, "Cannes Says 'Non' to *Marie-Antoinette*," www.MSNBC.com; Pam Cook, "Sofia Coppola: Portrait of a Lady," *Sight and Sound* 16, no. 11 (November 2006): 36–40; Roger Ebert, "*Marie Antoinette*," www.RogerEbert.com; Harlan Jacobson, "Coppola's Movie Booed at Cannes: Was Something Lost in Translation?" www.USAToday.com; Sony Pictures, *Marie Antoinette*, official website, http://www.sonypictures.com/homevideo/marieantoinette/index.html; Alexander Zevin, "Marie Antoinette and the Ghosts of the French Revolution," *Cineaste* 32, no. 2 (Spring 2007): 32–35.

MARY SHELLEY'S FRANKENSTEIN (1994)

Director: Kenneth Branagh. Screenplay: Steph Lady, Frank Darabont. Producers: Francis Ford Coppola, James V. Hart, John Veitch. Coproducers: Kenneth Branagh, David Parfitt. Executive Producer: Fred Fuchs. Photography: Roger Pratt. Editing: Andrew Marcus. Music: Patrick Doyle. Art Direction: Martin Childs, Desmond Crowe, John Fenner.

PRODUCTION DESIGN: Tim Harvey. COSTUME DESIGN: James Acheson.
CAST: Robert De Niro (Man), Kenneth Branagh (Victor), Tom Hulce (Henry), Helena Bonham Carter (Elizabeth), Aidan Quinn (Walton), Ian Holm (Victor's father), Richard Briers (Grandfather), John Cleese (Professor Waldman).
RUNNING TIME: 123 minutes. Technicolor.
RELEASED THROUGH: TriStar Pictures in association with Japan Satellite Broadcasting and the IndieProd Co. of an American Zoetrope production.
DVD: Sony Pictures.

This screen adaptation of Mary Wollstonecraft Shelley's classic 1818 novel was directed by Kenneth Branagh (who also starred in the title role of the mad scientist) and produced by FRANCIS FORD COPPOLA and JAMES V. HART. To portray the monster, a role previously essayed by Boris Karloff in the 1931 Universal Studios version, ROBERT DE NIRO was brought on board.

Coppola had expressed interest in filming *Frankenstein* as early as 1972; he finally was emboldened to do so after the success of his *BRAM STOKER'S DRACULA* (1992). The selection of Kenneth Branagh to direct seemed a logical choice, given the distinction Branagh had achieved with his Shakespearean adaptations *Much Ado about Nothing* (1993) and *Henry V* (1989). The Coppola/Branagh *Frankenstein* marked the first serious attempt at a close adaptation of Shelley's story (although the figure of the Frankenstein monster has appeared in more than fifty films, only a handful of these can be remotely considered adaptations of the novel), despite a few key departures. For instance, in her novel, Shelley devotes very little attention to the actual creation of the monster— a central trope in most of the film versions from 1931 onward, including this one.

When asked how this production would differ from other versions, Coppola told *Variety*: "First of all, with the talent. De Niro is the creature. It won't be reminiscent of Boris Karloff. But it has the same origin as 'Dracula'—we're doing the book [Mary Shelley's]. And in the book he learns to speak. It's the story of the 'unwanted child.' But he's still fabricated from the dead. People credit Mary Shelley as being the first writer of science fiction. It's a real classic story and a good script. We go from the Arctic to England with tremendous scenes—and no super-digital filming."

Variety characterized the film as a "lavish but overwrought melodrama . . . in many ways less compelling" than some of the previous adaptations. Budgeted at $40 million, the film pulled in a disappointing $22 million at the U.S. box office.—RODNEY HILL

References

Army Archerd, "Stakes Raised for Coppola, Hopkins," *Variety*, September 1, 1993, www.variety.com; David Blakesley, "Frankenstein; or the Modern Prometheus," in John C. Tibbetts and James M. Welsh, eds., *The Encyclopedia of Novels into Film* (New York: Facts On File, 1998), 132–34; Brian Lowry, "Mary Shelley's Frankenstein," *Variety*, October 31, 1994, www.variety.com.

MASTERSON, MARY STUART (1966–)

Actress who plays the role of Rachel Field in *GARDENS OF STONE* (1987), whose husband (played by D. B. SWEENEY) is a soldier determined to go to Vietnam. Born on June 28, 1966, in New York City, the daughter of writer-director and actor PETER MASTERSON and Tony Award–winning actress Carlin Glynn, Mary Stuart Masterson made her motion-picture debut at the age of seven in *The Stepford Wives* (1975). Raised in New York City, where she attended the Dalton School, and later majored in anthropology and film at New

York University. Masterson studied acting with Gary Swanson, spent two summers at the Sundance Institute in Utah, and became a member of the New York Actors Studio. In motion pictures she appeared opposite Eric Stoltz in *Some Kind of Wonderful* (1987, written and produced by John Hughes), starred in the Arthur Hiller feature *Married To It* (1992), and was voted Best Supporting Actress by the National Board of Review for her role as Lucy Moore in *Immediate Family* (directed by Jonathan Kaplan in 1989). In 1991 she starred as the headstrong Idgie Threadgoode, supporting Kathy Bates, Mary-Louise Parker, and Jessica Tandy in *Fried Green Tomatoes*, adapted by director Jon Avnet and Fannie Flagg from her novel, *Fried Green Tomatoes at the Whistle Stop Café*. In 1993 she appeared opposite Johnny Depp in *Benny & Joon*. Masterson also appeared in the New York stage productions of *Been Taken*, at the Ensemble Studio Theatre, Horton Foote's *Lily Dale*, at the Samuel Beckett Theatre, and Beth Henley's *The Lucky Spot*, at the Manhattan Theatre Club.—James M. Welsh

MASTERSON, PETER
[CARLOS BEN] (1934–)

American actor, writer, producer, and director, born in Houston, Texas, on June 1, 1934. FRANCIS COPPOLA cast Masterson with his wife, Carlin Glynn, to play the parents of Rachel Field, played by their daughter, MARY STUART MASTERSON, in *GARDENS OF STONE* (1987). Years before, Masterson had played Walter Eberhard in *The Stepford Wives* (1975), in which his actual daughter, then only seven years old, also played his daughter. As a writer, Masterson is probably best known for having written the book for the hit musical *The Best Little Whorehouse in Texas*; he also wrote the screenplay for the film adaptation of that musical, starring Dolly Parton and Burt Reynolds. Masterson is best known as a director for his work on the film *The Trip to Bountiful* (1985), which Masterson's cousin, Horton Foote, adapted from his play. Under Masterson's direction, actress GERALDINE PAGE won the Academy Award for Best Actress in that film.
—James M. Welsh

MATHISON, MELISSA [MARIE] (1950–)

Coppola protégée who worked as production assistant on *THE GODFATHER: PART II* and executive assistant on *APOCALYPSE NOW*. Melissa Mathison was born the daughter of a journalist in Los Angeles on June 3, 1950, grew up in Hollywood Hills, and was educated at the University of California, Berkeley, where she was majoring in political science when she went to work for Coppola on the *Godfather II* project. Through Coppola she became a screenwriter, adapting Walter Farley's children's novel *THE BLACK STALLION*, working for executive producer FRANCIS COPPOLA in 1979. In 1981 she dated the actor HARRISON FORD and later married him on May 14, 1983 (the couple separated in 2000). Her most famous achievement, however, is as the screenwriter for Steven Spielberg on the alien-visitation "classic" film *E.T.* She also scripted another children's film, *The Indian in the Cupboard* (1995) and in 1997 she wrote the screenplay for Martin Scorsese's *Kundun*.—James M. Welsh/Gene D. Phillips

MAURA, CARMEN (1945–)

Veteran Spanish actress who portrays the eccentric theatre critic, "Alone," in FRANCIS FORD COPPOLA's highly personal art film, *TETRO* (2009). On working with Coppola, Maura told the *New York Times*: "It was an amusing and entertaining experience. . . . He's a completely different kind of director. I liked his craziness. He was very friendly, simpatico and respectful, but you never know what he is going to ask, and he was full of surprises."

Maura was born in Madrid in 1945, into a conservative family, the grand-niece of the politician Antonio Maura, who served multiple terms as the prime minister of Spain. She studied philosophy and literature in Paris, at the École des Beaux-Arts, where she worked in the university theatre. She eventually gave up her studies to pursue a stage career, and in the 1970s she obtained several small cinematic roles. Through her work with the renowned Madrid theatre company, Los Goliardos, she met Pedro Almodóvar and appeared in several of his films throughout the following decades. Their more notable collaborations include: *What Have I Done to Deserve This?* (1984), the first Almodóvar film to receive international distribution; *Matador* (1986), with Antonio Banderas; *Law of Desire* (1987), revolutionary in its unbiased portrayal of homosexuality; the uproarious *Women on the Verge of a Nervous Breakdown* (1988), for which Maura won her first Goya Award, as well as a Felix Award as Best European Actress; and *Volver* (2006), considered by some critics their finest effort to date.—RODNEY HILL

References

American Zoetrope, "Carmen Maura," *Tetro* official website, www.tetro.com; "Carmen Maura," *Variety* Profiles, www.variety.com; Larry Rohter, "Family Dynamics, without the Bullets," *New York Times*, June 3, 2009, www.nytimes.com.

MILIUS, JOHN (1944–)

Writer and director who wrote the first draft of the screenplay for *APOCALYPSE NOW* then established himself as an action director with *Dillinger* (1973), his debut picture, which he wrote and directed, and nearly a decade later, *Conan the Barbarian* (1982). Born in St. Louis, Missouri, on April 11, 1944, and raised in Southern California, Milius met GEORGE LUCAS and his *AMERICAN GRAFFITI* colleagues WILLARD HUYCK and Gloria Katz at the USC film school. His first student project, a short film entitled *Marcello, I'm So Bored*, a spoof of Italian arthouse features, won the National Student Film Festival Award. Hired as a writer for American International Pictures, Milius cowrote the screenplay for *The Devil's 8* (1969), his first screenplay, and went on to collaborate on the screenplays of *Evel Knievel* (1971) and *Jeremiah Johnson* (1972, coscripted with Robert Redford). For John Huston he wrote the story and screenplay for *The Life and Times of Judge Roy Bean* (1972). Other screenwriting assignments included *Dirty Harry* (1971, uncredited) and the sequel, *Magnum Force* (1982). *Geronimo: An American Legend* (1993) and *Clear and Present Danger* (1994). Other feature films directed by Milius include the popular *The Wind and the Lion* (1975), nominated for a Writers Guild Award, and the presumably autobiographical portrait of the artist as a surfer, *Big Wednesday* (1978), but his most politically irritating picture was probably *Red Dawn* (1984), a paranoid fantasy about a group of red-blooded, patriotic teenagers in Colorado, led by a quarterback and fighting for freedom in the face of a Soviet/Cuban invasion of the United States. In 1990 Milius directed *Flight of the Intruder*, adapted by Robert Dillon and David Shaber from the novel by Stephen Coonts, set on an aircraft carrier in the South China Sea and in enemy airspace above North Vietnam in 1972.

Milius began his script for *Apocalypse Now* while in film school at the University of Southern California, after his professor told him about the many failed attempts to adapt JOSEPH CONRAD's novella, "HEART OF DARKNESS," into a film. For his adaptation, Milius borrowed the novella's plot, a journey up-river toward Kurtz, a man who has "gone native" and given in to primitivism and savagery; but Milius updated the setting from the Belgian Congo in the 1890s to Vietnam in the 1960s. In the film, Willard, a CIA assassin in America's Vietnam War, is assigned to travel up the Nung River by navy patrol boat and locate the stronghold of Walter Kurtz, a Green Beret colonel who had been about to be arrested for ordering the murder of suspected Vietcong. Kurtz escaped into the jungle, however, with a private army of Montagnard tribesmen and began fighting a savage war against the Vietcong and North Vietnamese Army, without regard for the rules of conventional warfare. The officers in Nha Trang who assigned this job to Willard argue that Kurtz has gone insane and is "out there operating without decent restraint, totally beyond the pale of any acceptable human conduct." Willard is instructed to "terminate" Kurtz "with extreme prejudice." In addition to Kurtz, other characters in the film are based on those in the novella. The accountant in "Heart of Darkness" is Colonel Kilgore in the film, the novella's Black helmsman is the film's Chief Phillips, for example, and the Russian harlequin in the novella is the photographer played by DENNIS HOPPER in the film.

Milius drew on the articles on Vietnam that journalist MICHAEL HERR wrote for *Esquire* and later collected in his book, *Dispatches* (1977) as a source for material on the war. WALTER MURCH, who designed the sound for the film and edited it, claimed that Herr was hired to write the voiceover narration for the film because Milius had borrowed so much from his articles. Herr's work influenced the way the war is portrayed in the film, as a drug-soaked, rock-'n'-roll, "psychedelic" war. Herr described Vietnam as "a California corridor cut and bought and burned deep into Asia." Taking this cue from Herr, Milius described Vietnam as "a California war," involving "an ancient Asian culture being assaulted by this teenage California culture," accounting for all the references in the film to Southern California and its culture—especially surfing, but also Charles Manson, the music of The Doors, Disneyland, and Beverly Hills (as the command bunker at the Do Lung Bridge is called).

In his articles for *Esquire* Herr told stories of "irregulars" in the Vietnam War who were "lost to headquarters," on their own, without supervision, who exercised absolute authority over hamlets in which they operated; of people driven insane by the war, including "mad colonels" who were "nonchalant about the horror"; and of those Americans who wanted to drop the bomb on Vietnam, who "wanted a Vietnam they could fit into their car ashtrays." These references suggest the Vietnam story in *Apocalypse Now* that was grafted onto the plot of "Heart of Darkness." Specific scenes in the movie that were taken from Herr's essays include the opening sequence in a Saigon hotel room, and the scene at the Do Lung Bridge, in which an American soldier locates by sound an enemy caught in the wire and kills him with an M-79 grenade launcher.

Another source for the Vietnam story of *Apocalypse Now* was the "Green Beret murder case." In 1969, Colonel Robert B. Rheault, head of the Green Berets in Vietnam, was arrested for the murder of a suspected Vietcong double agent, a charge similar to the one made against Kurtz in the film. Rheault himself had contempt for the regular army and was one of the critics within the military who believed committing conventional ground forces in Vietnam had been an error and that the war in Vietnam could be won through "dirty war" tactics. That kind of "dirty war" was being fought in Vietnam by the CIA with the help of the Green Berets employing tactics that included the assassinations of suspected Vietcong. Those assassinations took place under the Phoenix Program, controlled by the CIA and headed by William Colby, which began as a program to identify and arrest suspected Vietcong but ended in such excesses as beheadings of suspects. These decapitations became a signature of the program. Significantly, in the film the name of the first assassin sent to kill Kurtz but ends up joining him is "Colby," and Kurtz's compound is littered with severed heads. Rheault had been expected to be in line for promotion to general but had been warned that he jeopardized his chances for advancement if he remained in the Green Berets. He rejected that advice, however, and stayed in the unit he loved: "To hell with my career," he said. Kurtz does the same in the film. "He could have gone for general," Willard says of Kurtz, "but he went for himself instead." Critic Peter Lev has demonstrated that Milius had this case in mind when writing *Apocalypse Now*. Rheault is mentioned by name in early versions of the script, and Lev argues that Milius probably got a good deal of the story, including details of Rheault's life, from the news coverage that was widespread at the time Milius was working on the screenplay in 1969. The news coverage in fact contained the term "terminate with extreme prejudice" as a euphemism for assassination.

Milius has explained the origin of the film's title: "The title came from the button hippies wore that said *Nirvana Now* with a peace symbol. I made one with a tail and engine nasals, so the symbol became a B-52, and read *Apocalypse Now*." In fact, Milius believed that the decision to go to war in Vietnam was a mistake, but that once in the war, the United States should have done whatever was necessary to win, quickly and decisively. Milius has said that Kurtz is crazy, but that he is also telling the truth, and that he has wisdom. For Milius that wisdom is contained in the manuscript Kurtz has written: "Drop the bomb. Exterminate them all." In Milius's favorite

version of the film, the one first released in theatres, the closing credits are shown over an airstrike that destroys Kurtz's stronghold, implying that Willard has acted on the manuscript's advice.

Frances Fitzgerald has described the episode in the film in which Colonel Kilgore and his men carry out a helicopter assault on a Vietcong village in order to surf "Charlie's Point" as "black comedy" and Peter Lev sees it as a "satire of the Vietnam war." For Lev, the Kilgore episode raises a question of Milius's attitude toward the war. Milius, Lev says, "is pro-war but also a satirist of war." Milius himself has explained that seeming contradiction. He acknowledges the origin of the Kilgore episode in black comedy. He has said that he wrote Kilgore as "a wildly drawn character—straight out of *Dr. Strangelove*," the quintessential satirical black comedy about war. Milius is a self-proclaimed "militarist," but he has also said, "In order to be great, a movie has to be true. It must stay loyal to certain ideals and challenge them at the same time. *Apocalypse Now* challenged the inanity, the total unreasonableness of war."—Donald M. Whaley/James M. Welsh

References

Frances Fitzgerald, "*Apocalypse Now*," in *Past Imperfect: History According to the Movies* (New York: Henry Holt, 1995); Michael Herr, *Dispatches* (New York: Knopf, 1977); Peter Lev, *American Films of the 70s: Conflicting Visions* (Austin: University of Texas Press, 2000); Walter Murch, "Apocalypse Then and Now," *Film Comment* 37, no. 3 (2001); Jeff Stein, *A Murder in Wartime* (New York: St. Martin's, 1992); Donald Whaley, "Adaptation Studies and the History of Ideas: The Case of *Apocalypse Now*," in *The Literature/Film Reader: Issues of Adaptation* (Lanham, MD: Scarecrow Press, 2007).

MORELLO, GIUSEPPE (D. 1930)

Early leader of the American Mafia from Corleone in Sicily who immigrated to

New York's Italian community in 1892 and chose to pursue the *mala vita*, the life of crime, setting up shop in East Harlem. *Washington Post* reporter Jonathan Yardley suggested that it was Morello rather than Vito Genovese or Al Capone or Lucky Luciano who was "the true father of the American Mafia." According to Morello's biographer, Mike Dash, the first Mafiosi who came to America "were not sent there by their superiors as part of any worked-out plan to expand the influence of the fraternity," though they did attempt to pass themselves off as "benefactors, even defenders of the poor." They were in fact "parasites who terrorized their fellow countrymen, exploited the weak, and dealt in fear." As Jonathan Yardley pointed out, correcting the Mafia myth, Dash proved "conclusively that the received wisdom about the American Mafia—that it arose in response to the rich opportunities for corruption presented by Prohibition—is simply wrong. The Mafia had existed here for at least a quarter-century before then" and therefore was able "to capitalize spectacularly as control of the vastly profitable alcohol industry transferred from legitimate businesses to the underworld." By the 1930s, a new Mafia was emerging "from the first generation of Mafiosi," able "to dominate organized crime" nationwide, and not simply in Italian neighborhoods. This was the Mafia of Lucky Luciano, "shrewd and ruthless, but more of a businessman than he was a man of action," and this was the image of the Mafia romanticized by FRANCIS COPPOLA in the *GODFATHER* films.—JAMES M. WELSH

References

Mike Dash, *The First Family: Terror, Extortion, Revenge, Murder, and the Birth of the American Mafia* (New York: Random House, 2009); Jonathan Yardley, "Meet the Real Godfather," *Washington Post*, August 16, 2009, B8.

MURCH, WALTER (1943–)

He coined the term "sound design" to replace the traditional title of sound editor, to emphasize that sound editing is an integral part of the filmmaking craft. Murch has long been associated with the movies of FRANCIS COPPOLA, who first engaged him to mix the soundtrack of *THE RAIN PEOPLE* (1969), the first feature Murch worked on. Coppola installed Murch in his state-of-the-art postproduction facility at his office complex, AMERICAN ZOETROPE, in San Francisco, where Coppola set up shop to be far removed from the watchful eyes of the studio executives in Hollywood. Murch soon became part of Coppola's independent film unit. Accordingly, Murch was a sound technician on Coppola's next film, *THE GODFATHER* (1972), an epic gangster movie; and he made some notable creative contributions to the soundtrack of *The Godfather*.

In one of the most riveting scenes in the picture, Michael successfully carries out his plan to gun down two men in a Bronx restaurant. Walter Murch remembers that Coppola wanted musical accompaniment to this scene only after Michael has committed the murders and is leaving the restaurant. So Murch decided to add a sound effect just prior to the murders. He was aware of the elevated train tracks near the restaurant, so he employed the "screeching effect as the train turns a difficult corner" to symbolize Michael's state of mind. He is irrevocably turning a difficult corner: "This is the first time he has killed anybody face-to-face." In short, the grating sound of the train's brakes is a metaphor for Michael's anxiety, implying his apprehension as the moment of the massacre draws near.

Murch's superior work on *The Godfather* and other Coppola films placed him at the head of his profession. Murch also collaborated, as a sound designer and a film editor, on *THE GODFATHER: PART*

II (1974) and *THE GODFATHER: PART III* (1990). The epic sweep and complex sequences of both movies challenged his technical and artistic skills.

Coppola's next film, after *The Godfather*, was *THE CONVERSATION* (1974). Coppola needed an inventive sound technician like Murch for this film because several scenes in the movie were sound oriented. The plot concerns Harry Caul, a professional surveillance expert, who bugs a conversation between Mark and Ann, as they converse about Ann's husband. It seems that Ann's husband has discovered their illicit affair and may be planning to kill them.

Murch was a "full collaborator on this film," says Coppola. He edited the picture, assisted by Richard Chew, and mixed the soundtrack. This was Murch's first assignment as a film editor on a feature picture. (See the entry on *The Conversation.*) David Thomson writes that *The Conversation* is "a showcase for the brilliant editor/sound man Walter Murch." Murch likewise made some inventive contributions to *APOCALYPSE NOW*, Coppola's epic film about the Vietnam War.

Apocalypse Now, as released in 1979, opens with a riveting scene, a hypnotic montage of a phantom helicopter flying through the jungle amid smoke and napalm flames, accompanied by the whirling of a chopper's rotary blades. The image dissolves to Willard, a burnt-out intelligence officer lying drunk and nearly naked on a rumpled, sweat-soaked bed in a Saigon hotel, while a ceiling fan slowly revolves above him. He is groggily awakening from a nightmare about the war, which was prompted by the thump of the ceiling fan sounding like a helicopter.

Coppola notes in his audio commentary on the DVD of *Apocalypse Now* (released 2006), "Walter Murch elided the helicopter sounds with the shirring of the overhead fan in Willard's hotel room to blend the images together." Barton Palmer writes that this sequence "demonstrates the incredible talent of Murch and his contribution to the art of the cinema." Indeed, Murch won an Academy Award for his sound design of *Apocalypse Now*.

Murch also had a pivotal role in the creation of *APOCALYPSE NOW REDUX* (2001). Coppola explains in his "Director's Statement," issued when *Apocalypse Now Redux* was released, that he limited *Apocalypse Now* to two and a half hours for its original release in 1979 because he feared that the movie would otherwise be "too long and too strange" for the mass audience. In releasing an expanded version of *Apocalypse Now*, Coppola banked on the fact that audiences would welcome an extended version of a picture that had enjoyed such enormous critical and popular success over the years. So Coppola and Walter Murch resurrected fifty-three minutes of original footage that had been cut from the film the first time around and dispersed it throughout *Apocalypse Now Redux*, which was unveiled at the CANNES INTERNATIONAL FILM FESTIVAL in May 2001.

Continuing his creative association with Coppola, Murch collaborated with the director on *YOUTH WITHOUT YOUTH* (2007) and *TETRO* (2009).—GENE D. PHILLIPS

References

Michael Jarrett, "Sound Doctrine: Walter Murch," *Film Quarterly* 53, no. 3 (2002): 1–9; Walter Murch, "Stretching Sound to Help the Mind See," *New York Times*, October 1, 2000), sec. 2: 1, 24–25; Michael Ondaatje, *The Conversations: Walter Murch and the Art of Editing Film* (New York: Knopf, 2002); Barton Palmer, "Walter Murch" in *International Dictionary of Film and Filmmakers*, ed. Nicolet Elert (New York: St. James Press, 2000), 4:600–601; David Thomson, *Have You Seen . . . ?1,000 Films* (New York: Knopf, 2008).

NAPOLEON CONQUERS AMERICA (1981)
CBS cable TV show written by Mary Bell and Brooks Riley, directed and edited by Jim Painten, and produced by Mary Bell for Films 88 in conjunction with Zoetrope Studios and Images Film Archive. The title of this film could have been "Napoleon Conquers the World," but the focus is on the astonishing success of the restored epic *Napoleon*, first at Radio City Music Hall, and then in Los Angeles and other major American cities. This documentary was obviously made to promote the spectacular revival of ABEL GANCE's 1927 masterpiece. It prominently features interviews with FRANCIS FORD COPPOLA, who brought the film to national attention, CARMINE COPPOLA, his father, who composed the music for the American exhibitions and conducted the orchestras, ROBERT HARRIS, who saw the potential of Gance's work and went about purchasing the American rights, KEVIN BROWNLOW, who devoted a lifetime to locating lost footage to bring the film first to four and a half hours, and later to over five hours, and (briefly) Claude Lelouch, the French director who collaborated with Gance on the 1972 remake of Napoleon entitled *Bonaparte and the Revolution*. The film spends rather too much time with Francis Coppola, whose role was significant as impresario but whose knowledge of the film is far surpassed by Brownlow's. Carmine Coppola speaks interestingly and

at length about his score, his use of Revolutionary songs, such as "It Will Be," his borrowings from Mozart and Beethoven, the choices he had to make between Romantic and contemporary themes. But the film succeeds best when it speaks through Gance's own images. The film incorporates footage from Brownlow's own 1968 documentary, *The Charm of Dynamite*, footage Chris Menges had shot of Gance for that film, a sequence recovered from the 1928 MGM version that had been shortened from five hours to seventy-five minutes by Frank Hull for American distribution. The film is a worthy tribute to Gance's genius, Brownlow's determination and knowledge, and Coppola's artistic initiative.
—JAMES M. WELSH

"NEW" HOLLYWOOD
During the 1960s, the times they were a-changin' for Hollywood and its studio system. A bellwether of this change was Fox's *Cleopatra*, which lost $40 million in 1963. Although *The Sound of Music* grossed $100 million in 1965 over a production investment of $10 million, later big-budget pictures failed at the box office. Just as the "New Wave" of younger, fresher talents had swept over French cinema during the previous decade, a parallel movement was soon evident in America, bringing unconventional, up-from-television talents, such as Robert Altman, later including FRANCIS

COPPOLA and a host of others: Arthur Penn, Stanley Kubrick, Bob Rafelson, Hal Ashby, Brian De Palma, Terrence Malick, Martin Scorsese, GEORGE LUCAS, and, of course, Steven Spielberg. As Richard Martin wrote in his book *Mean Streets and Raging Bulls* (1997): "Their filmic interests were inspired as much by Europeans as by classical Hollywood." (And, in fact, many European talents escaped to Hollywood during the Cold War: for example, Roman Polanski from Poland, cinematographers Laszlo Kovacs and Vilmos Zsigmond from Hungary, and Miloš Forman from Prague.) Moreover, "the early films of the so-called 'movie brat' generation were targeted at a like-minded audience, a cine-literate baby boom generation of filmgoers, who, during the late sixties, were embroiled in the rise of the counterculture and the 'New Left.'" Consequently, the failure "of several blockbusters during the sixties prompted a widespread experimentation and innovation, resulting in the assimilation of European art cinema filmmaking techniques into the American mainstream cinema." Such a shift in taste, accompanied by the new *Code of Self-Regulation* introduced by the Motion Picture Association of America (MPAA) in 1966, resulted in hitherto "unprecedented levels of violence, sexuality, and profane language." The most popular treatment of the New Hollywood was written by Peter Biskind, one of the first historians of the New Hollywood, whose book *Easy Riders, Raging Bulls* (1998) no doubt influenced later, lesser writers attempting to follow his lead, even if his own clever title echoed an earlier one.—JAMES M. WELSH

Resources

Peter Biskind, *Easy Riders, Raging Bulls* (New York: Simon & Schuster, 1998); Richard Martin, *Mean Streets and Raging Bulls* (Lanham, MD: Scarecrow Press, 1997).

NEW YORK STORIES (1989)

After finishing *TUCKER: THE MAN AND HIS DREAM*, Coppola went on to contribute a segment to an anthology film entitled *New York Stories*. This omnibus movie was the brainchild of Woody Allen, who proposed to fellow filmmakers Martin Scorsese and FRANCIS COPPOLA that they each create a self-contained urban story, about a half-hour in duration, that could be filmed in a month.

The only cord linking the three short films together would be the common New York City setting. Naturally Coppola jumped at the chance to be associated with a film that involved two other important directors. Furthermore, Coppola had shot films like *YOU'RE A BIG BOY NOW*, *THE GODFATHER*, and *THE COTTON CLUB* in New York and was to that extent identified with the city. Given the trio of distinguished directors, Allen and producer Robert Greenhut easily found the $15 million needed to back the movie and enlisted Touchstone Pictures, a subsidiary of Walt Disney Pictures, to distribute the picture.

After casting around for a subject, Coppola came up with the idea of doing his segment along the lines of writer-vocalist Kay Thompson's children's books. Thompson had penned four books in the 1950s about Eloise, a precocious child who lives in the Plaza Hotel in New York, and Coppola wanted to deal with a similar little girl in his short film. Writing a script about a youngster gave him the chance to collaborate with his seventeen-year-old daughter Sofia on the screenplay. The scenario was about an eleven-year-old child named Zoe, who lives at the exclusive Sherry-Netherland Hotel on Fifth Avenue, dines at the posh Russian Tea Room, and has her own credit cards. It would be entitled "LIFE WITHOUT ZOE."

Scorsese contributed a forty-five-minute episode, "Life Lessons," a tale of a macho painter (Nick Nolte) and his assistant-lover, who wants to fly the coop. Woody Allen's thirty-nine-minute segment is entitled "Oedipus Wrecks," in which a hapless son is dominated by his nagging Jewish mother. Sandwiched between these short films is Coppola's thirty-four-minute "Life without Zoe," about a "poor little rich girl" (Heather McComb) who lives it up in a New York hotel while her parents are globetrotting.

Pauline Kael judged Scorsese's entry "intensely enjoyable" and Allen's segment a vaudeville sketch "with some genuine laughs." But she dismissed Coppola's piece as merely "forgettable." All told, Kael scored the movie "a two-base hit."
—GENE D. PHILLIPS

References

Leslie Halliwell, *Film Guide*, ed. David Gritten (New York: Harper Collins, 2008); Pauline Kael, *Movie Love* (New York: Penguin Books, 1991); Michael Schumacher, *Francis Ford Coppola: A Filmmaker's Life* (New York: Crown, 1999).

NICHOLSON, JACK (1937–)

Notoriously gifted Hollywood bad-boy actor, director, superstar, and lothario, who was offered the role of Kurtz in *APOCA-LYPSE NOW*, which Nicholson declined through his agent. Nicholson had also been offered the role of Willard. Nicholson worked with FRANCIS COPPOLA who was second-unit director on ROGER CORMAN's *THE TERROR* in 1963. But Jack Nicholson, born in Neptune, New Jersey, on April 22, 1937, became famous on his own, without assistance from Coppola. Like so many of the talent of the New Hollywood, they both began with Roger Corman. In 1958 Nicholson played the lead in Corman's *The Cry-Baby Killers* and was also featured in *The Little Shop of Horrors*, but he wasn't properly "discovered" until his breakthrough performance, replacing RIP TORN, in the iconic *Easy Rider* (1969). In succeeding years, the triumphs fell like dominoes, as Nicholson was sought out by top directors: Bob Rafelson's *Five Easy Pieces* (1970, garnering an Oscar nomination); Mike Nichols's *Carnal Knowledge* (1971); Hal Ashby's *The Last Detail* (1973, and another Oscar nomination); Michelangelo Antonioni's *The Passenger* (1975), and Miloš Forman's *One Flew over the Cuckoo's Nest* (1975, which hit the Oscar jackpot for Nicholson, who won the Best Actor Academy Award). Nicholson turned in another signature performance as the insane, murderous father in Stanley Kubrick's *The Shining* (1980), adapted from Stephen King's best-selling horror novel. Then, in 1983 he won the Best Supporting Actor Academy Award for *Terms of Endearment*; nine years later he was again nominated for Best Supporting Actor for his stellar performance in *A Few Good Men* (1992). But the Motion Picture Academy is not necessarily the best index to any actor's genius. Who could forget, for example, Nicholson's down-and-out portrayal with Meryl Streep in Hector Babenco's adaptation of WILLIAM KENNEDY's Albany novel, *Ironweed* (1987)? No Hollywood actor is so adept at going over the top as Nicholson, as witnessed by his paradigm performance as The Joker in Tim Burton's *Batman* (1989) or his signature performance as The Devil in *The Witches of Eastwick* (1987), a performance that AL PACINO could not quite equal in *The Devil's Advocate* (1997). After playing the lead for Roman Polanski in *Chinatown* (1974), Nicholson went on to star in and direct its sequel, *The Two Jakes* in 1990; but this was not his first turn at directing. The first picture Nicholson directed was *Drive, He Said*, adapted from Jeremy Larner's novel in 1970, followed by *Goin' South* (1978), a western graced by amusing performances by Nicholson and Mary Steenburgen. Perhaps no one has better defined

Nicholson's importance than *New Republic* film critic Stanley Kauffmann, who wrote: "Any future history of American film must, if it is to be adequate, treat Nicholson as more than a star. A box office draw, to be sure, but unlike most stars, he has done as much in his lifetime as any American screen actor to blazon, in itself, the art of acting. It used to be a theater adage that only great roles—meaning the classics—create great actors. Nicholson has shown that, in an age when the vernacular has become prosody, a great talent can create great roles."—JAMES M. WELSH

References

Stanley Kauffmann, "About Nicholson," *New Republic*, January 13, 2003, 22; Donald Shepherd, *Jack Nicholson: An Unauthorized Biography* (New York: St. Martin's Press, 1991).

NOTES (1979)

These "notes" constitute the diary ELEANOR COPPOLA kept while with her husband in the Philippines making *APOCALYPSE NOW*, a long, difficult, and arduous process. She explains that she wrote these "notes for myself without intending that they be read by anyone else." When FRANCIS COPPOLA read them in 1978, he "recognized that they could be a book" and encouraged her to publish them. FRED ROOS put her in touch with "the perfect editor, NAN TALESE," and Simon & Schuster published the book in 1979. The "notes" she captured, from Manila to Napa, not only give a behind-the-scenes account of the film production but also served as a useful source for her documentary about the making of *Apocalypse Now*, entitled *HEARTS OF DARKNESS: A FILMMAKER'S APOCALYPSE* (1991). "When I started making notes over a year ago," she confides on October 24, 1977 (p. 215), "I tried to make them like photographs. I wanted to leave out the adjectives, the judg-

ments. Just make little snapshots that all together would give a picture of my experience. I was the camera, outside the events, just trying to record them." Though she ended up a participant as well, this was her original intent.—JAMES M. WELSH

NOTES ON A LIFE (2008)

Autobiographical memoir written by ELEANOR COPPOLA and published by NAN TALESE and Doubleday in 2008. This book is Eleanor Coppola's second installment of her continuing adventures with her extravagant husband. Her first book was entitled *NOTES ON THE MAKING OF* APOCALYPSE NOW, and consisted of her "notes" that were eventually combined with documentary footage she had shot while her husband was directing that train wreck of a production in the Philippines to become an award-winning documentary film. One imagines it may be easier to write about the making of a single film, even one as tempestuous as *APOCALYPSE NOW*, than to compose "notes" on a whole life. It would be very easy to hit a wrong "note," for example, but this woman is enough of an artist to avoid discord, even when her life is not so harmonious. The tragedy of her life that most outsiders might be aware of would be the death of her son, Gio (Gian-Carlo, 1963–1986), in a Memorial Day boating accident near Washington, D.C., where Gian-Carlo was helping his father shoot a funereal film involving the honor guard at Arlington National Cemetery, adapted from NICHOLAS PROFFITT's military novel, *GARDENS OF STONE*, in 1986. That tremendous loss understandably overshadows the opening section of the book. Even so, there is more to this life than this one, awful tragedy, and the mother is certainly attentive to the needs of her other children. When daughter Sofia becomes a filmmaker, for example, and goes to Japan to shoot *LOST IN TRANSLATION*, the mother is also there, at her side. In fact, she has been conditioned to be at the side of the creative people in her life, but the book gives ample evidence that she is also quite creative herself, as she presents herself not only as a matriarch but also as a successful businesswoman (as she and Francis develop a profitable winery as well as a line of eco-friendly boutique hotels), and, finally, as an artist. Notes on a film might follow a definite trajectory from beginning to end. Notes on a life, however, cannot be so neatly organized. Autobiographical flashbacks come and go so quickly they are hardly noticed. "Francis and I married quickly in Las Vegas," she confides (p. 57). "I hadn't met Francis's parents. When I did I learned he was from generations of Italian men who believed a woman's life work was caring for home and children and supporting her husband's career." This she reveals without an apparent sense of regret. And, earlier (p. 28): "Francis and I met while I was the assistant to the art director" on his first feature film, *DEMENTIA 13*. All she promises in her "Prologue" is a "selection from my notebooks, both old and recent." The book ends just as Francis is about to film *YOUTH WITHOUT YOUTH* in Romania. Readers will learn much more, however, about the filming of *MARIE ANTOINETTE* in France. Eleanor Coppola is of course proud of her husband, but she virtually glows over the success of her daughter. This book is not just for movie fans and Coppola addicts. It is a touching family account, sensitively written and observed.—JAMES M. WELSH

NOTES ON THE MAKING OF APOCALYPSE NOW (1979)

Edited and published diary by ELEANOR COPPOLA written during the time her husband fought his demons in the Philippines while making his Vietnam epic. —JAMES M. WELSH

NOVELLO, DON (1943–)

Actor and Coppola regular who appeared in the following roles: Stan, the promo filmmaker, in *TUCKER: THE MAN AND HIS DREAM* (1988), Dominic Abbandando, public relations and media coordinator for Don Michael Corleone in *THE GODFATHER: PART III* (1990), the bartender in *JACK* (1996). Born in Lorain, Ohio, on January 1, 1943, Don Novello was the son of Eleanor and Dr. Augustine J. Novello, a physician. He graduated from the University of Dayton and then began his career as performer on *The Smothers Brothers Comedy Hour* in 1965. Novello produced *SCTV*, the Toronto-based comedy show, starring Martin Short, John Candy, Eugene Levy, and Catherine O'Hara. He is probably best known, however, for his *Saturday Night Live* character, Father Guido Sarducci, a priest who works as a gossip columnist. —JAMES M. WELSH

THE OLD GUARD

An elite U.S. Army ceremonial unit honored in FRANCIS FORD COPPOLA's film *GARDENS OF STONE* (1987), based near Washington, D.C., whose duties include burying the war dead in Arlington National Cemetery with meticulous precision. The title of the film refers to the tombstones of Arlington. The film is primarily about these military traditions and rituals. It is also of course "about" the heartbreak of Vietnam, as seen from the perspective of professional soldiers who had served there. The main character, a deeply patriotic, loyal soldier, played by JAMES CAAN in one of his very best roles, is against the war because he had served in Vietnam and knows the war cannot be won the way it is being fought. Coppola told the *New York Times* it was "not his intent" to make an antiwar movie: "Obviously, there is a message there, that we are sworn to protect our children and we keep putting them in situations that make that impossible, that you want to save your kids but you end up burying them, all dressed up in ritual. But I didn't associate *Gardens of Stone* with *APOCALYPSE NOW.*" Because the film stresses the "critical importance of family ties, ritual, honor, tradition and loyalty," Coppola believed it had "at least as much in common with *THE GODFA-THER*" as it did with *Apocalypse Now.* "I went to military school, and I've always been fascinated by the role of ritual in the military, particularly the code of honor," Coppola told reporter Robert Lindsey. Coppola had the full cooperation of the U.S. Army on this project (unlike *Apocalypse Now*) at Ft. Myer and Ft. Belvoir, Virginia, as well as at Arlington National Cemetery. The army's liaison officer for the film project, Lieutenant Col. John Myers, told the *New York Times*: "From the Army's standpoint, the film's depiction of the military is beyond reproach." Novelist NICHOLAS PROFFITT who wrote *Gardens of Stone* had served as a war correspondent for *Newsweek* in Vietnam, but had also served in the Old Guard at Arlington at the time that President John Fitzgerald Kennedy was buried there. There are 109 other national cemeteries, but Arlington, built on what was once the estate of Robert E. Lee, is the only one under the control of the army. During the American Civil War, 16,000 soldiers were buried there, but over 200,000 people have been buried at Arlington since 1864.—JAMES M. WELSH

Reference

Robert Lindsey, "Coppola Returns to the Vietnam Era, Minus Apocalypse," *New York Times*, May 3, 1987, sec. 2: 19, 34.

OLDMAN, GARY (1958–)

Distinctive actor who played the title role in *BRAM STOKER'S DRACULA* (1992) and helped conceptualize the count as an

Gary Oldman as Dracula.

oddly sympathetic fallen angel. Born in the inner-city neighborhood of New Cross, South London, on March 21, 1958, he studied drama with the Greenwich Young People's Theatre, followed by a scholarship to the Rose Buford College of Speech and Drama, then found work at London's Royal Court Theatre, and later performed with the Royal Shakespeare Theatre. He originated the role of Corman in Caryl Churchill's *Serious Money* on stage, and appeared in several British television dramas before making his feature film debut in 1986 playing punk rocker Sid Vicious in *Sid and Nancy*.—JAMES M. WELSH

ONE FROM THE HEART (1982)

DIRECTOR: Francis Coppola. SCREENPLAY: Armyan Bernstein and Francis Coppola, based on a story by Armyan Bernstein. PRODUCERS: Gray Frederickson and Fred Roos. PHOTOGRAPHY: Vittorio Storaro and Ronald V. Garcia. EDITING: Anne Goursaud, Rudi Fehr, and Randy Roberts. MUSIC: Tom Waits. PRODUCTION DESIGN: Dean Tavoularis. ART DIRECTION: Angelo Graham. SET DECORATION: Gary Fettis and Leslie McCarthy-Frankenheimer. COSTUME DESIGN: Ruth Morley. CASTING: Jennifer Shull.
CAST: Frederic Forrest (Hank), Teri Garr (Frannie), Raul Julia (Ray), Nastassja Kinski (Leila), Lainie Kazan (Maggie), Harry Dean Stanton (Moe), Allen Goorwitz (Restaurant Owner), Jeff Hamlin (Airline Ticket Agent), Italia Coppola and Carmine Coppola (Couple in Elevator). RUNNING TIME: 107 minutes. Technicolor. RELEASED THROUGH: Zoetrope Studios. DVD: Fantoma / American Zoetrope.

More than a film, *One from the Heart* is also one of the key events in FRANCIS FORD COPPOLA's career. It is one of the principal *films maudit* of contemporary Hollywood cinema: rarely seen, legendarily savaged by critics, a commercial failure that destroyed Zoetrope Studios. In this, it parallels the equally legendary *Heaven's Gate* and stands alongside that film as a focal moment in the decline and fall of the auteur cinema of 1970s Hollywood. Thus, it can also be viewed in contrast to the successes of *Jaws* and *Star Wars* as a negative example influencing the more constrained, conservative environment Hollywood directors have navigated since the 1980s. The irony is that in several respects *One from the Heart* embodies or prefigures many of the characteristics of Hollywood style in the last few decades, albeit in an idiosyncratic fashion. For Coppola, its failure would remain an albatross around the neck of his career at least until *THE GODFATHER: PART III*.

Far from the epic scale of *Heaven's Gate*, all this drama turns on a film with a slight, fairytale narrative. *One from the Heart* concerns the romantic trials of an unmarried couple living in Las Vegas—

Hank, an auto mechanic, and Frannie, a travel agent—over the Fourth of July weekend. Hank and Frannie have a fight that leads to a breakup over the anniversary gifts they exchange, revealing their contrasting visions of the relationship: Frannie presents a pair of tickets to Bora Bora, Hank presents the deed to the house they have been renting. Frannie feels stifled by Hank, who can't understand her need for romance. Frannie leaves to stay with her best friend, Maggie, while Hank goes to his best friend, Moe, for succor. The next day, each tries to embrace the freedom of being single, shopping and preparing for a night on the town. Frannie is wooed by Ray, a waiter/pianist, while Hank flirts with Leila, a trapeze artist in a circus family; each of these couples spends the night together. The next morning, Hank searches for Frannie (while Leila, rejected, literally disappears), as Frannie and Ray plan an escape to Bora Bora. While Hank searches for Frannie, Moe and Maggie meet in another new coupling. Hank

confronts Frannie at Ray's hotel, and while he drags her home, it is to no avail; "He doesn't yell at me," she says, "he sings to me." That night, Hank intercepts Frannie and Ray at the airport, and sings her "You Are My Sunshine" but again is rejected. At home alone in the dark, Hank cries; just then, Frannie returns to him.

The very simplicity of this narrative of romantic trials and reconciliation would be a focal point of criticism of the film. But on the film's release, this story would be completely overwhelmed by two other spectacular narratives, each of which achieved much greater cultural circulation: one centering on the economics of the film's production and distribution, and the other on the technology used to make it. In both, *One from the Heart* would be inextricably tied to the narrative of Zoetrope Studios itself, and to Coppola's auteur persona.

The production of *APOCALYPSE NOW* had served to create a perception of Coppola as a gambler, and Zoetrope Studios

Frederic Forrest and Nastassja Kinski.

was his riskiest venture, with *One from the Heart* its flagship, the principal outcome of, as *Saturday Review* proclaimed, his "long-simmering ambition to mate the old Hollywood of solid craftsmanship, company loyalty, and sound-stage productions with the new Hollywood of computer wizardry, film-school graduates, and sophisticated story-telling." In its stylization, *One from the Heart* is emblematic of a larger trend in the early 1980s as directors turned away from the realism and genre revisionism that dominated the preceding decade, instead embracing self-conscious artifice and a nostalgia for classical Hollywood conventions. This encouraged a return to sound-stage filming, particularly urgent for Coppola after the struggles over the filming of *Apocalypse* in the Philippines. *One from the Heart* was initially budgeted at $15 million and would be distributed by Paramount (with a back-end deal enabling them to withhold funds contingent upon approval of the completed film, but also giving Coppola the collateral necessary to obtain funds from banks and other investors). Although it featured a modestly scaled story, Coppola would recreate Las Vegas on the Zoetrope stages, with mammoth sets entailing the employment of 350 construction workers; the neon lights alone would cost $1 million. Soon, revised estimates put the budget at $23 million, with a final tally of $27 million, and financial crises resulted in employees working without pay out of sheer loyalty to Coppola and his dream. Further loans would be necessary, one of which, from Canadian real estate magnate Jack Singer with the Zoetrope lot as collateral, enabled the production to conclude, with $4 million still needed for postproduction. Coppola spent the money, confident of being repaid by Paramount on completion, but Barry Diller, Paramount CEO, balked. Now Coppola was forced to offer both the studio and his personal assets as collateral (thus the failure of the film bedeviled Coppola for nearly a decade).

But his struggles were far from over. Paramount screened a rough cut (reportedly missing most of the visual-effects shots) to exhibitors; the negative response made the national press. Coppola retaliated in the press, and arranged a preview of a more polished print at the Radio City Music Hall without Paramount's permission (to a lukewarm reception at best); Paramount dropped the film three days later. In an environment tainted by bad press around these events, Columbia acquired it, and rushed it into limited release in February 1982. This strategy proved disastrous, and by April Columbia and Coppola chose to scrap a national release and shelve the film. It grossed just $1.2 million. By the end of the month, the Zoetrope Studios property was up for auction; by February 1984, Jack Singer bought it for $12.3 million (it had been appraised at a value of $17 million).

If the press around economics quickly spiraled out of Coppola's control, he remains largely responsible for the other major discourse around *One from the Heart*, centered on the technical innovations used in its production. Coppola spoke widely about the film as the product of an innovative "electronic cinema" process; this was the focus of *American Cinematographer*'s exhaustive coverage of the film, and of much of the national press as well (e.g., *The Boston Globe*: "Coppola's New Gamble: High Stakes on High Tech"), which saw Coppola heralding cinema's "greatest leap forward since the invention of sound," one that would "revolutionize the film industry." This entailed a "previsualization" process whereby storyboards were videotaped, accompanied by line readings from the performers, followed by taped run-throughs of the scenes with the actors on location. During filming, video cameras were attached to the film cameras to provide an immediate record of what was being shot (here appropriating Jerry Lewis's use of video-assist). These signals were sent to a trailer dubbed the "Silverfish," outfitted with monitors, a control board, and a microphone transmitted to a PA system on the soundstage, allowing Coppola to see and respond to footage as it was being shot. (Disagreement remains over the extent to which Coppola directed actors from the Silverfish, rather than simply monitoring takes.) Video recordings, including transfers of the footage shot, allowed Coppola and his team to edit almost instantly, and replicate their choices when cutting the negative. The process, central both to the making of *One from the Heart* and to Zoetrope's synthesis of the "old Hollywood" studio system with new technology, was intended both to give the director an extraordinary degree of control over the image manipulation during shooting, and to radically streamline the postproduction process. For Coppola, there would be no contradiction between his technological obsessions and his responsibilities as a storyteller: "There is and can be content in technology. New tunes that we've never heard before, because they've never been possible before."

Coppola was widely portrayed as a madman for comments such as these, at the Fifty-first Academy Awards: "We're on the eve of something that's going to make the industrial revolution look like a small out-of-town tryout. I can see a communications revolution that's about movies and art and music and digital electronics and satellites, but above all, *human* talent—and it's going to make the masters of the cinema, from whom we've inherited the business, believe things they would have thought impossible." (Today, this seems extraordinarily prophetic.) Much of the twenty-two-month production process and expense of the film involved developing this system. As Jon Lewis puts it, "Coppola's hype that

One from the Heart was a kind of trial run for *his* new technology just made matters worse. No studio wanted to fund Zoetrope's research and development without a stake in the technologies' future use and revenue." Coppola's predictions that video would liberate access to filmmaking and spell doom for the studios further helped to antagonize the studios. Moreover, in reviews, the narratives of technological and economic excess were folded together, helping to foment the idea that Coppola's ambitions had overwhelmed his storytelling. Pauline Kael described the film as "cold and mechanized": "This movie isn't from the heart, or from the head, either; it's from the lab. It's all tricked out with dissolves and scrim effects and superimpositions, and even aural superimpositions." Similar claims were made in each of the three write-ups of the film in the *New York Times*. On its opening, Vincent Canby wrote that this romantic comedy/musical was "about as frothy as *2001*," and, noting the widespread return to studio production, revisited the film's "failings" in a piece titled "Obsession with Technique": "*One from the Heart* has no characters, no performances, no story, no comedy, no romance, only what Hollywood calls 'production values.'" One of the very few major reviewers to praise the film was Sheila Benson in the *LA Times*: "A work of constant astonishment, Francis Coppola's new film is so daring it takes away your breath while staggering you visually. . . . Coppola's leap into years-ahead technology is sure and dazzling. 'It's artificial,' he seems to say. 'Isn't it gorgeous?' Indeed it is—sumptuous, sensuous, stunning."

At the same time, discussion of the technology utilized in the production was matched by an acknowledgment of its nostalgic roots in the classical Hollywood musical and in theatrical traditions. One journalist described Zoetrope as "a beautiful little repertory company growing right here in the fertile soil of Hollywood." *One from the Heart* draws heavily on theatrical techniques like the use of scrims and lighting to effect spatial transitions within shots ("live cuts"), allowing for long, uninterrupted takes (discussed further below). Coppola boasted that "The entire film has so many long takes—one goes on for ten minutes." Producer Gray Frederickson reinforced parallels to theatre on the level of performance rather than style when speaking of the advantages of this approach: "It's fun—the actors love it. It's like a live production. . . . They can run through a whole scene and really get into it."

This is but one of the many contradictions that characterize the complexities of the film. Generically, the film is a romance, but with moments of comedy and, especially in the closing segments, poignant emotion. In the context of a romance narrative, the setting functions as much more than a backdrop; as Coppola put it, "With its polarity of fantasy, glitter, reality, disappointment, and everything turning on the notion of chance, Vegas is the perfect place to set a love story." It is a musical, featuring a lavishly staged dance number on the Vegas Strip (featuring Frannie and Ray) with extradiegetic music, Hank's fantasy of Leila singing "Little Boy Blue," and Hank conducting an orchestra of wrecked cars at the garage while Leila does a high-wire act. But the only song sung by a major character that advances the narrative is Hank's forlorn "You Are My Sunshine." Otherwise, extradiegetic music sung by TOM WAITS and Crystal Gayle is used to comment on the action, particularly in the opening scenes (the line "Once upon a town" helping to establish the theme of chance that links Vegas to the vicissitudes of love), introducing Hank and Frannie, and the closing scenes of reconciliation (from "Oh baby, this one's from the heart" at the air-

port, to Gayle's "Come here, you silly boy" when Frannie returns to Hank).

It is a film with a simple, fabulistic narrative, but there is also considerable formal complexity, encouraging comparisons to Max Ophüls. Throughout, Coppola builds the film around alternation and parallel editing, extending his use of these techniques in all of his 1970s films. The opening shows Hank and Frannie, in turn, at work, then returning home. Once they break up, the film alternates between the two of them at their respective friends' apartments (with scrim and mirror effects and tracking movements taking us from one to the other). The next day, each prepares for their night on the town while relaying to their friends the story of how they met; again, alternation between them allows for comparisons to be drawn, demonstrating a residual emotional investment in their relationship. When each character hits the Strip on the night of July 4, Coppola cuts between them, showing them just missing each other in an intricately choreographed sequence of shots. Later, alternation allows for mainly contrasts (in their motives and desires) between Frannie's rendezvous with Ray and Hank's with Leila and the aftermath of their assignations, as a contrite Hank searches for a Frannie who remains determined to escape to Bora Bora with Ray.

This alternation provides the rationale for the filmmakers' use of theatrical transitions and highly artificial lighting and color effects. Like the songs, visual style here serves in part to comment on the action, and indeed is treated almost musically, its sheer lushness of design calling up notions of arrangement and orchestration. On this level, we can again observe seemingly contradictory, even dissonant, aims embodied by the film's aesthetics, between realism and artifice. Coppola told

Saturday Review that his intent was "to take a fable-like story and treat it almost the way Disney would approach a story in his animated films. . . . Treat it with very expressive sets and lighting and music that heighten the story." Thus, lighting effects and transitions are blatantly artificial and lacking in practical motivation; for example, when Frannie works on her Bora Bora window at the travel agency, the lights of the Strip appear, reflected in the glass, only when Ray appears. At the conclusion, Hank sits in a darkened living room at the end, yet the lighting rises when Frannie steps into frame.

But the level of decorative, pictorial stylization on offer here is used to convey a story about working-class people (begging a comparison to Demy's *The Umbrellas of Cherbourg*), and the dinginess of Hank and Frannie's house conveys a sense of lumpen-prole that contrasts sharply with the polished surfaces of Coppola's recreation of Las Vegas. The union of realism (on the level of characters and narrative) and artifice (on the level of style) justifies a comparison to Luchino Visconti's *La notte bianchi* (1957). Visconti recreates a dilapidated, rubble-strewn Verona on a soundstage; he uses scrims for atmosphere; and he builds discontinuous sets adjacent to one another so that he can range across Verona and from the present into flashback with a camera movement rather than a cut. Coppola, too, has rebuilt a city on a soundstage (though his Las Vegas is part realistic, part fantastically stylized); he uses scrims (and mirrors) to effect transitions between, and superimpositions of, discontinuous spaces (in the first instance, Hank at Moe's and Frannie at Maggie's), again constructed contiguously on his soundstage, and he uses camera movements to take us from the one to the other in carefully choreographed long takes. In this way, theatrical devices

replace editing in the construction of space, further allowing juxtapositions in the form of superimposed images to create parallels between the characters.

Indeed, *One from the Heart* represents Coppola's first sustained exploration of virtuosic tracking shots, in collaboration with principal cinematographer VITTORIO STORARO, with extensive use of the then relatively new Steadicam technology (operated by its creator, Garrett Brown). Bravura camera movements would remain a prominent trait of Coppola's later films, in particular *THE COTTON CLUB* (1984), *TUCKER: THE MAN AND HIS DREAM* (1988), and *BRAM STOKER'S DRACULA* (1992). Coppola's collaboration with Storaro on this and the preceding *Apocalypse Now* (1979) also gave rise to a sustained interest in color experimentation, particularly apparent in *THE OUTSIDERS* and *RUMBLE FISH* (both 1983) in addition to the above named. In this film, color, like music, functions to comment on the action, largely through a rigorous system of patterned contrasts. Storaro described the film as "a totally unrealistic picture. We are expressing subliminally the emotions of the characters—expressing them in a more theatrical way." Further, Storaro wrote a detailed manifesto for his contribution to the film, centered on color aesthetics. As the story concerned male/female conflicts, so the film would reflect these conflicts through color contrasts, which moreover, he felt, would have a direct impact on spectators: "The lights of Vegas break the equilibrium of nature, change the heartbeats, increase the metabolism. Colors such as 'RED,' the symbol of conquest, lights above the town, has the tendency of increasing the blood pressure; 'YELLOW' and 'ORANGE' stimulate the nervous vascular system," while green and blue "have a regenerative effect." In that the Strip setting calls for a profusion of colors, "Vegas has a *cata-bolic* effect," inducing "the increase of the metabolism and the endocrine secretions," and enabling a "conflict between 'PURPLE-BLUE-GREEN,' the reentering colors, and 'RED-ORANGE-YELLOW,' the going-out colors" that then represents through color "the emotions and state of soul that distinguishes our separate moments of life."

Though reds typically appear in moments of passion and high emotion (both romance and strife), generally color is not used according to a particular symbology but is driven by the notion of conflict itself. Red is dominant when Hank and Frannie make love, but also when they fight (both in the breakup and when Hank drags Frannie from Ray's hotel). When Hank and Frannie are cross-cut on the Strip, each is associated with red and blue in turn, but always in contrast with the dominant color used in shots of the other. Later, scenes of Hank and Leila are bathed in blues and greens, while scenes of Frannie and Ray are suffused with red (when they make love, and again when they make plans for Bora Bora). The range of saturated hues seen across the film then sets the final segment into relief: Hank's return from the airport is strikingly desaturated, almost black and white, while the bright *white* light that rises upon Frannie's return in itself suggests a reconciliation.

In all these respects, Coppola and his team engaged in a level of experimentation on *One from the Heart* that perhaps doomed it to failure, particularly in the context of blockbuster production. Its poor reception from critics and audiences is explicable at least in part as a response to the film's radical departure from the realist, art cinematic approach to genre seen in Coppola's preceding films, films that established expectations with which he has continued to struggle. Arguably, too, the film fell on blind eyes and deaf ears by virtue of its indulgence in hyperbolic stylization to a degree that would become increasingly conventional in later years. Certainly its failure, and the aftermath of that failure, would change the course of Coppola's life and career. But its innovations would also influence the aesthetics of Coppola's subsequent films, in terms of not only color and cinematography, but also the mise-en-scène and soundstage filming of *Tucker* and *Dracula*. In this respect, Coppola's comments at the time perhaps remain *One from the Heart*'s most pertinent epitaph. As he told Lillian Ross, "It's an unusual film, and it can be proved only by time. Maybe it's something only *I* cherish. Maybe the film doesn't make itself understood. All I know is that I got twenty-seven million dollars' worth out of making the film, because it represents everything I will want in the next thirty years. There's plenty to learn from that movie. . . . Few people seemed to look at the movie in just its own light, as a personal film a filmmaker had made in which he was maybe trying to find a new vocabulary for himself."
—PAUL RAMAEKER

References

Garrett Brown, "Steadicam and *One from the Heart*," *American Cinematographer*, January 1982, 44–45, 82; Thomas Brown, "The Electronic Camera Experiment," *American Cinematographer*, January 1982, 28–29, 76; Vincent Canby, "Coppola's *One from the Heart* Opens," *New York Times*, February 11, 1982, C25; Canby, "Obsession with Technique," *New York Times*, February 21, 1982, A13; Raymond Fielding, "Special Visual Effects for *One from the Heart*," *American Cinematographer*, January 1982, 30–31, 58; Wally Gentleman, "Visual Effects as a Cinematic Art Form," *American Cinematographer*, January 1982, 32–33, 80; Jeanne Goodman, "Coppola's New Gamble: High Stakes on High Tech," *Boston Globe*, August 30, 1981, 1; Scott Haller, "Coppola's Biggest Gamble: *One from the Heart*," in Gene D. Phillips and Rodney Hill, eds., *Francis Ford Coppola: Interviews* (Oxford: University Press of Mississippi, 2004); Jon Lewis, *Whom God Wishes to Destroy . . . : Francis Coppola and the New Hollywood* (Durham, NC: Duke University Press, 1995); Janet Maslin, "Preview of *One from the Heart*," *New York Times*, January 17, 1982, A56; "Mating Film with Video for *One from the Heart*," *American Cinematographer*, January 1982, 24–25, 92; Gene D. Phillips, *Godfather: The Intimate Francis Ford Coppola* (Lexington: University Press of Kentucky, 2004); Lillian Ross, "Some Figures on a Fantasy," in Phillips and Hill, *Francis Ford Coppola*; Robert Swarthe, "Of Miniatures, Mattes and Magic," *American Cinematographer*, January 1982, 38–39, 49.

ON THE ROAD (2011?)

FRANCIS COPPOLA's long-delayed production of Jack Kerouac's 1957 classic of "Beat" literature (originally optioned as early as 1968) is still facing delays as of 2010. The current production—originally set to begin in 2006, with Walter Salles directing from a script by Jose Rivera, produced by Focus Features, Pathé, and AMERICAN ZOETROPE— got pushed back to the fall of 2009, with a projected 2011 release. However, in September 2009, Salles told *Variety* that he was still seeking financing for the film.

In addition to Coppola himself, numerous other screenwriters over the years have tried their hand (unsuccessfully) at adapting *On the Road* for Coppola, including MICHAEL HERR, Russell Banks, and Barry Gifford. At one point, Coppola planned to direct the film adaptation himself, and he was considering shooting in 16 mm black-and-white. Later, his plans to have Joel Schumacher direct, with Colin Farrell starring, also fell through.

The most recent resurrection of Coppola's *On the Road* project came amid a flurry of films centering on the "Beat" generation: *Howl*, with James Franco as a young Allen Ginsberg, and *Kill Your Darlings*, about Kerouac, Ginsberg, and fellow "Beat" Lucien Carr (both films in development as of 2009), as well as the documentary *Corso: The Last Beat* (2009), narrated by Ethan Hawke, and Walter Salles's own "companion piece" documentary in which he follows the path traveled in the novel, interviewing people along the way who knew Kerouac.

Salles told CNN: "I am not really interested in doing a period piece that wouldn't have a correlation with what we are living right now. There is a strange modernity to the theme, and maybe *On the Road* is more contemporary today than it ever was." —RODNEY HILL

References

Steve Chagollan, "Directors Dig into Beat Era," *Variety*, May 29, 2009; Bob Morris, "The Night; for Actors a Casting Call and a Cautionary Note," *New York Times*, February 12, 1995; Nick Vivarelli, "Vatican Hands Bresson Prize to Salles: Director Seeks Finance for Kerouac's 'Road,'" *Variety*, September 7, 2009; Grace Wong, "Walter Salles: Back on the Road," CNN: Screening Room, http://edition.cnn.com, October 10, 2008.

O'SULLIVAN, MAUREEN (1911–1998)

Veteran star of film, stage, and television who played Elizabeth Alvorg, Peggy Sue's grandmother, in FRANCIS COPPOLA's *PEGGY SUE GOT MARRIED* (1986). Maureen O'Sullivan started her film career at Fox in 1930, after being discovered by director Frank Borzage. Two years later, at MGM, she found the role that made her famous, playing Jane (to Johnny Weissmuller's Tarzan) in *Tarzan, the Ape Man*. A number of sequels followed in the next decade.

In 1936, O'Sullivan married the director John Farrow, and in the early 1940s she took a hiatus from acting to raise their children (including future actresses Mia and

Tisa Farrow). Returning to the big screen after her six-year absence, O'Sullivan starred in two of her husband's film noirs, *The Big Clock* (1948) and *Where Danger Lives* (1950). In the 1950s she turned to television drama, appearing in such anthology series as *Fireside Theater*, *Matinee Theater*, and *Star Stage*.

From the 1960s until the end of her career, Maureen O'Sullivan turned increasingly to the stage, with roles in *Never Too Late* and revivals of *The Front Page* and *Mornings at Seven*. For her work in the latter, she won an Outer Critics Circle Award and a Special Drama Desk Award.

Maureen O'Sullivan's last two film appearances were in *Peggy Sue Got Married* and Woody Allen's *Hannah and Her Sisters* (1986), in which she plays the alcoholic mother of Mia Farrow's title character. O'Sullivan subsequently was cast in Allen's *September* (1987) but was unable to finish the film; Elaine Stritch was recast in the role.—RODNEY HILL

Reference

"Maureen O'Sullivan: Biography," *Variety* Profiles, www.variety.com.

THE OUTSIDERS (1983)

DIRECTOR: Francis Ford Coppola. SCREENPLAY: Kathleen Knutsen Rowell and Francis Ford Coppola (uncredited), from the novel by S. E. Hinton. PRODUCERS: Fred Roos and Gray Frederickson for Zoetrope Studios/Warner Bros. ASSOCIATE PRODUCER: Gian-Carlo Coppola. PHOTOGRAPHY: Stephen H. Burum. EDITING: Anne Goursaud. MUSIC: Carmine Coppola. PRODUCTION DESIGN: Dean Tavoularis. COSTUME DESIGN: Marge Bowers. SPECIAL VISUAL EFFECTS: Robert Swarthe. SOUND DESIGN: Richard Beggs.
CAST: Matt Dillon (Dallas Winston), Ralph Macchio (Johnny Cade), C. Thomas Howell (Ponyboy Curtis), Patrick Swayze (Darrel Curtis), Rob Lowe (Sodapop Curtis), Emilio Estevez (Two-Bit Matthews), Tom Cruise (Steve Randle), Glenn Withrow (Tim Shephard), Diane Lane (Cherry Valance), Leif Garret (Bob Sheldon), Darren Dalton (Randy Anderson), Michelle Meyrink (Marcia), Gailard Sartain (Jerry), Tom Waits (Buck Merrill), William Smith (Store Clerk).
RUNNING TIME: 91 minutes. Technicolor, Panavision.
RELEASED THROUGH: Warner Bros. PREMIERE: March 25, 1983.
DVD: Warner Home Video.

In the fall of 1980 FRANCIS COPPOLA received a joint letter from the librarian of Lone Star High School in Fresno, California, Ellen Misakian, writing on behalf of several of the students who also signed the letter. After the release of *APOCALYPSE NOW* Coppola had served as executive producer on *THE BLACK STALLION* (1980), which became a hit with the youth market. The librarian accordingly urged Coppola to bring another teenage story, *The Outsiders*, to the screen.

Coppola was struck by the fact that the novel had been turned into a bestseller by its devoted teenage readers. The book, which was required reading in some high schools, had sold 4 million copies since its publication in 1967. The author of *The Outsiders*, S. E. (Susan Eloise) Hinton, was only sixteen when she wrote the book. She had disguised the fact that the novel was written by a girl by using a pen name because she feared that her young readers might question the authenticity of her book about teenage boys if they were aware that the author was a female.

Coppola realized that he could easily design a film about teenagers on a much smaller scale than the big-budget movies he had made during the previous decade.

The Outsiders would be shot on location in Tulsa, Oklahoma, S. E. HINTON's hometown, where the story is set. In addition, he would cast promising young actors in the picture who did not yet command big salaries.

Kathleen Rowell, another young writer, was commissioned to adapt the book for film. The story involves the ongoing feud between two gangs of teenage boys living in Tulsa in the 1960s. One group is made up of underprivileged lads known as greasers, who are from the shabby north side of the city. The other group is made up of upper-class youngsters known as socs ("soc" rhymes with "gauche" and is short for "social"), who live on the prosperous south side of town. "*The Outsiders*," writes Lizzie Skurnick, "is *West Side Story* by way of Oklahoma." "All of the greasers were orphans, all outsiders," says Coppola, "but together they formed a family." Hence, the film touches on the theme of family so common in Coppola's work.

Coppola was disappointed in Rowell's adaptations of the novel. The two drafts of the screenplay she had done had meandered away from the book. Conscious that Hinton's readers would resent a movie that diverged too much from the novel, Coppola decided to do a wholesale rewrite of her screenplay, sticking as closely as possible to the literary source. When one examines the script, it is evident that Coppola's version is extremely faithful to the source material, even incorporating actual dialogue from the book at times.

Because of the substantial work he did in completely overhauling the script, Coppola petitioned the Screen Writers Guild to award him an official screen credit as sole author of the screenplay for *The Outsiders*. Coppola claims that he lost the arbitration battle because of the Writers Guild's "antiquated procedures." The Guild's decisions, he explains, always weigh heavily in favor

of the first writer to do an adaptation of a literary work for film because they establish the characters and the basic plot for the screenplay. He concluded, "Even though I sat down and wrote the script that I used, the Guild gave her *all* the credit. Yet that woman simply did not write the script of the film that I made."

"The book was a kind of *Gone with the Wind* for kids, an epic classic struggle between the greasers and the socs, i.e., the poor and the rich, during the 1960s," Coppola explains. Indeed, the dog-eared paperback copy of *Gone with the Wind* that the young hero carries around with him almost amounts to a talisman. Coppola told his father, CARMINE COPPOLA, that, since *The Outsiders* was a *Gone with the Wind* for teens, he wanted "a kind of schmaltzy classical score," similar to the one Max Steiner had written for the 1939 movie of *Gone with the Wind*. "It appealed to me that kids could see *Outsiders* as a lavish, big-feeling epic about kids." *The Outsiders* would be filmed in widescreen and color in order to recreate the world of romantic melodrama.

For his part, Coppola shrewdly chose what one observer termed an honor roll of hot young actors, including TOM CRUISE, EMILIO ESTEVEZ, C. THOMAS HOWELL, ROB LOWE, RALPH MACCHIO, and PATRICK SWAYZE. Coppola thereby launched a whole generation of young film actors with this picture. He converted the gym of an abandoned schoolhouse into a rehearsal hall, where he videotaped the rehearsals in order to aid the young actors in developing their characterizations. Emilio Estevez (the oldest son of MARTIN SHEEN, using his father's real surname), helped to bring his character to life as one of the greasers by devising his own ducktail hairdo, a style quite popular with teenage boys in the 1960s.

Shooting started on March 29, 1982. Once a scene was in the can, Coppola would review it on the video monitor noting down suggestions for film editor Anne Goursaud, who was doing a preliminary edit of the movie back in Hollywood while it was being shot. Shooting wrapped on May 15, as planned. Estevez, who had visited his father on the set of *Apocalypse Now*, commented that Coppola "is getting his credibility back as a director who can deliver on schedule."

The Warners brass were dissatisfied with the rough cut, however, insisting that young people would not sit still for a teen picture that clocked in at two hours of screen time. The studio decreed that Coppola should shorten *The Outsiders* to ninety minutes. He regretted that in condensing the film he was forced to delete some of the scenes devoted to character development in favor of keeping mostly the plot-driven scenes.

The movie opens with Ponyboy (C. Thomas Howell), the film's narrator, beginning to write a composition for his teacher about some recent events in which he has figured. We hear him recount what happened in a voiceover as the plot unfolds. Ponyboy is the youngest of the three recently orphaned Curtis boys. Darrel, the oldest (Patrick Swayze), works hard to support his two younger brothers, and argues with Ponyboy, the youngest brother, about his belonging to a street gang. Sodapop, the middle brother (Rob Lowe), plays the role of conciliator between his two brothers.

Ponyboy belongs to the greasers, most of whom are orphans like himself, boys who have consequently formed a surrogate family of their own. The gang member that Ponyboy looks up to as a father figure is Dallas (MATT DILLON), a streetwise young fellow who has just gotten out of jail. One night, Ponyboy and another chum, Johnny (Ralph Macchio), are accosted by some members of the rival gang, who are drunk. When the other boys attack Pony-

boy, Johnny panics and pulls a knife, stabbing one of them to death. Johnny and Ponyboy run to Dallas for help, and he advises them to hide out in an abandoned country church for the time being.

The film has no shortage of visual imagery. When Ponyboy and Johnny move into the ramshackle church, Coppola cuts to two bunny rabbits huddled underneath the porch—a metaphor for the two fugitive lads hiding out together.

Although these two adolescent boys bear visible masculine traits (reflected in "the outward trappings of fist fights and interest in athletics"), Johnny and Ponyboy repeatedly express affection for one another. Their comradeship, says Richard Corliss, is not only familial but "unselfconsciously homoerotic. Left to their better selves, they can easily go all moony over sunsets, quote great swatches of Robert Frost's verse, or fall innocently asleep in each other's arms. Their ideal world is . . . a locker room; no women need apply to this dreamy brotherhood."

Those critics who have inferred a hint of homosexuality in this film misconstrue the value that Coppola places on male companionship in his movies (one thinks of the soldiers' camaraderie in his two Vietnam movies). In the present instance, Ponyboy and Johnny have not yet experienced a deep relationship in their lives. Consequently, they are experiencing in their friendship a relationship that is fulfilling for them on an emotional level that has nothing to do with sex.

Dallas comes to their hideout later on to tell them that Cherry (DIANE LANE), a witness to the fatal stabbing, is willing to testify on their behalf, and they decide to give themselves up. Before they can start back to town, however, a fire breaks out in the dilapidated church, and the trio are suddenly called upon to save the lives of some children who happen to be in the old building when the blaze starts. Tragically, Johnny is severely burned during the course of the courageous rescue effort, and he dies shortly afterward. When Johnny expires, Dallas cries out bitterly, "This is what you get for helping other people!"

Later on Dallas, the ex-convict, lapses into his old ways, attempts to hold up a store, and is killed in a reckless scuffle with the police. Reflecting on the loss of his two best friends, Ponyboy hopes to come to terms with this double tragedy by writing down what happened in a composition for his teacher. After all, one of his brothers tells him, "Your life isn't over because you lose someone." And so the movie ends where it began, with Ponyboy writing the essay that forms the content of the film's spoken narration.

The Outsiders was a bona fide blockbuster, despite the fact that some critics dismissed the movie as a minor melodrama unworthy of Coppola's directorial talents. On the contrary, the picture deserves a respected place in the Coppola canon for various reasons, not the least of which is the host of consistently excellent performances he drew from his youthful cast.

On the technical side, Stephen Burum's camera work in the movie, which was filmed entirely on location in Tulsa, Oklahoma, is superb. For example, in the sequence of Johnny and Ponyboy's sojourn in the country, there are shots of the pair silhouetted against a blood-red sunset, reminiscent of similar images in *Gone with the Wind*, Ponyboy's favorite film.

By the same token, Coppola employs shots of some incandescently beautiful sunsets throughout the movie to symbolize the brevity of youth. "When you watch the sun set, you realize it is already dying," he explains. "The same applies to youth. When youth reaches its highest level of

C. Thomas Howell, Rob Lowe, and Patrick Swayze.

perfection, you can already sense the forces that will destroy it." Coppola's remark becomes still more meaningful when one relates the golden sunsets pictured in the movie to a poem by Robert Frost that Ponyboy recites to Johnny, in which the poet likens the innocence of childhood to gold. Johnny picks up on the poem's theme by offering his pal this advice: "Stay gold, Ponyboy; stay gold." This is Johnny's way of encouraging Ponyboy not to lose the fundamental wholesomeness of youth as he grows older and is forced to face more and more of the grim realities of the adult world.

After the overwhelming problems Coppola encountered in financing and marketing *Apocalypse Now* and *ONE FROM THE HEART*, some critics found it refreshing to encounter a Coppola film that, bless it, was only a conventional genre picture about teenage rebellion. What's more, the youth audience took the picture to their hearts. The film earned $12 million in its first two weeks in release and eventually reaped $100 million in profits.

After finishing the feature film of *The Outsiders*, Coppola followed it immediately with the screen adaptation of another Hinton novel, *RUMBLE FISH*. For her part, Susie Hinton continued to write novels aimed at the youth market. Indeed, in June 2008, she was the recipient of the annual *Chicago Tribune* Young Adult Book Prize.—Gene D. Phillips

References

Ronald Bergan, *Francis Ford Coppola* (New York: Crest Books, 1998); Richard Corliss, "Playing Tough," *Time*, April 4, 1983, 78; Scott Foundas, "Coppola Rising," *DGA Quarterly* 3, no. 1 (Spring, 2007): 1–9; Lizzie Skurnick, "The Brotherhood of S. E. Hinton," *Chicago Tribune Books*, May 30, 2008, 6–7; Elizabeth Taylor, "Interview with S. E. Hinton," *Chicago Tribune Books*, May 30, 2008, 7–8; David Thomson and Lucy Gray, "Idols of the King: *The Outsiders* and *Rumble Fish*," *Film Comment* 19, no. 5 (September–October, 1983): 61–75.

THE OUTSIDERS: EXPANDED VERSION (2005)

FRANCIS COPPOLA released an extended version of his 1983 movie *THE OUTSIDERS* on DVD in 2005. Coppola had trimmed twenty-two minutes of footage from the original release version of *The Outsiders*, which ran 91 minutes, because the studio felt it was too long for a youth-oriented movie. The story revolves around an ongoing feud between two gangs of teenage boys in Tulsa, Oklahoma, the greasers and the socs (pronounced *soshes*, for social). Over the years, Coppola says, "I would get letters from a new crop of fourteen-year-olds saying, 'I like the movie, but why didn't you have this or that scene from the book?'"

The main impetus for proceeding with the extended version of the movie came from Coppola's sixteen-year-old granddaughter Gia (the daughter of his deceased son Gio), when she asked him to show *The Outsiders* to her class. "I cobbled together a new version with additional footage that had been excised from the movie the first time around," Coppola recalled, and dispersed it throughout the picture. He did not want his granddaughter embarrassed by her classmates asking about the missing scenes.

"I simply put back the footage I had eliminated from the first version," Coppola explains. "It was not difficult to put it back, since it had all been in the film in the first place." After all, the scenes he had cut were complete and ready for inclusion in the restored version, which runs 113 minutes.

"One scene that kids often asked about," writes Nancy Ramsey, "is the scene that is now the opening of the film." Ponyboy Curtis (C. THOMAS HOWELL), one of the youngest of the greasers, is followed and harassed by the socs. "It's an elaborate introduction to the major characters that sets up the conflict between the greasers and the socs," says Coppola in his commentary on the DVD of the expanded version. This sequence leads into the one in which Ponyboy and Johnny, Ponyboy's best friend, meet up with Dallas (MATT DILLON), the leader of the greasers, which was the opening scene of the cut version.

Another scene jettisoned from the original film shows Ponyboy and Sodapop (ROB LOWE), his older brother, cuddling in bed, talking before they fall asleep. "I thought the scene was innocent enough," remarks Coppola; and it certainly did not imply that the boys were homosexual. "But I had a preview of the film, and there were some snickers in the audience. So I removed the scene from the movie. He reinstated the scene, however, in the expanded version. "The intimacy of the scene carries an undeniable frisson," Manohla Dargis comments, "largely because such physical closeness between straight males is nearly absent from our screens. There is . . . an innocence in the brothers' embrace."

Among the scenes Coppola had to jettison from *The Outsiders* in order to edit the movie to the length stipulated by Warners, the one that really enhances the picture by its inclusion comes near film's end. There is a rap session in which the Curtis brothers, Ponyboy, Sodapop, and Darrel, reflect frankly on the life lessons they have learned from their recent shared experiences. They renew their closeness as a family; as Sodapop says, "If we don't have each other, we don't have anything. If you don't have anything, you end up like Dallas," who was an unhappy loner. This scene underscores the film's affirmation of the young people's deep need to belong, and as such, its inclusion in the movie is important.

Coppola christened the restored version of the movie *The Outsiders: The Complete Novel.*—GENE D. PHILLIPS

References

Stephen Farber, "Directors Join the S. E. Hinton Fan Club," *New York Times*, March 20, 1983, sec. 2: 19; Manohla Dargis, "Coppola Pays a Return Visit to *The Outsiders*," *New York Times*, September 9, 2005, B3; Nancy Ramsey, "*The Outsiders* Touched Coppola," *Los Angeles Times Calendar*, September 18, 2005, 1.

P

PACINO, AL [ALFREDO JAMES] (1940–)

American actor of Sicilian descent who perfectly interpreted the role of Michael Corleone as heir to Don Vito in *THE GOD-FATHER* trilogy. At the time he was cast, Pacino was primarily a New York stage actor who had only played a major role in one film, *Panic in Needle Park* (1971). FRANCIS COPPOLA wanted Pacino to play Michael from the start, but he had to fight for his choice, since the studio thought Pacino was a runt and wanted Ryan O'Neal or Robert Redford for the role. Pacino was also considered for the part of Willard in *APOCALYPSE NOW* and even read the script, but, according to Eleanor Coppola's *NOTES*, Pacino concluded that he couldn't "do it because he wouldn't be able to stand 17 weeks in the jungle."

Alfredo Pacino was born on April 25, 1940, the son of Rosa and Salvatore Alfred Pacino in New York City's East Harlem; after his parents separated in 1942, Pacino moved with his mother to the South Bronx to live with her parents, Kate and James Gerardi, who had immigrated to New York from Corleone, Sicily. The boy attended Manhattan's High School of Performing Arts, affiliated with the Fiorello La Guardia High School of Music and the Arts, until he dropped out at the age of 17 to find work. Eventually he resumed his stage preparation, and was tutored by Charles Laughton at Herbert Berghof's acting studio. In 1966

he was admitted to LEE STRASBERG's Actors Studio, where, nearly twenty years later, he would serve as co-artistic director with Ellen Burstyn, from 1982 to 1984. He was also affiliated with David Wheeler's Experimental Theater Company in Boston, where he performed in Bertolt Brecht's *The Resistible Rise of Arturo Ui* and in Shakespeare's *Richard III*. He also performed in *Richard III* and *Julius Caesar* in New York and in David Mamet's *American Buffalo* in New York and London.

Pacino made his off-Broadway debut in two plays, *The Connection* and *Hello, Out There*. He won an Obie Award in 1968 for his performance in Israel Horovitz's *The Indian Wants the Bronx* and two Tony Awards for his starring roles in *The Basic Training of Pavlo Hummel* (1977) and *Does a Tiger Wear a Necktie?* (1969). He played Shakespeare's *Richard III* on stage and later made his documentary film about researching that role, *Looking for Richard* (1996).

Pacino's screen debut came about playing a minor role in *Me, Natalie* (1969). Most of Pacino's choices for film roles have been on target and successful, especially *Carlito's Way* (1993), *Frankie and Johnny* (1991), *Sea of Love* (1989), *Bobby Deerfield* (1977), and *Scarecrow*, winner of the Palme d'Or the CANNES FILM FESTIVAL in 1973. Pacino received Best Actor Oscar nominations for his roles in *. . . And Justice for All* (1979), *THE GODFATHER: PART II* (1974), *Dog*

Day Afternoon (1975) and *Serpico* (1973). He finally won the Best Actor Academy Award for his performance as Lt. Colonel Frank Slade in *Scent of a Woman* (1992). That same year he was also nominated for Best Supporting Actor for portraying Ricky Roma in the James Foley adaptation of David Mamet's *Glengarry Glen Ross*. Pacino has sometimes had a tendency to overplay characters, as he does to good effect playing the brash, over-confident Ricky Roma in *Glengarry Glen Ross*, a tendency that he took to another level as Cuban drug lord Tony Montana in *Scarface* (1983), and then to parody level in *The Devil's Advocate* (1997). Pacino also has demonstrated a real talent for portraying down-and-out characters, in *Dog Day Afternoon* (1975), for example, and, more recently, with his performance as Lefty Ruggiero, an over-the-hill, low-level Mafioso who recruits undercover FBI Agent Joe Pistone (Johnny Depp) in *Donnie Brasco*, directed by Mike Newell in 1997.

Pacino has been nominated for Golden Globe Awards too numerous to mention. He won BAFTA Awards from the British Academy for Best Actor two years in a row, in 1974 for *Godfather II* and in 1975 for *Dog Day Afternoon*. In 1996 he won the Director's Guild Award for Outstanding Achievement in Documentary for his *Looking for Richard*. In 2003 he earned an Emmy Award for Best Lead Actor for his portrayal of Roy Cohn in *Angels in America* and the Screen Actors Guild Award for that same performance. On October 20, 2006, Al Pacino was the recipient of the thirty-fifth AFI Life Achievement Award given by the American Film Institute. Such recognition gives credence to the claim that Pacino may be "one of the greatest actors in all film history." His talent has found roles for him with scores of top directors, from Francis Coppola to Oliver Stone in *Any Given Sunday* (1999).—JAMES M. WELSH

Al Pacino and Richard Bright in *The Godfather: Part III*.

PAGE, GERALDINE [SUE] (1924–1987)

Respected stage and screen actress who played Margery Chanticleer in *YOU'RE A BIG BOY NOW* (1966), FRANCIS COPPOLA's master's thesis project at UCLA, which also featured Page's husband, RIP TORN. Born November 22, 1924, in Kirksville, Missouri, she was the daughter of Edna Pearl Page and Leon Elwin Page, an osteopathic physician and surgeon.

Page studied at the Goodman School of Drama in Chicago from 1942 to 1945. In the late 1940s, she moved to New York City, supporting herself variously as a hat-check girl, a lingerie model, and a factory worker, while trying to find work in the theatre. Her big break came in 1952 in an off-Broadway revival of Tennessee Williams's *Summer and Smoke* at Circle in the Square. Thanks to positive reviews in that show, Page found herself on Broadway the following year, in *Midsummer*, for which she received critical raves and ultimately star billing. She appeared in several other Broadway shows during the 1950s, including Tennessee Williams's *Sweet Bird of Youth* in 1959, and eventually became closely identified with the obsessive, troubled heroines of Williams's plays. Williams once described her as "the most disciplined and dedicated of actresses." She was also closely associated with LEE STRASBERG and the Actors Studio.

In 1961 Geraldine Page received her first Oscar nomination, for her role in the screen adaptation of *Summer and Smoke*. The following year brought her another nomination, for the film version of *Sweet Bird of Youth*. For both films, Page was named Best Actress at the Golden Globe Awards. Over the years she would be nominated a total of nine times for the Academy Award and would finally win the trophy for *The Trip to Bountiful* (1985). She also received a BAFTA Award as Best Supporting Actress for her role in Woody Allen's *Interiors* (1979).

One of Geraldine Page's Oscar nominations came for her supporting role as the mother of Peter Kastner's Bernard Chanticleer, in Coppola's *You're a Big Boy Now*, a role which also won her some critical notice. *Variety*, for example, had praise for Page and fellow cast members JULIE HARRIS and Rip Torn: "Both Geraldine Page as the mother and Harris as the landlady go all-out in hilarious roles and Torn, too, delivers a sock performance as the father who has difficulty understanding his son."

Geraldine Page remained active in her career, chiefly on the stage, for the remainder of her life. At the time of her death in 1987, she had been appearing on Broadway in a revival of Noël Coward's *Blithe Spirit*. She died in her home in New York City's Chelsea district on June 13, 1987, from a heart attack.—RODNEY HILL

References

"Geraldine Page," Turner Classic Movies Database, www.tcmdb.com; Elizabeth Kolbert, "Geraldine Page, 62, Dies, a Star of Stage and Film," *New York Times*, June 15, 1987, www.nytimes.com; "You're a Big Boy Now," *Variety* staff review, 1966, www.variety.com.

PATTON (1970)

FRANCIS COPPOLA moonlighted as a screenwriter while he was pursuing a graduate degree in film at UCLA. He gained a reputation as a skillful script doctor during his tenure at Seven Arts, an independent film unit. In *IS PARIS BURNING?* (1966), the last film on which he collaborated for Seven Arts, Kirk Douglas did a cameo as General George S. Patton, who was involved in the liberation of Paris. This proved to be a harbinger of Coppola's next major assignment as a scriptwriter. In May 1965, Twentieth Century-Fox offered him $50,000 to write a script for a full-scale screen biography of the legendary General Patton, whose men had named him "Blood and Guts."

Producer Frank McCarthy had rejected several script drafts submitted by other writers and decided to infuse the project with some new blood by hiring Coppola, who would hopefully bring some fresh ideas to the project. Moreover, given the months he labored on *Is Paris Burning?* Coppola explains in Johnson's book, he was seen by the studio moguls as "a Second World War Specialist." However, since his military experience in actual fact consisted of a stint in military school, Coppola devoted himself to researching the life of the controversial general.

Coppola gradually realized that "Patton was obviously out of his mind." On the one hand, if he wrote a script glorifying Patton as a great American hero, as some of the previous scriptwriters had done, it would be laughed at. On the other hand, if he wrote a script that condemned Patton as a heartless martinet, the screenplay would be rejected out of hand. Consequently, Coppola opted to combine both approaches and focus on the duality of Patton's character—to show him as a medieval knight living in the wrong century, "a man out of touch with his time, a pathetic hero, a Don Quixote figure." The people who disapproved of Patton could say, "He was crazy; he loved war," while the people who believed him to be a hero could say, "We need a man like that now." Coppola concludes, "And that is precisely the effect the movie [*Patton*] had, which is why it was successful."

The most celebrated scene in the entire film, which was directed by Franklin Schaffner (*The Best Man*), is the opening, in which Patton, standing before an enormous American flag, addresses an unseen gathering of troops. Coppola comments that he was experimenting with the concept that if

a character just stands in front of the audience and talks for five minutes "the audience would know more about him than if you went into his past and told about his family life." In one memorable line, the outspoken Patton warns his men, "I want you to remember that no bastard ever won a war by dying for his country. He won it by making some other dumb bastard die for his country." Coppola composed this monologue by quoting from three of Patton's speeches and later opined that "it was the best scene in my script."

After devoting six months to the screenplay, which is dated December 27, 1965, Coppola moved on to other projects. In typical Hollywood fashion, his screenplay was passed on to other writers who altered it substantially. When the title role was offered to George C. Scott, he remembered having read Coppola's screenplay earlier. He stated flatly that he would accept the part only if they used Coppola's script. "Scott is the one who resurrected my version," says Coppola. Screenwriter Edmund North then made some modifications in the Coppola version, but the shooting script is essentially Coppola's work.

Coppola depicts both the triumphs and trials of the aggressive, eccentric general, just as he said he would. Thus the film presents Patton's decisive victory over German Field Marshal Rommel in the African campaign. But it also encompasses the scene in which Patton, while visiting a medical outpost near the war zone, accuses a whimpering soldier suffering from shell shock of malingering, calls him a "gutless coward," and slaps his face. The episode becomes notorious enough to reach Supreme Commander Dwight Eisenhower, who demands that Patton apologize in front of his troops.

Thus, the movie presents a portrait of this intriguing, complicated figure in an ambiguous fashion, showing him as a legendary commander committed to serving his country and also as a military leader who thirsted for fame and glory as the reward for his exploits on the battlefield. Accordingly, critics applauded the script for examining both the virtues and the faults of the general, without leaning too much in either direction—and that is precisely what Coppola intended to do from the start. In Coppola's screenplay, German film historian David Gaertner states, "Patton remains ambivalent to the very end."

This spectacular war epic (nearly three hours long), as it happened, did not reach the screen until 1970, when it won the Academy Award as the Best Picture of the Year as well as Oscars for Schaffner, Scott, Coppola, and North, who shared the official screen credit for the screenplay. By 1970 Coppola had already established himself as a film director in his own right.
—GENE D. PHILLIPS

References

David Gaertner, "*Patton,*" in *Movies of the Sixties*, ed. Jurgen Muller (Los Angeles: Taschen, 2005), 556–61; Robert Johnson, *Francis Ford Coppola* (Boston: Twayne, 1977).

PEGGY SUE GOT MARRIED (1986)

DIRECTOR: Francis Ford Coppola. SCREENPLAY: Jerry Leichtling, Arlene Sarner. PRODUCER: Paul R. Gurian for Tri-Star-American Zoetrope. EXECUTIVE PRODUCER: Barrie M. Osborne. PHOTOGRAPHY: Jordan Cronenweth. EDITING: Barry Malkin. MUSIC: John Barry. PRODUCTION DESIGN: Dean Tavoularis. ART DIRECTION: Alex Tavoularis. COSTUME DESIGN: Theadora Van Runkle. SUPERVISORY SOUND EDITING: Michael Kirchberger.
CAST: Kathleen Turner (Peggy Sue Kelcher [Bodell]), Nicolas Cage (Charlie Bodell), Barry Miller (Richard Norvik), Catherine Hicks (Carol Heath), Joan Allen (Maddie Nagle), Kevin J. O'Conor (Michael Fitzsimmons), Jim Carrey (Walter Getz), Lisa Jane Persky (Delores Dodge), Lucinda Jenney (Rosalie Testa), Wil Shriner (Arthur Nagle), Barbara Harris (Evelyn Kelcher), Don Murray (Jack Kelcher), Sofia Coppola (Nancy Kelcher), Maureen O'Sullivan (Elizabeth Alvorg), Leon Ames (Barney Alvorg), Randy Bourne, Helen Hunt (Beth Bodell).
RUNNING TIME: 103 minutes. Color (DeLuxe).
PREMIERE: October 5, 1986 (New York Film Festival).
DVD: Sony Pictures.

After the financial failure of *THE COTTON CLUB*, Coppola had much better luck with his next venture, *Peggy Sue Got Married*. Independent producer Ray Stark, for whom Coppola had labored as a screenwriter in the mid-1960s at Seven Arts, was planning *Peggy Sue Got Married*, a time-travel fantasy, as an independent production to be released by Tri-Star Pictures. Coppola's financial straits resulting from *The Cotton Club* compelled him to direct the romantic fantasy film, which was not exactly his cup of tea. "*Peggy Sue*, I must say, was not the kind of film that I normally would want to do," he explains. Nevertheless, "the project was ready to go and they wanted me."

In July 1983, ARLENE SARNER and JERRY LEICHTING, a husband-and-wife screenwriting team, had brought *Peggy Sue Got Married* to the attention of producer Paul Gurion, who in turn interested Ray Stark in making the picture for his independent film unit. The title of *Peggy Sue Got Married* was derived from a popular song by the late rock-and-roller Buddy Holly. The scenario portrays Peggy Sue as a middle-aged woman whose marriage to her husband Charlie is on the rocks. She is magically transported back to her senior year in high school and comes to terms with her past life. KATHLEEN TURNER (*Body Heat*) was picked to play the title role because she was halfway between the ages of the younger and the older Peggy Sue, whom she would be portraying in the movie.

In reworking the screenplay along with the scriptwriters prior to filming, Coppola says that the model he kept in mind was Thornton Wilder's endearing play *Our Town*, in which the heroine "goes back and sees . . . her youth." He wanted to invest the movie with "that kind of small-town charm and emotion." *Our Town* is a work steeped in Americana that depicts the day-to-day lives of ordinary citizens living in a whistle-stop. Like *Our Town*, *Peggy Sue Got Married* is a paean to those mundane details of life that we take for granted—and that pass away all too fleetingly.

The kind of emotion Coppola helped to inject into the screenplay is evident in the scene where Peggy Sue encounters her mother (Barbara Harris) for the first time in her dream of the past, after the hands of time have been turned back to her teen years. Peggy Sue is touched to see Evelyn, her mother, looking so young. She hugs Evelyn and blurts out, "Oh, Mom, I forgot that you were ever this young!" Peggy Sue is pleased to have her mother restored to her, but Evelyn wonders why her daughter is embracing her so warmly. This scene, more than any other in the movie, was inspired by a parallel scene in *Our Town*.

Coppola was going for deeper characterization in the rewrites, so he developed the role of Charlie Bodell, Peggy Sue's wayward husband, in the revised screenplay. He shows how Charlie's failed career aspirations help to account for his unhappiness in his later life.

When it came to casting, Coppola conferred with Gurion. It was actually Gurion, and not Coppola, who chose Coppola's nephew, NICOLAS CAGE, to play Peggy Sue's unfaithful husband. SOFIA COPPOLA, the director's daughter, would appear as Peggy Sue's kid sister, Nancy. Coppola had discovered several promising young actors in his earlier films, particularly *THE OUTSIDERS*. In the present movie, Jim Carrey, whom he chose to play Peggy Sue's classmate Walter Getz, would go on to become a superstar, as would Helen Hunt, who played Peggy Sue's daughter, Beth.

Two staples of Coppola's production crew were on hand—production designer DEAN TAVOULARIS and editor BARRY MALKIN. The underscore was to be composed by John Barry (*Body Heat*), who was responsible for the background music in *The Cotton Club*. Coppola selected Jordan Cronenweth as director of photography because he was impressed with Cronenweth's work on Ridley Scott's *Blade Runner*.

Because the picture is essentially an extended dream sequence, Coppola had Cronenweth suffuse the movie with bright, saturated colors to give it a nostalgic glow. "The basic approach," said Cronenweth, was to make *Peggy Sue Got Married* "a contemporary *Wizard of Oz*, painted with broad strokes." After all, Peggy Sue is knocked into the middle of her high school years the way that Dorothy in *The Wizard of Oz* is knocked into the middle of next week. The present film is a fanciful picture of the past that is meant to crystallize for the viewer Peggy Sue's yearnings for her lost youth. Hence, the movie is bathed in a golden glow and amounts to a valentine for a vanished past.

As always, Coppola prefaced the shooting period with a couple of weeks of videotaped rehearsals. Principal photography commenced near the end of August 1985 and involved location filming in Petaluma, California, which Coppola and Tavoularis had selected to serve as Santa Rosa, the small California town in which Peggy Sue grew up. Setting the film in Santa Rosa is perhaps an homage to Hitchcock's *Shadow of a Doubt* (1943), which was cowritten by Thornton Wilder and which takes place in the same sleepy town of Santa Rosa.

The shooting phase lasted eight weeks, ending in late October, and it proceeded without any noticeable mishaps. Coppola, of course, collaborated closely with editor Barry Malkin on the final cut, and postproduction went as smoothly as the shooting period had. The premiere was set for the fall of 1986.

From the film's opening sequence onward, Coppola demonstrates that he is in total control of his material. The picture begins with a shot of a TV set on which Charlie can be seen doing a commercial for his hardware store. Coppola's camera pulls back to reveal Peggy Sue primping at her dressing table before departing for the twenty-fifth anniversary reunion of her high school graduating class. Her back is to the television set, indicating that she has, at this junction, turned her back on her philandering spouse. Like Natalie Ravenna in *THE RAIN PEOPLE*, Peggy Sue Bodell has walked out on her husband, for the time being, at least. She is separated from Charlie, and their two children, Scott and Beth, live with her.

At any rate, Peggy Sue manages to pour herself into her glittery prom dress, which is described as a "blast from the past." As she struggles into the outfit, she implies that it must have shrunk while hanging in the closet so many years, but obviously it is an uncomfortable reminder that her figure is not as slim as it used to be.

When she arrives at the party, which is being held in the school gym, she is chagrined to see an enormous blowup of a photograph picturing Charlie and her as king and queen of the senior prom. The photo captures them at a moment in time when their relationship was happy and

carefree, rather than sad and careworn, as it eventually became.

Visual metaphors of this sort abound in the movie. As a balloon floats upward toward the rafters of the gym, one of the alumni reaches for it, but it gets away. So too, many of the hopes and dreams that Peggy Sue and her classmates nurtured when they were young have eluded their grasp, driven off by the frustrations and disappointments of later life—epitomized, in her case, by her foundering marriage to Charlie. When Charlie himself makes his appearance at the reunion, he is at first barely visible in the shadowy doorway. He is but a dim figure from Peggy Sue's youth, someone whom she will get to know all over again as she relives the past and thereby will be able to come to terms with the present.

Peggy Sue passes out at the reunion and wakes up back at old Buchanan High in 1960, her senior year. But she has brought with her on her trip down memory lane her forty-two-year-old mind, and hence she views things from a more mature perspective than she possessed the first time around. Thus, when Peggy Sue tells her younger sister that she would like to get to know her better, she adds a perceptive remark that could only have come from her older self: "I have too many unresolved relationships."

One relationship she has failed to resolve in her later life is that with her estranged husband, Charlie Bodell, who, of course, is still a teenager when Peggy Sue meets him in the course of her return visit to her youth. She and Charlie married right after high school. Peggy Sue ultimately decides during her visit to the past that none of the young men in her life—including Charlie—are viable prospects for matrimony. Therefore, she decides not to marry anyone this time around. "Peggy Sue *got* married—case closed!" she states emphatically. "I don't want to marry anyone!"

Early in the movie, before she was transported backward in time, Peggy Sue had mused to herself during the reunion celebration, "If I knew then what I know now, I'd do a lot of things differently." But the question is, now that she appears to have the chance of a lifetime to change her destiny by altering her past, will she?

When Charlie comes to court Peggy Sue during her return trip to her adolescent years, her sour experiences with him in later life prompt her to break their engagement. "I'm not going to marry you a second time," she tells the uncomprehending Charlie. But their lovers' quarrel comes to an end when they kiss and make up—and make love. And this occasion turns out to be the time Charlie gets Peggy Sue pregnant, with the result that she does in fact decide once again to marry Charlie. In short, she winds up not doing things any differently the second time around after all.

Meanwhile, back in the present time, Peggy Sue has been taken to the hospital in the wake of her fainting spell at the reunion.

Charlie is at her bedside when she awakens, and begs her to take him back. Their daughter is there too, and the three of them embrace. For Peggy Sue, the high school reunion has proved to be a family reunion as well. The reconciliation of Peggy Sue and her husband at the fadeout challenges the viewer with the notion that, as Gene Siskel put it, "it is a generous and proper idea for us to accept the whole package, faults and all, of the people we care about." *Peggy Sue Got Married* thus reaffirms the need we all have to preserve strong family ties in life, a perennial Coppola theme.

Peggy Sue Got Married begins with a shot of Peggy Sue reflected in her dressing table mirror. It concludes with a shot of Peggy Sue, Charlie, and Beth appearing together in the mirror in her hospital room. Whereas Peggy Sue was a solitary figure in her bedroom mirror at the outset, at film's end she is surrounded in the hospital mirror by her husband and daughter. "Coppola's last mirror shot frames Peggy Sue in a cheerful family context," says

Kathleen Turner and Nicolas Cage.

Lee Lourdeaux. The last shot of the film matches the opening shot, thereby allowing the opening and closing images of the film to serve as bookends for the movie.

Peggy Sue Got Married was selected to be screened on the closing night of the New York Film Festival on October 5, 1986, and it was hailed as Coppola's spectacular return to form. *Peggy Sue* became his highest-grossing film of the decade. In its first three weeks of general release the picture grossed nearly $22 million.

Many reviewers were pleasantly surprised to find Coppola helming a light-hearted, humorous film, his first comedy since *ONE FROM THE HEART*. All in all, *Peggy Sue Got Married* was warmly applauded by the critics and the general public. Coppola managed to turn out a touching film that ranks among his best movies.—GENE D. PHILLIPS

References

Jeffrey Chown, *Hollywood Auteur: Francis Coppola* (New York: Praeger, 1988); Lee Lourdeaux, *Italian and Irish Filmmakers in America: Ford, Capra, Coppola, and Scorsese* (Philadelphia: Temple University Press, 1990); Gene Siskel, "Celluloid Godfather," *Chicago Tribune*, October 3, 1986, sec. 13: 4.

PENN, CHRISTOPHER (1965–2006)
American actor who played B. J. in FRANCIS COPPOLA's *RUMBLE FISH* (1983). Chris Penn was born October 10, 1965, the son of television and film director Leo Penn (1921–1988) and his wife, actress Eileen Ryan, and was the younger brother of actor Sean Penn and musician Michael Penn. He later costarred with his mother and his brother Sean in the film *At Close Range* (1986). After his performance in *Rumble Fish*, Penn, a charter member of the so-called "brat pack," appeared with his friend TOM CRUISE in *All the Right Moves* (1983)

and with Kevin Bacon in Herbert Ross's *Footloose* (1984). He also was featured in Quentin Tarantino's cult hit *Reservoir Dogs* (1992), with HARVEY KEITEL, with whom he also worked in *Imaginary Crimes* (1994), and in many other films helmed by legendary directors such as Robert Altman (*Short Cuts*, 1993), Clint Eastwood (*Pale Rider*, 1985), Paul Mazursky (*The Pickle*, 1993), and Tony Scott (*True Romance*, 1993). Christopher Penn died in Santa Monica, California, on January 24, 2006, at the age of 40. Sean Penn told *People* magazine that his brother died of heart failure because of his being overweight.—JAMES M. WELSH

PHILLIPS, GENE D., S.J. (1936–)
Knowledgeable film buff and dedicated film scholar and teacher who interviewed many of the writers and filmmakers whose work he later covered in many books, starting with Graham Greene in 1974 and following through with George Cukor, Fred Zinnemann, Alfred Hitchcock, Ken Russell, John Schlesinger, Stanley Kubrick, and many other film directors included in his book *The Movie Makers: Artists in an Industry* (1973). He also interviewed FRANCIS FORD COPPOLA and many of his collaborators in preparation for the critical biography, *Godfather: The Intimate Francis Ford Coppola* (2004). Father Phillips took his first college degrees at Loyola University of Chicago, where he later taught, and earned his PhD in English from Fordham University. Keenly interested in the process of adapting fiction and drama to film, Father Phillips served for over three decades on the editorial board of *Literature/Film Quarterly* and has written several books keyed to individual writers, such as *Graham Greene: The Films of his Fiction* (1974), *Fiction, Film, and Faulkner* (1988), *Fiction, Film, and F. Scott Fitzgerald* (1986), and *Conrad and Cinema* (1995).—JAMES M. WELSH

PLACE, MARY KAY (1947–)

Popular and steadily working actress, writer, singer, and director in film and television, who plays Dot Black in Coppola's film of *JOHN GRISHAM'S THE RAINMAKER* (1997). Upon graduation from the University of Tulsa with a degree in radio and television production, the Oklahoma native moved to Hollywood and was soon working behind the scenes in television, getting some onscreen experience as a dog on a children's TV show. While working in Norman Lear's office as a secretary for the writing staff of *Maude*, Place was overheard singing her own composition "When Communism Comes Knocking at Your Door." She was soon hired by Lear to perform the song on *All in the Family*. Place and her writing partner, Linda Bloodworth (later Linda Bloodworth-Thomason of *Designing Women* fame), sold their first script for the comedy series *M*A*S*H*, gaining an Emmy nomination for Comedy Writing in the process. Other scripts soon followed for *M*A*S*H* and *The Mary Tyler Moore Show*.

Place gained her greatest fame as aspiring country-western singer Loretta Haggers on Norman Lear's cult soap opera *Mary Hartman, Mary Hartman*, winning an Emmy and gaining a Grammy nomination for a tie-in album released under the title "Tonite! At the Capri Lounge, Loretta Haggers." When *Mary Hartman* went off the air, Place reprised her role in the follow-up series *Forever Fernwood*, but the show was not a success. Roles in major films followed, including Scorsese's *New York, New York*, *Private Benjamin*, *The Big Chill*, and SPIKE JONZE's *Being John Malkovich*.

Her sole performance for FRANCIS COPPOLA comes as Dot Black, the mother of the terminally ill boy in *John Grisham's The Rainmaker*. What might have been an overly sentimental white-trash stereotype in other hands becomes a moving and understated picture of a lower-class woman grappling alone with the slow death of her son, an apparently unwinnable lawsuit against a major insurance company, and her husband's inability to deal with these problems.

Place has continued to be a presence in television, with appearances in series like *Grey's Anatomy*, *The West Wing*, *My So-Called Life*, and *Big Love*; and she has directed episodes of *Friends* and *Arli$$*.

—TOM DANNENBAUM

References

Bob Lardine, untitled clipping, *NY News Sunday Magazine*, December 26, 1976; Michael Tolkin, "She's More Than Mary Hartman's Friend," *Village Voice*, June 21, 1976, 132.

PROFFITT, NICHOLAS (1943–2006)

Novelist who wrote *GARDENS OF STONE* (1983), a novel popular with Vietnam veterans, later adapted to film by FRANCIS FORD COPPOLA in 1987. Proffitt was born in Sault Ste. Marie, Michigan, on February 23, 1943, the son of a professional soldier, Sergeant First Class Stanley Proffitt (1915–1963), to whom *Gardens of Stone* was dedicated. Growing up on U.S. Army posts, Nicholas Proffitt himself served as a sergeant in THE OLD GUARD in Fort Myer, Virginia, in 1962–1963, after dropping out of West Point. In 1968 he earned a degree in journalism from the University of Arizona then later worked as a war correspondent for *Newsweek* in Vietnam in 1971–1973, advancing to bureau chief. He was a friend of the Vietnam journalist and novelist Phillip Caputo. After serving as bureau chief for *Newsweek* in Beirut, Lebanon, he returned to Vietnam to cover the fall of Saigon in 1975, departing on the last helicopter to leave the roof of the U.S. Embassy. He retired from journalism in

1981 to write *Gardens of Stone*, which was in part autobiographical, based on his service in the Old Guard. Two subsequent novels, *Embassy House* (1986), a CIA thriller, and *Edge of Eden* (1990) were not as successful as *Gardens of Stone* had been, and in 1991 Proffitt gave up writing fiction for day trading on the stock market. He died at his home in Naples, Florida, on November 10, 2006.—JAMES M. WELSH

PUZO, MARIO (1920–1999)

The author of *THE GODFATHER* (1969), which became an internationally best-selling novel that inspired the film by FRANCIS COPPOLA, Puzo also became one of the screenwriters for the *Godfather* trilogy. Puzo's popular Mafia-related novels include *The Last Don* and *Omerta*, as well as *The Fourth K*, *The Sicilian*, *Fools Die*, *The Fortunate Pilgrim*, and *The Dark Arena*. Puzo's novel *The Sicilian* was adapted to the screen in 1987 by Michael Cimino, though Puzo himself had no hand in writing that screenplay. In his lukewarm review of Cimino's film for *The New York Times* (October 23, 1987), Vincent Canby described *The Sicilian* as an "extended insert" to the *Godfather* epic, since it was set during the two years that Michael Corleone was hiding in Sicily, even though the story concerns the legendary Sicilian bandit Salvatore Giuliano, whom Michael might have escorted to America had not Giuliano been murdered at the age of 27 in 1950 by his own men. At the time of his own death in 1999 Puzo was writing *The Family*, a historical novel centered upon Roderigo Borgia, the future Pope Alexander VI, and his son, Cesare Borgia. *The Family* was later completed by Puzo's novelist companion, Carol Gino, and published in 2001. This papal fantasy seems to have been imagined as a sort of spiritual prequel to *The Godfather*, involving a similar but differently ambitious and corrupt "family." According to Carol Gino, Puzo "believed the popes were the first Dons," with "Pope Alexander the greatest Don of all," an opinion perhaps not shared by the Vatican. Puzo thought that Lucrezia Borgia "was a good girl," and that Cesare was "a patriot who desired to be a hero," but that Pope Alexander was "a true family man." Given these imaginative peculiarities, the novel, though besotted with incest and cruelty, was potentially engaging in its way.—JAMES M. WELSH

R

THE RAINMAKER (1997)

DIRECTOR: Francis Ford Coppola. SCREEN-
PLAY: Francis Ford Coppola, based on
the novel by John Grisham. NARRATION:
Michael Herr. PRODUCERS: Michael Doug-
las, Steven Reuther, and Fred Fuchs for
American Zoetrope, Paramount Pic-
tures. COPRODUCER: Georgia Kacandes.
ASSOCIATE PRODUCER: Gary Scott Marcus.
PHOTOGRAPHY: John Toll. EDITING: Barry
Malkin. MUSIC: Elmer Bernstein. PRO-
DUCTION DESIGN: Howard Cummings.
ART DIRECTION: Robert Shaw, Jeffrey
McDonald. COSTUME DESIGN: Aggie Gue-
rard Rodgers. SOUND: Nelson Stoll.

CAST: Matt Damon (Rudy Baylor), Claire
Danes (Kelly Riker), Jon Voight (Leo
F. Drummond), Mary Kay Place (Dot
Black), Mickey Rourke (Bruiser Stone),
Danny DeVito (Deck Shifflet), Dean
Stockwell (Judge Harvey Hale), Teresa
Wright (Miss Birdie), Virginia Madsen
(Jackie Lemancyzk), Andrew Shue (Cliff
Riker), Red West (Buddy Black), Johnny
Whitworth (Donny Ray Black), Danny
Glover (Judge Tyrone Kipler), Wayne
Emmons (Prince Thomas), Adrian Rob-
erts (Butch), Roy Scheider (Wilfred
Keeley), Randy Travis (Billy Porter),
Michael Girardin (Everett Lufkin), Ran-
dall King (Jack Underhall), Justin Ash-
forth (F. Franklin Donaldson), Michael
Keys Hall (B. Bobby Shaw).

RUNNING TIME: 135 minutes. Color
(Deluxe).

PREMIERE: November 21, 1997.
DVD: Paramount.

In April 1996 FRANCIS COPPOLA signed
with Paramount to write the screenplay and to direct the picture. MICHAEL
HERR, who had provided the narration for
APOCALYPSE NOW, would take on the
same task for *The Rainmaker*. (Coppola's
Rainmaker should not be confused with the
1956 movie of the same title starring Katharine Hepburn.)

The story revolves around Rudy Baylor,
an idealistic Southern lawyer who endeavors to maintain his integrity in a profession
filled with too many sellouts. The main
plot concerns the battle young Rudy, an
eager-beaver attorney, wages against a huge
insurance company that has cheated Dot
and Buddy Black, a poor Memphis couple,
out of the benefits they need to finance a
critical operation for their desperately ill
son Donny. Along the way Rudy assists an
elderly widow, Miss Birdie, in coping with
her greedy son, who wants to badger her
into leaving him all her money. He also
aids a battered wife, Kelly Riker, in escap-
ing from her sadistic husband.

Coppola put together an impressive
production team, engaging cinematographer John Toll, who had garnered an
Academy Award for photographing *Legends of the Fall* (1994), to lens the movie. In

addition, composer Elmer Bernstein, another Oscar winner for *Thoroughly Modern Millie* (1967), contributed the score. BARRY MAL-KIN, veteran of several Coppola movies, was secured to edit the picture.

The director elected to people his cast with dependable veterans and promising newcomers. Jon Voight (*Midnight Cowboy*) was called upon to play Leo Drummond, the slick, fancy-suited chief attorney for the insurance company, Great Benefit. ROY SCHEIDER (*Jaws*) won the part of Wilfred Keeley, the sly, corrupt CEO of Great Benefit. MICKEY ROURKE (*RUMBLE FISH*) took the role of a venal shyster lawyer named Bruiser Stone, who hires Rudy right out of law school; and DANNY DEVITO (*Tin Men*) enacted the role of Deck Schif-flet, Rudy's wily, down-at-the-heels mentor in the law office. Miss Birdie was to be played by Hollywood icon Teresa Wright, who won an Oscar for the classic film *Mrs. Miniver* (1942).

Coppola had a record of giving fresh young talent a boost dating back to *THE OUTSIDERS*. Running true to form, he selected MATT DAMON to play Rudy and CLAIRE DANES to play Kelly Riker. Neither of them had had a major role in a film up to that time.

Coppola has a long-standing predilection for shooting films on location whenever possible. Therefore it is not surprising that he opted to take his cast and crew to Memphis, Tennessee, where he shot a large part of the picture in and around the local courthouse, thereby adding to the authentic flavor of the film. ELEANOR COP-POLA filmed a "making of" documentary during the shooting of *The Rainmaker*. It was the fourth such documentary that she had made about her husband's films; it is included on the DVD of the film, released in 2007.

As filming progressed, Coppola aimed to make it clear that an inexperienced young attorney was up against a high-priced corporation lawyer that he would find it hard to beat. Hence, Coppola cleverly reworked the last forty pages of the

Coppola with Claire Danes and Matt Damon on the set of *The Rainmaker*.

script. In the rewrites Rudy makes some tactical errors that jeopardize his chances of winning the case. In his revisions of the screenplay, Coppola thus injected a greater degree of uncertainty and suspense into the courtroom scenes.

For example, Rudy presents in open court some incriminating documentation against Great Benefit, which was turned over to him by an embittered former employee, Jackie Lemancyzk (Virginia Madsen), who had stolen it from the firm's files when she was unjustly fired. Drummond maintains, much to Rudy's embarrassment, that stolen evidence is not admissible in a court of law. But Deck subsequently saves the day by finding a loophole, whereby evidence that has been stolen can legitimately be presented in court, provided that it was not stolen by the attorney who makes use of it!

Like the narration Michael Herr wrote for *Apocalypse Now*, the running commentary he composed for Rudy in *The Rainmaker* casts somewhat of a jaundiced light on the events in the story. At one point Rudy quips sardonically, "What's the difference between a hooker and a lawyer? A hooker stops screwing you once you're dead. Everybody loves lawyer jokes."

During the postproduction phase, Coppola returned to AMERICAN ZOETROPE in San Francisco to collaborate with Barry Malkin in producing the rough and final cuts of the film on Coppola's state-of-the-art equipment. The picture previewed well, so Coppola felt he was home free.

The Rainmaker starts out with Rudy Baylor, a greenhorn attorney with lofty ideals who still believes in Justice, although he finds himself operating out of a law office in a strip mall, working for a disreputable lawyer named Bruiser Stone. Mickey Rourke comments in the documentary that Bruiser, a flamboyant shyster, appropriately wears flashy clothes. "He dresses like a pimp."

Rudy takes on a major league insurance company, Great Benefit, which is bent on cheating a low-income family, the Blacks, out of the insurance benefits that might save the life of their son Donny Ray, who is suffering from leukemia. Indeed, the medical coverage that Great Benefit has denied Donny Ray would provide funds for an operation that could very likely save his life.

In the scene in which Rudy pays a visit to the bedridden Donny Ray at home, there is a ventriloquist's dummy lying on the bed next to him. "When I was nine," Coppola recalls, "I was bedridden with polio; and I had a ventriloquist's dummy to keep me company. So I thought Donny Ray should have one too."

Rudy soon becomes involved with Kelly Riker, who is in the hospital recuperating from a beating that she endured from her husband, a professional baseball player. It seems that his aluminum bat is his weapon of choice.

Rudy's other clients include Miss Birdie, a pixilated elderly woman who is determined to disinherit her ungrateful son. She soon becomes Rudy's landlady. So Rudy takes Kelly to stay with Miss Birdie in order to provide Kelly with a sanctuary from her heartless husband. In harmony with the theme of the significance of family so pervasive in Coppola's films, Rudy establishes a surrogate family, with Miss Birdie as the mother figure and Kelly and himself as her two "kids."

Rudy's chief opponent in the Black case is Leo Drummond, a high-priced, amoral attorney, backed up by a battery of lawyers. By contrast, Rudy's sole colleague is his seedy sidekick Deck Shifflet, an intrepid would-be lawyer who has failed the bar exam six times. Be that as it may, Deck knows his way around courthouses and teaches Rudy the ropes. Their give-and-take is at the heart of the film. Moreover, their deft interplay exemplifies how Coppola "allows his actors, rather than his showmanship, to carry the scenes," as Bruce Diones notes. Following the book, Coppola's skillful screenplay is filled with the kind of behind-the-scenes legal maneuverings that keep the story from becoming a battle of words instead of a battle of wits.

Meanwhile, Rudy keeps one eye on Kelly's case. Kelly has a final battle royal with Cliff, her abusive husband. The terrified Kelly finally picks up Cliff's baseball bat and administers what turns out to be a death blow with a resounding thud. Kelly has killed her husband, but Rudy eloquently convinces the district attorney that she did so in self-defense.

In the movie's deeply moving climax, Rudy presents documentation that proves that the life of Donny Ray Black—who has died in the course of the trial—could have been saved by the operation that the criminally negligent insurance company patently should have funded. Rudy shows in open court the videotape of Donny Ray's deposition, made shortly before his death. Rudy shrewdly freezes the image of the haggard, pale young man on the screen in the courtroom, and Donny Ray seems to be staring plaintively, with dark circles under his eyes, directly at Wilfred Keeley, the CEO of Great Benefit.

The jury ultimately sees through the slick and manipulative legal tactics of the shyster lawyer, Leo Drummond, while at the same time the jurors are favorably impressed by Rudy's sincere, straightforward defense of his client. The jury, accordingly, awards the Black family $50 million in punitive damages. Consequently the movie's title refers to a lawyer who causes a deluge of cash to rain down on his client. In short, Rudy Baylor is a latter-day David, who has vanquished Goliath in the person of big-time attorney Leo Drummond, whose client, Great Benefit, is bankrupted

by the verdict. As the movie ends, Rudy and Kelly are driving away from Memphis, preparing to build a new life somewhere else.

The Rainmaker opened on November 21, 1997, to critical hosannas and big box office. It earned $46 million in domestic rentals. *The Rainmaker*, Michael Wilmington contends, is "a richer, deeper, more enjoyable work" than most films about court cases. "Working near the top of his form, Coppola and his extraordinary cast and company turn an expert, crowd-pleasing best seller into a film of greater warmth, humanity, and humor." As such, the picture richly deserves to be called, in this writer's view, one of the best courtroom dramas ever made.—GENE D. PHILLIPS

References

Mark Caro, "Francis Coppola: An Interview," *Chicago Tribune*, November 20, 1997, sec. 5: 11; Bruce Diones, "The Current Cinema: *The Rainmaker*," *New Yorker*, January 5, 1998, 22; Kent Jones, "Mythmaker: Francis Ford Coppola," *Film Comment* 38, no. 2 (March–April, 2002): 30–36; Deborah Solomon, "Independent Streak," *New York Times Magazine*, December 16, 2007, 20; Michael Wilmington, "Courting Success: *The Rainmaker*," *Chicago Tribune*, November 21, 1997, sec. 7: 15.

THE RAIN PEOPLE (1969)

DIRECTOR: Francis Ford Coppola. SCREEN-PLAY: Francis Ford Coppola. PRODUCERS: Bart Patton and Ronald Colby for Warner Bros.–Seven Arts (An American Zoetrope production). PHOTOGRAPHY: Bill Butler. EDITING: Barry Malkin. MUSIC: Ronald Stein. ART DIRECTION: Leon Ericksen. SOUND: Nathan Boxer. SOUND MONTAGE: Walter Murch. PRODUCTION ASSOCIATES: George Lucas, Mona Skager.

CAST: James Caan (Kilgannon), Shirley Knight (Natalie), Robert Duvall (Gordon), Marya Zimmet (Rosalie), Tom

Aldredge (Mr. Alfred), Laurie Crews (Ellen), Andrew Duncan (Artie), Margaret Fairchild (Marion Sally Gracie (Beth), Alan Manson (Lou), Robert Modica (Vinny).
RUNNING TIME: 101 minutes. Technicolor.
PREMIERE: August 27, 1969.
DVD: Warner Bros. Archives.

Warner Bros.–Seven Arts was pleased with FRANCIS COPPOLA's direction of *FINIAN'S RAINBOW* (particularly of the musical numbers). And the front office was therefore willing to finance the picture he wanted to make next, a modest production based on an original scenario of his own, entitled *The Rain People* (1969).

The plot of this tragic drama concerns Natalie Ravenna (Shirley Knight), a depressed young housewife with a child on the way who impulsively decides to walk out on her husband one rainy morning and to make a cross-country trek in her station wagon. She takes this rash course of action in the hope of getting some perspective on her life. Natalie at this juncture feels stifled by the responsibilities of married life, epitomized by the prospect of having a child. In the course of her journey she picks up a hitchhiker, an ex-football player named Jimmy "Killer" Kilgannon (JAMES CAAN), who turns out to be mentally retarded as a result of a head injury he suffered in his final game. In effect, Natalie now has yet another "child" on her hands, and, almost in spite of herself, she gradually comes to care for him more and more as they travel along together. In brief, Jimmy becomes the surrogate for the child she is carrying.

In a sense, both Natalie and Jimmy qualify to be numbered among the rain people of the film's title. The rain people are tender, vulnerable types who, as Jimmy himself describes them at one point, are "people made of rain; when they cry they disappear, because they cry themselves away." Like the rain people, Natalie and Jimmy are easily hurt, and, sadly, they will both end up wounding each other deeply.

Natalie is aware that she is a mother figure for Jimmy. For her part, Natalie is touched by Jimmy's disarming vulnerability. But she is also wary of his growing emotional dependence on her and wants to break off their burgeoning relationship. She consequently secures him a job on an animal farm they happen to come across during their trip, in order to be able to move on without him. But the childlike Jimmy spoils everything by releasing all the animals from their cages, because he simply cannot stand to see them penned up. Jimmy is fired, of course, and Natalie is enraged at him for continuing to be attached to her. She accordingly abandons him on the road and forthwith takes up with Gordon, a state highway patrolman (ROBERT DUVALL). Gordon, whose wife is dead, invites her back to the trailer park where he lives with his younger daughter, Rosalie.

Jimmy surreptitiously follows Natalie to Gordon's trailer and furiously bursts in on them in order to save her from Gordon's

Shirley Knight as Natalie in *The Rain People.*

advances. Rosalie also shows up unexpectedly; when she sees the hulking "Killer" Kilgannon attacking her father, she frantically grabs his patrolman's pistol and shoots Jimmy. The movie ends abruptly, with Natalie sobbing inconsolably as she cradles the mortally wounded Jimmy in her arms, futilely promising to care for him from now on. "I'll take you home and we'll be family," she murmurs as Jimmy expires.

For the first time, Coppola's overriding theme, which centers on the importance of the role of a family spirit in people's lives, is clearly delineated in one of his films. "I am fascinated by the whole idea of family," he says, adding that in his films this theme "is a constant." Thus, as ROBERT JOHNSON notes in his book on Coppola, Natalie takes to the open road to escape the responsibilities of family life, only to find that she has taken them with her. This fact is strikingly brought home to her when she reflects that her unborn child, the very emblem of her marriage, is always with her, accompanying her wherever she goes. And this reflection in turn ultimately leads her by the end of the picture to reconcile herself to her responsibilities as a wife and mother; for she realizes that in trying to escape the obligations of family life she has brought nothing but misery to herself and others. Hence the movie ends, Coppola emphasizes, with an implicit "plea to have a family."

Coppola assembled a handpicked cast and crew to make the movie, which he planned to shoot entirely on location. Together they formed a caravan consisting of five cars, as well as a Dodge minibus that had been remodeled to carry their technical equipment. Making the film while traveling cross-country reminded Coppola of his experience working on ROGER CORMAN'S *YOUNG RACERS*, which was shot while the crew migrated across Europe in a minibus.

They traveled for four months through eighteen states, filming as they went. Coppola did not set out with a finished screenplay in hand but continued filling it out as shooting progressed. When he spied a setting that appealed to him along the way, the group would stop, and he would work out a scene for the actors to play. Thus, while in Chattanooga, Tennessee, Coppola heard tell of an Armed Forces Day parade and incorporated it into a sequence.

GEORGE LUCAS, Coppola's friend and colleague, went along as production manager. Coppola wangled some money from Warners-Seven to enable Lucas to shoot a documentary about the making of *Rain People*, entitled *Filmmaker: a Diary by George Lucas*. The crew also numbered cinematographer BILL BUTLER, administrative assistant Mona Skager, and editor BARRY MALKIN—the film was edited en route on the Steenbeck, which was on board the Dodge minibus. The director of photography for the picture was Bill Butler. His experience in making TV documentaries had taught him how to shoot quickly and efficiently with a small crew. "I told Coppola I could shoot just about any kind of scene that he could dream up," Butler says. Butler followed the same procedure on the present film as he had on his TV documentaries, filming the location scenes as much as possible with the natural light available at the location site.

Because the script for *The Rain People* was developed in a piecemeal fashion, the story does not hang together as coherently as one would like. As a matter of fact, Coppola is the first to concede that the killing that climaxes the movie is a kind of deus ex machina he concocted in order to resolve the movie's plot. The lack of a tightly constructed plotline made for a slow-moving film, and hence *The Rain People* did not win over the critics or the mass audience.

Still there are some fine things in the film: for example, the key scene in which Jimmy liberates the animals from their captivity is a symbolic reminder that Natalie at this point still feels cooped up by circumstances and likewise yearns to be set free from the emotional entanglements in her life. Another neat Coppola touch is having Gordon live in a mobile home, an indication of the transient nature of his life since he lost his wife and, by the same token, a foreshadowing of the sort of rootless existence Natalie is opening herself to if she opts to forsake her husband for good. Indeed, the desolate small towns, the bleak, endless turnpikes, the seedy motels, and shabby roadside diners visually underscore this point. It is a world in which a woman with a past can encounter a man with no future in the depressing atmosphere of a tawdry trailer park.

When the convoy got back to Los Angeles, George Lucas suggested WALTER MURCH, a fellow film student at USC, as sound engineer to mix the soundtrack of the film. Like Barry Malkin, Walter Murch would continue to collaborate with Coppola on his subsequent films.

Because *The Rain People* did not fare well at the box office, Coppola experienced some difficulty in launching another film project—until the release of *PATTON* (1970). Coppola won an Oscar for cowriting the screenplay for this epic World War II movie, which he had worked on just before he made *Big Boy*. Coppola's stock had now risen in the industry. Moreover, Coppola could take some solace in the fact that *The Rain People* captured both the Grand Prize and the Best Director Award at the San Sebastian International Film Festival. Furthermore, more than one feminist critic has singled out *Rain People* as one of the first films to come out of Hollywood that addressed the constricting role of the housewife in modern society. —GENE D. PHILLIPS

References
Robert Johnson, *Francis Ford Coppola* (Boston: Twayne, 1977); Gabriella Oldham, *First Cut: Conversations with Film Editors* (Los Angeles: University of California Press, 1995); Michael Pye and Linda Myles, *The Movie Brats: How the Film Generation Took Over Hollywood* (New York: Holt, Rinehart, and Winston, 1979); Dennis Schaefer and Larry Salvati, *Masters of Light: Conversations with Contemporary Cinematographers* (Los Angeles: University of California Press, 1984).

REDFORD, [CHARLES] ROBERT (1937–)
Iconic American actor, director, and superstar who was considered for key roles in *APOCALYPSE NOW* but declined because of other work commitments. According to ELEANOR COPPOLA's *NOTES* (1979), Redford read the script and liked "the Kurtz part, but can't consider the Willard part because his film is not finished and he has promised his family that he will not leave for a long location the rest of this year." Redford had starred as Jay Gatsby in the film adaptation of F. Scott Fitzgerald's novel scripted by FRANCIS FORD COPPOLA for director Jack Clayton in 1974. Born in Los Angeles on August 18, 1937, Redford attended the University of Colorado and the Pratt Institute in Brooklyn and later studied at the American Academy of Dramatic Arts. His breakthrough film role came in 1969 in *Butch Cassidy and the Sundance Kid*. His breakthrough film as director was *Ordinary People*, released in 1980, which won Academy Awards for Best Picture and Best Director.—JAMES M. WELSH

REEVES, KEANU (1964–)
Actor who plays Jonathan Harker in *BRAM STOKER'S DRACULA* (1992), departing

from the teenaged roles that had established his screen career: *River's Edge* (1987) and *Bill and Ted's Excellent Adventure* (1989). Reeves then went on to play Don John in Kenneth Branagh's *Much Ado about Nothing* (1993). Reeves was born in Beirut, Lebanon, and raised in Australia and New York. He attended Toronto's High School for the Performing Arts but dropped out at age seventeen. He appeared in several television series for the CBC before being cast in a small role alongside ROB LOWE and PATRICK SWAYZE in *Youngblood* (1986). The experience emboldened Reeves to pack up and move to Los Angeles. He starred with River Phoenix for Gus Van Sant in *My Own Private Idaho* (1991) and he played young Danceny in Stephen Frears's *Dangerous Liaisons* (1988). In 1993 Reeves traveled to Nepal to work with Bernardo Bertolucci on the film *Little Buddha*. Reeves proved himself a capable and bankable action hero in *Speed* (1994) alongside Sandra Bullock, and he continued in that vein in the wildly successful science-fiction film, *The Matrix* (1999), and its sequels (2003), costarring LAURENCE FISHBURNE. Reeves's more recent work includes Richard Linklater's *A Scanner Darkly* (2006), a digitally "rotoscoped" adaptation of a Philip K. Dick story, and the 2008 remake of *The Day the Earth Stood Still*.—JAMES M. WELSH/ RODNEY HILL

References

"Keanu Reeves," Internet Movie Database, www .imdb.com/name/nm0000206/; "Keanu Reeves," *Variety* Profiles, www.variety.com.

REMAR, JAMES (1953–)

American actor, popular on film and television, who played the psychopathic Dutch Schultz (aka Arthur Flegenheimer) in Coppola's *THE COTTON CLUB* (1984). Born December 31, 1953, the Boston native dropped out of high school to tour with a rock band. When the group disbanded, he relocated to Florida as a housepainter. He worked in summer stock and moved to New York, studying acting at the famed Neighborhood Playhouse. His first major role came in a touring production of *Grease*. He made his Broadway debut in *Bent*, Martin Sherman's play about Nazi persecution of homosexuals, playing the lover of his future *Cotton Club* costar RICHARD GERE. Assorted small film roles followed, leading to his featured role as Ajax in Walter Hill's *The Warriors*, and his breakout role in Hill's wildly popular *48 Hrs.*, as the villainous Albert Ganz, before being cast in Coppola's film.

Remar's performance as the thuggishly unpredictable Dutch Schultz is remarkable for its brutality, even in an oeuvre as well stocked with psychos as Coppola's. Remar's Schultz is presented as something of a throwback to the classical Hollywood gangster: loud and blustery and violent, committing bloody murder over slights to his honor, or the honor of whomever he feels has been slighted. His particularly brutal slaying of another gangster over a casually tossed-off racial slur is startling, not least because gangsters are not generally known for political correctness, and it becomes clear that Schultz's sensitivity has its limits. His early statement that he needs some good Irishmen in his gang doesn't stop him from complaining about "all these fucking Micks!" toward the end of the film (and the character's life). The idea seems to have been to strip Schultz of all possible dignity, especially in comparison to the other businessmen in the film, particularly JOE DALLESANDRO's elegant Lucky Luciano, whose rise to power is contrasted with Schultz's fall. The film's contempt for Schultz can best be seen in his final moments: surely no other character has ever been shot to death while at a urinal.

Remar has worked consistently in the years since *Cotton Club*, balancing film work in with television roles in *Walker: Texas Ranger* and *Dexter*. His highest profile role has probably been in the HBO series *Sex and the City*, as Richard Wright, the successful but frustratingly commitment-phobic boyfriend of Kim Cattrall's Samantha.—Tom Dannenbaum

References

Films and Filming, October 1987, uncredited clipping.

REYNOLDS, JONATHAN [RANDOLPH] (1942–)

Award-winning playwright and author of *GENIUSES* (1982), a satire involving a group of zany filmmakers on location in the Philippines, with only ten minutes "in the can" and twenty-eight days behind schedule while making a film called *Parabola of Death*. Reynolds spent three months working on *APOCALYPSE NOW* with FRANCIS FORD COPPOLA. The play was successful off-Broadway in 1982, but less so at Arena Stage in Washington, D.C., in April of 1983. Jonathan Reynolds was born in Fort Smith, Arkansas, on February 13, 1942. Reynolds has written a monthly column on food for the *New York Times Magazine*. His plays include *Dinner with Demons* and *Stonewall Jackson's House*, which received a Pulitzer recommendation. In 2004 he received a Guggenheim for playwriting. His screenwriting credits include *Micki & Maude* (Columbia, 1984), *Switching Channels* (TriStar, 1988), and *The Distinguished Gentleman* (Buena Vista, 1992).—James M. Welsh

"RIP VAN WINKLE" (1987)

DIRECTOR: Francis Ford Coppola, from the story by Washington Irving. Produced for Showtime's "Faerie Tale Theatre"
series by Shelley Duvall. PHOTOGRAPHY: George Riesenberger.
CAST: Harry Dean Stanton (Rip van Winkle), Talia Shire (Rip's wife), John P. Ryan (Henry Hudson) Sofia Coppola, Hunter Carson.
RUNNING TIME: 50 mins.
PREMIERE: March 23, 1987.

Before starting *PEGGY SUE GOT MARRIED*, Coppola found time to direct a fifty-minute film for SHELLEY DUVALL's cable TV series, *Faerie Tale Theater*. Duvall, a veteran actress (*The Shining*) was executive producer and host of the series that featured TV adaptations of classic fairy tales. She offered Coppola "Rip Van Winkle," the last of the twenty-six episodes in the series. Coppola was drawn to the project because the stakes were low and the salary quite reasonable.

Coppola began collaborating on the teleplay of "Rip Van Winkle," based on the Washington Irving short story, with writers Mark Curtis and Rod Ash in late November 1984. Irving's tale, first published in his *Sketch Book* (1820), depicts how Rip Van Winkle woke up from a twenty-year nap to find that he had missed the American Revolution. The schedule called for a six-day shoot with a $650,000 budget. Coppola rehearsed the actors for a couple of days, starting on November 28, before shooting commenced.

Coppola was not dismayed by the frugality of the production. He was revisiting the days when he was turning out "no-budget" pictures for Poverty Row producer ROGER CORMAN. "The bigger the budget, the less freedom you have," he explained. He thought that he was well suited "to a medium where the budgets are smaller and yet the imagination is bigger."

Coppola cast HARRY DEAN STANTON (*ONE FROM THE HEART*) in the title role; TALIA SHIRE (the *GODFATHER* films) as Wilma, Rip's shrewish wife; and John P. Ryan, who played a gangster in *THE COTTON CLUB,* as the ghost of the ancient mariner, Henry Hudson.

Coppola instructed director of photography George Riesenberger to favor primary colors in shooting the picture: deep blue for nightfall, glowing scarlet for sunset, and an eerie green for the apparition of Henry Hudson and his ghostly crew.

As the telefilm opens, a pair of gnarled hands take a book off a cobwebbed shelf, while the narrator intones, "This story takes place in the early Dutch settlement of New York, before this country was a country." We then meet Rip Van Winkle, an amiable Dutch loafer who is regularly scolded by his peevish wife for loitering at the local tavern and going hunting in the Catskills instead of toiling on their little farm. Talia Shire, decked out in a fearsome black wig, recalls Connie, the disgruntled wife she played in the *Godfather* films.

One evening, Rip goes off hunting in the upper reaches of the Catskills to escape his nagging wife. As he wanders deeper into the woods, a ghost suddenly materializes from the murky green fog. "I am Commander Heinrich Hudson," the spectral figure declares to Rip. Hudson is dressed in a traditional Dutch naval captain's uniform, which is tattered with age. He then introduces to Rip his band of merry men, the crew of the good ship *Half Moon,* which foundered off the coast some one hundred fifty years before. "We discovered this land at the time, and it is sacred to me," Hudson explains. "I return every twenty years to see if future generations are taking care of it."

Rip is appointed cupbearer to the crew. He is given a keg of a mysterious brew and told to keep their flagons filled as they engage in a spirited game of ninepins (bowling). Rip samples the tasty draught himself and eventually imbibes copiously from the keg. The revelers finally disappear, leaving Rip behind, sound asleep. As a mat-

ter of fact, the magic beverage causes Rip to sleep for twenty years. When he awakes, he is sporting a straggly white beard, and he finds the village much changed.

For one thing, the sign over the village inn, which once bore the likeness of King George III, has been replaced by one with the image of George Washington, thereby indicating to the viewer, if not yet to Rip, that the American Revolution has transpired while Rip slept. When he inquires at the tavern if anyone knows Rip Van Winkle, the customers point to Rip Van Winkle, Jr. (also played by Stanton). The young man is dozing on the porch (like father, like son). Young Rip informs his father that Wilma "broke a blood vessel screaming at a traveling salesman a couple of years ago and died."

Rip regales the group with the tale of his fantastic experience with Henry Hudson and the crew of the *Half Moon.* The narrator adds in a voiceover on the soundtrack, "In time he became a legend in the village, and he never grew tired of telling the children his story." A shot of Rip and the village children freezes into a picture in the same book the narrator was holding at the beginning of the film. He then closes the volume and replaces it on the shelf, and we see his face for the first time: it is Henry Hudson, grinning at us at the fade-out.

Since Coppola's episode of *Faerie Tale Theater* was slotted as the last segment of the series to be televised, it was first aired after *Peggy Sue Got Married* had opened. Some critics noted a link between the telefilm and the feature: In *Peggy Sue* the heroine is transplanted into the past—in "Rip Van Winkle" the hero is transported into the future. Moreover, "Rip Van Winkle," like *Peggy Sue,* got uniformly good notices, and deservedly so. Coppola's telemovie was described as a slightly fractured but never totally Grimm fairy tale.

In bringing Irving's storybook classic to life, Coppola tackles the material with antic glee and serves up engaging, warm-hearted whimsy. His direction is spry and imaginative, and it is evident that he cares about actors and performance—Harry Dean Stanton, Talia Shire, and John P. Ryan could not be better. "Rip Van Winkle," in short, is an unqualified artistic success. Happily, the *Faerie Tale Theater* TV series has not sunk without a trace, as so many television series do. The telefilms in the series were released on DVD in 2002. The most prominent filmmaker to direct a segment of the series is clearly FRANCIS FORD COPPOLA.—GENE D. PHILLIPS

References

Stephen Farber, "Francis Ford Coppola Sallies into TV on a Fairy Tale," *New York Times*, December 27, 1984, C20; "Washington Irving," in *The Cambridge Guide to Literature in English*, ed. Dominic Head (New York: Cambridge University Press, 2006), 560–61.

ROOS, FRED (1934–)

FRANCIS COPPOLA's casting director since *THE GODFATHER*, believed to be one of the best in the business. Fred Roos was responsible for casting JACK NICHOLSON in Bob Rafelson's *Five Easy Pieces* (1970), for example, a role that earned Nicholson an Academy Award nomination. A Coppola regular and insider, Roos was executive producer for *YOUTH WITHOUT YOUTH* (2007) and *TETRO* (2009) and has served as producer on several other Coppola pictures (*APOCALYPSE NOW, THE BLACK STALLION, ONE FROM THE HEART, THE OUTSIDERS, RUMBLE FISH, PEGGY SUE GOT MARRIED, GARDENS OF STONE*), and other films. Roos also coproduced *THE CONVERSATION, THE GODFATHER: PART II, THE COTTON CLUB,* and *TUCKER: THE MAN AND HIS DREAM*. His credits as casting director include (besides *Five Easy Pieces*) *The King of Marvin Gardens* and *Fat City*. Born in Santa Monica on May 23, 1934, and a native of Southern California, Roos

graduated from Hollywood High School and then attended UCLA, majoring in theatre arts and motion pictures. He served with the United States Army in Korea and wrote and directed a documentary series for the Armed Forces entitled *The Story of Korea*, intended as an orientation film for soldiers stationed there. After being released from the army, Roos produced two films in the Philippines, *Back Door to Hell* and *Flight to Fury*, both directed by Monte Hellman in 1965 and starring Jack Nicholson, who also wrote *Flight to Fury*. Roos worked with Nicholson on several pictures and was associate producer of *Drive, He Said*, which Nicholson directed in 1972. *The Conversation*, which Roos coproduced, was nominated for a Best Picture Academy Award and was winner of the Grand Prix at the 1974 Cannes Film Festival. Besides having served as Production Executive of Zoetrope Studios in Los Angeles, Roos also helped Coppola's daughter Sofia cast several parts for *LOST IN TRANSLATION*. He served as executive producer for all of her films—*THE VIRGIN SUICIDES* (2000), *Lost in Translation* (2003), and *MARIE ANTOINETTE* (2006).—JAMES M. WELSH

ROTA, NINO (1911–1979)

Distinguished composer of several film scores for Italian director Federico Fellini—such as *La Dolce Vita* (1960)—and the background music for the first two *GODFATHER* films. During his long career Rota composed 145 film scores. He also wrote four symphonies and eight operas, plus ballets and concertos. The prolific composer wrote his film music in a hurry, sometimes on a train, often by only reading the screenplay, but without seeing the film. In the case of *The Godfather*, Coppola flew to Rome for conferences with Rota, during which Rota picked out melodies on the piano for the movie's music. Coppola then returned to Hollywood with audio tapes of Rota's principal themes for the movie.

Rota furnished the underscore for *The Godfather*, utilizing a symphonic structure to comment on characters and situations. ROBERT EVANS, studio chief, initially feared that the score was too highbrow and operatic, but Coppola as usual stuck to his guns and insisted that the Rota score be used in the film. CARMINE COPPOLA, however, composed the incidental music for the dance band at the film's wedding reception.

Coppola was convinced, Larry Timm notes in his book on film music, that Rota's score added "an air of authenticity to the needed Italian flavor of the film." Since Francis Lai's score for Paramount's *Love Story* had been popular, Evans had wanted something similarly "accessible" for *The Godfather*.

Exteriors of a movie studio and a Hollywood estate were shot by a second-unit crew as a lead-in to the "horse's head" sequence; Coppola had nothing to do with this material, so Evans stuck on a music track from the studio's sound library that was precisely the kind of hokey music he had wanted for the whole film. Happily he did not get his way. Subsequent critical reaction to Rota's music was unanimously positive. "The score was laced with intricate melodies, Italian-tinged passages, and hauntingly tragic themes," Lebo comments. Some of the themes are among the most memorable in film history—for example, "The Godfather Waltz," first played by a lone trumpet during the opening credits and repeated throughout the film in various combinations of instruments.

Rota was nominated for an Academy Award for Best Original Score for *The Godfather*. When the members of the Music Branch of the Academy learned that Rota had incorporated into his score a love theme from an earlier film, amounting to seven minutes of music, his nomination was withdrawn. The Academy made

the technical point that this love theme was not original in the *Godfather* score. Rota pointed out that he had recycled the melody from a picture called *Fortunella* (1957), a huge flop in Italy and unseen outside Italy; the melody, after all, was his own composition. To no avail.

Rota was vindicated when he received the Oscar for his score for *THE GODFATHER: PART II*, which introduced some new music, but also resurrected some themes from the first *Godfather* film. For example, the waltz Don Corleone and his daughter Connie dance to at her wedding reception in *The Godfather* is again played by the dance band at the party following young Anthony's First Holy Communion in *Godfather: Part II*.

Rota also reused the love theme from *Fortunella*—now known as the love theme from *The Godfather*—which had caused Rota's score for *The Godfather* to be disqualified for Oscar consideration two years earlier. This time the inscrutable Academy jurors simply disregarded their previous objection to the tune. Carmine Coppola also received an Oscar for the Italian songs he wrote for the dance band in the extended party scene mentioned above.

Rota's daughter Nina writes that her father's film music recalls the lush, late-Romantic music of film composers like Miklos Rozsa (*Ben-Hur*) and Erich Korngold (*The Adventures of Robin Hood*), which served Hollywood so well in the heyday of the studio system. "Rota was especially adept at scoring for comedy," Richard Dyer comments, "a gift probably best known from the music for the sequence in *Godfather-II*, when Clemenza takes the young Vito Corleone along to steal a carpet."

Rota always deplored the snobbish attitude of some music critics that film scores do not qualify as serious music because they are subservient to the images on the screen. He was justly proud of his contribution to the art of cinematic music.—GENE D. PHILLIPS

References

Richard Dyer, "The Talented Mr. Rota," *Sight and Sound* 14, no. 9 (September, 2004): 42–45; Jenny Jones, ed., *The Annotated Godfather: The Complete Screenplay* (New York: Black Dog and Leventhal, 2007); Harlan Lebo, *The Godfather Legacy* (New York: Simon & Schuster, 1997); Nina Rota, *The Symphonic Rota-Fellini Scores*, CD liner notes (New York: Silva Screen Records, 1997); Larry Timm, *The Soul of Cinema: An Appreciation of Film Music* (Upper Saddle River, NJ: Prentice Hall, 2003).

ROTH, TIM (1962–)

British actor born in London, who starred as Dominic in Coppola's YOUTH WITH-OUT YOUTH (2007). Roth lived up to his early promise on the London stage by earning favorable reviews for films like *Made in Britain* (Alan Clarke, 1983) as a juvenile delinquent. "He is and always will be a terrific piece of South London," writes David Thomson, "rancid and yet fresh, treacherous yet driven by his own punk integrity." He has "the total authority of the hopeless outsider who refuses to give a fuck." In Robert Altman's *Vincent and Theo* (1990) Roth played Vincent van Gogh, and was a hotheaded thief in Quentin Tarantino's *Pulp Fiction* (1994).

Roth was cast as Charles Marlowe in Nicholas Roeg's TV version of "HEART OF DARKNESS" (1994), opposite John Malkovich as Kurtz. The television adaptation is significant for sticking to Conrad's period setting, whereas Coppola's APOCALYPSE NOW updated the story to the Vietnam War. Otherwise the telefilm is not particularly noteworthy. In fact, the critics' assessments of the telemovie were essentially polite but reserved, although most of them singled out Tim Roth and Malkovich as turning in fine performances. Perhaps the strongest endorsement for the cable film came from Ken Tucker: Filmmaker Nicholas Roeg "doesn't seem to have approached the material with awe or trepidation," he wrote; Roeg has made a movie about a man's "disillusionment and ruin that also works as an adventure story." In the last analysis, however, Roeg's cable adaptation of "Heart of Darkness" is simply not in the same league with *Apocalypse Now*, which will continue to be the yardstick by which subsequent screen versions of the novella will be judged.

In Coppola's 2007 film *Youth without Youth*, Roth played the lead role. *Sight and Sound* commented, "Tim Roth, as Dominic Matei, an elderly Romanian philologist who is restored to youth after being struck by lightning in 1938, gives a surprisingly subtle, deeply felt performance." Dominic subsequently falls in love with a young woman (Alexandra Maria Lara) who reminds him of the lost love of his youth. But she does not possess his gift for remaining young and pathetically ages before his eyes.

As James M. Welsh notes, the film "makes unusual demands on the viewer's imagination and powers of concentration." Roth proves his resourcefulness as an actor by consistently holding the viewer's attention throughout this complex, thought-provoking movie.—GENE D. PHILLIPS

References

Scott Founder, "Coppola Rising," *DGA Quarterly* 3, no. 1 (Spring, 2007): 1–9; David Thomson, *Have You Seen . . . ? 1,000 Films* (New York: Knopf, 2008); David Thomson, *New Biographical Dictionary of Film*, rev. ed. (New York: Knopf, 2004); Ken Tucker, "*Heart of Darkness* on Cable," *Entertainment Weekly*, March 11, 1994, 40; "*Youth without Youth*," *Sight and Sound* 17 no. 7 (July, 2008): 87.

ROURKE, MICKEY [PHILIP ANDRÉ ROURKE, JR.] (1950–)

Tough and charismatic American actor who plays Motorcycle Boy in FRANCIS COPPOLA's *RUMBLE FISH* (1983) and Bruiser Stone in *THE RAINMAKER* (1997). Rourke was born in Schenectady, New York, in 1950, but grew up poor in Miami, Florida, moving there at the age of ten when his parents divorced. Rourke learned to box in his teens at Miami's Fifth Street Gym, and boxed as an amateur before catching breaks that allowed him to move to New York to study acting with Sandra Seacat at the Actors Studio. Moving then to Los Angeles in 1980, Rourke got cast in a made-for-television movie, *City in Fear*, starring David Janssen. Roles followed in Spielberg's *1941*, Michael Cimino's *Heaven's Gate*, Lawrence Kasdan's *Body Heat* (1981), and Barry Levinson's *Diner* (1982). In 1984 he advanced his career further in performances in *The Pope of Greenwich Village* and in Nicolas Roeg's *Eureka*, before playing the small-town biker in *Rumble Fish*. In 2008 this Brat Pack Bad Boy got his first Oscar nomination playing Randy "The Ram" Robinson, a beat-up contender in *The Wrestler*. Roger Ebert praised Rourke in the *Chicago Sun-Times* for delivering "the performance of a lifetime," seconded by *Variety*'s Todd McCarthy, who claimed that his "galvanizing, humorous, deeply moving portrait . . . takes its place among the great, iconic screen performances."
—JAMES M. WELSH

RUMBLE FISH (1983)

DIRECTOR: Francis Ford Coppola. SCREENPLAY: S. E. Hinton and Francis Ford Coppola, based on the novel by S. E. Hinton. PRODUCERS: Fred Roos and Doug Claybourne for Zoetrope Studios. EXECUTIVE PRODUCER: Francis Ford Coppola. ASSOCIATE PRODUCERS: Gian-Carlo Coppola and Roman Coppola. PHOTOGRAPHY: Stephen H. Burum. EDITING: Barry Malkin. MUSIC: Stewart Copeland. PRODUCTION DESIGN: Dean Tavoularis. SOUND DESIGN: Richard Beggs. COSTUME DESIGN: Marge Bowers. CAST: Matt Dillon (Rusty James), Mickey Rourke (The Motorcycle Boy), Diane Lane (Patty), Dennis Hopper (Father), Diana Scarwid (Cassandra), Vincent Spano (Steve), Nicolas Cage (Smokey), Christopher Penn (B. J. Jackson), Larry Fishburne (Midget), William Smith (Patterson, the Cop), Michael Higgins (Mr. Harrigan), Glenn Withrow (Biff Wilcox), Tom Waits (Benny), Herb Rice (Black Pool Player), Maybelle Wallace (Late Pass Clerk), Nona Manning (Patty's Mom), Domino (Patty's Sister), Gio Coppola (Cousin James), S. E. Hinton (Hooker on Strip). RUNNING TIME: 94 minutes. B&W. PREMIERE: October 7, 1983 (New York Film Festival). RELEASED THROUGH: Universal. DVD: Universal.

After making *THE OUTSIDERS*, Coppola next filmed *Rumble Fish* (1983), based on another S. E. HINTON novel. "While I was shooting *The Outsiders* in Tulsa, I said to Susie Hinton, 'Have you written anything else I can film?' She told me about *Rumble Fish*, and I read it and loved it. I said to her, 'On our Sundays off from filming *Outsiders*, let's write a screenplay of *Rumble Fish*; and then as soon as we can wrap *Outsiders*, we'll take a break and start filming *Rumble Fish*.' And so we did." Coppola shot the dark tale in stark black-and-white.

In the novel, Rusty James, a disadvantaged teenager from a broken home, looks up to his older brother, who is known only as Motorcycle Boy, the leader of a local gang. The relationship of the two brothers struck a chord in Coppola. His brother, August, who is five years his senior, included young Francis in his activities and provided a strong role model for him when they were growing up. August Coppola "was my idol," Francis Coppola says, "just took me everywhere when he went out with the guys because he was the leader of the gang," which was called the Wild Deuces. "He always looked out for me." A dedication to August Coppola, who eventually became a college professor, appears in the end credits of *Rumble Fish*; "To August Coppola, my first and best teacher." As it happened, Coppola hired August's son Nicholas to play a gang member named Smokey in *Rumble Fish*, but Nicholas Coppola took the professional name of NICOLAS CAGE in order to obscure the family connection with the director of the film. Still, in the movie Nicolas Cage wore his father's own jacket from high school days, with Wild Deuces displayed on the back.

Coppola planned to go from one film right into the other. He reasoned that he could make *Rumble Fish* with the same production team and equipment he had assembled in Tulsa for *The Outsiders*. Director of photography Stephen Burum and production designer DEAN TAVOULARIS were carryovers from *The Outsiders*.

Never one to repeat himself, Coppola took a radically different approach to *Rumble Fish* from the one he had employed on *The Outsiders*. The latter was a romantic melodrama along the lines of *THE GODFATHER*, while he envisioned *Rumble Fish* as an art film, designed more in the direction of *APOCALYPSE NOW*. The shooting script for *Rumble Fish* follows the novel quite faithfully. The screenplay, which is on file in the Script Repository of Universal Studios, the distributor of the film, is dated May 4, 1982.

Motorcycle Boy, Rusty James's burned-out older brother, is color blind, due to the brain damage he has suffered in numerous fist fights and rumbles. His color blindness is also a symbol of the disil-lusioned young man's view of the somber world in which he lives. This confirms Coppola's decision to shoot the movie in black-and-white, with a few judiciously chosen color overlays, as in the shots of the Siamese fighting fish that give the film its title.

The director opted to have a background score that relied heavily on percussion and so commissioned STEWART COPELAND, the American drummer for the British rock band the Police, to provide the score. Copeland did principally use percussion for the background music for the film, but he also recorded Tulsa street sounds—such as traffic noises, police and ambulance sirens—and wove them into his score, which included not only drums but a piano and a xylophone. Copeland's spare percussive score was as far removed as it could be from the saccharinity that sometimes marked CARMINE COPPOLA's music for *The Outsiders*.

Two of the lead actors in *The Outsiders* reappear in *Rumble Fish*: MATT DILLON was signed to play Rusty James and DIANE LANE (who played Cherry, the girl with whom the Matt Dillon character had a brief flirtation in *The Outsiders*) would be Patty, Rusty James's girl in *Rumble Fish*. MICKEY ROURKE, who had auditioned for *The Outsiders*, was selected to play Motorcycle Boy. From *Apocalypse Now*, Coppola brought in DENNIS HOPPER as the drunken father of Rusty James. Finally, VINCENT SPANO took the part of Steve, Rusty James's naive but likable sidekick. Rusty James's good-hearted best friend has the same sort of dogged devotion for Rusty James that Rusty James has for Motorcycle Boy.

Coppola spent two weeks videotaping rehearsals for *Rumble Fish* in the school gym where he had rehearsed the cast of *The Outsiders*. By the end of June, Coppola had cut a distribution deal with Universal, with release set for the fall of 1983. Filming accordingly started on July 12, 1982, only a few weeks after the production of *The Out-siders* was finished.

The filming of *Rumble Fish* went off as efficiently as the shooting of *The Outsiders*, and production finished in October. Once more, Coppola was on schedule and on budget. Since *Rumble Fish* was thought to be an art film, it was considered too sophisticated to attract the same wide youth audience that saw *The Outsiders*. So Coppola decided to premiere the movie at the New York Film Festival on October 7, 1983, in order to bring it to the attention of a more mature audience. The critics who saw the picture at the Festival screening, however, were by and large unresponsive to the movie.

Rumble Fish begins with clouds hurtling across a darkening sky (by means of Burum's speeded-up photography). The swiftly moving clouds, coupled with the frequent images of clocks—including one huge clock without hands—are meant to express a feeling of urgency, of the unstop-pable passage of time—a fact of life Coppola says young people find hard to grasp. He particularly wished to heighten the effect of time running out for the disenchanted and self-destructive Motorcycle Boy, whose hour of doom may be approaching.

There is a sign spray-painted on a brick wall, "The Motorcycle Boy Reigns." It reminds Rusty James how much he misses his older brother, Motorcycle Boy, who had been the leader of the street gang Rusty James belongs to until he left town a couple of months earlier.

Rusty James is challenged to fight with Biff Wilcox, the leader of another gang. During the slugfest Motorcycle Boy suddenly appears out of nowhere, astride his bike, and breaks up the fist fight. Motorcycle Boy is a bored and aimless nonconformist, "the quintessential teen anti-hero," determined to beat the system or die trying, says Jon Lewis. In any case, the lad's alcoholic father is glad to see the return of his prodigal son.

Matt Dillon taunts a cop while Mickey Rourke watches in *Rumble Fish*.

Motorcycle Boy is fascinated by the Siamese fighting fish in the local pet shop; he calls them "rumble fish" because they possess a fighting instinct that drives them to attack each other. "Motorcycle Boy senses a kinship between these hostile creatures and the rival gangs, who have rumbles to fight with each other," Coppola explains. He is revered by his youthful peers for his stubborn attitude, which is antiestablishment and antiauthority. Motorcycle Boy's basic flaw, says Coppola, "is his inability to compromise, and that's why I made him color-blind. He interprets life in black-and-white."

Rusty James, an inarticulate, confused young man, is discouraged because the other gang members, who unabashedly admire his brother, constantly remind him that he is no match for Motorcycle Boy. "He's like royalty in exile," one of them opines. But Motorcycle Boy no longer has any such delusions of grandeur about himself. He has the nagging feeling that he has let his younger brother down, both as a role model and as a gang leader. "If you're gonna lead people, you've gotta have somewhere to go," he reflects. He implicitly realizes that he is a lost cause.

One night Motorcycle Boy takes Rusty along with him as he breaks into the pet shop. He opens all the cages and releases the animals. This scene recalls Killer Kilgannon's similar action in *THE RAIN PEOPLE*, which Hinton says she saw before she wrote *Rumble Fish*. Motorcycle Boy tells his kid brother that he intends to set the rumble fish free in the nearby river. Officer Patterson, who all along has thought Motorcycle Boy a menace to society, seizes the opportunity afforded by the pet shop break-in to shoot Motorcycle Boy dead. He is gunned down at the climax of *Rumble Fish*, just as Dallas was shot in cold blood in *The Outsiders*, in both instances by trigger-happy cops. Society, Coppola implies, has no place for rebellious loners like Dallas and Motorcycle Boy.

Patterson throws Rusty James up against a police car and frisks him, and Rusty James sees his own reflection in the car window in color—the only color image in the film besides that of the rumble fish. He smashes the window in anguish and frustration. Since the rumble fish are a symbol of self-destructive teenagers trapped in urban poverty, they represent Rusty James's determination to escape the narrow existence in which he feels entrapped.

Coppola employs some extended takes impressively in this movie. At the end, for example, the camera tracks slowly from Motorcycle Boy's corpse, past the curious onlookers to Steve, Rusty James's loyal friend, who shares his grief. Then it passes on to the brothers' fuddled father, who turns away from his son's dead body, downs a swig of whiskey, and stumbles away from the tragic scene. This panning shot is much more effective than a series of quick cuts to various bystanders would have been, since the solemn, slow pan underlines the funereal sadness of the occasion.

The shooting script ends much differently than the film. The last scene as described in the shooting script concludes with Motorcycle Boy lying dead on the ground, "with the rumble fish flapping and dying around him, still too far from the river, . . . as the police car drives off with Rusty James." In the movie as released, Rusty James silently carries the fishbowl to the nearby river bank, then he fulfills his brother's last wish by throwing the rumble fish into the river. Remembering his deceased brother's advice that he should get out of town and follow the river clear to the sea, Rusty James mounts his brother's motorcycle and roars off into the night.

There follows a brief epilogue that is also not in the shooting script and, therefore, like the wordless actions of Rusty James just described, must have been invented by Coppola during filming. The movie concludes with Rusty James in silhouette, astride the cycle on a California beach, silently watching seagulls flit over the Pacific Ocean.

Rusty James, writes Lizzie Skurnick, has finally realized that he cannot be the tough legend in the neighborhood that his brother was, "once he realizes that his brother wasn't either." He is now liberated from hero worship of his brother and is no longer living under Motorcycle Boy's shadow. He is now prepared to get a fresh start in life—alone. Several reviewers across the country subsequently condemned the movie as hopelessly obscure and pretentious. They pointed to the fantasy sequence in which Rusty James passes out after he and his buddy Steve are pummeled by muggers. Rusty James has a rapturous "out-of-body experience," in which he believes he is dead. As he floats above the city, he sees his comatose body stretched out on the ground below. He even imagines his own wake in a pool hall, as his grieving friends offer a toast "to Rusty James, a real cool dude."

This fantasy sequence is surely relevant to the film, since it patently reflects a pathetic wish fulfillment on Rusty James's part: he pictures himself being esteemed by his old buddies as a legend like his older brother, which is sadly not the case. David Ehrenstein observed that it seems that Coppola, still the maverick, simply will not behave. Prodded by "the suits" who run the studios to turn out another crowd-pleaser like *The Outsiders*, he instead followed up that picture that had captured the youth market with a baroque film, more likely to appeal to the much smaller art house set. Still, *Rumble Fish* attracted a larger audience in Europe than it did in the United States.

Coppola's faith in *Rumble Fish* as a significant film has been vindicated to the extent that it has over the years achieved the status of a cult film. Indeed, it was rediscovered by critics and filmgoers alike when it was released on DVD in 2005,

augmented by Coppola's audio commentary. Summing up, *Rumble Fish* proved that Coppola was not content to make genre movies in a conventional way, but, instead, breathed new life into the old formulas.—GENE D. PHILLIPS

References
Ronald Bergan, *Francis Ford Coppola* (New York: Orion Books, 1998); David Ehrenstein, "One from the Art," *Film Comment* 29, no. 1 (January–February, 1993): 27–30; Jon Lewis, "The Road to Romance and Ruin: *Rumble Fish*," in *Crisis Cinema*, ed. Christopher Starrett (Washington, DC: Maison Elve Press, 1993), 129–46; Lizzie Skurnick, "The Brotherhood of S. E. Hinton," *Chicago Tribune Books*, May 30, 2008, 6–7; Elizabeth Taylor, "Interview with S. E. Hinton," *Chicago Tribune Books*, May 30, 2008, 6–7; David Thomson and Lucie Gray, "Idols of the King: *The Outsiders* and *Rumble Fish*," *Film Comment* 19, no. 5 (September–October, 1983): 61–75.

RUSTY JAMES
French title of *RUMBLE FISH* (1983), named for the Matt Dillon character.

RYDER, WINONA [WINONA HOROWITZ] (1971–)
Remarkable American actress who disappointed FRANCIS FORD COPPOLA when she walked off the set of *THE GODFATHER: PART III* and had to be replaced, though she would later work with Coppola and others of his generation. The actress told Harold von Kursk of *Time Out* that she "wasn't happy about a lot of reports that I was having a nervous breakdown on the set of *The Godfather III* or that I was freaking out. I was exhausted," she admitted, "and I did have a serious sinus infection, but I wasn't the hysterical bitch that the rumours said I was." She had developed a bad cold shooting *Mermaids* in cold weather in Boston and then had to fly directly to Rome for the Coppola project. "My doctor told me that I was crazy even to have taken the plane to Italy.

He said I could have lost my hearing. Then the gossip comes out that I was having a nervous breakdown. It's a wonderful life, isn't it," she concluded. Winona Horowitz was born in Winona, Minnesota, on October 29, 1971, the daughter of Michael Horowitz and Cindy Palmer. Encouraged by her parents to take classes at San Francisco's American Conservatory Theater, she was "discovered" by a talent scout and screen-tested for the film *Desert Bloom*, but finally cast with CHARLIE SHEEN in the film *Lucas* (1984), at which point she adopted "Ryder" as her stage name. She would later star in *BRAM STOKER'S DRACULA* (1992), however, as both Mina and the (extrapolated) fifteenth-century Elisabeta, who commits suicide when she gets word that the Turks have killed her beloved husband, Vlad. Biographer and journalist Dave Thompson claims Ryder discovered JAMES HART's screenplay for *Bram Stoker's Dracula* and brought it to Coppola's attention. She had been cast to play the count's love interest for a TV movie that was to be directed by Michael Apted. But the actress had problems working on

Dracula with Coppola, who hired acting coach Greta Seacat to help Ryder with her role. Ryder told the British periodical *Time Out* that Coppola was "very insistent about what he wants, but he's not precise about the way he tells you he wants you to do something, and he doesn't have a lot of patience. It's like he testing you at times, forcing you to go further than you want, and that's very difficult to handle." Interviewing Ryder before *Dracula* opened in London, Harold von Kursk wrote that *Dracula* "has been a huge hit in the States, but success means little to Winona except greater choice in scripts and directors." Her success with Martin Scorsese was sensational: Ryder was nominated for an Academy Award for her wonderfully nuanced portrayal of May Welland in Martin Scorsese's *The Age of Innocence* (1993).—JAMES M. WELSH

References

Dave Thompson, *Winona Ryder* (Dallas, TX: Taylor Publishing Co., 1996); Harold von Kursk, "Winona Takes All," *Time Out* (January 13–20, 1993), 16–18.

Keanu Reeves and Winona Ryder in *Bram Stoker's Dracula.*

SANDERS, THOMAS (N.D.)

Production designer favored by FRANCIS COPPOLA for *BRAM STOKER'S DRAC-ULA* (1992). Sanders designed the "grand Victorian mansion" ELEANOR COPPOLA marveled over in her memoir, *NOTES ON A LIFE* (2008). He also recycled some of the sets that had been constructed for Steven Spielberg's *Hook*, which still remained at the studio.

SARNER, ARLENE

See LEICHTLING, JERRY.

SCHEIDER, ROY (1932–2008)

Leading and supporting stage and screen actor who played Wilfred Keeley in *JOHN GRISHAM'S THE RAINMAKER* (1997). Born on November 10, 1932, in Orange, New Jersey, Scheider studied at Rutgers University and at Franklin and Marshall College, in Lancaster, Pennsylvania, where he majored in history, his college education interrupted by three years of service in the United States Air Force. He made his stage debut playing Mercutio for Joseph Papp's 1961 Shakespeare Festival production of *Romeo and Juliet*, and appeared in over eighty plays during the following decade, gathering critical accolades, such as an Obie Award for his off-Broadway performance in James Joyce's *Stephen D.* in 1968 and his Drama League of New York Award for his Most Distinguished Performance

of 1980–1981 in the Broadway production of Harold Pinter's *Betrayal*. His film roles were also memorable, most notably, perhaps, in the Steven Spielberg blockbuster *Jaws* (1975), adapted from the best-selling novel by Peter Benchley, in which Scheider played the sheriff of Amity, a beach resort town. But for discriminating viewers, Scheider was even more effective as Dustin Hoffman's conflicted brother in the John Schlesinger thriller *Marathon Man* (1976), his Oscar-nominated performance with GENE HACKMAN in *The French Connection* (1971), or his Oscar nomination as Best Actor for his remarkable portrayal of Joe Gideon, an ailing Broadway director in Bob Fosse's *All That Jazz* (1979). Scheider died on February 10, 2008, and was survived by his wife, documentary filmmaker Brenda Siemer.—JAMES M. WELSH

SCHULMAN, ARNOLD (1925–)

American actor, author, playwright, and screenwriter for *TUCKER: THE MAN AND HIS DREAM* (1988). Born in Philadelphia, Pennsylvania, on August 11, 1925, he attended The University of North Carolina, Chapel Hill, where he studied writing. After serving in the U.S. Navy, he moved to New York, where he found work in theatre and, later, television and films. During the mid-1950s he wrote for the television series *Omnibus*, *General Electric Theater*, and *The Kraft Television Theater*. He studied with playwright Robert Anderson (best known, perhaps, for *Tea and Sympathy*) at the American Theatre Wing, then became a member of the Dramatists Guild. Schulman was one of the original members of the playwriting unit at the Actors Studio, and his first play was directed by LEE STRASBERG. His many screenwriting credits include Frank Capra's *A Hole in the Head* (1959), *Wild Is the Wind* (which earned a Writers Guild Award nomination in 1957), *Love with the Proper Stranger* (1963, nominated for a Best Original Screenplay Academy Award and also nominated for the Writers Guild Award), *Goodbye, Columbus* (nominated for Best Adapted Screenplay for 1969), *Funny Lady* (1975, with Jay Presson Allen), and *A Chorus Line* (directed by Richard Attenborough in 1985), among others.—JAMES M. WELSH

SCHWARTZMAN, JASON (1980–)

Actor/musician (and nephew of FRANCIS COPPOLA) who appears in several Coppola-produced projects, including *MARIE ANTOINETTE* (2006) and *CQ* (2001). In 1996, during one of Francis Coppola's regular family "creativity camps," SOFIA COPPOLA directed a play based on the F. Scott Fitzgerald short story, "Bernice Bobs Her Hair," staged in a converted barn. According to reporter Frank Bruni, Sofia was "so impressed with one cousin's performance that she recommended him to a friend who was casting a project titled 'Rushmore.'" Thus began the screen career of Jason Schwartzman, son of TALIA SHIRE. "He totally stole the show," said the younger Coppola of Schwartzman's role in her amateur production; "Hysterically funny."

It would be a full decade before Sofia Coppola would direct her cousin Jason again, as the feckless Dauphin in her film *Marie Antoinette*, produced by her father. In that stylized period piece, Schwartzman gives what *Variety* calls "a slyly detached

performance" as the young Louis XVI. The relatively few (but high-profile) critics who admired the film made note of Schwartzman's understatedly bumbling performance as the sexually inept King of France.

As for Schwartzman's film debut in Wes Anderson's *Rushmore*, as the eccentric high school sophomore Max Fischer, Todd McCarthy calls the performance "sensational," adding that Schwartzman's "droll, deadpan delivery subtly suggests Max's impatience with fools . . . and his unerring sense of timing bespeaks a natural gift for comedy." Both McCarthy and Roger Ebert note a remarkable similarity between Schwartzman's Max Fischer and Dustin Hoffman's Benjamin Braddock from *The Graduate* (1967).

Schwartzman also appeared in ROMAN COPPOLA's feature directorial debut, *CQ*, about a struggling director in the heyday of the European art cinema of the late 1960s. Schwartzman portrays an American horror director, a character described by the *New York Times* as "a brash party boy . . . a wild windup toy of an egomaniac who's so busy chasing women and sensations that he doesn't really get around to doing much work." Although the film received mixed reviews at best, GENE D. PHILLIPS observes that Jason Schwartzman "stands out in a good cast," which also included Gérard Depardieu, GIANCARLO GIANNINI, Billy Zane, and DEAN STOCKWELL.

Despite his success in the film industry (which he calls "the family business"), Schwartzman's first love has always been music. At the age of fourteen, he cofounded the rock band Phantom Planet, for whom he was the drummer. Their debut album, *Phantom Planet Is Missing*, came out on Geffen Records in late 1998, shortly before *Rushmore* was released. Schwartzman left the band in May 2003 to write songs and pursue a solo career and has since released two solo projects, *Nighttiming* (2007) and *Davy* (2009). His musical influences include the Beatles, the Beach Boys, the Kinks, Neil Young, and Smokey Robinson. Schwartzman's song "California" got wide exposure for its use in the successful independent film, *Orange County* (2002), and he composed much of the original music for Judd Apatow's *Funny People* (2009), in which he also appears in a supporting role.

In 2004 Schwartzman was cast as the star of the sitcom *Cracking Up*, a midseason replacement show on the Fox network, playing a student who moves into the guest house of a seemingly picture-perfect, but apparently crazy, Beverly Hills family. Despite some critical notice, the series was not renewed. His other major credits include David O. Russell's *I (Heart) Huckabees* (2004) and Wes Anderson's *The Darjeeling Limited* (which he also cowrote, along with cousin Roman Coppola).

As an actor, Schwartzman has been influenced by another important family member, his cousin NICOLAS CAGE. Schwartzman told the *New York Times*: "I looked up to him as a kid; he was a big influence on me. But ooph, I love them all. It really is a clan. We were all encouraged to pursue what made us happy, and it just so happens that this is what makes me happy. It's a circus family, you know what I mean? The flying trapeze."—RODNEY HILL

References

Roger Ebert, "*Rushmore*," *Chicago Sun-Times*, February 5, 1999, www.rogerebert.com; Nic Harcourt, "Tête-à-Tête: Jason Schwartzman," *Los Angeles Times*, May 1, 2009, www.latimes.com; Alexandra Jacobs, "He's That Guy from 'Rushmore' and More," *New York Times*, March 7, 2004, sec. 2: 22; "Jason Schwartzman," *Variety* Profiles, www.variety.com; Todd McCarthy, "Also Playing: *CQ*," *Variety*, May 12, 2001; Todd McCarthy, "*Rushmore*," *Variety*, September 11, 1998, www.variety.com; Elvis Mitchell, "*CQ*: How Contradictory Parts Go Together," *New York Times*, May 24, 2002, www.nytimes.com; Gene D. Phillips, *Godfather: The Intimate Francis Ford Coppola* (Lexington: University Press of Kentucky, 2004).

SEIDLER, DAVID (N.D.)

Cowriter with ARNOLD SCHULMAN for the screenplay of *TUCKER: THE MAN AND HIS DREAM*. A naturalized American born in London, England, Seidler was educated at Cornell University (BA) and the University of Washington (MA) before becoming a playwright in residence at the San Francisco Actors' Workshop. Before working on *Tucker*, Seidler had scripted *Malice in Wonderland* (1985), a Hollywood biofantasy concerning gossip columnists Louella Parsons and Hedda Hopper. After *Tucker* he scripted several made-for-television features and biopics, including *Dancing in the Dark* (1995), *Lies He Told* (1997), *Time to Say Goodbye?* (1997, an Alzheimer's drama), and *Come On Get Happy: The Partridge Family Story* (1999); animated features such as *Quest for Camelot* (1998) and *The King and I* (1999, an animated adaptation of the musical); and two martial-arts features for David Carradine, *Son of the Dragon* (2007) and *Kung Fu Killer* (2008).—JAMES M. WELSH

SHEEN, CHARLIE
[CARLOS IRWIN ESTEVEZ] (1965–)

The younger brother of EMILIO ESTEVEZ and the son of MARTIN SHEEN, born Carlos Irwin Estevez in New York City on September 3, 1965, the third of four children, all of whom, as James Cameron-Wilson has written, "went on to film careers, with varying degrees of success. Emilio Estevez [born 1962], is an actor, writer and director; Ramon Estevez [born 1963] is an actor," as is sister Renee Estevez (born 1966). Their mother, Janet Sheen, meanwhile, "turned associate producer on the domestic satire *Beverly Hills Brats.*" At the age of nine in 1974 Charlie Sheen acted in the cast of the television production of *The Execution of Private Slovik,* which starred his father, Martin Sheen, as a World War II soldier who faced a firing squad for desertion, and later worked with his father as an extra in the cast of *APOCA-LYPSE NOW* in 1979. His first starring role came with *Red Dawn* (1984), costarring with PATRICK SWAYZE and C. THOMAS HOWELL, who had worked with his brother in FRANCIS COPPOLA's *THE OUTSIDERS.* Always interested in sports, he won a baseball scholarship to the University of Kansas early on and later starred in the baseball feature *Eight Men Out.* A turning point in his career came when his older brother, Emilio Estevez, had to turn down the lead in Oliver Stone's *Platoon* (1987), due to a prior commitment, and Stone chose Charlie Sheen to replace him as Chris, the film's reluctant hero and narrator. This role made Sheen an instant star

after *Platoon* won four Academy Awards (including Best Picture). Sheen went on to play Bud Fox, in the shadow of Gordon Gekko in Stone's next picture, *Wall Street,* the following year, 1988.—JAMES M. WELSH

Reference

James Cameron-Wilson, *Young Hollywood* (Lanham, MD: Madison Books, 1994).

SHEEN, MARTIN
[RAMON GERARD ESTEVEZ] (1940–)

Gifted and popular Emmy- and Golden Globe–winning actor who has starred in more than seventy feature films, including *APOCALYPSE NOW* for FRANCIS COPPOLA (playing Capt. Benjamin L. Willard) and *Wall Street* for Oliver Stone, but whose record as a political activist almost matches his filmmaking achievements, with sixty-seven arrests for nonviolent peace demonstrations. He perhaps became most popular for his long-running, Emmy-nominated role as President Josiah Bartlet on the NBC

Marlon Brando and Martin Sheen in *Apocalypse Now.*

series *The West Wing*, since, at the time, Josiah Bartlet seemed to many viewers a better presidential model than the actual president who was serving. Sheen was born in Dayton, Ohio, the seventh son of a Spanish father and an Irish mother. Out of high school, Sheen went to New York City, where he earned acting credentials off-off-Broadway at the Living Theatre. In 1964 he played the lead in the Broadway production of *The Subject Was Roses*, then later played the lead in the 1968 screen adaptation. A breakthrough screen performance came in 1973 in Terrence Malick's *Badlands* and in 1974 on television in *The Execution of Private Slovik*. The stress of working with Coppola on *Apocalypse Now* induced a heart attack and a nervous breakdown when Sheen was thirty-eight years old. A spiritual turn toward India and Roman Catholicism helped Sheen weather this storm. —JAMES M. WELSH

Reference

Nancy Perry Graham, "Interview: Breaking Through," *AARP* (July–August 2008): 42–43, 73.

SHIRE, DAVID (1937–)

Born in Buffalo, New York, Shire wrote and performed the musical score for FRANCIS FORD COPPOLA's film *THE CONVERSATION* (1974). Shire is also Coppola's brother-in-law, having married Talia Coppola, who appeared as Connie Corleone in the *Godfather* trilogy and as Adrian in *Rocky I–V*. (They were divorced in 1978.) As a film composer, Shire's credits include *Drive, He Said* (1971), *The Taking of Pelham One Two Three* (1974), *All the President's Men* (1976), *Saturday Night Fever* (1977), *Straight Time* (1978), *Norma Rae* (1979), *Max Dugan Returns* (1983), *'Night, Mother* (1986), *Paris Trout* (1991), and *Zodiac* (2007). He won an Academy Award for Original Song, "It Goes Like It Goes," lyrics by Norman Gimbel, for *Norma Rae*

(1979), and was nominated for another, "I'll Never Say Goodbye," lyrics by Alan and Marilyn Bergman, for *The Promise* (1979). He also won a Golden Globe for Original Score, shared with Barry, Maurice, and Robin Gibb, for *Saturday Night Fever* (1977). His television work includes the series *The Virginian* (1969–1970), and *McCloud* (1970–1977). He won Emmys for his work on the television special *The Defection of Simas Kudrika* (1978), and the television series *Do You Remember Love* (1985), *The Kennedys of Massachusetts* (1990), and *Rear Window* (1998).

For *The Conversation*, Coppola decided to forego the use of an orchestra, limiting Shire to the use of one instrument. Shire wrote and performed a hauntingly poignant, jazzy piano score, with a recurrent melody that works as a counterpoint to the recursive narrative, the replaying of the tape of the title conversation between the adulterous lovers (FREDERIC FORREST and Cindy Williams) as they walk through Golden Gate Park in San Francisco discussing their plans to kill her husband (ROBERT DUVALL). Shire also wrote the jazz compositions that the main character, Harry Caul (GENE HACKMAN), listens to in his apartment, including the saxophone solos that Caul improvises to the recordings. Coppola used Shire's score as an early experiment in the use of synthesized elements, manipulated by the film's editor, WALTER MURCH, to enhance the performance. Shire's score has come to be regarded as a textbook example of the use of minimalism in scoring a motion picture.—JASON MOSSER

SHIRE, TALIA (1946–)

American actress and younger sister of FRANCIS FORD COPPOLA, featured in *THE GODFATHER* and its sequels but perhaps even better known for her role in Sylvester Stallone's *Rocky* series, for which she was named best supporting actress of 1976 by both the New York Film Critics Circle and the National Board of Review. She is the mother of actor JASON SCHWARTZMAN and musician Robert Carmine.

Born Talia Rose Coppola, she was offered a scholarship to the Yale School of Drama but dropped out after just a couple of years and headed to the West Coast. There, she landed a few bit parts in films produced by her brother's mentor, ROGER CORMAN, including *The Dunwich Horror* (1970) and *Wild Racers* (1968), credited as Talia Coppola.

In 1969 she became involved with DAVID SHIRE, an emerging composer and songwriter, best known for his film scores for *The Taking of Pelham 123* (1972), Coppola's *THE CONVERSATION* (1974), and more recently, *Zodiac* (2007). They were married in 1970 and have one son together, Matthew. In a *New York Times* interview, Talia Shire told Chris Chase that she approached her first marriage in a rather traditional manner. She set aside

her acting ambitions for a time, believing that a woman should be first and foremost a good wife and mother. "I was determined to choose sheets and set a table in a most rigorous fashion," she quipped.

Talia Shire's breakthrough role came, as it happened, with her brother Francis's breakthrough film, *The Godfather* (1972), in which she plays the youngest of Don Vito's children (and his only daughter), Connie Corleone. According to *Variety*, Shire initially was reluctant to approach her brother for a role in the film. "He was trying to make some interesting casting decisions which weren't considered commercial by the studios," Shire explains. "The last thing you need is, 'Can I give my sister a job?'"

When Paramount's production chief, ROBERT EVANS, decided on his own to hire Talia Shire, Coppola objected strongly at first, protesting that his sister was "too pretty" for the role (and perhaps also concerned about the appearance of nepotism). However, because he already had butted

Eli Wallach and Talia Shire in *The Godfather: Part III.*

heads with executives over the casting of MARLON BRANDO and AL PACINO, Coppola relented. His sister got the part, receiving credit for the first time as Talia Shire, but her payment for the performance amounted to a mere $1,500. (As the character of Connie became more prominent in the sequels, Shire's fees got progressively better, at $30,000 plus a $10,000 bonus for *THE GODFATHER: PART II*, and $500,000 for *THE GODFATHER: PART III*.)

Her reprise of the character of Connie in *The Godfather Part II* (1974) earned Shire her first Oscar nomination. Another contribution that Shire made to the sequel was her suggestion that Kay's "miscarriage" should turn out to be an abortion—a surefire way to alienate that character from Michael Corleone. As Coppola explained, Kay (DIANE KEATON) "knew that Michael would never forgive her, and she wanted out of her mafia marriage."

Throughout the 1970s Shire could be seen in numerous telefilms, as well as features such as John Frankenheimer's horror pic, *Prophecy* (1979). In 1978 she separated from David Shire and in 1980 married producer Jack Schwartzman (1932–1994), the head of Lorimar Pictures. Shire's second husband gave her a renewed sense of confidence in her ability to make the career that she had always wanted. She told the *New York Times* in 1982, "It takes a very powerful, centered man to give a woman permission to be strong. I used to feel guilty; I thought a strong woman was a castrator." Together she and Schwartzman formed a production company, TaliaFilm, and Shire has served in a producing capacity on a number of films, including *Never Say Never Again* (1983) and *Lionheart* (1987). Her first directorial effort was 1995's *One Night Stand*, produced by Schwartzman and Roger Corman.

Talia Shire further worked with her brother Francis on numerous occasions over the years, including roles in Coppola's "RIP VAN WINKLE" episode of SHELLEY DUVALL's *Faerie Tale Theatre* (1985), his episode in *NEW YORK STORIES* (1989) entitled "LIFE WITHOUT ZOE," and in his final installment of the Corleone family saga, *The Godfather: Part III* (1990).—RODNEY HILL

References

Peter Castro et al., "Family Reunion," *People*, March 24, 1997, 48; Chris Chase, "At the Movies: Growing Up in a Family of Achievers," *New York Times*, May 28, 1982, C8; Peter Cowie, *The Godfather Book* (London: Faber and Faber, 1997); Gene D. Phillips, *Godfather: The Intimate Francis Ford Coppola* (Lexington: University Press of Kentucky, 2004); "Talia Shire," *Variety Profiles*, www.variety.com.

SLATER, CHRISTIAN (1969–)

Popular American actor who plays Junior Tucker in *TUCKER: THE MAN AND HIS DREAM* (1988). Christian Slater was born on August 18, 1969, in New York, the son of stage actor Michael Hawkins (born Thomas Knight Slater) and casting director Mary Jo Slater, so it follows that he began acting at the age of seven on the television soap opera *One Life to Live*. He performed in the touring company of *The Music Man* with Dick Van Dyke and on Broadway before taking his first film role in *The Legend of Billie Jean* in 1985. He attended the Dalton School and the Professional Children's School in Manhattan, and the Fiorello H. LaGuardia High School of Music & Art and Performing Arts.

As luck would have it, Slater was cast at the age of sixteen to play a medieval monk opposite Sean Connery in director Jean-Jacques Annaud's film adaptation of Umberto Eco's *The Name of the Rose*

(1986), which, apparently, he considered a learning experience. He is perhaps best known for his starring roles in two critically acclaimed teen films: his portrayal of high school outsider J. D. in *Heathers*, with WINONA RYDER in 1989, and as charismatic Arizona student-DJ Mark Hunter in *Pump Up the Volume* (1990), a very good coming-of-age film. This remarkable performance set Slater up for many other popular roles, in such films as *Young Guns II: Blaze of Glory* (1990), *Robin Hood: Prince of Thieves* (1991, playing Will Scarlett), *Mobsters* (1991, playing Charles "Lucky" Luciano, after MATT DILLON had rejected the role), and a cameo in *Star Trek VI: The Undiscovered Country* (1991). In 1993 Slater got top billing with Patricia Arquette in Tony Scott's *True Romance*, with a supporting cast that included DENNIS HOPPER, GARY OLDMAN, Brad Pitt, Val Kilmer, and Christopher Walken. By 2010 he was starring as the lead investigator of the television series *The Unforgotten*.
—JAMES M. WELSH

Reference

James Cameron-Wilson, *Young Hollywood* (Lanham, MD: Madison Books, 1994).

SMITH, DICK (1922–)

Legendary film and television makeup artist whose work is featured in FRANCIS COPPOLA's *THE GODFATHER* (1972) and *THE GODFATHER: PART II* (1974). Smith is considered a pioneer in the specialty field of aging makeup, and he applied the technique of "old-age stipple" (which involves layers of latex makeup) to MARLON BRANDO for his role of Don Vito Corleone. Smith used similar aging techniques in other outstanding films such as *Little Big Man* (1970), *The Hunger* (1983), and *Amadeus* (1984), which won Smith his only Oscar, as well as a BAFTA Film Award.

In the field of television makeup, Smith was also a pioneer, as one of the first makeup artists hired at NBC (his earliest listed credits go back to 1948). Smith received his only Emmy (though he was nominated for several) for his work in transforming Hal Holbrook into the aged Samuel L. Clemens in *Mark Twain Tonight!* (1967).

Dick Smith is perhaps best known for his special-effects makeup design, for such films as *The Exorcist* (1973), *Altered States* (1980), and *House of Dark Shadows* (1970). The veteran makeup artist continued to work well into his seventies, on such films as *Death Becomes Her* (1992) and the remake of *House on Haunted Hill* (1999).—
RODNEY HILL

References

"Dick Smith," Internet Movie Database, www.imdb.com/name/nm0004615/; *Variety* Profiles, www.variety.com.

SPANO, VINCENT (1962–)

Italian American actor who plays Steve in FRANCIS COPPOLA's *RUMBLE FISH*. Spano was born in Brooklyn, New York, on October 18, 1962. He began acting at the age of fourteen, while attending Stuyvesant High School, awarded the part of Steve, a dying man's son, in the Long Wharf Theatre production of *The Shadow Box*. After its transfer to Broadway, the play won the 1977 Pulitzer Prize and the Tony Award for best drama. Spano made his feature film debut in Jonathan Kaplan's *Over the Edge* in 1979. In 1983, besides his role in *Rumble Fish*, Spano worked with John Sayles in *Baby, It's You*, as a working-class Italian lad who calls himself "The Sheik" after Rudolph Valentino. Spano later worked with Sayles again in *City of Hope* (1991). Among many other film roles, Spano worked with the Taviani brothers in *Good*

Morning, Babylon (1987). For television Spano was cast as Mafia chieftain Mark Ciuni in Showtime's *Blood Ties* (1986) and was nominated for Best Actor for the Cable Ace Awards for his performance.

In *Rumble Fish* Spano took the part of Steve, the naive but likeable sidekick of Rusty James (MATT DILLON). Spano was a swarthy, darkly handsome young man. Recalls Coppola, "I asked Vincent, who had black hair, to dye his hair blond," as a contrast to Matt Dillon. Vincent Spano gives an immaculate portrayal of Steve, Rusty James's good-hearted best friend, who has the same sort of dogged devotion for Rusty James that Rusty James himself has for Motorcycle Boy, his older brother. Spano effectively projects the inner turmoil of modern young people.

A highlight of Spano's later career was *City of Hope* (1991), directed by John Sayles, which focuses on crime and corruption in the strife-torn inner city. Spano was cast as a troubled young man with the cards stacked against him.—GENE D. PHILLIPS/JAMES M. WELSH

References

Leslie Halliwell, *Film Guide*, ed. David Gritten, rev. ed. (New York: Harper Collins, 2008); Ephraim Katz, *Film Encyclopedia*, ed. Ronald Nolan, rev. ed. (New York: Harper Collins, 2008); Leonard Maltin, ed., *Movie Guide*, rev. ed. (New York: New American Library, 2009).

SPRADLIN, G. D. (1920–)

Character actor who appeared in two FRANCIS COPPOLA films. Spradlin pursued a career in politics until he turned to acting in his late thirties. His first film was *Will Penny* (1967), a western. Coppola commandeered the former politician to play Senator Pat Geary in *THE GODFATHER: PART II* (1974).

Geary, says Coppola, represents the sort of high-profile politician that Michael Corleone likes to bribe. What's more, when Geary proves intractable about becoming involved in one of Michael's dirty deeds, Michael arranges to blackmail Geary into submission by having him framed for the murder of a prostitute in a Las Vegas brothel. Coppola comments that he had once read about a similar episode in the press and thought it might make "a creepy scene" in the picture. Pauline Kael says that the scene is poorly staged; on the contrary, it is riveting, with the nearly naked Spradlin muttering, "I can't understand how she died; we were just having fun." Still, Kael writes that the casting of Spradlin as Geary is "a juicy bit of satire; he looks and acts like a synthesis of several of our worst senators."

In *APOCALYPSE NOW* (1979) Spradlin plays General Corman, named after Coppola's early mentor, filmmaker ROGER CORMAN. It is General Corman who sends Capt. Willard on his top-secret mission to find U.S. Army officer Col. Kurtz and assassinate him. Corman woos Willard to take on the task with a roast beef and scotch dinner in the middle of the jungle. He explains to Willard that Kurtz has gone totally insane and is commanding a rogue army, which he maintains for his own unauthorized and savage attacks on the enemy. Though Spradlin appears in only one scene in this film, David Thomson singles him out for his fine performance.

Spradlin never worked for Coppola again, but he continued his acting career in movies for another twenty years, appearing in films like the thriller *The Long Kiss Goodnight* (1997) opposite Samuel L. Jackson.—GENE D. PHILLIPS

References

Leslie Halliwell, *Who's Who in the Movies*, ed. John Walker, rev. ed. (New York: Harper Collins, 2006); Jorn Hetebrugge, "Apocalypse Now," in *100 All-Time Favorite Movies* (Los Angeles:

Taschen, 2008), 2:234–39; Pauline Kael, *Reeling* (New York: Warner Books, 1977); David Thomson, *Have You Seen . . . ? 1,000 Films* (New York: Knopf, 2008).

STANTON, HARRY DEAN (1926–)
Stanton was born in West Irvine, Kentucky, July 14, 1926. He attended the University of Kentucky in Lexington, where he studied journalism and radio arts. He is a veteran of World War II and studied at the Pasadena Playhouse in Pasadena, California.

Stanton's prolific career began in television in the 1950s in series such as *Inner Sanctum* (1954) and a variety of westerns such as *The Adventures of Rin Tin Tin, The Texan, U.S. Marshall, Laramie, Have Gun Will Travel, Bat Masterson, Zane Grey Theater*, and *The Rifleman*. He also appeared in tough-guy crime series such as *The Lawless Years*. Even in his thirties, Stanton's appearance and laconic style conveyed the same suggestion of a unique, weathered, rough character that has kept him working in popular films and television series into his eighth decade.

One of Stanton's earliest notable films was the western *Ride in the Whirlwind* (1965), written by JACK NICHOLSON, produced by Nicholson and Monte Hellman, and directed by Hellman (*Two-Lane Blacktop* [1971] and *Cockfighter* [1974], in both of which Stanton also appeared). *Whirlwind* marked the first time Nicholson and Stanton worked together, and their friendship has persevered. According to Stanton, they met in the mid-1960s at a MARTIN LANDAU acting class. Later, Stanton stood up as best man for Nicholson and shared his Laurel Canyon home with him for three years after Nicholson's divorce. At Nicholson's 1994 American Film Institute Lifetime Achievement Award ceremony, Stanton and Art Garfunkel serenaded the star actor, at his request, with a rendition of the Everly Brothers'

"Dream." The Internet Movie Database lists seven Nicholson films in which Stanton has appeared.

While Stanton was landing small film roles in the 1960s, his television résumé continued to expand, including roles on such series as *Bonanza*; *The Fugitive*; *Combat!*; *Rawhide*; *Gunsmoke*; *The Guns of Will Sonnett*; *The Virginian*; *Mannix*; *The High Chaparral*; *The Untouchables*; *Cimarron Strip*; *The Wild, Wild West*; and *A Man Called Shenandoah*. Apart from this impressive variety, his preponderance of "type" work in western or gangster roles clearly stands out.

After *Whirlwind* (1965) Stanton's film roles, although still minor, became associated with bigger box office titles and stars, beginning with Paul Newman in *Cool Hand Luke* (1967) and with Clint Eastwood in *Kelly's Heroes* (1970). After reuniting with Monte Hellman for *Two-Lane Blacktop* (1971), he was picked up by Sam Peckinpah for *Pat Garrett and Billy the Kid* (1973) and by FRANCIS FORD COPPOLA to play an FBI agent in *THE GODFATHER: PART II* (1974). Coppola called on Stanton again for *ONE FROM THE HEART* (1982) and later again to play the lead role in the *Faerie Tale Theater* version of "RIP VAN WINKLE" (1987), in which Stanton also plays Rip's grown son.

Stanton began to see larger roles, costarring with JEFF BRIDGES in *Rancho Deluxe* (1975), playing a detective in the remake of *Farewell My Lovely* (1975) starring Robert Mitchum, rejoining Jack Nicholson in Arthur Penn's *The Missouri Breaks* (1976), and working with Dustin Hoffman in *Straight Time* (1978).

Stanton's most visible role in a blockbuster film came in 1979 with Ridley Scott's *Alien*. His portrayal of the spaceship's working-man mechanic Brett, alongside Yaphet Kotto, endeared him to audiences, despite—or because of—the fact that his character is the first to be killed in the *Ten Little Indians*–style horror film. His next hit venture was also in the sci-fi genre, as the character Brain in John Carpenter's *Escape from New York* (1981).

Stanton's most critically praised dramatic role came in WIM WENDERS's *Paris, Texas* (1984). Stanton plays Travis Henderson, a man who is as empty at the start of the film as the desert around him. In the opening portion of the film, Stanton's quiet style of acting perfectly reflects someone without memory and without any purpose other than to keep moving. Stanton himself described his interpretation of the role: "It wasn't odd to be in the lead; I took the same approach as I would to any other part. I play myself as totally as I possibly can. My own Harry Dean Stanton act . . . I don't know . . . whatever happened to Travis, I'd say . . . it's me." Near the end of the film, Travis explains, through a one-way mirror, to his young wife (NASTASSJA KINSKY) why he left her, in a scene that Roger Ebert has called "one of the great monologues of movie history."

The same year as his powerful performance in *Paris, Texas*, Stanton submitted another of his memorable quirky roles, costarring with EMILIO ESTEVEZ in Alex Cox's *Repo Man* (1984). Although not a box office hit, *Repo Man* has become a cult favorite. With these films in the mid-1980s, Stanton's popularity in the industry was at its highest, and he followed with more mainstream work, such as playing a suburban father in John Hughes's *Pretty in Pink* (1986), working again with Francis Ford Coppola in "Rip Van Winkle" (*Faerie Tale Theater* 1987), as the apostle Saul/Paul in Martin Scorsese's *The Last Temptation of Christ* (1988), and as a private investigator in David Lynch's *Wild at Heart* (1990). After their initial work together, Lynch used Stanton again in 1992 in his cult television series *Twin Peaks*.

Stanton's next work in popular films came at the end of the 1990s with Terry Gilliam's Hunter S. Thompson biography *Fear and Loathing in Las Vegas* (1998) and the Stephen King short story *The Green Mile* (1999). However, at the same time, he worked on a notable smaller-budget film, again with David Lynch, in the critically praised *The Straight Story* (1999), playing the ailing brother that Richard Farnsworth's character sets out to see, traveling by tractor over hundreds of miles, throughout this unique odyssey film.

The 2000s have seen Stanton's career continue in the same pattern, working with friends (Jack Nicholson, *Anger Management* [2003]), and doing strange and comic projects (*Alien Autopsy*; *You, Me, and Dupree* [2006]). But he has also discovered the strongest television series role of his career in HBO's *Big Love*, as Roman Grant, the self-proclaimed prophet and ruthless leader of the polygamous religious group, for which he was nominated for the 2007 Satellite Awards' Best Actor in a Supporting Role.

Throughout his long career in television and film, in westerns, crime dramas, science fiction, in virtually every genre, Harry Dean Stanton's work has been a reliable favorite of his fans, his peers, and Hollywood's most respected directors.— THOMAS CLANCY

Reference

Roger Ebert, "Paris, Texas," *Chicago Sun-Times*, December 8, 2002, http://rogerebert.suntimes .com/apps/pbcs.dll/article?AID=/20021208/REV IEWS08/212080301/1023.

STEELE, TOMMY (1936–)

A zesty English cockney actor and pop singer, who appeared in FRANCIS COPPOLA's *FINIAN'S RAINBOW*. Steele starred in the film version of *Half a Sixpence* (1967), in which he had played on the London and the New York stages. But the movie was a lame, overlong version of the stage show.

Coppola then cast him in *Finian's Rainbow* as Og, a leprechaun whose magical pot of gold has been stolen by Finian McLonergan (FRED ASTAIRE). *Finian's Rainbow* was originally produced on the Broadway stage in 1949, and its plot was considerably dated. Pauline Kael complained that, for the sake of some pretty songs one must endure the fairy tale pot of gold, not to mention "hypertense Tommy Steele's Puckish leprechaun."

As a matter of fact, Coppola was dissatisfied with Steele's performance in the movie: "The performance I'm really unhappy about was Tommy Steele, because I think I could have done better with him. When we were doing the rehearsal, Tommy was doing his *thing*. And I said to him that I really felt we were going in the wrong direction. Everyone loved him and told Tommy he was so great. But I felt the leprechaun should be more shy and timid and bewildered. I wanted it to be an introvert leprechaun, a guy who speaks in this quiet voice and then suddenly becomes a human being.

"And at my insistence Tommy started to do just that in the rehearsal, and he really was good at it. But actors are funny people. They have certain crutches that they rely on. And they're very unwilling to let those crutches go when they feel insecure. And somehow during the actual shooting, little by little, he slipped back into his familiar character. And you don't notice it because you're shooting little pieces. And that's the whole game of directing. Directing takes a lot of concentration and being able to be blind to certain problems and just focus where you should be focusing. I did that in some cases. In some cases I failed. With Tommy, I wanted a different kind of performance and he eluded me."

Finian's Rainbow was a failure, both with the critics and with audiences. Kael, damning the movie with faint praise, wrote that, compared with *Half a Sixpence*, *Finian's Rainbow*, "as a big, clean, family musical, wasn't so bad." Steele made one more film, *Where's Jack?* (1969), in which he was miscast as eighteenth-century highwayman Jack Sheppard, after which he retired from the screen and devoted himself to his career as a pop singer.—GENE D. PHILLIPS

References

Joseph Gelmis, "Francis Ford Coppola: Free Agent within the System," in *Francis Ford Coppola: Interviews*, ed. Gene D. Phillips and Rodney Hill (Jackson: University Press of Mississippi, 2004); Pauline Kael, *Going Steady* (New York: Boyars, 1994); Leonard Maltin, ed., *Movie Guide*, rev. ed. (New York: New American Library, 2009).

STOCKWELL, DEAN (1936–)

New Yorker reviewer Terrence Rafferty described "the remarkable Dean Stockwell" as the actor who plays Howard Hughes, meeting PRESTON TUCKER and his youngest son in a spooky deserted airport hangar in *TUCKER: THE MAN AND HIS DREAM* (1988); Stockwell later portrayed Judge Harvey Hale for FRANCIS COPPOLA in *THE RAINMAKER* (1997); he also appeared as Homer Thomas in *GARDENS OF STONE*. Stockwell was born in North Hollywood on March 5, 1936, the son of actor Harry Stockwell and dancer-actress Nina Olivette. Noticed by an MGM talent scout after appearing at the age of seven in a Theatre Guild production of *The Innocent Voyage*, Stockwell became a child star, performing in more than twenty pictures, playing Gregory Peck's son in *Gentlemen's Agreement* (1947) and playing the lead role in the allegorical film *The Boy with Green Hair* (1948). On television Stockwell appeared in many popular series, including *Climax, Playhouse 90, The Twilight Zone, Columbo*, and *Chicago Hope* (in 1994). On Broadway, he starred in the play *Compulsion*, a role he repeated for the screen version in 1959, for which performance he was named Best Actor at the CANNES INTERNATIONAL FILM FESTIVAL. He was later honored again at Cannes for his work in *Long Day's Journey into Night* (1962, with Katharine Hepburn and Jason Robards). As a mature actor, Stockwell made a memorable appearance as DENNIS HOPPER's friend, Ben, in David Lynch's *Blue Velvet* (1986) and was nominated for a Best Supporting Actor Academy Award for his performance as Mafia boss Tony Russo in *Married to the Mob* (1988).—JAMES M. WELSH

STOKER, ABRAHAM "BRAM" (1847–1912)

Author of the novel, *Dracula* (1897), Stoker was born in Dublin in 1847, the son of Abraham Stoker, a civil servant who worked in the chief secretary's office at Dublin Castle for over fifty years. His mother was a social worker devoted to equalizing the sexes.

Educated at Trinity College, Dublin, Stoker graduated with honors in mathematics in 1868 and went to work as a civil servant. Much enamored of theatre, he became the unpaid drama critic for the *Dublin Mail* in 1871. In 1875 he published his first horror story, "The Chain of Destiny." In 1876 he met Sir Henry Irving, considered the greatest English actor of his era, and the first actor to be knighted. Stoker became the actor's confidant and would work for twenty-eight years as Irving's acting manager, presiding over his productions at the Lyceum Theatre, London.

In 1878, Stoker married Florence Balcombe, who bore him a son, Noel, in 1879. In failing health, Henry Irving signed the Lyceum over to a syndicate in 1900; the theatre closed in 1902 and Irving died in 1905. Stoker lived on to write the two-volume *Personal Reminiscences of Sir Henry Irving*

in addition to novels and short stories, producing a total of seventeen books.

Stoker wrote *Dracula* in the British Museum, where he could also research the first nineteenth-century fictional vampire, John Polidori's Lord Ruthven, and Dion Boucicault's play, *The Vampire*. His working title for the novel, published in 1897, was "The Un-Dead." While Stoker was on vacation at the Yorkshire port of Whitby in 1890, he came across a book in the Whitby Library written in 1820 by William Wilkerson, who had served as British Consul in Bucharest. In Wilkerson's book, entitled *An Account of the Principalities of Wallachia and Moldavia*, Stoker read about the fifteenth-century Wallachian Voivode, Prince Dracula, and the account fired his imagination. Stoker's literary creation might have been considered Hungarian rather than Romanian, since he refers to himself as "*Szekely*," a Hungarian descended from Atilla. Stoker's biographer speculates that the mesmeric and exploitive genius Sir Henry Irving actually inspired Stoker's bloodsucking creation, and even describes Stoker as Renfield to Irving's Dracula: "I am Your slave, and You will reward me, for I shall be faithful. I have worshiped You long and afar off."—JAMES M. WELSH

References

Barbara Belford, *Bram Stoker: A Biography of the Author of "Dracula"* (New York: Alfred A. Knopf, 1996); Clive Leatherdale, *Dracula, the Novel and the Legend: A Study of Bram Stoker's Gothic Masterpiece*, rev. ed. (London: Desert Island Books, 1985).

STORARO, VITTORIO (1940–)

Award-winning cinematographer, born in Rome in 1940, the son of a movie projectionist who worked for Lux Film. Completing his studies at the Duca D'Aosta technical photographic institute, Storaro became an apprentice in a photography studio, then became assistant cameraman to director Bernardo Bertolucci, with whom he worked on *The Conformist, Last Tango in Paris, 1900, Luna,* and *The Last Emperor.* Storaro won Academy Awards for his work on *APOCALYPSE NOW, Reds* (for Warren Beatty), and *The Last Emperor* (for Bertolucci). His work as director of photography for FRANCIS COPPOLA includes *ONE FROM THE HEART* and *TUCKER: THE MAN AND HIS DREAM.*

Storaro's cinematography for Bertolucci's films attracted Francis Coppola, who hired Storaro for *Apocalypse Now.* His sweep and his ability to vividly depict the ambiance of surroundings are highlighted in sequences "such as the napalm bombardment, the Playboy Bunny show, and the nocturnal firing on the Do Lung bridge," according to M. S. Fonseca.

MARLON BRANDO arrived at the Philippine location to play Kurtz overweight. "He was already heavy when I hired him," says Coppola in the documentary *HEARTS OF DARKNESS: A FILMMAKER'S APOCALYPSE,* but by now he had ballooned to 250 pounds. "He had promised me he was going to get into shape, but he didn't. So he left me in a tough spot," because Kurtz is supposed to be wasting away from malaria. Coppola therefore had cinematographer Vittorio Storaro shoot Brando immersed in the cavernous darkness of his murky quarters, where Brando's girth would not be obvious. Actually, Storaro thought it dramatically right to photograph Brando as a disembodied voice so that Kurtz materialized out of the black void. "The Marlon Brando character represents the dark side of civilization," he explains. "[H]e had to appear as something of a pagan idol." Accordingly, Storaro filmed Brando "in the shadows or partially lit," and that gave him an air of mystery. Storaro won an Oscar for his eye-filling lensing of *Apocalypse Now.*

In photographing *One from the Heart* Coppola asked Storaro to shoot many unbroken takes, lasting up to ten minutes apiece. Storaro kept the camera on the go during these extended takes, as it unobtrusively glided from one character to another, closing in at times to capture a key gesture or remark, then falling back for a medium or long shot as the action and dialogue continued. In this fashion, the camera would draw the filmgoer into the scene and explore the action at close range and not simply remain a remote observer watching the action from a distance like a spectator at a stage play. One thinks, for example, of the quarrel scene early in the movie that peaks with Frannie walking out on Hank, which was done as a long take.

In order to capture the ambiance of Las Vegas during a festive Fourth of July celebration, Coppola and Storaro gave the film a bright look, often using saturated colors—pulsating magentas and gaudy oranges. Indeed, the film is sumptuously shot, and Storaro's virtuosity and visual flair are never in doubt.

Storaro also photographed *Tucker,* Coppola's movie about the maverick automobile inventor PRESTON TUCKER. The film's opening credits are superimposed on Coppola's facsimile of a promotional short made by the Public Relations Department of the Tucker Corporation. It has a cheerful voiceover narration, snappy 1940s Big Band music, and snapshots from the Tucker family album.

Storaro employed lush colors throughout the picture to give it the lustrous, lacquered look of an auto industry promo film. The credit sequence sets the tone for the film to follow, Coppola explains. "I had the desire to make the movie in the style of a 1940s promo film that had been produced by Tucker's Public Affairs office—with a great deal of showmanship. After all, this was a kind of Horatio Alger story."

Coppola, in concert with Storaro and his other collaborators, gave the entire movie the brash, peppy flavor of a promotional documentary, with sunny exteriors and glowing interiors, plus warm, earthy colors in the costumes. Coppola's films, says Fonseca, "benefit from Storaro's presence behind the camera as a true master of light."—GENE D. PHILLIPS/JAMES M. WELSH

References

John Belton, *American Cinema/American Culture*, rev. ed. (New York: McGraw-Hill, 2009); M. S. Fonseca, "Vittorio Storaro," in *International Dictionary of Films and Filmmakers*, ed. Nicolet Elert (New York: St. James Press, 2000), 4:792–94; Ric Gentry, "Vittorio Storaro in Conversation," in *Projections Six: Filmmakers on Filmmaking*, ed. John Boorman and Walter Donahue (Boston: Faber and Faber, 1996), 265–76; David Thomson, *Have You Seen . . . ? 1,000 Films* (New York: Knopf, 2008).

STRASBERG, LEE (1901–1982)

Legendary acting coach, born November 17, 1901, in Budanow, Austria-Hungary, who made his screen acting debut for FRANCIS FORD COPPOLA playing mobster Hyman Roth in *THE GODFATHER: PART II* (1974). In the United States since 1910, Strasberg studied for the stage with Richard Boleslavsky and Maria Ouspenskaya at the American Laboratory Theatre in New York. Utterly a man of the theatre (as actor, director, producer, and teacher) for most of his life, Lee Strasberg began his theatrical career as assistant stage manager at the Garrick in New York in 1924, made his acting debut in 1925, and in 1930 became one of the founders of the Group Theatre in New York. Starting in 1947 as the artistic director of the renowned Actors Studio in New York, Strasberg became mentor to many of the most highly respected Hollywood talents, including AL PACINO, who suggested to Francis Coppola that Strasberg be cast as the Jewish racketeer and crime syndicate treasurer Hyman Roth. The role was modeled on the notorious Jewish gangster Meyer Lansky. His performance for Coppola earned an Academy Award nomination. In 1969 he established the Lee Strasberg Institute of the Theatre in New York and Los Angeles.—JAMES M. WELSH

Reference

Ian Herbert, et al., eds., *Who's Who in the Theatre*, 16th ed. (London: Pitman/Gale Research, 1977).

SWAYZE, PATRICK [WAYNE] (1952–2009)

American actor who played Darrel Curtis in *THE OUTSIDERS* (1983). Patrick Swayze, the son of drafting engineer Jesse Wayne Swayze and dancer and choreographer Patsy Swayze, grew up in Houston, Texas, where he was born on August 18, 1952. His mother was a dance teacher and choreographer who created the dance sequences for the film *Urban Cowboy* (1980). Swayze concentrated on dancing and gymnastics growing up, and attended San Jacinto College in Houston on a gymnastics scholarship.

He went on to study with the Harkness and Joffrey Ballet Companies and then joined the Eliot Feld Ballet as principal dancer. He appeared in a dancing role with Joel Grey in the Broadway production of *Goodtime Charley*, then in 1978 took over the lead, replacing Barry Bostwick, who originated the role of Danny Zuko in the Broadway production of the hit musical *Grease*.

Swayze made his film debut in the roller-disco drama, *Skatetown, U.S.A.* (1980) and played a demolition derby driver in *Grandview, U.S.A.* In 1983 roles followed in Coppola's *The Outsiders* and in *Uncommon Valor*; Swayze played one of the youngsters in *Red Dawn* in 1984 (in fact the quarterback leader of the pack) and a Confederate soldier, Orry Main, in the Civil War miniseries *North and South* in 1985. Two years later, Swayze earned a Golden

Globe nomination for Best Actor for his performance with Jennifer Grey in *Dirty Dancing*, his breakthrough picture. *Washington Post* film critic Rita Kempley breezily described Swayze as "a cross between Brando and Balanchine." Another Golden Globe nomination would follow in 1990 for his performance with Demi Moore in the box office hit *Ghost*.

In addition to starring in *Dirty Dancing*, Swayze wrote and performed the hit single "She's Like the Wind" for the film's soundtrack album, which rose to the number three position on the pop charts. He also cowrote and performed the song "Brothers" for the *Next of Kin* soundtrack in 1989, a film in which he starred as Truman Gates, a police officer transplanted from Appalachia to the streets of urban Chicago, intent on avenging his brother's murder. In 1992 Swayze earned critical acclaim for his portrayal of Max Lowe, an idealistic American doctor serving the poor in Calcutta in director Roland Joffé's *City of Joy*. The actor prepared for that role by volunteering to work with the dying at Mother Teresa's clinic in Calcutta. Other daring but less successful roles were to follow, such as drag queen Vida Boheme in *To Wong Foo, Thanks for Everything! Julie Newmar* (1995) and his born-again role in *Donnie Darko* (2001).

Diagnosed with pancreatic cancer in 2008, Swayze continued to act while undergoing chemotherapy and received good notices for his portrayal of an undercover FBI agent in the A&E cable network drama series *The Beast* (2009). Swayze, who missed only one day of work while that series was being filmed, died the following year, on September 14, 2009, survived by his wife, Lisa Niemi, whom he married in 1975.—JAMES M. WELSH

SWEENEY, D. B.
[DANIEL BERNARD] (1961–)

Actor who made his film debut in 1987 as recruit Private Jackie Willow, patriotic, idealistic, and eager to fight in Vietnam, but frustrated by his assignment to THE OLD GUARD at Arlington National Cemetery, in FRANCIS COPPOLA's *GARDENS OF STONE*. Sweeney was born on Long Island, New York, on November 14, 1961, and raised in Shoreham, Long Island. He was educated at the Shoreham/Wading River High School, at Tulane University in New Orleans, and at New York University at the Tisch School of the Arts, graduating in 1984. His acting debut on Broadway was in a 1981 Broadway revival of *The Caine Mutiny Court Martial*, followed by a widely seen U.S. Army commercial and a small role in Sidney Lumet's film, *Power* (1986).

On television, Sweeney guest-starred in two series, *The Edge of Night* and *Spenser for Hire* and played the first victim of Son of Sam in the television drama *Out of Darkness*, which also starred MARTIN SHEEN as the cop who caught the notorious killer and also featured CHARLIE SHEEN in a cameo.

Sweeney's role in *Gardens of Stone* was his breakthrough film performance that led to *No Man's Land* (1987), a police drama directed by Peter Warner, and also starring Randy Quaid and Charlie Sheen. Following *No Man's Land* Sweeney again costarred with Charlie Sheen in *Eight Men Out* (1988), playing the legendary Shoeless Joe Jackson of the 1919 Chicago White Sox, the only team ever to throw a World Series title, in the unforgettable sports film directed by John Sayles. In 1989 Sweeney was cast in another breakthrough role as Dish Boggett in the television series *Lonesome Dove*. In 1992 Sweeney played a disabled hockey player turned figure skater in *The Cutting Edge*, a surprise hit that grossed $24 million. In 1993 he played Travis Walton, an Arizona logger who claimed to have been abducted by a UFO, in *Fire in the Sky*.—JAMES M. WELSH

Reference
James Cameron-Wilson, *Young Hollywood* (Lanham, MD: Madison Books, 1994).

T

TALESE, NAN A. (1933–)

New York editor and wife of the writer and journalist Gay Talese who edited her friend ELEANOR COPPOLA's first book for Simon & Schuster, then later published *NOTES ON A LIFE* under her own colophon, currently an imprint under the Knopf/Doubleday umbrella. Nan Talese, a graduate of Manhattan College in 1955, was born on December 19, 1933. She married Gay Talese in 1959. She worked at Random House and then Simon & Schuster, before becoming executive editor at Houghton Mifflin in 1981. In 1988 she became senior vice president at Doubleday, where she was granted her own imprint. Her imprint became part of the Knopf division in December 2008. She has handled many celebrity writers besides Eleanor Coppola, including Ian McEwan, Margaret Atwood, Antonio Fraser, Peter Ackroyd, Paul Newman, Mia Farrow, and Gus Van Sant, among others.—JAMES M. WELSH

TAVOULARIS, DEAN (1932–)

Production designer, born the son of Greek immigrant parents in Lowell, Massachusetts, educated at the Otis Art Institute in Los Angeles, where he studied architecture before working at the Disney Studios. Tavoularis earned an Academy Award for his work on *THE GODFATHER: PART II* and was nominated for his work on *THE GODFATHER*, *Bonnie and Clyde*, and *Lit-*

tle Big Man. His other work for FRANCIS COPPOLA includes the following films: *THE CONVERSATION, APOCALYPSE NOW, RUMBLE FISH, THE OUTSIDERS, ONE FROM THE HEART, PEGGY SUE GOT MARRIED, THE GODFATHER: PART III*, and *TUCKER: THE MAN AND HIS DREAM*, for which he won a British Academy Award in 1988. Tavoularis married the actress Aurore Clement, who appears in the French plantation sequence of *APOCALYPSE NOW REDUX*.

Dean Tavoularis, who was responsible for set design of *The Godfather*, had a harmonious relationship with Coppola. *The Godfather* was his first Coppola film, and he went on to design the two sequels, as well as *Apocalypse Now*. Tavoularis was glad that Coppola had held out for setting the movie in the postwar period, because he finds period films challenging—he has to be vigilant, so that every detail of the sets fits the historical setting of the story. In fact, Tavoularis's attention to historical detail gave the film the authentic look of the decade covered by the story, from 1945 to 1955. "You can't, for example, just put a can of soup on a shelf," he says. "It has to be the right can of soup." Being a stickler for detail and thus vividly creating the historical era in this film and his subsequent Coppola films placed Tavoularis at the head of his profession.

While making *Godfather: Part II*, the film unit moved on to New York City in late January 1974, where Dean Tavoularis cordoned off East Sixth Street in Lower Manhattan, between Avenues A and B, and systematically transformed it into Little Italy in 1918, with old-fashioned store fronts and a dirt road replacing the pavement of later times. Tavoularis would deservedly win an Academy Award for his production design on *Godfather: Part II*.

Press reports about the turbulent shooting period of *Apocalypse Now* continued to circulate long after the film wrapped. One dispatch concerned corpses of North Vietnamese regulars killed by Kurtz's renegade army, which are strewn around the grounds of his temple compound. It was alleged that there were some real cadavers mixed in with the dummy corpses on the Kurtz compound set. The film's press office vigorously denied this news story. More precisely, Dean Tavoularis points out that he had obtained a lot of bones from a restaurant, which he piled up in Kurtz's courtyard. When the crew noticed the stench and the rats crawling over the bones, one of them surmised that they were human remains, which was decidedly not the case.

The temple set was modeled on Angkor Wat, an ancient temple still preserved in Angkor, Cambodia. Tavoularis explains that Kurtz's macabre compound, complete with its decaying temple, was meant to reflect Kurtz's descent into madness and barbarism—and the depths of human depravity: there are altars covered with plastic skulls as well as heaps of bones scattered around the set and an eerie mist that envelops the compound. "I was living in the house of death that I was making," Tavoularis remembers, and growing depressed because of the grotesque atmosphere as time went on. The whole picture, he concluded, "was a nightmare."

Once Coppola was committed to shooting *One from the Heart* on the sound stages at Zoetrope Studios, Dean Tavoularis got going on constructing a number of mammoth sets. He employed 350 union construction workers, including 200 carpenters, to build a residential neighborhood, a section of McCarran Airport, and a desert motel. The most fabulous set that Tavoularis created was the mind-boggling replica of the Vegas Strip of casinos along Fremont Street. It encompassed miles of neon lights and a paved intersection. Tavoularis also had a detailed scale model of Las Vegas made for use in long shots. The sets covered nine sound stages in all. Without a doubt, Tavoularis's cityscape added a touch of gloss to the movie.

While making *The Outsiders* in Tulsa, Oklahoma, Tavoularis chose abandoned, deserted areas of Tulsa for location sites, in order to convey the juvenile delinquents' sense of being outsiders. For *Rumble Fish*, the companion movie of *The Outsiders*, Tavoularis selected locations in Tulsa that were even grimmer and grimier than those used in *The Outsiders*. Because *Rumble Fish* is a darker movie than *The Outsiders*, he wanted locations marked by dampness and humidity, in order to create the ambience of a desolate wasteland sweltering in the heat of high summer.

What's more, Tavoularis's seedy sets encompassed thick coats of dust, peeling paint, cracks in the walls, and crumbling stairways in the slum dwellings where the gang members live. As the camera explores the cramped living quarters the boys share with their families, the viewer gets a sense of the confinement the boys who live there must endure.

For *Tucker*, Tavoularis selected location sites in the San Francisco Bay Area, in easy commuting distance from Coppola's Napa home. In Sonoma, in northern California, they found an enormous manor house that was subsequently turned into Tucker's home in Ypsilanti, Michigan. Tavoularis converted the ballroom of the senior citizens' hotel in Oakland into the courtroom where Tucker's trial for fraud took place. He built several of the sets in a huge abandoned factory that had once been owned by the Ford Motor Company, on Harbor Way in Richmond, California. The ground floor became the Tucker plant, while the second floor housed the factory's offices. Little wonder that Tavoularis won a British Academy Award for *Tucker*.

As Gregory Votolato writes, Tavoularis's "masterful handling of a subdued color range" and "his sophisticated use of telling details" support Tavoularis's position as an outstanding production designer.—GENE D. PHILLIPS

References

John Belton, *American Cinema/American Culture*, rev. ed. (New York: McGraw-Hill, 2009); David Thomson, *Have You Seen . . . ? 1,000 Films* (New York: Knopf, 2008); Gregory Votolato, "Dean Tavoularis," in *International Dictionary of Films and Filmmakers*, ed. Nicolet Elert (New York: St. James Press, 2000), 4:813–14.

THE TERROR (1963)

DIRECTOR: Roger Corman. PRODUCERS: Roger Corman and Francis Ford Coppola. SCREENPLAY: Leo Gordon, Jack Hill. SECOND UNIT DIRECTOR: Francis Ford Coppola. PHOTOGRAPHY: John Nickolaus. MUSIC: Ronald Stein.
CAST: Boris Karloff (the baron), Jack Nicholson (Lt. Duvalier).
RUNNING TIME: 91 minutes. Color.
DVD: Echo Bridge Home Entertainment.

While pursuing a master's degree in film at UCLA, FRANCIS COPPOLA worked for independent producer-director ROGER CORMAN in various capacities, from scriptwriting to sound recording. After Corman finished shooting *The Raven* in 1963, he discovered that the film's star, Boris Kar-

loff, had no immediate commitments. Corman accordingly decided to make another horror quickie with Karloff and a young actor named JACK NICHOLSON, who had also appeared in *The Raven*. Corman arranged to shoot three days with Karloff in the studio. He appointed Coppola second-unit director and gave him a week to film location scenes with Nicholson along the California coast, which was standing in for the Baltic coast of Northern Europe, where the film takes place. The film is set during the Napoleonic era and centers on a mad baron (Karloff) who has spent the last twenty years in his eerie castle, mourning the death of his wife. Corman spent three days shooting all of Karloff's scenes while the sets from *The Raven* were being torn down around them!

Meanwhile, when Coppola and his small film unit arrived on location, he suggested to the cast that they rehearse that night for the scenes scheduled to be shot the following day. Nicholson, a veteran of some of Corman's previous low-budget epics, grumbled that Corman was not in the habit of rehearsing scenes in advance and Coppola was taking his job far too seriously. In retrospect, Coppola says that Nicholson and the other actors considered him an inexperienced young director who was too much of a perfectionist for his own good. As a matter of fact, Coppola was supposed to shoot for a week on location and actually stretched the shoot to eleven days. In one scene, Coppola instructed Nicholson, as Lt. Duvalier, to wade into the surf offshore while searching for a character who has mysteriously disappeared. Nicholson was knocked over by a huge wave: "I couldn't stand up," he remembered. "I was pinned to the ground by the weight of the uniform." Finally, he got to his feet and ran toward the shore in a panic, "and just threw that fucking uniform off while I ran." At that point, Coppola decided that he and

his film unit had had enough; and they all headed back to Los Angeles. The trade papers understandably dismissed *The Terror* as a shoddy horror flick. Nevertheless, Coppola maintains that he gained invaluable practical experience in filmmaking while serving time as Corman's production assistant. He never regretted the time he spent slaving in Corman's salt mines.
—GENE D. PHILLIPS

References

Beverly Gray, *Roger Corman: An Unauthorized Biography* (Los Angeles: Renaissance Books, 2000); Michael Schumacher, *Francis Ford Coppola* (New York: Crown, 1999).

TETRO (2009)

DIRECTOR, PRODUCER, AND SCREENPLAY: Francis Ford Coppola. EXECUTIVE PRODUCERS: Anahid Nazarian and Fred Roos. PHOTOGRAPHY: Mihai Malaimare Jr. EDITING: Walter Murch. ORIGINAL MUSIC: Osvaldo Golijov. PRODUCTION DESIGN: Sebastián Orgambide. SET DECORATION: Paulina López Meyer.
CAST: Vincent Gallo (Tetro), Maribel Verdú (Miranda), Alden Ehrenreich (Bennie), Klaus Maria Brandauer (Carlo), Carmen Maura (Alone).
RUNNING TIME: 127 minutes, Black & white and color.
RELEASED THROUGH: American Zoetrope. PREMIERE: 14 May 2009 (Cannes International Film Festival).

Tetro, a family drama, was FRANCIS COPPOLA's first original screenplay in thirty years (*YOUTH WITHOUT YOUTH* was an adapted screenplay) involving a highly complex interweaving of story lines, staged dance sequences, a play-within-the-film, music by Puccini, orchestral performances of Brahms's First Symphony, and references to E. T. A. Hoffmann's "Coppelia" story. Underlying all this is a gorgeously melo-

dramatic family saga of the Tetrocini family. No *GODFATHER* mafia family this, but an almost equally vicious and inbred family circle that is closed, tormented, and deadly.

Seventeen-year-old Bennie Tetrocini (ALDEN EHRENREICH, a gifted newcomer) has left a cruise ship on "leave" (while the ship undergoes repairs in Buenos Aires, Argentina) in search of his older brother, Tetro (VINCENT GALLO), who left New York eleven years earlier to get away from his oppressive and tyrannical father. Bennie finds Tetro living with his protective girlfriend, Miranda (MARIBEL VERDÚ), in an apartment in the bohemian "La Boca" neighborhood of Buenos Aires. Tetro, who at first refuses to see Bennie, has recently been involved in an auto accident and is hobbling about with a cast on his leg, suggesting a rather obvious Oedipal motif. He is not exactly overjoyed that Bennie has crossed the equator to seek him out. We learn that Tetro was once a promising playwright who passed through an asylum (where he met Miranda); although he has currently been reduced to running lights for local theatricals, he at least seems functional. There is an immediate though oddly unexplained tension between the two brothers, occasionally intermediated by Miranda. We also gradually learn about the brothers' father, Carlo (KLAUS MARIA BRANDAUER), an internationally acclaimed orchestra conductor. Carlo has recently suffered a stroke in New York and has requested his sons to come to his bedside in America.

In the meantime, more accidents accumulate about this family, one involving Bennie being struck down by a car, leaving him also constrained by crutches, and wearing a cast on his leg. To say this family is "accident prone" would be an understatement. Before he left New York, Tetro was involved as the driver in an automobile accident that killed his mother. More "accidents" will later be revealed, such as the penultimate revelation, to Bennie's consternation, that he is not Tetro's brother, but his son. Flashback scenes anticipate this: We see the young Tetro bringing his new girlfriend, a dancer, to meet Carlo after the death of Tetro's mother. Well, Carlo takes one look at the dancer and fairly devours her with his gaze. Indeed, he steals her away from young Tetro. However, the dancer is already pregnant with Tetro's child. So Carlo allows everyone to believe that the baby Bennie is his own child. Eventually, Tetro decides to leave the family, while Bennie grows up in this strained, conspiratorial atmosphere without knowing the truth about his parentage.

Back in the present, Bennie, still ignorant of the situation, has determined he must kill his father. But when Tetro shows up with a hatchet and delivers the news to Bennie about his paternity, he invites Bennie to use the ax on him. Bennie refuses and instead is reconciled with Tetro—but not before almost incurring his own death in yet another traffic accident (he strides into oncoming traffic and is rescued in the nick of time by Tetro). "Don't look into the light," Tetro advises him, leading him away. This family melodrama seems to be tragedy bordering upon farce. Bennie discovers an autobiographical manuscript written by Tetro, which Bennie then appropriates for use as a play that is entered into competition at a drama festival in Patagonia. Bennie is getting the accolades that should properly belong to his brother, who turns out to be his father.

Prior to *Tetro*, Francis Coppola's last original script was for *THE CONVERSATION* in 1974, and he seems to be trying to find his way into this swarmy family melodrama without total success. Without having been contextualized, Tetro's sullenness toward Bennie cannot be understood, for example. Of course, Tetro (whose very name in Italian means "gloomy") has good reasons for being angry, for hating his father, and for leaving home, but these are only suggested in surreal, colorful flashbacks (which Andrew Sarris likened to the "vivid color palette of Michael Powell and Emeric Pressburger") that draw attention to themselves against the background of the main story, which is gorgeously shot in black-and-white wide-screen cinematography by MIHAI MALAIMAMARE, JR., who had worked with the director on his Romanian film, *Youth without Youth*. The film nicely captures the noirish atmosphere of the "La Boca" neighborhood in contrast to the icy and shimmering outdoor mountain shots in Patagonia, where Bennie's play is to be featured at an arts festival. In one of his last *New York Observer* reviews, Sarris pointed out that this story of two brothers in conflict recalls *RUMBLE FISH* (1983), also shot in black-and-white, "which Mr. Coppola adapted from one of S. E. HINTON's series of young adult novels, with MATT DILLON living in the shadow of older brother MICKEY ROURKE."

The film *Tetro* is crippled (like its male characters), however, by the heavy-handed Freudian and Oedipal symbolic framework, which is almost laughably overdone. Likewise unconvincing is the "famous" impetuous drama critic, absurdly named "Alone," played "for maximum campiness" (as one reviewer noted) by the Spanish actress CARMEN MAURA, and costumed to resemble Hollywood figure Edith Head. Critics were taken by the "highly promising" performance of young Alden Ehrenreich, but less so by Vincent Gallo in the titular role. According to Todd McCarthy, the seventeen-year-old Ehrenreich, a New York University freshman, was "discovered" by Coppola's "longtime casting ace and producer, FRED ROOS."

Critically, *Tetro* did better than Coppola's *Youth without Youth* (2007), which was too overly drenched in Romanian mysticism to please mainstream American "critics," but it is as though the industry establishment wants Coppola to fail as an independent filmmaker and therefore treats him dismissively, and shamefully. *Variety's* Todd McCarthy criticized the film for its "small, particular story that's been inflated to immodest proportions," making the film feel "old-fashioned and labored," because Coppola "lacks the writerly flair to make the big scenes soar or resonate with multiple meanings and dimensions." *Washington Post* reviewer John Anderson sneered that the film aspires to be grand opera, and might be considered successful, "given how often grand opera is confusing, hysterical and/or illogical, and with enough plot lines to hang itself. No one cares that *Tosca* is a bloody mess, of course, because it has a score by Puccini. *Tetro* doesn't." The older and wiser Andrew Sarris was far more generous: "despite all its longueurs and extreme aggravations, *Tetro* deserves to be seen as the late work of one of the cinema's most accomplished masters of mise-en-scène." In France Coppola's *Tetro* was selected to open the Forty-first Directors' Fortnight (May 14–24, 2009) at the CANNES INTERNATIONAL FILM FESTIVAL: "We loved it," organizers told *Daily Variety*. "And our enthusiasm convinced Coppola that an opening Fortnight slot would be the ideal place to debut the film." Shouldn't a serious attempt by a seventy-year-old proven filmmaker to turn his talents in a new creative direction be so applauded?—JAMES M. WELSH/JOHN C. TIBBETTS

References

John Anderson, "*Tetro*: Angst and the Artiste," *Washington Post*, June 19, 2009, C5; Manohla Dargis, "Sons and the Father Who Made Them," *New York Times*, June 11, 2009, C1, C6; Nathan Lee, "*Tetro*," *Film Comment* (May–June 2009): 69–70; Todd McCarthy, "Cannes: Tetro," *Daily Variety*, May 14, 2009, 11–12; Jordan Mintzer, "Coppola's *Tetro* to Open Fortnight," *Daily Variety*, April 27, 2009, 1, 10; Larry Rohter, "Family Dynamics, without the Bullets," *New York Times*, June 7, 2009, sec. 2: 18–19; Andrew Sarris, "Oh, Brother! Coppola Goes Back to the Family for Indie Treat," *New York Observer*, June 15, 2009, 40.

THIS PROPERTY IS CONDEMNED (1966)

While he was still a graduate student in the Film School at UCLA, FRANCIS COPPOLA was hired as a screenwriter by Seven Arts, an independent producing company. He recalls that "the day I got my first job as a screenwriter, there was a big sign on the film school's bulletin board saying, 'Sell out!'" Some of his fellow students treated him with a resentment grounded in jealousy. "I was making money," he explains. "I was already doing what everybody was just talking about."

The first screenplay on which he received a screen credit as cowriter while working for Seven Arts was for the 1966 film *This Property Is Condemned*, to be released by Paramount.

This Property Is Condemned is a one-act play by Tennessee Williams that can be acted on the stage in about twenty minutes. Coppola was familiar with the play, since he had directed it on the stage while he was still in college at Hofstra University. The play simply presents a thirteen-year-old girl named Willie Starr who has been deserted by her parents. Willie recounts for a lad named Tom the sad story of her sister Alva, who took care of her until Alva's untimely death from lung cancer. And so it is Alva whom Willie idolizes and wants to imitate. Unfortunately, since Alva was a prostitute in her mother's boarding house/brothel for railroad men, Willie naively but firmly believes that the kind of life Alva led is the only truly glamorous existence for any girl. Consequently, there is little doubt by play's end that Willie is condemned to take up her sister's sordid way of life.

An enormous amount of expansion was imposed on the play's slender plot to bloat it into nearly two hours of screen time, which is fairly obvious when one views the movie, directed by Sydney Pollack (*Out of Africa*). The three principal authors of the 1966 film version—Fred Coe, Edith Sommer, and Coppola—elaborated Williams's slender little tale far beyond his original conception. The basic format the screenwriters hit upon was to make Williams's play the framing device for the picture. Accordingly, they broke the one-act play roughly in half, presenting the first portion as a prologue to the film and the remaining segment as an epilogue. In this way they utilized almost all of the play's original dialogue in their screenplay. In the prologue of the film, Willie, played by Mary Badham (*To Kill a Mockingbird*), describes her family and present situation to the boy Tom, and in the epilogue she wraps things up by telling Tom what happened to each of them. The scriptwriters then had to devise a full-blown story told in flashback to fit between the prologue and the epilogue. Several of the characters in the picture are derived from people to whom Willie refers in the one-act play.

The one character who is cut from whole cloth in the movie, and who has no discernible counterpart in the play, is Owen Legate (ROBERT REDFORD). He is a railroad inspector who hopes to marry Alva (Natalie Wood). But before Owen can make an honest woman of Alva, her life is tragically cut short by lung cancer. Williams accurately assessed the film as a "vastly expanded and hardly related film with the title taken from a very delicate one-act play. The movie was hardly deserving of the talents of Robert Redford and Natalie Wood." Or, one might add, the talents of Sydney Pollack and Francis Coppola.

It was not uncommon in Hollywood for a platoon of writers to work on the same script. As writer-director Preston Sturges (*The Miracle of Morgan's Creek*) once quipped, writers worked in teams, like piano movers. This was a system Coppola deplored. He estimates that after the script he had prepared with Coe and Sommer was submitted to the front office an additional dozen script doctors tinkered with the screenplay before it was finally completed. Yet Ray Stark, Coppola's immediate boss at Seven Arts, continued to see him as competent and dependable. Coppola became known around Seven Arts as a "clutch writer, a troubleshooter salvaging movies that were teetering on the brink of catastrophe."—GENE D. PHILLIPS

References

Joseph Gelmis, *The Director as Superstar* (Garden City, NY: Anchor, 1970); Michael Goodwin and Naomi Wise, *On the Edge: The Life and Times of Francis Coppola* (New York: Morrow, 1989); Gene Phillips, *The Films of Tennessee Williams* (East Brunswick, NJ: Associated University Presses, 1980).

THX 1138 (1971)

DIRECTOR: George Lucas. SCREENPLAY: George Lucas and Walter Murch. STORY: George Lucas. PRODUCER: Lawrence Sturhahn. ASSOCIATE PRODUCER: Ed Folger. EXECUTIVE PRODUCER: Francis Ford Coppola. PRODUCTION COMPANY: American Zoetrope PHOTOGRAPHY: David Myers and Albert Kihn. EDITOR: George Lucas. MUSIC: Lalo Schifrin. ART DIRECTOR: Michael Haller. SOUND MONTAGES: Walter Murch.

CAST: Robert Duvall (THX 1138), Donald Pleasence (SEN 5241), Maggie McOmie (LUH 3417), Don Pedro Colley (SRT), Ian Wolfe (PTO).

RUNNING TIME: 88 minutes (director's cut). Technicolor and Techniscope.

RELEASED THROUGH: Warner Bros/Seven Arts.
DVD: Warner Home Video.

THX 1138 was the first film produced by AMERICAN ZOETROPE, FRANCIS FORD COPPOLA's dream of a studio dedicated to supporting an auteurist U.S. cinema in the late 1960s. It might well have been its last, given the mystified reaction of its distributor, Warner Bros., as well as an indifferent response from the public to this bleak science fiction tale cowritten and directed by GEORGE LUCAS. Warners had agreed to back a feature-length version of Lucas's award-winning student short *Electronic Labyrinth THX 1138 4EB* (1967), made while he was at USC, after seeing an expanded script that Lucas wrote with sound designer WALTER MURCH. At this time, the major studios were struggling to adjust to new demands for more innovative content and style in the commercial feature, the result of industry and sociopolitical changes, the impact of European art cinemas, and shifts in audience demographics. Promoting authorial individuality over corporate formulas was the order of the day, and Warner Bros. hoped that their subvention of projects by the young film-school grads at Zoetrope might result in popular genre reworkings like *Bonnie and Clyde* (1967), *Butch Cassidy and the Sundance Kid* (1969), or, better yet, a repeat of the youth-oriented smash hit *Easy Rider* (1969).

Genre revisionism was indeed overtly positioned as a goal of *THX 1138*, with its brief prologue featuring a silver-suited Buck Rogers in a serial trailer from the 1940s, with a new voiceover placing our hero not in the distant future, but rather "in the twentieth century." This introduction contrasts with the first narrative sequence, a series of disconnected, abstract shots: An extreme close-up of a digital clock, its num-

bers flipping down with mechanical precision, is followed by a flickering video image of a man reaching inside a medicine cabinet, expressing his ennui to a disembodied voice who gently asks, "*What's wrong?*" A blur of lines on a computer printout then whirls through the feed followed by another flickering video image, this time of a woman who reaches inside the medicine cabinet, only to suddenly withdraw her hand and respond, "Never mind," to the repeated computer-generated query, "*What's wrong?*" Then there is a close-up of an oscilloscope screen translating her phrase into sonic-wave form. Just as all verbal information is instantaneously converted into the code-languages of machine apparatuses in *THX 1138*, so does the motion picture camera mediate between "reality" and the images thus produced—and so from the start of the film, Lucas offers not merely a reworking of the premises of popular science fiction but implicitly reminds the viewer that the foundation of cinematic practice is itself mechanical reproduction, and inherently voyeuristic (Telotte 2001). In this way, *THX 1138* both revises genre and incorporates the contemplative, reflexive qualities of art cinema, which was highly influential upon the entire generation of "New Hollywood" directors.

The formal aspects of *THX 1138* run counter to the classical Hollywood model in several ways, eschewing the visual polish of a studio feature (such as Kubrick's *2001: A Space Odyssey*, released in 1968) in favor of a cinema verité aesthetic, while adopting some of that classic film's focus on scenic detail and lack of affect rather than plot trajectory. Lucas and Murch sought to create a science-fiction work not situated within the contexts of the late 1960s but a "science fiction film *from* the future," a document sent back in time as a caution (or tutorial?) to the inhabitants of a late-capitalist, consumer culture. *THX 1138* follows a long tradition in futurist literary and cinematic narratives by creating a dystopian society of which humans' needs and desires comprise not the center but rather the margins of a complex technocracy, chiefly designed to keep a vast electronic network operating at any expense. As the frayed ends of well-worn circuits that can be replaced quickly, all characters have license-tag names (the film's title is the identification code for ROBERT DUVALL), sport closely shaved heads and identical white uniforms, and are constantly medicated to negate any rebellious thoughts or emotions, under threat of "prosecution for criminal drug evasion." Individuals who feel a need for counseling may visit a phone booth–size chapel to confess their discomfiture to "Omm," a Christ-like image illuminated by a fluorescent glare, reeling off a prerecorded message of homilies such as "blessings of the state, blessings of the masses" in response to any confession. Retail therapy is provided via the mindless, albeit mandated, purchase of geometric shapes called dendrites, available in all three primary colors; these are immediately disposed of via a chute in one's living quarters, presumably returned to the store for sale to others. Pharmacological control of this society's members has not eliminated sexual desire; as Duvall returns to his quarters after a difficult work shift spent assembling a robot torso, he seeks quick release not with his assigned "mate" LUH 3417 (Maggie McOmie) but by watching a hologram of a nude woman dancing; he then sedately enjoys a climax provided courtesy of a device resembling a Cuisinart suspended from the ceiling.

Like other dystopian fiction, in *THX 1138* surveillance of all subjects is ubiquitous, and thus infractions are immediately addressed. However, the enforcement is by rather benign police robots that resemble very tall CHiP officers with silver metal heads and that (despite their size and wield of nightsticks) are fairly easily dispatched by a blow to the face. Supplying a moment of wry humor in the film, one directionally confused cybercop repeatedly walks into a wall, apparently unable to change course. In a chaotic scene set in the robot factory, THX's biomedical sensors reveal that he has "severe sedation depletion," and thus his human monitors immediately subject him to a "mindlock"—disabling him completely just at a moment when he is about to carry out a delicate procedure inside a robot cranium. In these scenes, Lucas visualizes a central premise of *THX 1138*, the senseless operations of an indifferent technology whose entrenched routines and subprocesses are neither accountable to the humans who presumably invented them nor able to fruitfully pursue a unified course of action. Thus there are no real villains in the movie, no sinister cabals or computer colossus (staples of the science fiction genre) against which THX might rage; even the early introduction of British character actor Donald Pleasence (SEN 5241) as a possible foil does not materialize.

The dramatic conflict between good and evil so central to Lucas's subsequent *Star Wars* trilogies is nowhere in evidence in *THX 1138*, which while following a traditional three-act structure (identified as such by Lucas in his DVD commentary to the film) presents events in an offhand, ambiguous way. In the first act, we discover that THX's roommate, LUH, has been secretly replacing THX's daily course of medication, and soon he begins to feel dissatisfaction and fear at work and (what's worse) passion for LUH at home. The couple's rebellious act of making love is surreptitiously observed, and THX's failure to take his sedatives has already been detected at work. Repercussions follow in short order: LUH is suddenly gone from the apartment, replaced by SEN 5241, and THX is arrested and sentenced as an "incurable erotic" who requires conditioning. This treatment comprises the second act, set largely in what is probably *THX 1138*'s most famous image, a blindingly white detention environment, against which white-suited internees appear as so many floating heads in space. The stages of THX's therapy run the gamut from gentle pokes by cybercops brandishing long sticks, followed by a quite amusing scene in which technicians effect various physical distortions of THX's body as they bumble about trying to figure out their own "torture" equipment, culminating in a tender love scene with LUH, who arrives to tell THX that she is pregnant. Ultimately, THX's greatest torture is his consignment to a group of fellow internees, including SEN 5241, who sit and engage in what Lucas describes in the DVD commentary as an "abstract philosophical exercise," full of platitudes and slogans (SEN's dialogue was taken from Richard Nixon speeches) but devoid of agency. Restless, THX simply walks off, with SEN trailing behind; they soon encounter a black character named SRT, a former hologram now seemingly human, who shows them the way out. This begins the third act, a somewhat more conventional escape sequence in which THX and SRT (now separated from SEN, who has decided he doesn't want to leave after all) try to get out of the underworld city. On the way, THX discovers that LUH has been "consumed" (that is, harvested for her transplantable biological parts) and her fetus transferred to an artificial womb; we also learn that the costs to the state for THX's conditioning and capture are being continuously tabulated. THX and SRT steal two supercharged automobiles, but ironically the hologram cannot handle the operational controls and only THX escapes. Close to the top of the city shell and the outer world, THX abandons the car, and although more police are dispatched, they are abruptly recalled when the pursuit of

THX goes "over budget." In the film's final shot, THX climbs out of the ground, now on *terra incognita* as he faces a huge, glowing sun at dusk, a bird flying overhead.

As noted by one reviewer, *THX 1138* achieves much of its intended impact because of "the total absence of artifacts and images that are not contemporaneous" (Beck 1971, 60). Aside from a small set constructed for THX and LUH's apartment, all scenes were shot in more than twenty locations in and around San Francisco, perhaps most notably the then in-construction Bay Area Rapid Transit (BART) system, but also the Oakland Coliseum, the San Francisco Pacific Gas and Electric Building, the Marin County Civic Center, and a tumor research center in San Jose. These sites were chosen for their graphic, modernist qualities as well as strikingly illuminated interiors, since Lucas wanted to use available light wherever possible, anticipating the use of a fast film stock. As a result, *THX 1138* is grainy and very shallow in its spatial compositions, a look the director felt was well suited to its documentary approach while conveying the emotional isolation of its characters. But to fully achieve a particular tonal effect, Lucas is best served by the extraordinary work of collaborator Walter Murch, today the dean of U.S. sound designers. As Murch himself suggests on the DVD commentary, "the appeal [of *THX 1138*] is in the texture and the collision of images and sounds," and the complex aural montages he created for the film—snippets of conversation heard offscreen, phrases repeated like mantras, rhythmic cadences of electronic blips and beeps—offer the viewer a mesmerizing counterpoint to the meticulously designed mise-en-scène. The Special Features on the 2004 DVD rerelease contain two elements specifically devoted to the film's sound: "Theatre of Noise," a sound effects–only track, and "Master Sessions," in which Murch discusses with his usual insight and clarity the sound design of individual scenes.

The creative energies devoted to realizing *THX 1138* as an innovative "document from the future" resulted in its current cult status, but as noted above, Warner Bros. executives were aghast at the rough cut. Over Coppola's and Lucas's strong objections, the studio cut about four minutes of footage and released *THX 1138* with scant promotion in anticipation of low financial return. More seriously, Warners scuttled their support of American Zoetrope and rejected all submitted scripts, assuming they were similarly noncommercial. Only the huge success of *THE GODFATHER* (made for Paramount and released in 1972) provided Coppola with the funding to make the next Zoetrope project, *THE CONVERSATION* (1974). Lucas left Zoetrope and used profits from *AMERICAN GRAFFITI* to establish LucasFilm, the core of a media production conglomerate that now includes an array of companies (such as Industrial Light & Magic) that provide the skilled labor and technological expertise required by the special effects–driven fantasy, science fiction, and action films of the twenty-first century. If *THX 1138* seems light-years away from the *Star Wars* franchise, they shared an origin in Lucas and Coppola's commitment to a filmmaking practice rooted in the signature of the auteur.—Heidi Kenaga

References
Bernard Beck, "The Overdeveloped Society: *THX 1138*," *Society* 8 no. 11 (September 1971): 60; Raymond Cormier, "The Closed Society and Its Friends: Plato's *Republic* and Lucas's *THX-1138*," *Literature/Film Quarterly* 18, no. 3 (1990): 193–97; Sally Kline (ed.), *George Lucas: Interviews* (Jackson: University Press of Mississippi, 1999); Matthew Leyland, "Life before Luke," *Sight & Sound*, 14, no. 12: 76 (December 2004);

J. P. Telotte, "The Science Fiction Film as Fantastic Text: *THX 1138*," in *Science Fiction Film* (Cambridge: Cambridge University Press, 2001), 123–41.

TONIGHT FOR SURE (1962)

Director: Francis Ford Coppola. Screenplay: Jerry Schaeffer and Francis Ford Coppola. Producer: Francis Ford Coppola. Photography Jack Hill. Editing: Ronald Weller. Music: Carmine (credited as Carmen) Coppola. Art Director: Albert Loctelli.
Running Time: 75 minutes. Color.

FRANCIS COPPOLA enrolled in the Master's Program in Film at the University of California at Los Angeles (UCLA) in 1960. He was perennially broke and feared he could not pay his tuition. He saw some light at the end of the tunnel when a friend suggested he make a skin flick.

At age twenty-one Coppola was entering the film business on the very bottom rung of the ladder by making a short entitled *The Peeper*. It was the only chance he had, Coppola explains, to actually "fool around with a camera and cut a film."

The movie had a "cute" little premise, he recalls. Benjamin Jabowski, a would-be voyeur, hears about a photographer who is shooting pin-up pictures in the building next door to his apartment. The flimsy plotline deals with Ben's efforts to sneak a peek at the photo sessions. But all of his attempts to do so backfire in a farcical fashion. Coppola constructed some simple, minimal sets in an abandoned department store in Venice, a seaside area of Los Angeles. The sets consisted of four flats with pictures hung on them.

When he sought a distributor to release *The Peeper*, Coppola found no takers for his soft-core, slapstick flick. Finally he showed it to a small-time distributor who already had a rather silly western skin flick on hand called *The Wide Open Spaces*. This little item was about a drunken cowpoke who gets conked on the noggin by a rock. Afterward he sees naked girls instead of cows sauntering around the prairie. The company asked Coppola to intercut his film with theirs in order to have a saleable commodity. Coppola accordingly devised some new material in order to combine *The Peeper* with the topless western.

The plot gimmick that Coppola dreamed up to provide the narrative frame for the two stories he was knitting together into one film is built around a character from each film who shares his tale with the other. The resulting movie, eventually entitled *Tonight for Sure*, was first released in 1961.

Coppola later described the expanded version of his original film as "an inane comedy, in which you saw a couple of boobs once in a while." Some commentators on Coppola's work who have not seen *Tonight for Sure* have assumed that there is full frontal nudity on display in the film, which is certainly not the case. The picture qualified as a "nudie" because of the succession of topless girls who parade through the movie. Consequently, it comes across as an extended version of a bawdy burlesque skit rather than a porno flick.

Although both the Cowie and Johnson biographies of Coppola assert that *Tonight for Sure* is a black-and-white movie, all of the footage is in color (albeit muddy, dingy color), with the color photography for the Coppola segments shot mostly by his classmate Jack Hill. CARMINE COPPOLA (listed in the credits as Carmen) supplied the jazzy score for the picture and would score other Coppola films in the future.

Coppola was so eager for screen credits at the beginning of his career that in the film's opening credits he generously gave himself sole credit as director of the entire

movie—although he estimates that only about half of the complete film was his work.—GENE D. PHILLIPS

References
Peter Cowie, *Coppola: A Biography*, rev. ed. (New York: Da Capo, 1999); Robert Johnson, *Francis Ford Coppola* (Boston: Twayne, 1977).

TORN, RIP
[ELMORE RUAL TORN, JR.] (1931–)
Established film actor who played I. Humphrey Chanticleer, curator of rare books and the father of the lead character in FRANCIS COPPOLA's master's thesis film project at UCLA, *YOU'RE A BIG BOY NOW* (1966). In 2006 he was also cast in *MARIE ANTOINETTE*, directed by SOFIA COPPOLA. Playing as his wife in the Francis Coppola film was GERALDINE PAGE, whom he married. Born in Temple, Texas, on February 6, 1931, the son of economist Elmore Rual Torn and his wife, Thelma Mary, he was educated at Texas A&M University, graduating in 1962. He studied acting with LEE STRASBERG at the Actors Studio in New York and studied dancing with Martha Graham. He made his film debut in an uncredited role in the 1956 drama *Baby Doll*. However, Torn has said that his first love is the stage. He made his Broadway debut in 1959, staring as Chance Wayne in *Sweet Bird of Youth*, earning the Theatre World Award for his portrayal. Years later, his work in the film adaptation of the Marjorie Kinnan Rawlings memoir *Cross Creek* (1983) earned an Academy Award nomination for Best Supporting Actor. Early on in his movie career he played opposite Gregory Peck in *Pork Chop Hill* (1959). Other feature film credits include *Cat on a Hot Tin Roof* (1958), the film adaptation of *Sweet Bird of Youth* (1962), *The Cincinnati Kid* (1965), *Tropic of Cancer* (1969), *The Man Who Fell to Earth* (1976), *The Seduction of Joe Tynan* (1979), *Extreme Prejudice* (1987), *RoboCop*

3 (1993), *How to Make an American Quilt* (1995), *The Wonder Boys* (2002), and *Men in Black* and its sequels (1997 and 2002). For his work on television Torn won an Emmy, the CableACE Award, and the American Comedy Award for his portrayal of the beleaguered producer of *The Larry Sanders Show*.—JAMES M. WELSH

TROPIC THUNDER (2008)

Hollywood spoof movie directed by Ben Stiller about a spectacular Vietnam war movie gone wrong directed by a (fictive) British director named Damien (Steve Coogan) and starring a temperamental five-time Academy Award winner Kirk Lazarus (Robert Downey, Jr., in blackface), along with Stiller and Jack Black. *New Yorker* reviewer Anthony Lane wrote that anybody wanting to see an exposé of a "combat movie, strewn with compromise and creative sacrifice" would be better advised to watch ELEANOR COPPOLA's *HEARTS OF DARKNESS: A FILMMAKER'S APOCALYPSE* (1991), about the making of *APOCALYPSE NOW*. (Cf. *GENIUSES* [1982], which similarly attempted to satirize such filmmaking trials on stage.)—JAMES M. WELSH

TUCKER, PRESTON THOMAS (1903–1956)

American inventor and entrepreneur celebrated by FRANCIS COPPOLA and mythologized in *TUCKER: THE MAN AND HIS DREAM* (1988). Coppola had ties to Detroit, where he was born, and where his father played flute for *The Ford Sunday Evening Hour* radio show, hence the middle name for Francis *Ford* Coppola. Tucker, the man (apart from the myth or the "dream" or the Hollywood bio-fantasy and would-be parable) has been criticized as suffering from overblown enthusiasm, inadequate financing, and chaotic business practices. Brock Yates, a screenwriter perhaps moti-

vated by envy, wrote that the car "was actually designed by Ben G. Parsons and was styled by Alex Tremulis, not by a handful of devoted craftsmen working in a backyard in Ypsilanti, Michigan." At full capacity, the Tucker Corporation employed 2,200 people, and, according to Yates, "failed because there was not enough money and management skill to bring [the car] to market." The truth of the story is eclipsed by the movie "drama" concocted by screenwriters ARNOLD SCHULMAN and DAVID SEIDLER. In fact, Yates advises, Preston Tucker never spoke at the trial that ultimately acquitted him of "31 counts of mail fraud, SEC violations, and conspiracy." Coppola constructs the movie myth that Tucker "was a visionary crushed by an evil cabal of Detroit carmakers and their lackey, ruthless Michigan Senator Homer Ferguson [played by LLOYD BRIDGES in the film], not to mention the U.S. government in the form of the Securities and Exchange Commission and a corrupt court system." Brock Yates rejects this construction as "nonsense," adding that "sadly, because of the myths Coppola has fed us," the reality of the situation "will be blurred forever."

Reviewing *Tucker* for the *New Yorker* (August 22, 1988), Terrence Rafferty groused "there's a lot more dream than man in *Tucker*," that the distinction between the man and the dream becomes "dangerously fuzzy" because "Tucker himself can't distinguish between the image he's projecting and the person he really is." So what else may be wrong with this picture? Lawrence Van Gelder asked Anahid Nazarian, librarian for Zoetrope Studios, and was told: "He didn't really have an assembly line; there's one in the film. He actually had five kids; there are only four in the film. Our story takes place in one year; the real story took place over four years." Also, "the president of the Tucker Company was a good guy really, but we needed a villain, so we made him a villain." And Tucker himself was an "honest man with a great idea but bad business sense." The Tucker Torpedo, "The Car of the Future," introduced in June of 1948, lives on in the minds of those 200 members of the Tucker Automobile Club of America, who have preserved and cherished 47 of the 51 cars Preston Tucker originally produced. (Coppola himself owns two of them.) Brock Yates describes the car, capable of speeds up to 130 miles per hour, as being "tail-heavy," with 58 percent of the weight of this rear-engine vehicle suspended over the rear axle. (Would Ralph Nader have approved?)

For the record, the "real" Preston Tucker died a broken man at age fifty-three, on the day after Christmas in 1956, a conclusion not shown in Coppola's visionary movie. As early as 1975 Coppola showed interest in Preston Tucker in his *Playboy* interview with William Murray: "Traditionally, our greatest heroes have been creators and inventors," Coppola told *Playboy*. By the 1940s, however, "after the United States had demonstrated that the ultimate result of this ingenuity was our emergence as the most powerful nation in the world, we were being run by huge, entrenched institutions completely hostile to that kind of inventiveness. By 1941 Henry Ford couldn't have built his cheap car. We might have *had* a Henry Ford in the forties. His name was Preston Tucker." Coppola believed Tucker "had designed a car that could be built for a fraction" of the cost Detroit was spending on new models, "a safe car, a revolutionary car in terms of engineering, . . . a beautiful car." Yet Tucker was called a fraud, and he was destroyed," Coppola claimed: "I'm going to make a film of Tucker's story someday." And a dozen years later, he did exactly that.—James M. Welsh

References

Gene D. Phillips and Rodney Hill, eds. *Francis Ford Coppola Interviews* (Jackson: University

Preston Tucker.

Press of Mississippi, 2004); Terrence Rafferty, "Family Business," *New Yorker*, August 22, 1988, 61–63; Lawrence Van Gelder, "Reinventing the Wheels," *New York Times*, August 7, 1988, 19; Brock Yates, "Hollywood Gets It Wrong— Again!" *Washington Post Magazine*, September 11, 1988, 81–82.

TUCKER: THE MAN AND HIS DREAM (1988)

Director: Francis Ford Coppola. Screenplay: Arnold Schulman and David Seidler. Producers: Fred Roos and Fred Fuchs. Executive Producer: George

Lucas. PHOTOGRAPHY: Vittorio Storaro. EDITING: Priscilla Nedd-Friendly. MUSIC: Joe Jackson. PRODUCTION DESIGNER: Dean Tavoularis. ART DIRECTION: Alex Tavoularis. SET DECORATION: Armin Ganz. COSTUME DESIGN: Milena Canonero. CASTING: Janet Hirshenson and Jane Jenkins.

CAST: Jeff Bridges (Preston Tucker), Joan Allen (Vera Tucker), Martin Landau (Abe Karatz), Frederic Forrest (Eddie), Mako (Jimmy), Elias Koteas (Alex), Christian Slater (Junior), Nina Siemaszko (Marilyn Lee), Anders Johnson (Johnny), Corin Nemec (Noble), Marshall Bell (Frank), Jay O. Sanders (Kirby), Peter Donat (Kerner), Dean Goodman (Bennington), John X. Heart (Ferguson's Agent), Don Novello (Stan), Patti Austin (Millie), Dean Stockwell (Howard Hughes), Lloyd Bridges (Senator Homer Ferguson, uncredited).

RUNNING TIME: 110 minutes. Technicolor.

RELEASED THROUGH: LucasFilm/Paramount Pictures.

DVD: Paramount.

For Timothy Corrigan, FRANCIS FORD COPPOLA exemplifies authorship in postmodern Hollywood. Corrigan writes that authorship has been commodified, functioning as a brand name for studios to differentiate product, and thus is self-consciously enacted by directors in promotional material, interviews, commentaries, and so on. In Coppola's case, the performance of authorship-as-spectacle dramatizes a Wellesian persona as an artist oppressed by his industry, trapped by commercial expectations, and proving his authority by expending it in spectacular sacrifices of effort (fraught productions, attempts to resist the studios) and personal finances (using his own assets as collateral for Zoetrope Studios). For Corrigan, this commodification means that authorship now is primarily extratextual, but studying Coppola's films arguably demonstrates that

it is precisely because authorship has been commodified that it is incumbent upon ambitious directors to self-consciously craft auteur films, films with some discernable signature that can both differentiate those films in the marketplace and differentiate the directors themselves as prospective employees. *Tucker: The Man and His Dream* is a clear instance of a film that in its subject, themes, and style promotes certain conceptions of Coppola as author.

Tucker is a biography of PRESTON TUCKER (1903–1956), framed as a promotional film made by the Tucker Corporation, and centering on his short-lived automobile company (roughly 1946–1949). Tucker is seen from the outset as a restless dreamer, hopeless optimist, and devoted family man who designs a car incorporating such significant innovations as fuel injection, disc brakes, a rear motor, seat belts, pop-out windshields, and a "Cyclops" headlamp that turns with the steering wheel. He advertises his "Tucker Torpedo" without having first built a prototype and enlists the help of Abe Karatz to build a company to manufacture it. They obtain a government contract on a disused factory to house his plant (on the proviso that they produce fifty cars by a set date), with Tucker arguing that the Big Three American auto manufacturers are "guilty of manslaughter" for their refusal to incorporate safety features similar to his. Tucker and his team complete a "prototype" built from junked parts in time for the plant opening, albeit one that doesn't actually function.

Meanwhile Karatz raises funds, installing auto industry veteran Robert Bennington as company president to reassure investors. After the opening ceremony, Tucker is sent on a promotional tour while the board abandons his innovations. Tucker's struggle to build the car of his dreams is further frustrated by the opposition of the Big Three (eager to squelch the competition), and their lackey Sen. Homer Ferguson. Tucker and team produce a fully functioning prototype and take over the plant, leading to the resignation of Bennington and the board. They produce the required fifty cars, but, thanks to Ferguson, the Securities and Exchange Commission files suit against Tucker for fraud (based in part on the failure of the initial prototype), and the media portrays him as a charlatan. In the trial, Tucker gives his own closing argument, defending free enterprise and invention against bureaucracy and big business crushing the "little guy with the new idea." He is acquitted, but the Tucker Motor Company is dead. Tucker remains optimistic; it is the idea that counts, he says, and they built his idea.

It is a narrative of a dreamer who makes an innovative product, is accused of being a con man, and sees his company crushed by a conspiracy of his competitors without even having had a chance in the marketplace. The parallels between Tucker,

his car, and his corporation, and Coppola, *ONE FROM THE HEART*, and Zoetrope Studios are pervasive and exacting enough to suggest that the film is a figurative autobiography. For example, much of the drama surrounding Zoetrope and *One from the Heart* centered on Coppola's profligacy. Early in *Tucker*, Vera speaks to Eddie:

> VERA: How can we kid ourselves into thinking anyone would give us a loan? All we've got are debts and more debts, all of them so far past due. . . .
>
> EDDIE: How does he do it, the genius you married? No matter how much he makes, he always manages to spend twice as much!

Virtually no commentary on the film by reviewers, scholars, or the filmmakers themselves fails to note these parallels and to read the film as autobiographical. Coverage in *American Film* had the cast and crew

Jeff Bridges as Preston Tucker.

"seem[ing] at times to think they are shooting Coppola's autobiography." In the DVD documentary "Under the Hood," executive producer GEORGE LUCAS testifies, "I see parallels between Tucker and Francis. Both are flamboyant characters and are very creative; both like innovation—thus Francis likes interesting camera techniques." Janet Maslin noted that Coppola had returned to his "best subject—the underside of American business" but now with a "ruefully personal dimension." Here, a particular persona, Coppola-the-dreamer, takes center stage. In more *New York Times* coverage, Robert Lindsey explored the parallels: "A creative, if impractical, dreamer comes forth with a better idea that is quashed by the powerful establishment in order to maintain the status quo. But what comes through, though unintentionally, is the isolation the creator must endure as his vision is slowly stripped from him." Richard Schickel embellishes this in his *Time* review: Coppola "too is a merchant of slightly skewed dreams, a tilter at his industry's conventional wisdom, and a man who is himself a typical American genius, half visionary, half humbug." Ultimately the film is a celebration of an American Dream "which involves not the invention of products but the invention of self" (the invention of the self as film author, perhaps?).

Others further emphasized Coppola's personal connection to the material beyond the directly autobiographical. As a child, Coppola worshipped inventors, and his father took him to see a Tucker on the promotional tour. The film is dedicated to his son Gian-Carlo (Gio), who had recently died, and "who loved cars." The relationship between Coppola and Gio (an aspiring filmmaker who directed second-unit and supervised montage segments for *THE COTTON CLUB*) is mirrored by that of Tucker and Preston Jr., who rejects college to work on his father's cars. Just as Cop-

pola has worked with his family throughout his career, so Tucker is surrounded by his family throughout (and loses control to Bennington precisely when he is separated from them). This theme of family itself raises a parallel between Tucker and Zoetrope. Tucker's dreams are born in a familial environment, and the car is an intensive collaboration between Tucker, Preston Jr., and his team, itself a quasi-family: Abe, Eddie, Jimmy, Alex. Coppola has always prized his collaborators, including not only family members, but also the likes of FRED ROOS and DEAN TAVOULARIS, and Zoetrope was the apotheosis of this. The Zoetrope idea was to recreate a classical Hollywood studio, led by an artist instead of businessmen, to take advantage of the close-knit, long-term collaborations the studios enabled by virtue of their contract system and internal production facilities. *Tucker* is in part a celebration of collaborative creation.

For all the Tucker Corporation/Zoetrope parallels, the reading of the film as autobiography is complicated by the circumstances Coppola found himself in during the 1980s in the aftermath of Zoetrope, precisely in relation to collaboration and authority. Coppola had been planning a Tucker biopic since acquiring the rights in 1975, at one point planning a "Brechtian musical" using the Tucker story as a counterpoint to that of other inventors, like Edison and Henry Ford. Coppola imagined a film much more along the lines of *Citizen Kane* (furthering a widespread doubling of Welles and Coppola), as he discusses on the DVD commentary: "I wanted my film about Tucker to be an exposé, stark and heavy, about the man and the company being destroyed by larger corporate interests." But by the late 1980s, in order to produce the film, he was reliant on his much more successful former protégé, Lucas, which he acknowledged at the time.

"I'd lost some of my confidence. . . . I knew George had a marketing sense of what people might want. He wanted to candy-apple it up a bit, make it like a Disney film. He was at the height of his success, and I was at the height of my failure, and I was a little insecure. . . . I think it's a good movie—it's eccentric, a little wacky, like the Tucker car—but it's not the movie I would have made at the height of my power." By contrast, Lucas asserted, "I wanted to make it an uplifting experience that showed some of the problems in corporate America, and Francis didn't resist." Lucas responded to Coppola's wistfulness on the "movie [he] would have made" this way: "The truth of it is, Francis and I worked on the movie together, and he made the movie he wanted to make. Who knows what it would have been like if he'd have made it 'at the height of his power'?"

In the event, Coppola's discussion of the Tucker film he was no longer able to make reads as an attempt to reassert an authorial persona, Coppola-the-martyr, ironically by highlighting his diminished authority over his work. Yet his outlook on the material remained pessimistic: "I personally feel it's a tragedy." This survives despite the optimism of the presentation, for example in Tucker's courtroom assertion of his belief in the American spirit, a spirit that would keep America from sinking to buying its cars and radios from its "former enemies"—which of course is exactly what had come to pass by 1988. Moreover, the optimistic spirit and sentimentality of the film is held in check by its framing as a promotional film for the Tucker Corporation. While the promotional film conceit recedes after the opening credits, it recurs, particularly after the sequence of the plant opening; even though later in the film, Tucker watches a screening of the "completed" film-within-the-film (directed, incidentally, by an Italian), it remains unclear whether it ceases to function as a framing device. The Tucker emblem seen in the opening of the promo film is seen again under "The End" at the film's conclusion. As Steven Kovacs observed in *Film Quarterly*, "At times the distinction between promotional film and narrative dissolve since Tucker's enterprise is driven by self-promotion." Indeed, self-promotion on Coppola's part may be the key to the film. *Tucker* can be read as an alternate history, from the "loser's" perspective, wherein Coppola counters the perception of Coppola-the-madman, widely circulated during the failure of *One from the Heart* and the Zoetrope debacle (as Coppola reminisced, "The description you heard most often was that the inmates had taken over the asylum"), with the martyr, an artist and genuine innovator crushed by the forces of capital. Fundamentally, the autobiographical reading serves to reinforce the notion of Coppola-the-auteur, not least in light of the compromises required by Lucas, and the marketplace.

Another major theme in the reception of the film was Coppola's hyperbolic, pictorial stylization, a prominent feature of his work following *One from the Heart* (1982), particularly evident in *RUMBLE FISH* (1983) and *The Cotton Club* (1984). In an interview, JEFF BRIDGES said that working with Coppola was "like acting in a Rembrandt painting. . . . I've never done a film that is this complicated as far as camera movements and lights." For some critics, Coppola's exploration of cinematic innovation was a persistent debit of his 1980s films, with *Commonweal* bemoaning *Tucker*'s "stylized overstatement." Because of Coppola's evident personal investment in the film, *Tucker* garnered his best reviews in years, and writers who had difficulty with his stylization previously began to be more receptive now. Janet Maslin wrote, "*Tucker* combines the elaborate showmanship of the director's recent work with an urgent sense of purpose, and the combined effect gives his work a weight it has long been missing." In line with the promotional film device, the film is heavily influenced by period advertising aesthetics, with Coppola frequently referring to the influence of ad graphics from that era. GENE D. PHILLIPS has aptly described a use of "ultrasaturated colors to give the film the lustrous, lacquered look of an auto industry promotional film." An additional touchstone is the rich color and bold graphic style of WPA mural art, incorporated into Washington, D.C., interiors.

The centrality of color to *Tucker*'s style extends that of previous collaborations between Coppola and cinematographer VITTORIO STORARO. Scenes in and around Tucker's Ypsilanti home are bathed in a golden glow, with a strong orange tint in the "barn" (machine shop) next to the house. These hues are set off by blues and greens in exterior night scenes, such that warm interior colors frequently conflict with cooler colors through windows, bringing into play the contrasts seen in *One from the Heart*. Color is also used to highlight the gap between the golden colors of home and the cold grays of industrial sets, radio stations, and the like (the world of business that finally destroys the dreams fermented in Tucker's home and among his family). Another carryover from *One from the Heart* is a theatrical use of lighting, as when the orange light of the machine shop fades, without realistic cause, following an accident that might have killed Alex. Color saturation in some instances is such that it effectively obscures limitations on focal depth, facilitating an approximation of Wellesian deep focus. Elsewhere, as in the plant opening, we see a profusion of saturated primary colors (particularly the red of the model car). Throughout, in the manner of 1940s Technicolor, the use of bright colors is set in relief by the khakis, browns, and

wood-tones that form the baseline of color in the film (in costuming, interior office sets, etc.). Likewise, the frequent combination of saturated color and low-key lighting recalls not so much ad art as Russell Metty's cinematography for Douglas Sirk in the 1950s.

The influence of classical Hollywood is evident elsewhere in the film, and Kovacs notes that Coppola's approach to the subject here is "in the style and spirit of American cinema of the forties." Though Capra is often invoked in reference to the verve and sentimentality of the film, ORSON WELLES is, again, an obvious antecedent. The film as a whole can be read as an inverse of *Citizen Kane*, with Tucker failing spectacularly as a capitalist but surrounded by family and friends to the end. The most obvious tribute to *Kane* can be seen as a photo of the Tucker Corporation board of directors dissolves to a graphic match of the board in a meeting, reminiscent of a graphic match in *Kane* from a photo of a group of reporters Kane wishes to hire to the same reporters posing for his photographer once he's hired them. Following Welles and Toland, Coppola and Storaro make extensive use of high and low angles and frequently achieve striking deep-focus effects (despite the limitations of the anamorphic lens used here) in boardroom scenes and, most notably, when Tucker and Noble meet Howard Hughes, there producing an eerie effect emphasizing Hughes's isolation and paranoia.

Perhaps the most striking instances of style in *Tucker* continue and extend Coppola's experimentation with set design and theatrical transitions in *One from the Heart*. In one instance, set design enables a Wellesian elliptical jump cut. Karatz lays out multiple possibilities for the plant location to Tucker and family around the kitchen table, explaining that one option is absurdly large for their needs. Coppola cuts to Tucker's reaction shot, with a section of the kitchen set clearly visible behind him. Tucker replies, "It's perfect!" He rises, puts on his hat, and walks directly onto the plant floor. Coppola also uses connected sets representing noncontiguous spaces to eliminate the need for alternation during telephone conversations (elsewhere he will use superimposition). Vera talks to Tucker in D.C., and the camera glides past a wall in the Tucker house to Tucker's hotel room in Washington. Later, Tucker, in the plant, takes a call from Karatz in a diner; the plant set and the diner set are built side by side, and during the conversation the camera centers on the wall dividing them, Karatz talking on one side and Tucker replying on the other.

The use of such techniques is theatrical, highly artificial, reflexive, and hyperbolic, manifesting Coppola's ongoing experimentation in film style for its own sake. That many critics were more receptive to this here than in *One from the Heart* may be related not only to the narrative context—Coppola's investment in the subject and the use of innovative style to reflect the innovative car—but also to the changing contexts of Hollywood cinema in the 1980s, specifically its increasing stylization. Style had become the principal outlet for authorial innovation in a climate in which experimentation with narrative form had become economically unfeasible. Then as now, some reviewers remained skeptical toward such stylization, but as Jon Lewis reminds us, "For Coppola, working in a genre-based cinema like Hollywood, style *was* the determining factor of authorship. By affirming Coppola's attention to style, the critics were merely remarking that Coppola was, despite all the money and all the battles with the studio, still an *auteur.*"

In the end, *Tucker* did much to restore Coppola's critical reputation, but despite Lucas's input, it did little to restore his commercial reputation: the film cost $25 million, and grossed only $19 million. In response, he finally caved in to pressure to make *THE GODFATHER: PART III* (1990), the success of which did much to alleviate his post-Zoetrope woes. It was his next film, *BRAM STOKER'S DRACULA* (1992), that finally restored his commercial status. Ironically, it was also the film that saw him take his experimentation with film style to its most delirious extreme, in the process definitively reestablishing his credentials as a film author.—PAUL RAMAEKER

References

Kim Aubrey, producer, "Under the Hood: Making *Tucker*," DVD feature, 2000; Jill Kearney, "The Road Warrior," *American Film*, June 1988, 20–27; Steven Kovacs, "Tucker," *Film Quarterly* (Summer 1989): 26–28; Jon Lewis, *Whom God Wishes to Destroy . . . : Francis Coppola and the New Hollywood* (Durham, NC: Duke University Press, 1995); Robert Lindsey, "Francis Ford Coppola: Promises to Keep," *New York Times*, July 24, 1988, A22; Janet Maslin, "Two Directors Put Their Stamp on Their Dreams," *New York Times*, August 21, 1988, A21; Tom O'Brien, "Myth America," *Commonweal*, August 12, 1988, 430–32; Gene D. Phillips, *Godfather: The Intimate Francis Ford Coppola* (Lexington: University Press of Kentucky, 2004); Richard Schickel, "*Tucker: The Man and His Dream*," *Time*, August 15, 1988, 68–69.

TURNER, [MARY] KATHLEEN (1954–)

Popular blonde actress and star, whose role as Peggy Sue Kelcher against NICOLAS CAGE's Charlie Bodell in *PEGGY SUE GOT MARRIED* (1986) earned an Oscar nomination. She was also later directed by SOFIA COPPOLA in the role of the mother of the beautiful Lux sisters in *THE VIRGIN SUICIDES* (1999). In her FRANCIS COPPOLA film, Peggy Sue is able as a grown woman to revisit her teen years. Her performance charmed *Newsweek*'s David Ansen to write: "Imagine a paint-by-numbers comic book put in the hands of a Rembrandt; the bold comic outlines remain, but the subject is transformed by the dark palette and subtle brushwork into a tale reverberating with complex, adult emotions. So it is with *Peggy Sue.*" Originally, in 1984, the picture was to have been directed by Penny Marshall, with Debra Winger set to star in the lead. The project stalled over a script dispute until Coppola took over, with Kathleen Turner in the lead, and, as *Variety* reported, "the result is one terrific matchup," since Turner was "a natural for playing Peggy Sue, the grown up all-American girl with a rebellious streak."

Kathleen Turner was born in Springfield, Missouri, on June 19, 1954. Since her father, Allen Richard Turner, was a U.S. Foreign Service officer, she grew up in Cuba, Venezuela, Canada, and the United Kingdom, where she graduated from the American School in London in 1972 and attended classes at the Central School of Speech and Drama. Before going on to earn a Bachelor of Fine Arts degree from The University of Maryland, Baltimore County in 1977, she attended classes at Missouri State University, where she was a classmate of John Goodman. Her acting debut on television was for NBC in 1978.

Turner's breakthrough film role was as the femme fatale in Lawrence Kasden's neo-noir thriller, *Body Heat* (1981); she was so effective in that film as Matty Walker that

her performance drew comparisons with Lauren Bacall and made her an immediate and sensational sex symbol. Her later performance as Joan Wilder in *Romancing the Stone*, one of the top-grossing films of 1984, won a Golden Globe, so she reappeared with Michael Douglas and Danny DeVito in the sequel, *The Jewel of the Nile* (1985). She would appear again with Douglas in DeVito's *The War of the Roses* (1989); in 1991 she played the lead in *V.I. Warshawski*, adapted from the fiction of Sara Paretsky, a role that did not help her career. In fact, Turner's acting career became complicated by illness (rheumatoid arthritis) during the 1990s, but was later revived by Sofia Coppola and others, leading to her being cast in *The Virgin Suicides* in 1999. In 2000 she played Mrs. Robinson on the London stage in a spectacularly popular production of *The Graduate.* And in 2005 on Broadway she played Martha in Edward Albee's *Who's Afraid of Virginia Woolf?* beating out competitors Jessica Lange, Frances McDormand, and Bette Midler, and earning her second Tony Award for Best Actress, as well as the respect of Albee himself.
—JAMES M. WELSH

References

David Ansen, "Back to the Future," *Newsweek*, October 6, 1986, 73; Brit., "*Peggy Sue Got Married* (Color): Smashing Return to Form by Francis Coppola," *Variety*, September 24, 1986, 13.

UPTON, [RICHARD] MORGAN (1930–1991)

American character actor who played Mr. Gilford in *PEGGY SUE GOT MARRIED* (1986) and Turnbull in *TUCKER: THE MAN AND HIS DREAM* (1988) for FRANCIS COPPOLA; he also appeared in the WIM WENDERS film *HAMMETT*, produced by Zoetrope Studios in 1982. Morgan Upton was born on August 11, 1930, in Massachusetts, and died December 22, 1991, in San Francisco, California. He was active in the San Francisco Bay Area theatre community. His television work includes appearances on such popular series as *Hawaii Five-O, Columbo*, and *Laverne & Shirley.*—JAMES M. WELSH

VAMPIRES: THE LEGEND
BEFORE COPPOLA

Derived from a Magyar word, *vampir*, meaning "blood-sucker," *vampire* denotes a genus of Central and South American bats, but the first dictionary definition comes from folklore and popular culture, not biology, and describes a "preternatural being, commonly believed to be a reanimated corpse," believed to feed upon the blood of sleeping victims. The literary legend arises from notions of the sublime, and from romanticism and the gothic. Freud was interested in the *Unheimlich*, the "uncanny" (with further connotations of the *weird* and the *sinister*), of the familiar turning into the unfamiliar, which pretty well describes the visual style of FRANCIS COPPOLA's *DRACULA* film, with its echoes of F. W. Murnau, Carl-Theodor Dreyer, and ABEL GANCE, who never animated a vampire but certainly knew how to construct spectacular epic legends.

The "unofficial" film version of Stoker's novel was F. W. Murnau's silent classic *Nosferatu*, loosely adapted by Murnau in 1922, that changed the story substantially because Murnau had not obtained the rights to the novel from the Stoker estate. BRAM STOKER himself had worked on an unsuccessful stage adaptation that was simply too long and cumbersome until it was reshaped by Hamilton Deane's stage adaptation, set entirely in England. The Deane version toured England in 1926 before opening in London in 1927. The later American stage version was revised by the London-based American journalist John L. Balderson. This version opened on Broadway on October 5, 1927, and was the basis for the 1931 Tod Browning film, starring the forty-six-year-old Hungarian expatriate actor Bela Lugosi (Bela Blasko), whose appearance epitomized the image fabricated by Deane, and became the "classic" portrayal for decades in American movies.

Coppola set out to make a bloody good vampire film, one that would eclipse Bela Lugosi and out-bad John Badham's adaptation. But Coppola takes a page from Badham's book, as critic Gary Arnold pointed out in his *Washington Times* review: "John Badham's sumptuous, whirlwind 1979 *Dracula*, contrived for maximum erotic impact and elegance by screenwriter W. D. Richter, saved narrative drudgery by concentrating the story in Yorkshire," a gimmick taken straight from the stage adaptation upon which the Richter screenplay was based. In that version, Frank Langella and Kate Nelligan as the Count and Mina had breathtaking charisma surpassing anything that GARY OLDMAN and WINONA RYDER could achieve for Coppola. As Stephen Hunter joked in the *Baltimore Sun*, "*BRAM STOKER'S DRACULA* is about the naked and the dead—together at last." Coppola's film had very little, really, to do with the literary tradition, and, despite the absurd backstory incorporated into the film, little to do with the historical VLAD DRACULA. Instead, the Coppola film reversed the tradition by redefining lust in late-twentieth-century terms and working up vampirism as an AIDS metaphor. In the nineteenth century, harmful body fluids would have been associated with women rather than men. The film works in references to venereal diseases in Van Helsing's lecture to the medical students. In fact, one might argue that Werner Herzog's *Nosferatu* is closer to the spirit of Bram Stoker than Coppola's film, even though Herzog's film looked more to F. W. Murnau for its inspiration, and Murnau had pretty much stolen Stoker's fantasy, which critic Vincent Canby generously called Murnau's "unauthorized 1922 adaptation of the Stoker novel."

Certainly, Coppola's adaptation wisely ignored the campy Tod Browning/Bela Lugosi *Dracula* (1931), adapted from the stage adaptation of Stoker's novel rather than from the novel itself. *Baltimore Sun* critic Stephen Hunter suggested that "No doubt Coppola wanted to stay away from the by-now preposterous Transylvanian lounge lizard thing, pioneered campily by Bela Lugosi." Canby claimed that JAMES V. HART's treatment was an "unusually faithful screen adaptation of the novel," which only demonstrates that Vincent Canby really didn't know Stoker's novel. Or was this simply a failure of logic? Canby called "the film's vivid precredit sequence in Transylvania shortly after Constantinople's fall to the Turks in 1462" something that Bram Stoker somehow "saw fit to omit." But, then, Constantinople fell to the Turks in 1453, didn't it? Indicating that Canby's sense of chronology was as flawed as his judgment. If fidelity is an issue here—and it most assuredly is not—then the Coppola film may indeed be the nearest screen

adaptation to the source novel, but, regardless, many gross liberties have been taken. —JAMES M. WELSH

References
Gary Arnold, "'Dracula': Anemic Offspring in the Bloodline," *Washington Times*, November 13, 1992, E1, E5; Vincent Canby, "Coppola's Dizzying Vision of Dracula," *New York Times*, November 13, 1992, C1, C19; Stephen Hunter, 'Dracula': The Old Boy Never Looked So Good," *Baltimore Sun: Maryland Live*, November 13–19, 1992, 4.

VERDON, GWEN (1925–2000)
Popular American dancer and actress who played Tish Dwyer, the mother of characters played by RICHARD GERE and NICOLAS CAGE in Coppola's *THE COTTON CLUB* (1984). Daughter of an ex-vaudevillian dancer and an electrician at MGM, Verdon took dancing lessons as a child to strengthen her legs after a case of rickets necessitated orthopedic shoes and leg braces. The eventual winner of four Tony Awards in six years made her big splash on Broadway in a supporting role whose big moments were cut back at the demand of a temperamental star who didn't like the attention Verdon was getting from audiences. Verdon's remaining number in Cole Porter's musical *Can-Can* stopped the show on opening night, requiring an encore. Other shows soon followed, including *Damn Yankees*, in which she played the devilish temptress Lola, a role she repeated in the film version. *Yankees* marked her first collaboration with choreographer Bob Fosse, her eventual husband. Other Broadway triumphs included *Redhead*, *New Girl in Town*, *Sweet Charity*, and her last Broadway musical, Kander and Ebb's *Chicago*.

After her dancing years were behind her, she continued behind the scenes on Broadway acting as supervisor of Fosse's full-length dance piece, *Dancin'*, and later as artistic advisor for *Fosse*, an evening-long compilation of Fosse's best known dance work. She also began increasing her film and television work, appearing in such television series as *All My Children* and *Magnum, P.I.*, as well as films like *Alice* and *Cocoon*. Her role in Coppola's *Cotton Club* is unfortunately little more than a few isolated appearances, but she makes an impression nonetheless: her enthusiastic break into a full-out tap dance is one of the highlights of the film's final sequence. Verdon kept working in film and television consistently for the remainder of her life. Upon her death on October 18, 2000, the lights on Broadway were dimmed in her memory.—TOM DANNENBAUM

Reference

Robert Berkvist, "Gwen Verdon, Redhead Who High-Kicked Her Way to Stardom, Dies at 75," *New York Times*, October 19, 2000.

VERDÚ, MARIBEL [MARIA ISABEL VERDÚ ROLLÁN] (1970–)

Spanish actress who portrays Miranda, the title character's therapist and life partner, in FRANCIS COPPOLA's *TETRO* (2009). Miranda holds a central importance in the film's plot as the mediator between the frustrated playwright Tetro (VINCENT GALLO)—an Italian American who has moved to Buenos Aires in order to estrange himself from his entire family—and his younger brother, Bennie (ALDEN EHRENREICH), who has come to try to mend the broken ties. Miranda also gives Bennie access to Tetro's fiercely guarded journals and notes, which hold the secrets of the long-standing rift between Tetro and his father, the brilliant but egotistical and overbearing conductor, Carlo (KLAUS MARIA BRANDAUER). Furthermore, in a film dominated by fraternal and paternal conflict, critic Manohla Dargis characterizes Miranda as a much-needed "warm presence who embodies the sensual and the maternal."

Coppola described the part as the glue that holds the movie together; or, as Verdú told the *New York Times*: "From the start he was clear in telling me that I had to provide the heart, to bring a bit of light between these two brothers and their tormented relationship."

Maribel Verdú first gained critical notice at the age of sixteen in the film *27 Hours* (1986), after having appeared in numerous print ads and TV commercials. Through the 1990s she continued to build her reputation by working with some of Spain's most respected directors, including Carlos Saura in *Goya en Burdeos* (1999), and Fernando Trueba in *Belle Epoque* (the 1994 Oscar winner for Best Foreign Film).

Verdú's international breakthrough, however, came with Alfonso Cuarón's *Y tu mamá también* (2001), one of the biggest hits of the "New" Mexican Cinema. She received further recognition for her performance as Mercedes in Guillermo del Toro's *Pan's Labyrinth* (2006), which won her the 2007 Ariel Award as Best Actress.

Tetro marked Verdú's first role in an English-language film, a prospect that made her understandably uneasy at first. She told the *New York Times* that she was initially "nervous, worried that I couldn't do this, wasn't up to it." Coppola, however, soon put her at ease, she said: "I've been at this for 25 years, and never before had a director go to the airport to await me and take me to his home. . . . It was a gesture that made me feel comfortable and protected from the start."—RODNEY HILL

References

Manohla Dargis, "Sons and the Father Who Made Them," *New York Times*, June 11, 2009, movies.nytimes.com; American Zoetrope, *Tetro*, official website, "Maribel Verdú," www.tetro.com; Todd McCarthy, "Tetro," *Variety*, May

14, 2009, www.variety.com; Larry Rohter, "Family Dynamics, without the Bullets," *New York Times*, June 3, 2009, www.nytimes.com.

VIDAL, GORE (1925–)

Celebrity wit, novelist, playwright, critic, screenwriter, and National Book Award–winning essayist who collaborated with FRANCIS COPPOLA on the screenplay of *IS PARIS BURNING?* (1966), a film about the liberation of Paris, directed by René Clément. At the time, Coppola was under contract as a screenwriter with Seven Arts. Several writers had tried to produce a workable script for the film, but the producer, Ray Stark, was unhappy with what they had turned out, so he gave the script to Coppola to work on and brought in Gore Vidal to help. Vidal wrote about the experience in his memoir, *Point to Point Navigation* (2006): "I found Francis to be encyclopedic on anything that had to do with filmmaking," Vidal wrote. "He was truly post-Gutenberg. Film was where *it*—all of it—was at. For him the written culture had passed into night, making him the first member of the total-film generation that I was ever to meet." Gore Vidal was born in West Point, New York, on October 3, 1925, the grandson of Senator T. P. Gore of Oklahoma. A hugely multitalented writer, famous for his liberal opinions, he ran for public office and was frequently a liberal sparring partner for William F. Buckley on national television.—JAMES M. WELSH

THE VIRGIN SUICIDES (1999)

The first feature film written and directed by SOFIA COPPOLA, daughter of FRANCIS FORD COPPOLA, *The Virgin Suicides* was adapted for the screen by Sofia Coppola from the 1993 novel by Jeffrey Eugenides. Francis Coppola served as a producer on the film, which was produced by his AMERICAN ZOETROPE production company.

As Francis Coppola's daughter, Sofia Coppola grew up around film sets and the business and art of filmmaking. In talking about working as a director on *The Virgin Suicides* she has said, "It just feels familiar to me. I can't really imagine not doing this." But she didn't come to filmmaking naturally or eagerly. The experience of acting in her father's film *THE GODFATHER: PART III* (1990) at the age of nineteen soured her for a while on making movies, and she pursued work in photography, fashion design, and modeling. In 1995, she became enamored with Eugenides's novel, *The Virgin Suicides*, and pursued the movie rights, asking her father (unsuccessfully) for help in purchasing them. Against her father's advice, Coppola wrote a screenplay of *The Virgin Suicides* without having the rights, her status as a novice screenwriter allowing her to effectively adapt the novel without worrying about traditional screenplay structure. As her father has stated, "She took a wonderful novel . . . an acclaimed novel, that basically no one knew how to adapt. When she read the book, it impressed her so much that she said all she wanted to do was to get what the book had." Sofia Coppola was ultimately able to team up with the production company that owned the rights, Muse Productions, which hired her to direct her own adaptation of the novel. Francis Coppola, impressed with his daughter's script, joined the project as a producer.

The production of *The Virgin Suicides* was a Coppola family affair. In addition to Sofia's leadership as the film's writer/director and her father's involvement as a producer on the film, Sofia's brother, ROMAN COPPOLA, served as a second-unit director (a role he has filled on several of his father's films, on Sofia's two subsequent films, and on two Wes Anderson films). Their mother (Francis's wife) ELEANOR COPPOLA spent time on the set filming documentary footage of the production (which she has also done on some of her husband's films). A couple of Coppola family cousins worked on *The Virgin Suicides* as well—Robert Schwartzman in a small acting role and Chris Neil as an acting coach for the film's many young actors. Part of the family atmosphere during shooting stemmed from Francis's mentorship of novice director Sofia. "It's just great to have my dad as a mentor and producer because it's someone whose opinion I respect," Sofia has said. Her mother, Eleanor, agreed: "It was really touching for me to see Francis mentoring Sofia, and her mature enough to accept it."

The Virgin Suicides went into limited release on April 21, 2000, with wider release coming a few weeks later. Prior to its general release, the film had played first at the CANNES FILM FESTIVAL (in May 1999) and the Sundance Film Festival (in January 2000). While not a huge success financially, the film received a reasonably good critical reaction. The film stars James Woods and KATHLEEN TURNER as the parents of five teenage girls (the virgins of the title), with the lead teen portrayed by Kirsten Dunst. Josh Hartnett plays a teenage boy who tries to woo Dunst's character, while Scott Glenn and DANNY DEVITO fill cameo roles. The film's story concerns the lives of the five virginal girls and their lyrical, yet adolescently constrained life as seen through the perspective of a group of teenage boys. The story begins with the suicide of the youngest sister and reaches its climax with the collective suicide of the remaining four.—CHRISTOFER MEISSNER

References

Graham Fuller, "Sofia Coppola's Second Chance," *New York Times*, April 16, 2000, 29; "The Making of *The Virgin Suicides*" (supplementary material on DVD release of *The Virgin Suicides*), Paramount Home Video, 2000.

VOIGHT, JON (1938–)

Distinctive American actor and star, cast to play Leo F. Drummond in *THE RAINMAKER* (1997). From 1960 to 1964 in New York he studied acting at the Neighborhood Playhouse. While acting in Arthur Miller's *A View from the Bridge*, Voight met Dustin Hoffman, who later recommended him for his breakthrough movie role as Joe Buck in the film *Midnight Cowboy* (1969), which earned Voight an Oscar nomination. His role as a paraplegic Vietnam veteran in *Coming Home* (1978) earned Voight an Oscar, and his role in *The Rainmaker* earned a Golden Globe Award for Best Supporting Actor. More recently, Voight was a newsmaker as the father of the celebrity star Angelina Jolie and as a celebrity Republican critic of Barack Obama in the right-wing *Washington Times* (August 5, 2008).—JAMES M. WELSH

WAITS, TOM (1949–)

Composer (*ONE FROM THE HEART*); songwriter (*THE OUTSIDERS*); and actor, who played Buck Merrill in *The Outsiders*, Benny in *RUMBLE FISH*, and Irving Stark in *THE COTTON CLUB*. Waits also played an especially distinctive and memorable Renfield in *BRAM STOKER'S DRACULA*. The score Tom Waits wrote for *One from the Heart* in 1982 was nominated for an Academy Award.—JAMES M. WELSH

WALLACH, ELI [HERSCHEL] (1915–)

Celebrated American "Method" actor considered one of Hollywood's finest character actors, who played Don Altobello in *THE GODFATHER: PART III* (1990). Eli Wallach was born in Brooklyn on December 7, 1915, the son of Bertha and Abraham Wallach. He was educated at the University of Texas, Austin, and went on to earn an MA (in education) from the City College of New York. An alumnus of the Neighborhood Playhouse in New York and a charter member of the Actors Studio, Wallach also studied acting with the German director Erwin Piscator at New York's Dramatic Workshop of the New School.

Serving in the U.S. Army during World War II, Wallach coauthored a play called *Is This the Army?* spoofing Irving Berlin's *This Is the Army*. He made his Broadway debut in 1945 in *Skydrift* and later was in the two-year run of *Mister Roberts*, starring Henry Fonda. In 1951 Wallach earned a Tony Award for his performance in the Tennessee Williams play *The Rose Tattoo*. His film debut was in Elia Kazan's *Baby Doll* in 1956, a performance that earned Wallach a British Film Academy (BAFTA) Award. Later films included *The Misfits* (1961), *The Magnificent Seven* (1960, playing the Mexican bandit Calvera), and Sergio Leone's *The Good, the Bad and the Ugly* (1967, playing Tuco, the "Ugly"). Rumor has it that Wallach was originally cast to play Angelo Maggio in Fred Zinnemann's adaptation of *From Here to Eternity* (1953), but was replaced by Frank Sinatra, perhaps because of underworld influences. Wallach and his wife, actress Anne Jackson, produced and starred in the 1965 film adaptation of the Murray Schisgal play, *The Tiger*, retitled *The Tiger Makes Out*, featuring the screen debut of actor Dustin Hoffman. Eli Wallach appeared in just about every prestige television drama during the "Golden Age" of the 1950s: *Studio One*, *The Philco Television Playhouse*, *The Armstrong Circle Theatre*, *Playhouse 90*, and *The Hallmark Hall of Fame*, among others. He won the 1966–1967 Emmy Award for his role in the telefilm *The Poppy Is Also a Flower*. —JAMES M. WELSH

WELLES, ORSON (1915–1985)

Filmmaker and actor, who wrote a screenplay derived from JOSEPH CONRAD's

"HEART OF DARKNESS," which was not filmed.

In 1975 FRANCIS COPPOLA announced that he planned to make a film based on Conrad's "Heart of Darkness" (1899), but updated to the Vietnam War. A great fan of Orson Welles, Coppola was well aware that Welles had written a screenplay based on the same novella, which had gone unproduced. As for Conrad's novella, the story is narrated by the seaman, Marlow. He is charged with investigating the life of Kurtz, an ivory trader whom Marlow tracks down in the jungle. Gradually, Marlow unearths the hideous facts about Kurtz by inquiring about him from those who knew him.

In Kurtz's case, once he was on his own in the jungle, he became guilty of the most appalling behavior. In the course of the novella, Kurtz becomes ruler of a tribe of savages whom he allows to worship him as a god, and in this manner he keeps them subservient to him. In fact, he has engaged with the tribesmen in the most barbaric pagan rites, which have been offered in his own honor.

The jungle, then, becomes a metaphor for the heart of darkness that lies within each of us: our inclination to evil. In short, the story represents a journey into the dark heart of a human being.

The first attempt to bring "Heart of Darkness" to the screen was made by Orson Welles (*Citizen Kane*), who had originally hoped that his film adaptation of Conrad's story would be the first film he made in Hollywood for RKO, the studio with which he signed a contract in 1939. Welles wanted to begin shooting the film in the fall of 1939 (he had planned to be the voice of Marlow, the narrator of the story, in voiceover on the sound track, as well as to appear on-screen as Kurtz). Unfortunately neither the script nor the budget of the film was ready at that point. When Welles finally turned in his proposed budget for the production, it ran to more than one million dollars—much to the dismay of RKO's front office, since that was exactly twice the budget for the average RKO film. The studio brass accordingly insisted that Welles cut his budget in half, and he responded that he would do his best to be obliging.

The draft of Welles's screenplay for "Heart of Darkness" was literally taken from the source story. As a matter of fact, Robert Carringer notes in his book on Welles that Welles actually tore pages of the story out of the paperback edition of the novella "and pasted them onto sheets of typing paper; and he worked his way through these, marking the passages that were to be retained and crossing out the rest." Occasionally, however, Welles "changed or added a line or two," and made other alterations in the screenplay. Thus he updated the story to the present and made Marlow, the film's narrator, an American; but Welles maintained that whatever changes he made in the original story Conrad himself would have desired, were he alive at the time the film was being made.

Welles told Peter Bogdanovich that he planned to film the story in the first person: "The camera was going to be Marlow." Welles had insisted on the use of the subjective point of view; virtually everyone and everything would be seen through Marlow's eyes. Marlow himself would be visible in the course of the movie when his image was reflected in a mirror or in a windowpane. He would also be visible in the early scenes when Marlow is aboard his boat in New York Harbor, prior to his voyage.

Since Conrad employed first-person narration in the novella, Welles wanted to direct the film so that the subjective camera would serve as the eyes of the main character. In essence, the filmgoer is supposedly looking through Marlow's eyes at the action as it transpires. That is why, as Jonathan Rosenbaum points out, Welles states in the prologue for the film (in which Welles planned to demonstrate the use of the subjective camera in the movie to follow) the following remark, addressed directly to the moviegoer: "You aren't going to see this picture—this picture is going to happen to you."

Rosenbaum comments on the prologue: "It serves the ingenious function of demonstrating the . . . gimmicky aspects of the technique *before* the story begins, thus clearing the way for its subsequent use as a serious narrative device."

An excellent example of the subjective camera occurs in the climactic scene when Marlow disembarks from his boat at Kurtz's outpost in the jungle. As Welles conceived this shot with the "first-person camera" in mind, Marlow walks up the hill from the dock, enters Kurtz's compound, and proceeds to his lair. Kurtz is ensconced in a decaying temple, sitting regally upon a throne, and the camera tracks forward as Marlow walks toward the throne. This shot was to be accomplished in an extended take, employing the subjective camera, with the filmgoer seeing exactly what Marlow sees.

In sum, by employing the subjective camera, Welles thus provided a visual corollary to Conrad's first-person narration in the book. Moreover, Welles in his script evoked the first-person feel of Conrad's novella by accompanying his use of the seeing-eye camera with Marlow's running voiceover on the soundtrack, which was to be spoken by Welles himself in the person of Marlow.

The opening scene has Marlow about to set out from New York Harbor on his journey to find Kurtz. He has been employed by an unnamed government to bring Kurtz back from some unspecified country in South America to assume some kind of political leadership role. Carringer points out that "parallels are repeatedly drawn between Kurtz's leadership style and contemporary fascist regimes in Europe." As a matter of fact, while Welles was preparing *Heart of Darkness*, Hitler invaded Poland and World War II got under way. Indeed, in Marlowe's confrontation with Kurtz, the latter's despotism is clearly linked to the tyranny sweeping over Europe at the time. Kurtz symbolizes fascism by lording it over the natives, and he also refers directly to Hitler in the dialogue. In fact, Welles says in Simon Callow's book, "The picture is frankly an attack on the Nazi system."

Thus Kurtz says to Marlow, "There is a man now in Europe trying to do what I've done in the jungle. He will fail. In his madness he thinks he can't fail, but he will." By contrast, Kurtz is confident that, in creating a kingdom in the jungle, he has succeeded. "I'm above morality," he declares. "I've climbed higher than other men and seen farther. I'm the first absolute dictator." He implies that he will not be the last. As in Conrad's book, Kurtz has fallen seriously ill by the time Marlow reaches him; and he dies before Marlow can bring him back to America.

Unfortunately plans to film *Heart of Darkness* were finally abandoned by the studio when it became obvious that *Heart of Darkness*, with its elaborate jungle sets and "casts of thousands," could never be made for $500,000. In fact, Welles's script called for three thousand black natives to be seen bowing down to Kurtz in one sequence, which caused one dismayed RKO executive to point out to the front office that there were only four or five hundred black extras in all of Hollywood. Welles then turned his attention to making *Citizen Kane*; and the rest, as they say, is history.

Coppola, who was a great aficionado of Welles's films, was to some degree inspired to make a film adapted from Conrad's novella by Welles's aborted project. Moreover, Peter Cowie points out the many affinities between the films of Welles and

Coppola, suggesting that it is not surprising that both filmmakers would be attracted to the same literary source. "The two men are tightly linked by their fascination with the diabolical," he writes; "the notion of man as fallen angel." Their antiheroes "arouse a tantalizing sympathy in the audience." There is a distinct kinship between Welles's ruthless, despotic Charles Foster Kane and Hank Quinlan, the corrupt cop in *Touch of Evil*, on the one hand, and Coppola's Mafia bosses Vito Corleone and his son Michael Corleone in the *GODFATHER* trilogy. Not surprisingly, then, both Welles and Coppola were drawn to Conrad's Kurtz, yet another fallen angel.

The screenplay for Coppola's film *APOCALYPSE NOW* was by JOHN MILIUS, MICHAEL HERR, and Francis Coppola. The script updated the story to the Vietnam War and turned Kurtz from an ivory trader into a Green Beret officer who defects from the American army.

On the surface, Welles's scenario is very different from Coppola's film. Yet, although the settings and backgrounds of the two adaptations are quite different, there are some notable similarities. For example, both Welles's version and Coppola's version begin with the protagonist's explanation of how he got the appointment that necessitates his excursion upriver. Captain Benjamin Willard (MARTIN SHEEN), who is the central character and narrator of Coppola's movie, is mandated by his superior officers to penetrate into the interior of the jungle and track down Colonel Walter E. Kurtz (MARLON BRANDO), a renegade officer who has raised an army composed of deserters like himself and of native tribesmen, in order to fight the war on his own terms. When he locates Kurtz, Willard is to "terminate his command with extreme prejudice," which is military jargon meaning that Willard should assassinate Kurtz. Colonel Kurtz, it seems, has taken to employing brutal tactics to attain his military objectives.

Coppola also has Willard narrate the film (with narration written by Michael Herr), in much the same way that Welles has Marlow narrate the story (although Coppola does not employ the subjective camera in the fashion in which Welles had planned to utilize it in *Heart of Darkness*). Hence both *Apocalypse Now* and Welles's *Heart of Darkness* remain faithful to their common source by depicting the action through flashback, with the narrator's comments on the action heard in voiceover.

In 2001, Coppola released *APOCALYPSE NOW REDUX*, the director's cut of *Apocalypse Now*, with fifty-three minutes of additional footage added to the film as originally released. Coppola thereby brought fresh acclaim to his version of Conrad's "Heart of Darkness." In his article on *Apocalypse Now Redux*, Howard Hampton mentions the Welles version, and that Welles not only planned to play both Kurtz and Marlow in his adaptation, but also "to shoot the entire movie in first-person POV, with the camera showing everything through Marlow's eyes." He adds, "If it had been green-lighted instead of *Kane*," it would have been interesting to see "Orson Welles playing Citizen Kurtz." In some ways Coppola realized Welles's dream of doing a screen adaptation of Conrad's story set in modern times: updated to World War II in Welles's version and to Vietnam in Coppola's *Apocalypse Now*.—GENE D. PHILLIPS

References
Simon Callow, *Orson Welles: The Road to Xanadu* (New York: Penguin Books, 1997); Robert Carringer, "*Heart of Darkness*," in *The Making of Citizen Kane* (Los Angeles: University of California Press, 1985), 1–15; Peter Cowie, *The Apocalypse Now Book* (New York: Da Capo, 2001); Peter Cowie, *Coppola: A Biography*, rev. ed.

(New York: Da Capo, 1994); Howard Hampton, "*Apocalypse Now Redux*," *Film Comment* 37, no. 3 (May–June 2001): 36–42; Jorn Hettebrugge, "*Apocalypse Now*," in *100 All-Time Favorite Films*, ed. Jurgen Muller (Los Angeles: Taschen/ BFI, 2008), 2:674–79; Jonathan Rosenbaum, "The Voice and the Eye: A Commentary on the *Heart of Darkness* Script," *Film Comment* 8, no. 4 (November–December 1972): 24–26; Orson Welles, "Introductory Sequence to the Unproduced *Heart of Darkness*," *Film Comment* 8, no. 4 (November–December 1972): 27–28; Orson Welles and Peter Bogdanovich, *This Is Orson Welles* (New York: Da Capo, 1998).

WENDERS, WIM (1945–)

German film director, born in Düsseldorf on August 14, 1945, who studied medicine and philosophy before enrolling in the Hochschule für Film und Fernsehen in Munich in 1967. Following the path of the French New Wave filmmakers, Wenders wrote film criticism for the *Süddeutsche Zeitung* and for the journal *Filmkritic* as his interest in cinema developed. He went on to become one of the founders of the production cooperative, *Filmverlag der Autoren*, and consequently of *Das neue Kino*, the German equivalent of the French New Wave, and comprising the most gifted German filmmakers: Werner Herzog, Volker Schlöndorff, Wolfgang Petersen, and R. W. Fassbinder.

Wenders worked with experimental novelist Peter Handke on his adaptation of *The Goalie's Anxiety at the Penalty Kick* (1972). His early career peaked with a trilogy of films: *Alice in the Cities* (1974), *The Wrong Move* (1975), and *Kings of the Road* (1976), followed by an even more impressive film, *The American Friend* (1977), adapted from the Patricia Highsmith novel, *Ripley's Game*, and starring DENNIS HOPPER and BRUNO GANZ, along with his favorite American directors, Sam Fuller and Nicholas Ray in key roles.

In 1978 FRANCIS COPPOLA invited Wenders to Los Angeles to discuss a biopic project based on the life of the crime-fiction novelist Dashiell Hammett, based on the novel by Joe Gores (who worked on the screenplay with Thomas Pope), a project that took much longer than anticipated, partly because of the demise of Coppola's Zoetrope distribution outlet. The film *HAMMETT* was not to be completed until 1982, and the Wenders visit to the United States lasted until 1985, after Wenders had made another American film, *Paris, Texas* (1984), which earned the Golden Palm Award at Cannes. By 1987 Wenders had returned to Germany to work again with Peter Handke and Bruno Ganz on *Wings of Desire*, which earned Wenders a Best Director Award at the CANNES INTERNATIONAL FILM FESTIVAL.

While on hiatus from directing *Hammet*, Wenders made *The State of Things*, a film about a film director working on a troubled production. This led to speculation that *The State of Things* was really "about" the problems Wenders was having with Coppola and Zoetrope Studios, but Wenders told interviewer John Gallagher that was not the case: "For those people who still insist it's my comment on the making of *Hammett*, they still have to realize there's only two people who really get along with each other in *The State of Things* and who are really friends, and that's the producer and the director."—JAMES M. WELSH

Reference

"Wim Wenders: An Interview by John Gallagher," *Films in Review* 34, no. 6 (June–July 1983): 355–61.

WILLIAMS, ROBIN [MCLAURIN] (1952–)

Gifted stand-up comedian who became a celebrated, Oscar-worthy actor, capable of moving beyond comedy to drama in films directed by Robert Altman, Steven Spielberg,

Woody Allen, and FRANCIS COPPOLA, who chose Williams to play Jack Powell in the film *JACK* (1996). Robin Williams was born in Chicago on July 21, 1952, the son of Lincoln-Mercury automobile executive Robert Fitzgerald Williams (1906–1987) and Laura (Smith) Williams (1922–2001). He grew up in Bloomfield Hills, Michigan, and Marin County, California, where he attended Redwood High School and then Claremont Men's College. In 1973 he was admitted to the Juilliard School to study acting and then was accepted by John Houseman into the School's Advanced Program. Though he would later find work and fame as a stand-up comedian, Robin Williams played Estragon on stage with Steve Martin in Samuel Beckett's *Waiting for Godot*, and much later performed an astonishing cameo as Osric in Kenneth Branagh's extended 1996 film version of *Hamlet*.

Initially, however, Williams found work on television, first as part of the cast of *The Richard Pryor Show* on NBC before being cast by Garry Marshall as the alien Mork in the popular television series *Happy Days*; that portrayal carried him over to the spin-off sitcom *Mork and Mindy* (1978–1982). His feature film debut came in 1980 when Robert Altman cast him to play the lead in his peculiar and stylized *Popeye*; more serious roles were to follow in *The World According to Garp* (1982), with Williams playing the lead character, T. S. Garp, and *Moscow on the Hudson* in 1984. He earned Academy Award nominations for his serious roles in *Good Morning, Vietnam* (1987), *Dead Poets Society* (1989), and *The Fisher King* (1991).

Williams finally won the Best Supporting Actor Oscar for his portrayal of Sean Maguire in *Good Will Hunting* (1997). Equally significant, perhaps, he won the Screen Actors Guild Award for Outstanding Performance by a Cast in a Motion Picture for his portrayal of Armand Goldman in *The Birdcage* (1996) and in 1997 he won the Screen Actors Guild Award for Outstanding Performance by a Male Actor in a Supporting Role for *Good Will Hunting*. Earlier on, in 1987 Williams had won the Golden Globe for Best Actor for his portrayal of Adrian Cronauer, the lead character in *Good Morning, Vietnam*.

But gifted though he may be, the presence of Robin Williams as Jack Powell, a ten-year-old boy "who's growing four times faster than normal," could not make Coppola's film *Jack* a critical success (though in fact it did well enough at the box office, earning over $58 million). The film was roundly dismissed by reviewers in Philadelphia and Washington, D.C., but Janet Maslin of the *New York Times* found "some unexpected flashes of real emotion" in the film and praised Coppola's sensitive direction. Maslin noted that the film "was dedicated to the daughter of the director's late son," Gian-Carlo, who was killed in a boating accident at the age of twenty, and thought the film was made sincerely, "from the heart." Coppola himself told the Associated Press that he regarded Jack's disease as a metaphor, rather than "literally a genetic disease."—JAMES M. WELSH

WILLIS, GORDON (1931–)

Cinematographer, *THE GODFATHER* (1972), *THE GODFATHER: PART II* (1974), and *THE GODFATHER: PART III* (1990). Willis also photographed eight of Woody Allen's movies, beginning with *Annie Hall* (1977), starring DIANE KEATON. With films like *Klute* (1971) behind him, Willis assumed quite gratuitously that Coppola, who was, after all, an alumnus of the UCLA graduate program in film, knew little about the technical aspects of moviemaking. Coppola found Willis "a grumpy guy" to work with.

A major bone of contention between them was Coppola's penchant for encouraging the actors to improvise during rehearsals, with a view to making some last-minute revisions in the script before finally shooting a scene. "I like to lay a thing out and make it work with discipline," Willis explains. Whereas, in his mind, Coppola spent an exorbitant amount of time improvising with the actors on the outside chance that he might improve the scene as written. "You can't shoot the whole movie, hoping for happy accidents," he concludes. "[W]hat you get is one big, bad accident."

When Willis pointed out that *The Godfather* was falling behind schedule because of the extra time Coppola was spending on improvising during rehearsals, Coppola replied that he had requested an eighty-day shooting schedule and was given fifty-five days by studio chief ROBERT EVANS. It was therefore inevitable that he would fall behind schedule. (In point of fact, the shooting period was finished in sixty-two days.) Camera operator John Chapman, who would later be a cinematographer (*Taxi Driver*), remembers what he calls "the marvelous operatic fights" between Willis and Coppola. The camera crew knew that Willis had small confidence in Coppola. He appeared insecure to the tough New York crew.

Gradually both men gained a modicum of respect for each other's talents, but Coppola says that they did not really get along well until *Godfather: Part II*. "I agreed with Gordy on how the film should look," states Coppola. For example, in order to evoke the films of the 1940s, the movie's time frame, they used grainy film stock like old period photographs. Willis says the overall look of the picture is a sort of "1940s New York grit." The low-level lighting of several scenes emphasizes the deception and secrecy of this dark underworld.

The murky, under-lit look of these scenes was daring and unconventional. As the rushes were shipped to the studio in Hollywood from the New York locations, the report came back, "The camera is always focused on the dark." Studio moguls, accustomed to ultrabright lighting in films, were disturbed by such scenes. In fact, Willis earned the nickname "The Prince of Darkness" in the film colony.

Coppola brought back Willis to work on *Godfather: Part II*. "I got along with Gordy Willis on this film," Coppola says. "I didn't feel I was up against this crotchety schoolmarm who wanted things done his own way. Of course, I was producer as well as director, so I really had no one to answer to but myself."

The second *Godfather* movie not only chronicles Michael Corleone's subsequent career as head of the "family business," but also presents, in flashback, Don Vito Corleone's early life in Sicily, as well as his rise to power in the Mafia in New York City's "Little Italy" after his immigration to the United States. As Pauline Kael says, "We only saw the middle of the story in the first film; now we have the beginning and the end."

Working with Willis, Coppola conceived a visual scheme to keep the two plotlines in the picture distinct: The flashbacks to Vito's youth would be photographed in what Willis terms nostalgic "golden amber" tints, to give these scenes a period flavor as they portray Vito as a "Lower-East-Side Robin Hood" who steals from the rich and gives to the poor (in cahoots with Peter Clemenza [BRUNO KIRBY], a young hood). In the flashbacks, says Willis, "the imagery is softer and not as sharply defined." The scenes about Michael set in modern times would be filmed in a spare realistic color scheme featuring cool blues and grays in order to suggest how Michael becomes colder and more ruthless as time goes on.

In order to ensure continuity between the third *Godfather* film and its predecessors, Coppola reassembled a team of regulars, including Gordon Willis. Willis was nominated for an Academy Award for *Godfather: Part III*—belatedly, since he deserved to be nominated for the first two films of the trilogy as well. He received an honorary Oscar on November 14, 2009, at a special awards presentation sponsored by the Academy of Motion Picture Arts and Sciences.

Janet Lorenz and David Levine write that "Willis's true talent lies in his ability to translate a director's concepts into precise and compelling visual terms." He has stated that his job is "to make movies *with* directors; ultimately it is *their* ideas that I am executing."—GENE D. PHILLIPS

References
Pauline Kael, *Reeling* (New York: Bantam Books, 1977); Vincent LoBrutto, *Principal Photography: Interviews with Cinematographers* (New York: Praeger, 1999); Janet Lorenz and David Levine, "Gordon Willis," in *International Dictionary of Films and Filmmakers*, ed. Nicolet Elert (New York: St. James Press, 2000), 4:896–97; Dennis Schaefer and Larry Salento, *Masters of Light: Conversations with Cinematographers* (Los Angeles: University of California Press, 1984).

WISE, NAOMI (N.D.)
Coauthor with MICHAEL GOODWIN of *On the Edge: The Life and Times of Francis Coppola* (1989), an unauthorized biography, but the first book-length biography of FRANCIS COPPOLA. At the time the book was published she was described as film critic for *San Francisco Focus*. —JAMES M. WELSH

WYNN, KEENAN (1916–1986)
Likable American character actor who plays Senator Billboard Rawkins in FRANCIS COPPOLA's *FINIAN'S RAINBOW* (1968); son of the famous vaudevillian and screen comedic actor Ed Wynn and actress Hilda Keenan (who was the daughter of theatrical luminary Frank Keenan). Keenan Wynn attended the St. John's Military Academy and then started his stage acting career with the Maine Stock Company. After some success on Broadway and radio, Wynn landed a movie contract in 1942 at MGM, where his first notable success was in *See Here, Private Hargrove* (1944).

Wynn continued to be a staple at MGM into the 1950s, mostly portraying sidekicks to the male stars in the films in which he appeared. In the 1960s, he made numerous memorable screen appearances, including his brief but iconic scenes in Stanley Kubrick's *Dr. Strangelove, or: How I Learned to Stop Worrying and Love the Bomb* (1964) and roles in Disney films such as *The Absent-Minded Professor* (1960) and *The Love Bug* (1968).

From the 1950s onward, Wynn also made dozens of television appearances, in such series as *Studio One, Playhouse 90, The Twilight Zone, Alfred Hitchcock Presents, The Untouchables, Route 66, 77 Sunset Strip, The Mod Squad, Cannon, Hawaii Five-O, The Bob Newhart Show, Fantasy Island, The Love Boat,* and *Dallas*. Wynn was the father of screenwriter Tracy Keenan Wynn and actor Ned Wynn.—RODNEY HILL

References
Hal Erickson, "Keenan Wynn," All Movie Guide, http://www.allmovie.com/artist/keenan -wynn-77747; "Keenan Wynn," Internet Movie Database, www.imdb.com/name/nm0943978/; "Keenan Wynn," *Variety* Profiles, www.variety .com.

THE YOUNG RACERS (1963)

DIRECTOR: Roger Corman. SECOND UNIT
DIRECTOR: Francis Ford Coppola. SCREEN-
PLAY: R. Wright Campbell. PRODUCER:
Roger Corman. PHOTOGRAPHY Floyd
Crosby. EDITING: Ronald Sinclair. MUSIC:
Les Baxter. ART DIRECTION: Al Locatelli.
CAST: William Campbell (Joe Machin), Mark
Damon (retired racer).
RUNNING TIME: 87 minutes. Pathécolor.

FRANCIS COPPOLA served as a production assistant to independent filmmaker
ROGER CORMAN while he was enrolled
in the Masters Program in film at UCLA.
One day Corman inquired if Coppola could
recommend a sound engineer he could
hire for *The Young Racers* (1963), a movie
he planned to direct about sports car racing that would follow the Grand Prix racing circuit across Europe and incorporate
footage from various racing meets. With
youthful bravado Coppola volunteered,
"I'll do the sound." With that, he says in
Corman's autobiography, "I immediately
got the Nagra sound recorder out of the
closet at the office and went home to read
the manual." Coppola proceeded from
there to master the art of sound recording.

"I had always thought a Grand Prix
film would be fun to shoot with the races
and the crowds," says Corman. Coppola
was not only sound engineer but second-

unit director as well. In the latter capacity
he was working at times with Floyd Crosby,
the distinguished cinematographer on the
film, who had shot *High Noon.* "Working as
a team for the races was quite exhilarating
for me," Coppola comments. As second-
unit director, he shot most of the actual racing footage that was incorporated into the
picture. According to William Campbell,
who played a champion racer in the picture,
Coppola would go out onto the race track
in the middle of a race with his handheld
camera, "shooting pictures of these damn
racing drivers, driving past him within six
feet!" As a matter of fact, Coppola's exploits
were somewhat less perilous than Campbell imagined. He would take his camera
to trackside, lie on the ground, and photograph the racing cars as they whooshed by
him, but he was not lying on the track, as
Campbell suggests.

Variety summarized "the hackneyed
story" as having to do with Joe Machin
(William Campbell), a daredevil Grand
Prix champion and womanizer, "with a girl
in every pit stop," who turns out to have
"a heart of gold beating beneath the grease
and goggles." But the feeble plotline about
Joe's multiple affairs is soft-pedaled in favor
of following him from one racing event to
the next. The movie engages the viewer's
attention only intermittently, when it
thrusts the spectator into the cockpit with
the driver to go careening around the race

track at championship speeds—thanks to Coppola's handheld camera. So there were just enough thrills and spills amid the atmosphere of screeching tires and roaring crowds to satisfy the drive-in trade.
—Gene D. Phillips

References

Ronald Bergan, *Francis Ford Coppola* (New York: Orion Books, 1998); Roger Corman, *How I Made a Hundred Movies and Never Lost a Dime*, with Jim Jerome (New York: Random House, 1990); Beverly Gray, *Roger Corman: An Unauthorized Biography* (Los Angeles: Renaissance Books, 1999).

YOU'RE A BIG BOY NOW (1967)

> Director: Francis Ford Coppola. Screenplay: Francis Ford Coppola from the novel by David Benedictus. Producer: Phil Feldman for Warner Bros.– Seven Arts. Photography: Andy Laszlo. Editing: Aram Avakian. Music: Bob Prince. Songs: John Sebastian (performed by the Lovin' Spoonful). Art Direction: Vassele Fotopoulos. Costume Design: Theoni V. Aldredge. Choreography: Robert Tucker.
>
> Cast: Peter Kastner (Bernard Chanticleer), Elizabeth Hartman (Barbara Darling), Geraldine Page (Margery Chanticleer), Julie Harris (Miss Thing), Rip Torn (I. H. Chanticleer), Tony Bill (Raef), Karen Black (Amy), Michael Dunn (Richard Mudd), Dolph Sweet (Policeman Francis Graf), Michael O'Sullivan (Kurt Doughty).
>
> Running Time: 97 minutes. Eastmancolor.
> Released through: Warner Bros. Premiere: March 20, 1967.
> VHS: Warner Home Video.

FRANCIS COPPOLA served a term as a screenwriter in the mid-1960s for Seven Arts, an independent production company. The experience that the neophyte filmmaker

had gained from making *DEMENTIA 13* for ROGER CORMAN and from collaborating on various other movies helped him convince the newly formed Warner Bros.– Seven Arts production company to allow him to write and direct his first important film, *You're a Big Boy Now* (1967), which he shot on location in New York City. In due course, Coppola submitted the finished film to UCLA as his master's thesis and thereby gained his degree of Master of Cinema in 1968. The movie, which he adapted from a novel by British writer David Benedictus, is a freewheeling comedy about a young fellow on the brink of manhood who takes a giant step toward maturity when he finally gets out from under the control of his domineering parents and endeavors to make it on his own in the big city.

Coppola cast newcomers Peter Kastner and KAREN BLACK as the hero Bernard and his girlfriend, Amy. He then took the bull by the horns and bypassed the agents of the experienced actors he wanted for supporting roles and contacted the actors directly. He phoned JULIE HARRIS, and RIP TORN and his wife GERALDINE PAGE himself and coaxed them into reading the script. Geraldine Page spoke for the others when she said, "I get scripts daily, but this one really made me laugh." She thought Coppola was a marvelous young talent and trusted him implicitly.

Warner Bros.–Seven Arts assigned to Coppola a twenty-nine-day shooting schedule and a budget of $800,000—a meager budget by studio standards.

In his screen adaptation of the novel Coppola transplanted the setting from London to New York, where he had himself grown up. In Coppola's screenplay, Bernard Chanticleer (Peter Kastner) works in the stacks at the New York Public Library, where his father, Humphrey Chanticleer (Rip Torn), is curator of rare books. Bernard's raffish friend Raef (TONY BILL), who also is employed at the library, often attempts to make the naive Bernard a bit more worldly in his outlook on life. Humphrey Chanticleer, over the protests of his wife Margery (Geraldine Page), decides that Bernard should move out of their Long Island home and into an apartment of his own in New York City. Bernard apologizes to "Mummy" and "Daddy" for his failure to live up to their expectations in the past, thereby indicating that he is still in essence their little boy—he is not a big boy yet.

The apartment house Mummy and Daddy choose for him is presided over by the sexually repressed Miss Nora Thing (Julie Harris), who readily agrees to Margery's request that she report to Bernard's parents any partying Bernard indulges in with the opposite sex. Another tenant is a burly cop called Francis (after the young director), who likewise keeps a suspicious eye on Bernard, whom he views as a young punk. As things develop, Bernard becomes interested in Amy Prentiss (Karen Black), a coworker at the library. But he soon transfers his attachment to Barbara Darling (ELIZABETH HARTMAN), one of the library's patrons, an actress in offbeat, off-Broadway plays. The promiscuous Barbara eventually sheds Bernard for the more attractive Raef.

To his dismay, Bernard learns that his father, who maintains a respectable facade, is really a lecher who has made a pass at Amy and has even endeavored to work his wiles on Miss Thing when he corners her in the secret library vault he has filled with erotic art. Disenchanted with his father, Bernard defies Humphrey by stealing a prized Gutenberg Bible from his father's rare book collection. After a chase led by Humphrey through lower Manhattan, Bernard is captured and jailed—and bailed out by Amy.

The picture ends with the couple merrily romping through a pretzel factory (Bernard had earlier opined that what this country needs is a good five-cent pretzel). They are accompanied by the 1960s rock group the Lovin' Spoonful singing, "Go on and take a bow, 'cause you're a big boy now," while a conveyor belt sends a cascade of nickel pretzels toward the camera.

Benedictus's novel concludes with Bernard having lost both Barbara and Amy, but Coppola's screenplay reunites Bernard with Amy. Benedictus points out that his book concludes with Bernard living a solitary life, whereas Coppola supplied a happy ending: "Instead of being scarred for life by this sadistic Barbara Darling, the young hero will get a nice girl in the end. . . . Still I think there have been fewer concessions to public taste than in most American films."

A stand-out location sequence in *Big Boy* begins in Humphrey's office, where nearly all of the principals in the cast (even Barbara) meet for a showdown. It is at this point that Bernard impulsively steals the Gutenberg Bible and is pursued down Fifth Avenue by a posse led by his father. En route, they wind up in Macy's department store. Coppola explains that he wanted to see what would happen when this "madness" hit Macy's at 11:00 AM, with no one outside the film's cast and crew having the remotest idea of what was transpiring. Three cameras were concealed in delivery carts and shopping bags.

When he was shooting on location around New York City, Coppola and his cinematographer Andrew Laszlo utilized Eastman's high-speed color film stock so that they could film with natural light, even at night. Consequently, when shooting in Macy's, Coppola and Laszlo, as usual, filmed the scene with the natural light available, in this case a mixture of the fluorescent lights overhead and sunlight coming in through the windows. Kastner and his pursuers were running up and down the

Elizabeth Hartman and Peter Kastner.

aisles, "and they started a riot," Coppola remembers.

All in all, *You're a Big Boy Now* is a winning amalgam of quirky comedy and serious drama. On the one hand, there is the slapstick chase through Macy's department store. On the other hand, Coppola's script does have a serious dimension underlying the plot, despite the happy ending. Like the novel, the script presents a young fellow on the brink of manhood who matures by finally summoning the gumption to defy his overbearing parents and outgrow their influence.

At the film's denouement Bernard is jailed for stealing the Gutenberg Bible. While he is behind bars he admits to a guard that he has been imprisoned by his domineering parents, who have caused him to be "filled with self-doubt, frustration, and perpetual guilt. I've been in my parents' custody all my life. From now on

I'm going to be in my own custody." Significantly, it is Amy who bails Bernard out. She not only liberates him from prison but ultimately helps to free him from his parents' control.

You're a Big Boy Now reflects Coppola's theme, already enunciated in *Dementia 13*, that the family is a source of strife and emotional problems. He states, "I'm fascinated with the whole idea of family." In his work, "it is a constant." Indeed *Big Boy* is the first of his movies to explore a father-son relationship, a theme that would surface prominently in films like *THE GODFATHER*.

Big Boy was taken seriously by the film community. It was chosen as the only official U.S. entry at the CANNES INTERNATIONAL FILM FESTIVAL and gained Geraldine Page an Academy Award nomination. Still the picture merited a mixed bag of reviews, both at Cannes and in the American press.

Goodwin and Wise cite *Newsweek* critic Joseph Morgenstern as stating that not since ORSON WELLES went riding out of town "has any young American made a film as original, spunky, and just plain funny as this one." By contrast, other reviewers complained that Coppola photographed the movie in a rather showy fashion, with frenetic handheld camerawork during the chase in Macy's. The freewheeling cinematography is marked by the wild camera movement and gaudy colors reminiscent of TV commercials and, hence, draws attention to itself. Coppola, commenting on his style of cinematography in the picture, told me, "*You're a Big Boy Now* is a flashy movie to some extent. I have since been more subtle than that. But flashy films do attract attention, and that was what I wanted to do when I was making my first film for a studio."

Although budgeted at $800,000, the picture eventually cost closer to $1 million, which it never recouped during its original release. The film was not a commercial success because, besides the mixed reviews, the two leads were unknowns who had not yet established themselves in the movie world and lacked marquee value for the youthful filmgoers at whom the film was targeted. The young principals in *Big Boy* continued to pursue film careers. Elizabeth Hartman's career never really got off the ground, and she finally took her own life in 1987. The picture is in some ways light and slender; but it nevertheless indicates the stirrings of a major directorial talent.—GENE D. PHILLIPS

References

Jeffrey Chown, *Hollywood Auteur: Francis Ford Coppola* (New York: Praeger, 1988); Michael Goodwin and Naomi Wise, *On the Edge: The Life and Times of Francis Coppola* (New York: Morrow, 1989); Lee Lourdeaux, *Italian and Irish Filmmakers in America* (Philadelphia: Temple University Press, 1990).

YOUTH WITHOUT YOUTH (2007)

DIRECTOR: Francis Ford Coppola. SCREENPLAY: Francis Ford Coppola, adapted from the novella "*Tinereţe fără de tinereţe*" (literally, "Youth without Youth," but also translated as "Rejuvenation by Lightning") by Mircea Eliade, translated by Cristina Tirulnic. PRODUCER: Francis Ford Coppola. PHOTOGRAPHY: Mihai Malaimare Jr. EDITING: Walter Murch. MUSIC: Osvaldo Golijov. PRODUCTION DESIGN: Calin Papura.
CAST: Tim Roth (Dominic Matei), Alexanndra Narua Kara (Veronica/Laura), Bruno Ganz (Professor Stanciulescu), André M. Hennicke (Dr. Josef Rudolf), Marcel Iures (Professor Tucci), Alexandra Pirici (Woman in Room 6), Adrian Pintea (Pandit), and Florin Piersic Jr. (Dr. Gavrila).
RUNNING TIME: 126 minutes. Color.
RELEASED THROUGH: Sony Pictures Classics.
DVD: Sony Pictures.

A decade after filming *BRAM STOKER'S DRACULA*, FRANCIS COPPOLA returned to Romania to film his low-budget adaptation of MIRCEA ELIADE's novella, "Youth without Youth" in 2007. The novella by Eliade (1907–1986), written in 1976, recounts a metaphysical story about time and consciousness that Coppola told *Time* magazine (August 21, 2006) he found provocative: "It starts in 1938 and runs through the Second World War and goes from Bucharest to Switzerland to India to Malta. It's a big movie in terms of tackling the production. But I financed it through my wine business, and I took a page from Sofia's— my daughter's—book where she had made *LOST IN TRANSLATION* for just a modest amount."

The screenplay for Coppola's *Youth without Youth* was based on a translation by Max Linscott Ticketts published in the "Commemorative Edition" of *ZOETROPE:*

ALL-STORY magazine in the Fall of 2007 (vol. 11, no. 3). Other English translations exist of Mircea Eliade's novella "*Tinerețe fără de Tinerețe*": the story had earlier been translated into English by Ana Cartianu as "Rejuvenation by Lightning," though "*Tinerețe fără de Tinerețe*" translates literally as "Youth without Youth"; the alternative title makes sense, however, since the linguist Dominic Matei in that story (played by TIM ROTH in the film) is touched by the finger of God metaphorically while literally being struck by lightning. The story is fabulous, even miraculous, as Dominic Matei, a teacher of Latin and Italian at the Alexandru Ioan Cuza High School in the city of Piatra Neamț, is anointed for a higher purpose in his seventieth year, on the night of the Resurrection. Dominic is struck by lightning near the Gara de Nord in Bucharest in 1938, lifted several feet off the ground (as portrayed in Coppola's film), and severely burned; but then, miraculously, he begins to recover and heal in the hospital, and as he recovers, he seems to become progressively younger. At the same time, his intellect develops superhuman abilities, enabling him to master languages, ancient and modern, with supernal ease. Dominic assumes a new identity and travels the world, absorbing languages and wisdom. At the end of the story, he is led back to Romania and visits the Café Select, where his friends tell him, "We've been looking for you everywhere. . . . We heard you were in Bucharest, and that they took you for someone else." Matei attempts to tell his friends the truth, then makes an awkward departure into a snowstorm to go to his parental home in Piatra Neamț, at number 18 Episcopal Street. The next morning, "a very old man, a stranger, was found frozen to death" in front of no. 18 Episcopal Street, wearing an elegant suit and a rich fur coat." In the pocket of the coat was found "a wallet

with foreign currency and a Swiss passport to the name of Martin Audricourt, born in Honduras, on 18 November 1939." This is a strange conclusion to an even stranger story.

Eliade's story would seem to be an allegory of human potential imaginatively stretched to magical and metaphysical proportions. The symbolic implications are quite elegant and provocative. The unreceptive may reduce the literal story to a farfetched death-dream and therefore comfortably dismiss it. This is not a film made for a youthful demographic. It makes unusual demands on the viewer's imagination and powers of concentration. It is complicated in a way that most mainstream movies would not dare to be.

Eliade's story of Dominic seems to be optimistic, until the very end, when Dominic is brought back to "reality" at the Café Select in his home town of Piatra Neamț in the northeast of Moldavia, suggesting that he can't go home again, as time transpires against him. Dominic's goal as a linguist is to trace languages back through time and prehistory to an Ur-language. In the process of following that dream, however, he has to lose his identity, for who would believe, late in the story, that this ageless centenarian could inhabit the body of a forty-year-old man? The trajectory of his life is therefore mythic and symbolic, surely informed by Eliade's own fascination with the idea of eternal return, as defined in his study of *Le Mythe de l'eternel Retour* (1949).

In the Commemorative Issue of *Zoetrope: All-Story* magazine, Coppola records an imagined conversation with an alien visitor, amusingly attempting to explain what on one level the film is "about" (the mystery of human consciousness) and why he made this movie: "I used to say I was interested in consciousness and time because film is so adept at working in those areas; but now I think I'm most captivated by consciousness, because time is an invention of consciousness. That's what this story is all about. The reality in which we live is beyond our immediate perceptions." So the alien asks him: "Then what is the true nature of reality?" and he responds: "It's a kind of changing tapestry of illusion, and that's also this movie: a tapestry of illusion."

The "message," therefore, is that this is not the sort of "movie" likely to be embraced by mainstream viewers and reviewers. But Coppola also attempts to explain that "the movie's also a beautiful love story and a mystery of a kind. I've tried to build the story so that people don't have to immediately occupy themselves with the examination of consciousness. But then later, seeing the film again, if they want to consider it from that perspective, they can, and they'll discover additional dimensions to the story. That's the kind of movie I like to make: one that gives more as people give more of themselves to it." The problem is that many viewers may not be willing to make that kind of commitment and may balk at the notion of seeing a film more than once.

Therefore, perhaps predictably, the film was not a commercial success and encountered some puzzling and even hostile reviews in the popular press. Owen Gleiberman of *Entertainment Weekly*, for example, dismissed the film as a "patchy and ponderous mystico-historical disaster," consisting of "one soporific, depressed, deadeningly vague scene after another," and concluded that Coppola had "forgotten the language of storytelling," an absurd contention. Although he confessed that half the time he "had no idea what the movie was about," the more generous David Edelstein of *New York* magazine (no fan of Coppola's in the past, as evidenced by his review of *TUCKER: THE MAN AND HIS DREAM*) still believed that Coppola "was deeply in

tune—and having a hell of a time—with the material. (But if he didn't know what the movie was "about," how could he tell?) Edelstein was happy to see Coppola back to work after ten years of movie inactivity, and, though puzzled, guessed that the "movie [was] about memory that is always in the present tense," which always seems to be the case in film viewing. The core event was, of course, that Coppola had returned to filmmaking, and that, in itself, should have been reason enough to celebrate.

When Deborah Soloman of the *New York Times* asked Coppola if this "fable about an age-defying linguist and his lover who is reincarnated as a seventh-century Indian" was "intended for a mass audience," Coppola responded, "Not at all." But if it was intended for the art-house circuit, then it should have been produced thirty years earlier, when it might have reached a more tolerant and patient audience. The film unexpectedly demanded audiences to make an effort to understand it. But that is not the way of the American cinema, even though it once seemed, hopefully, that the so-called film generation of the 1960s might have been moving cinema in that direction. In his reflections on the film for *Zoetrope: All-Story*, Coppola's friend and colleague WALTER MURCH quotes the French filmmaker Robert Bresson, who stated (in keeping with Coppola's own metaphor): "The filmmaker is making a voyage of discovery on an unknown planet."

Youth without Youth is important for what should be obvious reasons: It marks a new direction in Coppola's creative career and a willingness to attempt a different kind of avant-garde filmmaking. It is also as if the director has discovered a new aesthetic. He certainly discovered a new cinematographer. As Coppola explains in *All-Story* magazine: "Each time I shot a test with an actor, I'd use a different photographer. They were all

good, but I chose MIHAI MALAIMARE, JR. The movie is about becoming young again, and I liked the fact that Mihai is so young, has a gentle personality, and is tremendously talented. When I told him the camera would remain stationary throughout, he said 'That's great!'" Mihai Malaimare would follow Coppola into the director's next intensely personal independent film, *TETRO*, but certainly the earlier film, *Youth without Youth* is "about" becoming young again, and should represent for Coppola a magnificent second chance, if not a "rejuvenation through lightning," then at least a "rejuvenation through cinema."
—James M. Welsh

References

Manohla Dargis, "The Folks You Meet on the Border Between Consciousness and Dreams," *New York Times*, December 14, 2007, B13; David Edelstein, "And Opening This Week," *New York*, December 17, 2007, 53; Mircea Eliade, *Mystic Stories: The Sacred and the Profane*, trans. Ana Cartianu (Bucharest: Editura Minerva, 1992); Owen Gleiberman, "Youth without Youth," *Entertainment Weekly*, December 21, 2007, 59; Ian Mohr, "Fountain of 'Youth.'" *Variety*, September 26–October 2, 2005, 7; Deborah Soloman, "Independent Streak," *New York Times Magazine*, December 16, 2007, 30; "*Youth without Youth* Commemorative Issue," *Zoetrope: All-Story* 11, no. 3 (Fall 2007).

Z

ZINNER, PETER (1919–2007)

A prominent editor, primarily of American theatrical films but also of television movies, Peter Zinner edited *THE GODFATHER* (1972), for which he was nominated for an Oscar, as well as *THE GODFATHER: PART II*; he also handled foreign postproduction on both films. In his review of *The Godfather* for the *New York Times*, Vincent Canby makes note of one of the film's most outstanding qualities: "*The Godfather* plays havoc with the emotions as the sweet things of life—marriages, baptisms, family feasts—become an inextricable part of the background for explicitly depicted murders by shotgun, garrote, machine gun, and booby-trapped automobile." What Canby doesn't point out is that the film achieves these extraordinary juxtapositions of emotion largely through the brilliant editing of Zinner and his collaborators. For example, in the signature montage sequence near the end of the film—in which all of Michael's enemies are vanquished as he presides as godfather over the baptism of his nephew—Zinner not only contrasts the sanctity of the ceremony with the horrors of murder, but through his use of graphic matching he also suggests that the murders have a ritual quality similar to that of the sacrament. The sequence is one of the most iconic (and ironic) in the film.

During World War II, Peter Zinner fled his native Austria and moved to Los Angeles in 1940. His earliest film work, dating back to the late 1950s, was as a music editor and music supervisor. Zinner's first credit as film editor came in 1962 with *Wild Harvest*, followed by Richard Brooks's *The Professionals* (1966); and he worked with Brooks again on *In Cold Blood* (1967). Zinner's other notable editing credits include: *A Star Is Born* (1976); Michael Cimino's *The Deer Hunter* (1978), which won Zinner the Oscar and the BAFTA Award for Best Editing; *An Officer and a Gentleman* (1982), starring RICHARD GERE, for which Zinner received another Oscar nomination; and episodes of the miniseries *The Winds of War* (1983) and *War and Remembrance* (1988). The latter earned Zinner an Emmy for his editing, as did the TV movie *Citizen Cohn* (1992); he also was the winner of several A.C.E. "Eddie" Awards for editing.

Over the years Zinner made a few forays into producing and directing, and he even acted in a small role in *The Hunt for Red October* (1990). His daughter, Katia Zinner, is also a film editor, with more than twenty-five films to her credit. Peter Zinner died in Santa Monica, California, in 2007 of complications from non-Hodgkins lymphoma.—RODNEY HILL

References

Vincent Canby, "The Godfather," *New York Times*, March 16, 1972; "Peter Zinner," Internet Movie Database, www.imdb.com/name/

nm0957038/; "Peter Zinner," *Variety* Profiles, www.variety.com.

ZOETROPE
See AMERICAN ZOETROPE.

ZOETROPE: ALL-STORY
Also known as *Francis Ford Coppola's Zoetrope: All-Story*, the director's "quarterly, fiction magazine," established in 1997, "dedicated to bridging the worlds of fiction and film." FRANCIS COPPOLA was both founding editor and publisher. The editorial board consisted of Coppola, FRED FUCHS, WILLIAM KENNEDY, TOM LUDDY, Daniel Menaker, and NAN TALESE. The Fall 1998 issue featured a typical mixture of new and older talent: Philip K. Dick's source for the film *Total Recall* (directed by Paul Verhoeven in 1990), a story entitled "We Can Remember It for You Wholesale," originally published in the April 1966 issue of *Fantasy and Science Fiction*, paired with the first chapter of the Gabriel García Márquez memoir *Vivir Para Contario / Living to Tell the Tale*, in Spanish and in English (translated by Edith Grossman). A later issue, vol. 3, no. 2, designed by David Bowie, followed the same pattern and featured a novella by the award-winning author Melissa Bank, three new short stories, and a translation of Julio Cortázar's "Blow-Up," the story that inspired Michelangelo Antonioni's film that won the Palme d'Or at Cannes in 1967. In a "Letter to the Reader" published in this issue, Coppola explains that *Zoetrope: All-Story* "was a project hatched out of our Crazy Idea Dept.," since Coppola believed that throughout his career "it has been the craziest ideas that proved enduring." Coppola gives this advice to young artists: ideas only seem "crazy because they are out of the ordinary, don't go down smoothly, and stick out. Creativity, after all, is the ability to see connections between seemingly dissimilar elements." By 2009 the magazine was in its thirteenth volume and still going strong, having published top-flight writers and filmmakers (Margaret Atwood, John Barth, Sherman Alexie, Rick Bass, Cynthia Ozick, Mario Vargas Llosa, Neil LaBute, Kurt Vonnegut, Hanif Kureishi, Edward Albee, Don De-Lillo; Gus Van Sant, John Boorman, Neil Jordan, Abbas Kiarostami, Steven Spielberg, WIM WENDERS, etc.). Coppola's *TETRO* was covered in the Summer 2009 issue and *YOUTH WITHOUT YOUTH* in Fall 2007.—JAMES M. WELSH

SELECTED BIBLIOGRAPHY

Baker, Fred, ed. "Francis Coppola on the Director." In *Movie People*. New York: Lancer Books, 1973.

Belton, John. *American Cinema/American Culture*, 3rd ed. Boston: McGraw-Hill, 2009.

Bergan, Ronald. *Francis Coppola Close Up: The Making of His Movies*. London: Orion Media/Orion Books, Ltd., 1998.

Biskind, Peter. *Easy Riders, Raging Bulls: Coppola, Scorsese, and Other Directors*. New York: Simon & Schuster, 1999.

———. *Godfather Companion*. New York: Harper-Collins, 1990.

Blake, Richard. *After Image: The Catholic Imagination of Six Filmmakers*. Chicago: Loyola Press, 2000.

Browne, Nick, ed. *Francis Ford Coppola's "The Godfather" Trilogy*. Cambridge: Cambridge University Press, 2000.

Cameron-Wilson, James. *Young Hollywood*. Lanham, MD: Madison Books, 1994.

Cardullo, Bert. "Re-Viewing *The Rain People*." In *Indelible Images: New Perspectives on Classic Films*. Lanham, MD: University Press of America, 1987.

Chaillet, Jean-Paul, and Elizabeth Vincent. *Francis Ford Coppola*. Trans. Denise Jacobs. New York: St. Martin's Press, 1984.

Chown, Jeffrey. *Hollywood Auteur: Francis Coppola*. New York: Praeger, 1988.

Coppola, Eleanor. *Notes*. New York: Simon & Schuster, 1979.

———. *Notes on a Life*. New York: Nan A. Talese/ Doubleday, 2008.

Coppola, Francis Ford. "Journal: 1989–93." In *Projections: Three Filmmakers on Filmmaking*, ed. John Boorman and Walter Donohue. Boston: Faber and Faber, 1994, pp. 3–43.

Coppola, Francis Ford, with James V. Hart. *Bram Stoker's Dracula: The Film and the Legend*. New York: Newmarket Press, 1992.

Corman, Roger, with Jim Jerome. *How I Made a Hundred Movies and Never Lost a Dime*. New York: Random House, 1990.

Cowie, Peter. *The Apocalypse Now Book*. New York: Da Capo, 2001.

———. *Coppola: A Biography*. New York: Da Capo, 1994.

———. *The Godfather Book*. London: Faber and Faber, 1997.

Evans, Robert. *The Kid Stays in the Picture: A Memoir*. Beverly Hills: Dove, 1995.

Fitzgerald, Frances. "*Apocalypse Now*." In *Past Imperfect: History According to the Movies*. New York: Henry Holt, 1995.

Gallagher, John. *Film Directors on Directing*. New York: Greenwood Press, 1989.

Gelmis, Joseph. "Francis Ford Coppola." In *The Film Director as Superstar*. Garden City, NY: Doubleday, 1970.

Goodwin, Michael, and Naomi Wise. *On the Edge: The Life and Times of Francis Coppola*. New York: William Morrow & Co., 1989.

Gray, Beverly. *Roger Corman: An Unauthorized Biography of the Godfather of Indie Filmmaking*. Los Angeles: Renaissance Books, 2000.

Grobel, Lawrence. *Above the Line: Conversations with Robert Evans and Others.* New York: Da Capo, 2000.

Johnson, Robert K. *Francis Ford Coppola.* Boston: Twayne Publishers, 1977.

Jones, Jenny, ed. *The Annotated Godfather: The Complete Screenplay.* New York: Black Dog and Leventhal, 2007.

Keyser, Les and Barbara. *Hollywood and the Catholic Church: The Image of Roman Catholicism in American Movies.* Chicago: Loyola University Press, 1984.

Kline, Sally, ed. *George Lucas: Interviews.* Jackson: University Press of Mississippi, 1999.

Kolker, Robert Phillip. *A Cinema of Loneliness: Penn, Kubrick, Coppola, Scorsese, Altman.* New York: Oxford University Press, 1980.

Lebo, Harlan. *The Godfather Legacy.* New York: Simon & Schuster, 1997.

Leitch, Thomas. "*The Godfather* and the Gangster Film." In *Crime Films.* New York: Cambridge University Press, 2002.

Lewis, Jon. *Whom God Wishes to Destroy: Francis Coppola and the New Hollywood.* Durham, NC: Duke University Press, 1995.

LoBrutto, Vincent. *Sound on Film: Interviews with Creators of Film Sound.* New York: Praeger, 1994.

Lourdeaux, Lee. *Italian and Irish Filmmakers in America: Ford, Capra, Coppola, and Scorsese.* Philadelphia: Temple University Press, 1990.

Madsen, Axel. "Bogdanovich and Coppola." In *The New Hollywood.* New York: Thomas Y. Crowell, 1975.

May, John R. "The Godfather Films: Birth of a Don, Death of a Family." In *Image and Likeness: Religious Visions in American Film Classics*, ed. John R. May. Mahwah, NJ: Paulist Press, 1992.

McNally, Raymond T., and Radu Florescu. *In Search of Dracula: The History of Dracula and Vampires.* Boston: Houghton Mifflin Co., 1994.

Meissner, Chris. "Francis Ford Coppola." In *The Encyclopedia of Great Filmmakers*, ed. John C. Tibbetts and James M. Welsh. New York: Checkmark Books, 2002.

Messenger, Chris. *The Godfather and American Culture: How the Corleones Became "Our Gang."* Albany: State University of New York, 2002.

Milius, John, and Francis Ford Coppola. *Apocalypse Now Redux: The Screenplay.* New York: Hyperion, 2000.

Oldham, Gabriella. *First Cut: Conversations with Film Editors.* Los Angeles: University of California Press, 1995.

Ondaatje, Michael. *The Conversations: Walter Murch and the Art of Editing Film.* New York: Knopf, 2002.

Palmer, William J. *The Films of the Seventies: A Social History.* Metuchen, NJ: Scarecrow Press, 1987.

Phillips, Gene D. *Godfather: The Intimate Francis Cord Coppola.* Lexington: University Press of Kentucky, 2004.

Phillips, Gene D., and Rodney Hill, eds. *Francis Ford Coppola Interviews.* Jackson: University Press of Mississippi, 2004.

Puzo, Mario. "The Making of *The Godfather*." In *The Godfather Papers.* Greenwich, CT: Fawcett, 1973.

Pye, Michael, and Linda Myles. *The Movie Brats: How the Film Generation Took Over Hollywood.* New York: Holt, Rinehart, and Winston, 1979.

Schaefer, Dennis, and Larry Salvati. *Masters of Light: Conversations with Contemporary Cinematographers.* Los Angeles: University of California Press, 1984.

Schumacher. Michael. *Francis Ford Coppola: A Filmmaker's Life.* New York: Crown, 1999.

Shadoian, Jack. *Dreams and Dream Ends: The American Gangster Crime Film.* Cambridge, MA: MIT Press, 1978.

Thomson, David. "The Discreet Charm of *The Godfather*." In *Overexposures: The Crisis in American Filmmaking.* New York: William Morrow & Co., 1981.

———. "Francis Ford Coppola." In *A Biographical Dictionary of Film.* 3rd ed. New York: Alfred A. Knopf, 1994.

Tomasulo, Frank P. "The Politics of Ambivalence: *Apocalypse Now* as Prowar and Antiwar Film." In *From Hanoi to Hollywood: The Vietnam War in American Film*, ed. Linda Dittmar and Gene Michaud. New Brunswick, NJ: Rutgers University Press, 1990.

Treptow, Kurt W. *Vlad III Dracula: The Life and Times of the Historical Dracula*. Iasi: The Center for Romanian Studies, 2000.

Von Gunden, Kenneth. *Postmodern Auteurs: Coppola, Lucas, De Palma, Spielberg, and Scorsese*. Jefferson, NC: McFarland, 1991.

Whaley, Donald M. "Adaptation Studies and the History of Ideas: The Case of *Apocalypse Now*." In *The Literature/Film Reader: Issues of Adaptation*, ed. Peter Lev and James M. Welsh. Lanham, MD: Scarecrow Press, 2007.

Ziesmer, Jerry. *Ready When You Are, Mr. Coppola, Mr. Spielberg, Mr. Crowe*. Lanham, MD: Scarecrow Press, 2000.

Zuker, Joel S. *Francis Ford Coppola: A Guide to References and Resources*. Boston: G.K. Hall, 1984.

INDEX

ABOUT THE AUTHORS

James M. Welsh, PhD, was educated in Bloomington, Indiana, and Lawrence, Kansas. Besides founding the Literature/Film Association and coediting *Literature/Film Quarterly* for thirty-two years, he has authored and edited more than sixteen books dealing with drama, literature, and film. In 1973 he hosted a television series, *The Films of the Gatsby Era*, originally broadcast on East Coast PBS stations from Boston to Miami, and for seven years thereafter he was arts editor for the CBS affiliate in Salisbury, Maryland, where he now writes as professor emeritus of Salisbury University. Welsh served two terms as Fulbright Lector of American Studies at the Universitatea "A. I. Cuza" in Iaşi, Romania, in 1994 and 1998.

Gene D. Phillips, PhD, teaches fiction and film at Loyola University of Chicago and is a contributing editor for *Literature/Film Quarterly*. He is coauthor of *The Encyclopedia of Stanley Kubrick* (2002) and has also contributed to *The Encyclopedia of Novels into Film* (1998) and *The Encyclopedia of Stage Plays into Film* (2001). A prolific writer and critic, Phillips is the author of several books on film directors—Ken Russell (1979), John Schlesinger (1981), George Cuckor (1982), and Alfred Hitchcock (1984). He has authored books treating the films adapted from the works of Graham Greene, Joseph Conrad, F. Scott Fitzgerald, William Faulkner, and Tennessee Williams. He is also author of *Creatures of Darkness: Raymond Chandler, Detective Fiction, and Film Noir* (2000), *Beyond the Epic: The Life and Films of David Lean* (2006), and *Some Like It Wilder: The Life and Controversial Films of Billy Wilder* (2009).

Rodney F. Hill, PhD, lives in Atlanta and teaches film studies at Georgia Gwinnett College. He is coeditor of *Francis Ford Coppola: Interviews* (2004), coauthor of *The Encyclopedia of Stanley Kubrick* (2002), and a contributor to *The Essential Science Fiction Television Reader* (ed. J. P. Telotte, 2008) and *The Stanley Kubrick Archives* (ed. Alison Castle, 2005). His essays have appeared in *Cinema Journal*, *Literature/Film Quarterly*, *The Quarterly Review of Film and Video*, and elsewhere.

Thomas Clancy graduated from Oklahoma State University in 1988 with a PhD in English, with his dissertation concentrating on hard-boiled fiction and film noir. His teaching career has focused on composition, literature, and film studies at colleges in Illinois, South Carolina, and Georgia. Currently, he coordinates a Writing across the Curriculum program at Albany State University in Albany, Georgia.

Tom Dannenbaum is a graduate of the film program at Brooklyn College. He lives in New York City.

Heidi Kenaga teaches writing and media courses at Wayne State University and has also taught at the University of Memphis and Clemson University. Her primary research interest is early U.S. studio history and business culture; and she has published essays in anthologies in the United States and Great Britain. Dr. Kenaga is the coeditor (with Diane Carson) of *Sayles Talk: New Perspectives on Independent Filmmaker John Sayles* (2006).

Christofer Meissner is currently a librarian/archivist and film and media instructor at Lake Region State College in Devils Lake, North Dakota.

Jason D. Mosser received his BA and MA in English from West Virginia University and his PhD in English from the University of Georgia. He has taught at West Virginia University, the University of Georgia, the Georgia Institute of Technology (where he was a Brittain Fellow in Writing), the Atlanta College of Art, Rockford College, and Gainesville State College. He is currently an associate professor at Georgia Gwinnett College.

Paul Ramaeker is a lecturer in film and media studies at the University of Otago in Dunedin, New Zealand. He is currently at work on a study of the influence of the international art cinema on Hollywood from the mid-1960s.

Manuel Pérez Tejada is a Marion L. Brittain postdoctoral fellow in the School of Literature, Communication, and Culture at the Georgia Institute of Technology. He teaches introductory media studies courses and English classes with an emphasis on film and media.

Fernando Arenas Vélez holds a PhD and MA in film studies from the University of Kansas in Lawrence. He has taught at the University of Kansas, the Georgia Institute of Technology in Atlanta, and universities in Colombia, South America. He has contributed to *Kinetoscopio*, a film magazine published in Medellin, Colombia, since 1990.

Billy Budd Vermillion is visiting instructor in media and cinema studies at the University of Illinois at Urbana-Champaign. His dissertation examines East European art cinema from 1956 to 1981.

Donald M. Whaley is professor emeritus of history at Salisbury University in Maryland, where he also served as coordinator of American studies. A Vietnam veteran trained at the University of North Carolina and Princeton University, Whaley edited a special issue of *Literature/Film Quarterly* dealing with films of the Vietnam War and also helped to organize a conference at Salisbury marking the anniversary of the Tet offensive. He has written numerous essays on such topics as the history of the South, soul music, Elvis Presley, jazz, Aldous Huxley, and anarchism. He is currently at work with Jim Welsh on *The Encyclopedia of Oliver Stone* for Scarecrow Press.